To My Pittsburgh Pal
Blain Kerkhoff

I know you will
enjoy many of
Beano's Stories –

Respectfully
Beanie Kish

HAVEN'T THEY SUFFERED ENOUGH?

An Unbelievable Career in
Sports, PR, and Television

BEANO COOK
and
JOHN D. LUKACS

White
Valley
Press

White Valley Press

Cook, Carroll H. and Lukacs, John D.
Haven't They Suffered Enough? An Unbelievable Career in Sports, PR, and Television
John D. Lukacs
ISBN: 979-8-6888-7060-2

Printed in the United States of America

Unless otherwise credited, all photos are from the personal collection of Carroll H. "Beano" Cook.

For our mothers,
Mary Kennedy Cook
Anita J. Lukacs

Contents

Introduction	*Take the points at home.*	1
1	*I'll court martial you.*	12
2	*Insult Duke.*	34
3	*A note from the Redhead.*	107
4	*One bus does it.*	145
5	*Nothing but U-boat commanders.*	178
6	*Honeymooning at Pitt Stadium.*	239
7	*The one I am most proud of.*	306
8	*Pull out the driver.*	320
9	*Under snacks for crew.*	356
10	*People are going to be disappointed...*	367
11	*One long coffee break.*	385
	Acknowledgments	411

HAVEN'T THEY SUFFERED ENOUGH?

INTRODUCTION

Take the points at home.

The story of how I came to have my name on the cover of this book is, like pretty much every story associated with the late, great Beano Cook, a good one.

The story starts with my first conversation with Beano, which took place on a February afternoon more than 25 years ago. I had mailed a letter to him at the Pittsburgh headquarters of the old *KBL* Entertainment Network, which beamed local sports programming to the greater Pittsburgh area and surrounding states in the late 1980s and early 1990s.

Although I had grown up watching Beano talk college football on *ESPN* and he appeared much more frequently on *ESPN* than on *KBL*, I felt my letter would have a better chance of finding its way to him via the cable operation in my own backyard rather than the one located in Bristol, Connecticut.

The fact that Beano lived in my own neck of the Western Pennsylvania woods was one reason why I decided to write him. As a soon-to-be high school graduate who wanted to be a sportswriter and perhaps do TV/Radio work as well, I was hoping the local legend would provide a neighbor and fellow college football fanatic with some advice and guidance.

I was delighted to discover a reply in my mailbox a few weeks later. It was my first introduction to Beano's special scrawl. More hieroglyphics than handwriting, and as colorful as the personality of the individual behind the penmanship, it was the first time I had seen my name printed in purple permanent marker!

Typed on a narrow note card inside the envelope was Beano's home phone number and a few brief sentences regarding his schedule and appropriate times to call.

The call was another first. In this case, my earliest, first-hand encounter with Beano's eccentricity. The phone rang ten times. I was surprised that no answering machine clicked on. I almost set down the receiver when someone finally picked up.

The voice on the line was unmistakable. It sounded, just like the writer Tom Callahan famously suggested, "like a plumbing fixture gargling Drano."

Yet it wasn't hearing the voice of one of my professional idols for the first time over the telephone that startled me as much as his unusual greeting.

"McGarrett! Five-O!" the voice yelled into my ear.

"Hello. Is this Mister Cook?"

"No."

"Oh," I replied. "I'm sorry."

Talk about confusion. I hadn't dialed the wrong number. The voice on the other end of the line was without a doubt the voice of the guy whose segments on "College GameDay" I looked forward to every fall Saturday.

It was during this first conversation that I learned that the Beano Cook we watched on television wasn't all that different from the Beano Cook that existed in real life. He had a lot of Walter Mitty in him. While many readers know him as a college football commentator and historian, those of you who have never enjoyed the experience of calling him at home don't know that he moonlighted quite a bit.

Sometimes, he was running an elite crime-solving unit on Oahu. He worked as a brilliant, but disheveled homicide detective, too. On a few occasions, he played the part of a Los Angeles County medical examiner with a knack for solving murder investigations.

Out of the countless phone calls we shared over the years, there was only one time I remember him answering the phone with a simple "hello." That was the last time I spoke with him. The call took place about a day before he passed away. But let's return to the first call.

"I'm not Mister Cook," snapped the voice. "Let's get that straight. Call me Beano."

I paused to collect my thoughts.

"Okay, Mister...no, Beano. This is John Lukacs. I'm a really big fan of yours. I wrote you a letter a few weeks ago and you wrote back telling me to call you. I want to get into sports journalism. I'm hoping you could give me some advice that I could apply towards pursuing a successful career."

At that moment I was sitting at the dining room table, my pen hovering steadily above paper, ready to primitively download and record all the wisdom and advice I expected Beano to begin transmitting.

What was I expecting? College recommendations, classes to take, his thoughts on how to land a spot on the school paper, internships, etc. Standard stuff.

Starting from the top, I learned that Beano Cook had his own idea of standard.

"You want a successful life and career?" asked Beano.

"Yes, sir."

"Are you writing these things down?"

"I am."

"Well, the first thing I want you to write down is to not get married."

I still crack up when I remember and replay the exchange in my head all these years later! It wasn't long before I got to know Beano better, and learned his strong feelings on bachelorhood, marriage, and a number of other subjects.

With the ice broken, I excitedly launched into my prepared introduction. It started with my accomplishments thus far, which were basically none, so that part didn't take long. I did have some plans or thoughts on education.

"I'm going to visit Missouri and Kansas," I told him. "Both have really good undergraduate journalism programs. Maybe Northwestern for graduate school. So far, I've been accepted at Penn State."

There was an audible groan.

"Yeah, I know how you feel about Penn State," I laughed. "In all honesty, though, my dream is to attend Notre Dame."

"No-trah Dame. Christ, it gets worse," he sighed. "It doesn't matter where you go to school. Don't get hung up on college. I barely got out of Pitt and I turned out okay. It's not what some piece of paper says you know, it's who you know. And journalism programs are overrated. Degrees – graduate, undergraduate – don't get caught up in all that. What you need to do is start writing. Just write, okay?"

"Okay. About what?"

"Anything. You want to write sports. There's no better way of practicing than doing. Watch games on TV, baseball, basketball, whatever. Then write your own game story, like the ones you read in the paper, the way you think it should be written given what you saw happen on the field and what else you know about the circumstances under which the game was played. I'll tell you what. Mail some of your stuff to me, I'll read it and let you know what I think."

"Wow, thanks."

"Kid, talent is all that really matters. The only way you can sell that talent to someone is by displaying it. You have to build up a file of clips. Gotta get the clips."

"Clips?"

"Published stories. Bylines. Newspaper clippings. Clips."

"Oh, ok. To put with a résumé. I understand."

"Yes. But let's back up a bit. You're a blank slate. I'm not knocking you. It's not a bad thing. Don't worry about getting published right now. First, you have to learn how to write. And by write, I'm talking about telling stories. Anybody can give you the stats and the salary cap. Forget that shit. Before you do anything, anything else, you first need to learn how to become a storyteller, then a great storyteller."

The way you become a great storyteller, Beano proceeded to tell me, was by studying other great storytellers.

"Read writers who have a lyrical quality to their work. Good writing flows like a catchy song. Transitions are key," Beano said.

Strangely, he didn't mention a single sportswriter to study or try to emulate. Instead, he rattled off a long list of popular historians, prolific novelists, and journalists.

At the top of the list were his two personal favorite authors, Thomas Wolfe and Willie Morris. Next, he added the historian, William Manchester.

Although I'd always been a reader, had this conversation never occurred, I'd have probably just kept reading *Sports Illustrated* and the sports sections of the local papers. His advice opened my eyes. It's not enough to read a lot, you must expand your intellectual horizons and read for and with a purpose.

That call was the beginning of a nearly two-decade long friendship. Although I didn't know it at the time, it was also something of a job interview.

Over the years, Beano had acquired a small support staff. He had a regular driver, Bobby Morrow, who took him shopping and to doctor appointments.

He had a housekeeper, a grandmotherly matron from his high-rise building named Marie who I imagine reminded him of his beloved mother. When Marie straightened up Beano's disaster of an apartment, thus wrecking his personal filing system, sitcom-style comedy typically ensued.

There were several of us on the payroll. A generous employer, he even paid health insurance premiums and made his two pairs of Steelers' season tickets available.

Before I was promoted to co-author, I worked my way up the ladder at Beano, Inc. At various times, I was everything from a researcher to bellhop. Chauffeur was perhaps the best duty. Out of many, one adventure stands out.

One early weekday in November 1997, Beano asked me to drive home from Notre Dame, pick him up in Pittsburgh and take him to State College, Pennsylvania. Since there were two games involving four top-five teams this Saturday, *ESPN* had decided to put on a special production featuring two "College GameDay" sets in Chapel Hill, North Carolina, and State College. The network, which wanted Beano to help anchor coverage of the Michigan-Penn State game while the regular "GameDay" crew covered Florida State-North Carolina, was promoting the dual-set doubleheader as "Judgment Day."

I jumped at the opportunity. Notre Dame had a bye, plus with payment in the form of a sideline pass to one of the biggest games of the year and a $500 check, who wouldn't have?

"Judgment Day" delivered two blowouts and while the money was great for a college kid, my enduring memories of the weekend are of the time we spent in transit.

Road trips with Beano were something else. Before you put the vehicle in drive, the music had to be ready. His favorite traveling tracks were college fight songs and anything from Frank Sinatra's catalog.

On this journey, the Chairman of the Board accompanied us from Blairsville to Altoona. Then we put on the marching bands. I'll never forget Beano singing along, word for word, while simultaneously conducting the Yale Band in "Bulldog" as we passed through sleepy Port Matilda.

Winding through the hinterlands of Central Pennsylvania, our conversations took a corresponding series of twists and turns. In addition to an incomparable memory, Beano possessed an incredible intellect. Mountains and topics, up and down we went:

sports; military history; politics; movies.

As the road went from four lanes to two, we narrowed our focus, compiling lists ranging from the greatest college football games he attended to the greatest conquests of Hollywood starlets by Sinatra and Howard Hughes, respectively.

The following week, I returned home from class one afternoon to the off-campus house that I shared with four other guys in South Bend to find the light blinking on the answering machine. I hit the playback button.

"We forgot Lana Turner," mumbled Beano between bites of his lunch. "Put her in the Sinatra column."

End of message.

I began writing material for Beano when I was in college. It was like being a presidential speechwriter who also wrote jokes for a comedian, someone along the lines of Rodney Dangerfield. I was good at it because I knew college football and history, as well as his other interests, his mannerisms, his delivery, and his sense of humor.

He used my stuff on *ESPN's* Saturday night college football scoreboard show and on other programs. After graduation, I contributed to his work on the "SportsCentury" series and did other things, like writing forewords for books that people asked him to do.

It was fun, gratifying work for two reasons: 1) he paid well and 2) on those occasions when he really liked a line but didn't think it was a good fit for him, he made sure I got the credit for it. He mentioned my name on the air many times to give me a plug.

As you'll read in this book, receiving proper credit – whether it was for a good line, for coming up with an innovative production concept, or for taking a big risk in some way, shape or form – was extremely important to Beano.

Beano was thrilled when Michael MacCambridge invited him to do a feature for *ESPN's* massive college football encyclopedia which was published in 2005. He was happy because his name would be appearing alongside that of his friend, Dan Jenkins, in the table of contents. Beano considered Jenkins the best college football writer of all-time.

The piece that we partnered up on was titled "Ten Days that Shook the Sport." Beano was so pleased with the finished product that he wanted my name to be put on the article, too. For whatever reason, it wasn't.

I don't know whether MacCambridge outright ignored Beano's request or if it was an honest error or omission, but Beano was pissed off privately. I shrugged it off as no big deal. After all, MacCambridge was paying for Beano Cook's notoriety, not the byline of John Lukacs. But to Beano it was a big deal.

"You wrote the whole damn thing," he said.

Beano called MacCambridge and insisted that my name be included on any future publications of the material. That gives you an idea of the kind of stand-up person he was.

While we're at it, it's only fair that I give credit where it is due, too. Beano, more than anybody else, taught me how to become a storyteller. Now how I ended up telling

Beano's stories, that's another tale that requires explanation.

In spring of my junior year, he put me to work digging up stats on historically great college football teams, players, and coaches. Then the focus of my research became the biographies of network television executives, producers, and on-air personalities.

Sometimes, he asked me to call certain individuals to clarify specific details regarding a story or event. When I mentioned the magic words – "I'm with Beano Cook" – heavily-guarded doors swung open, putting an assortment of legendary athletes, iconic sportswriters, and Emmy Award-winning sports television producers at my disposal.

When one task was completed, the material was shipped to Pittsburgh. Shortly thereafter, another assignment and advance check arrived in my mailbox. I hadn't the slightest idea of what he was doing with this material or what it was for.

One afternoon shortly after my graduation from Notre Dame in 1999, we got together for lunch at Yovi's Hot Dog shop on Liberty Avenue in downtown Pittsburgh. Yovi's was located right next door to the building in which Beano lived, Midtown Towers.

"The two questions people ask me the most are: 'Who do you like tonight?' and 'When are you going to write a book?' he said. "You and I are going to see if we can figure out an answer to the second one."

I nearly choked on a French fry. It was reminiscent of the revelatory scene in the 1984 movie "Karate Kid" when Daniel LaRusso finally understands why Mr. Miyagi had him doing all that presumably meaningless manual labor. It was at that moment I learned that there had been a much bigger purpose behind all of Beano's busy work.

I was even more surprised to learn that not only was I going to be part of the project, he intended for me – a nobody – to write it!

From underneath his clipboard and stack of newspapers, he produced a manila file folder fat with papers, pages of notes both handwritten and typed, yellowed newspaper clippings, old letters, and media releases, as well as my own extensive research.

There existed roughly one dozen of these folders, each one containing materials for a chapter that would correspond with a certain job or period of his life and career in sports, PR, and television. Others housed materials on subjects near and dear to Beano's heart, such as sports betting and expense accounts.

As I leafed through the contents of this first folder, Beano explained that he had begun putting together the book's basic outline in 1975, after he had left the Miami Dolphins. Indeed, some of the notes were typed out on the backs of old media releases from the 1974 season.

He also said that he had attempted to partner with a handful of individuals over the years but had never been able to make any substantial progress on the project. Just about the only parts set in stone would be the titles of the individual chapters, each of which would end with a funny or else personally meaningful line. Everything else was open to discussion.

"I can't fucking write, John. I've accepted it. I don't have the patience or ability to sit down and type and hammer the narrative out," he admitted. "You have the talent. You know how I think and what to say. You'll figure out how to make it flow."

Beano worked around my schedule, and I worked with his; he famously refused to touch the material during football season. As a result, we played with the project on and off for the better part of the next dozen years. At the time of Beano's death, somewhere between one-half to two-thirds of the manuscript was completed.

Why did I decide to finish it? And why now?

First, I had promised Beano during his last days that I would finish the book. And since Beano left me his notes and I had plenty of other materials to draw from, I knew that I could finish it. Yet it wasn't until recently that I realized that I should finish it. And that I needed to finish it fast.

The major catalyst behind the decision came when *ESPN* launched a special series in the fall of 2019 for the 150th anniversary of college football. Although the series as a whole was very well-done, I felt the production fumbled a scoring opportunity to honor Beano. He was only briefly mentioned and sadly, was portrayed as a clownish figure, college football's court jester.

In my opinion, despite all that Beano had done for *ESPN*, the network he was so proud to have been a part of sold him, his contributions to the sport of college football, as well as his entire extraordinary career, short.

Now *ESPN* was correct in labeling Beano as one of the sport's most well-known "Voices," but he was so much more than a voice.

He forgot more about college football than any other human being will ever know. As sections of this book certify, he's almost singlehandedly responsible for some extremely significant developments in both sports and sports television history.

Then there are the stories. And the names. Beano had the ears of network presidents, NCAA officials, NFL commissioners and team owners. As you're going to read, the number of famous people in the worlds of sports, media, politics, and entertainment he interacted with throughout the course of his life is absolutely staggering.

And in typical Beano-fashion, the way he tells you about these encounters and relationships isn't name-dropping. Given the untidy way his life was organized, it's more like name-spilling. The material was just too good to keep to myself.

Perhaps most importantly, I felt the project needed to be completed, both for Beano and for his legacy. By telling his incredible life story, the unknown details of his exceptional career and all his unique accomplishments would be understood by both college football fans and future generations.

Again, giving credit where it was due was one of the foundational principles of Beano's life. He had worked tirelessly on behalf of others for most of that life, from trying to get All-America recognition for Pitt athletes to good space for co-workers at *ABC* and *CBS*, as well as square deals for his *VISTA* clients. He had written countless recommendation letters, secured employment for and sang the praises of many men and women for sixty years – it was high time someone did right by him.

The first thing I did before jumping back into the material was to go back and read the obituaries and stories written on the occasion of Beano's death in October 2012. As I re-watched the retrospectives and tributes and re-read the tweets, I cataloged the various and unique titles that were associated with the man.

Analyst. Broadcaster. Commentator. Historian. Pundit. Prognosticator. Publicist. SID. Sportswriter. The "Cardinal" or "Pope of College Football."

Howard Cosell famously called him an "unmade bed." Cosell was perhaps closest to the mark. It's not only unfair, but perhaps impossible, to attempt to classify Beano with a conventional title. To better explain to you what the guy was like, I've come up with some unconventional titles for an unconventional guy.

It's fitting that he made his home in a city known for its rivers and bridges. The man was, when you truly think about it, a bridge himself. Born less than six months after Knute Rockne's death, his lifetime spanned the final gilded days of the golden era of sports to a new millennium.

To many of us, "The Four Horsemen" was a famous newspaper lede. Honus Wagner was a guy on an ultra-rare, expensive old baseball card. "The Chief," Art Rooney, Sr., was a cigar-chomping character on *NFL Films*.

To Beano, these people were friends.

His one-liners, observations and anecdotes were the girders, stanchions and columns connecting us to legendary, long-gone watering holes like Gustine's, Runyon's and Manuche's.

In much the same way, his memories and stories continue to bridge us with places like Forbes Field, Pitt Stadium, the Polo Grounds, the Orange Bowl, and countless other famed sports venues that have since vanished.

To the public, Beano was a dropkick in human form, a holdover from a bygone era. He bounced and booted deliveries, swearing his way through take after take – I'm sure that even in heaven he can hear Chris Fowler - but eventually what he was trying to say, in a way only he could say it, sailed through the uprights.

As you will read in these pages, he was a real pioneer, the first ever non-coach, non-jock, non-traditional commentator to talk college football on the tube. A real-life Oscar Madison in a world of vanilla former players and coaches and journalism school grads, he was truly colorful long before television was.

Beano was a key. His name literally opened doors. Whenever I needed tickets to a big game, all it took was one call from Beano and within 24 hours, I was in touch with an SID asking how many I needed.

I can't remember how many recommendation letters he wrote on my behalf, but I know what the most important one was. It was the one he sent to the admissions department at Notre Dame. When I received my letter of acceptance, he was the first person after my parents to hear the good news. It was then I learned that he had gone out on a limb with another prediction.

"I told them I might have gotten Powlus wrong," he said, "but I was one-hundred percent certain you would succeed at Notre Dame."

I believe that Beano was singlehandedly responsible for nearly all the important introductions, internships, and jobs that I received early in my career.

First, when no editors reciprocated my interest in writing for either of the student publications at Notre Dame, he took it personally.

"Fuck 'em," he growled. "You're good enough to be getting paid. Let me call somebody."

That somebody was the late Lou Somogyi at *Blue and Gold Illustrated*, who, along with Tim Prister, hired me at the age of 19 solely on the strength of Beano's glowing recommendation.

A few weeks later, *ESPN's* "College GameDay" show brought its traveling circus to town for Ohio State's first visit to Notre Dame Stadium in sixty years.

"Go over to the truck and ask for Steve Vecchione, the producer, Chris Fowler or Lee Corso," commanded Beano. "Tell them you're a friend of mine."

I was treated so well by everybody that weekend, I suspect that many of the people associated with "GameDay" believed that I was related to Beano. The following week, I drove to Columbus, Ohio to watch the crew do the show from outside the old horseshoe on the banks of the Olentangy River for the Penn State-Ohio State game.

A cop, noticing that I didn't have an official pass or *ESPN* identification, moved to deny me entry to the set, but Chris Fallica, one of the best college football and wagering minds in the business, jumped to my rescue.

"It's okay. He's Beano Cook's nephew," stated Fallica. "He's with us."

The cop apologized, asked me to say hello to Beano for him, and waved me by.

Beano was an only child. He had no nephews nor nieces. Although he often referred to me – many times with a hint of exasperation in his voice – as his "surrogate son," it wasn't until much later, until we started working on this book, that I learned why he did everything he did for me.

As many close to Beano knew, he was an extremely generous, loyal friend, but I now understand he did all these things for me specifically to fulfill a promise he made to his own mentor, the Pirates' play-by-play man, Bob Prince. The "Gunner" told Beano many years ago that "some kid is going to find you and ask you for advice or some help. Help him out like I helped you."

At times, Beano's name was a credit card. Like the old American Express advertisements told us, you didn't leave home without it.

One evening during my internship with *ESPN The Magazine* in New York City, I called Beano and asked if the famed Runyon's sports bar still existed. He regretfully told me that it had closed, but suggested I visit the descendant joint called Runyon's on 2nd.

I was delighted to find that there were still some holdovers, on both sides of the bar, from the old place at the new site. After a great meal and even better conversation, I placed my credit card in the check holder and left to visit the men's room. I returned to find only the card and no slip needing my signature.

"For a friend of Beans," said the bartender, "it's on the house."

Most of the nation, in the end, insisted on calling him a media personality. The more I got to know him, the more I came to understand that he put a special priority on the word personal.

I think that everybody that knew him will attest that no matter how the conversation began or ended, at some time during your discussion of scheduling, winning percentages and polls he always made it a point to inquire about your parents, your wives, your girlfriends, your children. Your holiday plans. Your doctor's appointments. Your vacations. Your life.

And then, without fail during the course of the call or dinner, he would tell a story, impart some wisdom, fill in some blank. So, strange as this may sound, to me the title that makes the most sense when you're talking about Beano Cook is educator.

If you worked in sports, PR, or television over the last fifty, sixty years, you were most likely a student at BC – Beano College – either part or full-time, or else had taken correspondence courses of a sort.

For many of us writers, he was the literary equivalent of a golfer's swing coach.

He taught us enterprise, how to look for and find stories.

He taught romance and sex ed: watch "Casablanca."

He taught us about expense accounts and how to deal with the Internal Revenue Service.

And perhaps most importantly, he taught us how to treat people. All people. I noticed early on that he made an effort to get to know postal workers and parking lot attendants, cops and corporate leaders, delivery men and athletic directors, bookies, and big money donors alike.

When you get right down to it, education might just be Beano Cook's enduring legacy. I know few people who possessed such a love for and unflinching loyalty to an educational institution that could rival Beano's for Pitt and The Kiski School. Nor do I know anyone else who backed up their beliefs with every cent of their hard-earned money.

Once we started working on this book, I learned the reason for his outlook. It was during his brief stint with the Miami Dolphins that he got to know Joe Robbie, the team owner, and Robbie impressed upon Beano his belief that an individual of means without any children has a responsibility to educate the children of others who are less fortunate.

So, in keeping with the theme of education, I think it would be appropriate that you, the reader, think of the material in this introduction and in the larger book itself as a commencement address. Typically, the end of a commencement speech is marked by the guest speaker imparting some valuable advice. There's no better, nor more valuable, advice for this guest speaker to impart than Beano's.

Please read the following, italicized exhortations as you will the pages that follow

– in Beano's voice. They are the four commandments by which he lived his life. He shared them with me not long after that first, unforgettable phone call and I've tried my best to follow them throughout the course of my own existence on this Earth.

Never miss an opportunity to tell your parents that you love them.

Don't be a slave to a pension.

Have fun.

Beano's most common lament, especially late in life, was that nobody has fun anymore. While he was referring to the sports and media businesses in today's world, he also felt it was true for most people in general, regardless of one's line of work. I think he'd be happy to know that this book will provide, in addition to some great stories, insight and predictions, a lot of laughs and a lot of fun.

Oh, and as one of Beano's favorite television characters, Lieutenant Columbo, would say, "just one more thing."

Always take the points at home.

John D. Lukacs
September 1, 2021

CHAPTER 1

I'll court martial you.

I've never been able to write a decent lede. Any editor who has survived hand-to-hand combat with my copy can tell you this. And at this point in my life, it's probably wishful thinking that I'm going to magically conjure up something clever or creative.

I've always been more of a storyteller than a real writer, so I'll steal some inspiration from the guy who wrote the greatest lede of all-time, Grantland Rice, on Notre Dame's "Four Horsemen," and jump right into what I do best, telling stories. Let's start with the nickname.

In dramatic lore, I'm known as "Beano." But that is only an alias. My real name is Carroll Hoff Cook. I was named after my great uncle, Carroll Cook, a judge in San Francisco. My father's side of the family is from San Francisco.

The credit for the nickname goes to a guy named Frank Leary, who gave it to me when my family moved to Pittsburgh in 1937.

We had arrived from Massachusetts, specifically a place called Duxbury, but that brought blank looks from the crowd gathered around the moving truck. Once it was explained that our former home was some thirty miles south of Boston, Frank Leary nodded understandingly and said, "ah, Boss-ton, like the baked beans."

At that fateful moment in history, the new neighbor boy was christened "Beans." Sometime shortly thereafter, "Beans" became "Beano." That's it, Fort Pitt, as the old beer slogan went.

We lived on Thomas Boulevard and the Learys lived on Meade Street in the neighborhood of Point Breeze. It's just east of downtown Pittsburgh, between two communities called Squirrel Hill and Wilkinsburg.

We moved maybe a year or two later, so I have only foggy memories of that period, mostly of the pigeons that lived in the Learys' garage and the alley between the two streets that served as our playground.

In fact, for many years I thought the man's name was John O'Leary. It wasn't until I moved back home to Pittsburgh again, this time from New York City, that I learned his real name. This was in April of 1982.

To celebrate my homecoming, my good friend Myron Cope had me on his radio show and one of the Leary brothers, Bill, called in. For the next thirty, maybe forty-five minutes, he filled in a lot of the gaps of my childhood and caught me up on everything that had happened in the old neighborhood and with his family.

This was on live radio. It was unbelievable. I felt like I was on an episode of "This Is Your Life." I was saddened to learn that Frank had been killed when his LST was torpedoed by the Japs during the war, but I was glad Bill called in. More than forty years later, I finally got this essential bit of biographical information sorted out.

After a lifetime of listening to and appearing on radio shows throughout the country, I'm convinced this sort of thing could not have happened anywhere but in Pittsburgh. No way it happens in New York where twenty guys would have lit up the switchboard to bitch that we weren't talking about the Yankees. Or in San Francisco, where I was born, nor some of the other places I have lived like Providence, Rhode Island and Lake City, Florida.

Pittsburgh is a special place. It is and always will be home. Moving from Point Breeze, we lived in Duquesne Heights and in Chatham Village on Mt. Washington. After the aforementioned breaks in other towns and cities, I've lived downtown ever since, for the better part of the last thirty years, in hotels and apartments from Stanwix Street to Liberty Avenue.

Thanks to these different perspectives, I truly believe that Pittsburgh is not so much a big city, but really just one big ethnic neighborhood. And everybody knows that in those neighborhoods, nicknames are forever.

If my mother had only known that the nickname would have stuck, she'd have never let me out of the house that day. She would not have let me anywhere near the Leary boys. My mother hated Beano. Absolutely hated it.

A fun exercise to do is to ask your parents what name they had picked out if you had been born the opposite sex. I asked my mother that question and she said that if I had been a girl, I'd have been named Kathleen. The way I, a kid growing up in the 1930s and 1940s, saw it, there wasn't much difference between Kathleen and Carroll.

Carroll made grade school difficult. Then it got worse. When I turned 18, I started getting advertisements in the mail for ladies undergarments. When I was in the army, I got more laughs at mail call than Bob Hope at a USO show.

As I got older, I realized I wasn't the only Carroll out there. There was strength in numbers. The Green Bay Packers had a receiver named Carroll Dale. Carroll Hardy played both pro football and baseball. Carroll Rosenbloom would own two NFL franchises, the Colts and the Rams, in his lifetime.

There was the racer, Carroll Shelby. One time at the Charlotte 600, I met a guy named Carroll and we spent the entire race sharing funny stories. And then there is the most famous Carroll of us all, Archie Bunker, the late Carroll O'Connor.

I use my initials on my bills and checks, but every now and then I have an occasional laugh when I get my mail. Just a few years ago I got a questionnaire concerning breast cancer. It was addressed to "Ms. Carroll Cook." The postage was prepaid, so I filled it out and sent it back.

I once told my mother that I had survived Carroll and that she would survive Beano. It could have been worse, I added, and shared with her a great story told to me by a chick I dated in New York whose given name was Priscilla. Growing up in Kansas, her nickname as a little girl was "Pussy." Everybody called her that. That nickname, as you can imagine, was getting increasingly problematic for Priscilla's mother as her daughter got older.

During a sleepover party the night before the first day of junior high, Priscilla's mother called the group to attention: "You are now young ladies, and as such, you should dispense with the childish names and call my daughter by her proper name."

A few seconds of silence followed. All of the sudden, you hear a room full of schoolgirls screaming in unison, "But Mrs. So-and-So, everybody loves 'Pussy'!"

My mother wasn't amused.

When I got out of the army in 1956, she asked me to do two things: give up hitchhiking and please do not to use Beano professionally.

The former was easy. The latter was impossible. By that point, it was too late.

To be honest, I'm thankful for Beano. And not just because it was an alternative to Carroll. There is no doubt in my mind that it aided my career. It's short, it's catchy, and it's been mine my entire life.

Well, it was all mine until one of my colleagues at *ESPN*, Betsy Ross, named her dog Beano. I didn't know what to think of that at first, but she assured me that it was an honor. When the damn gas pills came out, that wasn't much of an honor.

For the most part, Beano's been a good thing. Look at history, how many famous people are known exclusively by only their first or last names, by their initials or their nicknames. You've got Caesar and Cleopatra. FDR and the Fonz. Michelangelo. Napoleon. Cher. Kramer. I'm in good company.

My generation learned identities, history, sports, and news through nicknames – "Bambino," "Gipper," and "Honest Abe" are just a few examples – before we learned Thomas Jefferson gave us the Declaration of Independence. To young boys certain facts come first.

I don't know where Beano ranks all-time, probably somewhere between Frederick the Great and Ivan the Terrible, but I feel like I'm a part of television history in some small way because of it.

I've always had a thing for nicknames. Maybe it was the era I grew up in. Or maybe it was where I grew up. At one time, it was almost a job requirement to have a nickname if you were involved in sports, media, or politics in Pittsburgh. Everybody had one.

Albert "Rosey" Rowswell was the Pirates' play-by-play guy and when he died, my great friend and mentor Bob Prince, "The Gunner," took his spot in front of the mic.

Some say Prince's broadcast partner, Jim Woods, aka. "The Possum," started calling him Gunner because of his rapid-fire speech patterns and the way he called games. Others believe that it stemmed from the time a jealous husband accused the broadcaster of hitting on his wife and pulled a gun on Prince. The hopeless romantic in me likes that story better.

Along with a ton of catchphrases and other lines that are part of Pirates' lore, Prince came up with some lasting nicknames himself. He ordained Vern Law as "The Deacon" and called Dick Stuart "Dr. Strangeglove" because of his spotty fielding prowess. His best-known call in this regard is probably "Cobra," his nickname for Dave Parker.

The public thinks the nickname came from the way the great Pirates' outfielder could strike at moment's notice, the way he uncoiled his powerful swing at the plate or bit an overconfident baserunner with his lethal arm. Another story goes that Prince was taking a piss next to Parker and glanced over.

"Christ," exclaimed Prince, "that thing is like a cobra!"

Everybody called Art Rooney, Sr., the patriarch of the Rooney family, owners of the Pittsburgh Steelers, "The Chief."

It's no surprise that the most feared defense of all-time, "The Steel Curtain," was led by someone with a fearsome nickname like "Mean Joe" Greene.

Then you've got "Rocky" Bleier, who is perhaps the most beloved player in Steelers history. A big part of that is because of his military service in Vietnam and his incredible comeback story. But you can't discount the nickname. I'm sure if you asked Rocky, he'd agree that Robert or Bob Bleier just doesn't sound the same.

Once upon a time, boxers all had nicknames and Pittsburgh had some of the best, both boxers and nicknames. Joey Diven was considered the best pure fighter, street fighter, in boxing history. He was "The White Knight of Oakland" or "The Bear." Harry Greb was "The Pittsburgh Windmill" and the great Billy Conn was "The Pittsburgh Kid."

I got to know Conn through Prince. When Conn had you on the ropes telling stories, he knocked you out with laughter. He was the most bluntly honest person I've ever met. It didn't matter whether he was talking to a U.S. President or some guy at the corner bar, he said whatever popped into his mind.

Conn once told me how, after being introduced to Grace Kelly's mother while in the presence of her in-laws – the royal family of Monaco - he immediately asked the question that every Irish-American kid in the country wanted an answer to in the late 1950s: "Why'd ya daughter marry that greaseball?"

You can't forget Pitt's biggest cheerleader, "Tiger Paul" Auslander. Auslander's Duquesne counterpart was Maurice "Mossie" Murphy.

"Radio Rich" Glowczewski was Bob Prince's devoted man Friday. Lawrence "Deuce" Skurcenski has attended thousands of local high school games over the years.

I did high school football and basketball games with local media personality "Chilly Billy" Cardille on *KQV* radio and on *WQED*, the public television in Pittsburgh, in the early 1960s.

Bernard "Baldy" Regan was a fixture in Pittsburgh politics. The voice of disc jockey George "Porky" Chedwick filled radio airwaves for decades.

Some years ago, a Pittsburgh writer named Bill Modoono wrote a profile of me and called me the "last Pittsburgh character." I took offense to that at the time. I didn't like being thought of as the last of anything. Who wants to be called a dodo bird? But I guess it's better than being called an institution, which for me is too close an association to mental hospital.

I've never considered myself a character, but I'll admit my personality helped my career, especially in getting on the air. After all, I wasn't a former player and, let's be honest, I didn't get on TV because of my looks.

I look more like Max, the chauffeur on "Hart to Hart," than I did his boss, Jonathan Hart. Some of the women I've dated would probably say I bear a closer resemblance to Freeway!

I'd like to think there was more to it than being a character. I had a different perspective, different material, a different voice and definitely a different delivery. Yet in my mind, there's no mistaking that the nickname was the secret ingredient.

My friend Jimmy "The Greek" once told me he felt the same way. He doubted that plain old Jim Snyder, or Dimetrios Synodinos, his given name, would have gotten him on the air no matter how many winners he picked.

I am the only child of the late Mary Kennedy and Mills Cook. My dad, a Stanford alum, was a securities broker. I wouldn't say we were well-off, but we were better off than a lot of other folks during the Depression. We used to take these leisurely Sunday drives that I thought were boring as hell. The lone benefit of Pearl Harbor, at least for me, was that wartime gas rationing ended that practice.

Despite my parents' heritage, we weren't Catholic. We were what they called "Orange Irish." We were officially Protestant, but we weren't church-going people. In our household, we worshipped the Democrats. At least my Chicago-born mother did, so my father and I had no choice in the matter.

My mother was a very proper and dignified woman, but when it came to politics, she had a bit of a nasty streak. I guess you could take her out of Chicago, but you couldn't take the Chicago out of her. She once kicked a neighbor out of our house because he called President Franklin D. Roosevelt a "crippled old son-of-a-bitch."

She even once slapped me in the face for booing Roosevelt when he appeared on screen in a newsreel. I was eight years old. The feeling was that Roosevelt was leading us into the war in Europe and I had just heard one of my earliest heroes, Iowa's Nile Kinnick, give his unforgettable Heisman Trophy acceptance speech on the radio.

Kinnick said that football players would "rather struggle and fight to win a Heisman than a Croix de Guerre," and if the "Cornbelt Comet" said it, well, I had to agree with him.

I don't know what got into me that day, but I never made the mistake of defaming FDR in front of my mother again.

"The three things we will never find substitutes for," she once announced, "are Edward Murrow, a fall October day in New England, and FDR."

If that sounds like something I'd say, it's probably because I got my sense of humor, my love of history and my skill at delivering lines from my mother.

As she got older, her loyalty extended to President Kennedy. Once, when a Republican friend challenged her to defend JFK's rampant infidelity, she feigned ignorance saying, "I thought he had a bad back."

My mother lived into her late nineties and never mellowed.

"Reagan is like a pretty girl," I once heard her snarl while we were watching the evening news. "He can get away with murder."

Me, on the other hand, I hate all politicians equally, regardless of party. Today, I just don't see much difference between the parties or their ideologies. The way I look at it, they're all thieves. Liberals want to steal our freedoms and conservatives, our money.

The dumbest thing we ever did as a country was rebuild Washington after the British did us a favor and burned it down in the War of 1812. Still, I believe in the foundational principles of our country, in our republican system of government, participating in the democratic process, donating, debating, and voting. What I don't like is that the politicians participate too much.

After FDR died, Congress passed an amendment limiting the president to a total of two four-year terms. That was a good start. It should have been followed by another amendment limiting the number of terms that senators and representatives could serve. People always seem to complain about the current occupant of the White House, but that individual is only there four or eight years.

Nobody seems to realize that the people who do the most damage are those who spend thirty, forty or even fifty years on Capitol Hill. They turn Congress into a lifetime job and public service into a path to accumulating massive personal wealth.

And they somehow do it despite having no real leadership skills whatsoever. The only talent these people have is an ability to win a popularity contest every few years. They're nothing more than glorified prom kings and queens. And yet we treat them like movie stars or royalty. The vast majority of these people have never succeeded at anything else in their lives. They barely deserve our respect, much less any adulation.

Few things piss me off more than when a reporter or talk show host addresses someone who has been out of political office for twenty years as "Governor," "Senator," or "Mister Speaker." You don't call a retired mail carrier, "Mister Mailman." They're all government employees. Why the hell are politicians so exalted?

Positions in our government should come with temporary titles. These aren't lifetime peerages, like in England. It's bad enough we pay a pension and lifetime benefits to somebody who served a single term in the House of Representatives.

What's next, does a former female senator from Michigan get to be called the Duchess of Detroit? A Congressman from Nebraska becomes the Lord of Lincoln for the rest of his life? I think we might have fought a war to avoid this.

My solution to fix our dysfunctional government would be to first eliminate the party system, limit future presidents to one, six-year term (because an incumbent usually starts his re-election campaign in the second half of his first term, you really only get six years out of these people) and then fill Congressional seats like we do juries.

I call it the "Beano Plan." Not because of ego or desire for notoriety, but only because all the really good names, like Marshall Plan and Operation Overlord, are already taken.

How would the Beano Plan work? Like jury duty, all adult American citizens, rich or poor, with no distinctions made for color, creed, or profession, would be required to report upon receipt of a summons.

The only exceptions would be for people who are either too young, too old, or too ill. Everybody else would be fair game. Movie stars, scientists and pro athletes would be treated the same as waitresses, construction workers and cashiers.

Like the military draft, we'd have induction centers, where you would navigate a screening process in order to weed out the idiots (you know, like former Congresspeople) and those who have demonstrated incompetence in their civilian careers (again, former Congresspeople) or an inability to handle their own financial affairs.

We'd also weed out those unfit to serve due to racial or religious prejudices, a long prison record or affiliations with organizations like the Communist Party or Ku Klux Klan.

Salaries? Sorry. Once sworn in as a legislative team member of the United States of America, you'd get a travel stipend for round-trip airfare to Washington, plus a per diem for your service to your country, enough to cover a room at the Holiday Inn, three reasonably priced meals per day and some other minor expenses. That's it. Under the Beano Plan, you're not going to become a Rockefeller or Vanderbilt.

The length of your term? As long as it took to conduct America's business for one fiscal year. If your Congress gets everything done in five months, your term is up. Everybody goes home and the last one out of Washington turns out the lights. Just like on juries, until everybody agrees on a verdict, nobody goes home.

Likewise, under the Beano Plan, unless you agree on a budget and address big picture problems like national defense, you stay put. In the meantime, no recesses. No campaigning. No continuing resolutions. No taxpayer-funded overseas junkets. No voting yourself a pay raise.

I think after some trial and error, we'd get a functional, true representative government that's a lot closer to what the Founders intended.

The Founders all had day jobs. They intended the best and brightest of the country's businessmen, shop keepers, lawyers, doctors, and Indian fighters to assume positions of leadership, serve briefly and then go back home to their lives and professions.

I think my plan would help us get back to that and weed out the professional politicians and all the hangers-on, like party flunkies and lobbyists.

With a shot clock on, there would be no time to waste. Natural-born leaders would eventually emerge, just like what happens in combat and in other emergency situations in real life, and actually lead, rather than wasting everybody's time posturing, holding press conferences and campaigning for the next term and future paydays.

Since there's no way to stay in office for life and make a lot of money, people would forget the old party loyalties and learn to get along in a hurry in order to get home to their families and resume making a living.

A big benefit of the Beano Plan would be that it would remove the possibility of buying a seat in Congress like many wealthy candidates do.

To paraphrase a line from one of my favorite books, "North Toward Home," "anybody who can raise the money necessary to be elected to Congress, doesn't deserve to be in Congress."

It would also effectively kill off family political dynasties. No matter which side of the fence you sit on, I think we can all agree that the country doesn't need any more Kennedys, Clintons, and Bushes.

And not only would my plan eliminate nepotism, gridlock, and corruption, as a temporary position, it would eliminate the need for large staffs, transportation costs, big pension packages, lifetime medical benefits and all the other expensive perks we shell out for.

As for potential drawbacks, I understand that there might be concern that the Beano Plan would prevent us from staffing the government with the "best and the brightest."

I've got some news for you – the government isn't staffed by the best and brightest now. It probably hasn't been for some time. A lot of people think that because Senator So-and-So went to Harvard, he is intelligent. Don't fall into that trap of thinking.

The more Americans that wake up to this reality like Al Davis did, the better we all will be. My friend and former roommate, Sandy Padwe, told me that when Davis got done testifying before Congress, I think it was regarding the NFL's anti-trust suit, he was in disbelief. Nobody had ever seen Davis so shaken up, not even after a bad loss by the Raiders or in the midst of a difficult contract negotiation.

"I thought those people I read about were so smart!" Davis told Padwe.

"It's no different there," Padwe replied. "In fact, there might be a bigger concentration of idiots in Washington than in any other city on the planet."

Could the Beano Plan work? Maybe. Would I tune in? Definitely. A big bonus would be the entertainment it would provide. For example, instead of "Who wants to be a Millionaire?" we could have a gameshow called "Who wants to be Speaker of the House?"

At the very least, *C-SPAN* would become much more interesting because you'd have real blue-collar people at these hearings saying what's on their minds, not professional politicians reading prepared remarks and talking out of both sides of their mouths. So, we might have to loosen FCC rules on profanity, too.

I could also see the networks bidding big bucks for the rights to air Congressional hearings like they do now for the Olympics.

While we're at it, let's start a regular rotation of responsibilities for national political commentators and media members, too. Let them cover sports, courts, or work the enterprise desk every once in a while. I'd love to see James Carville, Chris Matthews or Bill O'Reilly cover a Redskins game or a gang shooting in D.C. for a change.

The political media class is a big part of the problem since journalists today are no longer public watchdogs, but rather loyal lapdogs of the politicians they are supposed to be covering objectively.

Too many live just as extravagantly as the pols. They live in the same gated neighborhoods, are members of the same country clubs, go to the same parties, their kids go to the same elite Washington schools, and they all vacation in Martha's Vineyard together.

It's gotten so bad, some families inhabit both worlds: a wife works in the White House and a husband runs a news division at a major network. It's basically incest.

Don't get me wrong, I still enjoy the Sunday shows, especially "Meet the Press," but I feel like I'm watching reruns anymore. Being the booker of one of these shows must be a lot like being Captain Renault, the French police chief in "Casablanca." Every week you just round up the usual suspects.

Before you read too much into the Beano Plan, understand that I am not obsessed with politics. Everyone has their Walter Mitty moments when they pretend to be someone else, someone important or famous. Rather than be a star quarterback, Hollywood actor or fighter pilot, in my daydreams I've always fantasized about being a conference commissioner, a television executive, or a publishing magnate.

Anyone who has read the many memos I put together at various networks over the years knows that I've always had a thing for schedule-making, conference re-alignment and brainstorming ideas for shows. The Beano Plan is largely a fun exercise in this same sort of fantasy, my way to try on the powdered wigs of James Madison and John Adams.

It's a sign - a bad one - of the times that people today care so much about politics. It's unhealthy. Unless you cover politics or work in politics, no regular American should know who the Chairman of the House Appropriations Committee is, or be able to recite the names of all nine members of the Supreme Court like it's the starting lineup of the '55 Brooklyn Dodgers. Things didn't use to be this way. If you had asked me who Felix Frankfurter was when I was 30, I'd have probably guessed that he was a hot dog vendor at Fenway Park.

When I was growing up, nobody's world, except for maybe my mother's, revolved around politics. I didn't have any interest in it, to my mother's dismay. I didn't have much interest in school, either, to the dismay of both of my parents, not to mention my teachers.

Although it has absolutely nothing to do with scholastic success, I am nevertheless very proud of the fact that I am probably the second-most famous alum of Pittsburgh's Linden Avenue Elementary School. The historian David McCullough was two grades behind me.

Like most American kids, sports were my world. The first three names I learned were Jesus Christ, George Washington, and Babe Ruth – and not necessarily in that order.

Starting around the age of ten, if there was a game or sporting event anywhere in the Greater Pittsburgh area, I was there. I spent more time at Forbes Field and Pitt Stadium and inside the Pitt Pavilion and Duquesne Gardens than I did in my own home.

I was hanging around so much, I got to know many of the city's sportswriters, athletes, coaches, and personalities on a first-name basis. People like Pie Traynor. Honus Wagner. The Chief, Mr. Rooney. When I tell younger Pittsburgh sports fans this, they look at me in disbelief, like I'm some kook claiming to have known people from the Bible.

Back then, these people weren't shut off from the rest of the world by agents, security guards or their entourages. I became something of a "minor" – pun intended – celebrity in town. Chet Smith, the longtime sports editor of the *Pittsburgh Press*, called me Western Pennsylvania's "most intrepid and enthusiastic fan."

When I was 14 or 15, this is right after the war and gas rationing had ended, I expanded my horizons by hitchhiking. Charles Kuralt and Jack Kerouac had nothing on me. I was always on the road.

I went to baseball games in Cleveland, Cincinnati, Philadelphia, Boston, New York, Detroit, Chicago and Washington, D.C. I took in the Penn Relays at Franklin Field. I attended big-time college football games like the Army-Navy game.

You could hitchhike back then. It drove my mother crazy, but hitchhiking probably drove all mothers crazy. They are wired to think that every motorist that stops to give a kid a lift was a serial killer. Usually, I was picked up by ex-GI's who told me I reminded them of a buddy from the service who they regretted not keeping in touch with after the war.

I used to keep track of the longest distances I had hitchhiked to games and when I finally quit in the mid-1950s, my personal records were pretty impressive: I had hitched 700 miles to see a baseball game, 600 miles to see a basketball game and 500 miles to attend a football game.

Call me short-sighted, sentimental, even senile. I agree with Edith and Archie Bunker, singing at their piano in their living room on 704 Hauser Street: those were the days! There was nothing like the late 1940s and early 1950s. The only things we were missing were air conditioning, civil rights and "The Mary Tyler Moore Show."

Sure, Pittsburgh was dark and dirty, but that's because the mills were running at full blast. Jobs were plentiful. Everything – food, gasoline, refrigerators, cars, and homes – was cheap. Crime was low. For a time, we were the only ones with the Bomb. After the war, America was the undefeated, undisputed heavyweight champ of the world. Life was good. What made it so good, I now understand, was that it was simple.

So simple that one of the biggest thrills of my youth was the time my friend Joe Knight found a pinball machine in the backroom of a bar in Pittsburgh's Bloomfield section.

The closest I've come to replicating this sensational event was fifty years later, when one of our gang who hung out at the Ruddy Duck at the Ramada in Pittsburgh found a magic (in other words, broken) payphone that permitted free long-distance calls.

You have no idea the excitement the former discovery generated. Believe it or not, for many years pinball had been banned in this country. It was some kind of bullshit about exposing children to gambling at a young age and truancy. It was like Prohibition, only for kids. And Joe didn't just find any old pinball machine – he found one that didn't tilt!

Only thing rarer, I discovered not long after, was finding a girl that put out. With the Pill still a decade off, things were so tough for a guy back then, a French kiss was considered a major conquest. Reaching second base? That was like hitting a three-team parlay. Getting laid was a home run, but for me, it was as difficult as hitting one out in straightaway center at the Polo Grounds.

Even if you were lucky enough to find a chick willing to fool around, you had to operate like you were a spy behind the Iron Curtain. We had code words and everything.

For example, if you asked somebody for a cigarette, you were just asking for a smoke. If you asked for cigarettes, plural, you were really asking if they had condoms.

All the cloak and dagger got pretty tiring. Pretty soon, there were enough of us who worked up the nerve to take a road trip to the whorehouses just over the state line in Steubenville, Ohio.

I remember the first one I went to, the fee was five bucks. That was in 1950. There were about five of us there in the waiting room, like a doctor's office, nervously waiting our turn. I don't know what we were more worried about, the cops raiding the joint or what to do once we got called back.

Looking back, half the fun was getting there. There was a popular song at the time called "Highways are Happy Ways." We'd be flying down U.S. Route 22 at seventy miles an hour, singing along with Jack Smith and the Clark Sisters while improvising our own lyrics: "Highways are happy ways when they lead the way to Steubenville."

I once told Jimmy the Greek, Steubenville's other famous native son next to Dean Martin, about our adventures.

"Some of us worked our whole lives to get out," he laughed. "And Beans couldn't wait to get into town."

* * *

The most important road trip I ever took wasn't to a game or a whorehouse. It was the first one I took in the fall of 1945 to the Kiskiminetas Springs School, an all-male boarding school located about 35 miles outside of Pittsburgh in rural Saltsburg, Pennsylvania.

Going to Kiski was one of the best things to ever happen to me. If I hadn't gone there, I doubt my life and career would have unfolded the way it did. It was at Kiski that I decided I wanted to be a sportswriter or work in sports in some capacity.

At first, prep school took some getting used to for this city kid. The campus, a former mineral spa and summer resort situated on the border of Westmoreland and Indiana counties, was pretty secluded. But that turned out to be a good thing.

Without distractions like movie theaters and girls, I actually concentrated on my studies. I became heavily involved in student activities, joining the staffs of the school paper and yearbook. I was class secretary, too.

I even curtailed my hitchhiking habit to a certain extent, but that was because I had a responsibility to attend school sporting events. That was probably the main reason I was there in the first place.

While Kiski's first-class academics impressed my parents, its storied athletic tradition was the big lure for me. At one time, Kiski had a reputation for being the cradle of college football's big stars. At last count, 11 members of the College Football Hall of Fame are Kiski alums.

You've got Andy Hastings, an all-American halfback on what was maybe the greatest Pitt football team of all-time in 1916. Tom Davies and Herb Stein, who played on Pop Warner's great post-World War I Pitt teams, were Kiski men, too.

Harry Stuhldreher, quarterback of the "Four Horsemen," was a member of Kiski's class of 1921. The 1928 Kiski team had ten future college football team captains on it.

Thanks to my father, a diehard Stanford fan, I had learned about "Bones" Hamilton and "Monk" Moscrip, two members of Stanford's legendary "Vow Boys" teams of the 1930s, at an early age. The two Kiski alums, along with a handful of other Stanford players, vowed that they would not lose to Southern Cal during the course of their four-year playing careers in Palo Alto and they never did.

Another Kiski alum was Cliff Montgomery, quarterback of the Columbia team that beat Stanford in the 1934 Rose Bowl. "Big Jim" Daniel of Ohio State and the first-ever captain of the Cleveland Browns, played at Kiski before the war.

I don't know if there was a day I was more proud of being a Kiski alum than November 10, 1951. My old man's alma mater was led to victory over Southern Cal by my friend and fellow member of Kiski's class of '49, Bob Mathias.

Mathias returned a kickoff 96 yards for a touchdown and Stanford intercepted a Frank Gifford pass and scored late to win, 27-20.

If the name Mathias sounds familiar, it should – he won the decathlon in the 1948 London Summer Olympics, and duplicated that feat in Helsinki in 1952. Mathias became a Congressman in California.

No one ever seems to agree with me when I say that his most noteworthy accomplishment was being a classmate of mine in prep school! I may not have had many academic highlights, but I had a knack for going to school with famous people.

While I played some varsity basketball and was captain of the tennis team one year, I knew I would never be a part of Kiski's football tradition. I just wanted to be around a big athletics program and gain experience anyway I could.

As it worked out, that experience wasn't playing football for Kiski, but covering its teams. Thanks to my previous relationships with several Pittsburgh sportswriters, I got a gig as a freelance correspondent. Mostly, I telephoned the results of Kiski athletic contests into the Pittsburgh papers. I also did a little bit of writing, which got me some attention – but not because people thought I was talented.

On one occasion, I wrote an editorial in the student paper that pissed off the school's headmaster so much he wanted to kick me out. He redoubled his efforts to get rid of me when I contributed a piece to one of the Pittsburgh papers that created a scandal on campus.

The story was about one of our athletes who was rumored to have been offered a scholarship to attend a prestigious eastern school. I don't remember all the details, but either the offer fell through or else the kid wasn't accepted. I don't think the publicity my story generated in any way influenced the school's decision, but perhaps I did jump the gun in my eagerness to score a "scoop."

The kid didn't seem too broken up about things, but our headmaster was a different story. He blamed me, suggesting my piece had somehow sullied Kiski's reputation. At his request, I was brought up on some kind of bogus charge in front of the student court. Making matters more interesting was the fact that the student who sat at the head of the court was the subject of my article! The court found me not guilty, but that wasn't the only happy ending.

The student in question would attend another college, where he met his future wife. He returned to Kiski and joined the faculty. He later thanked me and told me that if he had gone on to attend his first choice, he'd have never met the love of his life. I think it was more the forces of fate at work than it was anything I did, but of all the names I've been called in my life, Cupid is better than some of the unprintable ones.

I graduated from Kiski in June 1949, the recipient of the Latin Award and a scholarship to Brown University. Don't ask me how I mastered Latin. I took it because it seemed easier than French and German. To my ear, everything in French sounded dirty or sexual, and in German, everything sounded like "we march into France tomorrow."

At Brown, I was not so much big man on campus, but a man who was all over campus. I helped organize inter-fraternity sports for the athletic department and worked for both the school paper, the *Daily Herald*, and radio station.

I had my share of college fun, which included stealing a fire truck in a prank that thankfully I got away with. I didn't get away with everything, though.

In May 1951, I hitchhiked up to Boston to watch the Pirates play the Boston Braves in a Sunday doubleheader. I watched Warren Spahn toss a shutout in the first game and the Bucs' Cliff Chambers throw a no-hitter in the second. I couldn't believe my good luck – it was the Pirates' first no-hitter in 44 years, and I had been there to see it.

And then when I got back to campus, I couldn't believe my bad luck. I called my parents and told them that I had stayed in all weekend to study. My father said that he was surprised to hear that, since he had just read a nugget in Les Biederman's *Pittsburgh*

Press "Scoreboard" column about a Beano Cook sighting at Braves Field!

It probably wasn't much of a surprise to my parents that I didn't last very long at Brown. Due to my involvement in some other extra-curricular activities that I'll tell you about later on, my grades suffered.

I didn't have any regrets about leaving Brown, other than maybe the disappointment it caused my parents at the time, and I still don't. I believe that things happen in life at the right times, in the right places, and for the right reasons.

That right time turned out to be the latter half of 1951. The right place was Pittsburgh, and specifically Pitt, where I enrolled for the fall term.

The right reasons? Fatefully, my homecoming coincided with several special job opportunities, the start of some foundational friendships and my timely exposure to essential life lessons that I would have otherwise missed out on.

In my opinion, all of these things made for a complete education, one that probably far surpassed what I might have gotten at Brown or what would have accompanied any other school's diploma, for that matter.

For starters, if I hadn't come back home, I wouldn't have gotten what I consider to be the most important job I've ever had. I got really lucky when Larry Fagan, who spent thirty years as editor of the *Pittsburgh Press*, hired me as a copy boy.

Almost immediately, I was hooked on the newspaper business. I loved everything about it, the scent of fresh newsprint, the chattering teletypes, and especially the hustle and bustle of the newsroom. The atmosphere was intoxicating. I was put on the city desk, which, after my experiences on school papers, felt like a promotion to the *Daily Planet*.

Fagan was my Perry White. I'll never forget eavesdropping on a heated phone conversation between Fagan and what I could only surmise was a crooked public official. Fagan hung up and yelled into the newsroom, "no comment, boys." He immediately put three more reporters on the story. That, I learned, was how news was flushed out!

Working part-time, I made 75 cents an hour and sometimes as much as $30 a week, but the lessons I learned about both the news business and the business of life were priceless. At the *Press*, I got one of the best educations on people and the real world imaginable.

There was, however, a trade-off: my romanticized view of the newspaper business didn't last long. Being in the newsroom of a big city paper as a young kid in the early 1950s was an intimidating and eye-opening experience.

You are exposed to things you don't get at a prep school paper or even in journalism school. I'm talking about drinking problems. Gambling problems. Marital problems. Favoritism. Sexism. Racism.

I was on the desk late one evening when a three-alarm fire broke out in the Hill District, which is a neighborhood in Pittsburgh inhabited mostly by poor blacks. The reporter heading out to cover it wanted a photographer to accompany him, but one of the editors quickly overruled him. Because of the late hour, that would have meant paying the photographer overtime and, the editor explained, "we don't pay overtime for nigger fires."

I felt like Dorothy talking to Toto in "The Wizard of Oz." *I have a feeling,* I said to myself, *we're not at Kiski anymore.* It was the first time I had really heard that kind of talk. It was disgusting. I didn't know what to do or say. To be honest, as a part-timer, I wasn't even technically on the totem pole, so there was nothing I could do or say.

Just like how Dorothy's black and white world changed when she landed in Oz, the incident that night at the *Press* colorized my world, too. I learned that when it comes right down to it, there is ultimately only one color that matters in this world - green.

Everything boils down to money. It doesn't matter if you are talking about newspapers or television networks or some other business. That was the case at the *Press.* The paper wasn't run by racists. Even if it had been, they'd have been outranked by the bean counters. The fact of the matter was, in that pre-politically correct era, in a super competitive news town with three big dailies, bottom lines were bottom lines.

I grew up, professionally, pretty damn fast in that environment. I didn't like a lot of the things that I heard, but I learned how the world worked. I especially didn't like getting my ass chewed out, but I learned how to take it like a man, something kids don't get today.

I was thankful for those lessons, especially during my time in the army and later at Pitt, when I was called on the carpet nearly every other day by my bosses, and also when I got on the air, because it taught me how to handle critics and hate mail.

Although I spent a few summers working on a master's degree in journalism on Pitt's dime, I never got one. It took me two semesters at the University of Missouri and one at Northwestern to figure out that the free education I got at the *Press* was a doctorate.

That's largely due to the examples set by Fagan, Chet Smith, and writers like Biederman and Carl Hughes, who left the business and went on to be the president of Kennywood, a historic amusement park in Pittsburgh.

Those men were all great teachers, but I owe the most to the person who I believe is the best newspaperman in Pittsburgh history, Roy McHugh. The dean of Pittsburgh sportswriters and one of the best columnists I've ever read, McHugh remains one of the biggest influences in my professional life.

Despite being fifteen years older than me, McHugh was extremely patient, answering what had to be an annoying kid's endless series of questions.

He taught me the fundamentals, the small details that make or break a story and mean the difference between good writing and great writing, though I was never really able to use this knowledge to do any great writing myself.

A lot of what McHugh taught me would prove invaluable to my career in publicity. I'll never forget one memorable fall day in November 1951 when he showed me two pictures that had just come off the wire. One was of a Penn State football player with a good-looking coed and the other, the same player beside the Nittany Lion statue.

"Which one would you use?" he asked.

"The statue," I answered.

"Why?" asked McHugh.

"It's a school landmark that alums and fans know."

"Wrong answer," said McHugh. "Alums recognize the statue. But you're not working for Penn State alums, fans, or even directly for the readers, for that matter. You're first negotiating with people who work on the sports desk, and they ultimately decide which photos get in the paper. The guys who work on the desk, they all like pretty women."

I never forgot the lesson. When I was an SID and I was trying to get space in the paper for Pitt's wrestling or baseball teams, which was much more difficult than for the football or basketball teams, I would round up an attractive coed to pose with an athlete for a shot outside the Cathedral of Learning or some other campus landmark.

Then I'd call up the desk and say, "I'm sending over a shot of the team captain. Wait until you see this blonde." Sure enough, the photo would be in the next day's paper, and above the fold!

"I never should have told you that," McHugh later teased me. "You're singlehandedly turning Pittsburgh's newspapers into skin magazines!"

The best teacher I ever had was Bob Prince. If anybody knew anything about a well-rounded, worldly education, it was the Gunner. The son of a career army officer, he had crisscrossed the country countless times and had seen a lot of the world outside our borders, too.

By his own admission, Prince attended more than a dozen schools before graduating from Schenley High in Pittsburgh. For a time, he was on the swim team at Pitt and was rumored to have picked up credits at Stanford and Oklahoma. He even briefly attended Harvard law school.

I don't think anybody can say for sure where Prince ultimately got his bachelor's degree, but another great Pittsburgh character, the writer Jack Henry, was probably correct in his claim that "Prince's diploma has more handprints on it than Elizabeth Taylor's ass."

I got to know Prince by hanging around. Which is probably the best advice I can give to an aspiring sportswriter, reporter, announcer, SID, or anybody who wants to get into sports, sports media or media relations in some way, shape or form. Hang around.

I know sneaking onto press row or into a pressbox is a lot more difficult than it was when I was coming up due to all the security, but you can still hang around press gates and studio parking lots, as well as bars and restaurants that host remotes, and introduce yourself to some of your favorite writers, radio, or TV personalities.

Or you can write them. With e-mail, it won't even cost you a stamp. Just be respectful and sincere. You'd be amazed at the number of men and women who will remember the position they were in at your age and will write back to you and provide advice, friendship and who knows, maybe even help you out down the road with a recommendation letter or a job.

That's what happened with Prince. Years later, I wanted to thank him for taking me under his wing. I offered to take him out to dinner or buy him a few drinks. To my surprise, he flat out refused.

"You don't need to pay *me* back," he said. "One of these days, some kid is going to find you and ask you for advice or some help. Help him out like I helped you."

Prince opened doors for me all over town. I got a job as a student assistant doing publicity in Pitt's athletic department. I also worked for the Honus Wagner Leagues and thanks to recommendations from Prince and McHugh, tried to develop something of a reputation as a writer by contributing articles to community papers. I even got a few bylines in an old magazine called *The Pittsburgher.*

When I wasn't at work at a Pitt game or at the *Press*, in class or banging away at a typewriter, I could be found in Prince's shadow, taking notes.

Right away, I noticed that he never took himself seriously and wasn't afraid to go out on a limb in terms of trying out new material. Many lines bombed, but older Pirates' fans know that many "Gunnerisms" have stood the test of time. He wasn't afraid to laugh at himself or let others laugh at him. It was due to his example that I've never hesitated to ham it up on camera, sing a fight song on the air, or wear a crazy costume for a segment.

Prince floated around town, a blur of colorful sports jackets and cigarette smoke. In a way he reminded me of a mobster; his right hand was always outstretched, ready for a warm greeting and handshake.

He was extremely generous with both his time and money. He picked up more checks than anybody I've ever known.

And he knew everybody's name, everywhere you went. At Frankie Gustine's place. At Klein's. The Clock. The Home Plate Café. It was uncanny.

I'm not talking about sportswriters and athletes, but the regular, blue-collar people he came into contact with. The ushers at Forbes Field. Parking lot attendants. Doormen. Waiters. Barbers. Bartenders.

Prince had a reputation as a hard drinker, but he was more of a hard worker than anything else. Drinking was a way to network, a way to bridge personal lives to professional livelihoods.

Although I've never been a booze hound, I've tried to follow his lead in terms of making connections. I feel bad if I forget the name of the receptionist in my doctor's office or the guy working the press elevator at Heinz Field. It's not only a good way to pick up tips and stories and build up professional contacts and friendships, it's also a good way to go through life.

My willingness and ability to get to know and get along with people in all positions, at all levels of power, and from all walks of life, from PAs to producers, talent to television executives, interns, athletic directors, and university presidents alike, might be a reason why my career has lasted as long as it has.

I also owe Prince for instilling in me certain necessities of sound financial planning. The first of these was deferred compensation. It's something to think about. If you are presented with the option, don't take everything right away. Sometimes, such as when you're having a good year in betting or have some other income that's off the books, it's smart to stay in a lower tax bracket. And you never know when you might be out of work, so it's comforting to know you have deferred money to fall back on.

It was Prince who taught me to keep track of expenses. It's become a lifelong preoccupation which has saved me a considerable amount of cash over the years. For Prince, it was second nature. He always had some kind of action, a ton of business ventures, that reflected his wide variety of interests and also his love of longshot bets: TV stations; racehorses; South American oil wells.

He needed to offset the losers. The way he saw it, there was nothing that couldn't be expensed or written off. You just had to use your head, or, in some cases, your imagination. For example, "if you're at a bar or restaurant and you get up to go take a piss," Prince wisely counseled me, "put in for cab fare."

Expenses also are one of the few weapons you have with which to fight the Internal Revenue Service. I learned this particular lesson as a result of a gig I got renting out canoes at the North Park Boathouse in Allison Park during the summers. That job provided me with an occasional date, a few extra bucks and, most notably, my first battle with the I.R.S.

They decided I had made a mistake on my return and that I owed eight more dollars. When the letters showed up in my mailbox, I ignored them. It was eight bucks. No big deal, right? Wrong.

A few months later, an agent showed up at my door! I couldn't believe they'd go to such lengths, treating a college kid like Al Capone. I made it worse on myself by sharing those sentiments out loud. I'll never forget the agent's reply.

"Listen, kid," he said. "It's only eight bucks, but we'll spend a million dollars, if necessary, to get those eight bucks."

At that very moment, my lifelong rivalry with those bastards, as well as all state and local tax collectors, was born. It puts Pitt-Penn State, even North and South Korea, to shame. Every April I think of that smug agent when I give my accountant a mountain of ammunition in the form of expenses and send him off to war. Like Churchill's famous World War II speech about fighting the Germans on the beaches and in the hills, I shall never surrender.

You shouldn't, either. Now I'm not advising you to cheat on your taxes, but your long-term goal should be to keep your casualty numbers as low as possible. That's how you keep more of your money. After all, it's *your* money. You worked hard for it. If they want it, they should have to work just as hard, if not harder, for every penny they take.

I paid close attention to Prince's sermons and have used his teachings throughout my career. And I've tried to impart his wisdom to others. I'd like to think that I have my own disciples – writers, SIDs, TV talent and league executives – who still keep every receipt, pad their expense accounts and write-off as much as possible as a result of my example.

Prince also dispensed advice intended to help your love life. He was holding court at Gustine's late one night when someone asked him if he liked eating pussy. The Gunner was pretty well lubricated after a few Crown Royals with Coke – that was his drink – and his response was an all-timer.

"Do it like it?" he roared. "If it was air conditioned, I'd move in!"

All the advice in the world couldn't have helped me with the broads. I've never had much luck with women. But betting, that's another story. I've had some big wins in my life. And that's starting from the beginning. That big lottery in the sky, the birthday number I drew – September 1, 1931 – I hit the jackpot.

I remember very little about the Great Depression. I was too young to fight in World War II. I entered college around the time the war in Korea broke out. In a way, it was unfair that college students got deferments, but I'm going to be honest when I say that I'm glad I did. That might sound selfish, but it's a fact. And I would be too old for Vietnam, unless Ho Chi Minh had somehow launched an invasion of California.

Even so, when I graduated from Pitt in August 1954 the draft was still on, so I had a service commitment to fulfill. I learned that my number was coming up at my local draft board, so I had to decide in a hurry: should I enlist in another branch of the service or let the army draft me?

I used to get seasick on the canoes at North Park, so the Navy and Coast Guard were out. The Air Force? At this point of my life I'd yet to fly and was not as anti-air travel as I'd soon become, but I'd never been particularly interested in airplanes.

I've long believed that the only two groups in this country that know what they're doing and how to do it right are Catholic nuns and the Marines. I was only eligible for one of those groups and I knew I wasn't tough enough for the Marine Corps. That left one option.

I am pretty grateful for what the army has done on our behalf. Grant made sure "Dixie" didn't replace the "Star-Spangled Banner." Patton took care of the Nazis and MacArthur handled the Japs. And Ike would give us eight years of misused syntax, but only three-percent inflation. It was settled.

I was inducted into the U.S. Army the day after my 23rd birthday, on September 2, 1954. It would be a two-year enlistment, which according to my calculations meant that I would be discharged prior to the start of the 1956 football season.

I reported for basic training and just like in the movies, they cut off all your hair and assign you a serial number. I still remember mine: Cook, Beano, Private. Serial number five two dash three one nine dash four zero eight. If I am ever taken prisoner by Penn State fans, that's all they are getting out of me.

I was a city kid used to cabbing it or bussing it everywhere, so all the marching took some getting used to. I somehow got out of boot camp in one piece and got pretty lucky in that I never got sent overseas to some God-forsaken place like Greenland.

In fact, I spent the entirety of my hitch stationed in my own backyard, with a unit in an area of Pittsburgh called South Park that was charged with defending the city and the steel mills in the event of an air attack by the Soviets.

We started off with the older anti-aircraft guns like those used in World War II, and by the time I got out the 509th AAA Battalion was equipped with Nike surface-to-air missiles.

You'll probably be relieved to know that I wasn't in charge of shooting down Russian bombers. I was in headquarters company. I worked in public affairs and did clerical work, typing and filling out forms, that sort of thing.

I hated nearly every single minute of it. Twenty years later, during my brief stint on the sports staff of the *St. Petersburg Times*, Hubert Mizell joked that the army should have pardoned Eddie Slovik, the only U.S. service member shot for desertion during World War II, and shot me. At least I thought he was joking.

All of my former commanding officers would have agreed with Mizell. I was probably the biggest headache for the U.S. Army since Rommel.

A few years after I got out, my mother and I were watching a funeral for a big shot general on television and as the horse-drawn caissons were pulling the flag-draped coffin down the avenue in Washington, D.C., I had to laugh when she made the comment, "if only the army could do everything else as well as they do a funeral."

I wasn't in uniform very long before I learned that the guys that run the army don't do much of anything right except funerals. I also discovered that they don't like suggestions, especially from lowly privates.

"EM (enlisted man) is reluctant in adhering to and constantly criticized army policies, procedures and channels," wrote my battery commander in one of my fitness reports.

He was probably referring to one of my best ideas, at least in my opinion, which was the proposal I put together with the intention of getting my buddies and I more leave. Since you've already been briefed on the Beano Plan, we'll call this one "Operation Weekend Pass."

The way I introduced it to the brass, the army shelled out approximately X-amount of taxpayer dollars to feed Y-Y-number of soldiers in the 18th AAA Group on post each weekend of every month.

After conducting interviews with the cooks, as well as my buddies about their eating habits, I came up with some numerical dollar amount that could theoretically be saved if they let us go into town every other weekend since we'd be responsible for paying for our own meals. As you can imagine, it, along with all of my other crackpot ideas, was rejected.

Back in the barracks, one of my buddies thanked me for giving it a try and then told me a story relayed to him by a friend who was in the Navy. This guy was on an aircraft carrier and the skipper regularly ordered aviation fuel dumped overboard at year's end so that the carrier would be allotted the same amount of fuel the following year. I learned that no branch of the service was interested in cost-saving measures. It's no wonder our defense budgets have gotten out of control.

As much as I hated the dullness of duty, I didn't dare dream of going AWOL. But I never gave up trying to get off post legally. One of the few times I managed to succeed led to one of the most memorable trips of my life.

Planning for the mission began in late 1955, when I learned that Pitt was going to play Georgia Tech in the Sugar Bowl in New Orleans. The game would be historic because Pitt's Bobby Grier became the first black player to play in the Sugar Bowl. The occasion was personally historic for me, too: it was the first time I ever flew in an airplane.

A small handful of us, all Pitt alums, came up with a plan to go to the game. It was an interservice operation. We found these pilots in the Air Force reserves, also Pitt alums, who had to log some flight time. Pilots had to fly so many hours every month.

According to the flight plan, we wouldn't fly directly into New Orleans so the brass wouldn't figure out that we were using government aircraft to go to a football game. The pilots put us on the manifest and we made sure everything was set with the paperwork.

In the dark, early morning hours of January 2, 1956, we boarded a B-17 bomber in Pittsburgh. I quickly realized that we weren't flying first class. It was fucking freezing in there.

My stomach did a flip when I was handed a parachute. I started regretting the idea immediately. After putting it on, I took my seat inside the bare bones metal skeleton of the bomber. There were about six of us, including the two pilots.

Once we got airborne, the turbulence was awful. To this day, I have an extreme fear or, more precisely, an extreme hatred of air travel, and it probably started with this fateful first flight.

Anyway, to take my mind off of the cold and the chop, about halfway through the flight, as we were flying over these little flyspeck towns, I started pretending I was a waist gunner shooting at Messerschmitts during a bombing mission over Germany.

Next thing I know, we landed in Dallas. After taking on some fuel, we flew to Biloxi, Mississippi. From there, we took a bus into New Orleans, walked to Tulane Stadium, watched the Sugar Bowl, then got back on the bus, boarded the bomber in Biloxi, and flew home.

Pitt lost the game on a controversial call involving Grier, I didn't get to see Bourbon Street and the flights weren't much fun, but looking back, it's nevertheless nice to know that my first airplane ride was on the taxpayers.

The most heroic act I committed on behalf of my country didn't take place on a far-off battlefield, but in a Pittsburgh parking lot. Long story short, two guys in our outfit stole a bunch of rifles out of the armory with the intention of selling them to civilians. I knew that with the way the army typically handled things in terms of group punishment, we'd all get in hot water.

I did some detective work and found out these guys were hiding the rifles in a trunk of a car, got the guns and replaced them before anybody realized they were missing. The brass never found out about it and I never received so much as a thank you from anybody, much less a medal. But it was the right thing to do.

Maybe it's true that one good turn deserves another because right around the same time I learned that my enlistment would be ending early, the job of athletic publicity director at Pitt opened up. This was December 1955. Talk about perfect timing.

I got in touch with Pitt's graduate director of athletics, Frank Carver, who I had gotten to know when I worked in the athletic department, and he told me that I should apply for the job.

Next, I called everybody I knew and asked if they would put in a good word for me with Captain Thomas Hamilton, Pitt's AD.

Meanwhile, my mother typed up a cover letter. In fact, except for a couple of heartfelt paragraphs that I scribbled together, she largely wrote the thing. After we settled on the final draft, she insisted that I did not fold the letter and instead mailed it and the other contents inside a large flat envelope, which she thought looked more professional.

Today, I still advise young job seekers to first send an introduction letter in a large, flat envelope, to be followed by collection of newspaper clips or a demo reel.

Inside the envelope were recommendations from Chet Smith and Carl Hughes, as well as a glowing endorsement from my outfit's commanding officer, General Stephen Mellnik.

Mellnik, a West Pointer, was one of ten American prisoners of war, the only large-scale group of POWs, to escape from a Japanese prison camp during the war in the Pacific. These heroes brought the first word of the infamous Bataan Death March to the outside world. The escape was front-page news all over the country in 1944.

So, I was both proud and at the same time a little surprised to read Mellnik's recommendation: "Private Cook is a person whom I would be willing to trust with the reputation of my unit. I commend him to anyone who needs a highly motivated individual."

I later learned that Mellnik had delegated responsibility for the letter to one of his aides, a highly motivated individual in his own right as it pertained to this particular assignment.

As the story was recounted to me by a buddy who had been eavesdropping on the conversation outside the CO's office, Mellnik had ordered his aide to do everything humanly possible to make sure that I was successfully separated from the service and that I found employment in the civilian world so as to prevent my reenlistment.

"If you bring Private Cook back into the army," Mellnik threatened him, "I'll court martial you."

CHAPTER 2

Insult Duke.

When the army granted me an honorable discharge in early 1956, I raced home so fast with my separation papers, John Woodruff, the Pitt track star who won a gold medal in the 1936 Berlin Olympics, couldn't have caught me.

I was not waiting around for fear that Uncle Sam might change his mind about letting me become a free agent. I was ready to get on with my life and, as Paul Brown and Chuck Noll used to say, my "life's work" – whatever that was going to be.

When I look back on it, I realize my hitch in the service truly wasn't that bad. I didn't get shot at or have to shoot anybody. I had some fun adventures, like the Sugar Bowl mission, and I made some good friends. If not for the army, I would not have met John O'Connor, a University of Cincinnati grad who became my best friend.

The experience was even educational, as I learned how to make a bed with square corners. But since I haven't had an inspection of my bunk, either by an officer or a woman, in some time, I doubt I'll have any further need for that skill in my eighties.

I am still very proud to have served my country. I just couldn't stand the chickenshit. The politics. I remember thinking that something was very wrong during basic training when our company was forced to give money to the community chest so the battery commander could make points with the battalion commander with our dough.

If I had only known then that that kind of stuff was commonplace, I might have pulled a Corporal Klinger and bucked for a Section Eight. After all, I was already getting the ads for slips and brassieres. I'm kidding.

I did make up my mind, however, that once I was out, I was out. Even if World War III started and I was called back up, I wasn't going voluntarily or by myself. There would be three of us: me and an MP on each arm.

My new freedom, however, brought about a new kind of stress, the kind that accompanies unemployment. All my life, I've had a fear of being out of work. That anxiety started at this time. I was so desperate, I started applying for all kinds of jobs.

Some were out there. Really out there. For example, and I've never told anybody this before, I went through a lengthy interview process for some kind of mysterious position with the Central Intelligence Agency, but I didn't get the job. This proves that the C.I.A. does do things right on occasion.

For a long time I wondered what happened, so in 1976 I filed a Freedom of Information Act request to try to find out. According to the redacted file I was received, I didn't fail the tests or have any black marks on my record. The job I had interviewed for was eliminated. It was as simple as that.

The Russians and the K.G.B. never knew how lucky they were. Of course, the same could probably be said for our government. Secret agent Double-O Beano would have been an international incident waiting to happen.

Plunging ever deeper into the depths of my despair, I almost - almost - started missing the army. I recalled our last few weeks in uniform, when an officer approached O'Connor and mentioned a re-enlistment bonus, O'Connor joked that he could get more holding up a gas station. I had a good laugh at that memory, until I realized that the army didn't even bother with me, let alone offer a bonus to re-up. Feeling unwanted, even by the army, was an uncomfortable and unfamiliar feeling.

I began to worry that I may be working at a gas station, or worse, the one that O'Connor held up. And then the call came that I'd been hired as Pitt's new athletic publicity director. I'll never forget the date - June 20, 1956 - nor the sense of relief.

My luck was really running, too. July 1st was a Sunday, and the athletic department was operating on a half-week work schedule since the Fourth of July was that Wednesday. By the time July rolled around, I had already gotten paid for one day, and the first three days of the week, I had off. Being gainfully employed seemed pretty easy.

As was the case for many returning to work after a long holiday break, reality hit hard. I had been sitting alone in my new office in the Field House for maybe a minute on that first day when it suddenly occurred me that I had no idea how to be an athletic publicity director, or, as the job was more commonly referred to, a sports information director. We called each other SIDs back then.

At 24, I was the second youngest SID in the country, next to Jim Brock at Texas Christian. Bob Wycoff was my predecessor. A 1950 Pitt graduate, he was the school's first full-time SID. He became director of the university's main public relations office, which is why the SID job had opened up.

There was no training or orientation. Nobody introduced me to the coaches. As far as I know, John Michelosen, our head football coach, had no input on my hiring. I'm certain he would have objected had he only known what our working relationship would be like.

I found out that I wouldn't have much money to work with, either. There wasn't much in the budget for publicity. Back then, the whole athletic department was more or less a mom-and-pop operation. Actually, it was all pops. There were no women outside of the half dozen female secretaries who worked for the athletic department.

I didn't have my own parking space, but that was okay, because I didn't have a car. There weren't any students working in the office during the summer, so for the time being it was just me.

E.J. Borghetti, the current SID at Pitt, not only has a car and two offices in two different facilities on opposite sides of town, he has a staff bigger than Ike had to plan the D-Day landings. I imagine he has plenty of money to work with, too. Pitt also has its own studio in order to produce coaches shows and in-house content on its athletes – an idea I actually pitched Captain Hamilton on when I applied for the job some sixty years ago. E.J. doesn't need any of it, though. From what I've been told from people whose opinions I trust, people in TV and college sports, he's the best in the business.

Business is the best word to describe it. The world of college athletics is a lot different than it was when I was getting started. Today, coaches and athletic directors are paid millions of dollars. I think John Michelosen received a salary of around $24,000 a year from Pitt in the late 1950s. He also got a car, probably a Ford or an Oldsmobile, from the university. The big perk, this was before OPEC, was free gas because it was so cheap back then.

I don't know if coaches today get free gas, but they all drive luxury cars and SUVs. They probably fly first class when they're out recruiting, too. Our total recruiting budget for all varsity sports at Pitt in 1962 was $14,000. That wouldn't cover the monthly phone bill in any major college athletic department today.

It's a never-ending arms race. Perhaps appropriately, stadiums and practice facilities are bigger, more expensive, and tougher to get into than the NORAD nuclear bunker. When you add up all the coaches, secretaries, nutritionists, tutors, video technicians, and other support personnel, athletic departments now employ hundreds of people.

They're all issued computers and cell phones. In 1956, I rummaged around the Field House and found an old clipboard. It became my portable filing system. I used it to keep track of my schedule, organize appointments, notes, newspaper clippings, phone numbers and story ideas, pretty much anything that would pop into my cluttered head at any given moment.

I still have it. Anybody who knows me well knows about the clipboard and my attachment to it. Lieutenant Columbo wouldn't investigate a case without first putting on his raincoat. Likewise, I don't go anywhere without the clipboard.

Another old-fashioned tool that I had was my big mouth, which on occasion would do me more harm than good, but I considered it more of an asset than a liability. After all, I had basically talked myself into this job, so there was no reason I couldn't talk my way through it. And what I lacked in experience, money, and help, I figured I could more than make up for in energy and enthusiasm.

There was something else that I had. On "The NFL Today," the Greek used to have his checklists, and what I am talking about would fit under "Intangibles." It was an unconditional love for the University of Pittsburgh.

"I believe that I have something of far more value to contribute – an intangible asset that is a must for a job of this nature – a love of and an enthusiasm for the work," I explained in a letter to Captain Hamilton in March 1956.

"I live with every Pitt win and die with every loss. I love Pitt, something I believe necessary in the job I am applying for. To me, it would be more than just a place where I would work eight or nine hours and then go home. The job would be a part of me and I would be devoted to it every minute of the day."

I'm proud to say that I kept that promise. There were ups and downs, but that was exactly the way it would be for the better part of the next ten years.

Clipboard in hand and my heart bursting with Pitt pride, I hit the road that summer, traveling around Western Pennsylvania attending luncheons and giving what were essentially pep talks to booster groups.

I later found out that season ticket sales for my first football season in 1956 nearly doubled, from 9,144 in 1955 to 17,142. Part of it was that we were coming off a Sugar Bowl and were expecting to have a good team that year, but I like to think that my hard work and passionate sales pitches played a part in that success.

Thankfully, I had Frank Carver, too. He was my immediate boss. His official title was Graduate Manager of Athletics, which basically meant that he was the senior alum and our Assistant Athletic Director.

Carver had been at Pitt for more than 30 years. A member of the Class of '27, he had served as publicist for Jock Sutherland's great teams in the 1930s. He's the one who came up with the name of "Dream Backfield" to describe the Panthers' unstoppable quartet of Dick Cassiano, John Chickerneo, Marshall Goldberg, and Curly Stebbins during the 1937 national championship season.

I had gotten to know Carver when I was a student. I spent more time in his office listening to him tell stories than I did in class. He had the best stories.

He told me about the time he bet broadcaster Ted Husing ten dollars that Pitt would beat Army by three touchdowns in 1931. Ten bucks back in the Depression was like a $100 bill today, a huge bet, and he had to chase Husing down Cardiac Hill after the game to collect.

My favorite was his colorful description of Arnold Greene, Pitt's giant, 250-pound fullback, tumbling out of bounds in the 1936 Nebraska game and the groaning from the crowd when Greene slid into a huge pile of shit left by a team of oxen which had been pulling a covered wagon during the halftime show.

Carver reported directly to our AD, Captain Thomas Hamilton, who I will tell you about in greater detail later on. Hamilton, who had a storied career as a naval officer and in college athletics, ran a tight ship at Pitt and employed Carver much like his executive officer.

Carver was not only one of the classiest and most intelligent people I ever met in athletics, he was one of the most supportive and patient bosses one could ever ask for. He gave me two important pieces of advice that first day in 1956.

"Number one," he said, "no matter how much you mess up, kick off will be at one-thirty. Number two, they always have the last word."

He didn't have to identify the "they." I knew he was referring to the media. When I started at Pitt, there were about 120 full-time college athletic publicity directors in the country and the average annual salary was about $10,000. Though the universities paid your salary, and your boss was the school's athletic director, in reality you worked for the media. And by media, I mean sportswriters. Television was just getting started.

Your official standing orders were pretty simple: get all the good news in the paper and make sure that the bad news never leaked out.

It didn't take long for me to learn that unofficially, the job was traveling, telling half-truths, feeding hacks, nursing alcoholic, sex-maniac sportswriters and even teaching them how to spell players' names.

The job wasn't always easy, but it was enjoyable because relationships with media members were largely built on mutual respect and trust. Things were no where near as antagonistic as they are now between coaches, PR people and media members. For that, I blame television, television's money, and Woodward and Bernstein.

Back then, the members of the media, they wrote about bad news – scandals, recruiting violations, academic problems, players getting arrested, things of that nature. It was part of their job. They didn't enjoy it.

I get the feeling that their modern counterparts, the columnists, talk show hosts, and TV personalities, they enjoy it. They love digging up dirt. They truly love the bad news because it's an almost endless supply of material.

And they really enjoy being difficult to deal with. I'd never been very religious, but once I started doing PR at Pitt I began to believe in the afterlife. I'm not sure that decent media members go to heaven, but I figured there has to be a place for the bad ones, and that's obviously hell.

Like any other profession, there were good and bad writers. Early on, the hacks were pretty easy to spot. To give you an idea of how an SID's work week went, Friday afternoons before Saturday home football games, I'd take care of the out-of-town writers.

A good writer would come into the office and ask two questions: "Where's my press ticket?" and "What time does the nearest Western Union office close?"

The hack adds two more: "What time is the press party?" and "Do you have two comps (complimentary tickets)?"

I never went to the Friday practice, which they now call a walk-through, even though some SIDs thought it was important. The good writers and broadcasters went for themselves. The hacks never bothered and either made up quotes for their Saturday stories or else recycled the same ones they used the last time they were in town, which was probably sometime during FDR's second term.

Saturday mornings, I used to sit in my office and play the ticket game. This is when the local writers, late arrivals and pro scouts showed up. Back then, when there was a real rivalry between the pros and colleges, many schools adopted a silly policy of barring pro scouts from the pressbox, but I didn't and never would, despite some pressure from above. "We are in competition with the pros, but we shouldn't dislike them," Carver told me. "However, we shouldn't make it easy for them."

One of my many blunders at Pitt was the time I mentioned in my 1961 football media guide that Fred Cox, the long-time Minnesota Vikings kicker and inventor of the Nerf football, had been selected by the Vikings and Cleveland Browns as a junior in the futures draft.

This upset Carver, who felt I was helping publicize two pro franchises at Pitt's expense. "You don't advertise Chevys when you're selling Fords," he reminded me.

The last time I was in Pitt's state-of-the-art South Side football complex – which, incidentally, the Panthers share with the Pittsburgh Steelers along with Heinz Field – I had a good laugh when I saw the wall with all the NFL team logos and the names of the former Panthers who played for them. Today, being a pipeline program to the pros is a big selling point in recruiting.

I can only imagine what Frank Carver and Captain Hamilton would have to say about the arrangement if they were here today. Probably nothing, because both would have died of heart attacks when they were first told that Pitt Stadium no longer existed.

I've always considered myself a college guy, but the whole line about protecting the purity of the college game, amateurism, all that stuff, that was largely bullshit. I think it was Bobby Bowden who said that the "football program was the front porch of a university."

I agreed, adding that "every school also has a backdoor." What I meant was, there was a backdoor through which envelopes of money or test answers are handed to the players. Pitt had one. While there was no big-time funny business going on, it would be sanctimonious to claim otherwise. But many schools had or still have big back porches. And once upon a time in the SEC and the old SWC, nearly all the schools had parking lots!

We had good kids at Pitt and like players anywhere else our kids liked pro ball and wanted the opportunity to get paid professionally themselves one day. Personally, I never had anything against the pro game or anybody associated with it. In fact, I believed pro ball was destined to overtake college sooner or later. I've long had a theory as to why it happened. While we're talking about sportswriters, now is as good a time as any to discuss that.

It may be hard for younger people to wrap their heads around this, but at one time, this is long before "Monday Night Football" and the Super Bowl, pro football was not considered a good beat at a paper. It wasn't just not in the same class as baseball and college football, it was far beneath boxing and basketball in the pastime pecking order.

Younger readers from Pittsburgh, or those of you who are Steelers fans, won't believe this, but when I was a kid and basically up until the mid-1960s, the pre-game story for the Steelers was usually on page seven of the Sunday paper. There was no special Steelers Sunday section. That was partly because the Steelers stunk.

But it was also because pro football wasn't America's game yet. In the sportswriting business, it was a dead-end beat. That's why the senior writers from the 1920s through the 1950s let the young guys cover pro football.

By the 1960s and 1970s, however, those young writers were senior writers and columnists. And the sport they grew up covering, cut their teeth on, liked, and promoted, was pro football. It wasn't your father's sports section anymore.

Too many people have bought into the myth that it was the 1958 NFL title game between the Baltimore Colts and New York football Giants that propelled professional football to new heights of popularity. While that game, and the fact that it was nationally televised, was a big part of it, it wasn't the full story.

In 1958, pro ball was still largely a regional sport; there were only 12 teams in the league and all but two were located in the East and Midwest. Baseball was the same. The Dodgers and Giants had just moved to the west coast.

College football was the only truly national sport. In my opinion, it wasn't so much a case of the NFL seizing the high ground in this battle as it was college football abandoning it in the media.

For basically the first 100 years, from the game's inception in 1869 to the early 1960s, New York City – not New Haven, not Princeton, not West Point nor South Bend – was the capital of college football.

The major colleges all played big games in the Big Apple. The winners of the major trophies and awards, the Heisman Trophy, the Camp Award, the Lambert Trophy, and the MacArthur Bowl, for example, were announced or presented in New York.

That's because the nation's most powerful papers were located there. And at the end of every season, New York writers, like Moses, basically handed down the All-America teams on stone tablets to us.

The small handful of bowls were all played in the south on New Year's Day, but they didn't mean anything in the big picture since the national champion had already been crowned. The season had effectively been concluded in New York in December.

College football suffered a heavy blow when the New York teams like NYU and Fordham, along with Columbia and the other Ivy League schools, dropped big-time football in the 1950s. This left the New York writers, the country's most powerful influence group, with no home teams and no real reason to follow the sport. You could consider Army New York's team, but younger writers were turned off by antique autocrats like Red Blaik and later, Paul Dietzel. They weren't hip.

Right around the same time Army's football fortunes began fading, that seminal NFL championship game between the Colts and Giants was played – where else – in Yankee Stadium in the heart of the old college capital.

On the heels of that came the AFL. Then the pros basically dropped the A-bomb – the New York Jets signed an exciting quarterback from Beaver Falls, Pennsylvania who played his college ball at Alabama. Television was emerging as the dominant medium at precisely the perfect time in which to chronicle Joe Namath's incredible popularity as well as that of some of the other new pro superstars.

The colleges did nothing to fight back. In fact, behind the scenes, many major college ADs were very angry at the Ivy League schools, namely Cornell, Yale, and Princeton, for hosting pro exhibition games at their stadiums. This was in the late 1960s. They felt that as if dropping football wasn't bad enough, the Ivies were now collaborating with the enemy in order to hurt big-time college football. There may have been something to that claim.

At the time, I suggested that college football maintain a presence in New York by booking big games in Yankee Stadium, the Polo Grounds and even Shea Stadium when it was built, but the old guard ADs and university presidents viewed these venues, despite all the college football history that had previously taken place in them, as radioactive ground. The only people who took my advice were those who ran the small black schools in the South.

To be honest, the war was probably over long before the '58 NFL title game or before Namath ever arrived in New York. Nobody knew it yet. By 1962, I myself realized that the NFL's occupation forces were here to stay.

That year, when I traveled to New York for Pitt's game with Army in Yankee Stadium in the middle of November, a leading New York columnist shocked me when he told me he had yet to see a single college game that season.

In any event, that wasn't my fight. And pro scouts, unlike the hacks, never gave me any trouble. I remember one Saturday morning a guy came in and asked for two freebies. He said he worked for a local weekly. I can't remember the exact name of this paper, but it sounded fishy.

In one of his great books, Dan Jenkins made up a fictional paper called the *Fort Worth Light and Shopper*. In honor of Jenkins, my friend and favorite sportswriter, and my old neighborhood, we'll call this guy's paper the *Duquesne Heights Daily Coupon*.

I had a policy of refusing comp requests from weeklies, with the exception of the *Pittsburgh Catholic*, the *Jewish Criterion* and the *Pittsburgh Courier*, which was one of the top black newspapers in the country. We liked to keep all minority groups happy. This way, no one could write an editorial calling us anti-something. But the *Daily Coupon* didn't qualify and I turned him down.

"Then I will make sure that Pitt never gets another inch of space!" he declared.

I shrugged my shoulders as he stomped out of my office. I'd never seen so much as a sentence in his publication, anyway.

Then, just as now, too many people in the media have an entitlement attitude. I've known and still know a lot of creative, hard-working writers and broadcasters, but take it from someone who spent the second half of his career as a member of the media – the job is pretty damn easy. Especially for people who cover football.

That's definitely the case on gameday. Writers are given lineups, a play-by-play log of each quarter, halftime and game stats, and even print outs of post-game quotes. And that old line about a free lunch? There is such a thing in the pressbox. Everything is handed to them, yet most still struggle to come up with original material.

Now baseball writers, that's a different story. The worst job in media is being a war correspondent in a combat zone. The second worst is being a writer on a Major League Baseball beat. Coming up with 162 new ledes, not to mention off-day material, is grueling.

I give columnists a lot of credit, too. It's almost impossible for any human being to write a daily sports column and be good all the time.

It was hard to tell if some writers were purposely being difficult or else were just plain lazy. In 1964, I was pushing linebacker Marty Schottenheimer, who would go on to a long coaching career in the NFL, for All-America. It took forever to teach our local writers how to spell the name. The national writers were even worse pupils. Though I eventually succeeded in getting Schottenheimer some post-season recognition, it wasn't until I pulled out nearly all of my hair in frustration.

"No chance," Stan Isaacs, the *Newsday* columnist, told me about Schottenheimer's All-America potential. "His name won't fit in a headline."

That pissed me off. It was ridiculous. You're not going to consider somebody because of the number of letters in his last name? A *Sporting News* staffer agreed with Isaacs, but he at least made me laugh before the phone call ended.

"Nobody knows how to spell the name or pronounce it," he said. "And it's too long to fit into a headline. Ditka was perfect. Just five letters. Don't you have another Ditka around?"

Boy, I wished. Me and John Michelosen both.

I can put up with laziness or even stupidity, but not arrogance and vanity. Some in the media think they are more important than the event they are there to cover. Whenever I hear through the grapevine about a writer or broadcaster that had trouble parking his car, didn't like the food in the pressbox, had a poor seat or some other stupid complaint, I laugh.

Readers and viewers, especially the fans who do some kind of manual labor for a living, could care less about his problems. Worse than the constant complaints were some of the ridiculous requests these people made.

During the 1969 football season, my good friend Ernie Accorsi, who would later become general manager of the Baltimore Colts, Cleveland Browns, and the New York Giants, was working in PR as an assistant to Jim Tarman at Penn State.

Sometime during the week in the run-up to the 1970 Orange Bowl, Bill Conlin of the *Philadelphia Daily News* gave Accorsi an empty prescription bottle and told him to get it refilled. Accorsi went to Tarman and told him that this wasn't part of his job. Tarman explained, in so many words, that it was.

"Ernie, I've been trying for years to get the *Philadelphia Daily News*, which doesn't publish on Sundays, to cover our Saturday games. I've finally done that," said Tarman.

Accorsi got the prescription filled. I made trips to the pharmacy myself. I picked up dry cleaning. At various times, I was a bellhop, concierge, valet, travel agent and taxi driver.

During my first season in 1956, we played the University of Oregon at home and on the Friday afternoon before the game, Art Litchman, the Oregon SID, was sitting in my office. Litchman told that he would "do anything for a writer, except pimp."

A few weeks later, I found out that I'd do that, too.

A prominent national writer was in town for the Pitt-Army game and he said, "get me a girl." It took me a while, but I found him a hooker. It cost me two comps. I forget what paper I listed her on, but thankfully our ticket manager, Kenny George, never questioned it.

Right before leaving town, the writer barged into my office.

"Walton just lost a vote," he yelled. "That whore rolled me for forty bucks!"

I gulped. I had been pushing Joe Walton for All-America and needed to secure this writer's vote. Luckily, he had been kidding and Walton, of course, was voted a unanimous first-teamer.

Thankfully, neither Frank Carver nor Captain Hamilton found out about that one. That also wasn't the last time I helped a writer or broadcaster get laid. Eventually, I came to realize that a PR man must operate like a first sergeant in the army: get the job done one way or another. And if you have to break the rules - or, on occasion, the law - to do it, don't let the commanding officer know about it.

For the most part, I avoided breaking the law during my time at Pitt - for the most part. The rules, on the other hand, I began breaking them early and never really stopped.

The first one I broke was the rule on releases. It wasn't technically a rule, but it was established thinking back then that SIDs had to spend nearly all of their working hours writing boring press releases, all of which were eventually thrown into the trash can without being read.

Here's how it worked: you got the mailing list of writers that covered an opponent from the other school's SID before the season started. Before you played that team, you flooded media outlets with typewritten releases detailing information about your team. The material would include a general story on the upcoming game along with some information re-capping the previous week's game, the latest stats, a depth chart, numerical and alphabetical rosters, and tons of other stuff.

You put a lot of work into these things, but everybody tossed them away. The writers really hated them. That's because once you're on a mailing list, you can never get off.

"When I die," Ed Pope of the *Miami Herald* once told me, "the mailman will deliver the releases to me at the graveyard."

For the first few weeks in the fall of 1956, I didn't know any better so I dutifully went along with the arrangement. I wrote boring material, mimeographed a mountain of copies, mailed sacks upon sacks of releases, and maintained the status quo.

And then I had a revelation that I wasn't going to do it the way everybody else did. I came home with the idea after advancing my first away game. Well, not my first away game. My first road trip as an SID was West Virginia, which was only 70 miles away. The only thing you usually came home from Morgantown with was a busted tail-light.

I'm talking about my first big trip, all the way out to the West Coast, for the California game at Berkeley. Again, I've never been very religious, but the "it" I'm referring to was nothing short of what my Catholic friends call an epiphany. And I have a famous sportswriter to thank for it.

Back in those days, this is before fax machines, Federal Express and e-mail, an SID would advance the game. Depending on the distance, he would drive, take a train, or fly out to the college town or nearest big city about four or five days before the game.

Armed with photos of All-America candidates to hand out, plenty of stats and – most importantly – an expense account, an SID spoke at press and alumni luncheons, did radio and TV shows, and bought dinners for sportswriters. This was all done in the name of getting "space," as in column space in newspapers.

See, space created what we called "buzz," publicity, or hype, and buzz sold tickets and filled stadiums. Nowadays, schools aren't as concerned about space, buzz, or sellouts because television, the Internet and social media basically handle all the hype and because there's a ton of TV money to go around. Schools aren't living and dying by the gate anymore.

Back then, however, space meant everything. Space was the most important word in a publicity man's vocabulary. Space was the lens through which we viewed the world.

Many years ago, I was standing on the corner of Forbes Avenue in Pittsburgh with Myron Cope waiting for a light. We were checking out the headlines at Gus Miller's newsstand when at the same time our eyes settled upon one in particular, a big, eight-column banner: "KHRUSHCHEV ARRIVING IN THE U.S. TODAY."

Cope, the newsman, thought it was a momentous development. As a publicist, I had a different perspective. "Gee," I remarked, "that Russian guy gets good space."

Cope couldn't stop laughing. He got a big kick out of that one.

"To Beano 'good space' is better than a $60 dinner at the Chambord, a weekend in Paris and a date with Kim Novak," explained my friend Larry Merchant in the *Philadelphia Daily News*.

Merchant knew the score. In a way, you chased space like tail, and just like in that pursuit, you were usually exhausted and broke at the end of the hunt.

I remember when Pitt played at Minnesota my first year, I had to get up before 4 a.m. one day to fit all the events into my schedule because Minneapolis and St. Paul were large cities and the papers and radio stations were so spread out. In later years when television was catching on, I'd get plenty of exercise lugging reels of film around the country so local stations could run clips from our games during their newscasts.

Most of Pitt's road games, however, were in smaller towns like Lincoln and Syracuse. Those were much easier to navigate, but they didn't provide many opportunities for what we in the media call "creative writing," padding your expense account.

In 1958, Pitt played at Oregon and I really enjoyed Portland, namely because both newspapers were in the same building, making it much easier for me to pad my expenses, as Bob Prince had taught me, with cab fare.

Los Angeles was by far the best city for this trick. When the Democrats held their convention in LA in 1960, all the political reporters and commentators were complaining about the high cab fares. That was a gift. I sent Frank Carver copies of the stories and paperclipped them to a note which read, "now will you believe me when I make out those large expense accounts?"

I loved advances. Between all the expensed eating and drinking, I did quite a bit of sightseeing over the years, everything from touring historic sites to taking in Broadway shows.

I used the trips to advance my love life, too. See, whenever your AD signed a scheduling deal with an opponent, you could develop what I called "home-and-home relationships" with broads in other towns that you'd see every other year.

I have no idea who conceived the idea of a publicity director advancing a game for an entire week, but I think our professional organization, CoSIDA – College Sports Information Directors of America – should have built a monument in his honor.

Back to my first advance, on this trip in the first week of October 1956, I was young and inexperienced, which meant that I was all business. No broads. No booze. No sightseeing.

At first, riding the cable cars was a fun novelty, like commuting to work in a Rice-A-Roni commercial, but my patience started wearing thin because I wasn't getting much space. Everybody was writing about the Ohio State-Stanford game. The quarterback at Stanford was John Brodie, and since the Golden Bears had been down for a few years, nobody really cared about Cal-Pitt, despite the fact that we were ranked No. 7.

I decided to quit pestering the hacks and headed to the *San Francisco Examiner* to talk Pitt football with the best sportswriter in Frisco history. It took me awhile, but as I made my way through the Examiner's busy newsroom in the Hearst Building, I finally found someone to point me toward Prescott Sullivan's desk.

"You better hurry," added the staffer.

"Is he leaving town?" I asked. "What game is he going to?"

"Probably Stanford-Ohio State."

Although it was expected, I was still disappointed; I had been holding out hope that I could convince Sullivan to attend and write about our game, as well as Joe Walton.

"How do you know?"

"He has a toothbrush in his shirt pocket," the guy laughed.

I couldn't help but remember the line when I read Sullivan's obituary in the *New*

York Times some thirty years later. According to the obit, Sullivan was the model for the character of Oscar Madison, the slovenly sportswriter in Neil Simon's play "The Odd Couple."

I have no idea if it was true, or how or when Simon even met Sullivan, but Jack Klugman nailed the character. I saw Klugman in the original play at the O'Neill Theater in New York in 1966 and I loved it. Same with the television show.

When I found Sullivan in the newsroom, he did have a mangled toothbrush in his shirt pocket. The guy looked like he had been hit by a cable car. A houndstooth hat was perched precariously on his head, his shirt was untucked, his shoelaces were untied, and he had mustard stains on his tie.

His desk was an absolute fucking mess, too. It was covered with papers, used typewriter ribbons, dirty napkins and empty coffee cups. Although an aspiring slob myself, even I was somewhat taken aback at the scene. All I could figure was that Sullivan must have been very organized upstairs since he was one helluva columnist.

I introduced myself as Pitt's publicity director. Sullivan was polite, but he had no time to talk. He had a plane to catch and his ticket was buried somewhere under the releases. As he's pushing papers around, I heard him curse the releases.

"It's bad enough they keep sending this trash," he said. "But they aren't even remotely interesting! If just one was somewhat informative, or even a bit humorous, I'd give it a read."

I knew he wasn't talking about me specifically, even though my releases were in that pile. After thrashing around for a bit, Sullivan finally found his plane ticket, wished me and Pitt good luck, and shambled out of the newsroom, a living, breathing, manic pigpen of a man.

I stood there awestruck; I had just been hit with a lightning bolt of inspiration, so I just barely noticed that he didn't pick up his portable typewriter, much less a suitcase.

I wandered around Frisco for the rest of that day with two words, informative and humorous, as well as two questions cycling endlessly through my mind.

Was the great Prescott Sullivan really traveling all the way to Ohio with just a toothbrush?

And, more importantly, *how could I get people to read my releases?*

I don't know how, I said to myself, *but I'm going to get them to read mine.*

I didn't get much space that week, Pitt got shut out by Cal, and even though I didn't play a down, I was blamed for the loss by our coaches.

I even got my ass chewed out for talking on the team bus on the way to the game. I didn't know everyone had to be totally silent, as if we were on a landing barge headed for Omaha Beach.

It wouldn't be the last loss I was blamed for, either. That game was probably the start of my own "Odd Couple" relationship with John Michelosen – think Felix Unger with a whistle – but we'll get to that later.

The way I saw it, motivating players, calling plays, those were the coaches' jobs.

I had my job to do, a big part of which was getting people to read Pitt's releases.

I wasn't the first SID to try to tackle the problem. Fred Casotti at the University of Colorado used to write poetry. His releases would be four lines, about 18 verses. And everything would somehow rhyme. I don't know how he did it.

Harold Keith, the long-time SID at Oklahoma, had the most well-written releases in the country. Perfect prose. He was the Thomas Wolfe of SIDs.

I didn't have any kind of literary talent like Keith or Casotti so I had to come up with another way to be, as Prescott Sullivan requested, informative and funny.

One sunny fall day I was on my lunch break walking around Oakland, the Pittsburgh neighborhood where Pitt's campus is located. I ducked into Isaly's, a deli and dairy store, for an ice cream cone. Waiting my turn at the counter, I noticed the prices of various lunch meats and made a mental note that Isaly's famous chipped-chopped ham was 99 cents a pound.

When I got back to the office, I plugged that information in to the release I was working on. To this day, I don't know why I did it. Just for laughs.

To my surprise, a local writer found the line buried in the stats. He said his wife, who handled the grocery shopping, appreciated the tip. That got me thinking. Each successive week for the rest of the season, and throughout the remainder of my time at Pitt, I started putting more and more of this kind of material into the releases in order to break up the monotony of the stats and the boring quotes from the coaches.

In addition to lunch meats, I began to include the prices of lettuce and other types of produce at Pittsburgh supermarkets. I noted which filling stations had the cheapest gas and friendliest service attendants.

I included happy hour specials at local bars. Occasionally, I played food critic and rated restaurants ranging from the high-class Park Schenley (still the best prime rib I've ever had) on Forbes Avenue to the Home Plate Café next to Forbes Field.

Once I had a few long-distance advances under my belt, I started including which airlines had the best-looking stewardesses (American, hands down).

I rated road hotels. You know, four-stars, five stars. If you care to know, the Bear Mountain Inn, where we stayed when we played at Army, as well as the Hotel Syracuse, were both very nice. Neither, however, compared to the Balmoral on Miami Beach, the Miramar in Santa Monica and my personal favorite, the Ambassador in Los Angeles.

I made public service announcements. In a release that I sent out before one particular Labor Day weekend, I wrote, "Please drive carefully, for the life you save may be a Pitt tackle. We're already short at that position."

Prior the start of the 1962 season I had some fun writing up a release in which I described, using made-up stats and quotes and the kind of clichés employed by coaches, our optimistic outlook for the performance of our secretaries during the coming campaign: "Lucille Hui, who made only six typing errors in 1961, feels her skills will be much improved this fall. We look for a good season out of Lucille."

A lot of papers, some as far away as California, published that particular release in its entirety. It was all in good fun, a nice way to give some public recognition to our employees who worked behind-the-scenes, and the ladies loved it. If an SID tried it today, the feminists would be all over his ass. He'd probably be fired.

Since sportswriters ranked teams, I figured turnabout was fair play and started ranking sports sections in the releases. In the mid-1950s through the early 1960s, the Miami papers, the Dallas papers, Long Island's *Newsday*, the *New York Post*, and the *Philadelphia Daily News* were regularly in the hunt for the No. 1 spot. If memory serves me right, the New Orleans, Cincinnati and San Francisco papers seemed to be perennially poor.

Soon I was giving stock tips and writing reviews of plays and movies I had seen: "The two best performances I witnessed last week were Pitt's defense, which held No. 7 Penn State to a single touchdown in the Panthers' upset victory, and Charlton Heston in *Ben-Hur*."

Then I did the speed traps. That got a lot of attention. Pitt used to hold camp at Allegheny College in Meadville, a town ninety miles north of Pittsburgh. Before the interstate highway system was developed, you got places by taking two-lane roads everywhere. For the benefit of writers driving up to watch us scrimmage, I put the location of speed traps on Route 19 in the pre-season releases. As you can imagine, that really pissed off the local police.

I thought all the information, both football and non-football related, was useful. *Newsday's* Jack Mann thought it was all a stupid stunt. When he said, "I only want a fucking publicity man around when I want a useless stat," I knew the shot was directed at me and I felt duty bound to defend the honor of publicity directors.

So, I started titling my unique releases "Useless Notes for Useless Columnists." That got Mann pretty good. Everybody, both writers and SIDs, loved that.

Well, everybody but my bosses. They had mixed feelings on the releases. Myron Cope, in the feature he wrote on me for *Sports Illustrated*, described a typical workday at Pitt when Captain Hamilton was in command.

"Hamilton's office in the Pitt Field House was situated on the third floor of a layer-cake arrangement of athletic headquarters. Beano's was on the first floor," Cope wrote. "Arriving at work in the morning, Hamilton would light a cigar, pick up Beano's latest publicity release and lean back to study it. Frequently he would storm out to the catwalk that fronted the top floor, seize the railing as though he were back on the bridge of the *U.S.S. Enterprise*, and thunder, 'Bee-no!' All 30 employees in the athletic department would sit up, the hackles rising on their necks, and Beano would crash out of his office and clamber upstairs, falling three times on the way."

Cope pretty much nailed it. Once I got up there the "Bee-no!" was usually followed by a stream of other words that you couldn't print in *SI*.

Frank Carver wasn't as demonstrative or vocal when it came to chewing me out, but he let me know when I crossed the line. Still, both Hamilton and Carver must have realized that good or bad, all the space I was getting for Pitt was a net positive because neither ordered me to knock it off.

The releases became something of a phenomenon. At one point, I had Pitt alumni paying a $10 annual subscription for the releases during football season. The buzz was great, because it meant space for Pitt, my ultimate goal. All the space helped me, too. The releases put my name on the map.

"Beano has no equal," wrote Ron Paglia, the sports editor of the *Valley Independent*, a Pittsburgh-area paper. "He's a marching band, a sound truck, a sportswriter, a radio or TV announcer, a soap-boxer, a con artist all wrapped up into one big, controversial but lovable and big-hearted guy."

Sid Ziff, the longtime Los Angeles sportswriter, anointed me a "national celebrity." He wrote that my "weekly releases have become must reading in the trade."

Larry Merchant voted me a consensus "All-American Write End."

I was surprised to find out that thirty years after I wrote my last release at Pitt, people were still talking about them. The late, great Dick Schaap once told me that the only releases he ever read were mine.

"I read them," he explained, "because I didn't know what you would say next!"

As for the person's feedback I desired more than anybody else's, I will die with two of the most pressing questions of my life going unanswered.

See, Prescott Sullivan died in 1985. Our paths never crossed again, so I never learned if he read any of my improved releases, and if he did, if he found them both educational and entertaining, as per his request.

And I'll never know if he – and his toothbrush – made it to Ohio Stadium in time for kickoff.

* * *

Throughout my career, the good guys outnumbered the hacks by a wide margin. There were so many guys with whom I had a lot of laughs, guys who made the job fun.

Guys like Mickey Furfari. Mickey was sports editor of the Pacific *Stars & Stripes* during World War II, so he was literally battle-tested before covering fifty years of "Backyard Brawls" between Pitt and West Virginia during his long career with the Charleston and Morgantown papers. Whenever Mickey and I got together, it was more like a family reunion than a rivalry.

As far as laughs and lines go, nobody was more fun to trade them with than Dan Jenkins. I first met Dan when he was with the old *Dallas Times-Herald,* and I consider myself extremely fortunate to have been alive when he was covering college football for *Sports Illustrated.* Nobody at *SI*, or any other publication, will ever come close to his work on the sport again. He's one of the all-time great golf writers as well.

On that subject, reading the late Fred Russell's coverage of the Masters in the now-defunct *Nashville Banner* was an annual April tradition unlike any other. It was an honor to study under Fred and then later work with him on the Honors Court of the College Football Hall of Fame. Fred was 25 years older than me, so he didn't just know the "Golden Age of Sports" in the 1920s, he had lived it. I was in awe of the names he mentioned so casually in conversation and the countless legends of the game that he called friends. It's still hard to believe, all these years later, that I was able to call him one, too.

No discussion of golf writers is complete without the late Bob Drum, who worked for the *Pittsburgh Press* for nearly twenty years after the war. In the golf world, he is probably best-known for being the guy who discovered a teenaged prodigy from Latrobe, Pennsylvania named Arnold Palmer. But TV trumps all, so most people probably remember his great golf commentaries on *CBS* in the 1980s more than anything else.

I remember "The Drummer" first and foremost for being one of the few who could belly up with Bobby Layne and still be standing at the end of the night – or the next afternoon. The bar at the Pittsburgher Hotel was his favorite haunt. Everybody knew that you had a better chance of reaching him there rather than at the *Press* or at his home.

A hulk of human being, he was literally a larger-than-life character, definitely one of the most colorful in Pittsburgh, if not the entirety of sports media, history. Besides our hefty builds, Drum and I had several things in common. After the *Press*, he worked as an SID at VMI and later did PR for the Pinehurst Golf Club.

The knock on the Drummer was that he wasn't a good writer. In that way, I could relate to him. While neither of us could write, we somehow both ended up finding success in sports media because we could articulate our opinions on television.

There are individuals who are good reporters but poor writers, and vice-versa. Ed Pope in Miami was one of a very select few that could do both equally well.

Merchant is another example. Sadly, most young people don't know how great a writer he is because he's known primarily as a boxing commentator on *HBO*. Like Pope, he could report and write. Columns, magazine articles, books, you name it.

Jerry Izenberg is the country's greatest living sports columnist. He worked for Stanley Woodward and with Red Smith and Walter Lippman at the old *New York Herald-Tribune*. And you know what? He might've been the best writer in the group.

Furman Bisher was the best sportswriter in Atlanta history. And yes, I know that Grantland Rice spent time in Atlanta. That's how highly I think of Bisher.

Sinatra was "The Voice." Jerry West is "The Logo." I called the late Jim Murray "The Byline." Murray might be the greatest pure talent the business had ever seen. Every network I worked for, there were subscriptions to out-of-town papers, and it was always a race to be the first to get a hold of the copy of the *Los Angeles Times*. That was for one reason – to read Murray's latest masterpiece.

There were many other outstanding writers I got to know and befriend thanks to the Pitt job. Those relationships would come in handy when I came up with the idea for *Pittsburgh Weekly Sports* in 1963.

We'll get to that later, because I first want to talk a little about the local talent in Pittsburgh, which is something I don't think has ever been discussed, or at least as in-depth as it should have been. It was nothing short of extraordinary.

Right in my own backyard I had three of the greatest sportswriters of all-time covering Pitt during my first couple of years: Roy McHugh, Myron Cope and George Kiseda. That's not just my personal opinion. Bill Conlin said that this triumvirate was the greatest collection of writing talent to ever cover one team in any sport.

It's long been my opinion that the best writers are the Irish, Jews and Southerners. This opinion was formed early in my life due to my association with these legendary scribes.

The Irishman, McHugh, was the only one of the group who wasn't originally from Pittsburgh. McHugh came to Pittsburgh from Iowa after the war. Most of Pittsburgh knows him as a sportswriter but during one period of his career, McHugh wrote a general column. The writing was magnificent. I've said it before and I'll say it again here – if McHugh had been writing for the *New York Times* or the *Washington Post*, he would have won the Pulitzer Prize. That's how good he was.

Myron Cope, the Jew, grew up in the Squirrel Hill section of Pittsburgh. My first few years as SID, Cope was my roommate when Pitt played on the road. He remains my favorite roommate because he was a fun guy, but also because he was one of the few people who made me appear good-looking by comparison.

My least favorite roommate has to be Hot Rod Hundley, who I roomed with while doing some NBA games while I was with *CBS*. Now Hot Rod was a fun guy, too, but there wasn't much sleeping going on when Hot Rod was around. Plus, Hot Rod wreaked havoc on my expense account. The guy never paid for anything. And he was a walking *GQ* Magazine advertisement. He knew how to dress. I looked like a hobo standing next to him.

Back to Cope, I used to tease him that he was the second-best writer, behind Iris Rainer Dart, the author of "Beaches," to come out of Taylor Allderdice High School. In all seriousness, Cope was one of the all-time greats. He started on the staff of the *Post-Gazette* and then wrote for *Sports Illustrated* and the *Saturday Evening Post*. His work in *SI* is considered, at least among old-timers like me, among the best that the magazine ever published.

Like the case with Merchant, most people nowadays don't know any of this, because Cope's legacy is entirely intertwined with the Pittsburgh Steelers. Midway through his career, he stopped feature writing – he still did radio and television commentaries and wrote a couple of books – and became the color man on Steelers' broadcasts, working first with Jack Fleming then with Bill Hillgrove, the team's current play-by-play man.

As a broadcaster, Cope was to the Steelers what Prince was to the Pirates, an unabashed homer. He was perfect for the role. Like Prince, Cope loved the team unconditionally and was very creative with his catchphrases and nicknames.

Those of you who aren't from Pittsburgh or have never heard of Cope, I'm sure you've heard of the "Terrible Towel," right? Well, Cope invented it.

And Franco Harris's famous catch at the end of the 1972 AFC Divisional playoff game? Yes, Cope's the one who came up with the name "Immaculate Reception."

In a way, we were very alike due to our distinctive voices, our comic personalities, and our willingness to clown it up on camera, but I used to tell Cope that unlike me he could write. He didn't have to do the circus act. I guess in a way, I was kind of jealous of his amazing literary talent, or what I thought was his misuse of it.

George Kiseda wasn't a Southerner, but he was a native of Monessen, which is a town south of Pittsburgh. Kiseda, who was with the old *Sun-Telegraph* when I started at Pitt, was one of the greatest all-around talents ever to work in journalism.

Ask anybody who worked with Kiseda throughout the course of his career at the *New York Times*, *Parade Magazine*, the *Philadelphia Bulletin*, the *Philadelphia Daily News* or the *Los Angeles Times*.

Or ask anybody in the field, really. *GQ* Magazine called him one of the "all-time greats," lumping him in with Red Smith, Jimmy Cannon, Grantland Rice and Dick Young.

Sandy Padwe, a longtime newspaperman who became the dean of the journalism school at Columbia, used to say that he didn't teach sportswriting, he "taught George Kiseda."

Gene Collier, a Pittsburgh columnist, once told me that he's been hearing Kiseda stories his entire life. Funny thing is, Collier never met Kiseda or knew him. I did. And I'll tell you some of those stories.

After the Pirates won the 1960 World Series, Kiseda voted Eddie Dunn the Series MVP. If that name doesn't sound familiar, don't worry. Dunn didn't play for the Pirates. He was the groundskeeper at Forbes Field!

It was no big secret Dunn kept the infield as hard as concrete all season to benefit the Pirates, who were ground ball hitters. You can't fault Kiseda's logic. If you look at the stats, the Yankees had five errors in the four games played in Pittsburgh.

Other than Bill Mazeroski's famous home run, no play in the entire series was more important than the chopper hit by Bill Virdon in the eighth inning of Game 7 that bounced up off a rock and nailed Yankees' shortstop Tony Kubek in the throat.

I was there, up in the pressbox, when it happened. The ball was hit right at Kubek, and Gino Cimoli bolted for second. Every Pirates' fan's heart – mine, too, since it hadn't yet been broken by baseball – was in his throat expecting Kubek to vacuum up the routine grounder and start the double play. Instead, the injured Kubek would have to leave the game and the Pirates had new life, rallying for five runs and the lead.

Kiseda was just being Kiseda, but the Baseball Writers Association of America didn't appreciate his humor and kicked him out for writing in Dunn.

One winter, when the streets of Philadelphia were piled with snow, the mayor announced that public works crews were "working around the clock." The next day, Kiseda wrote, "the area around the clock at city hall is clean, but what about the streets?"

I loved that fearlessness in sticking it to those in positions of power or authority. During a strike, Kiseda once asked Michael Quill, the head of the city's transportation union, "Mr. Quill, why do you still have an Irish brogue? You haven't set foot in Ireland in fifty years!"

When somebody robbed a news stand at the 30th Street Station, the Philly cops asked for a description of the individual and the clerk said only that he was bald. Kiseda's lede: "If Yul Brenner had taken the 6 o'clock Paoli Express last night, he would be a suspect in the robbery of the newsstand at 30th and Market."

As the Sixers' beat writer, Kiseda was in Detroit to cover a game with the Pistons when a bad winter storm shut down the city. The weather was so awful that only one official was able to make it in for the game. Kiseda wrote that "Detroit is a one-whistle stop town."

Later, in his second career of sorts as a copy editor, he wrote one of the great headlines in the history of college football, and perhaps the greatest in the history of the *Los Angeles Times* sports section, after Anthony Davis scored six touchdowns for Southern Cal in the win against Notre Dame in 1972. The headline atop the *Times'* Sunday sports page: "DAVIS. DAVIS. DAVIS. DAVIS. DAVIS. DAVIS." I knew right away that was Kiseda.

Kiseda was really ahead of his time. In more ways than one. I don't know if anybody else knows this, but Kiseda was the first reporter to record a conversation with Casey Stengel. Unlike now when a press conference can't start until the members of the media put their tiny recorders and cellphones on the podium, tape-recording a coach or athlete was virtually unheard of.

The way Kiseda told it to me, he had been riveted to Stengel's rambling, entertaining testimony, captured on news cameras, in the hearing on baseball's anti-trust exemption before Congress in the summer of 1958. So, when the All-Star game came to Pittsburgh the following summer, Kiseda asked Stengel if he could record the interview. Stengel said fine and pretty soon, everybody was taping Stengel and "Stengelese" would be preserved for posterity. This goes to show that Congress occasionally has some good ideas.

When the *Sun-Telegraph* folded in 1960, Kiseda cracked that "it folded on merit." Neither the *Press* nor the *Post-Gazette* made a move to bring Kiseda aboard. That's because Kiseda had acquired a reputation as an activist. Kiseda was a true liberal, perhaps the first I'd ever really met.

I remember when Pitt had no black players in the late 1950s, Kiseda kept asking John Michelosen why. Tired of their sparring matches, Michelosen finally gave Kiseda a list of black players and told him to offer them all scholarships. Can you imagine a coach doing this with a beat writer now? Kiseda tried, but not one of the players signed with us.

At the start of the 1957 football season, Kiseda embarked on a crusade to get Army to move its November game against Tulane out of segregated New Orleans. According to Kiseda's logic, President Eisenhower had to call out the 101st Airborne

Division to integrate the schools in Little Rock, Arkansas, so why should the army stand for segregation elsewhere?

Kiseda wrote a controversial column in the *Sun-Telegraph* that brought national attention to the matter and then recruited a member of the House of Representatives from Western Pennsylvania to read it into the Congressional Record. Kiseda recruited me, too.

When Pitt played at Army that October, about a month before Army was supposed to play at Tulane, I brought up the subject with the Superintendent at West Point, General Garrison Davidson, at the press party. I'll admit that this took some balls on my part, seeing as how Davidson had three stars on his shoulders and had fought under Patton. I ended up being screamed at for the stunt by Captain Hamilton when I got back home, but the game was eventually moved to West Point. Not on account of me, though. It was all Kiseda.

A decade later, Kiseda was in a staff meeting at *Parade* to discuss the annual spring baseball cover. Kiseda said that it was an easy call. Frank Robinson, the first MVP in both leagues and the Series MVP of the defending world champs, Baltimore, should grace the cover. Someone higher up in the publishing hierarchy pulled rank and said, "We can't do it. We're in too many papers in the South." Kiseda blew his top and was shown the door.

Kiseda quit writing sports, threatening that he would "never" do it again. "And never is even longer than an NBA season," he added. He kept the promise, which was a real national tragedy. Maybe that was the ultimate protest by a lifelong activist. Instead of a sit-in or boycott, he decided to deprive the world of his talent.

I lost touch with Kiseda in later years, but I understood that he had issues with the ways in which the business of journalism was being conducted and after awhile he grew disillusioned with everybody and everything.

I'm convinced Kiseda was a liberal before it was fashionable, and that was the greatest detriment to his career. In those days, that was worse than being known as a drunk.

Contrast this with the way things are in today's media, where everybody leans left and you probably can't get hired unless you are a liberal. Kiseda was too far ahead of his time for his own good. He'd probably be the executive editor of a major paper or else be a VP at one of the networks now. He was that talented.

Kiseda was four years older than me, and Cope only two, but I looked up to them and considered them mentors much like I did McHugh and Prince. They were great teachers in their own ways.

I recall the time early in my career as an SID when I told Cope I liked a story about Pitt that he had written for the *Post-Gazette*. I'll never forget the look of horror on his face. He told me that something had to be wrong, that he had not done his job as a reporter and had missed some important fact or news item.

Once I assured him that he hadn't missed anything, he told me that it was a mistake for a PR man to get too comfortable with writers. While we were friends personally, he advised me to never take that friendship for granted professionally or relax my guard around anybody else in the media.

I never forgot that. During the remainder of my time at Pitt and at other stops during my PR career, I never again told anybody that I liked a story they had done.

Although I was never asked to lie to a newspaper, I was sometimes told not to tell the truth. There's a difference – I think. Most of the real writers knew the difference, and the hacks, I didn't care what they thought.

According to one columnist in the early 1960s, I was "an enigma in the field of press agentry...as forthright as a bayonet...writers respect him as the most honest, forthright man in this bizarre business."

That respect meant a lot to me because everything I did at Pitt was on the up-and-up. I felt this was the best, and right way, to do my job.

The trouble with being a PR man is that somewhere along the line you have to make a choice between truth and loyalty. I always tended toward truth. But that's because it was always just my ass on the line. If I'd had a wife and three kids when I was doing PR, I'd have probably chosen loyalty. Those people who brag about choosing honor over money? They usually have enough money and don't have to worry.

Einstein had his Theory of Relativity. Beano's Theory of Publicity was that if I was truthful at times when it wasn't advantageous for me to be, the press would likely believe me and help me out when I did have something to sell. So, I didn't play hide-and-seek. I was always available and if I told a writer something was off-the-record, I added that he could use it if he learned it from another source. As far as I know, nobody ever double-crossed me.

I doubt any college SID, network or pro league publicist now can say that. That's one reason I couldn't do the job today. I doubt my honesty would be reciprocated. Secondly, I hate to travel. Most importantly, nobody is having any fun.

Today, SIDs have these fancy titles like "Associate Athletics Director for Strategic Communications" and "Assistant Media Relations Director, Football," and they make a lot more money than we did, but they're not having any fun. At least the kind of fun we had.

I never joined a fraternity while I was in school, but I became a member of one about a year into the gig at Pitt, when CoSIDA was formed in 1957. Though some of the CoSIDA conventions did get a little wild, it wasn't quite "Animal House." Back then, though, there was definitely a brotherhood of publicity directors. I don't know if it's still like that now.

When I left Pitt I missed the conventions, the camaraderie, and commiserating about the coaches and the hacks. That's why I maintained many of my friendships with SIDs from my era, as well as got to know those of later generations. I knew how difficult the job was and what all it entailed. You leave the publicity profession, but it doesn't leave you.

Like their individual schools and conferences, these guys were unique and characters all. I'll tell you about some of the ones who made the biggest impressions on me.

It was said that only two SIDs in the entire country could get famed sportswriter Red Smith to return their calls immediately. One was Charley Loftus at Yale.

Loftus was something of an eccentric. He was one of those characters that you heard all these stories about. I wondered for years, right up until the day I finally met him, if he actually existed.

For starters, while the Yale head coach and team arrived with little fanfare, Loftus showed up at the Yale Bowl for games with a police escort. You thought it was the U.S. President or some dignitary. I never found out why he got that kind of treatment.

Also, Loftus never left town. Ever. He never attended away games. When he got married, he spent his honeymoon in the Taft Hotel in New Haven. And, if he was like everyone else in our profession, he probably put it on his expense account.

When he died, the headline in the *New Haven Register* was "LOFTUS LEAVES NEW HAVEN." That's pretty fucking good. Not as good as "HARVARD BEATS YALE, 29-29," but it's up there.

The other SID who got special treatment from Red Smith was Charlie Callahan at Notre Dame. Callahan was a throwback to the era when SIDs were called press agents. He's not only a legend in the publicity business, he's one of the legendary, leading characters in the story of my life.

Callahan graduated from Notre Dame in 1938 and after serving in the Army Air Force during the war, he returned to South Bend and became the SID in '46. He didn't see the Irish lose a game until his fifth year on the job. Five years! That's unbelievable.

Win or lose, nobody loved Notre Dame more than Callahan. Not even Frank Leahy. Whenever Pitt played Notre Dame, I made a habit of watching him during the pre-game ceremonies. He visibly squirmed if Notre Dame didn't win the coin toss. And after the playing of the anthem, everybody else took their seats. Not Callahan. He stayed at attention, even stiffened his spine a little bit more, during the Victory March.

He once put his life on the line, in a matter of speaking, for Notre Dame. In 1968, Callahan was in his third season with the Dolphins. He had been lured to Miami by Joe Robbie for the team's inaugural season in '66 and was the first publicity man in team history.

Anyway, on this particular weekend, Miami was playing in Denver. The day before the game, Notre Dame was playing at Michigan State. Callahan was a tortured soul: his body was in Denver, his heart was still in South Bend, and his mind, well, what was going in East Lansing was what was on his mind.

By the time Miami's practice ended, the Notre Dame game had already started and Callahan was so impatient to get in front of a TV, he jumped off the still-moving team bus, high-stepped through several lanes of traffic and was sideswiped by a car before staggering into the hotel lobby!

He never said a word about getting hit by the car. He was more upset about

Terry Hanratty being stopped just short of the goal-line on a run that, had it resulted in a touchdown, would have given Notre Dame the victory.

Callahan was the envy of pretty much everybody else in the business because selling Notre Dame football to the press is like selling the pyramids to archaeologists.

Even so, Charlie was one helluva salesman. He famously tried to sell No. 1 Notre Dame, with a straight face, as an overrated team at our luncheon before the '64 game. This was Ara Parseghian's first year. When his talk finished, I had to check the papers to confirm that Notre Dame was really undefeated.

"If this was the first game of the year," he announced, "Pitt would be favored."

Roy McHugh wasn't buying.

"And in 1776," McHugh laughed, "the British were the early favorites to win the Revolutionary War."

We all had some good laughs that day, but I started getting a sick feeling in my stomach when the Irish fans started pouring into Pittsburgh later that week. I remember reading a story by Bill Jauss in the *Chicago Daily News* in which he wrote that "the lobbies of the Pittsburgh hotels look like the Dublin bars."

The bastards are back, I thought to myself.

Sure enough, Notre Dame won a nail biter, 17-15. Late in the game, we had the ball inside the Notre Dame twenty. Instead of trying a field goal on fourth-and-inches, Michelosen called a quarterback sneak with Fred Mazurek that Notre Dame's defense read perfectly.

That one burned me up, just like all the other losses to Notre Dame, but the games took a backseat to the dinners. When I advanced games at Notre Dame, I would try to head out there early just to get some extra time with him. And when Callahan and the Notre Dame writers came to Pittsburgh, I always scheduled the press luncheon for Wednesdays and set aside Thursday nights for our dinners.

Every dinner would start the same way, with Charlie ordering a Miller High Life. Callahan was a loyal Miller drinker because Fred Miller, the president of the brewery, was an All-America end at Notre Dame and captain of the team that won the Army game for the Gipper in 1928. He stayed loyal because Frank Leahy, when he left coaching, sat on Miller's board. By the time the third or fourth bottle was finished, you had heard the entire history of Notre Dame football, from the 1913 victory over Army to last week's win over Navy.

As I grew older, we swapped our own war stories about the business, about our bosses, and about the trials and tribulations of doing publicity. Callahan once confided in me that the Notre Dame SID job wasn't as easy as it appeared.

When he went out to Philadelphia to advance the '53 Notre Dame-Penn game, there was a banner headline in one of the Philly papers early in the week that read "SEVENTY THOUSAND TO SEE QUAKERS-IRISH."

That weekend, the mid-Atlantic was hit with a massive snowstorm. Philadelphia got something like nine inches. The announced attendance was 68,000 and Notre Dame's athletic director, Moose Krause, turned to Callahan in the Franklin Field pressbox and said, "what the hell, Charlie! You came here to draw people, not drive them away!"

The conversations were largely one-sided. I was mesmerized, like a little kid, hanging on every word. Oh, could Callahan spin 'em. By the end of the night, I felt as though I knew Babe Ruth and Jack Dempsey, plus all the famous sportswriters Callahan knew and ran around with, legends like Stanley Woodward, Paul Gallico, Wilf Smith, and Bob Considine.

Somehow, the stories always came back, full circle, to Knute Rockne. Callahan had all the old Rockne stories. The Frank Leahy stories, too, the punchlines of which he delivered with a hint of Irish brogue in perfect imitation of Leahy.

The guy was a walking Notre Dame football encyclopedia. For example, he told me that the referee who called the crucial pass interference in the '48 ND-USC game, the 14-14 tie that cost Notre Dame its third consecutive national championship, was a Quaker from Kansas who hated Catholics. Only Callahan knew that kind of stuff.

I once asked Callahan why Notre Dame didn't retire numbers.

"Lad," he said while reaching out to gently pat my wrist, his habit when he wanted to make a point, "if we did, we wouldn't have any numbers left."

One day in early December 1956, Callahan sent a student to get Paul Hornung out of class. Thinking it was a family emergency, Hornung rushed across campus to Callahan's office. When he got there, Callahan was speaking to Hornung's mother on the phone.

"Yes, Mrs. Hornung, he's here. I'm going to hand the phone to Paul now."

Hornung's face turned pale. As Callahan extended the phone to the Notre Dame star, he covered up the receiver and gave Hornung some last-second instructions.

"Tell your mother," he said with a smile, "that you just won the Heisman Trophy."

My favorite is the Ratterman story. It's sometime in the late 1950s, the weekend of the annual Notre Dame varsity vs. old-timers' spring game. Callahan and a bunch of old Domers are up late drinking, celebrating the fact that nobody on the varsity had gotten hurt, and they decide to start picking an all-time Fighting Irish team.

Around 3 a.m., they get to quarterback. The verdict was unanimous: Johnny Lujack, the pride of Connellsville, Pennsylvania, hero tackler of Doc Blanchard in the '46 Army game and the '47 Heisman Trophy winner.

These guys are loaded, so they decide to put through a long-distance call – collect, of course – to Lujack to give him the good news. Well, Lujack refused to accept the charges.

Callahan and the lads went into a quick huddle: George Ratterman was the greatest quarterback ever to play for the Irish!

Sure, Ratterman was a great athlete, one of only four guys in Notre Dame history to letter in four different sports. He had a decent pro career, too. But he was a back-up at Notre Dame and he definitely wasn't on the same level as the legendary Lujack. Even so,

Callahan found a number for Ratterman and they woke him up.

"Hello?" answered a drowsy Ratterman.

"I got him on the line, lads!" yells Callahan.

In the background, there was a loud cheer and the clinking of High Life bottles.

"George, this is Charlie Callahan. I've got some great news. Are you sitting down?"

"No, Charlie, I'm laying down," murmured Ratterman. "Because it's three o'clock in the fucking morning and I'm in bed."

"George, we've just chosen you the all-time Notre Dame quarterback!"

"What's the matter with Lujack?" asks Ratterman.

"The hell with Lujack!" yells Callahan. "He wouldn't accept the charges!"

One time Callahan offered Lujack a deal: Callahan wouldn't call and bother Lujack for two full years if he would send Callahan's parents a congratulatory telegram on the occasion of their 50th wedding anniversary. Lujack sent the telegram. Exactly two years to the day, probably to the minute, later, Lujack's phone rings. This time, he accepts the charges.

"Times up," said Callahan.

Boy, Callahan was something else. When I got the news that he passed away in 1995, the feeling was almost the same as it was when my parents died. I miss him a lot.

My friend Roger Valdiserri took over for Callahan in 1966 and spent 22 years at Notre Dame. Roger and I had a lot in common. He got his start as a student intern at his alma mater like I did. He graduated from Notre Dame the same year I graduated from Pitt, in 1954. He also spent a season doing PR in the pros, with the Kansas City Chiefs, and was as miserable as I was when I served my one-year sentence with Don Shula and the Dolphins.

Sports fans know Valdiserri as the guy who convinced Joe Theismann to change the pronunciation of his name from "Thees-man" to "Thighs-man" at Notre Dame in order to rhyme with Heisman. Inside the business, Roger is considered one of the all-time good guys, but other than our friendship, I'll always remember him for his media guides. They were the best ever created. The three books that I always have at arm's length are the Bible, the Pitt media guide, and the Notre Dame media guide.

Valdiserri's successor was John Heisler, Notre Dame's current SID. Heisler carries the torch that was first lit by Arch Ward and George Strickler, two important early PR figures who helped publicize Notre Dame into national prominence in the 1920s.

If Miami of Ohio is considered the "Cradle of Coaches" due to all of the famous football coaches – guys like Red Blaik, Paul Brown, Weeb Ewbank, Woody Hayes, Ara Parseghian, Bo Schembechler, Carm Cozza and others – who practiced their trade in Oxford, Notre Dame is the Cradle of Sports Information Directors. There are so many who got their start working for Callahan and Valdiserri that went on to be SIDs at other schools and in the pros as well as do PR at the networks and in the corporate world.

Let's see, who else was there? The late Eddie Barrett at West Virginia. Eddie was the same age as me, but he was seen as something of an old-timer in the business since he'd been on the job since 1951, which was his junior year at WVU. As far as I know, he's the only major college SID to have been hired for a full-time position while still a student.

There was Frank Soltys at Arizona. He was president of CoSIDA for a time while I was at Pitt. Frank's brother Joe worked as the SID at UConn for many years. I got to know Joe's son Mike when I went to *ESPN*. Mike's been at *ESPN* since the beginning in 1979.

The class of the Southwest Conference was the great Jones Ramsey. He worked first at Texas A&M, when Bear Bryant coached in College Station, and then moved to Austin, where he and Darrell Royal made a great team for many years.

My friend Bill Little took over for Ramsey and continued the Longhorns' proud PR tradition.

Jim Brock at TCU pulled what everybody considered to be the biggest con job in the history of sports publicity by getting Sonny Gibbs on the cover of six preseason magazines one year. This was a big deal because back then, the preseason magazines were national. They didn't do regional covers. We all kidded Brock, but deep down, we were envious.

In the Big Eight, I told you about Fred Casotti and Harold Keith. There was Don "The Fox" Bryant at Nebraska, too. Oh man, the Fox! Don and I got along great due to shared love of good times and our mutual dislike of officers.

As the story goes, Colorado beat Nebraska one year and a couple of Colorado writers were celebrating loudly, a flagrant violation of the "no cheering in the pressbox" rule. Apparently, these guys had all been officers in the service and felt as though that gave them some kind of special privilege in civilian life.

When politely asked to pipe down, one by one they started pulling rank: one said he was a colonel in the army, another in the air force, and another a navy commander. The Fox had heard enough.

"I'm Sergeant Bryant of the United States Marine Corps," he yelled, "and I'm ordering you to get the hell out of my pressbox!"

Arnie Burdick at Syracuse was one of my good friends. Al Shrier at Temple was a lot of fun to be around. So was Gus Manning at Tennessee. The guys from the SEC all knew how to have a good time.

My friend Norm Carlson did a great job at Florida, including helping Steve Spurrier win the Heisman Trophy in 1966.

I got to know Kirk McNair at Alabama and Langston Rogers at Ole Miss after my SID career, when I was working with *ABC*.

I was convinced that the great Ted Mann at Duke owned stock in Western Union, because he sent out an unreal number of telegrams. Mann once went to bat for me during an incident that we'll talk about later on. To this day, I'm still grateful for what he did.

George Gallet at Miami of Florida was a great guy, but he was another strange one like Loftus. He never left Miami unless it was with the football team.

My only interaction with my Ivy League colleagues came at the CoSIDA conventions or at the New York Football Writers Association luncheon in Manhattan. Besides Charley Loftus, the two I remember most are Penn's Bob Paul, who I enjoyed being around, and Columbia's Phil Burke, who I couldn't stand to be around.

That's because Burke used to call players from Notre Dame, Southern Cal, and Pitt "animals." At first, I took offense to this, but later I felt some amount of pride that he was elevating the talent at Pitt up to the level of that at Notre Dame and Southern Cal.

Like with Valdiserri, the late Val Pinchbeck and I had a lot in common, too. He was my age and a Syracuse alum who started at Syracuse the same year I started at Pitt. And he left Syracuse at the same time that I left Pitt. He went to work for Al Davis, doing PR for the AFL, before becoming an NFL executive.

The Big Ten Conference generally had, and in my opinion still has, the most inferior publicity directors. Many people in the business may disagree, which is their right, but before you complain that I am biased against the Big Ten, you should know that it's also my opinion that the Big Ten has had the best athletic directors throughout the history of college athletics.

I had a lot of respect for guys like Iowa's Bump Elliott, Michigan's Fritz Crisler and Minnesota's Paul Giel, who had a cup of coffee with the Pirates in 1959-60.

For all but a few months of his tenure as AD at Penn State, my friend Jim Tarman led the athletic department when the Lions were an independent in football, but since he negotiated Penn State's membership into the Big Ten, I feel he belongs up there, too.

I rate my former bosses at Pitt, as well as Notre Dame's Moose Krause, Gene Corrigan, and Dick Rosenthal, very highly, but I sincerely believe that the best college AD of all-time was my good friend, the late Don Canham at Michigan.

Back to the Big Ten SIDs, for the most part, their jobs were easy, and I suppose, in a way, they still are. For many years, the schools these guys worked for were located in towns and cities that didn't have pro sports teams, so they had no competition for space.

I remember when the top beat at the Minneapolis and St. Paul papers was Minnesota football. That's because the Vikings, Twins and Timberwolves weren't around.

Now it wasn't just the Big Ten. It was the same way in other big cities like Atlanta, Miami, and New Orleans. I always felt like I had to work twice as hard as the Big Ten guys because I had real competition.

Although Boston College had to compete with the Red Sox, Bruins and the original Boston Patriots, the closest situation to Pitt was probably Northwestern, which was always below the Chicago Bears, Cubs and White Sox in the order of things.

In Pittsburgh, the order was the Pirates, Pitt and then the Steelers. The Penguins did not come into existence until a year after I left Pitt. Back then, Pittsburgh was a baseball town. The Pirates dominated conversations all year long. People were so into the Pirates, nobody now will believe this, they were the first major league team to finish last and still draw a million people. That was in 1947.

I considered every spring practice and fall camp story I got in the papers a win. And in all honesty, the gap between the Pirates and Pitt wasn't that close. I wasn't competing with the Pirates for space, I was competing with Beetle Bailey and Blondie Bumstead.

On the other hand, I guess in the interest of fair play I should point out that for some of the Big Ten teams there's a possible disadvantage being the only game in town. It means that you're covered too much. Everything you do, good and bad, is big news. But they basically owned the papers that covered their teams. They could control access.

And their games were always sold out. For someone who was never any good at math, I envied Ohio State's Wilbur "Bill" Snypp. While I had to look at walk-up sales and scan the stadium with binoculars and make all kinds of difficult computations, all he had to do each week to figure out attendance was simply count the three or four empty seats at Ohio Stadium and subtract the total from 83,000.

The Big Ten SIDs all just seemed so serious. They didn't crack jokes or appear to have any fun. When you entered Big Ten territory you weren't seen as an opponent, you were an enemy. It really got to be that way when I was doing publicity for *ABC*.

Maybe they were like that because their coaches, guys like Woody Hayes and Forest Evashevski, and later Bo Schembechler, treated winning and losing like it was life and death.

The lone exception was Fred Stabley, Sr. at Michigan State. When he started, Michigan State was an independent. But the Spartans became mighty good, mighty fast. I credit the administration. They realized that being a first-class athletic department meant more than just fielding good teams. So, they hired Stabley and gave him resources.

The end result was that the most efficient PR operation in all of football was the pressbox in Macklin Stadium, which is now called Spartan Stadium. Some writer called it the "Stabley Hilton," and the nickname stuck.

From the moment you got out of your car – I think they even had valet parking in the press lot – you felt like you were checking into a five-star hotel in a big city. Stabley was the best host in the country. He and his staff went out of their way to make you feel comfortable.

There wasn't a bad seat in that pressbox. And talk about amenities! They had phones everywhere. And six dark rooms, more than I've ever seen. The first time a sports photo was put on the wire service directly from a venue while the game was going on was at Macklin Stadium during the Notre Dame-Michigan State game in 1951. You can look it up. It was the first play from scrimmage, Dick Panin's 88-yard run.

And the food was the best. The best! People used to joke that Stabley was trying to get a Michelin rating. When I was at *ABC* and attended the famous 1966 Notre Dame-Michigan State game, they put on a full Thanksgiving dinner with turkey and all the trimmings for 700 accredited media members.

Stabley's assistant was Nick Vista, who took over the head job after Stabley retired. Vista was a first-class host and nice guy, too. It was a seamless transition of Michigan State legends just like it was when Duffy Daugherty took over for Biggie Munn.

Other than Stabley, Vista, Callahan, Loftus and perhaps Snypp, the only SID in the country that I was similarly somewhat envious of was West Point's Joe Cahill. Cahill got to work on a beautiful campus and enjoyed the best gameday experience in the country.

It was also one of Cahill's duties to deliver the film of the previous week's game to Army's No. 1 fan, who happened to live at the Waldorf-Astoria hotel in Manhattan. Joe would get off the elevator on the penthouse floor and knock on the door of Room 37A. You know who would answer the door, typically wearing an old West Point bathrobe? General Douglas MacArthur.

That was the only thing I was envious of Cahill for. He had to deal with all the brass at West Point on a daily basis. That couldn't have been any fun.

I know it wasn't for Budd Thalman, who was the SID at Navy when I was at Pitt. As if it wasn't bad enough dealing with the Baltimore and Washington, D.C. hacks, he had every admiral in the Navy trying to get in the pressbox when Roger Staubach was playing in Annapolis. "And they all look on me as an enlisted man," he once told me.

The admirals, though, were nothing compared to Wayne Hardin, who was the only coach in the country I disliked not just the day Pitt played Navy, but the other 364 days of the year as well. Hardin was a great coach. He won at Temple.

But Hardin, in my opinion, was a prick. I've met many famous coaches in my lifetime, some of the most infamous sideline despots of all-time, but none of them rubbed me the wrong way quite like Hardin.

When Navy played at Pitt, Thalman would show up in Pittsburgh with a suitcase full of booze for me. It was much cheaper at the Annapolis PX than in Pennsylvania, where liquor sales are controlled by the state and heavily taxed.

I was always very appreciative of Budd's bootlegging on my behalf, and am still grateful for his longtime friendship, which has surprisingly entered its sixth decade. I say surprisingly because we are rivals in two ways: Budd graduated from West Virginia and spent fifteen years of his career as the Penn State SID.

Some of us had more fun than others, but the only one who probably didn't have any fun at all was one of Budd's predecessors at Penn State, Jim Tarman. I felt bad for Tarman. He had to check every release he wrote with coach Rip Engle, who was a tyrant. I imagine that other than Hardin, Engle was probably the most difficult coach in the country to work with.

Not only would Tarman have to defend Engle, he'd also occasionally have to bail him out. This must have been incredibly difficult for a man with Tarman's integrity. For example, in a press conference at the Carlton House hotel in Pittsburgh before the Pitt-Penn State game in 1958, Engle said that "Hitler had started out with some good ideas."

I was there that day. Imagine a coach getting away with that line today! None of the writers who were present wrote about it. Which is probably a testament to Tarman's talent when it came to damage control, yet it also says something about the way Penn State once so thoroughly controlled the media, a subject we'll return to later.

Engle was a winner, there's no doubt about that. In sixteen years at Penn State, he never had a losing season. Incredibly, he was 3-0 versus Woody Hayes, with each win taking place in Columbus against an Ohio State team that was ranked in the top ten at the time. But win, lose, or draw, oh, was he fucking insufferable! Many other coaches, behind closed doors, said that he was devious and an abject moaner who was completely naked of class.

Here's an example why. In 1958, Penn State lost to Syracuse 14-6. After the game, Engle bitched about the officiating. He complained that Syracuse didn't deserve the victory, that it was impossible for a team to play an entire game without being assessed a penalty.

Well, a month later Penn State beat Pitt 25-21 and the Nittany Lions weren't called for a single penalty! At the time, I said "How come Engle isn't saying that he didn't deserve to win?" In my book, the only thing worse than being a crybaby is being a hypocrite.

When you added Penn State's athletic director, Ernie McCoy, to the mix, no, I didn't much care for that bunch. McCoy and I got into nose-to-nose shouting matches on several occasions, but it never escalated beyond that. From my perspective, everybody in State College was too tightly wound.

In the late 1950s I almost got in a fist fight with one of Engle's hot-headed assistants, a former quarterback from Brown named Paterno, at a bar in Pittsburgh. We'll talk about that incident, and about my relationship with Joe Paterno, later.

But Tarman and I, in a situation that was unique for SIDs at archrival schools, got along wonderfully in the early years. I'm willing to bet that no SIDs at Alabama and Auburn, or Ohio State and Michigan, ever had a relationship like we did.

Consider what happened in the 1958-59 basketball season, Don Hennon's senior year, when we were scheduled to finish the season at Penn State. I suggested to Frank Carver that we approach them about moving the game to Pittsburgh so that Hennon could play the final game of his storied career on his home court. Somehow, Penn State agreed. Today, such a thing would be impossible. It was all Tarman. I credit him for working McCoy around.

We were pretty close, almost like brothers in a way, and usually kidded ourselves as such. If a player would get hurt or in trouble or some other bad news would come out in the winter or summer, we'd call each other up and say, "You're killing me, you lucky so-and-so, you're getting offseason publicity!"

Unfortunately, our relationship changed when we both moved into new roles. When Tarman became the AD at Penn State and I went on the air, coincidentally at the same time in 1982, he took offense to a lot of the things I said about Penn State. Tarman, like many Penn State fans, thought that I went too far with some of my remarks. In some cases, I probably did. But it was never my intention to purposefully hurt Tarman, Thalman or Paterno. Things were always blown out of proportion because of the emotions that went along with the rivalry.

I've always spoken my mind. Jim knew that. I think he thought my opinions or our disagreements should be like they were in the old days, voiced in a private phone conversation, over dinner or in a letter, not aired on national television. If I'd done that, I'd have helped him in his job but I wouldn't have been doing my own.

The other part of it, I have come to understand after knowing Jim for some sixty years, is that he really believed it when he used to say that Penn State was different. "We do it the Penn State way," he used to crow. Oooh, that was annoying.

The whole "Grand Experiment" bullshit. It was non-stop. And it wasn't just me. Over the years, the attitude of people at Penn State rubbed a lot of people in college football, TV, and the media the wrong way.

Now I couldn't fault Tarman for being proud. He deserves credit, maybe as much as Paterno, for building Penn State into the powerhouse it is. When he started in State College, Beaver Stadium had only 45,000 seats and Lambert Trophies were hard to come by. When he retired, the stadium capacity was 100,000 and there are annual expectations of Big Ten and national championship trophies.

Unlike a lot of other schools, they did have clean-cut kids who didn't act like outlaws, but Tarman was effectively claiming that Penn State never did anything wrong. Not even Notre Dame pretended that its coach was the Pope or proclaimed that its players were altar boys. I could admit that Pitt was not perfect. But Tarman never could when it came to Penn State.

His statements echoed Paterno's controversial claim that he couldn't "leave coaching to the Barry Switzers and Jackie Sherrills of the world." There was definitely something in the water up there. That attitude, the arrogance – it all came back to bite Penn State in the ass, big-time, with the scandal.

So, it was no surprise that Tarman and I, in our post-SID years, were hot and cold, on and off more than Sinatra and Ava Gardner were in the 1950s. Yet the fights never lasted very long. Sooner or later, one of us would pick up the phone and make the call, or else put pen to paper, make a half-assed apology, and all would be forgiven.

Now I can't speak for Tarman, but I was always relieved when it happened. For two reasons. One, because Jim is one of the best friends I've ever had. Second, it meant that the next time I was in State College, he would be picking up the tab at the Nittany Lion Inn, which has the best breakfast buffet, as well as lobster bisque, I've ever had.

* * *

With a week's worth of work behind you, it was a huge relief to finally get to Saturday afternoon. When we played at home, I'd leave my office at the Field House about an hour before kickoff and start making my way over to Pitt Stadium.

My stroll down Allequippa Street was nothing like walking beneath the towering pines at North Carolina or through the Grove at Ole Miss. Worse, back in the 1950s, the smoke from the mills was sometimes so thick it seemed as though you couldn't see ten feet in front of your face.

Pitt fans of a certain age, however, will agree with me when I say that you didn't necessarily need to see Pitt Stadium. You sensed when you were near it. You felt it.

Those making the long hike up Cardiac Hill on De Soto or Lothrop Streets, when the massive façade suddenly appeared on top of you, probably had the same reaction I had when I first caught a glimpse of the stadium rim on gameday – your heart skipped a beat.

To our opponents and their fans, Pitt Stadium probably appeared to be nothing more than a giant bowl of concrete with splintery bleachers stuck in the middle of a smoky city. Going strictly by appearances, they were probably right. It may not have had any nationally-notable features like the famous hedges at Georgia or the beautiful backdrop of the San Gabriel mountains at the Rose Bowl, but it had character.

There was a lot of football history made in that building. There was a certain electricity and excitement in the air, especially for big games, in Oakland on those Saturdays that you couldn't understand unless you experienced it yourself. That energy and that environment will never, ever be replicated at Heinz Field, or anywhere else.

Pitt's beautiful basketball arena, the Petersen Events Center, now sits on the ground where Pitt Stadium once stood, but there's a hole in my heart that will never be filled. I don't get over to Oakland all that often anymore, but when I get close I feel like Patton in that scene in the George C. Scott movie, one of my all-time favorite flicks, when he's tramping around the ruins of the Roman battlefield in North Africa.

I can still feel Pitt Stadium. I hear the honking horns of the traffic and the brassy notes of the bands. I can smell the freshly cut grass. I'm taken back to the ancient battles with Penn State, West Virginia, Notre Dame, Carnegie Tech, Duquesne, and Fordham. Those games seem as though they were played last week, not fifty, sixty, or seventy falls earlier.

Our old pressbox, on the other hand, I won't wax nostalgic for that dump. For years, I begged our administration to fix up our facilities, but nothing came of it. It was hard to tell what Frank Carver was more apathetic about, the state of our basketball program or the decrepit football pressbox. When it mysteriously burned down in the 1970s, the joke around Pittsburgh was that I was responsible.

What I do miss, more than any other part or aspect of my career, were football gamedays at Pitt. Nobody came close to the atmosphere I created. Not even Stabley. Everybody had fun. If an SID tried it now, he or she'd probably be fired before halftime of the home opener. It was college football's version of Rick's Café Americain in *Casablanca*.

I imagined myself in the role of Rick Blaine, but I didn't wear a white tuxedo dinner jacket like Bogie. And of all the pressboxes, in all the college towns, in all the world, there was no chance Ilsa Lund would walk into mine; printed on our letters of transit, press tickets, were the words "no women and children permitted in pressbox."

That wasn't just a Pitt policy. It was like that everywhere.

You wouldn't be shocked to find that there was gambling going on. I never progressed to the point of craps and roulette, but I did run a regular pressbox pool for total points. It was illegal, yet I was never told to stop by my bosses, who I feared more than the cops. We had plenty of phones so writers could keep in touch with their bookies.

Everybody had a blast. Most of all, me. I loved the parade of characters, all the interesting people, the writers, broadcasters, coaches, and sports celebrities, that passed through. Between the cigarette smoke and laughs and all the famous people, often times you couldn't tell if it was an afternoon game at Pitt Stadium or an evening at Toots Shor's.

On any given Saturday I rubbed elbows with Roone Arledge, Bing Crosby, Curt Gowdy, Lindsey Nelson, Red Grange, Mel Allen, Bill Flemming, Chick Hearn, Jim Simpson, Ray Scott, and so many others.

The pro scouts and coaches might have been the most interesting pressbox patrons. My favorites were Gil Brandt, Al Davis, Bucko Kilroy, Don Klosterman and Emlen Tunnell.

When the service academies played at Pitt, we had more brass in our pressbox than they had on the deck of the *USS Missouri* on the day of Japan's surrender. Better them than Major Strasser! I met General Matthew Ridgway, the World War II and Korean War commander who later retired in Pittsburgh, at one Pitt-Army game.

Instead of a Sam, my right-hand man was my public address announcer. When I started making my pre-game rounds, my first stop was always to give him some last-minute instructions.

Your PA announcer is a very important member of your publicity team. If you're pushing a lineman for All-America, they can help make or break a campaign. For example, when Ditka played for us, I told our PA guy, "when Mike makes a key block, make sure it's announced loud." Like most fans, most writers watch the ball.

Unlike Monsieur Blaine, I did stick my neck out for a few people. After squeezing up and down the rows collecting cash for the pool, I would go check on the kids who worked for the student papers. While many schools discriminated against student writers, I went out of my way to make sure that the kids from our school paper, the *Pitt News*, and the visiting school's paper were treated right.

Being a student reporter is a tough gig. You've got to be objective in your coverage of players who are your classmates and, in some cases, your friends, too. Because you're young and not getting paid, coaches don't give you any respect. In my experience, every football coach considers the school paper a potential menace. They feel that it should be little more than a propaganda outlet for the athletic department.

Me, on the other hand, I always felt that school papers were created for one reason – to make sure coaches and administrators don't get delusions of grandeur. It angered me when our kids didn't get support from the faculty. Professors are the first to yell about the First Amendment and press freedom, but I noticed it's a different story when the school paper practices it. Any school that practices self-censorship should be ashamed of itself. Same with SIDs who don't protect their kids.

I don't know if it's still the case, but at one time the NCAA's treatment of school papers was downright shameful. Prior to the 1963 NCAA Basketball Tournament, the NCAA published a long memorandum about press tickets. I saw that there was no mention of school papers and it burned me.

In a way, I felt more obligated to the *Pitt News* than I did to the *Press* or *Post-Gazette*. It took three letters and two very heated phone calls, but I finally got Jim O'Brien, the *Pitt News* sports editor, a seat on press row at the Palestra.

"I might have to put a local writer in the stands if I give your school paper a seat," one NCAA flunky had the nerve to tell me.

"Damn it," I said, "Put him in the stands! This is our kid's team, not his."

There were a lot of sharp kids who became writers, columnists or editors at major papers and magazines. O'Brien, who I'm going to talk about in a little bit, is a great example. After he graduated from Pitt, he went on to a long writing career. He was on staff with the *Pittsburgh Press* and the *Miami News* and worked for *The Sporting News*, *Street and Smith's* and other publications. He held my old job as Pitt's SID for a few years in the mid-1980s. He now writes books on Pittsburgh sports history.

I took care of the small, suburban papers, too. That stemmed from a phone call I received in my first year from Johnny Bunardzya, the sports editor of the *Charleroi Mail*, which served a small Western Pennsylvania steel mill town in the Monongahela River valley.

"Cook," he said, "I would like a story on one of your kids who's on the third team."

At first, I thought it was a joke. Then I realized that he was serious.

"Yes, Cook," he explained. "It may not be big news in Pittsburgh, but when a player from a town like Charleroi is on a big-time football team, it's news here."

I learned how right he was. From that point on, unlike many other SIDs, I went out of my way to help out the guys putting out the small papers. The Johnny Bunardzyas at the *Charleroi Mails* and his counterparts at the *Butler Eagle*, the *Beaver County Times*, the *Jeannette News-Dispatch*, the *McKeesport Daily News*, and similar small-town publications.

Nobody in the business works harder than the sports editor of a small paper. These guys do everything but pour the ink and crank the presses. If they're lucky, it's a 60-hour work week with no overtime pay. I always hated the way the owners of these papers treated their staff. These people will not spend money.

I did what I could on my end to help these guys out. I found seats for them in the pressbox and tried to send a few comps their way. In return, they got me space in every paper in every mill town and coal patch from Youngstown, Ohio to Johnstown, Pennsylvania.

Few of our coaches understood that what I was trying to do by expanding Pitt's reach in publicity would help them, too. Lou "Bimbo" Cecconi, our backfield coach, was one who got it. One day in the early 1960s, Cecconi, a Donora native, asked me to get a story in the *Donora Herald-American* about one of our receivers who also happened to be from Donora, Mickey Rosborough.

"We are after a boy from there," Cecconi said, "and a little publicity would help."

The other coaches, however, were largely oblivious. I remember one asked why I treated the writers and editors from the small papers with as much respect as those who represented the big Pittsburgh dailies or the big city out-of-town papers.

"Anybody can be nice to Red Smith," I used to say.

That reminds me of the time in the late 1950s that I was approached by a balding, grandfatherly-looking gentleman wearing glasses in the pressbox at Pitt Stadium. Imagine seeing one of your idols walking right toward you. Now think how you'd react. He put out his right hand. Unconsciously, I extended mine.

"Hello," he said, "I'm Red Smith. I'm with the *New York Herald-Tribune*."

I knew who he was. Every fucking guy in the pressbox knew who he was! That's just how Red Smith introduced himself. He was a humble, first-class human being. I was so starstruck, I couldn't get out a word. I might've been less intimidated if Marilyn Monroe had walked up to me and struck up a conversation. That encounter was one of the few times in my life that I've been rendered totally speechless. What a thrill.

By the time I'd finished my rounds, it was usually a minute or two before kickoff. What came next was one of my favorite moments, one of the real highlights of the job. It made the ticket game, the ridiculous requests from the writers, dealing with the hacks, the hookers, the coaches, the freeloaders, the phonies, and everybody else all week, worthwhile.

I'd take my seat, light up a smoke and for a few, fleeting moments, quietly soak it all in: the sea of fedoras and waggling pennants in the stands; the clicking of typewriter keys; the muffled sounds of the marching bands on the other side of the pressbox glass.

I'd take a drag and exhale a puff of smoke and a sigh of relief. I had made it another week without incident, or, failing that, without getting fired. Outside of throwing together and distributing stat sheets, my job was more or less done.

As for the actual games, I can tell you the score of every one we played from 1956 through 1965. That would be pretty boring. And, since we weren't very good while I was at Pitt, it would be kind of depressing, too.

Instead, I'll give you the *Reader's Digest* condensed version – the highlights, main characters, and key events – of the John Michelosen era from the first-hand perspective of yours truly.

My first year in 1956 we finished 7-3-1. The tie was with Penn State. We had a really good defense. We typically had solid defenses while I was at Pitt and '56 was probably our second-best, just behind the defense we had in 1960. We held Syracuse's Jim Brown to 52 rushing yards and Notre Dame's Paul Hornung, the Heisman Trophy winner, to 59 yards.

We won our last game, on the road against a good Miami Hurricanes team, to get into a bowl. That turned out to be a rematch with No. 4 Georgia Tech, this time in the Gator Bowl. We lost once again to Tech, 21-14, and it wasn't as close as the score suggested.

We lost that game before kickoff. Bobby Dodd gave his team ten days off for Christmas and Michelosen murdered our guys in practice every single day for two weeks. By gameday, the Yellow Jackets were fresh, and we were flat. I had no way of knowing this at the time, but that was the only bowl we'd play in during my time at Pitt. In fact, it was Pitt's last bowl for nearly 20 years.

The following season got off to an interesting start. For me, at least. It was a weekday afternoon sometime in early August 1957. I'll never forget that day. Like Walter Cronkite used to say after the show "You Are There," it was a "day like all days, filled with those events that alter and illuminate our times. And you were there."

There, in this particular instance, was my office in the Field House. It was about the size of a phone booth, if anybody remembers what those were. I was sitting at my desk cutting stories about Pitt players out of newspapers and pasting them in a scrapbook, you know, like any normal five-year-old would, when my phone rang.

"Is this Mister Cook?" said the female voice on the line.

"It is. Can I help you?"

"Yes. I'd like a copy of the roster of this year's football team."

The young lady didn't identify herself. At first, I thought maybe she was a student staffer from the *Pitt News*. It didn't occur to me to ask why she wanted a roster.

"That's no problem," I replied. "But there are over 100 names on the list right now. We're going to camp soon and once we get through cuts we'll have it down to the final roster before the season opener. If you want to call back..."

"No," she interrupted. "I'd prefer to have it right now, if you don't mind."

Now I was wondering what was going on.

"I don't mind at all. But would you mind telling me why you want the roster?"

"I want to sleep with everybody on the football team," she said, matter of factly. I figure the sooner I have the list, the sooner I can get started."

"Well, then. Okay. Do you want it alphabetical or numerical?"

"Alphabetical, please."

"Do you have pen and paper ready?"

"Yes."

I took a deep breath.

"First name is Cook, comma, Beano. Guard. Next, Crafton, comma, Don. Tackle..."

I went all the way down the list. By now, pretty much everybody knows the roster story, but I think I should get credit for more than just my quick thinking. It was also solid thinking on my part to say I was a lineman. As athletes go, they're practically anonymous. I didn't have the nerve to pretend I was a running back or receiver.

I later found out the young woman's name, but I won't tell you how I did that, nor will I ever share her name with anybody else. It wouldn't be right. She's probably somebody's grandmother now.

Many people have asked me, did you get lucky as a result of that fateful phone call? I'm not telling you that, either. Or if she accomplished her goal. John "Frenchy" Fuqua of the Steelers has said he'll never tell anybody if the ball on the "Immaculate Reception" play hit him first. He maintains that he'll take that information to his grave. I plan to do the same regarding these details of the roster story.

As for the 1957 season, we started 3-1 with the only loss being in the opener to No. 1 Oklahoma, but we stumbled down the stretch, losing five of our last six to finish 4-6. The only bright spot was that that lone win was a narrow 14-13 victory over rival Penn State.

Despite our 5-4-1 record, the 1958 season was a very memorable one, and that's due to two games. One was our tie with No. 1 Army. That game featured a lot of firsts and lasts.

Although he caught a touchdown pass in our opener against UCLA, it was America's introduction to Mike Ditka since we had a ton of national media on hand and the game was televised on *NBC*. Ditka made a huge catch for nearly 40 yards from deep in our own territory when we were down 14-0 and also played a great game defensively.

Army was loaded. In addition to halfback Bob Anderson, a future College Football Hall of Famer, the Cadets had Bob Carpenter, "The Lonely End," and quarterback Pete Dawkins, who would win Army's last Heisman Trophy that year. The tie was Army's only blemish during an undefeated season, which was also Red Blaik's last at West Point.

I'll also never forget the game because it's been suggested that I had some small influence on the outcome.

When Army's plane landed in Pittsburgh before the game, Captain Hamilton greeted Blaik, who wasn't his typical surly self. He had an added edge.

"Listen, Tom," bitched Blaik, "from now on, whenever we play Pitt, keep your publicity man away from my scouts."

The previous week, I had been in Army scout Tommy Harp's ear the whole game. It wasn't the first time I had conspired to prevent the coach of a No. 1 team from scouting Pitt.

In 1953, top-ranked Notre Dame had an off week before playing us and Frank Leahy was evidently so concerned about Pitt after we tied No. 8 Oklahoma that he came to scout our next game, against Nebraska, himself.

I was working in the pressbox as a student assistant and introduced myself to Leahy. Strangely enough, he didn't shoo me away. I ended up conducting what would be one of my first interviews and it just happened to be with a guy that I believe is one of college football's greatest coaches.

Despite his reputation as a taskmaster, I found Leahy to be a really nice guy. He politely answered my many questions about Rockne, about his time as an assistant at Fordham and the scoreless ties with Pitt in the 1930s, and a handful of other subjects.

Just about the only time I sensed any agitation in his voice was when he said, and I'll never forget this, "Lad, Our Lady's university is pronounced No-trah Dame." That's why, to this day, I pronounce it that way. Because of Frank Leahy.

I know that the practice of head coaches scouting opponents in person is as dead as the drop kick, but to put this story in a modern perspective, imagine a student nowadays chewing the ears off Nick Saban or Urban Meyer for an entire game! It wouldn't happen.

Despite my efforts, Pitt's upset of Notre Dame the following week didn't happen, either. But Notre Dame didn't blow us out. It was 23-14. That Notre Dame team, with Heisman winner John Lattner and twenty other players who would eventually play in the pros, finished No. 2 in the country.

Maybe the score wasn't worse thanks to my scheming. Maybe not. But I know one thing: Leahy didn't get a good look at us. He was asked by some Pittsburgh writers his thoughts on Pitt after the game.

"Truthfully, I have none," Leahy told them. "I could not concentrate on the game. A large, gregarious chap sat next to me and talked to me all through the game."

Back to Army in '58, despite what's been said, I can't take even the slightest bit of credit for that result. It was the muddy field, which helped slow the speedy Cadets down, and the inspired play of our guys, especially Ditka, Dick Haley, John Guzik, John Flara, Bill Kaliden, and Ivan Toncic, that really made the difference.

The other game in '58 was our last-second victory over Notre Dame a few weeks later. I didn't have anything to do with the outcome of that one. It was what happened after the game ended that makes it unforgettable. We'll come back to that story later.

In 1959, we finished 6-4 and No. 20. I can't say we were good, but even though we were shutout twice, we weren't bad, either. It was another up-and-down season, the streaky kind that would come to characterize most of John Michelosen's tenure.

We won three straight to close out the campaign and it was personally satisfying to me that we pounded Notre Dame and Penn State in the last two. Those dominating performances, plus the play of the "C Boys," the three-headed backfield monster of Bob Clemens, Fred Cox, and Jim Cunningham, got my hopes up for a special season in 1960.

It was going to be Ditka's senior year and since I knew he would basically promote himself for All-America with his play, I spent most of the summer trying to figure out how to get space for the "C Boys" and promote them nationally.

Taking a lead, or rather lede, from Grantland Rice, I assigned them nicknames, "Calamity," "Catastrophe," and "Chaos," which sounded catchy, as well as a little more upbeat than Famine, Pestilence, Destruction and Death. Yet something was still missing. I needed another angle.

The idea finally came to me at camp. I decided we'd insure our entire backfield for a million dollars! Back then, a million bucks was a lot of money. I got the idea after reading about how the famously well-endowed burlesque dancer, Evelyn "Treasure Chest" West, had insured her tits with a big policy from Lloyd's of London.

When Frank Carver heard my idea, he looked at me like I was a boob. He always heard me out – he didn't always agree with me – but he always listened to me. For that I was grateful. I know it couldn't have been easy for him because my crackpot ideas probably gave him a few stomach ulcers over the years.

"Please don't tell anybody how you came up with this one," he asked me.

Deep down, he knew that was wishful thinking.

"I do not know what this season will bring," he told reporters before the season started, "but two things are certain. Beano will have us all over the papers, and he will have us deep in hot water."

I had a one-track mind when it came to space. I had seen only the headlines and the space I thought I'd get. Carver, who had taken over as our AD, saw red ink. Lots of it. He thought the premium payments would be too much of a strain on the athletic department's budget and, in retrospect, he was probably right.

I'm glad we didn't invest too heavily in 1960 because the season turned out to be, keeping with the theme, a big bust. I was successful in getting us in all the papers and creating some buzz nationally; we started out ranked No. 7 in the preseason AP poll. But that was as high as we would get. We got off to a really unlucky start, losing two of our first three by the grand total of two points, and finished a disappointing 4-3-3.

The lone highlight of 1960 was the Syracuse game. They were undefeated and ranked No. 3. We not only shut down Ernie Davis and shut out Ben Schwartzwalder's defending national champs at their place, we ended their 16-game win streak.

Out of all the years I was at Pitt, '60 haunts me the most. More so than '63, to be honest. Even though Ditka had a phenomenal year and was a consensus All-American, I wish we had done more with his senior year, both for Mike's and the program's sake.

We were terrible without Ditka in '61, going 3-7, and barely finished 5-5 in '62, so everybody wanted John Michelosen fired. The students, alums, boosters – everybody.

Michelosen tried to pacify both the public and the press by announcing that he would resign if he had two straight non-winning seasons. That wasn't good enough for Chancellor Edward Litchfield. In a meeting after the end of '62 season, he told Michelosen to open up the offense the following season. Told might be putting it lightly. It was basically an order.

This was a very big deal. Back then, other than signing off on hirings and firings, college presidents never meddled in the affairs of their athletic departments. And like most of the suits who run universities, Litchfield knew nothing about football. Previously, he had been busying himself by buying up land and buildings and holding press conferences to talk about the big expansion plans he had for the university.

If it was strange for the head of the university to suddenly switch gears and take an active interest in football strategy, it was shocking for one to come out and publicly tell the coach how to do his job. Especially a coach like Michelosen. I wouldn't say that Michelosen was used to doing things his way, rather, he was used to doing things Jock Sutherland's way. Michelosen played what they used to call "blocking quarterback" for

Pitt. He was the captain of Pitt's 1937 national championship team and Dr. Sutherland's protégé. Sutherland's idea of good field position was having the ball on his own 12.

Michelosen employed that same school of thought. To call Michelosen conservative would be an understatement. He was the coaching equivalent of Barry Goldwater. One New York writer said watching a typical Michelosen offense operate was a lot like watching some guy rake leaves.

Litchfield had had enough. He had been catching hell from the boosters, alums, students, and faculty who were tired of boring football, so like the C.E.O. of a company, he probably thought he needed to listen to his shareholders and customers and roll out a new and improved product.

I didn't doubt his authority to make such a demand, but I think he went about things the wrong way by leaking the details of the meeting to the press. And in later public comments, such as when he said that "like real estate, John needs redevelopment," he came off sounding like a jerk.

Why did Litchfield launch such a public spectacle? I can't say for sure. Maybe he saw our sinking attendance and season ticket sales numbers and became concerned that financial problems in the athletic department would torpedo his projects and, by extension, his legacy. In any event, the press was having a field day with all the material.

This all took place not long after the Cuban Missile Crisis. My first thought was to grab my clipboard, go into a fallout shelter and shut the steel door behind me.

Publicly, Michelosen took the directive in stride, but seeing as how he and I were already in a professional cold war and knowing that he couldn't lash out against Litchfield, I expected him to be even more difficult to deal with now behind closed doors.

To my surprise, though, his behavior towards me did not change. It was business as usual through the spring and fall camp. I came to realize that he knew that we were going to have a big year and would let the team's play be his response to Litchfield, the press, and our fans. What a response it was!

For the first time in 25 years, since the Sutherland era, Pitt won its first four games. We shut UCLA out on a Friday night in Los Angeles, beat Washington and blew the doors off a Marv Levy-coached Cal team. We escaped Morgantown with a win over West Virginia thanks to a long touchdown run by Paul Martha in the fourth quarter.

To the fans it probably seemed as though we were passing more, but it was an illusion. We employed some new formations and probably passed more often on first down than we had in previous seasons. In all honesty, I think the only thing Michelosen really changed was his predictability.

In the Washington game for example, our quarterback Fred Mazurek completed a pass for a key first down deep in our own territory in the fourth quarter. Passing in the shadow of our own goalpost late in a close game would have been as unheard of in 1962 as it was in 1932.

"Jock Sutherland is spinning in his grave," remarked a local writer after the throw.

John Underwood caught the exchange in a piece he wrote for *Sports Illustrated.*

"Jock Sutherland isn't buying season tickets," I replied.

I am convinced that Michelosen had not undertaken a complete overhaul of the offense, but instead had made some minor changes in his tactical approach in order to appease Litchfield as well as funnel increased traffic through the Pitt Stadium turnstiles.

The stats support my theory. We rushed for 1,000 yards more than we passed for, so we were still a run-first team. That hadn't changed. What had changed was the fact that we were finally putting our abundance of skill position talent to good use.

Exhibit A: Paul Martha. He was a Swiss Army knife wearing cleats. He could play every position on the field and as a result, I doubt he spent a minute on the bench that season. Martha was voted a consensus All-American at halfback in 1963 and was entirely deserving of the honor. Martha was a top-flight student as well. He went on to be a successful lawyer.

Fred Mazurek was our sparkplug. Mazurek, who also played centerfield for Pitt's baseball team, was a multi-purpose threat who led the team in both rushing and passing in '63. I think he's the last Pitt player to do that.

We didn't depend on a one-man receiving corps, a Ditka-type end who could single-handedly drag six defenders across the goal line. Mazurek had the triumvirate of Joe Kuzneski, Bill Howley and Al Grigaliunas, as well as an uncanny knack for knowing which would be open on any given play.

We also had a lot more team speed than we were used to, thanks to guys like Mazurek, Martha and Eric Crabtree, a sophomore from Monessen who was not only a weapon on offense and in the return game, but the team leader in interceptions and fumble recoveries.

With the legs those guys had, the same three-yard run from Michelosen's old playbook now had the potential to become, with a missed tackle or two, a 30-yard gain.

While these guys ran by defenders, our fullback, Rick Leeson, ran them over. Leeson, thanks to his power running style and kicking duties, was our leading scorer.

This team executed at an extremely high level. We were extremely disciplined and didn't miss many blocks or tackles or make mental errors. Our offensive line, which was led by guard Ed Adamchik and our outstanding tackles, John Maczuzak and Ernie Borghetti (the father of E.J., Pitt's current SID), manhandled teams.

And while the offense got all the press, our defense gave up only 13 points per game on average. That's really something when you take into consideration that our guys were playing ironman football; 1963 was the last year of pure, one-platoon college football before the NCAA changed the rules.

In some quarters, Litchfield got the credit for the team's success and that did Michelosen and his assistants a tremendous disservice. I know it pissed the players off. Michelosen was a lot like his mentor. He was sort of aloof. He definitely wasn't what they'd now call a "players' coach," but the players were pretty protective of him.

In the end, we didn't open the offense up to the extent the press or fans thought we had. I think the players not only resented Litchfield's meddling and public needling, they knew their embattled coach's job was on the line and they played harder, smarter and with greater focus because of it.

There's no doubt motivation played a major role in Pitt's success in 1963. It might also be one of the reasons why we didn't go undefeated or play for the national championship.

Which brings us to the Navy game and one of my biggest blunders at Pitt, which also led to one of the worst weeks I had on the job in ten seasons.

But before we get into all that, we have to go back a few months before the season started, to the spring of 1963 and the creation of *Pittsburgh Weekly Sports*.

As an SID you do a lot of traveling, which gave me the opportunity to read a lot of out-of-town papers. I'd been a newspaper enthusiast since I was a kid, but as I got older, I didn't just read the country's sports sections, I studied them. I learned how to tell the difference between the hacks and those who had talent. I noted up-and-coming writers whose work and careers I intended to follow.

I also compared artwork, photographs, layout, and design styles. I learned what I liked and didn't like, what I thought worked and didn't work. For example, I liked the photo spreads, the sequence shots, used by the Miami papers.

There were other examples, too many to mention here, of what I didn't like. I thought the majority of the country's sports sections were poorly written, poorly edited, and poorly illustrated. I was surprised anybody actually subscribed to these rags.

There were weekly magazines like *Sport* and *Sports Illustrated* that were much better overall products than the papers, but that's all they really were, products of Madison Avenue. They looked slick with their color covers and photo spreads, but the literary content was hit-or-miss. One week you'd have a great football feature by Myron Cope and the next there would be big spread on sailing by someone I never heard of.

The only constants week in and week out were the ads for booze and men's suits. When Dan Jenkins and Frank Deford came aboard in the early 1960s, and when they started with the swimsuit issue, that's when *SI* really took off.

Furthermore, the pieces most papers and magazines published were, in my opinion, boring. I knew what I liked to read – controversy. Lots of it. It's 1963, and the country's sportswriters were still cranking out the same "gee whiz" style of stories from the 1920s. I was tired of the status quo, and I suspected that the public thought the same way.

There had to be a way to do everything – writing, reporting, commentary, and art – right. Moreover, I had been the SID at Pitt for nearly eight years, yet I still hadn't given up hope of becoming a writer myself.

And then it hit me: if I couldn't find a paper that met my lofty expectations, and if no newspaper would hire me to write, why not put out my own paper?

It wasn't until the spring of 1963 that I finally got the guts to put my thoughts and plans into writing. The finished product, dated March 29, 1963, wasn't particularly well-written, but it was typed on Pitt Athletic Department letterhead, which I hoped would lend the memo some legitimacy in the eyes of the people who would read it.

There appeared in the copy more questions than answers, but it was inspiring – to me, at least. It was equal parts sales pitch, business plan and Jerry Maguire's manifesto.

"After traveling all over the country for seven years," I announced, "I am convinced the sports pages of this country, generally speaking, are a disgrace. Eighty percent of the writers are not qualified to be in this business. It isn't the quality of the writing that upsets me as much as the inability of so many individuals to see a good story which is in front of them."

My mission was to put out a paper that I'd like to read. I was going to publish a weekly sports paper in Pittsburgh, but it wouldn't be purely a Pittsburgh sports publication. It would feature fresh local content along with stories and columns supplied by the best sportswriters from across the United States. To recruit that national talent, I sent my memo to ten handpicked writers.

It was my "dream team" of sportswriters. Furman Bisher. Bob Broeg at the *St. Louis Post-Dispatch*. The *Boston Globe's* Bud Collins. Mel Durslag from the *Los Angeles Herald-Examiner*. I reached out to the *Philadelphia Bulletin's* Sandy Grady and the *Daily News's* Stan Hochman and dotted the "I's" with *Newsday's* Stan Isaacs and the *Newark Star-Ledger's* Jerry Izenberg. Larry Merchant and Jim Murray rounded out this list of living legends.

"I have definite ideas what a sports page should include. I believe in having as many columns as possible. I want my writers to say something. Here is the reason I am writing you," the memo concluded. "I consider you one of the best writers in the country."

I provided some financial details and asked if they were interested in joining me in this venture to clear it with their editors and get back to me. And then I held my breath. I honestly didn't know what to expect in the way of responses. It also occurred to me that the idea was so off-the-wall, I might not get *any* responses.

I was shocked when I started receiving the replies – telegrams, letters, and long-distance phone calls. One by one, each of these guys signed on. I went ten for ten. It was unbelievable! Not to mention overwhelming. I had somehow managed to recruit all this incredible talent and now what? I had no idea how to publish a paper. So, I called someone who did.

I had known Jim O'Brien since he was a freshman at Pitt. I was impressed with his work ethic. He reminded me of myself at Kiski and in college. He was a hustler.

By the spring of 1963, O'Brien had been the sports editor of the *Pitt News* for two years. He was the first non-senior to hold that position. I was confident he had the know-how and experience we needed, and he proved me right. I was the idea man, the public face of the venture, but O'Brien made it all work behind-the-scenes. Without him, there would not have been one single issue printed, much less nearly six years' worth.

Once I had my editorial staff, I turned my sights to advertisers. I signed up clients small and large, from Leo Brady's Ski Hut in Shadyside and Canter's Restaurant to Mellon Bank. I still remember the slogan for Frankie Gustine's place: "Major league atmosphere...Minor league prices!"

Out of financial necessity, ours was a small, family business. Literally. Our editorial office, where we put the paper together, was O'Brien's parents' home in the city's Glenwood section. Our business office was my parents' home on Mount Washington.

O'Brien's mother made sandwiches and was our proofreader. My mother's job, as usual, was keeping me grounded. "Don't be like Hearst," she lectured me.

We began publishing *Pittsburgh Weekly Sports* in the fall of 1963 and it was a hit from the beginning. Well, not in the financial sense. It was a huge hit with sportswriters. And not because of our pay scale. Our contributors were paid the princely sum of $2.50 per article. I don't think the money mattered to them. It was the creative freedom.

They enjoyed reading the work of their contemporaries, too. Each contributor was a subscriber, but they were paid subscribers. We didn't give them comps.

Pretty soon, writing for *Pittsburgh Weekly Sports* was like being a member of an exclusive fraternity. Everybody wanted in. I nearly fell off my chair when Red Smith called my office one day me asking why I hadn't invited him to contribute!

I signed Smith up right away. We also added Myron Cope, Ed Pope, George Kiseda, John Crittenden, Milt Gross, Jack McKinney, Lenny Shecter, and even Bill Veeck – yes, as in wreck – during that short period in the Sixties when he was out of baseball.

We established a reputation for publishing high quality prose, plus we received plenty of praise for our art and photography as well. Even when we didn't deserve it.

I remember one time we were having problems with photos, so O'Brien broke into the *Pittsburgh Press* at 2 a.m. to "borrow" some of theirs. I had a hard time keeping a straight face when somebody told me that the late Leo Koeberlein, the longtime managing editor at the *Press*, was overheard complaining to his staffers, "why can't we have photos like *Pittsburgh Weekly Sports*?"

Individual issues of the paper sold for twenty cents. We charged $2.00 for quarterly subscriptions. I don't think we ever raised the price higher than $2.50. A few months in, it became obvious we weren't going to get rich – in fact, some weeks we struggled to put out the paper on our shoestring budget – but the other rewards made our hard work worthwhile.

O'Brien built up a big file of clips and he was able to network with every big-time sportswriter in the country. He also gained valuable managerial experience coordinating our small staff.

Another Pitt student, Bob Smizik, a forty-year fixture in the sports sections of the *Pittsburgh Press* and the *Post-Gazette*, got his start at *PWS*. Bob's cousin Frank worked for the paper as well.

We used a number of students, as well as others with journalism backgrounds, guys like Rege Ebner and Chuck Lynch, as freelancers. I was an equal opportunity employer: we even had a Penn State graduate, Lou Prato, writing for us.

As publisher, I finally got to write, as much as I wanted and on any subject I wanted. I contributed a column or story to nearly every issue. My main contribution, however, seemed to be trouble.

One notable example was during the summer of 1967, when I got a tip from "Big Bob" DiPasquale, an usher at Forbes Field, about a clubhouse fight between Roberto Clemente and Willie Stargell.

It sounded like a big scoop, so O'Brien wrote up the story and we ran it on the front page. Unfortunately, we didn't take the time to do our due diligence in fact-checking. Not long after we learned that there had indeed been a big fight, only it was between Donn Clendenon and Maury Wills, not Clemente and Stargell.

A lawyer who represented both Clemente and Stargell was a subscriber and when he read the story, he filed suits on behalf of his clients against *Pittsburgh Weekly Sports.*

O'Brien came home one day to find his father sitting at the family's kitchen table, our news desk, with a sheriff who was there to serve us with the court papers. The claims in the suits totaled nearly two million dollars!

We settled out of court. A retraction coupled with a public apology was all it took. I felt bad about the headaches we created for O'Brien's parents, but I don't regret the call. Our marching orders, the creation of controversy, had been clear since day one.

Pittsburgh Weekly Sports was published in a tabloid format, roughly eight pages per issue, and it was eight pages of content that people were not used to. The content was designed to strike nerves and it usually did. The letters-to-the-editor page was overflowing with feedback every issue. After all these years, I can't say for sure whether the majority of readers liked the content or hated it, but they read it, they talked about it and they paid for it.

At the height of our operations, we had subscribers in close to forty states and shipped issues to American servicemen stationed overseas. NFL commissioner Pete Rozelle was a subscriber.

We also had a loyal, albeit somewhat captive audience of subscribers who were serving time in assorted midwestern jails. I was never able to determine if the paper was used to smuggle contraband or if they were simply sports fans who enjoyed great writing. If so, my columns might have constituted cruel and unusual punishment.

We successfully weathered staffing storms – Bob Smizik held the fort as editor for two years when O'Brien served his own stint in the army – postage hikes and other problems over the years, but it wasn't meant to last. The paper finally folded in 1969, three years after I left Pitt for New York to work for *ABC Sports*.

My mother needn't have been concerned. I never built a publishing empire. Still, *Pittsburgh Weekly Sports* remains one of the proudest accomplishments of my career. Red Smith said it was the best sports publication he ever read.

I don't know about the best, but it certainly was ahead of its time. Some thirty years ahead of its time, considering that *The National* came out in 1990. Of course, there were some differences between our paper and *The National,* but I basically came up with the idea of a nationwide sports newspaper first.

I have no doubt someone will try to resurrect the idea in the future. In fact, it would probably be much easier to try it today with the Internet because you'd have none of the printing or production costs that ate up our budget. I'm confident, however, that no one will assemble anywhere near the amount of sportswriting talent under one masthead that I did.

By now you're probably wondering, what does *Pittsburgh Sports Weekly* have to do with the outcome of the 1963 Pitt-Navy game? Here's the story. That was a big game in a lot of different ways. It was a top ten matchup. Pitt was ranked No. 3 in the AP poll and the Naval Academy was No. 10. The Navy preview issue was one of the first issues we published. I was looking to use the buzz around the game to make a big splash for the paper.

It was also a big game for Pitt because of what happened in the previous meeting between the two teams. In 1962, we played Navy in Norfolk at Foreman Field, the old Oyster Bowl, and they killed us. Wayne Hardin called a timeout with two seconds left in a 32-9 game in an effort to try to tally one more score and hit 40 points. But that wasn't what pissed off Pitt's players, coaches, students, and fans the most.

Earlier, Navy had scored on a trick play that began with halfback Jim Stewart limping toward the sideline with an apparent injury. Pitt's defense thought he was trying to get off the field. Instead, when the ball was snapped Stewart bolted up field and Staubach hit him in stride for a 66-yard touchdown. People at Pitt thought it wasn't just a trick play, it was a dirty trick play. You get the picture; there was more than poll position at stake. Pitt wanted payback.

Somebody likened the Stewart touchdown to a sneak attack and when you think of a sneak attack, you think of Pearl Harbor, right? I did. Somewhere along the line in our editorial discussions, I decided it would be a good idea to run a full-page photo of the half-sunken U.S.S. Arizona on the cover and pair it with a headline that asked, in so many words, will Navy launch another sneak attack on Pitt? I thought we'd get a lot of space.

We sure did. We got space in Navy's locker room, in the dorms, the dining halls, all over the grounds at Annapolis. I later heard from Budd Thalman that Hardin made a huge deal of it. He had copies put up everywhere.

Veterans' organizations like the American Legion and Veterans of Foreign Wars were in an uproar, too. At the time, it never occurred to me that I might have supplied Navy with some ammunition. I didn't think press clippings ever won a ballgame. I still don't. It wasn't like Bill Terry's old line, "Is Brooklyn still in the league?" made the Dodgers play any harder or better.

Maybe I'm naïve about the importance of bulletin board material, but I've always been puzzled as to why coaches think press clippings or quotes possess some kind of magic motivational powers.

Our ends coach, Ernie Hefferle, was one of those coaches. When I advanced games, Hefferle would corner me as soon the team got into town and ask for the local papers he knew I had picked up. He would cut out all the clips that made our opponent sound like the Green Bay Packers. It made me laugh. I don't think the clips ever made a difference in our record.

Navy in '63, however – that might have been an exception. You can't take anything away from Navy and especially Roger Staubach, who had a great game.

Freddie Mazurek, on the other hand, played his worst game of the season. He completed only four passes, two of which were to Navy defenders. In Mazurek's defense, he was battling a toe injury. Michelosen replaced Mazurek with Kenny Lucas in the second half and he tossed two interceptions as well. The final was 24-12, but it wasn't that close. We were down 17-0 at one point.

There was no doubt about it. Navy played inspired football for some reason. Coming off the rout and the trick play in '62, Pitt should have had the motivational advantage. Instead, I might have flipped the script with the *U.S.S. Arizona* cover.

I can remember at least two times previously that I had been blamed for losses by our coaches. The first, which I mentioned earlier, was the Cal game in 1956. At a luncheon before the game, I had listened to Cal coach Pappy Waldorf sandbag the local media about his team's lack of depth. He said he was concerned about Pitt grinding the Golden Bears down as the game went on. A typical coach's sob story.

When it was my turn, almost just to see if the writers noticed that I said the exact opposite of what Waldorf had just mouthed, I told the audience that we expected to be a strong second-half team. The way Michelosen reacted after we lost, you'd have thought I had passed Waldorf one of our playbooks along with dessert a few days earlier.

Two years later, Pitt traveled to Lincoln to play 2-6 Nebraska in the second to last game of the year with an Orange Bowl bid on the line. All of the writers in Lincoln were on the level when they told me that they thought the game would be a runaway Pitt victory. I went on a local television show and reassured Cornhusker fans that Michelosen was not the kind of coach who ran up scores against overmatched opponents.

Sure enough, we were upset, 14-6. It was a natural let-down spot after our comeback win over Notre Dame the week before, so I don't think my appearance on a TV show caused the loss. But the coaches did. They didn't speak to me for a month.

I still find it strange that none of the coaches blamed me for the Navy loss in '63, the one time I did do something that might have indirectly hurt the team and university.

Another surprise was the treatment I received from the students when I got home. The '63 Navy game was probably the first major college football game I did color on. And in this particular instance, I wasn't even technically on the airwaves. There were only a few thousand viewers, all Pitt students, and I had managed to piss off each and every one of them.

Here's what happened. That game was so big, some students had suggested to Litchfield that Pitt put on its own special broadcast of the game via closed circuit

Television for the benefit of those who couldn't travel to Annapolis. Litchfield gave the go-ahead and a group of students blacked out the Field House windows, set up a big screen and sold tickets.

I was paired up with a Pitt senior named Sam Zacharias who did the play-by-play on this one-of-a-kind production. We even did a halftime interview with Bobby Kennedy, who was U.S. Attorney General at the time.

Anyway, I came home to stories in the *Pitt News* complaining about my commentary. I got a lot of dirty looks on campus. The kids, who were disappointed in how the game went, felt that I had been a cheerleader for Navy. That wasn't the case. We played awful, Navy played well, and I was brutally honest in pointing that out.

It was an awful week. And the most bizarre part of this strange season was yet to come. Nobody could have predicted that within a few short weeks, the President of the United States would be shot dead and that a 9-1 Pitt team would be shut out of the bowls. For the time being, though, the world kept spinning on its axis.

O'Brien and I got back to work. After the Navy cover controversy, I told him that the *Chicago Tribune* kept publishing papers after "Dewey Defeats Truman" and we would, too.

The football team got back to the business of winning, with Mazurek leading one of the most electric second-half comebacks in Pitt Stadium history to beat Syracuse, 35-27. We easily beat Notre Dame and Army in successive weeks to get to 7-1. That brings us to the day Kennedy was killed and all the football fallout resulting from that historic tragedy.

A lot has been said and written about the controversial way Pitt's 1963 football season ended. To this day, that team is known as the "No Bowl Team." I'll give you my version of the story as someone who was inside the athletic department at the time. There were some difficult decisions made by people at Pitt and elsewhere, some I agreed with and some I disagreed with. For the record, I had no say or official vote in any of them.

On the morning of the shooting, November 22, I was in my office when I heard the news. Remember, it was a Friday. We were playing Penn State at home the next day. The whole campus, the city, everybody was in shock.

I still had a job to do. In the middle of all this, writers were arriving in town and picking up their press tickets. My phone started ringing off the hook. After awhile, I literally cut in on Cronkite. I stood in front of the TV that everybody was riveted to and asked, what the hell's going on? Are we playing or not?

I imagine the scene was the same in athletic departments across the country. College football wasn't like the NFL, where Pete Rozelle had the power and authority to make an executive decision that the pro games would be played that Sunday.

Since that day, I've been convinced that college football needs its own commissioner, someone with the leadership skills and authority to make executive decisions in times of emergency as well as to handle other business in the sport such as disputes between schools, disciplinary and eligibility issues, and financial deals.

I make a lot of predictions in this book and one I would bet the house on is that we will have an NCAA football commissioner sometime within the next ten years, perhaps even sooner. We're going to talk more about this idea later on and I'm going to name a few individuals who I think would be perfect for the job.

Back to November 1963, in the midst of all the chaos and without any executive leadership, the individual schools, and in many cases the conferences, made their own calls. Notre Dame was supposed to play at Iowa that weekend. Charlie Callahan told me that both athletic directors decided to go ahead with the game, but Moose Krause was overruled at the last second by Father Hesburgh, who made the decision to cancel after consulting with his predecessor, Father John Cavanaugh. Cavanaugh was a close friend of Joe Kennedy, Sr. I think some schools followed Notre Dame's lead.

Harvard and Yale didn't play. The Big Ten decided as a conference not to play. Nebraska and Oklahoma played. Auburn and Florida State played. Why did some schools play while others didn't? I don't know.

At Pitt, Frank Carver and Chancellor Litchfield conferenced with their opposite numbers at Penn State and a mutual decision was made to reschedule the Pitt-Penn State game. It was moved back two weeks, to December 7, because we had a game at Miami on November 30. That fateful decision was partly why we ended up not playing in a bowl.

There is no doubt in my mind if we had played that Saturday according to schedule, and if we'd won, we'd have been in the Orange Bowl. Everybody had us playing Bud Wilkinson and Oklahoma in the Orange Bowl. Nebraska upset Oklahoma, so the opponent would have changed, but our postseason destination wouldn't have. As it turned out, that was really our only chance to play in one of the major bowls.

There was some talk about Pitt playing No. 1 Texas in the Cotton Bowl, but that was largely wishful thinking on the part of the local media and our students, alums, and fans. I think that even if Navy had lost to Army, the Cotton Bowl still would have invited Navy because Staubach was such a big draw.

That left the Sugar Bowl and the Rose Bowl, neither of which we had a shot at. The Sugar Bowl was basically set with Ole Miss and Alabama, and the Rose Bowl had just started its exclusive agreement with the Big Ten and what was then known as the American Association of Western Universities, the forerunner of the Pac-10 Conference.

The decision not to play the Penn State game on November 23 was what cost us a major bowl bid. When we pushed the Penn State game back to December 7, the Orange Bowl folks got nervous. We were No. 5 in both polls going into Miami, but we still had two games left. They were concerned that they might get stuck with a three-loss team.

As a result, after Auburn beat Florida State and then upset Alabama, they picked Auburn. It was an unfortunate series of events for Pitt, but if I had been in charge of the Orange Bowl I probably would have made the same decision.

Now if I had been Frank Carver, I probably would have decided to play the Penn State game the day after Kennedy was shot. Granted, it's easy to say that now, knowing how everything turned out.

It's unfortunate that our schedule was arranged the way it was, with the Penn State game slated before Miami. If we had been in Miami that Friday there is no way we would have packed up our equipment and then returned to South Florida in two weeks. The Miami game would have gone on as scheduled or else it would have been canceled, like Notre Dame and Iowa was.

Since State College was only a three-hour bus ride away, there weren't any major travel costs or logistics issues to take into consideration. That made the decision to reschedule Pitt-Penn State easier. It cost us the Orange Bowl.

Of course, you can't look at the decision purely from a modern perspective because that perspective was much, much different than the one Carver and Litchfield had. They weren't looking at the decision with a bowl as the primary goal, as most ADs and administrators would look at it today.

Back then, bowls were big, but not nearly as big a deal as they are now. Academics played a big part in post-season scheduling. At least they did at Pitt. I wasn't present for all of the discussions, so I can't say for sure, but to me Carver and Litchfield were looking at things more from a patriotic, or even a public relations, perspective.

What ended up happening, we beat Miami and Penn State, finished 9-1 and No. 3 in the UPI poll, and we stayed home in January. The media blew the whole thing out of proportion and the players got watches inscribed with the word "Uninvited."

That wasn't true. We were invited to a bowl. Three of them. Unlike today, back then there were only a handful of bowls. There were the four classics played on New Year's Day, the Cotton, Orange, Rose, and Sugar, plus a half-dozen lower tier games played in late December. We turned down two of those, the Sun, and Liberty Bowls.

Then there was the Gator Bowl situation. The public doesn't know the story behind that. The Gator Bowl at that time was the most prestigious non-major bowl. They wanted Pitt pretty badly. We almost went. People don't know how close it was.

In the end, we didn't go because of segregation in Florida. We had two black players on our team that year, Eric Crabtree, a running back, and James Jones, a tackle. That fact probably prevented us from considering the Sugar Bowl, although I don't think we were ever seriously in the running for a trip to New Orleans.

Not only were memories of the '56 Sugar Bowl still fresh in the minds of people at Pitt, there was a prevailing thought among many schools that a Northern team, even one that didn't have black players, couldn't get a fair shake in the Deep South in terms of the officiating.

These things all came up in the negotiations. The Gator Bowl reps guaranteed us that there would be no problem with the black players staying at the team hotel, but then the administration got word that the black alumni were working with the NAACP to organize a big protest in Jacksonville. They didn't think Pitt should be helping the economy of a city that treated half of its residents like second-class citizens. I agreed with that sentiment.

What I didn't agree with was the way the protest organizers planned to use our players, both black and white, as pawns. They were going to make it national news. That scared all of the brass at Pitt. In the end, Pitt declined the invitation and North Carolina played the Air Force.

Everybody can deny it all they want, but that's what happened. Pitt was between a rock and a hard place. People today will probably say Pitt should have taken a stand. Maybe we should have. Maybe not. The brass at Pitt were concerned about the long-term effect any negative publicity might have on the future of the athletic department.

Back then, if you ran the show at a big-time school, you had to look at all of the consequences of your decisions. It's great to claim the moral high ground, but the other side of it is, if you bring baggage that gives the bowl committee and host city a black eye, you get a reputation as a problem school. You don't want that.

Like it or not, that was the reality of college athletics in the 1960s. You could get blackballed from future bowl bids or get sent to a basketball regional 700 miles away. Down the line, it might cost you some television money, too. This wasn't just a problem for schools like Pitt. It was widespread. It affected everybody. Almost everybody.

I never had the guts to bring this up with Charlie Callahan, and I've never talked about it on the air, but I have a theory that Notre Dame didn't play in bowls for fifty years because the collars understood that keeping Notre Dame insulated from controversy was good for business. The excuse that they didn't play in bowls because of academics or because the bowls were essentially exhibition games that didn't factor into the final polls, that was just too convenient for me. Notre Dame dodged responsibility, in my opinion.

For example, in 1953, when Georgia Tech asked Notre Dame not to bring its black players to Atlanta, Notre Dame reportedly wrote a check to make the problem go away; they paid Georgia Tech to move the game to South Bend.

If anything, with all its clout, Notre Dame should have been the one breaking down the bowl color barriers in Atlanta, Dallas, and New Orleans. When Notre Dame finally got into the bowl business on January 1, 1970, the school's timing, of course, was impeccable. Attitudes were changing in the country in regards to race, so there were no difficult decisions to make. Football was now a television game and they had a coach in Parseghian with movie star looks. Luck of the Irish, right?

As for Pitt, it's not a popular opinion, but I believe the people above my pay grade who made the decision made the right call. The university had a responsibility to its students – all of its students, not just the minorities – faculty, employees, everyone.

This was the era before big endowments. As I've said before, we were in a town with pro franchises and plenty of competition. People reading this now in an era where political correctness and moral posturing is placed before good business sense will be confused. We have the luxury of debating right and wrong today, but back then bottom lines and protecting livelihoods took precedence over everything else.

I'm reminded of what my boss at *CBS*, Van Gordon Sauter, once said: "Being idealistic is great so long as you don't have to meet a payroll."

Part of me is happy that we didn't go to that game because it would have put me, personally, in an uncomfortable position. Two years earlier, Penn State played Florida in the 1962 Gator Bowl and it was a big mess. Florida wore Confederate flag decals on their helmets in the game. Penn State practiced in St. Augustine and the black players were treated terribly. Jim Tarman told me that Penn State's All-America end and future Pro Hall of Famer Dave Robinson was refused service in a drug store when he tried to buy a Coke.

When I heard about this, I really gave it to the NCAA, which had already labeled me as a troublemaker, plus Penn State, for putting its athletes into such a position. I would have felt like a hypocrite, having to defend Pitt for playing down there after everything I had said.

To be honest, I don't think our players were bummed out about not playing in a bowl. They would have preferred to play top-ranked Texas or to have gotten another shot at Navy. Once those options went away, the allure of a bowl disappeared, too.

I can say with one-hundred percent certainty that none of them would have thought the time spent on bowl preparation and away from their studies would have been worth it. I'm not kidding. These were really smart kids who took school seriously. Out of the 61 players on the roster, an amazing number, 34, went on to get advanced degrees. There were 15 future dentists, five engineers, three doctors and three lawyers on that team. That's unbelievable.

In the end, the players were ambivalent and the administration didn't think a lower-tier bowl was worth our players' valuable time. They also thought it might cost the university in the long run. It was the media, as well as the alums and fans, who made the biggest stink about us not going to a bowl and that's why people still talk about '63 today.

Officially, we never said a word. Years before, when I started the job, Frank Carver told me that we should never complain publicly about something that doesn't go Pitt's way because it's a bad look. If we get screwed, he said, "we don't have to cry. The newspapers will do it for us." In the case of the '63 team, they've been doing it for us for going on fifty years.

I still think it's unfortunate that Carver was blamed for the way the season ended. Litchfield was unfairly blamed as well. I've even encountered people who thought I was the athletic director then and that the "No Bowl Team" was somehow my fault. If you are a Pitt fan and you have to blame somebody for 1963, blame Lee Harvey Oswald.

At the time, I didn't put much thought into what a trip to a major bowl would have meant to other people. Now, I regret we didn't go for John Michelosen's sake. If anybody truly got screwed in that whole deal, it was Michelosen. After everything he went through with Litchfield and the media before the season, the leadership he demonstrated that fall, not to mention his lifetime loyalty to Pitt, he deserved that reward.

He'd never have another shot. We went 3-5-2 in 1964 and 3-7 in 1965 and that was it for him. Frank Carver agonized over the decision, but he had no choice but to fire his good friend.

It was the end of two eras at Pitt; 1965 was my final football season in Oakland, too. We went our separate ways and I didn't give our relationship much thought until he died. Remarkably, Frank Carver and John Michelosen died on the same day, October 17, 1982. "There may be words to describe the fate that arranged for them to die on the same day. I wouldn't know. The coincidence is so bizarre," Roy McHugh wrote in the *Pittsburgh Press*, "it leaves me tongue-tied."

Standing on the porch of the funeral home following Michelosen's memorial service, I said to Jim Tarman, "it doesn't matter now that Carver hated basketball and Michelosen never passed on first down."

In a way, I attempted to cleanse my conscience, although through the years, I knew my behavior concerning the basketball at Pitt never claimed my endorsement.

As for Michelosen, I remembered what Jack Wiley, one of our assistants, said to me one evening at Frankie Gustine's in the 1970s: "you didn't hurt John, Bean, but you didn't do all you could to help him." Wiley spoke the truth, and his words will remain with me forever.

To be sure, there was no hatred or anything like that. Our relationship was more like one of those famous Miller Lite commercials. I thought Michelosen made my job more difficult than it needed to be – tastes great! He probably thought the same way about me – less filling!

We were two hard-headed people who were polar opposites in nearly every conceivable way.

I was young and stubborn and I also enjoyed pushing Michelosen's buttons. Before the start of each season, I set the over/under for how many times Michelosen would try to kill me in one of my releases. By the early 1960s, the number was around three, three and a half.

I remember one game, we were playing so poorly, I instructed the PA announcer at Pitt Stadium to start reading off Pitt's basketball schedule. This is right in the middle of the game. The coaches and players got so mad at me, they came back and won. You see, it was usually a good bet to take the over.

And Michelosen, well, he was a football coach. All coaches are, by nature, control freaks. They have to control everything, the practice schedule, the length of their players' hair, the curfew at the team hotel. Everything.

Coaches are so secretive, so neurotic, and so despotic, I imagine that it's only a matter of time until they start holding their annual conventions in North Korea.

Football coaches have long enjoyed authority and respect bordering on reverence. That's nothing new. One of the best stories I ever heard involved two former University of Tennessee players who nervously snuffed their cigarettes when legendary Volunteers' coach Robert Neyland approached.

"Why are you worried about him seeing you smoking?" a local writer asked. "You graduated ten years ago."

"We know that, and you know that," came the response from one of the former players, "but the General doesn't."

Michelosen was no different. He kept trying to control me, I resented it and I resisted it. Every week in the fall from 1956 through 1965 there was a new episode of Pitt's "Odd Couple." Our comedy shows usually opened with Michelosen standing in the doorway of my office. You could see the look of disapproval on his face before he ever opened his mouth. It was hard to tell what bothered him more, my messy office or my messy appearance.

Michelosen was always a picture of fitness, clean-shaven and conservatively dressed. Me, on the other hand, I've always had an affinity for funny hats, stripes, polka dots and purple socks. In the summertime, I sweated like a pig. I used to sit in the office in my underwear with a cold towel around my neck. With my hay fever, I'd be sneezing up a storm. My appearance, coupled with my attitude, probably drove him nuts.

It seemed like every other conversation was an attempt to persuade me to discontinue the practice of using coeds in press photos, my sure-fire method for getting space.

"I don't think it looks good," Michelosen would say while casting a disapproving glare at the pinup photos I had tacked up on the office wall.

"Broads mean space," I'd reply.

"And broads mean trouble."

And we were back to square one. Of course, I kept using the coeds, he'd inevitably return to my office and we'd revisit the topic a few weeks later.

Occasionally, he'd have new nits to pick. I remember one Monday morning he came into my office in a bad mood.

"Where did you get those weights for our players?"

"I took them on the first day of practice," I told him.

He grunted and left. For some reason, coaches feel that games are decided by the weights listed in a program. There was also the time he complained about the choice of words I used in a release.

"You used the phrase 'first team,'" he said. "I would prefer you to say, 'first unit.'"

I told him I would do it his way in the next release, but I didn't mean it and I certainly didn't do it. It went on like this, tit for tat, back and forth, week after week, season after season, for ten years.

When I left Pitt, I felt like an anthropologist that had lived with a tribe of primitives in the Amazon for a decade. Coaches are, when it comes right down to it, a tribe. All these years later I still don't understand them or their strange customs, beliefs, and rituals, but I'll share with you some of my observations.

For starters, coaches are very superstitious. I think they pick either heads or tails in the womb and never change their minds. They could lose fifty coin flips in a row and they still won't go the other way.

On road trips, I noticed early on that we stayed at the same hotel if we won the game the previous trip and some place different if we lost the last time we were in town.

Does your school's coach call the same stupid play in every crucial third and short situation? Coaches are notorious creatures of habit, which, when you add in how superstitious they are, means they are prone to making the same mistakes over and over.

Howard Waite, our trainer, made this observation. "If we made the same errors every year," Waite told me, "we'd be fired."

Coaches are devoted to rituals, and none is more sacred than the rite of practice. They treat every one like it is high mass on Easter Sunday at the Vatican.

They think everybody should take a vow of silence, too. I can't tell you how many times I was kicked out of a Pitt practice for committing the venial sin of talking too loudly. The coaches thought that what they were doing on that field was as important as what Dr. Salk was doing over in his lab.

If you've seen one football practice, you've seen them all. When the Steelers' carousel of coaches was going round and round in the 1950s, Jim Tarman asked Chet Smith, the sports editor at the *Pittsburgh Press*, if he was going to watch one of the new coach's first practices.

"Why?" asked Smith. "Are they doing it different?"

College or pro, it doesn't matter if it's a practice the week leading up to the Super Bowl, or the William & Mary game. They're all equally boring. I looked forward to the ones in the spring the least. It drove me crazy when people asked how Pitt looked in the spring game. You could say good, or bad, and be correct on both counts. Spring football is like jerking off – you have no idea how good you are when you're going up against yourself.

Coaches have their own language, too. At first, it was all Greek to me. I couldn't make out any of it on my first Picture Day, another time-honored ritual, in 1956.

Before anything else happened in the fall, you took the team pictures. At one time this was done on the first day of practice, but the country's publicity directors got worn out hearing their head coach say, "Damn it, when are these photographers going to finish?" so the NCAA decided to start practice one day earlier and give the day to the press.

It's now called Media Day instead of Picture Day. Besides the name change, the other difference is that the coach doesn't say "damn it" as much anymore.

Coaches like the pictures to be taken in dark uniforms, so the players won't look so big. Some don't permit shoulder pads to worn, either. Like fudging the weights listed in the program, they must think that it gives their team some type of psychological advantage to appear larger than advertised when they take the field.

Once you wrapped up the pictures, the coach addressed the media. It was tradition that every head coach across the country opened with, "We will miss..." before running down a list of starters and seniors lost to graduation. It's a solemn moment, like a general reading off a list of battle casualties.

As an SID, you learn that the coach does it for a reason: to create the built-in excuse of a shortage of talent in case of a losing campaign.

Upon hearing the name of a seldom-used senior, the writers will look at each other in confusion. One might even have the guts to say, "but Coach, he played only 20 minutes."

"He was a good influence on the team," the coach will reply. "He was a holler guy."

What does this mean, in English? Basically, it means that "holler guys," or players labeled good leaders, stink. It's the same as when a buddy fixes you up with a blind date and you ask him if the broad is good looking, and he says she has a "tremendous personality."

Next, the coach complains about the sophomores (this was back when freshmen were ineligible) because they lack experience. Many years ago, Knute Rockne told someone, "a sophomore in the lineup will cost you a touchdown," and ever since then all coaches have had an irrational hatred of underclassmen.

Then the coach will complain that the juniors don't have enough experience, at which time a writer will offer up the interesting observation that the team has plenty of experience in the senior class, 25 of whom are lettermen.

"But you know how seniors are," the coach counters, "they become complacent."

I don't think there's ever been a politician that could out-bullshit a football coach, which is saying something.

I also firmly believe that coaches hand out letters to all seniors for two reasons. One, so they can say they lost a ton of lettermen from last year's team and two, in hopes that if the former bench rider becomes a successful businessman, he will donate money to the ol' alma mater and build the coach a new practice facility.

In my experience, assistants were sometimes harder to work with than the head man. They were always jockeying for favor with the head coach or advancing their own agendas. A college coaching staff was full of court intrigue. They resented outsiders and tried to discredit me at every opportunity.

One of our assistants, for example, complained about my outside activities with *Pittsburgh Weekly Sports*. That made me angry because I kept quiet regarding their outside work. You may not know this, but college assistants used to be paid by professional teams to recommend players for the draft. This was before my friend Mel Kiper, and all the other talent evaluators and scouting services, came along. It was against the policy of most schools, but the coaches did it anyway because it was extra money.

When I was at Kiski, I learned a poem by Rudyard Kipling in which he wrote that "East is East, and West was West, and never the twain shall meet." At times, I wondered if football coaches and publicity men were from the same planet.

On Friday nights before Saturday games the home team usually held a press party in a hotel suite. Some schools called them "smokers" or hospitality rooms. The purpose was let the writers mingle with the coaches, but over the course of my ten seasons at Pitt, I noticed that every party ended up being the same.

After fifteen minutes the writers were all clustered in one corner, enjoying the free booze and talking to each other about everything except football, while the coaches were all sitting around a table, running plays with the salt and pepper shakers.

In my experience, college coaches were a little better than their pro counterparts, but most remained fairly ignorant of what was going in the world. At one of these parties, I remember talking with an out-of-town writer about Marlon Brando's phenomenal performance in *Julius Caesar*. One of the visiting team's coaches – who heard the words "play" and "phenomenal" – poked his head into the conversation and asked, "This Marlon Brando – who's he play for?"

I remember in one loss against UCLA in 1964, fumbles killed us. One of our assistants suggested that I keep the fumbles out of the stats. "It might hurt the confidence of the team," he told me. I couldn't believe he was serious.

A few weeks later, there was another game that we literally almost fumbled away. Leave the fumbles in, the same coach told me. "But don't forget to mention," "he added, "that we won the game despite fumbling all the time."

Translation: the kids were lousy, but the coaching was great!

The language barrier was especially evident when it came to damage control. Sometimes when my phone rings early on a Sunday morning, I think it's an assistant coach calling to tell me about some mischief a group of players got into the previous night. I haven't worked as an SID in forty years. That's how much you dreaded the calls, which always ended with a request to "keep it out of the papers." As if it was totally up to me!

I enjoyed a pretty good success rate when it came to running interference for our kids. On the rare occasion when I was unsuccessful and tried to explain to the coach that it was the doer, not the deed, that was news, they looked at me like I was speaking Japanese.

My favorite early morning calls from coaches were the ones I'd get when I was doing advances on the West Coast. The calls typically came from Ernie Hefferle. Hefferle played for Duquesne back when Duquesne played big-time football. He scored the winning touchdown in Duquesne's 13-12 victory over Mississippi State in the 1937 Orange Bowl. At Pitt, he coached Joe Schmidt, Joe Walton and then Ditka. Not a bad run at that position.

I liked Hefferle and the media liked him as well since he gave them colorful quotes, but I'm convinced he had no concept of time zones. And that since I was 2,000 miles away, he thought he had to yell into the phone so that I could hear him.

We played at Oregon one year, it was '57, and the phone rang in my hotel room at 4 a.m. local time in Portland. There was no hello. Just the Spanish Inquisition.

"Anybody hurt in the Brigham Young game?" Hefferle yelled into my ear. "How's the quarterback's knee? What else is happening?"

He must have thought the Oregon coaches invited me to attend their practices. The only thing worse than starting the day at 4 a.m. is starting a day at 4 a.m. with a headache.

There was one coach at Pitt whose calls and office visits I really enjoyed. That was the late, great Steve Petro. Petro came to Pitt from Johnstown to play football in the 1930s and didn't leave until he died. Everybody called him "The Rock." He was Mr. Pitt. Petro was on the coaching staff for decades, a holdover under a half-dozen different head coaches, then worked as an assistant to a few Pitt ADs well into the 1980s.

God doesn't make characters like Petro anymore. He was legendary for two reasons, the first of which was his appetite. He could eat three loaves of bread a day and not put on a pound. One of those guys.

The second was his wit. Nobody was quicker on the draw. In the 1937 Rose Bowl, Pitt was killing Washington and just before halftime a Husky player tried talking trash.

"I'm not surprised you guys are beating us," he said, referencing a rumor that East Coast schools were essentially fielding semi-pro teams, "because *our* players don't get paid."

"Well, after playing against you for a half," Petro snapped back, "I can see why you don't get paid."

Petro was our freshman coach and scout. When he presented his scouting reports at our Monday press luncheons, he had a way of making every opponent sound unbeatable. Jim O'Brien pulled me aside after one luncheon. "If Petro had scouted Custer for Sitting Bull," O'Brien said, "the Indians would have retreated."

When Pitt was embroiled in the midst of a scandal, Petro's was the lone voice of reason. I don't want to get into all the dirty details – it was a sex scandal. A gangbang. As far as I know, there were no criminal charges and whatever went on was reportedly consensual, but it made us look bad.

Other schools and coaches got ahold of the story and twisted it. It was being used against Pitt in recruiting. Naturally, we had to tell the public we did not condone this kind of behavior. Somebody suggested that we issue a statement that Pitt was instituting a non-fraternization policy between male athletes and female students.

"The hell we are!" yelled Petro. "We can't go around telling people Pitt's against fucking! We'd get no players! No red-blooded kid would come here. I'll be damned if I'm going to coach at a monastery and lose to Penn State with inferior talent every year."

And that, friends, is the little-known story of how Steve Petro saved Pitt football.

The only time I sympathized with Michelosen, and with coaches in general, was when it came to recruiting. It must be incredibly difficult as a grown man to have to kiss some 17- or 18-year-old kid's ass. I couldn't have done it.

Pitt's rigid academic requirements made the job that much harder. I didn't realize how much harder until I got the SID job. When we played Georgia Tech in the Gator Bowl after my first season, I was surprised to learn that we had more engineers on our squad than they did. I'd always figured everybody at Georgia Tech was a helluva engineer. It's a line in their fight song, for crying out loud.

I think it was starting in 1960, a recruit had to have a foreign language on his high school transcript to get into Pitt. That was ridiculous. To many, including myself at times, English is a foreign language. Roy McHugh used to say that Litchfield was trying to "grow ivy on the Cathedral of Learning."

Joe Namath, who was from Beaver Falls, wasn't just in our backyard, he was practically in our living room, but Namath couldn't even meet Maryland's standards for the college boards, so Pitt had absolutely no wiggle room at all.

To his credit, Michelosen didn't cry or complain about not being able to go after Namath or anybody else. He was a gentleman, and perhaps that led to his undoing. While other coaches jumped offsides with the rules, he never crossed that line of scrimmage. He adhered to Pitt's policy and did everything by the book.

We still managed to sign our share of great kids, though, and that's largely due to our coaches' hard work and a little bit of luck.

Al Grigaliunas, the captain of the '63 team, is a perfect example. Grigaliunas was born in Lithuania. His father was killed by the communists when he was a little kid. He spent six years in a displaced persons camp before coming to the United States with his mother and settling in Cleveland. Grigaliunas was not only a tough kid and a dependable receiver, he was a serious student. He went on to a graduate degree and a job with IBM.

Some may say that Al was lucky to live out the American dream, but it was Pitt that got lucky. I know I feel fortunate to have been able to work with a kid like him, as well as his teammates. Nearly all of the athletes we had during my time at Pitt were class acts.

That said, I don't like to play favorites, but Mike Ditka is my all-time favorite Pitt athlete. For a couple of reasons. One thing, he was the furthest thing from a phony. The Ditka I knew at Pitt is the same Ditka you saw on the sidelines in Chicago and the same Ditka you see on TV today. He's the same Ditka off-camera, too. With his personality, he's the epitome of what we call a "Pitt guy."

Ditka's legend at Pitt wasn't cemented by what the media or his own publicity man said about him. It was what his opponents said. When your opponents respect you (although in Ditka's case, I think fear was part of it, too), that carries more weight than a thousand All-America votes.

Back then, schools picked all-opponent teams. The players voted, SIDs tallied the results, and the information was shared between ourselves, the coaches and players. For the most part, it wasn't made public. After his senior year in 1960, seven of the ten teams on our schedule picked an all-opponent team and Ditka made all seven. He made Notre Dame's all-opponent team three straight years.

That had to have killed Terry Brennan. It was a three-horse race between Notre Dame, Pitt and Penn State and Notre Dame was out of the picture early. It was Penn State up to the very end. Thank God Mike picked Pitt.

Joe Paterno said that Ditka was his toughest recruiting defeat, as an assistant or as a head coach. We were lucky because there was no letter of intent back then. If there had been, he would have probably gone to Penn State. Ditka, the kind of guy he was, he would not have gone back on his word.

I never worried about Penn State. We lost kids to Penn State and it never seemed to come back to hurt us in a big way. When it came to football, before the mills and mines closed down and people started moving away in search of work, Western Pennsylvania was so rich in football natural resources, there was more than enough talent to go around.

In 1957, I went to Miami of Florida to do an advance and I listened to the Hurricanes' head coach, Andy Gustafson, complain about the discrepancy in talent between the two teams. This was on television. I couldn't believe he had the balls to bring up the subject, because everybody in college football knew that Miami had been winning the last three or four seasons thanks in large part to players from Western Pennsylvania. The Miami team we beat to get into the Gator Bowl the previous season was No. 6 in the polls.

"We have the Pitt publicity man with us tonight," Gustafson announced to his audience. "What do you think, Beano Cook?"

"I think you ought to know what you're talking about, Gustafson," I cracked. "You dig in the same coal mines."

Every school back then recruited the Pittsburgh area, but Notre Dame was the standard I judged our recruiting by. Not that I expected to beat them for players very often. I once asked Steve Petro, if there are ten kids, if it's down to Notre Dame or Pitt, how many would we get? He said one, maybe two. It was the affirmation. In other words, if Notre Dame also offered a kid we were after, that was a good sign the player was a legitimate talent.

I'll give you an example of how tough it was for us in recruiting. There were four kids we really wanted in 1959. We didn't get any of them. Denny Phillips was considered a major loss, but he never did anything at Notre Dame. Michelosen considered Ed Rutkowski his toughest loss, recruiting-wise. The other two went to Iowa. One was Matt Szykowny, who went to North Catholic High School in Pittsburgh.

For years, Pitt people have laughed at me for saying this, but I'll bring it up again here because I still believe it with every fiber of my being. If we had had Szykowny in 1960, Pitt would have won the national title. That's how good that kid was. Notre Dame recruited him. He started for Iowa right away at quarterback.

I think he would have been a good fit with our personnel. Minnesota won the national title that year with two losses. We had three ties and lost three games by a total of 13 points. Our defense gave up 77 points in ten games. All we needed was a damn quarterback. Even with an average offense, we'd have won nine games and probably all ten, plus a bowl.

Szykowny was a standout player on the hardwood, too, so that recruiting loss might have had an effect on Pitt's basketball program as well. God knows we needed all the help we could get. That's not a knock on head coach Bob Timmons or the kids who played for him. The whole time I was the SID, and for many years after, there seemed to be an administrative apathy, both inside the athletic department and from the larger university leadership itself, towards basketball.

While Pitt has had its moments over the years, the story of Pitt athletics is, for the most part, a story of what might have been. The '63 "No Bowl Team," and Szykowny are just a few examples. There were many games, calls, coaching hires and recruiting results, that, had they gone another way, might have completely altered Pitt's athletic history.

I'll share with you one of the big ones. It's one that the public is not aware of. Believe it or not, Ara Parseghian applied for the Pitt football job in 1955, the year Michelosen was hired. God – or his son, Touchdown Jesus – may strike me down if I'm lying. Frank Carver showed me the carbon of the letter of Pitt's answer.

Bobby Knight applied for the Pitt basketball job. It was sometime in the Sixties when he was at West Point. I can't precisely remember the year. He applied for the Pitt job one year, and the Penn State job the next. I don't know which was first, but he applied for both. Talk about another once-in-a-lifetime opportunity that Pitt screwed up.

I can't, however, argue with the Buzz Ridl hire. The creator of the "Amoeba Defense," Ridl was the best basketball mind Pitt's ever had, other than Doc Carlson, of course.

Then the boosters wanted Tim Grgurich, a good coach and tireless worker who put his heart and soul into the job, but the university still wasn't ready to commit to building a big-time program so Grgurich got screwed over.

Even if we had somehow gotten Knight, he probably wouldn't have stayed very long. Still, as a Pitt fan I get goose bumps imagining Parseghian pumping his fist on the home sideline at Pitt Stadium and "The General" in command at the Field House.

Likewise, I've spent a lot of time over the years wondering what might have been in regards to Pitt basketball when I was SID. As in football, we weren't consistently good. We had a few good teams, tall peaks between some long valleys. We went to the postseason four times in my ten years, the NCAAs three times and the NIT once.

We didn't have as much talent as the blue blood, basketball-first schools because we didn't spend any money and because Western Pennsylvania has never been a basketball hotbed. Still, there was more local talent back then than there is now.

Chuck Hursh, co-captain on our '57-'58 team, was from Irwin, Pa. Brian Generalovich, a two-time team captain from '62 to '64, was from Farrell. Generalovich played a little football, too, and made Notre Dame and Penn State's all-opponent teams his senior year. Generalovich's teammates, Dave Sauer and Cal Sheffield, were from Avonworth and New Brighton, respectively. Small towns were the lifeblood of Pitt basketball those years.

The greatest Pitt basketball player of my era, and maybe of any era, Don Hennon, came from the tiny town of Wampum, just north of Pittsburgh, near the Ohio border. If you've seen the movie "Hoosiers," Wampum High School, the smallest school in the state, was the Hickory of Pennsylvania. Don's dad, Butler, was a helluva coach.

Wampum won three state championships under his guidance.

People always like to ask, what if "Pistol Pete" Maravich had a three-point line? I say, what about Don Hennon? For the better part of two seasons, he was the best offensive player in the country. Imagine what Hennon's stat lines at Pitt would have been! He also played in an era when freshmen were ineligible to play on the varsity. If he had had four years and a three-point line, his records at Pitt might still be unbroken.

What if Pete's father, Press Maravich, who coached Ditka at Aliquippa High School, hadn't been offered the Clemson basketball head coaching job in 1956? What if we'd hired Press? Perhaps if Press had stayed in Pittsburgh, maybe Pete, even though his first choice was reportedly West Virginia, would have ended up at Pitt in the late 1960s instead of LSU.

The "what if?" game, of course, goes both ways. If there had been no segregation in Oklahoma, the great Julius Pegues would have gone to Tulsa, Oklahoma, or Oklahoma State. Pegues, Pitt's first black basketball player, wanted to be an engineer and was unable to attend those home state schools. Pitt was extremely lucky that a Tulsa oilman, a Pitt alum, found Pegues and pushed him in Pitt's direction.

Pegues was one of the few lucky breaks that we got. Even when we managed to put together a good team and make the postseason, the deck was still stacked against us.

For example, I thought it was ridiculous that we had to play No. 3 Kentucky on its home floor in Lexington in the regionals of the 1957 NCAA tournament. The NCAA, in a gesture of magnanimity, let us wear our home uniforms. It was a fucking joke. Even so, we gave Adolph Rupp and his Wildcats all they could handle, losing only by six, 98-92.

The following year in 1958, Hennon's junior year, we lost to Miami of Ohio at Northwestern in the first round. That tournament was one of the great tragedies in college sports. The regionals that year were again held in Lexington and the Final Four was in Louisville. Kentucky never had to leave the state to win the national title. Temple played Kentucky in the semifinal game and got robbed. The final was 61-60.

I was at the game and was almost thrown out of the gym for getting mouthy with the refs. The officiating was terrible. If that game had been played anywhere else except in the Commonwealth of Kentucky, Temple wins. Looking back, I shouldn't have allowed myself to get so worked up. I should have known better than to expect fairness. The NCAA men's basketball tournament is the sports equivalent of a Chicago election.

For reasons I was never able to figure out, both Captain Hamilton and Frank Carver were indifferent about basketball. I told you how little money we had budgeted for recruiting in all sports. The biggest chunk of it, of course, went to football. Basketball got pennies. There wasn't much in my budget to do more than the bare minimum in terms of publicity.

It was frustrating. Nobody will ever confuse the Pennsylvania Turnpike for Tobacco Road and Western Pennsylvania will never be as hoops crazy as Indiana. Pittsburgh was never a big basketball town, but it was a fun basketball town.

Duquesne, our crosstown rival, was good under Dudey Moore and Red Manning.

During that time, the Pitt-Duquesne rivalry was red hot. Every time we played, regardless of the records, there were fights on the court, in the stands and on the streets.

The Steel Bowl tournament was a big deal in Pittsburgh every December. Pitt and Duquesne were the hosts and two other teams from another part of the country, big name teams like Michigan and UCLA, would complete the field. Pitt and Duquesne would each play one of them first. Everybody hoped Pitt and Duquesne would win so they would face off for the championship.

Our crowds were nothing like they'd get at Allen Fieldhouse, Kentucky's Coliseum or Duke Indoor Stadium, but people came out because our kids played their hearts out every winter. It killed me that even on a meager budget we were so close and yet nobody in the administration seemed to care.

Over the years, I got pretty animated in my support of our athletic teams. As you'll read, there were times I didn't behave very professionally when representing Pitt. There was a fine line between being the school's publicist and being a passionate Pitt fan and I crossed that line quite a bit. It seemed to happen most often with basketball.

After one particularly tough loss, to Westminster College, I was so upset I called Frank Carver at his home at 12:30 in the morning.

Westminster was a small school powerhouse. They went to the NIT in the 1940s. But there's losing, then there is bad losing. There was no shame in getting run out of the gym by Hot Rod Hundley and Jerry West, but Pitt should not have been losing to Westminster. I was hoping it was the wake-up call the university needed.

"What are you going to do?" I asked Carver.

"I'm going to go back to bed," he replied.

While the administration slept on Pitt basketball, it seemed that I was the only person in the athletic department losing sleep over it. It became clear to me that we weren't going to devote any money or resources to the program, so I began thinking of ways that I could help. The result was my best publicity idea ever. Tragically, but I guess appropriately, just like Pitt's basketball teams over the years, I couldn't quite seal the deal.

It was the fall of 1958. The start of the 1958-59 basketball season. For nearly two years, I had been trying to get Dr. Jonas Salk, the hero virologist who developed the polio vaccine at Pitt, to pose for a photo with Don Hennon. I had the headline all written out: "Pitt's Two Greatest Shot Makers." I just knew that once that photo and headline hit the wires, it would be a hit. It would get space in every paper in the country.

Unfortunately, I wasn't getting anywhere with Dr. Salk. So I decided to put my request into writing and signed it "Carroll H. Cook." It had occurred to me that perhaps he wasn't taking the calls to his office seriously since they were coming from a guy who identified himself as Beano. I sent it via interdepartmental mail. About a week later, the phone rang.

A voice said, "Is Carroll Cook there?"

I said, "this is Carroll Cook."

"This is Dr. Salk."

I stood up! I don't think I ever jumped to attention that fast when I was in the army. Of course, who wouldn't stand up for the guy who beat polio? That was a lot tougher than beating Penn State.

We had a quick chat. He was soft-spoken. Very down to earth. You'd have never known I was talking to one of the most brilliant medical minds of the 20th Century. Then I explained the reason for contacting him. He listened patiently. There was a brief pause.

"This Don Hennon," Salk asked, "is he in one of my classes?"

The way he said Hennon's name, I immediately recognized that he had no idea who Hennon was. There was probably only one person on campus, maybe in the entire city of Pittsburgh, who hadn't heard of Hennon and I was talking to him. An uneasy feeling came over me as I told him no, Hennon was not one of his students.

"I'm sorry, I can't do your photo shoot then," Salk explained. "But I wish you good luck in your endeavors. Have a good day, Mr. Cook."

It was a bitter pill to swallow, although Salk's friendly bedside manner gave it the effect of having been administered with a sugar cube.

Hennon averaged 26 points per game that season, but I couldn't duplicate my feat of 1957-58, when I got him named a consensus first-team All-American alongside Elgin Baylor, Oscar Robertson, and Wilt Chamberlain. That was one of my proudest moments as Pitt's SID. Of course, let's not forget that he did all the work. He sank the shots. I hope Don doesn't mind if I credit myself with an assist.

This all makes for a great story, one that I'm sure will feature prominently in my obituary. It will also remain the biggest "what if" in my life, or at least in my publicity career. What if Hennon had been in one of Salk's classes? I could have gotten him first team again in '59 and that photo wouldn't have just been on the front page of every paper in the country, it would have made every paper in the world. In a final bit of irony, Hennon was drafted but spurned the NBA and went on to become a doctor himself, a surgeon.

All coaches have at least one game that causes them to wake up in the middle of the night in a cold sweat, one game that they never get over. Joe Paterno, for example, never got over the '79 Sugar Bowl against Bear Bryant and Alabama. A lot of men get hung up on a certain woman, you know, "the one" that got away.

I still think about Salk, Hennon and the Fall of '58 every now and then. That photo was the Holy Grail of publicity stunts and it was almost mine. It was the space that got away.

*   *   *

As an SID, you didn't just handle football and basketball. You promoted baseball, wrestling, gymnastics, swimming, soccer, tennis, track, darts, beanbag, shuffleboard, spin the bottle, and whatever else the university deemed a varsity sport. There were no intercollegiate women's sports when I was at Pitt. They were part of intramurals.

The other big difference between then and now is that today, sports information departments have at least one staffer, sometimes even two, assigned to every sport. I did them all myself. I didn't mind all the work. The kids on these teams were as dedicated to their sports as the football and basketball players were and in some cases, more so. I wanted to see everybody and everything associated with Pitt succeed.

The work, however, wasn't easy and it definitely wasn't all that enjoyable. That wasn't because of the kids. It was because of the coaches of what we used to call these minor sports. Now, because of political correctness, we have to call them non-revenue sports.

They were basically good people. Perhaps I would have gotten along with them better if not for the professional arrangement that bound me to them. There's no denying, however, that they were delusional. To a man, these coaches shared a false, collective belief that I was personally screwing them over when it came to publicity. They had no idea how difficult it was to negotiate with the papers for space for their sports.

They also hated football. It should be understood that without football, soccer, track, tennis, all these other sports, they would be non-existent at the collegiate level. These coaches lived off football, but at the same time resented the idea that football got all the publicity.

One by one, they'd come by my office demanding publicity. Some, like Ben Grady, our swimming coach, and Warren Nagler, our gymnastics coach, were easier to get along with than others. I liked Bobby Lewis, our baseball coach. He never complained about me using coeds to get pictures of his players in the papers. He knew the score.

But some of these coaches, there were times when I'd hear the knock at my door that I hoped I'd see John Michelosen instead of them. That should tell you something.

Every SID had his non-revenue sport nemesis. I think it was Jones Ramsey at Texas who once said, "the only thing I hate more than track is field." Jim Tarman had a running feud with Chick Werner, Penn State's track coach. I had something similar with Rex Peery, our wrestling coach.

Peery was a legend in wrestling. As a student, he won three consecutive NCAA titles at Oklahoma A&M, which is now Oklahoma State. Captain Hamilton, when he wanted to start a wrestling program at Pitt, aggressively recruited Peery to be our coach. I liked Peery. He was a good guy. Unfortunately, you couldn't reason with him when it came to publicity.

I tried to explain to him that wrestling wasn't as big in Pittsburgh as it was in Oklahoma. Sometimes, he'd come into my office waving copies of the Morgantown and State College papers to show me all the coverage West Virginia's and Penn State's programs got. I told him that we weren't in Morgantown or State College. We had the Pirates and the Steelers to compete with.

Peery was like Michelosen. He'd complain every time I used a coed to get a photo of a wrestler in the paper. I knew of an SID who had a big wrestling tournament at his school and in order to promote it, he got seven coeds, all knockouts, and posed them for pictures. Each one was photographed demonstrating a different move and in the captions, he gave them names like "Miss Take Down," "Miss Full Nelson," and "Miss Double Reverse."

I thought about copying the idea, but Peery probably would have put me in a choke hold. Although he was 20 years older than me he probably could have whipped my ass. I was also afraid he'd bring Bruno Sammartino by my office. Sammartino, who hung around the Field House with Peery quite a bit back then, this was when "Studio Wrestling" was a big hit on television, was much closer to my weight class.

I'll admit that sometimes, these coaches had legitimate reasons to be upset with me. For example, I remember this one Saturday afternoon, it was sometime during either the 1962 or 1963 football season. I was heading over to Pitt Stadium and on my way out of the Field House, I happened upon a small crowd.

When I stopped to investigate what was going on, I saw one of our trainers attending to an injured athlete. A man and woman were standing close by. They seemed pretty concerned about the situation.

"What happened?" I asked.

"He broke his leg during a drill."

I leaned over a little closer and noticed it was a soccer player. The starting goalie.

"Whew," I said, relievedly. "Thank God it wasn't Paul Martha!"

I was running late, so I didn't stick around for the ambulance. When I went into work Monday morning, Leo Bemis, the soccer coach, was waiting for me outside my office.

"Do you have any idea who you said that stupid little joke in front of?" he asked.

"Leo, I honestly don't know."

"You said it to the kid's parents!"

I looked at him confused.

"The soccer player, you idiot!"

Bemis stormed out. Was he fired up.

About 30 minutes later, Frank Carver came in. That conversation went about as well as the one with Bemis.

"Leo Bemis was in my office waiting for me this morning," Carver said.

I tried to say something, but Carver cut me off.

"How could you say that?" he yelled. "What in the hell is wrong with you?"

"Frank," I said, "I didn't know it was the kid's parents."

He walked out of there shaking his head. Christ, was he pissed off at that one.

Incredibly, there were several other times that I did much worse. On each of these occasions, I probably deserved to be fired for my behavior, or else for what I said. How the administration put up with me and my antics, I'll never know.

I was extremely lucky that I had understanding bosses. That's probably the only reason that I lasted as long as I did at Pitt. Both of them should be candidates for sainthood, as patient and understanding as they were with me. Especially Tom Hamilton.

There are few people in the history of college football that had a greater influence on the sport than Hamilton. In addition to serving as Pitt's AD, he twice filled in as interim head football coach at Pitt. He was a player, coach and athletic director at Navy, the commissioner of the Pacific-8 Conference, and also spent a number of years on the U.S. Olympic Committee and as vice president of the National Football Foundation.

Hamilton played on the 1926 Navy team that tied undefeated Army, 21-21, in front of 110,000 fans at the Soldier Field dedication game. For many years, that was the largest crowd in college football history.

Hamilton also coached at Navy for a total of five years in two different stints that bookended World War II. For those who aren't aware, he is the guy who coined the famous saying, "a tie is like kissing your sister" after the Army-Navy game in 1946.

Hamilton was one of our earliest naval aviators. During the war, Hamilton developed the Navy's V-5 pre-flight training program and was executive officer on the *U.S.S. Enterprise* during the Battle of Leyte Gulf, the largest naval battle in history, in 1944.

Despite all that experience in both combat and athletics, Hamilton probably had no idea that he'd hired a kamikaze pilot to be his SID. When Myron Cope was putting together the *Sports Illustrated* piece on me, he interviewed Leo "Horse" Czarnecki, the head of maintenance in the athletic department.

"Listen," Horse told Cope. "I seen the brass here so mad at Beano their eyes was popping out of their heads."

That was Hamilton. Nobody could chew your ass out like he could. Nobody. It was by design, though, not because he was a ball buster. You could make mistakes, but never the same mistake twice. He wanted you to learn from your mistakes.

I was admittedly a slow learner. There were a few times that I thought I had fucked up so badly I was going to be fired. One that stands out was the 1959 Pitt-Duke basketball game. I remember it was a Saturday. January 31, 1959. Don Hennon's senior year. We were treading water at .500 for the first couple of weeks of the season and then started a long losing streak. By the time we got to Durham, my nerves were shot.

We played decently the first half and were in the game despite the fact that the officials were completely in the bag for Duke. At halftime, they had called 13 fouls against Pitt and only five personals on Duke. One official in particular seemed to enjoy blowing his whistle on Pitt. His name was Joe Mills. He was a Southerner with a thick drawl.

I was getting pretty hot and started letting Mills have it from close range, my seat near the scorer's table. I called him a bum, a homer, and probably some other, less family-friendly names that I shouldn't have.

Some of our players on the bench followed my lead and started razzing Mills pretty hard. That, in turn, got the home crowd fired up. Right before the half, Mills hit our bench with a technical and that almost blew the roof off of the gym.

I was so worked up, as Mills walked off the floor at the half I hit him with another barrage. He didn't acknowledge any of it until I wheeled out the heavy artillery.

"You must still be mad about Gettysburg!" I yelled.

That one was a direct hit. Pretty soon we were chest-to-chest, going at it as Elton Casey, the longtime Durham sportswriter, described it in his story on the incident, "in the Leo Durocher-umpire style."

Things escalated. Mills wanted me kicked out of the gym. A cop was summoned to the scorer's table. He told me that if I didn't leave, I'd be arrested. Rebelliously, and perhaps somewhat stupidly, I sat down and refused to vacate the premises.

Then Footsie Knight showed up. Just my luck, Knight, the ACC's director of officials, happened to be in attendance. Now, there was no chance Mills would back down in front of his boss and risk both personal and professional humiliation. It was a standoff.

All the while, the crowd was yelling and booing. Years later, I found out that Ken Simpson, who was doing play-by-play, told his listeners that there was a commotion on press row and started describing the action on the air.

Thankfully, Ted Mann, Duke's SID, arrived on the scene and brokered a peace treaty. I didn't have to leave the building, but I had to leave press row and spend the rest of the game in the stands. I didn't think the terms were particularly fair, but I realized this wasn't Panmunjom. I was on enemy soil. And watching the second half from the bleachers sure beat listening to it on the radio behind bars.

Reluctantly, I stood up, snatched my clipboard, and headed up into the stands to a cascade of cheers and jeers from the home crowd.

"I've been thrown out of better places than this," I yelled, defiantly, over my shoulder.*

We ended up losing, 75-66. Mann said it was the first time in his 31 years in Durham that someone had been tossed from press row at Duke. As far as I know, I'm still the only one.

I felt I was upholding Pitt's honor. I felt further vindicated when a number of other SIDs whose teams had gone down to Durham and received similar treatment from the refs called the following week to express their solidarity.

I also heard that Mills had a brother who was a referee, too, and he recently got into it with the Notre Dame head coach, John Jordan. Apparently, many other teams had been victimized by the Mills brothers' hair-trigger whistles.

Before long, though, I began to worry. It occurred to me that Captain Hamilton probably wouldn't feel the same way I did about my behavior. He might think it reflected

---

* Out of all the joints that I've been kicked out of in my life, Cameron Indoor is without a doubt in the top five. Jack Lang, the New York sportswriter, had me thrown out of the Shea Stadium pressbox one time. In 1971, I was escorted out of the Orange Bowl pressbox after an altercation with some pro football people during the North-South Shrine Game.

badly upon Pitt. So when I got back to Pittsburgh that Monday, I was very nervous. This time it might not be a mere dressing down or reduction in rank. I was thinking more along the lines of a dishonorable discharge.

I was surprised I wasn't summoned to his office first thing in the morning. All day long, I waited for him. I was dreading it. I kept staring at the clock. Finally, about quarter of five, Hamilton walked into my office.

"I understand you had a little trouble with the officials down in Durham?"

Here it comes, I said to myself. Then I saw a smile creep onto Hamilton's face.

"When I was at Navy, we played a game there. I know how it is."

With that, he walked out! I didn't know if the Duke affair was forgiven, but for all intents and purposes it would be forgotten.

After that close call, I'd be on my best behavior for at least a little while, right? Wrong. That same year, a Pitt professor committed suicide by jumping out of a window on one of the higher floors of the Cathedral of Learning.

We were really thin at quarterback that year. The only capable, experienced signal caller we had was Ivan Toncic. In one of my releases, I wrote, "A few weeks ago a Pitt professor committed suicide by jumping out of a high window from the Cathedral of Learning. If anything happens to Ivan Toncic, coach John Michelosen might join him."

The public wanted my head for that one. Joking about suicide and all that. Thank God, Hamilton didn't give it to them. I later learned that a writer from *Sports Illustrated* wanted to publish a reprimand of me in the notes column, but was overruled by an editor. For that, I was grateful. The whole thing was largely confined to Pittsburgh and never became national news. I never found out who the editor at *SI* was. I would have liked to have bought him dinner. On the expense account, of course.

I was similarly grateful for the handful of friends and colleagues who knew when to tell me, diplomatically, to pull back on the reins. When Arnie Burdick, the former Syracuse SID who became editor of the *Syracuse Herald-Journal*, saw me later that year, he said, "Beano, we love you. We prove it by not using all the material in your releases."

Hamilton was more than a boss. He was a major influence on my life. The one thing that I didn't follow Hamilton's lead on, not until much later, was his respect for Notre Dame. He had the utmost respect for the people who ran the school and football team's special place in college football.

My shortsightedness, my recklessness, my inability to control my mouth, not to mention my blind hatred of Notre Dame, all of it led to what was undoubtedly the biggest screw-up of my career as an SID. We'll call it the Notre Dame incident.

It took place in late 1958, about three months before the Duke affair, but it was a much bigger deal than what happened at Duke. I almost singlehandedly ruined relations between Pitt and Notre Dame, which would have had major consequences for the athletic department, not to mention the effect it would have had on some long-time friendships.

It's impossible for me to explain just how much I hated Notre Dame at this time. I hated them more than Penn State. It wasn't only because we could never beat them in recruiting or on the field with any regularity. They not only had the media in their pocket, they had an entire religion behind their team. They had so many advantages.

I couldn't stand their fans, especially the subway alums, either, and barely tolerated friends who actually attended the school. I couldn't understand how anybody could root for Notre Dame. To paraphrase one of the legendary lines written by Heywood Broun, I felt that cheering for Notre Dame was "like cheering for Niagara Falls at the moment somebody was going over in a barrel."

I despised pretty much everything about the place and anybody associated with it. The lone exception, of course, being Charlie Callahan. Strangely enough, I was the only one in Pitt's athletic department who thought this way. The coaches liked Notre Dame. They wanted to beat them, of course, but there was a healthy respect between the coaches and schools.

Frank Carver, you didn't dare utter a negative word about Notre Dame's alums or administration in his presence. "High class," he used to say. "The most honorable school to deal with in the business."

I suspect his appreciation of Notre Dame stemmed from a big favor done for him by Elmer Layden, the former "Four Horseman" and Notre Dame head coach. Carver had gotten to know Layden when the latter coached at Duquesne in the 1920s and 1930s.

Layden was the commissioner of the NFL during the war. Carver was working in public affairs for the Army Air Corps at an air base in Tennessee when his commanding officer asked him to find a couple of pro teams to play a benefit game. This officer, like all officers, wanted the order carried out yesterday. Carver was in a bad spot; if he didn't pull it off, he was probably being sent to Alaska or some other cold, miserable assignment.

"Boy, you Pitt guys have all the luck," Layden informed Carver. "Just today I had Curly Lambeau of Green Bay and Greasy Neale of the Eagles here in my office wondering what to do with an open date on the same weekend that the schedules had given them."

Captain Hamilton might have been friendlier with some members of Notre Dame's administration than he was with some of our own people. At the 1957 Pitt-Notre Dame game in South Bend, I was shocked when I saw the two athletic directors, Hamilton and Moose Krause, sitting in the pressbox together and talking like old friends. It was like seeing FDR and Stalin sitting together at Yalta.

You'd never see that happen now. Today, athletic directors spend time with boosters and corporate buddies trying to get money. Not each other. Anyway, it made me uncomfortable. I guess I took the rivalry too seriously.

Hamilton had been competing against and dealing with Notre Dame since before I was born. He knew how important that football team was to an athletic department's finances, not to mention college sports in general.

When Army broke off relations with Notre Dame in the late 1940s after the war, the Pentagon called Hamilton when he was the AD at Navy and asked him to break off relations with Notre Dame, too. He refused to do it. He never specified if it was insubordination, but he left Navy to take the Pitt job in 1949, so read into it what you will.

Hamilton could have ended the series, but he stood his ground. In my opinion, both schools' fans should be thankful they play. As rivalries go, it's mostly one-sided and not as glamorous or near as important to the national championship race as Notre Dame-Southern Cal, but Notre Dame-Navy is one of the last pure rivalries we have left.

Okay. The Notre Dame game in '58. They came in ranked fourteenth in the country. It was Terry Brennan's last year as coach. Despite the fact that Notre Dame was in a period of deemphasis, they still had material. Our kids, though, were ready to go that Saturday. So was I. I couldn't sit still. It was a see-saw affair. If all the pacing I did in the pressbox could have counted towards the stats, I'd have been Pitt's leading rusher.

With under a minute left, Pitt was trailing 26-22 and had a first and goal on Notre Dame's five. We lost a yard after the first three plays. Finally, on fourth down, the late Bill Kaliden from Homestead tucked the ball under his arm and ran six yards to the right side for a touchdown. With the kick we went ahead, 29-26. There was pandemonium in Pitt Stadium!

I didn't start celebrating just yet, because there were 11 seconds left and Notre Dame had a quarterback, George Izo, who could throw the ball a mile. But we held on.

Here's where I come into the story. When the game was officially over, I didn't just celebrate, I went temporarily insane. I was so flush with adrenaline, I ran out of the pressbox screaming my head off. I was so caught up in the moment, to this day I can't remember exactly what it was that I said.

One variation of the story has me yelling "we beat the bastards!" Some say I was screaming "we beat the cocksuckers!" Other people present that day insist it was "we beat the motherfuckers!" It was probably some nasty, foul-mouthed concoction of all three.

I got a kick out of it when the media made such a ridiculous deal of an excited Tyler Palko blurting out the word "fucking" just one time in his post-game interview after Pitt defeated Notre Dame in a last-second nail biter in 2004. That was nothing compared to my behavior!

My explosion of expletives wasn't caught on camera and beamed out to TV sets across the country. What I did was actually worse. As fate would have it, my words were uttered in front of a tiny group of people. The wrong people at precisely the worst possible moment.

See, when the door to the pressbox flew open and I started flailing around and yelling all that foul language, a group of priests, some of whom represented Notre Dame's leadership, just happened to be crossing my profanity-laden path. Father Hesburgh was one of them. I vaguely remembered the white collars and black suits.

It was all a blur. I was so victory drunk, I nearly knocked these bewildered priests over and continued all the way down to the tunnel, ranting and raving and waving my arms like a lunatic the whole way.

The following Monday, Frank Carver came to my office. That wasn't a good sign. Captain Hamilton must have been so pissed at me this time, he sent Carver in his place. After a few years, I think they alternated the responsibility of dealing with me, like two parents who were absolutely worn out by a terror of a toddler.

Carver shut the door behind him. Another bad sign. I tried not to fidget.

"Beano," he said. "We got a call from Notre Dame's president. Do you know what it was about?"

Of course I did. But I didn't say a word. I was guilty, but I figured it would be best if I exercised my right to remain silent.

"He said that he and some priests were involved in a very unfortunate incident while they were guests of ours on Saturday," continued Carver, his voice now quivering. "They were almost attacked by, and I'll quote Father Hesburgh, 'a wildman who came out of the pressbox yelling obscenities about Notre Dame!'"

"I'm really sorry, Frank."

"Wildman!" he yelled. "Obscenities!"

Carver typically had a placid personality, so this was new and frightening.

"I know, I know," was all I could stammer out.

"How do you think this makes us look?"

The gentleman that Carver was, he caught himself before letting his own emotions get the best of him and, thankfully, letting his hands get too close to my neck.

Once he caught his breath, he went on to say that Hesburgh assured him that the relationship between the two schools would not change as long as future incidents such as the one on Saturday could be avoided. That was a relief. I was also relieved to hear that the priests had no clue as to the identity of the "wildman."

"I have an idea who it is," Carver told Hesburgh. "And I'll have a word with him. Father, I promise you that this will never happen again."

"This won't ever happen again," he said to me. "Will it?"

"No, sir."

Carver opened the door to leave. He was halfway through the threshold when he turned back with some final words of wisdom. I'll never forget what he said.

That day, I learned that in college football, every offense, probably up to and including first-degree murder – as long as the victim isn't the gate – was pardonable.

"This is the only time I'm going to say this so please pay attention. Notre Dame is a good friend of Pitt's and I believe we are a good friend of Notre Dame's. We want to keep things that way. Whether you like them or not, that's immaterial," Carver explained. "If you have to insult somebody, don't insult the one team that fills our stadium. Insult anybody else. Insult Duke."*

---

* Duke fans: I doubt Carver had any animosity towards Duke. It was probably the first school that popped into his head. I have nothing but respect for Duke, its administration, its players, its coaches, especially Coach K, who I saw play at West Point, and its fans. In fact, I have a Duke sweatshirt given to me by your AD, Kevin White, that I proudly wear when it gets cold.

CHAPTER 3

A note from the Redhead.

Of all the great advice that Frank Carver gave me over the years, there were some specific words of wisdom that always came in handy when I arrived at a crossroads in my career: "The job comes to the man."

It was the truth. When I think about all the jobs I've had, the opportunities that showed up out of nowhere, those typically ended up being the most rewarding experiences. With maybe one or two very notable exceptions, the jobs that I chased and lobbied for, the ones I tried very hard to make happen, those brought misery and disappointment.

It was a bittersweet moment for me in late 1965 when I told Carver that a job had come to me and that I had decided to leave Pitt. I had been offered the position of director of publicity for college sports at *ABC*. It was one of the toughest decisions I ever had to make because I loved being the SID at Pitt. It was, in many ways, the best job I'd ever have. I knew in my gut, however, that it was time to go. In fact, I had known for more than a year.

Veteran sportswriter Dan Parker of the old *New York Daily Mirror* called me "the greatest publicity man since Barnum – and, on second thought, Bailey, too." I didn't think it was true, but I appreciated the plug.

Thanks to that kind of high praise from the likes of Parker, Red Smith, Paul Zimmerman, and some others, plus all the notoriety I'd gotten from the releases, a line of suitors began forming outside my office door starting in the early 1960s.

None of these publicity gigs seemed like they'd be any fun or offered any real financial incentive, at least none worth leaving my alma mater for. Some of these jobs, though, were high-profile, so I flirted with a few of them.

In the spring of 1960, I was invited by Tex Schramm to apply for the job of publicist of the Dallas Cowboys. I had met Schramm while working as an errand boy for

CBS during the Winter Olympics in Squaw Valley that February. Schramm was wrapping up his duties as the assistant director of *CBS Sports* before taking over operations for the upstart Cowboys.

I didn't get the job, and, in retrospect, I'm glad I didn't. Building a franchise from the ground up is all work. There would have been no laughs.

Years later, I wrote Schramm and asked him why he didn't hire me. He called me and said, "Beano, we were just getting started and the things that came out of your mouth, well, I thought you'd be too controversial."

When I hung up the phone, I had a good laugh. Tex was full of shit. I always respected the guy. I consider him an important part of league history, a founding father of the modern NFL, but he was worried about the things that came out of my mouth?

I was a guest of Joe Robbie at the 1978 Cowboys-Dolphins game, which Dallas lost because they had a million turnovers. Despite that fact, Schramm stood in the Orange Bowl pressbox and called the officials "dirty cocksuckers" and the Dolphins "lucky cocksuckers."

Nowadays, pro football teams don't give a second thought to signing players who have been arrested for beating their girlfriends or wives. You can father ten kids with ten different women. Nobody cares. If Stalin showed up at the combine and ran the 40-yard-dash under 4.4 seconds, he'd probably be a middle to late first round pick.

In 1960, though, Beano Cook was too controversial for pro football!

In 1964, I was offered the Lakers' PR job. I was very close to taking it, but I didn't want to live in Los Angeles. I would have been too far from Pittsburgh and my parents.

By the time the '64 football season ended, I really regretted the decision. We got walloped by Penn State, 28-0, in the season finale in State College. The wind had a bite to it that November day and I couldn't help but wonder how warm and sunny Southern California probably was by comparison.

Back in Pittsburgh, the Field House was quiet that Sunday. John Michelosen came over to my office for a few words.

"Well," he said, "It's over. Sure went fast."

It did. Perhaps mercifully. It was a terrible year. There was a lot of optimism going into '64 after we went 9-1 in '63, but the season ended in disappointment and frustration. And I had no way of knowing at the time that '65 would be even worse.

Michelosen looked small and tired when he walked out, and I felt ashamed of myself for not showing a little more compassion during the season. Even so, when I glanced at the 1965 schedule on the wall, I dreaded the thought of another season with him and our annual arguments about the heights and weights in the media guide.

What happened next was nothing less than a sign. Just before I got up to leave, I looked down at my desk and I saw a lined piece of paper with "Shottenheimer" written on it. The name, of course, was misspelled. I felt sick to my stomach. This time, I didn't have any lazy sportswriters or copy editors to blame. The handwriting was my own.

I showed up at *ABC's* headquarters on Sixth Avenue in midtown Manhattan in March 1966 with my clipboard and mixed feelings. On one hand, I was excited for the opportunity. I was convinced that television was the future. This job was my foot in the door.

I was apprehensive because at the time I didn't think highly of the people who worked in television. I told someone that *CBS* was the country that fielded the biggest team for the '60 Olympics. And with the exception of Schramm, who did his job and didn't waste any time trying to impress everybody, they were the most obnoxious people I had ever met.

One of my jobs was to drag the winners over to do TV interviews. Sometimes it was hard to pry a medalist away from the writers. "Tell them to forget the newspapers," one of the producers sneered. "If he goes on television, fifty million people will see him."

The arrogance was like cheap aftershave; I could smell it a mile away and it made me nauseous. I left a day early, before the closing ceremonies, because I couldn't stand being around those people a minute more than I had to.

So, why did I willingly join their ranks? Why did I take the PR job at *ABC*? Those two questions can be answered with one word.

Roone.

Throughout his remarkable career in television, the only things Roone Pinckney Arledge, Jr. racked up more than honors and awards – he's credited with 37 Emmys, four Peabodys, and countless other achievement awards – were numerous nicknames, titles, and distinctions, both official and informal.

Many called him simply by his distinctive first name. Some remember him as president of *ABC* Sports and later, *ABC* News. *Life* Magazine was more extravagant, calling him one of the "100 most important Americans of the 20th Century" in 1990. When Roone died, Frank Deford wrote the obit in *Sports Illustrated* and called Roone "the most important person in the history of sports television."

Roone had two nicknames. The public one was "The Wizard." It had a double meaning. He was obviously a wizard when it came to television. It was also because, as the movie told us, nobody gets in to see the great Oz, not nobody, not no how. It was accurate, because Roone worked behind a wall of secrecy guarded by his secretaries.

Many of us inside *ABC* Sports called Roone something else, a secret nickname. I don't know who came up with it, but it was one of us who worked for him in the late 1960s. We called him "The Redhead." We would say amongst ourselves, "the Redhead's happy," or "watch out, the Redhead's pissed."

Since Roone rarely handled communications verbally, when someone received a compliment it was almost always in the form of a handwritten note. The recipient, beaming with pride, would say, "I got a note from the Redhead."

Whatever you called him, Roone was a legend. In my opinion, the two most innovative people in television in the last fifty years were Norman Lear and Roone Arledge.

Roone perceived the world of television through his own camera lens, a pioneer in production concepts and programming ideas who was years of ahead of his time. The lingering crowd shots. Freeze-frames. Field microphones. Split-screens. Cranes on golf courses. Cameras in every conceivable, as well as previously inconceivable, location. It was all Roone.

He brought historic events to people in real-time, and I truly believe he's the man responsible for setting the 24-hour news cycle in motion. He and his staffs at *ABC* Sports and News did simple stories and spectacles equally well. He broadened our view of sports with "Wide World" and made us look forward to, of all things, Monday nights.

While his skills as an administrator were questionable, he was undoubtedly a builder and a leader. The two greatest divisions in network television since the end of World War II were *CBS* News up until the day Cronkite retired, and *ABC* Sports, from the day Roone took over in the 1960s until the day he left in the 1980s. Roone spanned eras, from black and white floor consoles to the eve of high-definition flat screens.

And though he's been gone nearly ten years, his influence lives on. It's no stretch to suggest that there's a little Roone in every broadcast you watch. Every Super Bowl, every Olympics, every Triple Crown horse race, every Rose Bowl, every British Open, every nightly news, every magazine show, every live satellite feed, every "SportsCenter."

Roone lives on not only in the production concepts and programming ideas, but through the people who make these telecasts possible. Roone's knack for discovering talent was remarkable. In terms of on-air talent, the names are a veritable who's who in television history: Cosell. McKay. Gowdy. Schenkel. Jackson. Walters. Jennings. Sawyer. I don't have to give you the first names. Everybody knows them.

People in sports, especially when the subject is football, like to talk about "coaching trees," the coaches who cut their teeth working under a particular coach and went on to success on his own. For example, there's the Bill Parcells coaching tree, or the Bill Belichick coaching tree.

In the world of sports television there's an Arledge tree of directors, producers, and network executives. For years, I could tell just by the moves made that the individual had worked for Roone.

When I heard my friend Howard Katz, as president of *ABC* Sports, hired comedian Dennis Miller for "Monday Night Football," I said to myself, *"that's something Roone would have done."*

Some of Roone rubbed off Dick Ebersol, the current president of *NBC* Sports. During the 2008 Summer Olympics, Ebersol somehow convinced the International Olympic Committee to hold the swimming events at 9 a.m. Beijing time so America could see superstar swimmer Michael Phelps in primetime. Successfully negotiating with the IOC and the Chinese Communist Party is no mean feat, but Ebersol pulled it off in true Roone fashion.

I could go on and on. The Arledge tree is really the Arledge National Forest. So many of Roone's acorns and saplings grew into towering redwoods. These are people who either started at *ABC* or else spent time there under Roone and went on to do big things. In addition to Katz and Ebersol, you've got Sean McManus, Bob Iger, Geoff Mason, Don Ohlmeyer, Mike Pearl, Terry O'Neil and so many others who became legends in production and as executives.

And then there's me. I called Roone boss for a dozen years, most of which was spent doing PR for *ABC* Sports. But in 1982, he put me on the air as a college football commentator, kick-starting my career on television. I had a lot of fun doing PR, but it's my second career that brought me national notoriety and that's the real reason why you're reading this book.

Being on television is what made my name a household one. It changed my life. Once you are on television everything changes. There are perks. Not nearly as many as a Congressman gets, but there are perks. People do favors for you whether they like you or not. Phone calls are returned faster. Requests for tickets are taken care of.

And I've got Roone to thank for it. Of all the names in this book, all the people whose paths crossed mine throughout my life and career, none were as important to me, professionally, as Roone.

For reasons that I'll never know, Roone seemed to like me. He trusted me and he respected my opinions. He put up with my bullshit. He gave me a lot of freedom in my job.

He also gave me more responsibility, in regards to things like schedule-making and programming, than any network publicist had probably ever been given, or will ever be given. Because of Roone I participated in – and, on a few occasions, was a prime mover behind – some important moments in college football and sports television history.

"We're not trying to take the game into the living room," Roone used to say about *ABC's* event coverage, "we're trying to take people out of their living rooms to the game."

So according to Roone, there's only one way for me to tell my story. Throughout the course of this book, I'll to be taking you out of your living room and back, at various times, to the late 1960s, 1970s and 1980s, to the golden era of network television sports.

To paraphrase Charles Dickens, it was the best of times. It was an era of outrageously high salaries and out-of-this-world egos, of limousines, Lear jets and limitless expense accounts. Everybody was chasing something: power; pussy; betting losses. There were office politics, but political correctness hadn't yet ruined the party. We didn't have social media but that didn't stop us from socializing. At Runyon's. Mike Manuche's. Mister Laff's. Jimmy Weston's. Everywhere. Everybody had fun.

There's no better place to start than at what once was the center of the sports television universe, the *ABC* Building, 1330 Avenue of the Americas, New York, New York.

In this chapter, we're getting off the elevator on the 20th floor to a sea of mini skirts, tweed and tartan jackets. We'll start off by listening in on a few off-the-record conversations and phone calls. As you turn these pages, we'll sit in on production meetings, NCAA television committee meetings and rights negotiations.

I'll show you around the production truck. I'll take you on some remotes and we'll visit some stadiums, arenas, hotels, and bars that no longer exist.

We'll also take a few breaks with the guys around the coffee wagon. In addition to Cosell, Gowdy, McKay and the other names I mentioned above, there are some other interesting characters, people like Joe Aceti, Chet Forte, Howard Rothstein, Andy Sidaris, and a few others that I'd like you to meet.

First, though, I have to introduce you to Roone. Since he was such an important part of the story of my life and career, it's only fair that he helps me tell this part of it.

*   *   *

I first met Roone Arledge when *ABC* Sports came to Pittsburgh to do the Michigan State-Pitt game in September 1960. I was blown away with the whole operation. The entire crew. The giant stack of index cards that Curt Gowdy had in front of him in the booth. That was the first time I had seen an announcer so prepared. I'm not saying that other outfits were fly-by-night operations, but everybody from *ABC* stood out. Especially Roone.

He was probably the first television bigshot that didn't make me feel like I was a glorified usher. I noticed his genius, his vision, right away when he asked me about putting cameras on the roof of the VA hospital that overlooked Pitt Stadium. He was the first producer who had ever asked me about doing that. He literally had every angle covered.

As I'd learn when he hired me, one of the many secrets of Roone's success was his attention to detail. No event, no person - no task, done or undone - went unnoticed. That statement might surprise some people, because those of us who knew him well knew him to be terrible with certain details.

He was horrendous when it came to returning phone calls. I happened to be near Roone's office one day in the early 1970s when I heard his secretary say, "Yes, Mr. President. I'll give him the message."

President Nixon left a message for Roone to call him back. As far as we know, Nixon died waiting for the call.

He was often impossible to find. When he was made head of *ABC* News in 1977, I said "now Roone will have two offices where he won't be found."

His desk was always covered by piles of papers. That's because he preferred making decisions at the last possible minute. He drove his secretaries crazy when it came to expense accounts. He never kept receipts. So the guy wasn't perfect. But he was paying attention.

For example, Roone could be walking through the office and pass someone's unoccupied desk, and if the phone rang, he'd stand there. If it rang a third time, he'd pick it up himself. The secretaries got the message: he did not like to hear a third ring.

And Roone knew how to one-up the competition. Literally. When I first arrived at *ABC* in '66, I noticed that we had two receptionists. One came in early, another came on in the evening for relief. And this second receptionist did not leave until very late.

Ten years later, when I started working at *CBS*, I noticed there was only one receptionist and she left at five o'clock on the dot. I immediately thought of Roone and remembered something he once told me.

"I don't worry about *NBC*, Beano, but *CBS Sports*..." he had said, nodding his head towards Black Rock, directly across the street, "if they ever wake up..."

That's why he had two to their one! It was a pre-emptive move, and hardly a surprising one for a man known for his vision. As Roone explained in further detail, he considered *CBS* Sports a sleeping giant. The network had strong affiliates, solid programming, and the best news. I don't think anybody or anything kept Roone up late at night, but the Tiffany Network, as *CBS* was called, worried him the most because of what he perceived to be its incredible potential.

I remember another time Roone was walking around the office on a summer night, a Friday night no less, around quarter of seven. I'd say about sixty percent of the people were still in the office. He stopped in the doorway of my office and poked his head in.

"How many people at the other networks do you think are still at work?" he asked.

It was a rhetorical question. He walked away before I had the chance to answer.

I know Roone appreciated all the hard work. He understood being number one was a team effort. He made those trips through the office often just to say hello to people and to thank them for staying late.

Contrary to what a lot of people, such as Jim Spence, who considered Roone aloof and shallow, have said and written, Roone wasn't as cold and distant as many believed. He definitely wasn't a laughs guy, but he was a people person. By that, I mean that he understood people. How to treat them. How to motivate them. And especially how to deal with them. If Roone had gone into the foreign service, nobody would have heard of Henry Kissinger.

Sure, this was the era of big spending in network television, but Roone didn't just outbid or outspend the competition. He loved the art of dealmaking. When it came to brokering deals with everybody from league executives and corporate sponsors to foreign functionaries, no one was better. It was the same with team owners, commissioners, coaches, announcers, athletes, and anchors. Roone was one helluva diplomat. I saw it first-hand.

Red Auerbach once called Roone to complain about Jack Twyman, a great NBA forward who used to do color for our *NBA on ABC* telecasts in the 1960s and early 70s. The late Twyman, a Pittsburgh native, never said a bad word about anybody. Everybody liked him.

During one particular broadcast we did in Boston, Twyman commented about a couple of dead spots on the floor of the old Boston Garden. It was a quick comment that few, if any, viewers paid attention to. Oh, but Red Auerbach had been paying attention.

That man heard and read everything. He was one of the thinnest-skinned pro franchise owners around, right behind Art Modell. Once, the sportswriter Steve Hershey wrote an article that was critical of the Celtics. The next game he covered, the Celtics seated him almost up in the rafters of the Garden as punishment. The Celtics organization, in my opinion, lacked class, and maybe that was attributable to Auerbach's leadership. Anyway, I happened to be in the office when Auerbach called Roone about Twyman.

"Roone," said Red, "Tell Twyman to knock it off, talking about the dead spots."

He sounded genuinely pissed. As if Twyman was making up claims out of thin air.

"Oh," mused Roone, playing dumb. "I'm sorry. I didn't know there weren't any dead spots on the floor."

"Oh, no, there are dead spots," replied Auerbach.

"Well, Red," said Roone. "What's the problem?"

Auerbach was used to bullshitting or intimidating other broadcasters and network suits. That didn't happen with Roone.

I remember the time Roone wanted to move some Big Ten football games to alter the programming schedule. This was in the late 1960s. Roone called up Bill Reed, the commissioner of the Big Ten, on the phone. Right off, Reed didn't like the idea.

"There's a tradition in the Big Ten to kickoff at 1:30," Reed replied, solemnly.

"If you feel that way about the tradition, we just won't do as many games."

The games were moved.

Roone had been wanting to produce a big college football game in primetime on national television since I got to *ABC*. I didn't understand his preoccupation with the idea but looking back, it had to have been related to his big plans for "Monday Night Football." He probably wanted to experiment with some things, from production and technical standpoints.

We succeeded in airing the first nationally televised primetime college football game between Alabama and Miami at the Orange Bowl in November 1968, but the game didn't make as big a splash as Roone wanted.

So we went back to the drawing board for the '69 season and lined up Alabama and Mississippi to play their early October showdown under the lights at Legion Field. Back then, Alabama played all of its big games in Birmingham since Legion Field had a larger seating capacity than Denny Stadium, Alabama's on-campus facility in Tuscaloosa.

Right away, Roone ran into two roadblocks which would try his patience and test his skills as a negotiator. First of all, the lighting at Legion Field was terrible. We sent some people down there to check things out and they reported that there would be poor picture quality for the broadcast.

Nobody seemed to know how to remedy the situation, either. Our people were being jerked around by every official in Alabama. Stadium management said we had to talk to the mayor of Birmingham, the mayor's people said you had to talk to city council, and so forth.

I suggested Roone put in a personal call to the highest-ranking authority in the state of Alabama. And I don't mean the governor.

Bear Bryant called Roone back right away and told him not to worry.

"The mayor of Birmingham will put in new lights," Bryant growled, confidently. "Or he won't be re-elected."

Unfortunately, the second roadblock to Roone's plan wasn't as easily overcome. Roone put in another call, this time to Lawrence Welk, to ask him to move the time of his ballroom dancing show, which aired on Saturday nights on *ABC*, to accommodate the network's special football broadcast. It was a one-time thing, but Welk, whose contract gave him final say in such matters, refused. I could tell the conversation hadn't gone well.

"Adios and au revoir?" I asked as he put the phone back on the receiver.

"Auf wiedersehen and good night," Roone grumbled.

Roone reluctantly, but with little other recourse, went with an absurdly late kickoff, 9:30 p.m. Eastern, 8:30 in Birmingham, but that game turned out to be a high-scoring shootout between Archie Manning and Scott Hunter that the whole country tuned in to watch.

For what it's worth, Roone said he preferred dealing with prima donna performers and politicians rather than priests. Negotiating with Fr. Ned Joyce at Notre Dame, he once told me, wasn't particularly painful, but "you are at a disadvantage from the start because you must say 'Father' first."

Some negotiations were outright wars. The epic battle for the NCAA college football package in 1969 was one notable example. In 1965, a year before I arrived at *ABC*, the NCAA had granted the network exclusive rights to college football, but tried to attach a bizarre stipulation to the deal that *ABC* never televised pro football. Yes, never. Not in 1965. Not in 2065. Never again.

Although the request sounds absurd, it wasn't unusual if you knew anything about Walter Byers, the administrative dictator who ran the NCAA for nearly four decades like Castro runs Cuba.

Not only did Byers run the NCAA with an iron fist, he often behaved like a child. He would read the papers at TV committee meetings when Roone was talking because he thought it pissed Roone off. Once, after he had had too many martinis and signed an option on a deal, he blamed Roone for getting him drunk.

During the college football television negotiations in 1981, I was working at *CBS*. This was in the midst of the dual deal *ABC* and *CBS* were hammering out with Byers and the NCAA. At an impasse, *ABC's* Jim Spence, who had taken over for Roone, attempted to bring up the 16-year relationship between *ABC*, the NCAA, and Byers. Byers had no time for nostalgia or goodwill. "This is business," he said.

Then when *ABC* sued the NCAA because of its supplemental contract with Ted Turner's *TBS*, an NCAA lawyer said, obviously having conferenced with Byers, "you would think after a 16-year relationship *ABC* wouldn't act this way."

What I remember Byers for the most was his tremendous hatred for pro football. It was a phobia. Byers was one of those pigskin puritans who probably viewed the NFL first as a rogue league and later came to see the pros as a competitor. He'd been going out of his way to discredit professional football for years and had been accustomed to strong-arming the networks and getting what he wanted.

Lindsey Nelson once told me that when he was doing college games for *NBC*, he was forbidden from mentioning that John Michelosen had coached the Steelers prior to coaching Pitt. That was Byers. Imagine a broadcaster, when Bill Walsh came out of retirement to take the Stanford job, not being able to say that Walsh won four Super Bowls with San Francisco!

And think about the endless cross-promotion that goes on today. Back then, you couldn't do any of that. Today, you can't watch a Saturday night college football game on *ABC* without being reminded a dozen times, maybe more, of the following Monday night's NFL matchup on *ESPN*. There are fifty TV time outs during Saturday Notre Dame home games and *NBC* uses half of them to run promos for "Sunday Football Night in America."

When Roone announced "Monday Night Football" in '69, Byers went through the roof. His beloved sport sharing a network with the hated NFL? It was scandalous.

Things got so heated during contract negotiations in a hotel conference room near Chicago's O'Hare Airport that Byers erupted into a blistering tirade. I was there. It was shocking stuff.

The negotiations got off to a bad start when we showed a promotional film that demonstrated some of the technological advances that we intended to employ in our coverage of college football. Some of our most talented people put a lot of time into the film and Roone expressed his disappointment that the committee didn't comment on it.

"We voted 8-7 that we liked it," Byers sneered. It was a sarcastic, smart-ass line.

Things got really hot from there and very little was accomplished over the course of the following day. After so much back and forth, Byers finally exploded. He was ranting and raving about *ABC*, the NFL, you name it.

What was most surprising to me was Roone's self-control. Despite his trademark red hair, Roone rarely became flammable in these types of settings. He kept his cool and didn't say a word until Byers finally ran out of verbal ammunition.

"Walter," Roone said, "we took our own vote and you came in first in our personality contest. The vote was 3-2. Charles Manson came in second."

It took all the self-restraint I had not to laugh. When Byers tramped out of the room in his cowboy boots, I turned to Roone.

"How can you just sit there and put up with all of his shit?" I asked.

Roone replied that with Byers, the screaming wasn't a signal that the negotiations were finished. It meant that things were moving into the next phase. There was a next phase and that's all the mattered.

"What good would it do to yell back?" Roone explained. "We want college football."

In the next phase, Byers made disparaging remarks about *ABC's* programming and then presented Roone with an outrageous offer that could only be met with all the gold in Fort Knox. He then walked that back and said he could be convinced to give *ABC* a tremendous discount if only we'd ok a small provision in the contract that the network, would not televise pro football. Our lawyers nixed it. Other times, Byers got his way.

It was at the 1981 meetings that Byers made maybe his strangest demand yet: he wanted it put in writing that if World War III broke out, it would void the contract. *ABC* signed off on it. Looking back, I guess it was probably a prudent move. By that time, Roone had Byers all figured out. Leonid Brezhnev, however, was still a wild card.

Back to '69, after our meeting Byers secretly met with *NBC* functionaries to try an end run around Roone. Where did this meeting take place? In a remote hangar at JFK Airport. I got all the details from the late Carl Lindemann, Jr. the longtime *NBC* Sports and, later, *CBS* Sports executive. The story Lindemann told me sounded like something straight out of a James Bond movie. Byers was a real piece of work.

In the end, Roone agreed to promote the Saturday games on the Monday night broadcasts and he and Byers came to terms on the NCAA package. That deal, and 1969 in general, was a banner year for Roone. It was the culmination of five years of patience and planning. It was sweet revenge.

The way I heard the story, Pete Rozelle opened up bidding for the NFL television rights at $24 million in 1964. *NBC* already had the AFL contract. That left just *ABC* and *CBS*. *ABC* submitted a bid of $26 million right around the deadline and Roone felt confident since he had some wiggle-room – he was permitted to bid up to $28 million.

Bill McPhail, the president of *CBS* Sports, on the other hand, was concerned. He didn't want to raise his network's bid blindly, so he called Jim Aubrey. Aubrey, the network president, told McPhail to sit tight. Aubrey later came to McPhail's office and wrote "$28.1 million" on an envelope and pushed it over to McPhail. That turned out to be the winning bid.

The end result was that *ABC* had no football for several years. At the time, Roone had achieved some success and notoriety with "Wide World of Sports" and "American Sportsman," but still had no mainstream sport or product to put his stamp on. To say he was upset with how things transpired would be an understatement.

For many years, people at *ABC* believed there was a leak. After hearing the story, I believe it. Somehow Aubrey found out that $28 million was the number *ABC* wouldn't go north of. Roone never forgot. He handled all negotiations from that point forward.

No, you didn't cross Roone. "Superstars" was proof. The talk about "Superstars" – a sports competition show involving famous athletes competing in sports that weren't their own, a kind of Olympics featuring American pro athletes – started in the mid-1960s when Dick Button was shopping the idea to all three networks.

I want to make it clear that "Superstars" was Button's baby. Barry Frank, one of our execs who would later serve a short stint as *CBS* Sports president before going on to be a high-powered agent, often gets credit for the idea. Now Frank does deserve a little bit of credit for ultimately selling Roone on the show, but I think Roone's mind was already more than halfway made up on it because he wanted revenge.

See, Button had pitched Roone the idea before, but Roone never seriously considered it until the NBA, led by the ownership of the Los Angeles Lakers and the New York Knicks and Madison Square Garden, stabbed *ABC* in the back in the 1970s.

What the NBA and *CBS* did was make it impossible for *ABC* to match the terms of the current contract, which *ABC* had the right to do. The NBA wanted its Saturday games in November to tip-off between one and two o'clock. There was no way we could do that because we had college football.

ABC naturally sued and when they went to court, the NBA's lawyers pointed out to the judge that legally speaking, it was one-year trial, and that's what it ended up being – they didn't do it a second year. The whole thing was basically a ploy intended to make it impossible for *ABC* to match the terms so that *CBS* could jump in. You didn't have to be Perry Mason to figure that out. But the judge ruled in favor of the NBA.

When the NBA was planning its betrayal, Red Auerbach sat in the meeting and reportedly warned the other general managers and owners. "You don't think Roone," he said, "is just going to sit there and take this, do you?"

He certainly wasn't. At the time, the joke around the office was that someone was going to pay dearly even if just for getting Roone up early in the morning. Roone liked to come to the office late and the trial cramped his style.

There's no doubt in my mind that Roone, as forecasted by Auerbach, was plotting his revenge on the NBA and *CBS*. He was even more focused than usual during this time period. I was working on our NBA broadcasts then and I remember asking him something about the NBA one day and he said, kind of out of the blue, "we're going to do Superstars." I might have been the first person to hear of the decision.

"Superstars" went on the air in the winter of 1973, about a year before I left *ABC*, as a feature on "Wide World." It was a runaway hit. Don Ohlmeyer, a 1967 graduate of Notre Dame who worked on "Monday Night Football," produced the show. Roone and Ohlmeyer just pounded *CBS*. Pounded them. "Superstars" destroyed the NBA in the ratings and the long-term fallout cost the Association plenty of money.

Roone wasn't one to gloat, but when he did, he had a way of doing it discreetly. He was at the Polo Lounge of the Beverly Hills Hotel when the ratings for the first Sunday of head-to-head competition between "Superstars" and the NBA came in.

As luck would have it, Roone spied Walter Kennedy, commissioner of the NBA, across the room. Roone called the waiter over. He scribbled a short message containing only two things on a cocktail napkin, folded up the note, handed it to the waiter along with a nice big tip and instructed the waiter to deliver the message to Kennedy.

What two things, you're probably wondering, were contained in this brief note?

The ratings and Roone's signature.

*   *   *

Roone's battles with the NCAA, the professional leagues and the International Olympic Committee are legendary. Others have written extensively on the subject. What really impressed me, though, were his little-known in-house dealings, those with his own people. That goes for both superiors and subordinates.

As for the former, few people are aware that when *CBS* and *NBC* turned down the first Monday night package, the brass at *ABC* did, too. But Pete Rozelle had a bid from the Hughes Network – owned by the eccentric tycoon Howard Hughes, the network started out as the Sports Network Inc. in the mid 1950s, a primitive *ESPN* of sorts – for $10.4 million.

Rozelle, however, was wary. He knew if the concept of Monday night football failed on the Hughes Network, it would be another five to ten years, maybe longer, before it would ever be given another shot on a major network.

Roone reassured Rozelle that he would make it work at *ABC* and asked him to sit tight. "Give me a few weeks," he said. Rozelle, to his credit, was willing to wait because he knew the promotional value of *ABC*. And because he also knew the value of Roone.

In the meantime, Roone called the affiliates and conducted what amounted to an informal survey. He asked the affiliates, "what will you do if the Hughes Network has pro football on Monday nights?" The general response was, "we're going to take it. Your programming isn't very good on Monday night."

When Philadelphia, which at the time was the fourth-largest market in the U.S., said they would clear the football game, that was the turning point. Roone went back to the network brass with this information and this time they took it, thinking it was a defensive move. They had no idea that it would be the hit that it was. But Roone did.

Incidentally, this first year of the package, *ABC* paid $8.6 million. That's unbelievable. At this writing, *ESPN* and the NFL are currently in talks to extend the network's current agreement to carry Monday Night Football through the 2020 season, a deal that would pay the NFL nearly $2 billion annually. Yes, billion.

As for the way he interacted with subordinates, Roone seldom chewed *ABC* employees out in public, or when he was in the truck. If he was unhappy he usually pulled the individual aside and communicated his displeasure discreetly. And nobody knew anything about it unless that person told you.

There was, however, one notable occasion during the '76 Summer Olympics in Montreal. On the third night of the games, somebody spelled gymnast Nadia Comaneci's name wrong on the graphic. This was right after she had scored the first perfect ten score in modern Olympics history.

Roone was so mad he ordered producer Chuck Howard to fire the PA (production assistant) on the spot. To the best of my knowledge, that's the only time that anybody saw him blow up in public. When somebody asked why, he explained his decision.

"Look, on the first night nobody knew who she was," Roone said. "By the third night, everybody in the world knew who she was."

Roone chewed my ass out just one time. It happened in private and I totally deserved it. It was late November 1971. *ABC* had the Iron Bowl that year and I did something that I shouldn't have. I called a few sportswriter friends and asked them, as a personal favor to me, to vote Auburn into the top five. I wanted to be able to promote the Iron Bowl as a top five showdown. Auburn had been in the top five all season, but the week before, after a bye, the Tigers had dropped to No. 6 behind Penn State.

I probably didn't even need to do it since the entire country would have been watching anyway. Both teams were undefeated, Alabama was No. 3, and Auburn was a big draw because of Pat Sullivan, the eventual Heisman Trophy winner.

Until now, only two people ever knew about it. I told Roone, thinking he'd applaud my initiative, but instead he let me have it. He told me to never try to manipulate the polls or to do anything else that could be considered by the public to have been improper, even if my intentions were only to help the network.

When it came to outside complaints or pressure, Roone didn't throw his people to the wolves. The only action I can remember in this regard was the case of Warner Wolf. Wolf made some comments about Bear Bryant and we were flooded with calls and letters from Prudential agents in Alabama. Prudential sponsored the "College Football Scoreboard Show." Pretty soon, Wolf wasn't working for us anymore. I suspect there was another reason for Wolf's departure, but I won't speculate on the situation since that was above my pay grade.

Roone's behavior was much different than that of his contemporary counterparts who won't hesitate to fire somebody or even go so far as to ruin someone's career to save face, to impress the suits, the sponsors, or to be politically correct.

I remember during the Dallas Cowboys' "Monday Night Football" debut in 1970, a 38-0 humiliation at the hands of the St. Louis Cardinals, both Howard Cosell and Don Meredith made some remarks that upset Rozelle. Cosell was just being Cosell and Meredith, the former Cowboy, let his emotions contaminate his commentary. It was nothing, if you asked me, but Rozelle called Roone the next day.

Roone patiently listened to the complaints and then said, "Pete, I should be the one complaining about the way Dallas played." And that ended the conversation.

Early on during the "Monday Night Football" experiment, Rozelle complained to Roone quite a bit about Cosell, but Roone finally told Rozelle, flatly, "listen, you pick the games, we pick the announcers."

I didn't create anywhere near the amount of controversy that Cosell did at *ABC* – well, at least not until Roone put me on the air in 1982, and we'll get to those complaints later on – but when I did ruffle feathers, Roone had my back, too.

In December 1971, the late Charley Bidwill, owner and president of the St. Louis Cardinals, wrote a letter to Rozelle complaining about my behavior in the Orange Bowl pressbox at the North-South Shrine Game. Bidwill accused me of talking "in the worst way about professional football." It read like a police report. He listed George Boone, the Cards' personnel man, a CEPO scout, Jackie Graves, and Green Bay scout Baby Ray as witnesses.

Did I bash pro ball? Probably. Did what was essentially a heated argument between grown men need to be escalated in a letter to the commissioner of the National Football League? Of course not. It was complete chickenshit, but totally in character for Bidwill. He ran an organization that, I had been told, but have no way of verifying, if a player was awarded the game ball, sent that player a bill for the ball the following week.

Rozelle forwarded the letter to Roone who made sure I saw it. That was Roone's way of saying, "FYI. Carry on." I never heard another word about the incident again.

This wasn't the first, and definitely would not be the last letter that would be forwarded to my attention while I was at *ABC*. I didn't always know how all those things would shake out, but I could be sure of a fair trial as long as Roone was in charge.

In the early 1970s, I did color on a handful of *ABC* regional college football telecasts. I typically worked with Lynn Sanner, but on occasion got to share the booth with my good friend, the late Dave Diles. Diles was not only a wonderful person and a lot of laughs, he was an all-around talent who excelled at doing "Wide World" and covering big events like the Indianapolis 500 and the Olympics as well.

During this time, *ABC* had four, maybe five two-man broadcast teams doing college football. Chris Schenkel and Bud Wilkinson was our No. 1 team and Keith Jackson and Lee Grosscup our No. 2. The other crews were rounded out by names like Bill Flemming, Forest Evashevski, Merle Harmon, Dave Nelson, Joe Kapp, and several others.

When I first learned that I was being taken off the broadcasts, the decision didn't bother me. It would have been nice to have added another year of on-air service onto my pension, but it wasn't a big blow to my ego or my plans since I never really had a desire to do games. At this point of my career, I was having fun doing PR, but I still held out hope of one day becoming a writer or columnist.

What bugged me more than anything else were the rumors that I'd been bumped to make room for a minority. I later found out that they hired Ron Burton for my spot. I felt worse about what I said when I learned that it was Burton because Burton was a class act. I didn't want him to think my comments were aimed at him because they weren't.

As for being booted, it's one thing to be removed for being bad at your job, but I wasn't. I wasn't Schenkel or Jackson, okay, but I wasn't bad. I also felt that I knew more about college football and its history than all of our other on-air personalities combined.

If somebody, whether they were black, yellow, red or whatever, would have beaten me in an audition or been better suited for the job due to their talent or merits, fine. I resented the idea that I was considered expendable, that I had to be the one let go just to make some junior suit's experiment in political correctness possible.

As word got around, some writers asked how I felt about the decision. I'll admit that I was pretty pissed off. I tried to come up with a line that would be clever or funny, but what I blurted out was neither.

"I would rather be white," I said, "and not have the job."

There's no doubt in my mind that had I uttered that line today, I would have been fired immediately. There's a good chance, had the line been more widely reported or if I'd been a higher profile figure, I would have been fired even back then. But I wasn't. Because, thankfully, Roone was my boss.

"Look, Beano," he told me, "you gotta watch it." And that was it.

Everybody is familiar with the incident that got the Greek fired. I won't rehash all the details here, but I will say that what happened to him was a tragedy. It devastated him. The suits at *CBS* let it get out of control. Those of us who knew the Greek best knew that he wasn't a racist. I believe that had he been working at *ABC* he would have been suspended and that would have been the maximum sentence. Roone wouldn't have sacrificed the Greek at the altar of political correctness.

Roone, however, didn't put up with racism. In fact, compared to some of the other places I worked, *ABC Sports* was a model operation in regards to race relations, dirty jokes, the way women were treated, things like that.

Well, maybe not a model operation – this was still the 1960s and 70s – but it wasn't the wild locker-room atmosphere that other places were.

I recall the time Bud Palmer was doing the scoreboard show and, after giving the score of a game involving William and Mary College, flippantly mentioned that the school played more like its latter namesake than the former. Roone ordered Palmer to apologize during a future broadcast.

Palmer had a habit of making controversial remarks. I remember when I was working at the '60 Olympics in Squaw Valley, he referred to one Japanese competitor as "the Jap skier." Palmer's slip created a media firestorm. Finally, one New York columnist stepped forward to stamp out the blaze, commenting, "perhaps what Palmer said was wrong, but there are some of us who still remember Pearl Harbor."

I felt bad for Palmer. He was vilified because, like a lot of us, he was a member of a generation raised on wartime propaganda and acquainted with slang terms that were a big part of the American sports vocabulary back then.

At the Polo Grounds in New York, for example, homeruns down the right field line were called "Chinese homers" because the foul pole was only 258 feet from the plate and the shots were considered cheap, like the kind of goods manufactured in China at the time.

In 1958, LSU won the national championship in football because of its outstanding defense and special teams, nicknamed the "Chinese Bandits." Imagine being the poor SID trying to explain that one in today's world.

Would a current black heavyweight champ consent to being called "The Brown Bomber," as Joe Louis did in the 1930s? Of course not.

You'd never get away with using any of this stuff today. But it wasn't crude. Neither was Palmer. Palmer was a television pioneer, a pro's pro, and a good guy to boot. He left the business at a relatively young age, before turning 50, and literally headed for the hills, or mountains, in Colorado to run a ski lodge. I often wondered why such a talent would leave broadcasting. Perhaps he had seen all the PC bullshit coming.

Roone wasn't a big liberal, though. I remember when he told Don Meredith to stop making jokes about Nixon on the air during "Monday Night Football." Unlike some people, I didn't read too much into that. I think Roone realized that letting politics seep into programming was a bad idea.

I actually think it bothered him more when Meredith kept mentioning the Goodyear Blimp because Firestone was a sponsor. In the end, I don't think he leaned one way or another, politically. Roone, above all things, was a supporter of Roone.

One thing was for certain. He was definitely more forward-thinking than any of his counterparts at the other networks. Roone was often considered ahead of his time in terms of programming ideas and technical innovations, but I don't think he gets enough credit for the way in which he fought for equality in terms of television sports.

In college football, Roone started putting the historically black schools on television. He was the first to do this. Each year he made one game national, and did one regional game, too. I fielded a ton of complaints from affiliates who were upset about the programming.

In fact, I remember one station manager in Minnesota who regularly complained to me about what he called the "watermelon games." I told Roone and his answer was for me to find more of these schools and to do more games. "Are there any black schools in Minnesota?" he asked.

While Branch Rickey gets credit for breaking Major League Baseball's "color barrier" by signing Jackie Robinson, few know that Roone made Robinson the first black baseball commentator in television history. Roone hired Robinson to work on *ABC's* "Game of the Week" broadcasts for the 1965 season.

Even fewer people know that when Roone used Cosell on "Monday Night Football," he got heat from the *ABC* brass. It wasn't because of Cosell's bombastic style or the controversy he generated. It was because Cosell was a Jew.

Anti-Semitic attitudes were more prevalent back then than people understand. There's long been a myth that the Jews control television. I've been hearing it forever. There have always been a lot of Jews in television, in the media, and in Hollywood. The truth is, they didn't start being more outspoken and flexing their muscle until fairly recently, so that gives the illusion of them being a controlling influence.

I remember when the New York Mets came into the league, and the organization started putting together a broadcast team. The first team suggested was Les Keiter, Bill Mazer and Ralph Kiner. A friend who was in the know told me that the New York ad agency that was involved in polling public opinion dismissed the idea. "No. Two Jews," was all the report said. Team management ended up going with Lindsey Nelson, Bob Murphy and Kiner. If the Jews controlled everything, would that kind of stuff have gone on?

Ed Scherick, Roone's predecessor, went on the record saying that he had been told not to hire Cosell because he was Jewish. Roone told me that nobody above him at *ABC* ever said anything to that effect out loud, but he figured out what was going on. He stood firm and Cosell became, in my opinion, the biggest superstar that our business has ever had.

Roone also once said to me, and I don't think he ever said it to anybody else, "if we have Sunday afternoon football, I might not have used Cosell. It doesn't matter who does the games on Sundays. It's the game, not the announcers."

You couldn't tell Cosell that, but Roone was right. The better game will, ten times out of ten, get the audience. But I never forgot when he said that. It was one of those statements that registers. Sports television history could have turned out so differently.

You couldn't tell Howard Cosell much of anything, to be honest. It was hard to get a word in edgewise. I would know. I became something of a confidant to Cosell over the course of my two separate stints at *ABC*. The relationship provided me with not only a unique perspective of an extremely talented, yet troubled and complicated man, but some great stories that nobody's ever heard.

Before I go any further, before I share any of this material, let me first preface these remarks by saying that my sharing the stories in this chapter or anywhere else in this book isn't an attempt to present myself as having had a close relationship with Cosell or Roone.

I wasn't either's best friend. I wasn't Cosell's consigliere and I was the furthest thing from Roone's right-hand man. The chauffeur who rode Roone around in his Jaguar probably out-ranked me at *ABC*. I didn't have anything other than what I would describe as a very, very unique working relationship with each person.

It's important to me that we make this clear. Some people write "tell all" books and they're really just attempts to make their lives or careers look and sound more important than they really were. Anybody who knows me well knows how much I hate phonies, especially those who work or worked in TV and the media, and the last thing I want to do is come off as one of them. I merely want to share some of the great stories, lines, and observations that I have collected over the course of my life and career.

Now that we've got that out of the way, let me also say that this chapter in particular isn't intended to be a love letter to Roone. I can be truthful in claiming that when I worked for Roone I felt that I was in the presence of greatness, and I can revere him personally for what he did for me professionally, but at the same time I also reserve the right to say that the guy could, at times, behave like a big prick.

I also don't want to give the impression that working at *ABC* Sports was one big, never-ending party. It was fun, but it was also tough working for Roone. The only thing tougher was working against him.

In a way, Roone ran *ABC* Sports like he was a Roman emperor. He'd hire people and throw them into the Coliseum that is network television sports and then sit back and enjoy it all, like he was watching gladiators fight to the death.

With the money, the egos, and the backdrop of big-time sports this all made for a really challenging, pressure-packed work environment. I didn't envy the production guys, the directors, producers, and PAs, one bit. At *ABC* Sports in the glory years of the 1960s and 70s, everybody was hearing footsteps, like a 35-year-old wide receiver.

He was manipulative as hell with talent, too. I remember when Roone tried to get Curt Gowdy to co-host "Wide World." Jim McKay was slipping. Gowdy, who had a conscience, unlike many in television, was reluctant to stab McKay in the back. But Roone egged him on. "(McKay) would do it to you," Roone claimed.

What I disliked most about Roone's managerial style were the double standards. For example, Roone knew all about Chet Forte's gambling problem. He let him get away with it for years, while others were dismissed for other, lesser offenses.

As you'll read elsewhere in this book, I turned down several opportunities to cash in on inside information for fear of running afoul of Roone and his rules on gambling. I followed the rules, Forte didn't. Maybe I was a sucker for doing so.

There was one time, and to this day I can't figure out why, Roone got really riled up about my work for the *Football News.* I had been writing a column for several years and it didn't seem to bother anybody. I was careful to never write anything negative about *ABC* or anything that could be construed as a conflict of interest while I was an *ABC* employee.

Yet Roone reached out to Roger Stanton, the publisher, to try to stop me from contributing. I didn't get it. Roone never said a word to one of our racecasters, Chris Economaki, who owned the *National Speed Sport News*, not even when that publication took apart our announcers and our coverage of the Daytona 500 one year.

I never brought up Economaki's, or anybody else's side gigs, with Roone because I knew better. I knew that he must have considered me special enough, seeing as how in he let me get away with a lot of things, like Frank Carver and Captain Hamilton did at Pitt, that would have gotten a lot of other people fired.

His behavior towards me was confusing and irritatingly inconsistent at times, but I'm confident that on the big balance sheet of good and bad behavior, I came out well ahead.

As for Cosell, I don't flatter myself thinking we were pals, same as I don't think that Roone and I were. In fact, both men were masterful manipulators with big egos who, in all probability, provided me with the special access that they did because of what they thought I could do for them. I was a PR man, after all. I'm sure I was used to leak information to the press or to others in the business, or employed as a spy, maybe at times without my knowing it.

That said, my conversations with Cosell, maybe even more than those with Roone, remain some of the most enduring memories of my career.

"Bean-o Cook!" he'd yell from the other side of the office. You know the voice! You'd hear him coming a mile away. That was my signal to hurry and wrap up whatever it was I was working on.

Cosell would blow into my office in a cloud of cigar smoke, ready and rearing to go. He wanted to bullshit. He would inspect my messy desk, the coffee stains on my shirt, all the while shaking his head side to side, disgustedly, like John Michelosen used to.

"You – my – friend," he would exclaim in that same, staccato speech pattern that millions of Americans heard for so many years during a football game or a big fight, "you are the hu-man fuck-ing per-son-if-i-cation of an unmade bed!"

And then he would take a seat and launch into the topic du jour. He could talk about anything and everything. Cosell wasn't just playing an intellectual on television. He really was one. His vocabulary, all the big words, that wasn't an act. We'd talk books. He was very well read. Music. Politics. He'd give stock tips. Financial advice.

My main complaint about carrying on a conversation with Cosell was the same bitch I had about him when he was talking on television: he really does know a lot, but unfortunately he thinks we want to hear it all. If Robinson Crusoe had been on the island with Cosell instead of Friday, he'd have gone bananas and committed suicide. Cosell never shut up. But we listened. All of us.

At first, I thought Cosell was a purely a New York phenomenon. The television writers at the New York papers needed something to write about. I was reminded of something Roone once told me about television writers: "They only write about television because the papers already have enough hacks to write about what is happening in Washington and nobody cares what is happening at IBM."

It wasn't until I went on the road and heard the conversations in other parts of the country that I changed my mind. I'd overhear people at an airport or in a crowded bar saying, "I wish I could hear Cosell." Both men and women would strain their heads to get a better view of the television when Cosell was on it. I realized then that no other announcer had ever had this kind of following. And I don't think another ever will, to be honest.

Now there were people that hated him, but even those that hated him paid attention to him and listened to him. Anybody that said they didn't was, in my opinion, a liar. Cosell is probably the only television personality in American history who could be the country's most-beloved and most-hated broadcaster at the same time. There were polls that proved just that.

One evening, I was at Joe Healey's Runyon's, on 50th and Second, hanging out with a bunch of writers. The bar's namesake was the famous writer, Damon Runyon. Runyon's was a sports bar. The walls were covered with memorabilia, boxing gloves and autographed photos, but it wasn't a sports bar as people know them now, the big chain places with a thousand TVs.

It was the place where everybody who worked sports and media, sportswriters, TV producers, network executives, broadcasters, ballplayers and even PR flacks like myself, hung out. It was our "Cheers." A little wilder version of it, though. The people who hung out there were serious about drinking, betting and bullshitting about all things sports.

Any given night, you could see John Madden, Dan Jenkins, Mike Lupica and Jack Wilkinson of the *New York Daily News*, Pete Axthelm, Jack Dolph, John Walsh and so many other sports and media luminaries. And those you couldn't see in the crowd, you could hear, such as legendary *CBS* Sports publicist Bill Brendle. It was one of the great American joints.

Anyway, I was sitting at Runyon's when I said I didn't believe anybody who said they didn't masturbate or listen to Cosell. I got some laughs, but I knew the line it wasn't fit for print, so I thought on it for a second and sanitized it: "the biggest liars are people who say they don't watch "Dallas" and don't listen to Cosell."

I was working for *CBS* at the time, and since "Dallas" was a hit for the network, I figured my bosses would appreciate the plug. As was the case with some of my better ones, the line found its way into *Sports Illustrated.*

I saw a side of Cosell that few others knew existed. Contrary to what you've read and heard, Cosell wasn't so totally self-absorbed that he couldn't laugh at himself. I remember before the big "Battle of the Sexes" tennis match in 1973, he told me he was rooting for Billie Jean King over Bobby Riggs. "I can't stand loudmouths," he laughed.

I'll also never forget the time he stood in the doorway of my office, this was in October 1984, and said, "Bean-o, my boy, I've done it – I've accumulated enough 'fuck you' money!" I never asked him for details. I was just happy that I didn't have to use my expense account to pay for our lunch that afternoon.

Most of the time we talked about the business and the people in it. Nothing was sacred. Nobody was off-limits. Not even Roone. It's my opinion that Cosell respected Roone, but was envious of the Roone mystique, the way he was worshipped by the media.

"Roone wants only two things in life," Cosell once told me. "Number one, to be the most powerful man in the world, and two, to be the best-known man in the world."

I had heard Cosell's greatest line, "the horizontal ladder of mediocrity," direct from Cosell before Myron Cope immortalized it in *Sports Illustrated*, but it didn't resonate with me until much later, until I'd been around the mediocrity, the suits, the egos, all the talentless hacks that were in television, long enough myself. Until I went on the air, actually.

Once I started receiving hate mail and the television writers started ripping me, things he'd said began to make perfect sense. I had a much better appreciation for Cosell's talent, as well as an understanding of his insecurities.

I think back to the time that Tom Brookshier told me that Cosell "opened it up for us. He started to criticize and that made it possible for everybody else to criticize."

Brookshier had been right. All of us in the business, those who are on the air today, owe Cosell a debt of gratitude. Thanks to him, we no longer had to be cheerleaders.

I owe Cosell a lot. Almost as much as I owe Roone. I believe Cosell was the reason I got on the air. His success made it possible for Roone to take a chance on me.

I also believe that to this day, Cosell, Jimmy the Greek, and myself are unique.

None of us had television good looks or baritone voices. None of us fetched coffee at some station in Iowa and worked our way up through the ranks. We weren't jocks. We remain the only television personalities who somehow went around the system.

While I definitely have a soft spot in my heart for Howard, I have no problem admitting that a lot of what's been said and written about him was true. Like Roone, he had his flaws. His ego was super inflated. He could be surly. Condescending. What's been said about his drinking was true. A lot of people, like my friend Irv Brodsky, who did PR for "Monday Night Football," had to deal with the worst of Cosell on a regular basis.

Cosell would never admit it, but I think he was a lot like Roone in many ways. Most notably, in the way he liked to maneuver people into situations and then watch how they handled themselves. He lived for the reactions. All of life, for Cosell, was a big game and he enjoyed watching the plays unfold from his perch high in the pressbox.

There was the memorable time the subject of Muhammad Ali came up in one of our conversations. I went on something of a tirade. While I've never disputed Ali's status as the greatest heavyweight boxer of all-time, there's one thing I've never been able to square away: his refusal to complete his military service obligation. Many people consider Ali an activist or a hero, but deep down I'll always think of him as a draft dodger.

"I did my two years, I didn't enjoy it, but I did it," I told Cosell. "So did Elvis, for Christ's sake. Is he bigger than Elvis? Why should he be any different than the rest of us?"

Cosell, who served as an officer during World War II, didn't agree with me, but he said that I was entitled to my opinion.

And then there was the name change. I said that as someone who has spent most of his adult life doing PR, I knew a PR stunt when I saw one.

"If I ever meet him," I declared, "I'll call him Cassius to his face."

"And there you have it, ladies and gentlemen," Cosell laughed. "Bean-o Cook has gone on-the-record with an audacious, if not potentially perilous prediction."

I didn't think anything of Cosell's pronouncement until I showed up for our lunch at Manuche's the next week. I was startled to see a certain third-party, a guest, sitting next to Cosell at our usual table.

When this hulk of a human being stood and unfurled his right arm – half of his nearly seven-foot reach – to shake my hand, I extended my own hand and gulped. Hard.

"Nice to meet you, Muhammad," I sheepishly blurted out.

Cosell never said a word. He just sat there, grinning ear to ear, puffing on his cigar.

* * *

All the times I was in Roone's office, I don't recall ever seeing a crystal ball. Contrary to what the *NBC* people down at 30 Rock or the folks across the street at CBS probably thought, Roone didn't have a top secret, magic formula for creating hits.

There were a couple of things that made Roone different from everybody else. For starters, he didn't care if people laughed at him for taking chances or failing. Not even his own people.

Legend has it, the idea for "Wide World" was conceived during a late-night conversation between Roone and Curt Gowdy in a hotel room in State College, Pennsylvania. Roone and Gowdy were there for a Holy Cross-Penn State basketball game. I don't know which part of this story is more incredible, the fact that a Holy Cross-Penn State basketball game was nationally televised or that Roone and Gowdy had to share a room.

"How many sports are there?" Roone asked.

"Well," answered Gowdy, "Probably eight."

"There are more than that."

"Of course. But probably eight or nine real spectator sports. Baseball, football, basketball, hockey, golf, and a few others. Why do you want to know?"

Roone told him about this show he wanted to create. It wouldn't just focus on the "real" sports. The more Roone talked, the more Gowdy thought he was crazy.

"Roone," Gowdy laughed, "you better get some sleep."

But out of that conversation came "Wide World."

The critics laughed at "American Sportsman," too. They laughed when he put the Olympics on in primetime and professional football on Monday nights.

They laughed at him when he said he was going to show highlights at the half. When *ABC* got the Monday night contract, Roone initially had no idea what he was going to do at halftime. But he did promise that "we're not going to put the Shamokin High School band on in primetime." Which makes me think that someone had once televised a pro game in Philadelphia and used the Shamokin High School band as halftime entertainment. Roone, out of all people, would have known that. Again, the details.

They laughed when Roone went to news. He made some mistakes, but eventually he made *ABC* News, which, incredibly, at one time had no weekend newscast, number one.

I remember when he signed David Brinkley to do a new Sunday show. Everybody thought Brinkley was washed up. I told some friends, just wait. And watch. I was right. "This Week with David Brinkley" destroyed "Face the Nation" and "Meet the Press."

Roone was a brilliant judge of talent. How did he do it? I believe it's because he went with his gut instead of depending on input from his producers or bosses or letting one of the worst inventions of the 20th Century, focus groups, have any say in the matter.

Take Jim McKay. If you knew McKay's background like some of us did, you wondered why Roone hired him for "Wide World."

"Jim was a newsman, I knew that," Roone explained. "But I knew he could write and I thought that between that talent and his ability as a presenter he would be perfect."

One of the greatest understatements of all-time was when Roone told McKay about the requirements of the gig. McKay told me that Roone told him, with a straight face, "there will be some traveling." What a line.

Roone knew in his gut that the American public would like McKay. He also seemed to know what else American sports fans wanted, variety. They were, in effect, consumers. Like all consumers, they wanted options. He might have been a television executive, but I began to understand that fundamentally he was a salesman at heart.

I'm convinced Roone had this revelation after a trip he took behind the Iron Curtain in the 1960s. I don't know all the details, but somehow he was allowed in. It had to be something organized by the State Department due to the Olympics. He made a number of stops in places like East Germany, Yugoslavia, and Russia.

We got to talking about it one day during a discussion on world events and politics. I was mesmerized by his accounts of his travels, as well as the observations he made. The guy was pretty perceptive. On this particular trip, Roone said by the time he got to Russia, he was convinced that there was no way the West could lose the Cold War.

"We stayed at the best hotel in Moscow and it was a fucking mess," he said. "If their best hotel, which they polish up to impress foreign visitors, was a mess, what does their army look like once the big May Day parade is over? What about their supply chain and production capabilities? If they can't even do room service, they can't feed an army of a million men. If they can't even run a hotel right, they're not going to beat us in a war."

I had to admit, his theory made a lot of sense. Unfortunately, it took a few decades for his prediction to come true.

"Why do you think the communists put up the wall?" Roone asked me.

Contrary to what our media told us, East Germans weren't risking their lives to cross over due to their desire for political or personal freedom, he said. It was economics.

"Everyone in East Germany was spending their money in West Germany because the stuff they were making in East Germany was crap," he answered.

So Roone came home and, in a matter of speaking, decided to figuratively flood the shelves of the television market with high quality new products, new innovations. In turn, he built his own wall and kept the consumers, sports fans, on *ABC's* side of it for many years.

In the era before Roone, or what I consider the Dark Ages of sports television, televised sporting events were only a moderate improvement over radio broadcasts. They were televised in black and white. There was no instant replay and no slow-motion. The lenses that permitted closeups and panoramic views hadn't been invented yet, as were the microphones that allowed viewers to hear the sounds we now take for granted. Most switches wouldn't permit split-screens and the chroma key process was non-existent, too.

As a result, announcers just described the action and the viewer, who watched from one static perspective, received little else in the way of information. But once advances in technology caught up to Roone's vision, he started giving viewers more. A lot more.

When Roone was in the army, he worked in public affairs with the ordnance department, which was charged with testing new weapons, at the Aberdeen Proving Grounds in Maryland. So tinkering and experimenting was second-nature to him. Many of his television innovations would be tested and developed on "Wide World," but in my opinion it wasn't until he employed them in *ABC's* ground-breaking coverage of college football that he began to win the ratings wars with the other networks.

Roone's eye for on-air talent extended into the production ranks. He drew up the battleplan and let his trusted lieutenants execute it on college campuses around the country. *ABC* crews pioneered the use of isolated camera footage and ground level sequences, and that *ABC* was the first to use split-screens on replays and the first to set up a system for injury reporting.

Where other networks used graphics as a novelty, *ABC* was the first to make them an important part of the narrative of a game. Viewers were provided with a stream of information in the form of a running tally of stats, plus regularly updated scores from other games. Bud Wilkinson used animation instead of an old-fashioned blackboard and *ABC* announcers were the first to aggressively criticize officials on the air. At Roone's direction, microphones were strategically set up to pick up sideline chatter and cameras filmed coaches at practice and in team meetings and concentrated on defensive players before *NFL Films* popularized these things.

It was truly a team effort. Chuck Howard, our producer, Andy Sidaris, our director, and our technical director, John Allen, worked magic every Saturday while sitting inside *ABC's* sparkling-white control truck.

As press director for *ABC* Sports, I was intimately involved with many aspects of production. I did advances, but in addition to getting into town early and meeting with the press, I worked with ADs, SIDs, band directors, cheerleading coaches, you name it, in order to find some kind of hidden angle that I felt would improve the broadcast. Roone was adamant that every one of us did our part to take the viewer to the game.

Whenever I finished my official duties, I reported to Andy Sidaris. Sidaris was a sports television legend. He spent 25 years at the helm of "Wide World" and also did the Olympics and "Monday Night Football." He directed the football game in the movie "M.A.S.H." and he's also the guy who pioneered the "honey shot," the close-ups of cheerleaders or attractive coeds in the stands.

He'd give me a pair of binoculars and when I spied a good target from the pressbox I'd ring him up down in the truck. I felt like I was back in the army when our anti-aircraft units were out on maneuvers. The chatter on everybody's headset sounded a lot like it.

I'd eavesdrop on Sidaris as he checked in with all the cameramen, which he identified by camera number, before finding a moment to break in.

"Let me see some lovelies, six," Sidaris snapped. "Come in closer and show me the bench, four.... nod if you hear me, three...where are those Song Girls, six? A little wider on the bench, four...we're coming to you, blimp..."

"Andy, I've got two blondes in the student section, lower bowl, maybe a half-dozen rows back," I would say. Copy."

"Copy that, Beans."

He then relayed the information to our cameramen. Sidaris knew what the average American male viewer wanted. He profited on that knowledge when he left *ABC* in the 1980s and started writing and directing B-movies that starred *Playboy* models with machine guns.

As proud as I am to have been a small part of what I think is the best production and broadcasting unit in the history of televised college football, the teams that did the most notable work in terms of turning all of Roone's ideas and innovations into reality were those that did the Olympics for *ABC*.

Everything that was field tested on "Wide World" and tweaked during college football seasons, they perfected. I'm telling you, they turned event production into a fucking art form. *ABC's* Olympics, in my opinion, should be the most glittering part of Roone's golden legacy.

Two things in particular made *ABC's* Olympics stand out. First, there was the way our people masterfully captured the emotions of the competitors. The close-ups. During the '72 Olympics in Munich, when the little Russian gymnast Olga Korbut received a low score from the judges, she started crying. Roone was in the truck and when the camera started panning away, he made the call: "Hold up! Keep it on her. Stay there."

It was powerful stuff. It humanized the athletes and their lives and told their stories in a way that print media couldn't and that the other networks hadn't previously thought of.

Second, Roone was responsible for pushing for all the little vignettes on all the athletes. Before Roone, networks concentrated on the events. Now, competitors became more important than the competitions. You learned about their families, their hometowns, their backgrounds. Thanks to Roone, America realized that these foreign athletes were people, too, not just strange names that you couldn't spell or pronounce.

At the same time, however, there have been negative side effects to "up close and personal" and this, to me at least, is an unfortunate part of Roone's legacy. He wanted to take us out of our living rooms, onto college campuses and to faraway countries, but today's producers and executives have gone way too far.

No longer satisfied with the locker room or the coaches' meeting rooms, we're barging into bedrooms and courtrooms, too. We should have stopped at the sideline. Made that the 38th Parallel of sports. Coverage is overdone to the extent that viewers are given too much access. We're inundated with information.

Consider your average college football telecast. For decades, the viewer had no idea who a team's defensive coordinator or strength coach was. Throughout the 1960s, 70s and 80s, nobody showed an assistant coach's name with a graphic. Even a fat cat donor couldn't pick these guys out of a police lineup. Now, they're all the broadcast team talks about. Tune into a game today and you get to watch an interview with him at the team hotel, you learn what other coach or famous athlete he played Pop Warner with, what jobs he's in the running for, and maybe even what his favorite color is.

It's not just the information on the coaches. Every sporting event, even the drafts, has a cast of hundreds. You can't do anything without hearing from the owners, the general managers, the athletic directors, the coaches' wives and children, the players' parents, girlfriends, teachers, et cetera. They keep parading these people out. It's unbelievable.

Somehow we went from quick, interesting vignettes to grueling, full-length features on the most intimate details of an athlete's life. It seems like every time I turn on the TV, an announcer, sideline reporter or studio host is telling me about some athlete's mother's drug problem, the death of a little brother or some other depressing tragedy. There's no privacy or decency anymore. I wonder if Roone would have pushed for all these things if he had only known how intrusive and oversaturated with information television sports would become.

I've often wondered what he'd think about a lot of things. So far, I've tried my best to avoid putting words in Roone's mouth, but it's my personal opinion – this is due to things that he said to me and the way he said them – that of all the shows he created, all the legendary events he produced and supervised, Roone's personal favorite was "Wide World."

That's because he created it from scratch. It was his baby. He made sports that nobody cared about popular and in return, the show made him.

Amazingly, it almost never happened. The way Roone described the situation, "Wide World" was pitched as a 13-week show and a certain amount of advertising had to be sold before a certain date before it got the green light. At quarter of five on that Friday deadline, a cigarette company called up and bought into it. Fifteen minutes!

Today, Wide World never gets on the air because advertising of tobacco products on TV is banned. I don't think lung cancer was a good trade-off, but if that call hadn't come, one of the most iconic shows in sports television might never have gone on the air. Fifteen minutes might have been, for Roone's career, the difference between the "thrill of victory" and the "agony of defeat."

There's been plenty of speculation over the years as to who deserves the credit for writing the show's tease, but in my opinion the best story about those famous lines was this one relayed to me by Roone. He said that when Chuck Howard rolled the tease for one of the *ABC* suits, the guy was so underwhelmed he asked, "You're going to put that shit on the air?"

People probably said the same thing when Roone put me on the air in 1982. In fact, I know that there were people at *CBS* who felt that way. We'll talk about them and what they did later. I was angry at the time, but I now understand that they wanted me to fail to prove that Roone made the wrong call.

Many people, if they couldn't work for Roone, were obsessed with beating him. That was typically a tall order, because nobody else had Roone's brilliance and balls. In addition to being a deal maker, innovator, and visionary, he was a risk taker.

Yet of all the things that Roone was, there was one thing, in my opinion, he was not – a sports fan. I don't think he could have won a sports trivia contest if his life depended on it. When I got to *ABC*, I was shocked to find out how little Roone actually knew about college football. Of course, that was probably why he had hired me in the first place. I wasn't there only to do publicity.

I made a good first impression on him with my work ethic, or what must have appeared to be my work ethic. Pretty soon after I started, it got back to him that I came into the office on weekends. Between us, I wasn't really working six or seven days a week. Since long distance was so expensive, I came into the office on Saturday or Sunday afternoons to make personal phone calls. I'd call my parents, broads and buddies and run up *ABC's* phone bill instead of mine. Not only did it save me a lot of money, it made me look like a workaholic.

Somehow, Roone heard about these weekend sightings of me at the office. I kept up the practice when I worked at *CBS* and as far as I knew, none of my bosses, Roone included, ever figured out what I was really up to.

But that doesn't mean I wasn't a hard worker. I was. Roone realized that right away. He noticed that I studied future schedules, the ratings, and other reports religiously. I'm talking about the NCAA's materials and our own internal research.

When I started digging into this material, I felt like Daniel Ellsberg when he first got his hands on the Pentagon Papers. It blew my mind how much input and clout that too many largely incompetent people had. All these important programming and scheduling decisions were being handled by people who were totally clueless when it came to college football.

These people on the NCAA television committee might have been great at their jobs in production or athletics administration, but they had barely a fraction of my knowledge about the history, the coaches, the rivalries, the fans – all the things that make college football unlike any other sport.

I plugged all this information it into my head, cross-referenced it with my unique understanding of college football, and started spitting out some very interesting results in terms of scheduling that got Roone's attention.

I guess I should first explain that back then, this is fifteen, twenty years before the landmark Supreme Court ruling in 1984, scheduling for the networks was a lot different than it is now. We were limited to doing only eight national games in my first year in 1966.

That number rose, I think to 13 or 14 games, by the time I left *ABC* after the 1973 season. We were restricted to a select number of regional telecasts, too. The reason for these limitations is that NCAA member institutions didn't want a lot of games to be televised out of an irrational fear that television would drastically reduce attendance at games.

Remember what I said about advances and how important it was for an SID to get space in order to sell tickets? The gate was all that mattered. This was the mindset of the people who ran college athletics back then. They thought less college football, rationing it, was what was best for the sport. It's a far cry from today where, between the networks, cable channels and the Internet, you can watch fifty college games every weekend.

For me, it was a strange role reversal. Instead of chasing space to help sell tickets for one school, I was essentially working for all of the schools in the NCAA and *ABC* at the same time. I had to help the NCAA keep the stadiums full, while simultaneously getting good ratings and keeping the sponsors happy. It was a challenge.

My loyalty was with *ABC*, but my love was with college football. It's like picking your favorite parent. But I did the job and I did it well. Our ratings at *ABC* during this time remain among the highest in the history of televised college football.

We were successful because of our announcers, our production teams and, I hate to brag, because of me. But I was only able to do the job my way because of Roone. He trusted me, my knowledge, and my expertise.

Anybody with a basic understanding of college football could pick out the handful of national big games each season: Michigan-Ohio State, Texas-Oklahoma, and so on. Those games were big in 1969 and they'll be big in 2019. Even if one or both teams has an off-year, these games will always be highly anticipated and easy to promote.

The trick was to forecast which teams will come out of nowhere and plug those surprise teams and their games into our limited number of spots. That's where I came in. I knew every school's schedule five or ten years into the future.

I was able to predict Indiana and North Carolina State would have great seasons in 1967. I had a feeling about Kansas in 1968, and Air Force in 1970. My predictive powers and instincts told me Michigan State wouldn't be good in 1967. Same with Ohio State in '71.

I wasn't just making preseason predictions. I explained the intricacies of rivalries and fandom and how these things should influence game selection and coverage maps to both Roone and the NCAA television committee.

I remember telling the committee that I knew, probably better than anybody else in television, that when Ohio State appears on television, the attendance in the Mid-American Conference suffers. See, unlike Pennsylvania, where loyalties are evenly split between Pitt and Penn State, alums of the smaller Ohio schools will put aside their rivalries and come together to root for Ohio State in big games.

Say Penn State played Texas, Pitt fans would cheer for the Longhorns when the score was announced at Pitt Stadium. The same would happen in reverse in State College. Now if Ohio State was playing Texas, nobody would show up for Akron's and Toledo's games. Fans and alums of those schools would go to a bar or someone's house to watch it, and would both cheer for Ohio State. I learned this when I was in the army and would spend Saturday afternoons with my Ohio buddies watching games in the PX.

I put a lot of time and energy into writing long memos and drawing up detailed scheduling proposals chock full of this kind of information and sent these materials to Roone and the television committee. I don't think Walter Byers or anybody else much cared for my plans, nor the grandiose names I attached to them like "The Philadelphia Plan," but Roone was the only subscriber who mattered to me. He paid attention to me. For the majority of my first stint at *ABC*, for all matters related to college football, I was his Rasputin.

I honestly think Roone came to think of me as America's No. 1 college football fan. Somewhere along the line he realized that if *ABC* aired the games that Beano Cook wanted to watch, and dazzled them up with stats, graphics, honey shots and expert commentary, the rest of the country, being like me, would tune in. Now I wasn't always right, but my track record was such that the odds were very much in the network's favor that we'd pull big numbers.

To me, it was a sign of a great leader. So many suits in television would disregard the opinions of their subordinates due to their egos, but Roone was different. If there was something he didn't know, he was willing to listen to, as well as put power into the hands of someone who did.

There's no better example of his willingness to do that, and our relationship in this regard, than the 1969 Texas-Arkansas game.

Almost immediately after the success of the Notre Dame-Michigan State game in 1966 Roone and I started talking about trying to arrange another No. 1 versus No. 2 matchup late in the regular season that would determine the national championship. We were looking for a guaranteed ratings bonanza that we could build up to as the season progressed.

To us, as the network of college football, it made perfect sense to try to maximize the package and manipulate the ending of the regular season because the other networks televised the bowls. When I was at *ABC*, we had the Sugar Bowl. That's it.

And when it came down to it, those were all really just exhibition games. The AP poll wouldn't take the bowls into account for the national championship until '68. It wouldn't be until the mid 1970s for the coaches' poll.

Oh, and by "arrange," I'm not suggesting any sort of impropriety like my secret stunt with the voters in the run-up to the '71 Iron Bowl. Everything we talked about was above-board. We thought if we found a matchup that had the potential to be No. 1 versus No. 2, it couldn't hurt to reach out to both schools and float the idea of moving the date of the game to late November or early December for television.

Roone and I were essentially a two-man selection committee for a big-time college football championship long before anybody heard of the Bowl Coalition, Bowl Alliance or BCS.

In fact, while I wasn't the only one back then talking about the need to create a playoff to decide a national champion, I might have been the only one who put together a comprehensive plan laying out how a playoff would work. I was certainly the only one in a position to put it in front the most powerful man in television sports. So I did. This was in 1971. "The NCAA must devise a way to eliminate mythical championships and meaningless trophies," was my mission statement.

According to my plan, it would be an inclusive, 16-team playoff. It would feature the 11 conference champions and the five leading independents, which would be determined through criteria, basically records and strength of schedule rankings, established by voters from the Coaches' Association and Football Writers Association of America. The members of the FWAA made up the voters of the Associated Press poll.

I envisioned it to be something like a football version of the NCAA basketball tournament merged with the Indiana High School Basketball Tournament, in which schools of all sizes and enrollments were lumped together. I figured there would be less resistance to the idea if everybody were included.

Plus, it provided the best chance to create a format where upsets were possible. Could Arizona State, which won the WAC and finished No. 8 that year, have upset Nebraska or Oklahoma? Probably not, but you'd never know if the Sun Devils never had the opportunity.

I had the first round of the playoffs starting on Saturday, December 4, the second round played December 11 and both would have been telecast regionally. The third round would have been played December 18 and aired as a national doubleheader. The championship game would have been played two weeks later, on New Year's Day, 1972.

"Many of the playoff games could replace or be played as the various bowl games," I wrote, "which are profitable but essentially meaningless." I folded the idea into a larger memo that was chock full of ratings information, advertiser reports and all kinds of maps, charts, and graphs. In a unique display of foresight, I even included information on how pay-per-view television might eventually be worked into the equation. The whole plan was probably too ahead of its time to be taken seriously.

I wasn't surprised that nobody on the television committee read it or commented on it, but I was a little disappointed that Roone, someone who had made a career of being way ahead of his own time, didn't even want to discuss the idea.

Some day, there's going to be a playoff in college football, although I may not be around to see it. It will take awhile for everybody to get on the same page, but the schools won't be able to turn down the television money. Sometime in the near future, college football will catch up to me, or at least to where I was in 1971.

Back to the Sixties, Notre Dame-Southern Cal, already a national, made-for-TV matchup, was the first game we looked at, but since the schools decided to alter the home and home format of the series in 1960 (up until then the game had always been played the Saturday after Thanksgiving, no matter the location), we figured it wasn't going to work.

It made no sense for Southern Cal to agree to play in South Bend in late November or December with the national title on the line and Notre Dame wouldn't give up an October home date in an odd-numbered year since that would mean back-to-back trips to the Coliseum.

Stanford's recent re-emergence on the national scene made my father happy, but the former Indians weren't quite a top five team. Other than Southern Cal and UCLA, the pickings out west, in the old Pac-8, were slim.

Elsewhere, Oklahoma and Nebraska were still a few years from their epic Seventies' showdowns. Eastern football was really down. Army-Navy was already a big late-season game, but the matchup hadn't factored into the national championship picture since Roger Staubach left Annapolis.

Unless it was two conference teams, the Big Ten was out. There was no chance of setting up another Notre Dame-Michigan State game. Woody Hayes bitched so much after '66 – he was upset, and probably a little jealous, that Notre Dame got all the national attention – that the Big Ten decreed that there would be no more big non-conference games in November. I call it the "Woody Hayes Rule" and it remains in effect to this day.

There was some fun football being played in the Southeastern Conference, but the league's scheduling quirks, not to mention Bear Bryant's late Sixties slump, didn't help the SEC. The up-and-down play of the teams from year to year made planning nearly impossible on our end, too. Look at Georgia's record early in Vince Dooley's tenure as head coach. It seemed like the Bulldogs would be in the top five one year, then .500 the next.

Tennessee had a solid run in the late 1960s and early 70s so I would have loved to have tried to set up Alabama-Tennessee for No. 1 in late November, but I doubt we could have gotten the schools to sign off on the idea due to the tradition surrounding the date. Tradition matters more in the South than anywhere else and the last time that game wasn't played on the third Saturday in October, the late, great General Neyland was probably a private.

It was appropriate that after a lot of drilling elsewhere, I finally struck oil in the Southwest Conference. The '69 Texas-Arkansas game had been on my radar since January 1, when Texas destroyed Tennessee in the Cotton Bowl and Arkansas beat Georgia in the Sugar.

I spent that spring putting together a plan for what I thought was going to be the year's biggest college football game, and perhaps the year's biggest event. Well, biggest event not to take place in the Orange Bowl, the Sea of Tranquility, or on a farm in rural New York!

The timing was perfect; there was a big push by both the NCAA and the network to do something big to celebrate college football's centennial season. I went to Roone with my plan and explained to him not only how *ABC's* college football moonshot could work, but how we first sold it to the coaches and the schools, and then later, sports fans and viewers.

Of course, I first had to sell Roone. I told him that both teams finished the '68 season in the top ten and given the number of starters they had coming back there was no doubt in my mind that both would start the 1969 season ranked in the preseason top five. This dramatically increased their odds of finishing the season ranked somewhere in the close vicinity of No. 1.

Secondly, I thought the schedules were conducive for a matchup of undefeateds. Arkansas had an easy schedule and Texas, if the Longhorns could get by Oklahoma in Dallas, would have smooth sailing to a December showdown in Fayetteville.

"Now for the real variables," I said. "Coaches are creatures of habit and since the Texas-Arkansas game is always played in October, I'm not sure how either is going to react to the idea of moving the game. They don't like change, anything that ruins rhythm. But I know how rivalries work, so I've got a hunch that Texas might enjoy rubbing Texas A&M's nose in the fact that the Arkansas game would be played after their annual game and that it would be much bigger. Plus, if you play the game on October 18 as it's originally scheduled, Texas is going to have to play Oklahoma and Arkansas in consecutive weeks. I'd be sure to mention this to Darrell Royal when you talk to him."

Roone, listening and puffing on his pipe, nodded in agreement.

"The call, however," I continued, "isn't Royal's to make. Arkansas is the home team, so the decision is ultimately up to Frank Broyles. But the Razorbacks' only loss last year was to Texas. It's *the* game on the schedule. We should appeal to his coach's instinct. Tell him it would be best to build up to the most important game on the schedule. If it's played in mid-October, Broyles might have to worry about a letdown in the latter half of the season."

So far, so good. I could tell Roone liked what he was hearing.

"Plus, we're giving them free advertising," I added. "It's a chance to showcase his campus for recruiting. And it's not just a game. It'll be big for the entire state. Arkansas is the only team in that conference that isn't in Texas; they've always been the odd-man out in that league. Everybody in that state is very aware of all this. They hate Texas. You can tell Broyles, we're bringing the entire country to Arkansas for the afternoon. We're going to turn Fayetteville into the capital of college football."

When Roone spoke with Broyles, he read the lines almost directly from my script. Not surprisingly, we got the response that we wanted. I knew that Broyles, not to mention the whole state of Arkansas, was resentful that Texas was the flagship program of the SWC and that no matter how many times they won the league or beat Texas that would not change.

I called Arkansas' move to the SEC in the early 1990s before anybody else. Broyles couldn't wait to get out of the shadow of the Lone Star State. It was a long-awaited homecoming. Broyles was originally from Georgia and had played at Georgia Tech when that school was part of the SEC. Whenever I talked to him, I always thought he felt more at home with the other Deep South schools.

It's also widely believed that in return for moving the game, Broyles got *ABC* to televise Arkansas' 1970 season opener against Stanford. That, though, was not a concession. We already decided to air that game. Roone, the master negotiator, just made it appear to be a deal sweetener.

"But what about the other variables," Roone replied. "The other teams? Say Texas and Arkansas have the seasons you think they're going to have. How can we be sure they're going to be one and two? How do we know another team, maybe two other teams, aren't going to go undefeated and fuck this grand plan of yours up?"

He could have been talking about any number of schools, but I knew he was referring to Ohio State. Everybody was picking the Buckeyes in 1969. The defending national champs had a ton of returning talent and a very favorable schedule. In fact, when Roone phoned Royal, even the Texas head coach was genuinely surprised at Roone's confidence.

"You really don't think Ohio State is going to be number one?" he laughed.

"The football gods have spoken to me," Roone replied.

I knew Roone had a high opinion of me and my knowledge of college football, but I wouldn't call myself a football god! I'll admit that when I read Roone's account of the conversation in his memoirs, I was a little disappointed that he didn't give me a plug, at least some small amount of credit for assembling all the information that influenced his decision.

Or for putting a bow on it. See, at the end of my presentation I looked Roone right in the eyes and made what is probably the boldest prediction of my life.

"Ohio State's going to lose," I told him.

Roone raised his eyebrows. But it wasn't false bravado on my part. I truly believed Ohio State was going to be upset by somebody. My gut said Minnesota might do it. They also had to play Purdue and Michigan State, as well as Michigan, and that was in Ann Arbor.

"Okay," Roone said. "Let's do it!"

People have written that I was responsible for moving the game. Now in a way, yes, I was. But it wasn't my decision. My call. It was Roone's. He was the boss. I staked my reputation and my standing with Roone, but that was behind-the-scenes. If things hadn't worked out the way they did, I wouldn't have received any notoriety for my role, but I wouldn't have been taken apart by the press, either.

Roone took all the risk, therefore he should receive the credit. Still, I believe it was my research, my reasoning, my presentation, and my confidence, that inspired him to give it a go. Again, I don't think there was anybody else, another television executive, who would have trusted my instincts the way Roone did.

He was taking a leap of faith. Now it wasn't Ike getting the weather report on June 5, 1944 and saying, "let's go," but it was a pretty big gamble from a television perspective. Not only was Roone betting that these two teams would be playing for the national title, he was betting that the whole country was going to tune in. That wasn't guaranteed.

No offense to Texas or Arkansas and their fans, but the game wasn't Notre Dame-Southern Cal or Army-Navy. We were placing a big bet on a regional rivalry. Notre Dame-Michigan State in '66, believe it or not, wasn't even a national game. Some parts of the country didn't get it. People are surprised when I tell them that.

So for Roone to make Texas-Arkansas a stand alone national game, to bet that people in Oregon and Massachusetts who had no connection to either team were going to watch like it was college football's Super Bowl, this was a bigger deal than most people understand.

The game was scheduled for December 6, which, when you think about everything that could go wrong between now and then, injuries and other potential issues, all the moving parts that needed to fall into place, we were going to need some luck to pull it off.

To start, I was validated by the preseason rankings, which had Ohio State number one and Arkansas and Texas at two and four, respectively. And I couldn't have asked for more consistent play from both teams from start to finish. In racing out to identical 8-0 records, neither team had a margin of victory that was less than ten points.

And that luck we needed? We finally got it when Ole Miss shockingly shutout No. 3 Tennessee in Jackson and Bo Schembechler's first Michigan team pulled one of the great all-time upsets by beating No. 1 Ohio State in successive weeks in mid-November.

So that's how *ABC* got its one versus two, "Game of the Century" matchup in 1969. I don't want to say it all went exactly to plan, but I was pretty pleased with myself.

I have to admit, though, there was one thing I didn't see coming and that was the phone call from the White House that President Nixon would be attending the game. Contrary to popular belief, that wasn't part of the deal from the beginning. We only found out about it the week of the game.

We had done a great job promoting the game week after week, but when it was announced that Nixon was coming, it created so much buzz, it sent the hype over the top. This was right in the middle of Vietnam, so in our planning we had been primarily concerned about protests, but now we had security, the Secret Service, all that stuff, to take into consideration as well.

When I saw "Marine One" descending out of the gray clouds outside Razorback Stadium on the day of the game, I couldn't help but think about Dan Parker comparing me to Barnum and Bailey. I truly felt like I was responsible for creating a circus.

It seemed like every print, radio and television outlet in the country covered the game. Every sportswriter in the country was there, too. There were all kinds of celebrities present. Actors. Country music stars. Media people. One minute I was shaking hands with the Reverend Billy Graham and the next, with Colonel Sanders. Yes, *that* Colonel Sanders.

It seemed like every politician in Texas and Arkansas followed Nixon into town. But I guess it was better for the country that they were all in Fayetteville instead of Washington or the state capitals coming up with ideas to take our money.

As for Nixon, I don't care what your feelings are about the guy or your political loyalties, when you're standing ten feet away from the President of the United States like I was when a college marching band starts playing "Hail to the Chief," your heart would be pounding like mine was!

Schenkel interviewed Nixon at halftime. I was standing outside the booth, eavesdropping on the conversation. Up to this point, the game had been a snoozer. Nixon, to his credit, nailed the second half prediction. He said Texas would come back.

Now with the game ending the way it did, with James Street's bomb on 4th and 3 and Texas earning an improbable 15-14 victory after being down 14-0, you'd think that would be the end of the story, the icing on the cake, right?

Wrong. What happened after the game in the Texas locker-room, when Nixon handed that plaque to Darrell Royal and proclaimed Texas the national champions, that might have been the sweetest part of the whole story for this Pitt alum.

I could only imagine how pissed off Penn State fans must have been. And they're not going to believe me when I say this, but they had a right to be angry.

After going undefeated in 1969, Penn State's second consecutive undefeated season, the Nittany Lions had a claim to No. 1. Now I don't think it was as strong a claim as Texas's was since they only played one ranked team, West Virginia, but they had a claim. Their anger at Nixon, however, was totally misplaced.

They should have been mad at their head coach and players. See, Penn State put it, the bowl, to a vote. Actually, there were two votes, two team discussions. This happened right after Penn State beat Maryland to go to 8-0. Jim Tarman told me what happened. The players voted to play in the Orange Bowl.

And they ended up beating Missouri in Miami. I actually think that if they had played Texas, Penn State would have won. That's the truth.

To his credit, Paterno wanted to delay the decision and play the Texas-Arkansas winner in the Cotton Bowl. He felt you should always play the best or highest-ranked team and he was right. He wanted to go to Dallas. But where he screwed up was being too democratic. He let the players have a voice in the decision.

The team was swayed by several black players who were concerned about the way they might be treated in Dallas, which was segregated. I can't blame those players for thinking the way they did, but you have to weigh those concerns with what could be the once-in-a-lifetime opportunity to win a national title.

Plus, I would have thought that every player on the team would have jumped at the chance to go into Dallas and show up the segregationists by kicking Texas's ass. You only defeat injustice and evil by confronting it head on, not running from it. That's why I've always said Penn State ducked Texas. It could have been a historic game in several ways.

In any event, there's no way what happened in '69 with Penn State happens today. The coach and the AD make the decision and if the players don't like it, tough.

My main issue was in Joe's public handling of the situation. He let the perceived slight fester in the minds of Penn State supporters, even going so far as throw fuel on the fire with his remarks at the graduation ceremony a few years later, so many Penn State fans are still upset about it today even though they don't know all the important details. But now they have those details. So, Penn State fans, please quit complaining about 1969.

Back to "The Big Shootout," that game remains one of the fondest memories of my first tour at *ABC*. Despite all the challenges we were presented with, I'm extremely proud of the way our entire organization, our broadcast team, our production crew, and our PR people, performed.

Texas-Arkansas wasn't just a big football game. It was a major news event. It was like producing a Super Bowl, the Academy Awards, and a party convention at the same time. Everything went so flawlessly, and on the biggest possible stage, no less. When we got the ratings, the game got a 52 share, which meant that nearly half the country had tuned in. It might have been *ABC* Sports' finest hour when it came to college football coverage.

Darrell Royal later said Roone and I were "smarter than a tree full of owls" for making it all happen. Roone never said a word to me, but the big smile he had on his face in the pressbox at Razorback Stadium that afternoon told me all I needed to know.

The Redhead was happy. I knew right then and there that unless I somehow really fucked up, the job of NCAA press director at *ABC* Sports was mine as long as I wanted it.

The last time I saw that smile on Roone's face was, coincidentally, the last time I saw Roone. It was July 2001. I was sitting at a table at Tavern on the Green in New York City with Bob After, Howard Katz and Geoff Mason. Roone had prostate cancer and only a few months of life left, so someone decided to have a get-together, a grand farewell.

In order to be invited you had to be employed by *ABC* sometime before Dec. 31, 1972, since it's generally accepted that the peak of Roone's reign was the 1972 Olympics. The location was entirely appropriate as well, since Roone and others had decided on "Wide World of Sports" for the show's name over drinks at Tavern on the Green.

There were only three speakers and they are no longer with us. One was Andy Sidaris. The others were Jim McKay, and of course, Roone. I can't tell you what any of them said. I was too caught up in the memories.

I don't think there's another team in the history of sports, not among any of the great dynasties, in which the teammates feel as much pride as we do. If you worked at *ABC* Sports under Roone Arledge, it's like being able to tell people you played for the Yankees in the 1920s, or under John Wooden at UCLA.

Later in that decade, at McKay's funeral in Baltimore, Mason read off all the names of all the people who once worked at *ABC* Sports who were no longer alive. I could tell by looking around the room that it sent chills up nearly everybody's back.

As for our skipper, or head coach, feelings are probably mixed. Everyone is entitled to their own opinion of the man. I, for one, am extremely proud that I can say I worked for Roone. That declaration means a lot to me. It makes up for everything I've been through in my career, the firings, the turmoil, the hate mail, the bad press and the bad days.

I'll never know what Roone truly thought of me. In all honesty, although I worked for him for twelve years, I really didn't know the man. I remember reading an interview with Ingrid Bergman, who was asked about Humphrey Bogart. Bergman replied that she kissed Bogie – referencing "Casablanca," of course – but didn't know him. I knew exactly what Bergman was talking about.

I'll never know what Roone would have thought of this book or the fact that I basically devoted an entire chapter in it to him. I'd like to think that Roone would enjoy the read, but there's no way to really know for sure.

Even if he were still alive, there's no way he could be tracked down at his office for a comment.

A phone call? Definitely not. He wouldn't return it.

That's just as well. I'd have been pleased with simply a note from the Redhead.

CHAPTER 4

One bus does it.

Pete Rozelle was a very smart guy. Not rocket scientist smart. The minds behind the Manhattan Project, the polio vaccine, and the Apollo program – Albert Einstein, Dr. Salk, Wernher Von Braun – that's a whole different ballgame.

Rozelle was what I call "sports smart." He knew football. He knew business. He knew how to negotiate. He certainly knew publicity.

Rozelle got his start in football as the SID at the University of San Francisco. When San Francisco played Fordham in New York City in 1951, he arranged to personally chauffeur Grantland Rice to Triboro Stadium. He used the ride to plug halfback Ollie Matson for All-America and secure San Francisco some incredible space. It was a brilliant maneuver. An all-timer by an all-time great.

Howard Cosell told me it took the owners 23 ballots to come to a consensus on Rozelle as a compromise pick for NFL commissioner in 1960. The cardinals – the ones in Rome, not Arizona – never needed that many votes to pick a Pope.

Those of us who are old enough to remember what professional football was when Pete took over the NFL remain in awe of the empire he built. He took a popular sport, but one still below baseball and college football in the pastime pecking order, and turned pro football into America's biggest draw, the NFL into the country's most valuable professional sports league. I believe he is the greatest league executive in the history of professional sports.

Yet Rozelle, for all his brains and vision, once made a ridiculous statement that made me laugh. He said that only ten percent of the American public bet on sports.

If that's the case, they all must live on my block.

Everybody I know bets. Not necessarily with a bookie, but they bet in some way, shape or form. Look at the popularity of the Powerball and the instant lottery tickets. There are fantasy leagues and office pools, too.

In Western Pennsylvania, every corner bar, Amvets and VFW post has block pools, where you pay a buck, maybe five bucks, for a square during Steelers games. My mailman, Mike Pometto, knows the weekly NFL lines like he knows his route. Even your parish priest bets. He probably bets Notre Dame every week, but that still counts.

And I've got two words for you: March Madness. Every American, whether they are male or female, young or old, sports fan or not, if you say the word "bracket," they know what you are talking about.

I hear the conversations everywhere, from restaurants and parking garages to the waiting room at my doctor's office. It doesn't matter if it's the day after the Super Bowl, the Sugar Bowl, or the Southwest Regional of the NCAA basketball tournament. People used to ask each other "who won?" Now, it's "did they cover?"

When my friend Joe Gordon started working as publicity director for the Steelers in 1969, he told me that he was shocked to learn the number of regular people that bet. Back then, regular people didn't mean regular people as we know them now, the guys who worked in the steel mills and fixed cars.

Gordon was talking about doctors, lawyers, accountants and businessmen, the so-called white collar professionals. This was back when the subterranean world of gambling was just starting to surface in mainstream America, so it was a big surprise to him that these "regular people" had an interest in the Steelers that went beyond winning and losing. It wasn't news to me. It was a world I had been a part of my entire adult life.

Betting is no longer a social taboo confined to an underworld of back alleys and smoky pool halls like the one in which I made my first real bet at the age of 18. It was the winter of 1950. There was a pool hall located near a burlesque house called the Casino on Diamond Street in downtown Pittsburgh. Neither the pool hall nor the Casino nor Diamond Street are still in existence. Forbes Avenue runs right through the spot today.

As I made my way down Diamond Street, I passed the Casino and the posters outside advertising that week's stage acts. A young man on a mission, I didn't have enough time nor enough money to take in the milkman's matinee. With apologies to the tempting Miss Tempest Storm, I was looking for action, but not that kind of action!

You walked up a tall flight of stairs to enter this establishment and when I finally got to the top my eyes bugged out, much like they would have had I taken in the burlesque show. Clouds of cigar smoke and chalk dust floated by and, like a curtain opening, gradually revealed a giant chalkboard covered with team names and numbers. It was a primitive version of the big electronic setups that you see in the sportsbooks in Las Vegas now.

Ever wonder where the expression "chalk" comes from in betting? Back in the old days, they used chalkboards like this one I'm describing to list odds. Typically, only the favorites appeared on these boards, and as money came in they erased the numbers and updated the odds using more chalk. So if you were betting the favorite you were "betting chalk." Anyway, it was one of the most beautiful sights my eyes had ever seen.

Even though I was essentially a kid, I felt right at home. I wasn't the least bit nervous. When Bobby Kennedy was attorney general of the United States in the early Sixties, he said that gambling in large numbers couldn't thrive without the cooperation of corrupt policemen and politicians. I figured that must have been how this place stayed in business. It was probably the safest place in town other than police headquarters.

I made the first bet of my life in this joint. It was a college basketball game. I barely remember the name of my first kiss, but I still remember everything about the day I lost my betting virginity.

The date was February 4, 1950, No. 2 Duquesne was playing at No. 15 Louisville. Duquesne was a two-point underdog. For the life of me, I couldn't figure out how Dudey Moore's Dukes, led by Chuck "Silk" Cooper and Ed Dahler, were dogs.

I had rehearsed my lines on the way there, so when it was my turn at the counter, I delivered them flawlessly, like a pro.

"I would like to bet Duquesne," I said, confidently. "Eleven dollars to win ten."

The guy taking the bets didn't ask for identification. Money changed hands.

"If you win," he said, "come back. We're here tomorrow and we pay you."

I didn't have to go back. On February 5, Duquesne was no longer undefeated and I was out eleven bucks. That early experience showed me just how green the grass, actually the money, was on the other side. And, well, it got me thinking.

Arriving as a freshman at Brown University in the fall of that same year, I landed a job distributing pool sheets. Somebody in Pittsburgh – I don't know whether he was mob or not – told me where to go in Providence to find the action. It was the back room of a tailor shop in Federal Hill.

My reference must have checked out, since this outfit put me in charge of on-campus operations. I'd be sizing up and hemming in fellow students, more or less.

"Okay. This is what we do," the guy in charge told me. "You distribute the pool sheets on campus and we give you thirty pahcent."

Outside in the shop, you could hear the sound of a cash register ringing up a sale. That sound was echoing loudly in my head.

"Thirty percent of the profits?" I asked, excitedly.

"Nah, kid," he laughed. "Thirty pahcent off the top."

I caught on quick enough. I vividly remember the first week of the season because there must have been 150 guys playing and only two won. That shows you just how much of a chance the public has. My army buddy John O'Connor played the same sheets when he was in college. We use to joke about the heading: "For Amusement Only - Ties Lose."

The money was great for a college kid in the early 1950s, thirty cents on every dollar, on the gross. Each week I made about $70 in cold, hard cash. Adjusted for inflation, that's $500 bucks today, maybe more. And the best part? It was tax-free, baby.

After a while, I must have felt guilty and went to the Dean of Men at Brown and told him what was going on. He said that as long as my little racket was confined to campus he didn't care what happened, but if I went downtown and got caught by the Providence police or the Feds it would mean expulsion.

So I rarely left campus, much to the dismay of my three roommates, who came to hate Tuesday and Friday nights. On Tuesdays the sheets came out, and on Fridays the money had to be in. I started taking action on games, too. Football. Basketball. The phone was ringing off the hook.

The money was great, but after awhile the stress wears on you. I'm lugging a wad of cash to Atwells Avenue every week. The people I was working for, they treated me really well, but I knew they weren't the Chamber of Commerce. I was constantly worrying that I was going to get caught, that G-men with tommy guns were going to bust into my dormitory.

And I was on the profit side of the deal! Betting is even less fun when you are consistently on the wrong end of most of the transactions.

Some advice to consider if you are thinking of getting involved in betting: always remember that when a bookie travels, he flies first class. When a bettor travels, he flies coach, last row, middle seat, and probably sits next to a crying baby.

Betting is a lot like turbulence. When the pilot tells you there is nothing to worry about, don't believe him until you land. And in some extreme cases, until your baggage shows up. Nothing is for certain until you get paid.

As long as you gamble for fun, as a form of entertainment, and not as a means to pay the rent, you're okay. Once you start betting the rent, you're in trouble. "The Chief," Art Rooney, Sr., told me that. He also told me that the time to double up is when you win, and not at any other time. Don't ever chase.

And maybe the wisest advice he ever gave me was never bet a friend more than twenty bucks. If you win the bet on a fluke, the friend will hate you. Paying the juice to a bookie is better than ruining a friendship.

I left Brown after the spring semester in '51. Looking back, my time there was really my only association with organized crime other than watching "The Untouchables."

Once I got to Pitt, I went on the straight and narrow. I took my studies much more seriously. Joe Paterno, who graduated from Brown with honors the same year I enrolled, said he developed a lifelong love of the literary classics while he was a student there. Sometimes I think I should have spent more time in the library like Joe and less time in the tailor shop.

In any event, I'm extremely proud to be a Pitt alum, and a "Pitt guy." I never felt I fit in the Ivy League. Like Mr. Rooney, I've always felt most comfortable around people who worked for a living. People who didn't play by the rules. And especially people involved in betting.

That's probably why I have continued to associate with bettors and bookies for most of my life. Particularly bookies. In my experience, they're good people. All you really need in life is a good doctor, a good barber, and a good bookie.

Take my late Pittsburgh bookie friend Tony for instance. He had one standing rule: "If you want to bet, call me. If you start betting parlays, I'll call you. And if you start betting teasers, I will pick you up in a limo with a broad."

Tony always knew the word on the street, so I made it a point to keep in touch with him when I was the SID at Pitt. If there was anything fishy going on with Pitt's teams, he would know about it.

Early one Friday morning in the winter of 1959, I got a call from Tony at my office. Pitt was playing Holy Cross in basketball that night.

"What's going on there?" he asked. "How bad is the injury?"

"What are you talking about, Tony?"

"You opened as a two-point favorite, and now you guys are two-point dogs."

I immediately went to see Bob Timmons, Pitt's head coach. He told me that our starting center, John Mills, got hurt at practice the previous night and was sitting out. How that information got out so fast was mind-boggling. Tony knew about it before me, the school's SID, did.

The money poured in on Holy Cross that afternoon, but Pitt won easily, 83-71. So much for inside information.

Another call from Tony stands out. It involved an interesting proposition in the early 1960s. I had done color commentary for a handful of high school basketball playoff games on *WQED*, the Pittsburgh public television station. Tony called and asked why we didn't do more games. I told him that we could only get a sponsor for a couple of games. The money just wasn't there for high school sports back then.

Tony then asked me how much it would cost to do some more games. If I remember, $500 was the figure.

"Fine," said Tony, "I've got guys who are willing to put up the money."

If you put your ear close enough to the receiver, you could almost hear the gears turning in his head.

"See," he explained. "Once you are on TV, they will bet anything."

By "they," he meant the public. By "guys," I also knew who he was referring to.

I could just hear myself on the air: "Tonight's game is brought to you by the mob. Call them for all your cement mixing and heavy shoe needs." Tony tried to talk me into it, but I told him that we better forget the idea.

That conversation marked the exact moment I first realized the impact that television had on betting. Television is without a doubt the biggest reason behind the explosive growth of sports betting in the United States because it satisfies a natural curiosity. People like to watch what they are betting on. And the suits who run TV know this. It's no coincidence that we've seen the number of live televised games increase twenty-fold in virtually every sport over the past twenty years.

Thanks to *ESPN*, *Fox Sports*, *CBS Sports Network,* and other offshoots like the *NFL Network* and the *Big Ten Network*, there is action to be had every hour of every day. In my opinion, if it weren't for betting, the ratings for TV sports would be thirty, maybe even forty-percent lower. I firmly believe that of all the teams and all the sports, only Notre Dame and Southeastern Conference football could survive on sheer fandom alone.

In this era of skyrocketing contracts and scandals, there are not enough true fans left to drum up the promotional sponsorship needed to keep pro sports on the air for the entirety of their regular seasons, or, in other words, non-playoff action. Other than fans of the two teams in their respective markets, there would be no audience for national telecasts of November NHL or NBA games. It has to be betting.

Don't tell the NFL that. As an organization, the NFL gets very defensive about betting. That's because betting is one of the two foundational pillars the NFL was built upon. In two cases, quite literally. Two of the league's flagship franchises, the Giants and the Steelers, once had very strong ties to gambling.

Everyone knows that Tim Mara, the founder of the Giants, was a bookmaker. It's a big part of Steelers' lore that the Chief bought the franchise in 1933 with winnings from the horse track. That story may or may not be true, but for as long as I knew him, it wasn't exactly a secret that the old man was on the F.B.I.'s radar in regards to his purported connection to some local organized crime figures and a number of gambling-related activities.

So it's no surprise that the people who run the NFL have been trying for the better part of the last fifty years to distance the sport from its history, its humble, rough and tumble beginnings in the 1920s and 30s.

Unlike college football, which was based on institutional and generational loyalties, and a traditionalist attitude favoring amateurism, professional football had no pomp and pageantry, paid its transient players like military mercenaries, and, more importantly, was more violent than college ball.

Broken noses and busted jaws were almost built-in conditions of a pro's contract. There was a player-coach in Pittsburgh named John McNally whose nickname was "Johnny Blood." You can guess where he got the nickname. He was a helluva character.

Mr. Rooney hired McNally in the late 1930s to run the Pirates, which was also the name of the city's baseball team before he changed it to the Steelers in 1940. Helmet-to-helmet contact? Hell, today Commissioner Roger Goodell would fine Johnny Blood just for showing up at the stadium with a nickname like that.

Pro football was the kind of game that appealed to guys who didn't have a formal education, much less loyalty to a college or university, and worked for a living. Steelworkers in Pittsburgh. Miners in Pottsville, Pennsylvania. Meatpackers in Green Bay, Wisconsin. Longshoremen in New York. And these same guys, coincidentally, also liked to bet.

The way Jimmy the Greek told the story to me, the guy who invented the point spread in the 1940s, Charles McNeil, picked pro football as the sport to try his system, which he called "wholesale odds," for a very good reason. Prior to the point spread, the way you bet was on the moneyline. The math confused these guys. I'm not talking down on them. I have a college degree and basic arithmetic confuses the hell out of me.

By all accounts, McNeil was a certified genius. He was a math teacher, a University of Chicago alum. He taught at the prep school in New York that Joe Kennedy sent Joe Jr. and Jack to. For me, the definition of intelligence and being a great teacher is not all book smarts, or warehousing knowledge. It's being able to impart knowledge, making something difficult to understand simple for other people. That's what McNeil did. He made the numbers less intimidating.

The point spread opened up the world of wagering to the masses. It wasn't just the old-time sharps and degenerates anymore. Everybody, Walter Winchell's "Mr. and Mrs. America," was hooked. The business at his book was booming. McNeil started with pro football, and it was such a resounding success with the public he started making odds on college football and college basketball.

Together, violence and gambling built pro football, and the NFL, into the billion-dollar behemoth it is today. The NFL's recent efforts to bring awareness to head trauma and reduce dangerous injuries are admirable, but its decades-long denial of the sport's other foundational lure is laughable. That's probably why the League has been dogged by gambling-related issues and problems throughout its existence.

In 1963, Rozelle suspended two of the NFL's biggest stars, Green Bay's Paul Hornung and Detroit's Alex Karras, for betting on NFL games. I truly believe the whole affair was more about protecting the league's wholesome image with an eye to future TV deals than it was about betting.

I don't remember the specifics about Karras's part, but Hornung said he never bet against Green Bay. "I would have been an idiot to have bet against the Packers," he once told me, "because we covered the number every week."

I also believe Rozelle made an example of Hornung and Karras because they were high profile players. If he had been sincere in his concern he'd have investigated the entire league, but then he would have had to shut down the NFL because all of the players were betting.

The late Tom Brookshier once told me a good story about the time he had to call a timeout during an Eagles game in the late 1950s to deal with a distracted teammate. The opponent was moving the ball down the field in big chunks because this one player was missing tackles and seemed preoccupied with the scoreboard.

"What's going on?" Brookshier asked in the huddle. "You hungover? Wife problems?"

"My problem," the player answered, while gesturing to the out-of-town scoreboard, "is that the Rams are beating the Bears 7-0 and I have Chicago giving seven!"

I felt for those guys. They were blowing out knees, breaking legs and losing teeth and weren't getting paid millions like players today. Betting was a way to makes ends meet for some. The public, at least the betting public, sympathized with Hornung and Karras.

I especially sympathized with my friend Hornung, who just a year earlier had waged a legal battle against the I.R.S. in regards to a sports car he received for being named *Sport* magazine's most valuable player. To be honest, I don't know anybody who didn't side with Hornung. The I.R.S. is the most-hated alphabet government organization of all-time, just behind the K.G.B.

Hornung, however, got the last laugh on the NFL and Rozelle. He made me laugh, at least. Hornung and Sonny Jurgensen were doing a game in Washington in the 1970s and Jurgensen pointed out that two Redskins' players who played predominantly on special teams were getting $65,000 a year, which was above the league average.

"Wow," replied Hornung. "In my day, I would have had to miss three crucial field goals to make that kind of money."

It's no wonder bettors have been laughing at the league behind its back for years. The NFL's public stance on betting has always bordered on the absurd, but around the time of the merger, the government joined the farce as the NFL's bumbling sidekick.

Uncle Sam launched a federal probe in Detroit which put a dark cloud over Super Bowl IV – the last championship game between the old AFL and NFL – in 1970 due to the strange connection between the defendant and Kansas City's Len Dawson, who both shared the same last name. They were really reaching. Dawson had nothing to do with the investigation and the Chiefs were 13-point underdogs versus the Vikings that won outright.

I also remember in the 1970s, the NFL made a big stink about an episode of one of my favorite TV shows, "MacMillan and Wife," which starred the crime-solving team of San Francisco police commissioner Stewart McMillan, played by Rock Hudson, and his much younger wife Sally, played by actress Susan St. James.

The episode, "Death is a Seven-Point Favorite," was spun around a murder investigation involving sports betting and a fictional Frisco pro football team, but the show's producers used a 49ers helmet in the opening title card, so the NFL bitched.

Here's a prediction for you: sports betting will one day be legal in the United States. The NFL should not only accept that reality and embrace its history, but also take a leadership role in the legalization process.

Rozelle himself, in a 1976 deposition, admitted that there was no proof that betting harmed pro football. In fact, if you talk to individuals affiliated with the league – off-the-record, of course – they all say the same thing, that betting helps the NFL.

Look no further than the phenomenon of "Monday Night Football." The league experienced arguably its greatest period of growth in the 1970s and 80s, which was also the heyday of "Monday Night Football."

The idea of one professional football game in a prime-time slot on a weekday night was novel, but the rise in popularity of "Monday Night Football" wasn't solely attributable to this new novelty or even to Howard Cosell, for that matter.

It was because Mondays were redemption days for bettors, plain and simple. Payoff day used to be Monday. With the advent of "Monday Night Football," bettors gained a day. Weekend losers could chase, or cut their losses.

My friend John O'Connor was on a PTA board in Cincinnati in the Seventies and the board used to meet on Monday nights, so he missed the first half of the Monday night games. Raising motion after motion, he insisted that they switched to another day of the week.

He eventually prevailed and the PTA meetings were rescheduled to Tuesday evenings. It meant that he now missed *Happy Days*, then the No. 1 show in the country.

"But you can't bet on the Fonz," O'Connor told me.

In my opinion, credit for the success of "Monday Night Football" goes to three people. Roone Arledge, Cosell, and your neighborhood bookie – and not necessarily in that order.

The driving force behind television is the ratings game, and what drives ratings? Betting. That's why in addition to Monday night games, we now have pro games on Thursdays and college games on basically every night of the week. For the suits who run TV and sports to tell us otherwise insults the intelligence of Americans. And this idea isn't limited only to high-profile pro sports.

In March of 1986, Texas was playing Southern Cal in the NCAA women's college basketball national championship game in Lexington, Kentucky. The Lady Longhorns were three-point favorites. This was the first time I had seen a betting line on a women's college basketball game. As a result, I predicted that the game would be the highest rated in the history of the sport. Texas won, 97-81, covered the spread, and I was right about the ratings.

Today, four decades later, women's basketball games – both the pro and college variety – are televised regularly. You can watch every women's NCAA tournament game, not just the Final Four. Why? Is it because people are suddenly into women's hoops? No. It's because you can bet all the games.

For years, people decried sexism as the reason for the lack of interest in the women's game. They claimed that it wasn't as popular as the male brand because female players weren't as athletically-gifted or because they couldn't dunk. This was bullshit. Once the public began to bet women's hoops, the sport took off. You can't tell me that's not the case, because, well, most chicks still can't dunk.

The NCAA should have gone this route decades ago instead of wasting time with Title IX. Too many athletes, male and female, suffered from these bungled efforts at enforced equality. All you had to do was get Vegas on board and local bookies would have followed.

Not only would many colleges not have had to kill men's sports like wrestling, women would not have played in empty gyms for so long. Women's sports would have exploded in popularity naturally, thus helping girls get involved in youth leagues at earlier ages through true market demand, not through feel-good legislation that accomplishes little.

Here's some advice for all future would-be sports leagues: getting your sport on the line is priority number one. It was for the late Jack Dolph. When Dolph, the former director of *CBS* Sports, was named commissioner of the now-defunct American Basketball Association in 1969, he told me that his first duty was to get ABA games on the betting line. Think about that. It wasn't signing players. Wasn't a TV deal.

"I was able to get the finals on, but that's all," said Dolph.

When he told me that, I sensed the disappointment in his voice.

I once teamed up with the medium of television to influence a betting trend myself. It wasn't, however, a conscious effort. It was common sense.

There was a bookie in New York who went by the name of Captain Bligh. He was fucking brutal. He never smiled unless you went 0-10 on a football weekend. But he was a bookie, so we got along fine.

We used to have lunch on Fridays and one Friday in the fall of 1983, he told me that West Virginia was favored over Penn State. While it might have made sense to the guys in the desert, it made no sense to me whatsoever. I knew the history between the schools.

The following day on *ABC*, I said that to have West Virginia favored in State College was ridiculous. Even though West Virginia was undefeated and ranked No. 4, Penn State had not lost to the Mountaineers since 1955 and Joe Paterno's Lions were the defending national champs. I predicted that Penn State would win straight up.

Not only did they win, Penn State pounded WVU, 41-23. I remember getting a call from a *CBS* announcer following that game later in the afternoon, thanking me for the "advice." He left it at that.

The next time I saw Bligh, he was pissed. He explained that the minute I made that prediction, his phone started ringing off the hook. Everybody loaded up on Penn State.

I've always been very reluctant to be a tout. First of all, there's a big difference between going large on a game with your own money, and telling others what to do with their hard-earned cash.

I don't know how other network commentators did business, or how many of them even bet, but back when I was on the air regularly, you could be confident that I always put my money where my big mouth was. If I made a pick on the air or on the chat I did with *ESPN*, that was the way I was betting that game. Some bets were bigger than others.

The biggest bet I ever made happened to be on one of the biggest games I've ever attended, the Florida State-Notre Dame "Game of the Century" in 1993. I attended that game as part of the first-ever "College GameDay" regular-season road show with Chris Fowler, Lee Corso, and Craig James.

Out of all the big games I've seen or attended in my life, this game would definitely be in the top five for atmosphere. I didn't attend Nebraska-Oklahoma in 1971, but I think only that game, Texas-Arkansas in '69, and Notre Dame-Alabama in the '73 Sugar Bowl beat the '93 Florida State-Notre Dame game in terms of build-up and the game itself living up to the hype.

Nebraska was favored in '71, by one or a half-point. Some bookies had it as a pick. The betting line for Texas-Arkansas was roughly the same. The wise guys knew that those games were going to be classics.

That wasn't the case with Florida State and Notre Dame. Second-ranked Notre Dame was a seven-point underdog to the top-ranked Seminoles. You couldn't blame the wise guys, since Florida State looked like an NFL team up to that point of the season.

Me, on the other hand, I felt that the Fighting Irish had too many things (as usual) going for them. For starters, homefield advantage. One of my cardinal rules is never pick against Notre Dame when the Irish were getting points at home. It's like picking against Russia when that country fighting on its home soil in the middle of winter. You don't do it.

Factor in the way I'd seen Lou Holtz inspire underdogs over the years, it just seemed like the perfect situation for Notre Dame. I felt that Notre Dame would cover, so I called my bookie the night before the game and told him I wanted Notre Dame plus seven for $25,000. I was confident, but again, like Mr. Rooney had warned me, I wasn't betting the rent.

When we drove to campus the morning of the game, I realized I fucked up. It was still dark out and I saw all those Notre Dame fans milling around. Thousands of them. I knew I should have taken Notre Dame on the moneyline to win straight up.

I don't know if Fowler and the others knew that I bet the game, or for how much. By the time the scoreboard rang up triple zeroes and Irish fans were storming the field to celebrate the wild 31-24 victory, it didn't bother me that a longtime rival had won a big game because I had won big, too.

Later that evening, while walking through the parking lot, I even found myself humming the Victory March, like John McKay did while walking off the field after the '73 Notre Dame-Southern Cal game.

Speaking of the Victory March, I won a big bet five years earlier when Notre Dame upset No. 1 Miami, 31-30, in a similarly epic game in South Bend. But I didn't make any money on this one.

My good friend, Tim Brando, the first host of "College Gameday" and one of the most multi-talented on-air personalities I've ever worked with, didn't think the Irish had a chance. We made a bet on the show the week before that if Notre Dame beat Miami, he would sing the Victory March on the air. Not only did Brando honor the bet, he flew out to South Bend and did it in front of the entire Notre Dame team. Nobody confused him for Sinatra, but I'll admit that his rendition wasn't half bad.

To be honest, I wouldn't be a good tout. You have to nail every pick, yet no matter how many you get right, people are never satisfied. The Greek once told me that on a particular NFL Sunday one year, he went 3-0 on the one o'clock games. On the four o'clock game he was wrong. He went to the track the next day and everyone gave it to him. For a winning percentage of .750!

A similar incident happened to me in the spring of 1988. I predicted on our New Year's Day edition of "GameDay" that Michigan State would lose to Southern Cal 31-7 in the Rose Bowl. Of course, Lorenzo White ran all over the Trojans and the Spartans won, 20-17. Four months later, I was in Detroit doing an Arena football game and as I was walking across the carpet I heard some guy yell "31-7, asshole!" I didn't even turn around.

I've met people whose teams I picked against ten, twenty years ago and they bring it up. They never forget. What bugs me is that few remember the ones you get right. For example, I picked Penn State to upset No. 1-ranked Miami in the 1987 Fiesta Bowl. Sportswriter Rick Reilly was the only one to give me credit. "The only people who thought Penn State could win was a plumber from Altoona and Beano Cook," wrote Reilly.

The only guy who will be remembered more for his correct predictions than his misses is Nostradamus. The rest of us in the business just have to live with that.

The only people who can consistently get away with making bad picks and costing us money are politicians. That isn't the worst part. When it comes to betting, most are at best clueless, or at worst, insufferable with their holier-than-thou attitudes regarding what's long been considered a "vice."

And yet, strangely enough, some are just like the rest of us. One fall Sunday afternoon in the early 1980s, Kentucky Governor John Y. Brown, Jr. was in 206, the guest viewing room at *CBS* Sports, following that day's NFL action. Brown was waiting for his wife, Phyllis George, to wrap up her duties as co-anchor of "The NFL Today."

When Brown and George departed, my friend and co-worker Susan Nemeroff, the director of talent at *CBS* Sports, noticed that Brown had left a slip of paper at his seat. She brought it to me. Susan is an intelligent woman, but I had to explain to her what the numbers - Pittsburgh -7, Kansas City +6, and Cleveland -3 - written on the paper meant.

I started laughing my ass off. I remembered when Brown announced he was running, a Buffalo sportswriter wrote that "if John Y. Brown runs Kentucky the same way he ran the Buffalo Braves, we will have 49 states." The great Dave Kindred added that Brown had "wrecked two basketball franchises, now he plans to ruin a state." He wasn't very successful with the Celtics, either.

Brown might have been 0-3 running basketball teams, but he went 3-0 on the early games that day. Maybe he missed his true calling.

The important lesson, I guess, is that he was a politician who liked to bet and he didn't bother trying to conceal it. Politicians that understand gambling are increasingly rare. And that's going to be a problem. If history tells us anything, America's leaders will have no idea how to regulate sports betting when my prediction comes true.

Look at state lotteries. In Pennsylvania, lottery proceeds reportedly go to help the elderly. The politicians saw the cash pouring in and decided to expand. When they first started the lottery in Pennsylvania, they didn't do it on Christmas.

But they're greedy, as all politicians are, and now they do it on Christmas and most other holidays, too. And then they added the instant tickets, national games like the Powerball, and afternoon drawings as well.

I won't be here when it happens, but if the Second Coming takes place during a lottery drawing, the Book of Revelation will be relegated to the little box in the corner of your television screen until the Powerball is drawn. And that night's lead story on local news will probably be followed on the nightly news by a piece featuring soundbites from a politician talking about how we need to raise taxes to help our senior citizens.

Then came the casinos, another racket. Our legislature in Pennsylvania, which, incidentally, is the largest full-time lawmaking body in this country, decided to start building casinos across the state. The profits were supposed to reduce property taxes and fund schools and other programs, but property taxes keep going up instead. Bottomline, all the money raised by gambling is either squandered or used by the politicians for personal enrichment.

I told you I believe sports betting will be legalized everywhere in the United States. I'll take that prediction a step further and say that I think it happens sometime in the next ten years. If I had to bet, I'd take the under. It's going to happen sooner than people think.

But it's not going to succeed. Why? Because maybe not at first, but one day very soon after legalization, the pro leagues and the NCAA will start demanding their shares. That will tack on a kind of service fee to your bet.

The government will want its cut, too. It'll be a much bigger cut than the colleges, pro commissioners and players' unions take. The politicians will fail to realize that the state and federal governments can't tax bettors heavily.

I knew a guy who told me that if he can win $2,000 or $3,000 on football in the fall his family is going to have a great Christmas. Some years he only wins $500, but he makes sure he never loses big. He bets for entertainment, not as a profession. That's what the politicians will have to realize. They can't tax the small stakes bettors. But, on the other hand, the pro who wins $500,000 annually should have to report it. Some of it, at least.

If you win money with your bookie, no one knows about it. If you win money with the state, you can be sure that the I.R.S. is going to know about it. That's why people go with the bookies now and will whenever the government gets into the gambling business. The novelty of doing it above board will soon wear off. Governmental greed will kick in. Mark my words.

I saw this all coming decades ago. It was after a conversation I had with Larry Merchant. Merchant recounted the story for me of the time he testified as a character witness for a bettor who was being put on trial in Rhode Island on bookmaking charges.

Merchant met this man while researching his book, "NFL: The National Football Lottery," in the 1970s. Merchant spent a year in Las Vegas chronicling the stories and characters that surrounded an entire NFL season of betting. The material was incredible.

The man in question wasn't taking bets, he was placing them. And winning. Big. That's what got the government's attention. Even though betting was becoming more and more visible in the public eye, the government was so slow on the uptake, it was startling.

I asked Merchant for his impression of the whole situation and he told me that it was shocking to him that the government couldn't understand that this guy wasn't taking bets, that he was simply betting on games in Las Vegas, where you could do it legally.

"I told the prosecution, the government, that you have to let the bettors keep all the money they win," said Merchant. "And they said that they can't do that."

Back then, the government was trying to make some money off gambling but also trying to put a dent into organize crime. This time around, they'll try to raise revenue through legalization, while also trying to muscle the competition, the local bookies, out of business. And they'll fail in the future like they failed in the past.

It'll be entertaining to watch everyone find out just how clueless and incompetent Congress really is. But our so-called leaders better become competent quickly. Sometime in the future, the only people that don't bet will be the dead.

* * *

Another reason, besides television, for the increase in betting today is that you can get final scores so quickly. When I was growing up in the 1940s, I sometimes had to wait until the Sunday evening Sun-Telly, the *Pittsburgh Sun-Telegraph*, was delivered to get the scores of the Saturday night West Coast college football games.

Today, thanks to the Internet, you can get the scores on your cellphone anywhere, anytime. Sometimes, I feel like one of those old coots they used to bring on TV shows in the 1950s who was alive when Lincoln was assassinated. When it comes to getting scores, I spanned the Pony Express to the jet age.

Of course, the real secret in betting is getting the score - or, more realistically, something that could help you better estimate the final score - before the game. I'm talking, of course, about the subject of inside information.

Despite the fact that I am in the media, seldom do I get real inside information. But the public tends to think that I do. That's why people on the street ask me who I think is going to win a particular game. I don't kid myself that they care about my thoughts or opinions.

Let's get real. If I had consistent access to inside information I would be swinging on the Riviera with Stefanie Powers during bowl season, not sloshing through the slush on the sidewalks of Pittsburgh.

Some advice for everyone in sports media today: people don't watch pre-game shows and coaches' press conferences because they care about you. They are looking for information on injuries and tips that they think will help them beat their bookies.

I remember one memorable time I was being pumped for some inside information, only it wasn't by a sharp or some guy on the street. It was by two F.B.I. agents at the New York field office in the first week of January 1968. They had asked me to come in on my lunch break for an informal interview about some kind of investigation related to gambling.

The scene was as you'd imagine it. Phones ringing. Wanted posters plastered on the walls. An office full of G-men in dark suits with white shirts, heavy on the starch.

This is just like "The F.B.I." TV show, I said to myself as I took my seat. *Tonight's episode, 'Beano.'*

As the minutes dragged on and we waited for another agent to arrive, my mind began to wander. *What is this about, anyway? Did they know about what I did in Providence during my freshman year in Brown? Were they trying to sweat me?*

"Look, is Efrem Zimbalist getting here anytime soon?" I joked. "I'm not a vice president at *ABC*, I actually have to come back from lunch."

"Relax, Mr. Cook."

Now I started to panic. A million thoughts raced through my head. *Just great. How am I going to tell Roone that I'm going away to prison? The hell with Roone, what am I going to tell my parents? What if the Providence mob finds out I was here? I'm not going to flip. No way. I'm no stool pigeon.* I tried to stay cool.

Finally, the second agent walked into the room and we got started. I was relieved that the line of questioning had nothing to do with Providence or the pool sheets. The whole thing was about a publication called "Sports Journal" that this outfit in Miami put out.

It was a newspaper geared to sports bettors. It wasn't underground, but it wasn't *Sports Illustrated*, either. You could get it at certain newsstands around the country if the proprietor was hip. I had it delivered to my apartment on 47th Street. I didn't pay a subscription fee. I had worked out a deal with the publisher that in exchange for receiving my *ABC* releases, they would put me on their mailing list.

I was truthful when I told the agents that I knew the publication was used by bookies and bettors, but I lied when I said I didn't use it myself for betting. I told them it was a work saver for me for research purposes because it contained all the team schedules and kickoff times and things of that nature in one handy guide. I hope the statute of limitations has passed on this revelation because I'm too old to go to Sing-Sing.

I had learned of this rag from a buddy in Pittsburgh, a big bettor, and they seemed pretty intent on learning his identity, which I refused to give up, even after they vaguely threatened me by explaining the consequences of withholding information.

My impression was that they thought the publication was being used to transmit gambling information, maybe through some sort of code, throughout the country, or else they were trying to work their way through the mailing list in hopes of finding some leads they could use to implicate people in organized crime.

These are just guesses. In any event, it was a fishing expedition and since I was a guppy, they threw me back in the pond. I never heard from them again.

I was no crook and I've always considered myself to be a patriotic, law-abiding (for the most part) citizen, but my sense of relief turned to anger after I left the building.

It's 1968. We're losing good young men in Vietnam. God knows how many communists have infiltrated the government. There are riots in the cities, the rich are rigging the stock market, the politicians are robbing us blind and here these guys are, using the full weight of the F.B.I. to intimidate regular Joes looking to make a few extra bucks betting on sports. It pissed me off.

I wasn't a snitch that time. But I am going to spill the beans right here with some good inside information stories I've never told anybody else. Truth is, I've had plenty of opportunities to use my relationships with SIDs, front office-types, coaches, other media members, etc., to make a couple of extra bucks. I passed up a lot of hot tips over the years. I honestly don't regret missing out on those paydays. At this stage of my life, the memories and stories are more valuable to me than any money I could have won.

Most of these opportunities happened during my first stint at *ABC*, but I wisely avoided any compromising situations. Roone was adamant about not betting. Especially on *ABC* Sports events. Roone had two "Thou shalt not" commandments. One concerned betting and the other concerned hustling coeds on the road. Both rules were followed – to a point.

At times, adhering to the former of those rules was the more difficult of the two. You have to understand that the betting atmosphere back then was unbelievable. Some of the people I knew and worked with were betting on anything and everything.

Remember "The Dating Game?" A couple of *ABC* guys, led by the late Chester "Chet" Forte, would bet on the outcome of the show every week.

Forte was an All-American basketball player at Columbia in the 1950s, and the first director of "Monday Night Football." He was responsible for making the show as visually impressive as it was. He was a great talent. But Chet had a problem. He bet like nobody I've ever seen. It ended up costing him his job at *ABC*.

Anyway, Forte got tired of losing. So he found out who the producer of "The Dating Game" was and scored all the winners in advance one week. Although a degenerate gambler, deep down Forte was a good guy. He had a good laugh, then gave everyone their money back.

"It's too bad, Beans," Forte told me after he had refunded the last of his ill-gotten winnings to the gang, "that betting on the NBA isn't that easy."

When it came to real sports, Forte played for keeps. One Sunday afternoon when I was at *ABC*, the Detroit Pistons were playing the Los Angeles Lakers in Detroit. The Lakers had played a game the previous night and Jerry West had gotten hurt. The Lakers came out for the shoot-a-round and Forte spied West in street clothes.

All at once, Forte bolted from the arena, muttering something about checking the feed in the production truck. Of course, he blew past the truck and hit the nearest payphone, where he called the usual list of characters. The Lakers were favored by three, so Forte told everybody and his brother to bet Detroit.

It's ten minutes before two (*ABC* used to come on those days at two o'clock with NBA games) in the truck. In the truck there was a red phone. The only person who is supposed to have that number is Roone. Typically, when it rang, everybody in the truck froze. It meant something was wrong. Somebody was in deep shit. If Forte went to take a piss, whoever was next in the chain of command would have to pick it up. Most of the time, it was just a wrong number and everybody exhaled in relief.

So, about ten minutes before two that day, the red phone rings and Forte picks it up. Instead of Roone, it's Chet's bookie! Everybody could hear the screaming.

“What the fuck is going on there?” this guy yells. “I have all this money coming in on the Pistons. Everybody in the world is calling me about the Pistons.”

“You son-of-a-bitch, we're going to get even with you now," Forte laughed. “Watch the opening of the show."

Forte slammed the phone down with a look of satisfaction that I'll never forget. At two o'clock the show opens up with a shot of West sitting alone on the bench in street clothes. Chris Schenkel's somber voice narrated the scene: "Jerry West, he will not play today.”

The Pistons won straight up. Before all of that commotion in the truck, Forte pulled me aside and asked if I wanted in on the action. I told him no because if I would win this bet, it would be all over Sixth Avenue. Which ensured it would eventually get back to Roone.

The closest I ever came to a sure thing with the NBA and inside information almost exploded in my face. The Knicks were playing the Celtics at Madison Square Garden on a Saturday night. The game wasn't on *ABC* and I wasn't working, but since I lived close to the Garden, I was there hanging out on press row, talking to some writers.

I found myself eavesdropping on a conversation between two PR guys. The conversation faded in and out, but one sentence caught my attention: “Russell is out.”

Hmm, the Celtics were four-point favorites and Bill Russell was a late scratch? I had a press pass, so I went home to call a friend that would have appreciated the tip.

Imagine my surprise when the first thing I saw upon re-entering the Garden is Bill fucking Russell out on the floor going through warm-ups! I knew I wasn't seeing things because at a towering six-feet, ten-inches tall, Russell is not the type of guy you have a tough time picking out of a crowd. Bewildered, I made my way back down to press row and casually pulled aside one of the PR guys.

“I thought Russell wasn't playing?”

“He isn't,” the guy told me. “Cazzie Russell has (National) Guard duty.”

Oh, Shit, I said to myself. They had been talking about "Snazzie" Cazzie Russell of the Knicks, not Bill Russell of the Celtics!

It was about that time I contemplated suicide, but the betting gods were with me that night: Boston won by two. To this day, my friend never knew that Bill Russell played. He wasn't a fan, just a bettor. He won. He collected. That was that.

As for Bill Russell, everyone knew about his physical abilities, but the guy could flat out think. He was probably the most intelligent former professional athlete I've ever worked with. I say that even though he used to mistakenly call me “Bongo” instead of Beano.

One time, during a *CBS* production meeting before game six of the 1980 NBA finals, he showed off those wits. Los Angeles was leading Philadelphia 3-2 in a tight best-of-seven series and Kareem Abdul Jabbar wasn't going to play.

The line opened with Philly favored by five, then it jumped to five-and-a-half, then six. It kept on rising, finally peaking around eight points right before the tip.

The room was abuzz with one question: what are the Lakers going to do without Kareem? Then Bill Russell silenced everyone when he posed his own question: "What are the Sixers going to do with Magic in the pivot?"

When the meeting ended, everyone rushed for the phones and took Los Angeles. The final box score listed Earvin "Magic" Johnson as having 42 points and 15 rebounds. The Lakers won going away, 123-107, to claim the World Championship.

Our entire crew, Bongo included, cashed that one.

Another NBA game I remember was a game between the Lakers and the old Baltimore Bullets. The Bullets later moved to Washington and after another name change, they're now known as the Wizards. I was working for *ABC* at this time.

The morning before the game I ran into Eddie Einhorn, an independent producer with whom I would later work at *CBS*, at a Holiday Inn a block or two away from the Baltimore Civic Center.

Eddie looked like hell. He had done the Laker game the previous night and because of a late finish and some transportation issues, didn't get into town until four o'clock that morning. Eddie also told me that was the same time the Lakers arrived as well.

I knew the game was scheduled for two o'clock that afternoon so I figured Los Angeles would be flat. The experts can say what they want about athletes, sleep, and conditioning, but it's a proven fact that after staying up or out late, most of them don't play well the next day. Of course, there are exceptions.

The joke in Pittsburgh when Bobby Layne played for the Steelers in the 1950s was that if Layne went to bed early, you bet the opponent. If you knew that Layne had been out until five in the morning, you bet the Steelers because if he went to bed early, that meant he wasn't feeling well.

Anyway, Baltimore was a four-point dog that was probably dog-tired. *ABC* was televising the game, so I didn't bet it. I told one of our people in the truck, but I don't know if the guy bet it. I was tempted to call some people, but if Roone found out, it would be grounds for dismissal and rightfully so.

I stayed on the straight and narrow when it came to Roone's rules, but that didn't mean I couldn't take care of my friends. One occasion was a game between the Celtics and the old Cincinnati Royals in March of '69, Bill Russell's last season as head coach in Boston.

When I got into Cincinnati, O'Connor picked me up. I told him I had noticed that the Celtics had problems when they played two days in a row. It was a trend. They had played the night before, beating the Sixers in Philly in a high-scoring game.

Furthermore, they got into Cincy late. I told O'Connor I had a hunch that the Royals would pull away in the fourth quarter, but I couldn't bet because *ABC* was doing the game.

On our way to the game, we made a quick detour across the river to Newport, Kentucky and O'Connor went into a place much like the joint where I made my first bet and put some money on the Royals. If I remember correctly, the game was a pick. Just as I had thought, Cincinnati pulled away in the fourth quarter to win.

On the way back to Pittsburgh I ran into the late Richie Powers, who was one of the game's officials.

"In that fourth quarter," he said, "(The Celtics) kept saying 'Russ, get us out of here, we're exhausted.'"

That made me happy. I was getting good at noticing trends.

Another exception I made with inside information was for a friend who was a sports editor at a big metropolitan daily paper. This friend, who will remain nameless because he's still alive and has somehow managed to keep his betting secret from his wife all these years, asked me to let him know about any hot tips that I picked up on the road.

That hot tip landed in my lap in October 1970, when Alabama was playing Ole Miss in a nationally televised SEC showdown in Jackson, Mississippi on *ABC*. Alabama was a four-point dog and the game was being touted as another big quarterback duel between the Rebels' Archie Manning and the Crimson Tide's Scott Hunter.

It was a day or two before the game and myself and a half-dozen other *ABC* personnel were in a meeting in a room on the second floor of the Admiral Benbow Inn in Jackson when a PA burst in with big news: Hunter was injured and wouldn't even suit up.

All at once, seven guys had to make a phone call. I went back to my room and called a writer on the staff of the paper and told him to tell his boss that Scott Hunter was out. In other words, load up on the Rebels.

I thought of my editor friend when Alabama scored on a Johnny Musso touchdown catch to pull within 26-17 at the end of the third quarter, but Ole Miss recovered a fumbled punt on their way to defeating 'Bama easily, 48-23. I got a call from the editor that following Monday and he thanked me.

Later, I found out that the line on the game never changed despite Hunter's injury. This just proves that bookies always know what is going on.

When Notre Dame played at Michigan State in 1966, Notre Dame was a five-point favorite. A few people, namely media types, learned the night before the game that Notre Dame's star running back, Nick Eddy, had injured himself getting off the train and wouldn't play. But this fact wasn't released to the general public until game time.

I had this information on Friday night, but didn't do a thing because it was my first year working for *ABC*. Of course, everyone knows the final score of that game: Irish 10, Spartans 10. It's the most famous stalemate since the Korean War.

After the game, I was in Dan Jenkins's hotel room when he was writing his gamer for *Sports Illustrated*. He called me over, pointed to the paper sticking out of the top of his typewriter and asked, "what do you think?"

I leaned over his shoulder and when I read the lede, I laughed so hard I almost swallowed my cigarette. A jab at the Victory March, it remains one of the best ledes in recent sportswriting history: "Old Notre Dame will tie over all." And I was the first person to read it!

When I got back to Pittsburgh for the holidays, the guys in Oakland let me have it for not calling with the Eddy news. I told them that all I had to do was call them, and they would've jumped on the Spartans, won big and then bragged about it. Some may say I was paranoid, but news in the betting world travels faster than you can possibly imagine. I couldn't risk word getting back to Roone.

Bud Wilkinson, the famous coach of the Oklahoma Sooners, once told me, this was when we were both working for *ABC*, "if a coach doesn't know the line, he won't be around that long."

For many years you'd never hear an active coach make such a statement. It was an unwritten rule that you didn't talk about betting in public. By in public, I mean talk to the media about betting.

In September 1978, Pepper Rodgers was on the hotseat at Georgia Tech. He had lost three of his last four in '77 and started '78 0-2. Going into the third week of the season he told Furman Bisher that "I better beat Tulane and I better beat the spot."

Bisher told me what he said. This was back before you could talk about betting on the record, but it was nevertheless refreshing for me to hear a coach admit something I had known for years. Oh, and that Tulane-Tech game? The Yellow Jackets, favored by nine, won 27-17.

Lou Holtz is one of the great coaches in college football history. He might just be the sport's all-time greatest storyteller. One of my favorites is the one about the expectations of the boosters at Notre Dame.

"When I went there they said, 'Coach, we just want to be competitive.' The first year we lost five games by a total of 14 points, which I thought was competitive, and the alums said, 'no, you don't understand, competitive to us means to win, not just come close.' The second year we won eight games and went to the Cotton Bowl and they said, 'we don't just want you to win, we want you to win them all.' The third year we won them all and they said, 'You're still not getting it, coach. We meant you have to cover them all as well.'"

In the spring of 2002, when Steve Spurrier announced that he was leaving Florida for the NFL, *ABC's* Terry Bowden, the former coach at Auburn, remarked that Spurrier's decision would rankle all of the Gator faithful, but especially those who bet.

"UF fans are not only used to winning," said Bowden, "but winning big and most often bigger than the line, if you know what I mean." I was glad to see somebody mention this on the air.

One of the big untold stories in betting, especially in college sports, is the influence of the booster clubs and big shot donors. The fat cats want it all. They want the prestige and notoriety of getting their names on buildings when they donate money. They want to deduct their donations on their income tax. Then they want it all back in the form of winning bets on the school's teams. This is especially true in football. The coaches know this. All coaches.

At one time, the coaches from nearly every single major program would look at the film of a specific opponent and then would let everybody – the rich boosters and big money donors – know by Wednesday of that particular week that this was *the game*, the time to bet the house on the ol' alma mater. And they were right something like ninety percent of the time.

One Saturday afternoon in October 1959, the late Roy Simmons walked into the pressbox at Pitt Stadium. A scout and assistant at Syracuse, Simmons was a successful lacrosse coach as well. Syracuse was playing Navy that afternoon in Norfolk. I told Simmons that the Orangemen were going to have a tough game against the Midshipmen.

"We will win by four touchdowns," he replied with a smile.

That was his way of letting me know that this week was *the game* for Syracuse. I immediately went to one writer who liked to bet and let him in on the information. Simmons was only a few points off. The final was Syracuse 32, Navy 6.

When coaches pretend that they don't know the spread, I laugh. There is only one documented case in history that I know of in which a coach was totally oblivious to the line. It was Joe Paterno and the game was Pitt-Penn State in 1982.

I know for a fact that Paterno was very surprised at the volume of thank you notes he received from Penn State fans after he sent in the field goal unit late in the Lions' victory. Penn State, up 16-10, was giving seven that afternoon. They won, 19-10. Paterno actually had no idea how much betting there was on college football until that incident.

Paterno's naivete was a special case. Every college football coach is aware of the point spread. But even with relaxed attitudes toward betting nowadays, they still won't admit it publicly. So you have to read between the lines.

Pay attention to the press conferences. When told that their team is favored, a coach will shrug it off, or else he won't admit that he pays attention to those things.

Yet have you noticed that when they are underdogs they always somehow know the line? They use the spread to motivate their teams, fire up their fans and, when they win, brag about how the media and Vegas disrespected their team.

Coaches in pro football are no different than their college counterparts. They know. My single season working for the Miami Dolphins was eye-opening in many ways.

Don Shula and I didn't get along very well, but there is one thing I'll say about him, and in my view, it's a compliment. Off the record, Shula was extremely candid on a number of subjects. Betting being one of them. I found it incredibly refreshing.

For example, at the midway point of the 1974 season, there was an informal bullshit session between Shula, Charlie Callahan, writer Bill Braucher and my future New York roommate, Rich Podolsky, and myself before the start of one of Shula's pressers.

At some point, our conversation turned to point spreads and Braucher said he wished Atlanta had scored one TD less versus Pittsburgh in the Monday night game.

"You should never give that many points," Shula chided Braucher.

My ears perked up. I knew the Steelers had been favored by 11. What I didn't know was how Shula knew the number. I'd never known a coach to admit that he paid attention to those things.

Podolsky, a bettor who always studied the stats and the trends, agreed with Shula.

"Teams that are underdogs ten or more points," Podolsky said, "have beaten the spread seventy percent of the time this year."

"We haven't beaten a spread yet," admitted Shula.

Shula was correct. Our record was 5-2, but we were 0-7 against the spread.

"How do you know?" asked Podolsky.

"I read it in your paper last week," Shula laughed.

In January 1976, the Steelers played the Oakland Raiders at Three Rivers Stadium for the 1975 AFC Championship. Pittsburgh was winning 16-7 late in the fourth quarter of a turnover-filled game when Oakland's defense recovered its fourth fumble of the afternoon.

With 17 seconds left, John Madden sent in a nearly 50-year-old George Blanda to attempt a 41-yard field goal instead of going for the first down. Blanda converted the kick, making the score 16-10. The Raiders recovered the onside attempt, but 16-10 was the final.

Madden's move made sense because he needed two scores to win, but I know several bookies and bettors who insist to this day that Madden kicked the field goal first to fuck over Pittsburgh backers. The Steelers, see, were favored by six and a half.

Though Lou Holtz resigned from the Jets job before the 1976 season ended, the lessons he learned previously as a college coach helped him persevere as long as he did.

The Jets were playing the 9-2 Colts in Baltimore in late November. The Jets were 17.5-point underdogs that day and spent most of the game proving Vegas right. After they scored a seemingly meaningless touchdown late in the fourth quarter of a blowout, one of the Jets' players petitioned Holtz for permission to attempt an onside kick.

"That's ok," said Holtz, denying the request. "We covered. Our fans will be happy."

Paul Zimmerman, then of the *New York Post*, but later to be nationally-famous as "Dr. Z" with *SI*, told me that one.

There's another story involving the Jets and Colts, and this one features arguably the most famous coach in NFL history. The setting was a somewhat more memorable Jets-Colts game: Super Bowl III. As everybody knows, the Jets were three-touchdown dogs.

The late Morrie Siegel, a long-time Washington, D.C. newspaperman, told me that he asked Vince Lombardi his opinion about the game.

"You can't give Joe Namath three touchdowns," Lombardi replied.

Siegel called his bookie to put some money on the Jets. The amount was more than Siegel typically wagered, so the bookie was naturally curious.

"What gives, Morrie?" he asked.

"Vince Lombardi," Siegel explained, "says you cannot give Joe Namath three touchdowns."

There was a pause, and the bookie replied, "Maybe. Maybe not. I guess it depends how much Vince bets."

Unlike college football and the NFL, college basketball has never fooled around with elaborate fan dances when it came to betting. The popularity of college hoops has been tied to betting for as far back as I can remember, and that's a pretty long time.

The first newspaper with college basketball point spreads that I remember reading was the *New York Post* in the early 1950s. Perhaps coincidentally, the basketball team of the City College of New York was involved in the most famous point-shaving scandal in college basketball history at the same time.

CCNY got caught, but most of the college teams in New York were involved in the scandals back then. The only reason there were scandals was because the amount of betting was through the roof. The betting got to be so big that if the Knicks had a game scheduled at Madison Square Garden and a promoter could set up a big college doubleheader for the same day, the Knicks were banished to the State Armory to play.

The rest of the country is now addicted to college hoops the same way 1950s New York was, and once again betting is the reason. That's because if college basketball was a drug, it would be the most readily available drug for consumption.

Out of all the major sports, college basketball provides the greatest number of opportunities for action. There are upwards of 350 Division I-A men's hoops teams, so nearly every single night from mid-November until April there are men's college basketball games being played everywhere from Maui to Massachusetts. Thanks to cable, many of them are televised, too.

It's also the most exciting sport to bet. Well, other than the last two minutes of a game, with all the fouling and free throws, that is. The only thing that lasts longer than the end of a college hoops game is a PBS pledge drive.

All that action, though, can drive you mad. Especially when it's the other team going on a 17-0 run. Or when the "iron is unkind," as my buddy Tim Brando likes to say, to your team for an eight-minute stretch. Every bet, whether the game is a blowout or a nail biter, seems to come down to a free throw. It's incredibly difficult to win consistently. College basketball strains your nerves like no other sport. That's why, in my experience, college basketball has the absolute worst junkies, the most fanatical bettors, of any sport.

I attended arguably two of the most memorable basketball games, both involving Duquesne, in Pittsburgh history. To the public they remain significant for historic reasons, but to me, they are memorable because of the way the bettors went berserk.

Right before Christmas in December 1946, Tennessee traveled to Pittsburgh to play Duquesne. That 1946-47 Duquesne team was one of best in school history. It finished 21-2 and ended up losing to the eventual national champions, Utah, in the NIT. Back then, the NIT was more prestigious than the NCAA tournament.

The buzz for the game was so big that Duquesne officials decided to move it to a high school in a town outside of the city called McKeesport that could accommodate the crowd. Duquesne Gardens was obviously a bigger venue, but Duquesne had donated most of its bleachers to a scrap metal drive during the war. Everybody claims that there were 2,500 people crammed into the gym that night, but I think the number was closer to 3,000. I was one of them. You couldn't move.

All of us were disappointed because there wasn't any basketball played that night. After hours of deliberations, Tennessee refused to play because Duquesne refused to sit Chuck Cooper, who was black. I never saw a crowd so upset when an official announced that the game was canceled. People were livid. They had cops lined up everywhere.

Contrary to what was written in the papers, the police presence wasn't to stop people from attacking the Tennessee players or bus or anything. The conversations I heard on the way out had nothing to do with racism, but rather, refunds. People were asking each other whether or not the bookies would be refunding bets or not. I think every person in that gym that night had some kind of action on the game.

On February 11, 1952, No. 5 Duquesne was playing No. 4 St. Bonaventure at Duquesne Gardens. It was a Monday night. A showdown between the only two undefeated teams left in the country, it was the first college basketball game to be televised in Pittsburgh.

Normal Duquesne fans were happy because the Dukes won by six, 69-63. Duquesne bettors, on the other hand, were pissed because the line was six-and-a-half. I got out of there in a hurry. I thought some of the bettors were going to tear the place down.

Another Duquesne game stands out in my mind, this one was in the winter of 1959. Niagara was the visiting team and the Purple Eagles were installed as three-and-a-half point dogs. Duquesne had the game in hand, leading 75-70 with only a second or two remaining on the clock. In those waning seconds, Niagara threw up a desperation shot. The buzzer sounded, and a half-second after that, the ball swished through the net.

Everyone held their breath waiting to see referee Cliff Fair's ruling. Fair signaled that the shot was good, even though it was clearly after the buzzer had sounded. Duquesne 75, Niagara 72. As Fair, a strait-laced, conservative guy who never swore, struggled to get off the court amid a blizzard of profanity and popcorn, he couldn't understand the reason for the harsh treatment and foul language from the fans.

Later that night, I was eating in the upstairs room at Gustine's with a bunch of writers when Fair came in. Shaking his head, he was still confused at the night's events. I gently reminded him that the line was three-and-a-half.

"That's why they were blank-blanking me!" he exclaimed.

How rabid are Pittsburgh college basketball bettors? Ask Tim Grgurich, the former Pitt head coach and long-time NBA assistant. Grgurich is as Pittsburgh as it gets. He grew up in the Lawrenceville neighborhood of the city and graduated from Central Catholic High School in Oakland. That still didn't prevent the home crowd at Pitt from booing him one time after a win. And not just any win, a win over a hated rival.

On the evening of December 7, 1963, Pitt was playing Duquesne at the Field

House. The Panthers were two-and-a-half point favorites. The game was a wild, see-saw affair, with Pitt ahead by two points when Grgurich was fouled with a second left on the clock in overtime.

He missed the free throw, but it didn't affect the outcome of the game, as Pitt won 69-67. As Grgurich exited the court, he was booed by a sizable contingent of Pitt fans despite the fact that he had played really well and Pitt had won.

And as if beating cross-town rival Duquesne in hoops wasn't fun enough, earlier that afternoon we defeated archrival Penn State in football, 22-21.

It's been said that the greatest feeling in the world is hitting the lottery or having your team plus six-and-a-half in overtime in the Super Bowl, but as a Pitt alum and fan, I wouldn't have traded the way I felt that evening for anything. It's only one person's opinion, but I feel that December 7, 1963 was the greatest single day in the history of Pitt athletics.

Many bettors like to go on "gut" feelings, but I prefer using my head. That means basing my plays on certain criteria, like coaches, rest, and referees. For instance, in the 1966 NIT, San Francisco was playing Army in New York City. Both teams had won their opening round games on Saturday and this quarterfinal game was scheduled for the following Tuesday.

Army's young head coach, Robert Montgomery Knight, took his team back to West Point, about an hour or so north of the city, to prep for the game. I knew Knight was a good coach because I had seen Army play one other time that season, but his decision to go back to West Point caught my attention.

There were some people around the office at *ABC* who were going to the game, and they asked me who I liked. The Dons were seven-point favorites. I told them to bet Army. My reasoning was that Army had executed a tactical retreat from the distractions of the big city, whereas USF had been in town since the previous Thursday. Army would be rested and ready to go. And this Knight could flat-out coach. Final score: Army 80, San Francisco 63.

In betting, it potentially pays to pay attention to the officials. I was at the bar in the old Pittsburgh Hyatt when Houston played North Carolina State in the 1983 NCAA championship game. The Jimmy Valvano team.

The Cougars were ranked No. 1 and were huge favorites. Depending on where and when you got it in, Houston was favored by seven, seven-and-a-half or even eight points. For many years, that game was the biggest championship game upset, according to point spread, in the history of the NCAA tournament.

During the pre-game show, Brent Musberger announced that the officials for the game were from the Atlantic Coast Conference. I turned to the table behind me and casually remarked that with ACC officials working the game, you had to take NC State and the points. The guys at the table looked at me like I was some kind of genius, and ran to the phones.

They thought it was some special revelation, but to me, it was second-nature.

I've always paid close attention to the referees. At one time, you had to.

People today think that certain officials in the NFL or officials from a college conference have it out for their teams. I don't buy that at all. Some may be a little quicker than others to throw a flag or call a foul, but nowadays the refs are largely neutral. That wasn't the case in the 1950s and 1960s.

In 1957, Pitt played Southern Cal in football in Los Angeles. A split crew of officials did the game. The West Coast officials started penalizing us right away and one of the East Coast refs said, "Cut it out or I'm going to start hitting USC." One of our players told me this. He said that the refs were doing more fighting on the field than the teams were.

The most partial officials, this is both football and basketball, were the ones from the Big Ten. It wasn't how many they called, but when. They weren't dishonest, just unethical.

As you will recall from the Duke basketball incident, Southern officials were murder in intersectionals. Of course, Pitt's opponents probably thought Eastern officials were biased. Collectively, all officials seemed to look out for the home teams more back then.

Individually, I don't recall any one official being notoriously bad. The late Albie Booth, the old Yale football star, was generally an excellent official. Except when Pitt, Penn State or Syracuse played either service academy. Then he'd kill you. I never figured out why.

As a bettor back then, you learned to pay attention to the refs because the wise guys sure did. A great example is the Pitt-UCLA football game in Los Angeles in September 1960.

Before the game, Pitt was a one-point favorite. When it was announced in the L.A. papers the day before the game that the entire officiating crew was from the West Coast, there was a full two-point swing. By kickoff, UCLA was minus one. Pitt ended up losing 8-7, a push.

I remember another basketball game back in the late 1960s, Xavier was playing Duquesne in the Civic Arena on a Sunday afternoon. All week, the game was a pick. The day before, the *Pittsburgh Post-Gazette* printed the names of the officials who would be doing the game. There was no change in the line. One of the officials, however, didn't show up.

Minutes before the game was slated to start, he was replaced by a local guy, John "Red" Mihalik. Mihalik, a native of Ford City, which is just north of Pittsburgh, was at one time widely considered one of the best officials in all of basketball. He did NCAA Final Four games, including the West Virginia vs. California final in 1959. Mihalik could be counted on to call a fair game, but he had a reputation as being a homer for local teams.

Upon hearing the Mihalik news, bettors rushed for the phones. This was before cellphones, so every pay phone within three blocks of the Civic Arena was in use. People were shouting to each other in the parking lot, then from one street corner to the next. I heard that gas station attendants on the other side of town were telling drivers. At tip, Duquesne was minus four. This all took place in a matter of a few minutes. It was unbelievable.

Back during the Cold War, there was something called CONELRAD, which was the forerunner of the Emergency Broadcast System. It was a civil defense communication network in case the Russians attacked us. All radios had the special frequencies labeled.

I used to say that CONELRAD was a waste of taxpayer money. All the government had to do was ask bookies and bettors to get the word out and it would travel faster than any radio transmission.

* * *

Friends who know this particular story swear it's true. Minnesota was playing at Detroit. The Vikings' bus was stuck in traffic, so the driver drove up onto the median to try to get the team to the stadium in time. Next thing you know, he sees the flashing lights in the mirror and is pulled over. The cop asks for his license.

"You don't understand," said the anxious bus driver. "I've got the Vikings."

"I don't care who you have," replied the cop. "I've got the Lions plus three."

Ever hear the one about the loser who can't win? All his life, he's been betting football, baseball, and basketball.

Finally, somebody asked him, "Why don't you try hockey?"

"What do I know about hockey?" he replied.

Some sports are just plain impossible to bet and hockey is one of those for me. The NHL's archaic practice of not releasing injury news makes the sport too difficult to cap. Which is a hindrance to bettors. There's no transparency.

And the action is too fluid and disorganized, making the games hard to follow. Others may disagree with me, but I don't enjoy watching it. The late, great Pete Axthelm, one of the biggest lovers of all kinds of betting action known to man, said it best: "If you bet hockey that means you have to watch it. And hockey is not worth watching even if you are going to win."

Now I do have a good hockey betting story. In the mid-1990s, I bet Pittsburgh Penguins chairman Howard Baldwin a grand that the Penguins would leave town. I made it a public bet not because I was looking for a stunt, but because, as previously stated, I liked to go on record with my picks. That, and I thought I was going to win!

I was convinced that he would move the team out of Pittsburgh. As you know, the Pens are still in Pittsburgh today. And playing in a brand new arena, to boot. To be honest, I didn't feel all that bad paying up because the Pens staying ultimately helped the city, so it was one of those rare occasions when a loser bet has a happy ending.

I've got some good NBA stories, but it's another sport I avoid betting nowadays. The regular season has always been too hard to handicap. In the NFL, there are the "any given Sunday" trap games. But the NBA has any given Mondays, Tuesdays, Wednesdays,

Thursdays, Fridays, and Saturdays. It's the only major sport in which a playoff-caliber team can out of nowhere lose by thirty points at home to a cellar-dwelling club on any night of the week.

The playoffs, though, just like in hockey, present a different, much more exciting version of the sport. Playoff basketball was something I used to enjoy betting. One time, I was even able to write it off.

In the late 1970s and early 80s, while I was working for *CBS*, Rich Podolsky and I shared an apartment in New York City. For the longest time, we put off getting cable television and only decided to do it one year when the NBA playoffs started in order to watch the games.

"The I.R.S. will understand," I argued, "that we would never watch NBA games during the season unless we could deduct them as a business expense."

Strangely enough, the I.R.S. agreed with us.

As for amateur athletics, just because the athletes aren't paid doesn't mean big payoffs aren't involved. Take the '72 Olympics. New to the network as a researcher, Terry O'Neil was assigned to gather track and field data for *ABC*.

I first got to know O'Neil, a native of Natrona, Pa., which is just outside Pittsburgh, when he joined us after graduating from Notre Dame. We later worked together at *CBS*. O'Neil became a top-flight producer who won fourteen Emmys, the majority of which he collected while working for Dick Ebersol at *NBC Sports*.

Like with Ebersol, I could tell O'Neil was going places early on. Especially after I heard about the work he did in the run-up to Munich. While canvassing the practice locations of participants, O'Neil compiled volumes of material about the world's best track and field athletes for his supervisors. All that great stuff for the vignettes that Roone loved so much.

It was during this time that he discovered John Akii-Bua, an unknown Ugandan runner whose practice times were out of this world. Akii-Bua was training to compete in the 400-meter hurdles event, but it wasn't his specialty. He had only run the event in competition five or six times and he didn't even get fit for shoes until six weeks before the Olympics.

Now here's the really interesting part of the story: O'Neil also found out that Akii-Bua's day job in Uganda was law enforcement, and since he didn't have a car or horse to use, he trained for the Olympics by chasing criminals on foot. Plus, he had 19 kids at home, so his whole life was pretty much spent on the run, jumping one type of hurdle or another.

O'Neil wrote all of this information down and then gave it to some *ABC Sports* talent and executives who pooled their money, called Ladbroke's, the betting parlor in London, and put money on Akii-Bua, a big longshot.

Akii-Bua dominated the event, beating the world record time by a half-second. O'Neil was out in the field, but he could hear the celebrating taking place in the truck. That was one time that Roone's rule regarding betting on *ABC* events was conspicuously violated. As for O'Neil, he never saw a farthing of the money his hard work and research had earned.

Another good Olympics story is the time a guy came into Runyon's and asked the bartender, Doc, if he could put the opening ceremonies of the Olympics on the television.

"We don't do parades here, pal," Doc explained, "unless there's a line on 'em."

If you are thinking about betting boxing, don't. Save your money. Corruption and the greed of promoters have hollowed out boxing. It's a shell of the sport it once was. When I was working for the Dolphins, I went to see some fights at the Miami Beach Convention Center one night and as soon as I entered the building I knew that every fight on the card was fixed. There were more seedy characters sitting around the ring that night than there were in the docks at Nuremberg.

Baseball is fixed too, but legally. Until there's a salary cap, small market teams are nothing more than minor league teams that charge major league prices for beers and hot dogs. And baseball is one of the few sports that, sometimes, even when you win, you lose.

See, in the early years of the Mets, New York bookies, even Captain Bligh, gave runs to bet. Now, you bet baseball on the moneyline. But back then, you could take the Mets plus three, plus four runs. Just like football. The Mets were so fucking bad in the early 1960s that people were doubling up on them when they went on the road. A major stipulation, however, was that the game had to go the full nine innings. I remember one game, the Mets were winning 7-1 after seven innings and the game ended up being called because of rain. All bets were off.

Speaking of no-win situations, you can't forget marriage. When Phyllis George married Hollywood producer Robert Evans in 1977, the wire story stated that they were married under sycamore trees that were 400 years old. This prompted the Greek to say, "don't expect the marriage to last 400 days." When he was pressed to give it a line, he told us, "even money it doesn't last two years." Sure enough, George and Evans divorced in 1978.

When Dick Ebersol got married in 1981, I figured I'd try my hand at setting odds. Oh, and who did Ebersol marry? None other than Mrs. Sally McMillan, Susan St. James. I made two predictions. First, I said the bride was going to get more action in one week as Mrs. Ebersol than she did in six years as Mrs. McMillan. Hopefully, you can figure that one out.

Secondly, when I was introduced to the newlyweds she said that she had heard that I had set the over/under at three years. "We will see about that, Mister Beano," she said with that thousand-watt smile of hers. Needless to say, that was a bad call. The Ebersols have been happily married for decades.

There was another friend of mine who used to call his bookie too often and it almost cost him his marriage. But it's not what you think. See, it was a long-distance toll call to his bookie and he had a lot of explaining to do when the phone bill arrived. His wife thought he was calling another woman. In order to prove to his wife that he wasn't cheating on her, he had to tell her he was betting behind her back!

Perhaps the best betting relationship story was one told to me by Captain Bligh. He was such a sicko that he used to tag along with a friend to meetings of Gamblers Anonymous. He'd relay some of the incredible stories to me. My favorite involved one guy who stood before the group and told this meandering tale of how his marriage caused his gambling woes.

"I had three games last Sunday and at halftime was ahead on all three," said the poor mush. "I was feeling good so I took my wife into the bedroom and we had sex. I came out in the middle of the fourth quarter to check the scores, and all of my teams were behind. I lost all three bets and now my wife's filing for a divorce. It's all her fault."

I'll never blame a woman for my bad luck, but maybe that's because in my experience, betting is better than sex. In most cases the main event lasts longer, with the exception of horse racing.

On the subject of racing, my Southern friends would probably disagree, but to me, auto racing is boring. I guess in a way it's a lot like marriage in that you remember only the beginning and the end.

The same can be said of politics. We remember inaugural speeches like FDR's and JFK's, and Nixon's resignation, but not much in the middle. Over the years, however, elections have provided us with opportunities to cash.

It's fairly well-known that the Greek made a bundle betting on Harry Truman to defeat Thomas Dewey in the 1948 Presidential election. Another of his big wins was when he predicted that Walter Mondale would be Jimmy Carter's running mate in 1980.

"How did you know?" Mondale later asked the Greek.

"You're shorter than Carter," was the reply.

Mondale started laughing. He thought the Greek was kidding. He wasn't.

I remember another of the Greek's big wins, which followed a serious operation.

"What are the odds, doc," he asked his surgeon, "of my making it?"

"Even money, Jimmy."

"Doc, I'll give you 4 to 1."

People think that timing bets became popular when the books began offering the length of the national anthem at the Super Bowl as one of the props. That's not true. These kinds of bets have been around for a long time. It's just that the recreational bettor hasn't been aware of them until fairly recently.

One of my all-time favorites in this regard was when I heard that people started betting on the amount of time it would take Pat Summerall to read promos for *CBS* shows during that network's NFL telecasts. Everybody's favorite play was trying to estimate his hangtime between "Murder" and "She Wrote."

Other broadcasters were harder to handicap, but I had known for years that Keith Jackson hated doing promos, so he read them as fast as possible.

When I worked for the Dolphins, I didn't have to start any pools like I did at Pitt. The Orange Bowl pressbox had been a casino long before I showed up. The most popular bet was the one for the length of the invocations that preceded each Dolphins' home game.

An invocation is basically an opening prayer. Joe Robbie, a serious Catholic, would invite a local priest, bishop, or other man of faith to give it. This was back in the wholesome days of the NFL. It would be right before the anthem.

"As Robbie grows older," sportswriter Hubert Mizell explained, "he is starting to pay more attention to the guy above." And as the years went on, Robbie gave the speakers all the time they wanted, so the invocations got longer and longer.

I like two things to be short, wars and invocations. Nobody could do anything about it, so all the writers finally embraced it and it became everybody's favorite prop.

"The record is 3:42," Ed Plaisted of the old *Hollywood Sun-Tattler* told me when I first got to Miami. "Of course, that's not official because it was a pre-season game."

It was my job to time the invocation and the bettor that came the closest to the length won the pot. It was only a buck to get in, but the whole thing was very competitive. Everybody was looking for an edge.

Once, the announcer Bob Halloran, when he was working for the *CBS* affiliate in Miami, bumped into Archbishop Coleman Carroll a few hours before kickoff.

"Gonna be a long one tonight, Bishop?" Halloran asked Carroll.

"No, Bob, a short one. About 30 seconds."

The archbishop had no idea that he had just given Halloran some inside information.

"I didn't want it to seem too obvious," Halloran later told me when I handed him his cash, "so I took 33 seconds."

A big argument followed the invocation before the second Dolphins-Colts game in November 1970. There was the usual invocation, but then there was a moment of silence for Les Bingaman, the Detroit Lions' star and former Dolphins' assistant coach who had recently passed away. Nobody could decide whether the moment of silence should count as part of the length of the invocation or if it was separate.

Ernie Accorsi, the Colts' PR man, was asked to resolve the situation as an impartial arbiter. I don't remember how Accorsi ruled, but the Baltimore writers and those in the stands had to be confused by all the arguing coming from the pressbox after a moment of solemnity for a departed colleague. This just goes to show that not even the dead are spared when it comes to betting.

Speaking of which, some people are offended by the celebrity death pools on the Internet, where bettors try to predict when and in what gruesome manner certain celebrities will die. That's a consequence of what happens when you mix a celebrity-crazed culture with a bet-happy public.

Honestly, those pools are nothing. The public has no idea to what levels some bettors will sink to for a fix, or what bookies will do to provide them with it.

Consider 1978. That exciting college football season started with upsets and concluded with close rivalry games and controversy. In the Heisman Trophy voting,

Oklahoma's Billy Sims edged Penn State quarterback Chuck Fusina, despite the fact that Fusina had more first-place votes, and Alabama and USC ended up split national champions.

The NFL season was similarly memorable, thanks mainly to off-season rules changes implemented to aid passing attacks and increase scoring. The league also added two more games to the regular-season schedule and expanded the playoffs with a second wildcard team.

But the buzz in the underground betting world had nothing to do with what happened on Saturdays and Sundays in the fall of 1978. A lot of the talk was about the developing situation in Guyana – Jonestown.

I don't remember how or when the bet went up "on the board" so to speak, but it might even have been as early as late 1977, when the media started covering the craziness pertaining to Reverend Jim Jones and his People's Temple commune.

When the Congressman from California, Leo Ryan, announced that he was going to South America on a fact-finding trip, action really ramped up. I think the final death count was 918 people and the over/under had been set somewhere around 950. These people were right on the number. The military was tasked with bringing the bodies home and every time a plane landed at Dover Air Force Base, the board was updated.

A little more than three years later, Bobby Sands, a 27-year-old Irish Republican Army leader, starved himself to death along with three other IRA inmates in Her Majesty's Prison Maze in 1981. Sands had embarked on the fast in an effort to force the British government to regard IRA internees as political prisoners rather than criminals. While the rest of the world agonized over Sands' fate, it was business as usual in the underground betting world.

Captain Bligh got in touch with some doctors and did some research on hunger and metabolism. He calculated odds and fixed an over/under. It was 71 days. If I remember correctly, Sands had to go at least 45 days for the bet to the count, which Bligh thought was the equivalent of 4.5 innings in baseball. If he died on the 46th day and you had the under, you won. If he died on day 12, it was no bet.

Sands died on May 5, 1981 after 66 days of only water and salt and the bookies ended up winning more than they lost. And no, I didn't bet the hunger strike nor Jonestown.

The only thing that could possibly top those stories was this really wacko outfit, I think it was in Chicago, that "estimated" how many people would die in automobile accidents on the nation's highways on a particular weekend. They usually picked holiday weekends. For example, how many people would die across the continental United States over the Memorial Day or Labor Day weekends.

These guys would have an over/under for you and had a guy who worked for the National Transportation Safety Board on their payroll to get quick, certified results. It was sick stuff, but I guess there were some degenerates for whom March Madness and all the Super Bowl props had lost their luster.

Dan Jenkins once asked me if I ever bet this gruesome game. As we've previously established in these pages, Jenkins is the most talented sportswriter I've ever known. That's due to his lightning quick wit. He was one of the most spontaneously funny people I've ever met. He had no real rivals. Not even the professional comedians.

I remember the time he went on Carson and stole the show. Jenkins told me that during a commercial, one of the producers pulled him aside and warned him: "Listen, buddy – Johnny tells the jokes."

Despite his late night television appearances and all of his work in *SI* and *Golf Digest* and his bestselling books, I believe that his best lines never made print. There's a good reason why. He has a pretty peculiar, sometimes shockingly dark sense of humor. I mean dark.

Jenkins, during one of our discussions on bowl matchups in the early 1970s, once remarked that "Wichita State should play Marshall in the Radar Bowl."

After completing a piece on the Steelers for *SI*, he informed me that "Bo Rein, in his present state, is a better interview than Chuck Noll." Rein was a college coach that died in a plane crash in 1980.

Jenkins was naturally intrigued when he heard about the highway accidents prop and we had a memorable chat about it. I've never told anybody this story, about this conversation, until now. His response is a classic.

"No, Dan, I've never bet it," I told him. "And I won't ever bet. Because if you take the over and not that many people are dead by Saturday or Sunday night, you're upset because you don't have much of a chance to win, not to mention the fact that the cheering factor makes you an absolutely awful human being."

"All true," said Jenkins. "But if you do bet, it's probably a good idea to take the over."

"Why?"

"Because," he explained in his trademark, Texas twang, "one bus does it."

CHAPTER 5

Nothing but U-boat commanders.

I'm a newspaper man. I have been all my life. When I was a kid, I used to go to the train stations in Pittsburgh and pick up the out-of-town papers that travelers discarded. I'd check the benches, rummage through trash cans and occasionally sneak onto the Pullman cars to search for folded treasure. I later found out that I wasn't the only one collecting papers.

Forty miles away in Steubenville, Ohio, at roughly the same time, Jimmy the Greek was doing something similar. Only he wasn't an amateur, adolescent scavenger like myself. Born in early September 1918, the Greek was exactly 13 years older than me and even though he was only in his early 20s, his was an advanced, highly-organized paper procurement operation. He had the porters and conductors that came through Steubenville on his payroll. He told me they brought him the sports pages from the big papers published on the coasts. The Greek was always in search of an edge in betting.

I didn't know anything about or care about betting yet. I was a collector. I collected newspapers like other kids collected baseball cards or stamps. I loved the way the different papers looked. The mastheads, the styles of type. And the names!

To an eight or nine-year-old kid, the names were magical. The *St. Louis Globe-Democrat* and the *New York World-Telegram* sounded worldly. The *Sioux City Tribune & Journal* sounded like something out of the Old West. The *Baltimore News-American* and the *Brooklyn Eagle* evoked patriotism. These papers are long gone.

Unlike the case with most childhood hobbies and pursuits, I didn't lose interest in newspapers as I got older. If anything, I became more passionate about papers. When I was the SID at Pitt, I had subscriptions to twenty, maybe even twenty-five papers. My office was filled, from floor to ceiling, with stacks of everything from the *New York Times* to the small, suburban Pittsburgh weeklies.

When I did advances, I packed lightly in order to leave room in my suitcase for the papers I brought home from the road. At each network I worked, I expensed subscriptions to all the big dailies, plus *Sports Illustrated* and a few other magazines.

Those who know me well know that in addition to the clipboard, I'm usually carrying at least one newspaper with me at any given time. Seventy years on, it's a love affair that's still going strong. At my age, a whiff of Chanel No. 5 is not guaranteed to turn my head but the smell of fresh newsprint still has a hold over me. Perhaps above all else, I enjoy the physical act of reading the paper: the crinkling sound when you turn the pages; getting the ink on your hands.

I still subscribe to maybe a half dozen papers. I might be the last person in America who does. It bothers me that newspapers are dying. Part of the problem is technology. Young people prefer the Internet. I understand that.

Another big part of it, at least in my opinion, is that storytelling is a lost art. Nobody appreciates long-form writing anymore, so nobody writes it or publishes it anymore. Everything in print has been reduced to nuggets, just like how the sound bite took over and eventually ruined television. So newspapers are basically an antiquated form of television.

People don't have any patience. Everyone's in a hurry. As a result, they don't sit down to read and exercise their minds anymore. The same reason we'll never see another Charles Kuralt on TV is the same reason we'll never read another Red Smith in the sports pages. Maybe it's not that nobody cares what they have to say, it's that nobody can sit still long enough to listen to or read what they're saying.

Once upon a time, you could put a sports story in front of me, cover up the byline and I could tell who the writer was just by reading the lede. This was any paper in any city in the country. Nowadays, with the exception of some of the Pittsburgh writers, I can't tell one writer from another. To me, their work all reads the same. It's cookie-cutter commentary.

I've noticed two things disappear in recent years: long-form writing and formal dress. When I started, coats and ties were mandatory attire in the pressbox. Now I see writers wearing jeans and shorts. I suspect they'll be wearing pajamas before long.

The one thing I will say about the writers today, I don't know if it's the same thing as taking the job seriously, but they take the games seriously. Much more seriously than I ever did. I enjoyed the bullshitting, hanging out before and after the games, more than I did the games themselves. I used to enjoy going over to the Civic Arena, Three Rivers Stadium or Heinz Field, getting a bite to eat and telling stories. I quit going a few years ago because everyone was in a big rush to get to their seats and their computers.

I feel sorry for today's generation of writers, broadcasters, and media personalities. They'll never know that it's not the games, or the work, that matters – it's the stories. The friendships. The laughs.

I don't mean to drag anybody who is working in the business today, but I think most of the good writers are either retired or dead. I know I'm biased because of my age and because of all the legendary writers who I've been lucky to call friends and colleagues throughout the course of my life.

I will, however, admit that I'm probably missing out on some good writers because I'm not online. I don't read any blogs or websites. A lot of talented writers have made the transition online. My friend Ivan Maisel, who started out in papers and also worked for *SI*, is one of them.

My younger friends print out copies of stories on the Internet and mail them to me, which I appreciate because I'd never see them otherwise. I'm never going to buy a computer. Or a cell phone. Or an answering machine. I tell people, it's fairly simple to figure out: if you call and I don't answer, I'm either not home or I'm dead.

I don't have cable, either. I don't need it. I watch the Sunday political shows, "60 Minutes," "Seinfeld," re-runs of "Hawaii Five-O" and "Columbo," and that's it.

Most of the football games are on the three legacy networks, so I don't miss too many games. If I have action on a game that's on cable, I'll call a friend for the score. It's a pretty reliable practice, unless you have Catholic friends who attend mass on Saturday evenings, so they don't catch you up on the late afternoon games until they get home. I've never been a patient person, but it beats an expensive monthly cable bill.

I remember when I told people that I didn't have cable when I was working for *ESPN*, they looked at me funny. Yet I wasn't the only one back then. In the early years of *USA Today*, the big shots who ran the paper told Rudy Martzke not to write about cable in his television column because they didn't have it.

I've never been big on gadgets or machines. I have no mechanical skill whatsoever. I can't fix anything if it breaks. More importantly, in my experience, these things are bad investments. That's why I haven't owned an automobile since Reagan's first term. Between depreciation and parking (a major expense for people like me who have lived in cities all their life) and all the repairs and maintenance, a car will break the bank. Vehicle ownership is like having a gambling problem; the house, the mechanic, always wins. You can't even get lucky on a missed extra point.

Another reason for the decline of newspapers is a talent shortage. On one side of it, I think people who are born with writing talent aren't pursuing writing jobs because they no longer pay well. The people that own the publications are cheap. George Kiseda was adamant that a skilled writer should be able to make a living solely through writing. To him, writing was a vocation, a spiritual calling, not merely a profession. The people who signed the checks didn't feel the same way. So while the suits get stingier, many people gravitate to other fields.

I can't blame them. Not only is the pay poor, it seems like the people who call the shots nowadays are stamping originality and creativity out of everyone. I remember when we called certain people in the business who were free spirited, "Runyonesque." They aren't making any Damon Runyons anymore. Or George Kisedas, Bob Drums and Dan Jenkinses, for that matter. The people in charge have all but eliminated those kinds of personalities. Why?

Because if you control the personalities, you control the message and avoid costly controversy. I feel as though it's like this in everything now. Not just in the media. It's in business. Politics. Even the military. Our service academies seem to be factory assembly lines for robot officers who all look, act, and sound alike. We'll never see another MacArthur with his corncob pipe and sunglasses, or a Patton with pearl-handled pistols. They are all trained to not rock the boat and not question, let alone challenge, the politicians. This is probably why we haven't won a war since 1945.

Don't get me wrong, there's definitely controversy in sports media, but it's all controlled controversy. Today, everything in sports media is scripted. On television, they pair two or three over-the-top personalities and have them pretend to scream at each other, but the viewer is unaware that the arguments were pre-planned in the production meeting.

Sports talk radio is heading in the same sad direction. Some hosts would rather humiliate and hang up on a caller than listen to what he has to say.

Sportswriters file columns or write stories not with an eye towards accuracy, they do it, as the new saying goes, for clicks.

Writers get their marching orders from editors, who get theirs from advertising, management, and ownership. And everybody follows them enthusiastically and with little regard to where it's leading the industry as a whole. That's another big problem.

Some of the greatest advice my mother ever gave me was when she warned, "Don't ever be a slave to the three P's." The three p's are Pablum, which was an old brand of baby food, the PTA, and a pension.

Basically, don't let the fact that you have mouths to feed affect your core beliefs and don't become someone's serf because they control your retirement. Don't ever get so beholden to a life, or lifestyle, or worse, so far in debt, that you'll stay shackled to a job that isn't right.

Everyone has their own definition of happiness and while I never had a family or any responsibility to anybody but myself, I can say that following her advice led to a fairly happy existence. There were many times that I worried about being unemployed, but I never let a boss or job run, much less ruin, my life.

In my opinion, papers are going under for three reasons. The first is because storytelling talent is so low on the list of priorities in hiring nowadays, it's barely on the list at all. There are fundamentally sound writers out there, and because of the emphasis on numbers and analytics young people today are great with the stats, but that reminds me of Stanley Woodward's great line: "I want writers, not people who memorize batting averages."

I'm thankful that I came up with the idea for *Pittsburgh Weekly Sports* in 1963, not now. Diogenes would find an honest man on Capitol Hill before I found any true talent. Few young writers today, it seems, have that special talent for turning a phrase, for writing a really clever lede, or for finishing a piece off with a killer closer of a line.

For this, I blame Woodward and Bernstein. I think contemporary editors are placing an emphasis on investigative reporting rather than storytelling skills. The reality of the never-ending, 24-hour news cycle requires reporters to keep breaking stories, to dig up dirt. So sports editors, they're going after people who are experts on producing exposés on sex scandals, recruiting violations and incidents of domestic violence, not the wordsmiths capable of producing the colorful columns and beautifully-written features of yesteryear.

The end result is, we have entire generations of young people that have grown up wanting to be the crusading reporter who takes down Nixon. Only today, in sports journalism, Nixon is a head coach at State U., or a pro team owner or some other individual in a position of power.

I'm not the only one who has noticed this alarming trend. I recall a conversation I had with Sandy Padwe, who worked as deputy sports editor of the *New York Times* and as a senior editor for *Sports Illustrated.*

Padwe, on the talent shortage of the sports staff of the *New York Times*: "it's like being in the seventh game of the World Series in the eighth inning and you want a pinch-hitter, and you look down your bench and all you see are pitchers."

Maybe it's my age, but I don't think the public particularly wants to read what's considered modern sportswriting. People can only take so much lecturing, political posturing, negativity, and muckraking. Readers are starving for real stories and storytellers to tell them.

I believe this to be the case in sports as well as in every other department of the paper. Unfortunately, those old-fashioned kinds of pieces don't win awards and awards are pretty much the only reason most papers seem to be in business today. The way I see it, these people should be worrying about losing subscribers, not winning Pulitzers.

I'm also convinced that a lot of talent is being shut out of the system. I'm talking about the crusade for diversity. It's not a popular opinion, or politically correct to talk about, but I'm going to talk about it anyway. I'm not going to let newspaper owners keep blaming everything on television, the Internet, or the reading habits - or lack thereof - of young people.

Too many people with little experience, lesser or even no talent whatsoever, are being elevated to prominent positions they aren't qualified for because of their ethnicity, their sex, their sexual orientation, or even their good looks.

Look, there have always been hacks. We had them in my era. You'll never get rid of them. But people without creative writing talent weren't in the majority because back then, bottom-lines - not political correctness - came first.

Sandy's analogy resonated with me. When I was publishing *Pittsburgh Weekly Sports*, I envisioned myself as Yankees' skipper Miller Huggins managing Murderers' Row. Huggins's only goals were to put the best team on the field in order to win the pennant and then the World Series. He didn't fool around with his lineup card for the sake of diversity.

Back then I didn't know of any minority sportswriters or women journalists. I can honestly say that I would have read their clips and hired them if I thought they could write. But back then, there weren't very many Diane Shahs, Lesley Vissers or Jackie MacMullans.

Of course, back then, the things people discriminated against in the business were different. There were ways you could discriminate against a white guy. But I didn't pay attention to them, either. I didn't care where a writer went to school, if he was a Democrat or a Republican, a Protestant, Catholic or a Jew, or nobody ever saw him with a broad.

Likewise, if you're a sports editor today, your staff should be loaded with the best creative writing talent from top to bottom in order to entertain readers and sell papers, nothing else. It shouldn't resemble a meeting of the United Nations because some focus group or gaggle of angry activists thinks it should.

Some people may call me over the hill, out of touch, a racist or a sexist – so be it. None of it is true. I've collected a lot of résumés in my life, from people of both sexes and of all colors, beliefs and backgrounds and tried to get them jobs. I still do.

The only thing I've ever discriminated against anybody for was a lack of talent. I refuse to put my reputation on the line for anybody or for any cause, to advance affirmative action, to address racism, sexism, feminism, or any other fucking "ism."

In fact, I'm willing to bet I've probably done more for women professionally – in sports media – than NOW, the National Organization for Women, has. I've provided a fair number of female writers and broadcasters with recommendations. In fact, one of the first individuals who I tried doing this book with was a woman.

I'm going to talk about women in sports media in greater detail later on, but when it comes to the fairer sex, I've never had a problem with women in pressboxes and locker rooms, as reporters on the sidelines, as producers or even as executives. I only have a problem with women being in one place, really, and that's in a foxhole on the front lines of a combat area.

At one time, because of all the papers I read, I knew a good many of the country's up and coming writers. I may not have any talent myself, but I've always been good at recognizing it, like a baseball scout who knew about players in obscure leagues.

I was typically in a good position to recommend talent when some of my editor friends from big city papers called. I've helped fill a lot of positions over the years. The calls still come, but lately, the editors are asking only for women and minorities rather than asking me to recommend great writers. That's troubling.

Fairly recently, I got a call from a longtime friend who runs the sports department at one of the top metro papers in the country. We'll call him Joe. Joe asked if I could recommend any writers for a position at his paper that opened up. After he told me what the beat was, I rattled off two or three names before he interrupted me.

"Beano, look, I'm sure they're all great," he said, "but I need a Hispanic."

"Joe, why the hell do you even bother asking me anymore?" I said. "I live in Pittsburgh, not El Paso."

Look, good writing is good writing, whether you are male or female, black, white, yellow, or green, or if your family hails from Mexico or Mars – the town in Western Pennsylvania, or the planet. My argument is, and always has been, true writing talent trumps everything. Especially politics.

That's the third reason why newspapers are failing. It's actually the biggest issue I have with the newspaper and publishing industry today because I've seen first-hand how the ever-widening political divide affects people professionally, how it's affecting print publications financially, and how I think it's affecting our country collectively.

I told you about George Kiseda and what happened to his career. Another example is the late Bill Roeder. One of those nights when I was working the desk at the *Pittsburgh Press* in the early 1950s, Roy McHugh called me over and handed me a story written by Roeder that had come over the wire.

"You want to be a sportswriter?" he asked. "Read this. He's going to be a great one."

A few years later, Roeder wrote an aggressive piece about the greed of the Yankees for the *New York World-Telegram*. The Yankees were pissed. The team's brass called Roeder's bosses and he was kicked out of sports and reassigned to the city side.

A few weeks later, Roeder wrote a story about Forest Hills Country Club denying membership to the diplomat Ralph Bunche because he was black. That got Roeder into even hotter water. He landed on his feet, however, taking a job with Newsweek where he wrote the "Newsmakers" column for many years.

The *World-Telegram* folded, but in my opinion it was policies like the one used to run Roeder off the paper that caused the paper's downfall, not the printers' union or competition, or whatever other excuse management used.

It still bothers me what happened to guys like Kiseda and Roeder and I get upset because I see it happening again. Only it's reverse discrimination. I've noticed that the people making the hires nowadays lean oppositely from the way the people who blackballed Kiseda leaned. Now they're all left or far left. They want diversity of sex and race and basically everything else under the sun, but not of political views, thoughts, and opinions.

Now the owners are free to slant coverage whichever direction they see fit. As a former publisher myself, I know that is a prerogative of ownership. Their business is none of my business, but ultimately, I don't think hiring only people who see things your way is good for the country. I don't, however, expect them to care or change. The people and the conglomerates that have been running newspapers for the better part of the last fifty years are some of the dumbest individuals and outfits in the country. They're worse than Congress – if you can imagine that.

For too long they've been prioritizing partisan politics, on both sides, instead of pure talent in their hires. They lost out on Kiseda's talent decades ago and if they keep at it, I predict they're going to end up losing out on tons of talented writers in the future. Not only writers, but subscribers and readers, too.

I feel strongly about the survival of newspapers for a number of reasons, namely because I believe a free press, a real free press that provides equal access to all viewpoints, is essential to the survival of the First Amendment and the country itself.

Beyond patriotism, it's also personal. While I'll always be a newspaper man, I've never been able to come to grips with the fact that I'll never be a newspaperman. See, for the longest time, the first forty years or so of my life, what I wanted more than anything else in the world was to be a sportswriter or a columnist on the staff of a big city paper.

From the moment I started working on the copy desk at the *Pittsburgh Press* as a teenager I knew that was what I wanted to do with my life. Right up until the mid 1970s, every job I took, every decision I made professionally, it was all done with an eye toward landing a job on a newspaper.

I can't say what my motivation was. Maybe it was the romanticized vision of being a sportswriter, following in the footsteps of Grantland Rice and Red Smith, that I'd clung to since I was collecting papers during my childhood.

Or maybe it's just a natural desire to create, to leave something of intellectual value or worth behind as proof of one's existence. The Bible tells us that the greatest thing in life is to save another. I think somewhere in there it says the second greatest thing is to right a wrong. The third greatest thing in life, for me at least, is to beat Notre Dame and Penn State.

The fourth? To be able to take an empty sheet of paper and write something on it that has meaning. I've always just wanted to be – and be considered by others – a good writer.

I've hung out with writers my entire life for two reasons. First, they tend to be great conversationalists. I have been fortunate to get to know quite a few of the greatest scribes in American history. And I'm not talking only about sportswriters.

One of the great thrills of my life was the day in April 1984 when Jack Whitaker came into my office at *ABC* and handed me a letter. It was from Willie Morris, the author of one of my all-time favorite books, "North Toward Home," thanking me for helping him promote his book "The Courting of Marcus Dupree."

I've also associated with writers due to more selfish reasons – in hopes that talent is contagious. At this writing, I'm sorry to report that it isn't. Or perhaps it is, and I'm immune.

By the summer of 1974, I had finally figured out what another of the all-time greats, Oscar Wilde, meant when he said, "in this world there are only two tragedies. One is not getting what one wants and the other is getting it."

A few months earlier, I had finally gotten what I wanted: I was hired as a sportswriter on the staff of the *St. Petersburg Times*. At one time, it was the best all-around newspaper south of the *Washington Post*. It's now called the *Tampa Bay Times*. I signed on for about $300 a week. It was a fraction of what i had been making at *ABC*, but I didn't care because I desperately wanted out of the television business and because I had finally landed my dream job.

Roone wished me good luck and told me to be myself. Stay unconventional, he said, and don't try to be like all the other sportswriters out there. In his opinion, I needed to take the same approach he did with "Wide World." He advised me to focus on attracting the fringe readers of sports.

"Forget the fucking fanatics," he told me. "They'll read anything, even a quick brown fox jumps over the lazy dog."

By taking the advice of my old boss, I got off on the wrong foot with my new bosses. My first assignment was to cover a Harlem Globetrotters game. I didn't include the score in the lede and they weren't happy. I couldn't understand it. It was a fucking Globetrotters game. Everybody knows they always win!

"Someone broke into the Globetrotters' office," I wrote in my lede, "but all that's missing are the box scores for next season's games."

I had stolen the line from Paul Zimmerman, who told me that early in his career he was assigned to cover an election in New Jersey, which, if you think about it, is a lot like a Globetrotters game. The results are preordained. In order to have some fun, he wrote that candidate so-and-so had won, but the paper couldn't certify by how much because some guy had broken into the office of the Democratic party in New Jersey and stolen the results.

This was right around the time of Watergate, so I thought it was both a funny and timely reference to both the break-in and it illustrated the absurdity of thinking that Globetrotters' games were real, competitive sporting events.

My story was very unconventional. I ignored the players and instead interviewed people in the crowd and asked them why they came to the game. I thought I made the big splash I had been looking for and that the lede was the perfect touch. I ended up being the only one at the paper who thought that way.

If people wanted to criticize me for not having the score in the piece, okay. But the score in the lede? That struck me as ridiculous. Now if the Globetrotters had lost, it would have been the first line. Even I'm not that dumb.

I nibbled around the plate with a few decent articles, but I couldn't quite seem to find the strike zone with my material. It wasn't for lack of effort. Not by me, and certainly not by my co-workers, who took turns tutoring me. Some of the most revered names in newspaper history tried their damnedest to teach me the fundamentals of good writing.

One was the late Van McKenzie, a brilliant editor whose layouts were works of art. I'll never forget how patient and helpful he was with me. McKenzie later worked at the *Atlanta Journal-Constitution* and at *The National.*

Another was our staff ace, Hubert Mizell. Mizell was literally a giant in the sportswriting business – he was 6'4, 300 lbs. – who won every award imaginable.

The paper's editor, Gene Patterson, a Pulitzer Prize winner who fought in the Battle of the Bulge, tried, too.

My beat, or area of expertise, was sports on television. I was supposed to write about broadcasters, producers and executives, things that happened behind-the-scenes. I remember writing about Joe Garagiola when he started doing play-by-play for *NBC's* baseball telecasts, and on some juicy items from my old stomping grounds at *ABC* that were fed to me by my "Deep Throat," my friend and successor as *ABC's* NCAA press director, Donn Bernstein.

Bernstein, or "Double N" as everybody called him, is one of the all-time great guys in the PR business. I remember the time he was mugged outside of his co-op on 78th street on Manhattan's Upper West Side. One of his neighbors was the late actor, Christopher Reeve. I called Bernstein to see how he was doing and to cheer him up and instead, in typical Bernstein fashion, he ended up making me laugh.

"I'm fine," he said. "But where the hell is Superman when you really need him?"

None of my stories created any controversy or got any attention and that wasn't anybody's fault but my own. My writing stunk. Patterson suggested that I talk into a tape recorder in order to "write" my stories instead of laying siege to a typewriter.

"Don't hold back your conversational salt," he used to say. He thought I got too hung up on grammar and syntax (which I did), and if I went with my instincts and whatever words first fell out of my mouth it would let "the real Beano through."

It was sound thinking, but it didn't work. For whatever reason, I've never been able to articulate my views in my writing the way I've been able to do it on camera or on the radio. Patterson won a Silver Star at Bastogne, but eventually surrendered in the face of my blitzkrieg of bad writing.

If anybody deserved a medal for the Battle of St. Petersburg, it was my good friend Buddy Martin, our sports editor. Martin is a great writer and a consummate media professional who has been there and done that. There includes stints with the *New York Daily News* and the *Denver Post* and that means newspapers, television, books - everything.

For a guy with his talent and experience, trying to teach me must have been a lot like Kotter trying to get through to the Sweathogs. One time, he was so exasperated with me and my copy, he threw down his red pencil, then threw up his arms in disgust.

"This stuff is terrible," he grumbled. "You have Jesus Christ and Mary Tyler Moore in the same sentence!"

"What's the bitch, Buddy?" I asked. "I've put Christ in good company."

I did break six stories on TV sports which made the wire. I also think I still hold one record at the paper, but it had nothing to do with writing. It was for the highest number of WATS line calls, 56, made in a single month. WATS stood for "wide area telephone service." A long time ago, big businesses, including newspapers and television networks, had WATS lines. They provided flat-rate long distance for employees to make calls. I'm sure that record didn't endear me to management.

It took me only a few months to come to the painful conclusion that I just wasn't cut out to be a sportswriter. Among the likes of Mizell and Martin, I was the missing link.

In retrospect, I realize that I never should have reached that rarified air. That's one of the reasons I'm so dead set against papers hiring anybody for any other reason but talent. I was a prime example of somebody getting a job they weren't qualified for. Only I didn't get the job due to affirmative action, because I was black or because I had a nice rack. It was my Rolodex, my relationships with bigshots in television and sports, that got me hired.

I wasn't going to be a hack or be a burden on Buddy or anybody else, so I quit. My stay in St. Petersburg lasted all of about five months. The whole experiment was about as short as the average length of an Elizabeth Taylor marriage and probably just as rocky. I didn't think anybody at the paper was sad to see me go. Now that I think about it, I wasn't even there long enough to learn my zip code.

Now I did learn two things thanks to St. Petersburg. Number one, the difference between doing PR and writing was that spreading bullshit was much easier than creating it. Second, just because your plan or dream job doesn't work out, that doesn't necessarily mean you've reached the end of the road. In reality, you've arrived at another intersection in life. Now what? Which way do you go from here?

At first, I considered putting my career into reverse, figuratively speaking, and trying to get a job as a college SID. Then I thought about heading north to New York. I figured I might be able to do PR for a company. The way things worked out, I ended up heading south, to Miami, and got mixed up in professional football.

I had gotten a call from my old friend Charlie Callahan, who was working for the Dolphins. Callahan said that there was an opening with the team he wanted to discuss. Right around the early 1970s, teams started employing two people to handle publicity. Callahan, who had been with the Dolphins since the franchise was born, was going on sixty and the workload and the travel demands were wearing him down. He would remain the publicity director and, "if I was interested," I would be the director of public relations.

Was I interested? I couldn't believe my luck! Not only was the timing absolutely perfect, it was a fantastic opportunity to work with someone who I loved being around and had looked up to most of my adult life.

Now I had some reservations about working in the NFL, but there was something about the team's maverick owner, Joe Robbie, that put me at ease. He wasn't a warm and fuzzy guy, but I felt he was an honest individual. I sensed that if I would be loyal to him and the organization, he'd be loyal to me.

We wrapped up the interview in an elevator inside the building on Biscayne Boulevard that housed the Dolphins' administrative offices. Robbie hired me just as the doors opened to the lobby, so I like to tell people that I got in the NFL on the ground floor.

My first day of work was August 4, 1974. I'll never forget it. It was the day after the team's first exhibition (sorry, Pete Rozelle, I mean pre-season; he hated when you called them exhibitions) game. I was still stung by what had happened in St. Petersburg, but I had managed to avoid the unemployment line once again and my future, just like the dazzling Florida sunshine on that summer day, still seemed bright.

As I pulled into the Dolphins' palm tree studded compound at Biscayne College, I specifically remember that the song "Chevy Van" was playing on the radio. It was one of those moments in time. I was in a wonderful mood.

A mere twenty minutes later, I learned that life in the NFL for a public relations director is nothing like making love in a Chevy van. I reached that conclusion shortly after being introduced to one Donald Francis Shula.

The introduction was made by the late Bill Braucher of the *Miami Herald.* It was Braucher, one of the best pro beat men ever, who served as the secret intermediary that brought Shula to the Dolphins from Baltimore. When we walked into Shula's office I felt about as welcome as the Germans did when they marched into Paris in 1940. I could see the veins in Shula's neck and face tightening when he stood up from his desk.

"I want you to know one thing," he snarled. "Robbie hired you without telling me and I'm not happy about it!"

"I know, coach," I replied, "getting me isn't like getting O.J. Simpson."

I probably shouldn't have said it, but the line just came to me and I liked it. Shula glared at me. So much for breaking the ice! He proceeded to ream my tail for five minutes. When he finally calmed down, I felt like I had been in there for two hours.

"I have heard stories about you," he concluded. "Your behavior at Pitt was lower than whale shit. You're supposed to be a wise guy and I don't like wise guys. So let's get one thing straight – I didn't want you here, I didn't ask you to come here, so I don't want to see you around here. At practice, anywhere."

"*Whale shit?*" I said to myself. I hadn't been chewed out like that since the army, or by Captain Hamilton. I was so shaken, I barely remember meeting our general manager, Bobby Beathard, or any of the other front office personnel or players that day. Braucher told me not to worry, that Shula would eventually come around.

"You're just an innocent victim," he explained, "of the feud."

A few months earlier at the team banquet, he went on to say, Shula and Robbie had exchanged some harsh words. Shula threatened to knock Robbie on his ass. And then, when Shula reportedly told a writer that Robbie had been drinking too much, any possibility of a reconciliation died.

It wasn't that I didn't trust Braucher, who would become a good friend, but I was so shocked, I couldn't believe it. I'd had no inkling whatsoever of these troubles in paradise. It just didn't make any sense. The Dolphins were winners. Big winners.

In the summer of '74, the Miami Dolphins were the preeminent franchise in pro football. In just nine years, Shula and the Dolphins had accomplished more than many other teams had in their entire existences. The Dolphins made the playoffs in their fifth season, Shula's first as head coach, made it to the Super Bowl in their sixth, won the Super Bowl and finished a perfect 17-0 in the seventh and won the whole thing again in their eighth. If this kind of behavior was going on behind closed doors with a winning team, I didn't want to know what it was like to be part of the day-to-day operations of a losing team in the NFL.

Soon enough, I saw the feud up close. Three weeks later, I was advancing our first pre-season road game versus the Rams in Los Angeles. I received odd instructions from Callahan which specified that under no circumstances were Robbie's and Shula's rooms to be on the same floor at the team hotel. "Trust me on this, please," Callahan said. I trusted him. He had worked for three legendary coaches, Frank Leahy, Ara Parseghian and Shula, in his career.

The situation became much clearer to me later following an incident that took place at Los Angeles International Airport after the game. The football game was over, but, as I was learning, that meant only that the other games could resume.

This particular pre-season game had been preceded by the latest skirmish in what was one of the other big feuds in football history, the one between Robbie and Rams' owner Carroll Rosenbloom. It was a dispute over where the game was to be played. We'll talk more about that feud later.

We were at the airport ready to fly home when an argument broke out, this is in front of dozens of travelers and airport personnel, between Robbie and Shula. The alphabetical travel roster contained all of the usual names, front office people, team personnel, et cetera, with one notable late addition: Robbie, Elizabeth.

Joe's wife had gone out to L.A. before the game, but was returning on the team plane. Her presence on the manifest, for whatever reason, pissed Shula off. It was a seemingly trifling matter, but he probably viewed it as a challenge to his authority. The franchise may have been owned by Robbie, but, like most coaches, Shula thought the team was his.

"In the contract I have the final say on who is on the plane," Shula complained.

I stood there in disbelief. This guy was going to tell the team owner his wife couldn't fly home on the charter? I felt awful for Mrs. Robbie. I would get to know her during my time in Miami and she was a very nice lady who I had a lot of respect for. In fact, the three wives I admired most for their grace were Mrs. Edith Bunker, Mrs. Emmy Cosell, and Mrs. Elizabeth Robbie – and not necessarily in that order.

In any argument related to X's and O's Shula of course held the upper hand, but you weren't going to beat Joe Robbie, a brilliant attorney, in any legal proceedings.

"That isn't what the contract said," Robbie reminded Shula. "You have *a* say, not the final say. I am not going to have my wife fly commercial with a three-hour layover in Dallas."

When everybody, Mrs. Robbie included, was boarded and accounted for, I took my seat and buckled up. "*Welcome to professional football,*" I said to myself. For once, the thought of turbulence didn't bother me. I was more concerned with how bumpy a ride the season was going to be. As foreboding as the feeling was, I knew I wasn't going anywhere. At any other time, the lack of laughs I found upon my arrival in Miami would have driven me to seek employment elsewhere. Anywhere, really, except the army.

But since I couldn't leave Callahan hanging, I decided that I had to stick it out for at least a season. I figured that at the very least I might get some stories – hell, maybe even a Super Bowl ring – out of it.

* * *

For the first few weeks, while I was hunting for an apartment, I slept on a cot in our office out at the training camp. I lived there for about a month and finally found a place in Coconut Grove just as the regular season started. I'd have plenty of sleepless nights in my year with the Dolphins, but not all of them were attributable to Shula and the stress that accompanies a madcap season full of controversy, close losses, suspensions, and injuries.

See, when I got the phone hooked up at my own place, the number they gave me was one digit off from the reservations line for Eastern Airlines. I can't even begin to estimate how many wrong number calls I got over the course of that year. After awhile, since the phone company refused to assign me a new number, I took it in stride. At all hours, day and night, I carried on conversations with friendly, but confused strangers about aisle and window seats. I'm convinced this kind of stuff only happens to me. Well, me and Cosmo Kramer.

In the office, I'd fall asleep by counting phone numbers. Callahan didn't have a Rolodex or appointment book. He had this strange habit of writing phone numbers on the wall. There had to be a thousand of them scribbled in pencil and pen on the aqua green paint. He had the home and office numbers of every sportswriter in the country. Those of announcers and other television personalities, too. All the Dolphins' players and coaches. He had politicians and public officials right next to pizza parlors.

If that room still exists at what's now called St. Thomas University, and if you peeled off a few layers of paint, it would be like unearthing a major archaeological find, the sports media equivalent of ancient hieroglyphics.

The food at the training table wasn't half bad. I ate a ton but didn't put on any weight because I got plenty of exercise playing hide-and-seek with Shula. The way I figured it, Shula disliked me not because of who I was, rather, because I wasn't Mike Rathet.

Rathet was a writer who had done publicity for the AFL during the league's early years before joining the Dolphins. Rathet was Shula's guy. They were close and co-wrote a book together. Rathet ended up as sports editor of the *Philadelphia Daily News*. Making matters worse, since Shula had no say in my hiring, he probably thought Robbie hired me to be a spy.

I didn't know how serious he was about not wanting to see me around, so at first I did my best to avoid him. I only entered the dining hall after I had been assured that he had already eaten. If I saw him coming, I'd dive into the bushes, duck into an equipment room, or throw up a newspaper in front of my face. More than once I tripped on a sprinkler or hid under some blocking pads. It was ridiculous. I felt like I was living in a "Three Stooges" short.

I wasn't there very long before I got the impression that Shula was unquestionably a martinet, but at the same time I have to admit that I was also very impressed with his operation. Our practice fields looked like the fairways at a country club. Practices and press conferences started and ended on time like clockwork. During business hours, the players were all business. To my surprise, there weren't many complaints from the writers. Maybe they were content with the access they received. Or maybe they kept quiet out of fear.

I couldn't find fault with Shula's management style. I decided that if I ever bought a professional football team or a concentration camp, I would hire Don Shula to run it.

One day, Joe Robbie asked me how things were going. I told him about Shula's welcome and how Shula said that he didn't want to see me at practice. Robbie got upset. He said he'd talk to Shula.

"Joe," I said, "let me tell you something, he's doing me a favor. You think I want to stand out there in the hot sun and watch practice?"

That's one of the great misconceptions that every coach, college or pro, has. They are convinced that practice is as big a deal to everybody else as it is to them. I realized that things were much worse in the pros. And it wasn't just Shula and the assistants. The players all thought that the sportswriters and everybody else were fans who wanted nothing more in life than to attend practice and to hang out with them.

Some years later, when Braucher was preparing to leave Miami to become a columnist at the *Cincinnati Enquirer*, Nick Buoniconti went up to him and said, "you're not coming out here anymore? That's too bad. You're going to miss us."

Braucher set Buoniconti straight.

"You think I like coming out here? That I like practice? Do you really believe that I enjoy watching you guys run drills? Waiting to get little nuggets of information? Let me tell you, Nick, I'd rather attend a hanging."

Everybody associated with pro football, I would come to understand, developed a certain gallows humor. Especially those doing PR in the league. Between dealings with the players, coaches, owners, and media, it was absolutely necessary in order to keep one's sanity. The job was, I soon discovered, a lot different than being a college SID.

For starters, the college job is much harder from an actual work perspective. With all the competition for space from pro teams, a college publicist must think. By think, I mean come up with clever promotional ideas.

In Miami, I didn't have to do any thinking whatsoever. I didn't have to dream up PR stunts like the Salk photo, or pose the players with good-looking coeds to get a story into the South Florida papers. With any pro football team, coverage is automatic. You don't really need good press. In the pros, your job is to head off bad press at the pass.

In pro football, all the paperwork makes it impossible to have time to think. The daily routine of press conferences and arranging player and coach interviews fell in Callahan's domain.

I handled the flight and hotel reservations for road games and, of course, the releases. While writing them up was like riding a bike - anybody who has done PR never forgets how to write a release – I wasn't allowed to have any fun with them like I did when I was at Pitt.

Putting together the releases and the mailing can take up the first half of the week. I think our mailing list had the names of about 1,300 media members on it. That might sound like a lot, but to be honest, if you were any good at your job, you were done with the releases on Monday.

I wasn't obligated to attend practice, Shula had stated that he didn't want me to attend, so I never did. In our division of responsibilities, I handled the advances and traveled with the team on the long-distance road trips. Our first three games of the season were on the road, so Callahan handled the season opening loss at New England and our week 2 game at Buffalo, a 24-16 victory.

My first regular season road trip was the following week, to San Diego. It was there I learned that like the releases, I wasn't going to have much fun doing advances, either.

Standing in the lobby of the Islandia Hyatt House, I probably looked like a sad little kid staring out of his bedroom window while the rest of the neighborhood gang went out to play. I watched Larry Csonka and Nick Buoniconti hop into a cab and head to town. Linebacker Doug Swift went to the beach.

Two of the dozen writers who traveled with the team, John Jolinski and Paul Bodi, were off to Tijuana. Bodi bought four cases of Coors beer, which you couldn't get in Miami at this time, and it was my job to find room for them in the baggage compartment on the flight home. Two more writers, Charlie Nobles of the *Miami News* and Rich Podolsky, with *Dolphin Digest*, drove up to L.A. and shot over to Vegas. They barely made it back for the game.

Everyone was having fun. Everyone except me. At one time, doing an advance was the best part of doing PR, a chance to get out of the office, get out of town, and live large on the expense account.

I discovered that an advance man in the NFL worries about other, more mundane duties and, thanks to the automatic coverage of pro football, has no meaningful interaction with the media. Instead of chasing space and tail and running around with sportswriters like in the good old days at Pitt, I was stuck playing a role that was something halfway between a hotel concierge and a general's enlisted aide.

One of the most important jobs that you do when you advance a game is to make sure the buses are there at the airport once the team plane lands. As a general rule, I scheduled the buses to arrive about two hours ahead of the plane.

My friend Hank Goldberg, a popular, long-time fixture on the Miami air waves known for his coverage of pro football and horse racing, asked me why I got so worked up about the buses. I told Goldberg that I knew that the wind doesn't flow from Miami to the West Coast, and the last thing I was going to do was have Shula get off the plane and the buses not be there.

I don't know why, but I'm convinced that a coach would rather get an offsides penalty on Third and Goal from the two in the Super Bowl than wait a single second for the buses. Forget scorned women. Hell hath no fury like a football coach delayed.

When it came to the buses, all coaches were the same. It was a mania, an incurable affliction that affected every coach in the NFL. Ernie Accorsi, who did PR for the Baltimore Colts in the early 1970s, told me that he used to call the bus company three times a day.

"They must have thought I was nuts," Accorsi admitted, "but I never really relaxed until I actually saw the buses with my own eyes."

Elliott Trumbull told me that when he retired from the Lions, he was going to write a book. "The title will be," Trumbull laughed, 'Where's the bus?'"

I'm sure one of Trumbull's successors, my friend Bill Keenist, now a senior vice president with the Lions, could add a chapter or two to that book.

Cincinnati was playing in Buffalo one year and when the Bengals' plane landed, there were no buses. The late Al Heim, the Bengals' publicity director, was sweating buckets. "You have no idea," he told me. "The last coach in the world you want to see step off the plane and the buses not be there was Paul Brown."

And Heim was one of Brown's buddies! From what many people have told me, Brown might have looked like Eliot Ness in that fedora, but he operated like Capone. You made one tiny mistake, it was the St. Valentine's Day Massacre. He was equal parts perfectionist and psychopath.

Just as the plane was taxiing in, the buses showed up. For an embattled PR guy, it doesn't get much better. "That was better," Heim told me, "than winning in overtime."

After what happened in Los Angeles back in August, I took no chances in San Diego. When the team landed prior to that preseason game, the buses I had ordered were not allowed to drive onto the runway. A few weeks earlier, the "Alphabet Bomber" had blown up the Pan Am terminal, killing three people and wounding nearly forty others. Security was so tight, the whole airport was on lockdown. Of course, Shula went bananas. He got even more agitated when I explained that it was by order of the F.B.I. How dare the Federal Bureau of Investigation pull rank on a professional football coach!

Shula was extremely upset that the players had to walk through the terminal just like all the other passengers and I could tell that in his mind, it was all my fault. In San Diego, I told the bus company to have the buses there two hours before the plane arrives and to park as close to the airport as possible. "I don't care if we have to pay you triple time or you get a ticket. I want to live," I told the dispatcher. "And if the buses aren't there, I'm dead."

If the buses were on time, that meant you survived to the next step and were around to hand out hotel room keys to the coaches, players, front office people and all the others who had made the trip.

Miami usually had a large road entourage. The Robbies had 11 kids, so in addition to the family, there were a number of other friends and guests that the team put up. Joe and his wife typically got a two-bedroom suite, and Shula a one-bedroom suite, which as previously discussed, had to be on different floors.

Shula, thankfully, wasn't too picky with the rooms. He was nothing like the late Hank Stram, who, I have been told, was the biggest diva in all of professional football.

According to Bob Sprenger, the Chiefs' PR man, *NFL Films* should have mic'd up Stram when he checked into hotels. Sprenger told me about the time he incurred Stram's wrath because the coach's suite was too small.

"Coach," pleaded Sprenger, "you're not on your honeymoon. You're going to be here for less than 18 hours. And you'll be sleeping about eight of those. Why the fuss?"

"I don't care," persisted Stram. "This suite is too small."

"It's not only the best one they have, it's all they have," explained Sprenger. "What do you want me to do?"

"Get a carpenter up here," yelled Stram.

I'm certain there were times that Sprenger wished Stram would matriculate his way off a cliff. I also have a feeling the late Joe Blair, the Washington Redskins' public relations director, would have liked George Allen to accompany Stram. I felt bad for Blair, who in his career also worked for taskmasters like Jim Tatum at Maryland and Vince Lombardi.

Blair told me about a conversation he had with a hotel manager during one advance.

"One last thing," Blair told this guy. "Please have somebody go immediately to Coach Allen's suite with a chocolate milkshake. And please, sir, make sure it's cold."

"A what?"

"A chocolate milkshake. And, again, it must be cold."

"I've had actors and millionaires request that a hooker be delivered to the room and a thousand other crazy demands," said the manager, "but these coaches seem like the weirdest bunch of all. I wouldn't want your job."

Amazingly, despite the low pay – pro PR directors made about an average of $23,000 a year in the early Seventies – many people wanted that job. The late Don Weiss, the head of the NFL's PR office and a member of Pete Rozelle's inner circle for many years, told me that he received hundreds of letters every year from job applicants who stated that they "would do anything to work for an NFL team."

I could only surmise that the job had appeal to those on the outside looking in. Kind of like marriage. Back then, if you were hired, you might just have to do anything.

One summer, when the Redskins reported to training camp at Dickinson College in Carlisle, Pennsylvania, Allen discovered that his wife had forgotten to pack his pajamas. He ordered Blair to go out and find him a new set, specifically requesting a set with the team's color scheme, burgundy and gold.

Blair put about 200 miles on his car driving throughout Pennsylvania and finally found a pair of burgundy and gold silk pajamas. Late that night, he proudly presented the pajamas to the head coach. The quirky Allen, not surprisingly, was not satisfied.

"You couldn't find any," he said, deflatedly, "with little Indians on them?"

Exasperated, Blair finally left Washington after ten years to do PR for Ed Garvey and the Players Association.

When you did advances, you weren't just at the coach's beck and call. The owners had their own strange demands. Take Carroll Rosenbloom. Jack Geyer, when he was doing PR for the Rams, told me he spent more time talking to delicatessen owners in various cities while searching for low fat goat's milk and lean meat than he did sportswriters and broadcasters. We're going to talk more about the owners in due time.

When Shula got to his suite, Callahan told me, he wanted cold beer and soft drinks waiting. Callahan said that 12 bottles of each would suffice. Why be satisfied with a first down when you can pick up twenty yards? I wasn't paying, so I told the hotel managers to make it two cases.

Some things, however, like the quality of the food or room service, were totally out of a PR man's control. I have concluded that there's a direct relationship between a coach's reaction to the food and service at the hotel and winning or losing.

After a brutal, last-second, 20-17 loss to Washington in week 5, I overheard a distraught Shula complaining to our promotions guy, Jim Johnson, that "the potatoes at the hotel were bad." So, let it be put in the historical record that Don Shula disliked the potatoes at the Washington Sheraton-Park Hotel.

The other bizarre NFL practice I became enlightened to on road trips was the rule about the squatter's right to the bar. It's not in the league's bylaws. Most teams prohibited their players from drinking in the hotel bar. Of course, they didn't permit women in the rooms, either. You can guess which rule was more strictly enforced.

At the same time, the owners frowned upon their coaches drinking before the game, too. So the players who wanted to booze had to find a bar near the hotel. If the coaches were already in that bar, the players must leave. If the reverse happens, the coaches must find another saloon. Neither group snitched on the other. Of course, since I got into town early, both groups often approached me to conduct reconnaissance on their behalf. At times, I felt like a double agent.

By the fall of 1974, I came to the depressing conclusion that between worrying about the coaches, the owners, the buses, the bars, the potatoes and everything else, the purpose of advancing a game – at least the way I knew it – was largely gone with the wind.

As for the game itself, I was never more grateful for a win than when Miami rallied from a 21-7 deficit to beat the Chargers, 28-27. I dreaded being on the same plane with Shula on a long flight after a loss. Thankfully, I only had to endure that twice. After we turned the ball over four times and lost a nail biter to Joe Namath and the Jets in New York in late November, I remember looking out the window on the flight home and thinking that D.B. Cooper had the right idea. I'd jump out and nobody, Shula especially, would ever find me.

In all seriousness, the job of doing PR in the NFL wasn't that tough. Tedious and at times humiliating, yes. Tough, no. But certain situations unique to pro football arise and they can make the gig much more challenging. One of them in the 1970s was the invasion of Howard Cosell and company for a Monday night game.

As my friend Irv Brodsky, the longtime publicist for "Monday Night Football," once said, "the place to be in America is inside *ABC's* booth at halftime on Monday night." Everybody, every athlete, celebrity, musician, and politician, wanted to be interviewed by Cosell in the booth on live television. It was a status thing in the Seventies and for a good part of the Eighties, too.

On the Tuesday before our Monday night game versus the Jets in October, Robbie started to receive calls from Senator Walter Mondale of Minnesota. Mondale, who wanted to be U.S. President, probably thought that Robbie, a former Minnesotan who had been active in Democrat party politics in the state, would be his way into the booth. Robbie told Mondale, point blank, "I don't have any say about who goes on at halftime."

But Mondale kept calling. Robbie started dodging him. Some of Mondale's calls were routed to me and it took all I had to be polite. The country had eight percent unemployment, double-digit inflation, and this guy is more worried about being on television than in trying to solve the peoples' problems? Typical politician. Typical bullshit.

As the week went on, I learned that Mondale was the least of my worries. When I heard that *ABC* wanted to interview Ed Keating, the sports agent, I called up Don Ohlmeyer. Keating had negotiated the landmark deal with the Cleveland Indians that week that made Frank Robinson the first black manager in major league history. It was the biggest sports news event of the week and Keating would have been an appropriate interview subject, but why did it have to be in Miami and on my watch? Keating, of course, was the agent who turned over Larry Csonka, Jim Kiick and Paul Warfield to the World Football League.

"Ed Keating?" I asked Ohlmeyer. "Have you lost your fucking mind? If you want publicity, sure, put him on. But when Robbie hears about it, you'll have the first murder on live television since Jack Ruby."

"Well," replied Ohlmeyer sheepishly, "you don't have to tell Robbie. Of course, when he hears about it, I guess your name will be added to the fatality list."

Despite my worries, I ended up having a pretty good week. I enjoyed catching up with Chet Forte, Cosell, Brodsky and Ohlmeyer, we beat the Jets, 21-17, and, to my great relief, neither Mondale nor Keating made it to "the place to be." Shula would be in a good mood for at least another 24 hours and Robbie seemed pleased with my work so far. In fact, the only person who might have had reason to be upset with me was Rhoda Morgenstern.

Let me explain. I did quite a bit of behind-the-scenes wrangling that week, so much so that by the time kickoff rolled around I felt like I was working for both the Dolphins and *ABC*. Everybody at *ABC* was all worked up because not only was the broadcast team still working through some kinks after Alex Karras replaced Fred

Williamson, *CBS* had a runaway ratings hit with "Rhoda" that was providing some very stiff competition to the Monday night game over the first few weeks of the season.

The way Ohlmeyer explained it, *ABC* felt that if the national anthem made it on the air, impatient viewers might switch over to "Rhoda" and never change the channel back to *ABC*. He appealed to me as a friend and former *ABC* employee to maneuver things so that the Star-Spangled Banner was played before airtime.

This was no easy favor to grant. Robbie loved seeing the song played on TV. He was a really patriotic guy - he saw a lot of action in the Pacific during the war - who took a personal interest in the pre-game schedule, who delivered the invocation, who the singer of the Star-Spangled Banner was. That sort of thing.

Everything was timed to the minute with precision in the pre-game, yet somehow, with the help of the Dunedin High School band, I pulled it off. I risked Robbie's wrath to help Ohlmeyer because I knew word would get back to Roone that I was still a team player.

Plus, I guess a part of me missed the old gang in the truck, too. I didn't want them to catch hell. It's one thing to get beat by "The Godfather," as the show would be in November when *NBC* and the Corleone family put out a contract on Cosell, but to lose a ratings war to a pretty, but neurotic Jewish broad from the Bronx on the prowl for a husband, well, that's something else entirely.

* * *

Everybody knows the Miami Dolphins of the 1970s were a loose, fun-loving, and mischievous bunch. Kiick and Csonka, you might remember, were nicknamed "Butch Cassidy and the Sundance Kid" for their off-the-field antics and adventures. Bill Braucher gave them the nickname. When the movie "North Dallas Forty" came out a few years after I left Miami, I thought the producers got the partying part of professional football down.

Home or away, these guys could put it away. On the road, the first thing many of the players did after I handed them the room keys was go and buy booze for their rooms. In our office out at Biscayne College during camp, Callahan and I had an ice box in the room that we kept full of cold Miller High Life beer, Callahan's favorite. When I went to bed, there would be maybe 18 or so bottles in there. The next morning they were invariably gone. During the night, players and coaches would sneak in and steal them.

Callahan used to hide two Hershey chocolate bars in the back and each morning, I'd hear the same sad complaint: "I don't mind those guys taking the beer, but why my candy bars?" Sorry, Charlie. He never knew that I was the chocolate bar thief.

I don't recall a lot of drug use. That doesn't mean that drugs weren't being used, just that I don't recall seeing them being used. These guys didn't need drugs. They were crazy enough.

Callahan told me that on our first road trip of the regular season, on the flight up to Boston, Jake Scott locked poor John Jolinski in the bathroom of the plane for 45 minutes. Scott pulled the same stunt on Strat Zammas, a producer for *WTVJ* Channel 4 in Miami, but somebody had to take a piss, so Zammas was stuck in there for only ten minutes. That night, Robbie and Jim Johnson spent 45 minutes with Jolinski over drinks trying to calm him down and talk him out of writing a story on what Scott had done.

The Dolphins might have been the back-to-back Super Bowl champs, but when it came to chasing tail, they were a middle of the road team. I knew because I had an interesting conversation with an airline stewardess who flew many of the team charter flights. She said the Redskins had the most aggressive, horned up players in the league. At the other end, the Atlanta Falcons were absolute gentlemen. The Falcons had only two winning seasons in their first 12 years of existence, so I guess losing hamstrings the libido.

The Dolphins had a reputation as being a brainy team, so maybe they just outsmarted the competition when it came to chicks. One the best stories in this regard concerns a married player who was dating a stewardess on the side. It was the week of one of the Super Bowls before I was with the team. The players' wives were scheduled to arrive later in the week, so this player asked his girlfriend if she could fly in on Sunday and leave Thursday prior to his wife's arrival. But the stewardess couldn't get off work. This player went to the team doctor and asked him for a favor: can you put a fake cast on my girlfriend's arm? The doctor played along and since the stewardess could not work with her alleged injury, she was able to make the trip.

One day Hank Goldberg took a seat in my office and proceeded to tell me about how he had managed to get a group of players to visit this club of his and talk football.

"How much did that cost you?" I asked.

"Nothing," Goldberg replied. "Everybody agrees to come for nothing."

I looked at him in amazement.

"How in the hell did you pull that off?"

"Simple," he said. "It's a club of women who want to learn about football."

I had to hand it to Hank. And to the players. I have no idea what went on at these clinics, but I'm certain that all of these chicks, especially the good-looking ones, were serious in their desire to learn all variations of the trap play.

Those women probably had more contact with the players than I did. I didn't spend much time around them. And to be perfectly honest, it didn't bother me all that much. Unlike some writers and PR guys, I wasn't trying to be buddies with the players. But I do want to tell you about a few of the guys on the team I enjoyed being around.

The first was my favorite Dolphin, the late Jim Mandich. Mandich was very easy to get along with. He was the kind of laidback, free spirit I liked. Somebody told me that at one of the Super Bowls, Mandich had been out all night partying and didn't get back to the team hotel until 7:30 in the morning. He was walking by Robbie's room, which was on the ground floor, and saw that Robbie and Shula were seated at a table. Most players would have ducked or taken an alternate route. Not Mandich. He knocked on the window, smiled, waved, and went on his merry way.

I remember watching an interview with Mandich after the game. Some reporter asked him how he planned to celebrate the win. "I'm going home, gonna order a couple truck loads of beer," Mandich replied, "and wait for the honeys to call."

The other player was Jim Langer, our center. He called me up at my apartment one day to thank me for a feature story on him that ran in a magazine. I told him I had nothing to do with it. The writer called me and I just connected you two, I said. "Even so," Langer said, "I wanted to thank you on behalf of myself and my family."

In my experience, linemen were always very happy to receive any notoriety, so I didn't think much of it when I hung up the phone. Later on, it hit me: in all my years of doing PR, nobody had ever gone to the trouble of tracking me down at my home to express their gratitude like he had. That impressed me very much, more so than anything Langer did on the field. Which is saying something because he's a member of the Pro Football Hall of Fame.

And then there's Larry Csonka. After our Monday night win over the Jets, I noticed Zonk slipped out of the Orange Bowl without talking to the media. He was probably late for some good times somewhere. When I read Braucher's story in the next day's edition of the *Miami Herald*, I was surprised to find that it contained a number of quotes from Csonka. When Braucher came by my office the following week I asked him how he did it.

"(Csonka) gave me two sets of quotes before the game," he explained. "One to use in case of a win and the other for a loss."

From that point forward, I looked at Csonka differently. I no longer thought of him as purely a punishing runner or as the Sundance Kid of South Beach. I considered him one of the smartest players on the team.

I wish more of them had been like Mandich, Langer and Zonk. Most of our kids at Pitt, as well as a majority of those at the other schools we played, behaved like real professionals when it came to interacting with the media.

Not long after I started working for the Dolphins, I found that most of the so-called professionals acted like spoiled brats. Some were deliberately difficult to get along with. A few could be nasty and intimidating. Others were quietly manipulative.

A good example of the deliberately difficult was Bob Griese. "I hate talking to Griese," one beat writer told me. "He's a complete bore. I have to do three stories on him a year and when I finish the third, I feel like going out and getting drunk to celebrate."

I had been out of the Dolphins' job only a year or so when my *Pittsburgh Weekly Sports* partner Jim O'Brien started working for the *Miami News*. When he told me that he had been assigned a Griese feature, I warned him that Griese always opens the conversation with questions of his own. No hello. No pleasantries. It was like being grilled by Judge Sirica. O'Brien did the interview then called me back.

"You were right," he said. "First thing out of his mouth was, 'how did you get my number?' I told him to cut the third degree. Answer a few and we'll get this over with."

Professional football players might be the most narcissistic, not to mention paranoid athletes on the planet. They think their home phone numbers should be a bigger secret than the Air Force's nuclear missile codes.

I can understand that some prefer to screen calls from the media and fans. But what about your own head coach? That was the problem Lou Holtz discovered when he took the Jets job in 1976. Frank Ramos, the team's longtime PR man, told me that Holtz asked for Joe Namath's phone number and he had to tell Holtz that he couldn't have it.

"I can't directly talk to my quarterback?" asked a flabbergasted Holtz.

"I'm sorry, coach," replied Ramos. "I'm just following orders."

Ironically, Ramos was one of the easiest guys in the business to work with. The first thing I did upon arriving in New York in 1966 was call Ramos to buy a pair of Jets season tickets. It was a tough ask because of Namath's popularity, but Ramos took care of me.

Unfortunately, he couldn't help Holtz. Ramos told him that he would have to go through Namath's agent, who would pass the request on. If and when Namath got back to Holtz, that was up to the quarterback. It was unbelievable.

The combativeness, the conceit – it's all due to money. The greatest thing to happen to sports in the last fifty years is television. And the worst thing to happen in the last fifty years is television's money. It ruined baseball. It's why we have utility infielders making more than the gross domestic products of some third world countries. It's why we have wildcard games and why the World Series doesn't end until Black Friday.

It's slowly compromised the integrity of college football and will eventually ruin that sport as well. For some reason, probably greed, it started ruining pro football almost immediately. Starting in the Seventies, there was a lot more of it to go around due to the merger and the sport's skyrocketing popularity. The first casualty was conviviality. As player salaries shot into the stratosphere, the players got more and more difficult to deal with.

The first indication I had that things were getting bad was when I heard that the Dallas Cowboys gave cashmere sweaters to each member of the team as a Christmas gift. The players showed little appreciation for the gesture, throwing the sweaters around the locker room while making sarcastic remarks.

Then I heard the story about a player who signed a contract for five years for $495,000. He kept giving the owner the cold shoulder at the team facility. Finally, the owner cornered him.

"Why couldn't you have agreed to five years at $500,000?" the player whined. "Now I can't go around saying that I'm a $100,000 a year player."

I shared this story with Joe Robbie and he nodded his head up and down in agreement.

"If you give five thousand here and five thousand there, it adds up," he explained. "It's the only business where you can give your employees 95% of what they want and they'll still call you cheap."

Robbie told me that when one player asked for a membership to an exclusive country club in South Florida, he had to explain to the agent that it was hardly, as the agent put it, "a small concession." Robbie explained that if he agreed to that concession, every player on the roster would want a membership, meaning that it would be fifty small concessions, not one.

Nothing pissed him off more than when the players who defected to the World Football League told the press they were doing it to provide for their families. Whenever anybody mentioned the WFL in his presence Robbie rolled his eyes and called it, contemptuously, the "World Family League."

I found it ironic that Robbie probably did more, at least indirectly, for the players' families than any other owner in the league. He told me when he paid for the wives of the married players to travel to the first Dolphins' Super Bowl, he caught hell from the single players who wanted their girlfriends, and in some cases their parents, comped, too. So he obliged on the second and third trips.

He suggested that if the Dolphins returned to the big game, he'd have to charter another flight just for the grandparents and family pets. I laughed at the line, but he didn't. He wasn't joking. The franchise wasn't even ten years old, but thanks to the never-ending succession of demands he had a certain weariness in his voice at times, like he had been running the team for a century.

"An owner pays for the success of his players on the field with their arrogance off it," Robbie once told me. "I'm 58 going on 116."

Due to the money, players started sticking around longer, too, which was a drag on owners, PR personnel and media members.

"When a player was over the hill 20 years ago, he quit," complained Callahan. "Now he sticks around for a few more years because of the big money. And since he figures the club owes him something, he doesn't think it matters whether he can help the team or not."

Throughout this book I've made a few predictions and here I will put another in writing: sometime in the not-to-distant future, in order to help pay the exorbitant salaries of the players, all NFL games will be on pay-per-view.

The exception will be the Super Bowl due to the insane amount of advertising money that always seems readily available, even during economic downturns. Some may laugh at me for this one, but over the course of the past forty years professional football has become America's new Sunday religion. Like it or not, the faithful are going to have to start putting something into the collection basket.

I had been hired in the middle of the '74 strike, so I was literally learning on the job about the league's labor problems. The NFL's public relations department kept in constant touch with each team's PR office. I was kept in the loop on the progress of the talks, given a rundown on the views of the national writers (they were mostly against the players), and instructions to follow if I talked to the press. Both Robbie and I were relieved when it ended.

"Nobody wins a strike," I recall him telling me that summer.

It wasn't until early November 1974, when the first real crisis of the season hit the team, that I began to see the effects of pro football's new-found wealth and prosperity first-hand. I began to wonder how the league would be able to withstand the damage that the players' sense of entitlement had created.

I clearly remember the day when Mercury Morris was suspended. A bunch of writers were walking down the hallway to Shula's office and since the doors to the locker room were open, you could hear one of our tight ends, Marv Fleming, hollering, "here come the vultures, here come the vultures."

And you want intimidating? That same afternoon, John Jolinski was standing by himself in the hallway when big, bad Bob Kuechenberg passed by and said to him, "you fuckin' parasite."

These guys talked tough, but I found that underneath that bulk and all those pads, they were extremely sensitive and emotionally fragile human beings.

Take the case of Paul Warfield and the Chargers game. We were playing poorly until Warfield got hurt. Rookie Nat Moore entered the game, sparked the Dolphins to victory, and was awarded the game ball. Braucher wrote that if Warfield hadn't gotten hurt, San Diego would have won.

The next morning when Warfield came to breakfast, he couldn't find the *Miami Herald.* His wife had hidden it. When he finally read the story, he was furious. Braucher made an observation and expressed an opinion, which was both his job and his right. But in pro football, I learned, feelings trump the truth. Everybody had to walk on eggshells around Warfield for awhile.

I can't blame Kooch, Fleming and the players for circling the wagons and sticking up for one of their own, a vet. Nor can I blame Merc, who I genuinely liked. He was hearing Benny Malone's footsteps. But he literally asked for it.

"Go ahead and suspend me," he dared Shula before strutting out of Shula's office.

He then had the balls to tell Charlie Nobles that he didn't like the "SUSPEND ME" headline that ran about eight columns in the next day's *Miami News*! I knew that Merc was frustrated, probably more so than anybody else over his injury situation, but I didn't think his behavior during the suspension affair was very professional.

And then, just when the storm seemed at its worst, it all blew over. Morris was reinstated almost immediately, he suited up for our week 9 win over the Saints and all seemed forgiven. I walked into Shula's Tuesday afternoon presser at 3 o'clock and thought I had the wrong room. There was no tension.

The press conference got started when Braucher tossed a copy of the *New Orleans Times-Picayune's* Monday sports section at Shula. Braucher pointed out a story by a writer who had mistakenly written the previous week that it was Warfield, not

Morris, who had been in Shula's doghouse. "And I thought we had horseshit writers here," Shula said. Everybody laughed.

Somebody reminded Shula of a funny moment captured by the cameras. "When I got home my wife and my kids couldn't wait to tell me that Mercury was picking his nose on television," laughed Shula.

Charlie Nobles strolled into the room at 3:25 p.m. and Shula, who was in the middle of answering another reporter's question, stopped, pointed to his watch and said, "what the fuck is this? You're late. You owe me some laps after practice, Charlie."

More laughter. I couldn't believe how quickly the mood had changed. A week earlier, World War III was about to break out between the team and the media.

After the presser ended, Nobles pulled me aside and told me that Morris made it a point to tell him after the game that he re-injured his knee when he was hit while standing on the sideline. It was almost as if Morris was trying to plant that news in the paper. After this soap opera, I could only conclude that if a player is getting used for eight column headlines in the NFL, the writers are parasites. If the writer is the one being used, well, it's just business.

The more prosperous the players got, the more they looked down on the members of the press as peons. Likewise, those in the press got more disenchanted by the day. I remember that around this same time, a writer who had covered high school sports for the Baltimore paper was promoted to the Colts beat. After one full season and three games into the second, he pleaded with his boss to return to the preps.

"These people are too much," he complained. "Get me back to a beat where I can have some fun and enjoy myself."

I will say one thing: even though they had to put up with the players, it's my opinion that the writers that covered the Dolphins were better off than their counterparts who covered the league's other teams. That's because of Don Shula. If that statement sounds strange coming from me, especially after everything I've told you thus far about my own contentious relationship with Shula, let me explain.

It's my opinion that no coach in the history of the NFL devoted as much time and energy to cultivating the media as Shula. As anybody who covered the team during that time period will probably tell you, Shula could at times be testy or intimidating, but nobody can say he didn't make himself available.

"I dare you to show me a coach who meets with the press three times and maybe four times a day during training camp," Callahan told me.

I noticed that even during the season, he was available for interviews at odd hours. He took phone calls at designated times from the out-of-town press. What really impressed me was the way he attempted to come up with fresh angles for the writers.

You couldn't appreciate the level of cooperation unless you visited the facility in the middle of the week. No team in the NFL had more press watching the daily practice sessions than the Dolphins. During the season, the four television stations in Miami did at least three interviews each day. We had every radio station and paper south of

Orlando and Tampa on site every week. Every day was like Super Bowl media day. I never saw anything like it. It was all by design. Shula's design.

Callahan had a theory. He said that in the run-up before Super Bowl III between the Colts and the Jets, the Jets' Weeb Ewbank dominated the daily press conferences. So, in the wake of that epic loss, Shula set out to not only become the NFL's best coach on the field, he wanted to be the best all-around coach in other facets, too.

I have to admit that he had the personality for the PR part of the job. There were times he could be so funny and personable, I almost found myself liking the guy. Almost.

I typically nodded off when he started rambling about the X's and O's, but my ears perked up when he used to tell stories that took place off the field.

For example, Shula and Carl Taseff, one of our assistants who was Shula's college roommate, played baseball in the service with Vic Janowicz, the 1950 Heisman Trophy winner. Shula and Taseff talked a major into going A.W.O.L. and driving them to Chicago to watch Janowicz play in an all-star game. He was great at telling those kinds of stories.

Another one of my favorite Shula stories was after the Redskins' loss, when he caught himself playing the "takeaway game."

"Takeaway that last minute and forty-six seconds and takeaway that cheapie they got when Scott slipped and...geez, I'm starting to sound like Weeb," he laughed.

"Once, Jimmy Brown scored five touchdowns against us and a few days later when we went over the films, Weeb said, 'sure he scored five. But takeaway that 90-yard run and that 60-yard run and that 45-yard run, he only averaged two yards a carry against us.'"

Then there was the presser in which the subject of the infamous '74 Jets-Giants game (won by the Jets, 26-20, in overtime at the Yale Bowl) came up. That was the game Giants' kicker Pete Gogolak swore up and down that he made a 42-yard field goal in OT, but the refs called it no good.

"You can't believe those Hungarians," Shula laughed.

After the media left the building, however, it was back to business as usual. It occurred to me that Shula, in a way, resembled a politician. He was like Hubert Humphrey in public. In private, around people like me, underlings, he behaved like LBJ.

I'll give credit where credit is due, however. At least Shula tried. Coaches today, this is in both the pros and college, don't even go through the motions anymore when it comes to treating the media with professional courtesy and respect.

Bill Belichick, for example, conducts press conferences with all the humor and friendliness of an East German border guard stationed at the Berlin Wall. But the members of the media have nobody but themselves to blame for the treatment they receive. They created the monsters.

"The trouble is, the media and the public puts these coaches on pedestals," Braucher once said during one of our weekly bull sessions in my office. "As a result,

America worries more about what happens on a fall Sunday afternoon than what is going on in Vietnam or Congress."

Braucher was right. The line is evergreen. Replace Vietnam with whatever foreign policy mess the country is currently involved in and add Congress and it holds up today.

Coaches have always been megalomaniacs, so when you consider that they're now getting a lot more money and more overall control of the teams, it's only logical to assume that their behavior would worsen, too.

Even so, I don't think it's any worse than what I had heard and experienced. In fact, I'd bet that the behavior of the coaches back then was much more outrageous. This isn't another case of an old man arguing that his era was better, or, in this particular case, worse. Thanks to the proliferation of cable television and networks like *ESPN*, the Internet and social media, the public is more aware of what goes on behind-the-scenes today. None of these things existed back then, so coaches could get away with a lot more.

In the old days, you had to read between the lines to get an idea of how things were. Myron Cope got along with Steelers' coach Chuck Noll, but when he nicknamed Noll "The Emperor," it wasn't exactly a term of endearment. Cope came up with something that sounded flattering on the surface but also served as a veiled reference to the way Noll ran the team.

At camp one year, the Washington Redskins almost didn't take a team picture. George Allen argued that it would have taken too much time away from practice. Allen, like most coaches, had no problem wasting Joe Blair's time sending him on a search for pajamas, but God forbid anybody use a few precious minutes of practice time for a time-honored team tradition. Team president Edward Bennett Williams had to pull rank on Allen and order the photo be taken.

If not for Bob Sprenger, I'd have never known that Hank Stram had his own photographer. I thought only presidents and movie stars had one. Stram also didn't allow his assistants to talk to the press, ostensibly to prevent them from divulging important information about the gameplan, but everyone figured that it was really because Stram didn't want anybody stealing his thunder.

When Kansas City axed Stram at the end of the 1974 season, the official party line was that Stram's failure to make the playoffs was the reason. But the truth was that Stram had dabbled too much in areas of the team's operations that weren't his. And since Lamar Hunt owned the franchise, he decided to take it back from Stram.

It's my opinion that Paul Brown was not only the all-time greatest coach in football history, he was the all-time worst autocrat, too. Why? It's because Brown, the celebrated coaching innovator, wasn't just intimidating at practices or in press conferences. Or, as I told you, at airports while waiting for the buses. Everybody knows that as both an executive and a coach he ran two franchises with an iron fist. But very few people know that he wielded an unbelievable amount of power even after he left the sidelines.

When *CBS* was looking for a color commentator in the early 1980s, I thought Mike Reid, the former Penn State and Bengals' standout, would be a good fit. Reid had been recommended to me by my Penn State friends so I recommended him to the producers.

Rich Podolsky, who was writing for "The NFL Today" at the time, recommended Larry Csonka, but Csonka was involved in a grand jury investigation so he did not receive a tryout. Apparently, Csonka (who was never charged with anything) was guilty until proven innocent.

So, Reid was a shoo-in, right? Not if Paul Brown had anything to say about it, and, evidently, he did. Brown had learned that Reid was going to get a tryout, so he called some higher-ups at *CBS* to voice his displeasure. Apparently, Brown was still bitter that Reid had retired, perhaps prematurely, in 1974. Reid probably had three or four good years left, but you can't fault someone for wanting to do something else with his life. Whatever Brown said, it was enough to sway the suits at *CBS* against Reid.

I remember talking to one vice president who said that "Paul Brown wasn't happy." I replied, "so what?" It made no sense to me how and why Brown, or any coach for that matter, could continue to exert influence over a former player's life, but I was outranked. It seemed as though everyone at *CBS* was a vice president but me.

The moral of the story is, these guys are not merely obsessed with their images and winning. In the end, I believe it's the power that motivates them. At the league's PR meetings in April of 1975 a bunch of us flacks were sitting around after lunch commiserating with each other about our respective coaches.

One of my colleagues wondered aloud, "what would happen if the NFL folded?" We all thought on the question for a few seconds.

"I don't know what would happen to us and the players, but the coaches would probably go to South America," somebody shouted from the back of the room, "and form the Fourth Reich."

There is no group of people in the United States, other than politicians, who live more insular existences than professional football coaches. For them, life is one big huddle that never breaks.

Consider this story involving a well-known coach who was born in the late 1930s. A few years back, at the league meetings in Hawaii, this coach bumped into a friend of mine, a team executive, and asked him what he was going to do before the next round of conferences.

"I'm going to visit Pearl Harbor and the U.S.S. Arizona," replied my friend.

The coach looked at him curiously.

"Are you going to be here for the meetings tomorrow?"

"Of course."

"But how are you going to get back from the Philippines so soon?"

If you think their grasp of history and geography is bad, wait until you hear about current events. Callahan told me this story and it's a good one. In the fall of 1973, everybody in the entire country was riveted to their televisions watching the Watergate scandal unfold.

One October afternoon, Spiro Agnew resigned the Vice Presidency because of improprieties during his term as Maryland's governor. One of the trainers went into the conference room and interrupted the meeting with the news.

"Agnew is out," the trainer announced.

The coaches, slowly lifting their faces out of their playbooks, all looked at each other, confused. Finally, one of the assistant coaches seemed to understand. Although not quite.

"Great!" he yelled. "Just what we need. Another fucking injury."

That's a true story. I'm not Neil Simon or Jerry Seinfeld. I'm not creative enough to make that stuff up.

Ed Pope told me about the time Shula was introduced to the actor Don Johnson. This was in the mid-1980s when the show "Miami Vice" was popular. Shula apparently did not know that Johnson was only playing a cop on TV. When they shook hands, he thanked him for his excellent work in getting drug dealers off the city's streets.

When I heard that story I knew it had to be true because in my experience, nobody was more clueless about pop culture and related things than Shula.

I'll never forget what happened in Shea Stadium after the loss to the Jets. James Michener had been a guest of the Robbies for the game. The late Michener, perhaps the most prolific novelist in American history, was doing research for his book, "Sports in America." I was anxious when Robbie took Michener into the Dolphins' locker-room. It was an honor to be in the presence of such a great author, so I felt bad when I tip-toed towards the door. I was hoping to get out of there before the bomb went off. I had no such luck.

Shula, still steaming about the game, exited the coaches' office and yelled, "who the hell is that?" When I tried to explain it to him, Shula, completely ignorant of the identity of the literary legend standing in his midst, cut me off.

"I don't care," he yelled. "Get (Michener) the fuck out of here." I felt awful for Robbie, who was horrified and embarrassed.

These guys ate, slept, and breathed football to such an extent that Biscayne College might as well have been a monastery. The coaches were so isolated from the outside world they reminded me of monks. There was no room nor time for books, newspapers, television, movies, music, or anything else. They spent so much time cloistered in the compound away from their wives, I sometimes wondered if they had taken a vow of celibacy, too.

One evening in mid-January of 1975, I walked past the coaches' film room. I saw the flickering light filtering out from under the door and when I heard the excitement in their voices it was hard to tell if they were watching a dirty movie or studying film of college kids for the draft. "Look at those legs!" yelled one coach. "Fantastic upper body!" added another.

That's the difference between football coaches and everybody else. They were probably getting all hot and bothered over some running back. I didn't even bother poking my head inside the room. I just kept on walking down the hall. After hearing that enthusiastic talent evaluation, any normal, red-blooded American male, especially an overstressed and undersexed director of public relations, could only assume that we were going to take Raquel Welch in the first round.

* * *

I didn't have much fun dealing with the coaches and players, but the job had both its moments and its bright spots. It was a once-in-a-lifetime opportunity to work with Charlie Callahan. I had a lot of laughs with writers like Bob Braucher, Ed Pope, John Crittenden, and others.

And each year that goes by – it's been twenty since his death – I'm further convinced that I was truly blessed to have had the chance to befriend Joe Robbie. Robbie was the most interesting person I've met in my life.

Many NFL team owners thought the same way about their team's public relations director as they did their caddy at their country club. Not Robbie. He was different. I think one reason we got along so well is because I wasted no time making sure he understood that I was different, too. My third day on the job I wrote an important memo to Robbie and my secretary, Mary Stansell, looked up from her steno pad with a concerned look on her face.

"You're pretty blunt," she said. "Are you absolutely sure you want to send this?"

"I'm telling him what I think should be done," I replied. "If he disagrees with me, and thinks I'm out of my lane, he can fire me."

In many ways, Robbie was like Roone. He listened to me. To a certain point. He didn't always agree with me or follow my advice, but listening, for a rich and powerful person, is probably the highest form of respect they can show.

I had no problem doing the same because Robbie might have also been the smartest person I met in my career. If he had ever gone on "Jeopardy!" I have no doubt he would have won. Like Cosell, he had a very well-rounded intellect. We talked about politics, literature, and countless other subjects besides football.

Unlike my relationship with Roone, however, Joe and I became close friends. He treated me not just as a publicity man, but at times as a trusted advisor. He bounced ideas off me and shared some insight and opinions about league matters and the other owners that I doubt he shared with anybody else.

Even after I left the team, I had an open invitation to attend any Dolphins game, home or away, as his guest. If I needed Super Bowl tickets, all I had to do was ask. We communicated regularly right up until his death in January of 1990.

What I liked most about Robbie wasn't that he treated me like a member of his inner circle. To me, the best thing about the guy was that he wasn't a phony. He was one of the most genuine and generous human beings I've ever met. He was so influential in my life, I decided to follow, in a matter of speaking, in his financial footsteps.

I once asked him why he was so active in giving money to colleges and universities for scholarships. Unlike many wealthy people, it had nothing to do with tax write-offs or getting good publicity. Robbie was fond of quoting Andrew Carnegie's line, "a man who dies rich dies a disgrace." He said that he felt that when a person of means has the capability to provide for the education of the less fortunate, no better investment can be made.

That's why when I die, I'm leaving all of my money to the two educational institutions that changed my life, Pitt and Kiski Prep. It's makes me feel good to know that I'll be helping some kids who need it long after I'm gone.

I've always been a staunch defender of Robbie. I hope that the material in this book will contribute something positive towards his legacy. Not that he ever needed me as a defender, but I feel that he was both misunderstood and underappreciated.

For starters, the fans never gave him a fair shake. Many Dolphins' fans thought Robbie was a jerk. There are two reasons for that. One was the way, as I explained earlier, Shula came off in public. He was a better actor than Robbie and since he won, he was the natural public face of the team.

Secondly, Robbie was constantly ripped by the writers and papers in South Florida because they all feuded with him one time or another. It was partly Robbie's fault; he committed some serious mistakes, such as writing letters to the editors and publishers in an attempt to get certain writers fired.

"The trouble with newspapers," Robbie once told me, "is simple. It's like plucking the feathers from a chicken. Unfortunately, you can't put the feathers back on if you are wrong."

Robbie was a very intelligent man, but once he got plucking, he just couldn't stop himself. It's not like he could have won these battles anyway.

The *Miami Herald* was Robbie's main media adversary. He told me how, in 1971, when the team unexpectedly hosted the conference championship game, the *Herald* criticized the way the Dolphins handled the distribution of tickets for the public. They felt the rank-and-file fans were being squeezed out.

The public never learned, however, that while the paper was bashing Robbie and pretending to be on the side of the little guy, there was no hesitation on the part of the *Herald's* ownership and management to call him for comps! They sent their errand boys over to the team offices, entered a side door and exited with tickets. It was extortion, but Robbie admitted that didn't have a choice but to pay up or else the paper would have kept pounding him.

There was one time during the year I worked for him that Robbie pretty much plucked every single feather off the *Herald*. Maybe this time the paper deserved it. I don't remember exactly what it was about, but it was a stupid skirmish that almost escalated into a war. I used my friendship with Ed Pope to resolve the situation.

I don't think Robbie ever got the credit he deserved for the laying the foundation for the Dolphins' dynasty of the early Seventies. He was the one, after all, who took a giant gamble on starting a team in Miami. If anybody complained about Robbie in his presence, Callahan would get very defensive. He would wag his pointer finger and say, "no Robbie, no Dolphins."

Callahan was right. The odds were stacked against Robbie and his partners, one of which was the actor Danny Thomas, from the beginning.

"There was a feeling in pro football that the sport couldn't succeed in the tropics," Robbie told me. "Many felt that only industrial cities with a blue-collar fan base could sustain a team."

Miami definitely wasn't like Detroit, Green Bay, Pittsburgh, or Philadelphia. The city's economy was based on three things: tourism, the airlines, and hookers – and not necessarily in that order.

Naysayers pointed to the failure of the Miami Seahawks of the All-America Football Conference in 1946 as further evidence. The city's first professional football team was hampered from the beginning by having the upstart league's least wealthy owner, poor attendance and tropical rainstorms that regularly washed out Burdine Stadium.

Football folks found South Floridians a problematic bunch, too. The locals, Robbie said, were "suspicious of new business ventures because every huckster on this earth has at some time or other passed through Miami to attempt to sell his scheme."

It's a town, in my experience, that shows little loyalty towards anybody or anything since everybody who lives there is a transplant. Out of our entire front office and promotions staff, only one of us, a secretary, grew up in Miami. Everybody was from somewhere else.

And I don't just mean from the north or from somewhere else in the U.S. Dade County was approximately fifty percent Spanish-speaking. That number is probably much higher now. Miami had a lot of Cubans and people from South America. Nobody had any idea how they were going to take to pro football or the things that made pro football popular, gambling and physical violence.

People may find this hard to believe because of how ritzy the area is now, but at the time, the average income of a Miami season ticket holder was the lowest in the entire league. There was a die-hard Dolphins fan who worked at the gas station near my apartment who I gave my comps to. He could not have afforded to go to the games otherwise. I used to stop in and buy a Tab on my way home from work and the smile on his face always cheered me up after another long day of dealing with Shula.

Against these long odds, Robbie won. Well, Shula coached the team, so technically he won, but you get what I'm saying. I'm not trying to take any credit away from Shula. He was the head coach, so he rightfully deserves a lot of credit for Miami's success. Although I don't consider him the all-time best coach in NFL history, as the league's all-time winningest coach he has no peer in terms of longevity and consistency.

Outside of Paul Brown and maybe Chuck Noll, no coach is more deserving of a gold jacket and a bust in Canton than Shula.

It's pure speculation to wonder if Miami might have eventually won a Super Bowl without Shula, but there is no arguing that Shula is the reason why they won so soon and so consistently. Without him they might have struggled, as most expansion teams typically do, for more than just a handful of seasons.

After Robbie heard George Wilson, the former Northwestern and Chicago Bears star he had hired to be the franchise's first head coach, deliver his first pre-game pep talk, he was fearful it would take decades to build a championship ball club.

"As our first pre-season game in old Balboa Stadium in San Diego was about to begin in early August 1965, George gathered the team in the locker room and said to them, 'the first thing that happens when you go out on the field is that the referee flips a coin to determine who kicks off and who receives. If you receive, be sure to recover the fumble. If you kick off, be sure to try to block the try for extra point.'"

Before Shula arrived, training camp for the Dolphins failed to measure up, both in terms of building toughness and team unity, against the league's other teams. In Shula's first year, everything changed. His first order of business was to tear down and then completely rebuild the team's culture.

Everything Wilson did was more divisive than helpful. Callahan said that Wilson would tell the veterans to take the rookies out the night before practice and get them drunk. Then the next day he would work the rookies to death and send the veterans over to the swimming pool.

Csonka told me that he used to find garbage in his bed and the veterans would send him to a place 15 miles away to get hamburgers. Good-natured hazing is one thing, but all Wilson did was inspire the rookies to hate the veterans and vice-versa.

Shula unified the team by getting them to hate him instead of each other. The practices at his first camp were brutal and, despite the fact that there were no lights yet installed at the practice fields, typically continued beyond dusk. When Braucher asked Shula if he was going to start handing out coal miner's lamps to the media, the players were too exhausted and too shell-shocked to laugh.

After one practice, Csonka bumped into Braucher.

"You and your damn Shula," he said, lamenting Braucher's role in bringing Shula to Miami.

"No more falling off bar stools at two in the morning for you guys," Braucher laughed.

"Shula doesn't need a curfew," yelled Zonk as he hobbled away toward an ice bath. "Nobody can move."

Shula, however, was not building a team of tough guys. He specifically designed the practices to be hell so that the games would seem easy by comparison. His only demand of the players on Sundays was for them to think.

"The Dolphins, you'll see," Hubert Mizell told me not long after I joined the team, "play with brains."

I believe that was part of the Dolphins' appeal, how they got popular. It wasn't just that they won, it was how they won, their style of play. The accent was on smartness and quickness, not brute strength. It made sense. Miami wasn't Chicago or Cleveland, so why try to play like a rust belt team? I think Shula purposely built a unique team for a unique town. It gave Miami fans their own identity, too. It was a smart marketing move.

Strict discipline was another of Shula's hallmarks. I had lunch with Jim Mandich one day after I first joined the team and he explained what it was like to play for Shula.

"Any player who piles on or hits somebody out of bounds better hide from Coach Shula like you're doing," Mandich laughed. "Outside of fumbles, especially deep in our own territory, there's nothing he hates more than a penalty for a cheap shot."

It's been rumored in some circles that Miami possessed another latent appeal, and this is something that has never been discussed in print, at least to the best of my knowledge. It wasn't something I considered until the day I took a long-distance call from a Miami fan in Eugene, Oregon who wanted to purchase a 1974 media guide.

"You live all the way out in Oregon and root for the Dolphins," I said. "Is it because we win?"

"Oh, that's part of it," he replied. "The other reason is that you're the only white team in pro football."

I wasn't expecting that answer. Furthermore, his assertion didn't seem right from a personnel perspective. I thought our roster had the same racial composition, more or less, as any other team in the league.

After I hung up, I checked the starting lineup. We had one black player on defense. There were five on offense. I recounted the conversation to Braucher.

"Is it an accident that we don't have that many blacks?" I asked.

"Look," Braucher said, "Shula doesn't do anything by accident. But the idea that Shula or anybody else associated with the Dolphins is racist is absolutely ridiculous."

Our draft the following spring provided evidence contrary to that fan's claim. Our first three picks were black and, outside of two linebackers, nearly all of the players we selected in the first ten rounds were black as well. We ended up trading some of them, but I doubt any team run by racists would waste valuable time evaluating and drafting black players.

There was some talk, privately, among the writers, that racial problems on the '74 team were partly responsible for the Dolphins failing to make it to their fourth consecutive Super Bowl. I didn't and I still don't subscribe to that theory.

Now there were some grumblings, I will attest to that. In the diary I kept that season I noted that the first signs of a "black and white problem" started on October 11. This was the week between the Monday night win over the Jets and our loss to Washington. The way I remember it, some of the white players felt that Shula didn't yell at the black players. He only chewed out the white guys. They told me that Marv Fleming worked hard but accused Mercury Morris and Marlin Briscoe of "loafing" in practice. Some were resentful that Paul Warfield didn't even show up for the Jets game.

However, as one white player, whose name I'll keep confidential, told me, "every team in the league has this problem. Pittsburgh, we hear, is a jungle."

I don't doubt that there was in-fighting in the ranks and maybe some animosity had developed between certain players, but that happens in any competitive situation involving egos, prestige, and money. It's not a realistic excuse, though. It's not like the bottom fell out of the season. After the Washington loss, we won eight of our next nine.

Personally, I attributed the loss to Oakland in the divisional game not to racial tensions or any kind of chemistry issues, but the fact it's damn near impossible to get to, much less win three straight Super Bowls. I'm not sure that any team will ever accomplish the latter feat.

As for Pittsburgh, the Steelers went on to win the franchise's first Super Bowl that year, so what's that tell you? You take those rumors with a grain of salt. It's a cop out when teams, coaches and players use excuses, whether we're talking about bad calls, allegations of cheating or even race problems to cover up the fact that they just couldn't get the job done.

I can appreciate Shula's greatness as a coach. My dislike for him is not so much rooted in the way he treated me, but the way he treated Robbie. Shula was so intense and at times so insufferable that the feud between the two men, as Callahan observed, "took the fun out of it for Robbie."

By "it," Callahan meant owning a team, winning Super Bowls, and probably sometimes even life itself. I know there are two sides to every story, and I don't want to paint Robbie as a perennial victim, but he did make Shula a rich man and gave him a lot of power. In any relationship between two people of such stature, there's got to be give and take. I felt Robbie did most of the giving and Shula most of the taking.

I also felt it was ridiculously unfair that Robbie was forced fight on the homefront, inside his own organization, while at the same time being constantly under attack from other owners, other leagues, the team's own fans, politicians and at times what seemed like all of South Florida.

Braucher once observed that "the owners have sacrificed every business principle they know in their determination to wear a Super Bowl ring at the annual owners' meeting."

I agreed with him for the most part, but not all owners were like that. Robbie wasn't in it to make money. Not that he wanted to throw money away, but he wasn't as cheap as people have said. Robbie really wasn't in it just to win, either. He wanted to win, but he wasn't desperate to win.

It was sometime in the early Seventies that Joe Gordon, the longtime Steelers' PR man, told me that he was certain that if Art Rooney, Sr. could "make a deal with the man upstairs for a Super Bowl, he would check out."

I'm glad the Chief never made the deal since he would have missed out on three more. Robbie didn't want anything that bad. He had a life and goals outside of business and football which were increasingly related to his philanthropy.

The more I learned from the other PR guys as well as friends who worked in several capacities for the other teams and for the league, the more I realized that the majority of the owners cared only about winning and money. A handful enjoyed the clout that came with ownership, the opportunity to wield power and influence, more than anything else.

To me, the NFL appeared to be a vast ocean inhabited by all kinds of strange creatures. It's too much of a stretch to say Robbie was a friendly, well-meaning dolphin – although highly intelligent, he was too cold-blooded and calculating as a businessman – but he was swimming against the current and, often times, with a bunch of sharks.

Some owners were merely meddlesome, others made demands that were downright dictatorial. Yet others still issued orders and commands to former employees as if they were indentured servants for life.

We'll start with the story of the wife of one of the Dolphins' owners, one of the minority partners, who thought the picture of her husband in the game program failed to show his best features. She supplied another photograph and instructed us that it be used in the future. When placed side by side, neither Callahan nor myself could tell the difference between the two photos.

Ernie Accorsi went to work for the NFL after he left the Colts. At one league meeting in Minneapolis, Accorsi spotted Georgia Rosenbloom, the wife of former Colts owner and at the time Rams owner Carroll Rosenbloom, across the room. Accorsi could tell she forgot his name and saw her asking somebody for it before making her way over to him. He sensed she was going to ask for a favor, probably something for her young son, Dale.

"Oh, Ernie," she said, "it's so good to see you again. I need some help. You've gotta find a skating rink for Chipper."

"No," replied Accorsi, turning to walk away, "I don't."

I remember the time the *Chicago Tribune*, a paper which prided itself on its guts and its reputation in standing up to corrupt Chicago politicians, caved to the incessant demands of George Halas and removed a writer from the Bears beat.

For a long time, Art Modell was the most vicious and vindictive man in the NFL. At his best, he just complained about everything. He read every single line of the league's releases and bitched if there wasn't anything in there about the Browns.

At his worst, he could be like Paul Brown, the way he harbored vendettas. He was rumored to have been responsible for *CBS* taking Jim Morse, who captained Notre Dame's 1956 team, off the network's NFL broadcasts. At the time, Morse moonlighted as a sports agent. The way I heard the story, Modell got upset when one of Morse's clients, I think it was Dave Costa, signed with the Chargers instead of Cleveland after leaving Denver. Modell reportedly said that Morse wouldn't broadcast any more NFL games. He didn't.

Modell also reportedly spied on Forrest Gregg and his coaching staff when

Gregg coached the Browns. Someone found a spy in the broom closet in the locker-room while Gregg was addressing the team after a loss to Los Angeles.

"If you ever say anything to anybody about what went on in Cleveland," Modell allegedly threatened Gregg, "you will never get another job in the NFL."

That is called blacklisting, which is against league rules, but Robbie thought Rozelle always looked the other way for Modell. People said Modell went around bad-mouthing Gregg when he took the Cincinnati job. The Bengals complained to Rozelle about the double-standard, but nothing came of it.

I've said many times that the three things that made the National Football League so successful were Pete Rozelle, television, and gambling. Rozelle was a perfect example of what a man with insight, leadership and PR skills can do for a corporation or professional league.

"Bert Bell gave the NFL guts," Ernie Accorsi once said. "And Pete Rozelle gave it class."

And yet today, some people, even in the league office, put the knock on Rozelle. It's an absolute disgrace. Yet Rozelle wasn't perfect. In my opinion, the favoritism he exhibited toward certain teams and owners is a detriment to his legacy.

It was Robbie who pointed this out to me. He said he understood he was an outsider. He wasn't a jock, a former player or coach, and he wasn't fabulously wealthy.

"I owned no oil wells, no hotel chains, had no financial inheritance," Robbie said. "They probably talked amongst themselves, 'what is a Minneapolis lawyer doing in professional football as an owner with management control?'"

Robbie was at times difficult to deal with, so I'm sure that in addition to these things Robbie's reputation as a financial whiz and his role as the vanguard of the "nouveau riche" might have rubbed some of the other owners the wrong way. But being not liked is different than being discriminated against.

For years, until he died probably, Robbie felt that Rozelle was secretly very partial to three franchises: Modell's Browns, Lamar Hunt's Chiefs, and the Dallas Cowboys when Tex Schramm was running the show. He told me he thought Rozelle went out of his way to help Atlanta, Denver, and Wellington Mara's Giants as well. Robbie called those six teams the "palace guard."

I didn't put a lot of stock into Robbie's claims until a phone conversation we had about a year after I left the Dolphins, when the NFL announced the addition of two expansion teams in Tampa Bay and Seattle.

"Mark my words, Beano," Robbie said, "one of three teams, Cleveland, Kansas City or Dallas, will get to play the expansion teams on the road in the first two years."

Robbie was right; the Browns played in Tampa in 1976 and in Seattle in 1977.

Robbie had been around long enough to know that people play favorites. He accepted it as part and parcel of doing business in this world. But in his mind, favoritism wasn't a victimless crime.

"If Rozelle wanted to help some people, that didn't bother me," Robbie said, "but when you do favors for certain owners, other owners get the short-end of the deal."

Yet Robbie never held a grudge. He wholeheartedly agreed with my prediction that Rozelle would one day be considered the greatest commissioner in pro sports.

Carroll Rosenbloom was not exactly a favorite of Rozelle's, but unlike Robbie he was a favorite of the press. This was because Rosenbloom knew the value of PR better than any owner in the league. Rosenbloom wined and dined members of the media and through that lavish treatment secured the loyalty of the press.

Rosenbloom also had a reputation of being generous with his players and they spread the word far and wide to keep the gravy train going. Unbeknownst to the press and the public, Rosenbloom's generosity did not extend to everybody, especially the other members of his organization.

When the Colts won Super Bowl V, Accorsi received a bonus of $750. Compare that to Robbie, who gave Charlie Callahan a bonus of $11,000 when the Dolphins won Super Bowl VII. Thanks to the press, Rosenbloom was one of America's most beloved, generous owners and Robbie's reputation as a cheapskate persisted.

It's my opinion you can trace the roots of the Robbie-Rosenbloom feud to two extremely important events. The first and more well-known of the two took place on January 12, 1969, when Shula lost to the underdog Jets in Super Bowl III, the game made famous by Joe Namath's prediction. "I ruined Carroll's party," Shula would say.

The most over-the-top comparison regarding a loss in sports when was when Rosenbloom, referring to that game, reportedly said to family friend Ted Kennedy, "I know how you felt when your brother was shot."

That's an unbelievable line. But Rosenbloom never got over that game. He never forgave Shula for it and that was a mistake. Their relationship deteriorated to a point that it became irreparable.

The second was when Bear Bryant turned down the Dolphins' job, forcing Robbie to look for another coach. Since speaking directly with Shula would have violated the league's tampering rules, Robbie enlisted Braucher to make contact. Shula, on the suggestion of his fellow John Carroll University alum and friend, decided it was the perfect time to get away from Rosenbloom, who he couldn't stand, and relocate to Miami.

Rosenbloom compounded his mistake by raising hell when it became apparent that Shula was as good as gone. See, prior to that, most of Baltimore's players and the majority of the media, not to mention Rosenbloom himself, thought Shula was an ordinary coach.

All the noise Rosenbloom made about tampering cost the Dolphins a first-round draft pick, but I'm convinced that it also effectively elevated the public's perception of Shula as an elite coach before he had really ever done anything. Rosenbloom's behavior increased the value of an asset that was basically already out the door, a bizarre blunder by an otherwise brilliant businessman.

In addition to being PR savvy, Rosenbloom was one of the few owners who understood the business aspect of football as well. I'll give you an example. At the end of

Alan Ameche's career, Weeb Ewbank cut Ameche right before the Colts were scheduled to play an exhibition in Chicago. Since road teams received a share of the gate, Rosenbloom hurriedly countermanded the coach's order before the news was released to the public.

"Half of Wisconsin is coming to this game!" Rosenbloom yelled. Sure enough, Soldier Field was filled with Badgers fans and on the first play from scrimmage the former Wisconsin star ran for a long touchdown.

Rosenbloom was right that time, but dead wrong on Shula and that caused him no small amount of mental anguish for the rest of his life. After Shula proceeded to build the Dolphins into powerhouse, it made him so angry he had to find somebody, anybody, to blame other than himself. That's where Robbie came in.

The Colts won the first post-merger Super Bowl, but I think Rosenbloom didn't realize the extent to which he had fucked up until Miami beat Baltimore in the second-ever AFC championship game in '71. Everybody thought that was going to be a close game. I remember Vegas had the game as a pick. Shula and the Dolphins won, 21-0.

Everything the Dolphins did after that drove Rosenbloom nuts. He fixated on Robbie for the rest of the decade. It started with petty chickenshit.

Early in Shula's tenure in Miami he went to Robbie to see about giving each member of the team a Christmas gift. "We can't," Robbie said. "It's a league rule."

They finally figured out a way to circumvent the rule book - apparently gifting food, under the heading of team dinners and functions, was okay - by giving each player at turkey. Even so, Rosenbloom found out and filed an official complaint with the commissioner's office.

It developed into a never-ending succession of personal attacks. Anytime Rosenbloom could say something bad about Robbie, he did. To the press and in private conversations. He habitually referred to Robbie as "that Lebanese cocksucker." It was behavior unbecoming of a gentleman or an NFL owner.

Robbie tried to ignore Rosenbloom, but Rosenbloom refused to back off. Miami's preseason game at Los Angeles my first year, that was just one of Rozelle's many attempts to mediate the feud. The game was originally scheduled to be played in Miami, but Robbie agreed to move it to Los Angeles after Rozelle extracted from Rosenbloom a promise that he would quit badmouthing Robbie. It didn't work. As far as I know, the two men never patched things up. The feud finally ended when Rosenbloom drowned in '79.

Robbie's altruism and his ability to turn the proverbial cheek were just some of the reasons why I admired him. Another reason why I generally took his side over Shula's was because I never saw him interfere with the team's actual football operations. By this, he never tried to call plays, sit in on staff meetings, or stalk the sidelines like some other owners. I felt Shula, after having escaped from Baltimore and his own feud with Rosenbloom, should have been more appreciative of Robbie's style of ownership.

Robbie had to be the most hands-off team owner in the entire league, seconded only by Art Rooney, Sr. I think the most successful owners, even those with playing and coaching backgrounds, are those who get out of the way of their head coaches and let them do their job.

Now Mr. Rooney wasn't always so hands-off. He liked to run the show. Sometimes, he made the right calls. Other times he didn't. A good example of the first was when one of the Steelerettes – yes, the Steelers once had cheerleaders, this was in the Sixties – got knocked up by a player and Mr. Rooney disbanded the squad. A serious Catholic in a traditional town, he didn't want the bad press that he thought would accompany the news if it ever got out.

As for the second, his short-lived experiment with play calling is one of my favorite Chief stories. It's sometime in the 1950s. Mr. Rooney had grown so tired of coach Walt Kiesling's super conservative play calling – Kiesling famously opened Pittsburgh's first offensive series of every game with a bland, up-the-middle run by fullback Fran Rogel – that he ordered the coach to launch a long pass at the start of one game.

Sure enough, quarterback Jim Finks threw a bomb to Jack McClairen, who took it all the way into the opponent's endzone. The crowd at Forbes Field was stunned – a long pass on first down! Rooney, watching from his perch high up in the pressbox, was ecstatic. And then he saw the flag. Offsides, Pittsburgh. After the game, Rooney learned that the lineman had jumped on purpose.

"If that pass play works," Kiesling had grunted to his charge, "(Rooney) will be down here every week giving us plays."

The penalty was a message from head coach to team owner that certain boundaries needed to be respected. Message received. "A philosophical man," Myron Cope later wrote in *Sports Illustrated*, "the Chief never again makes the attempt."

I've often wondered if that seminal event wasn't the turning point for the Steelers' fortunes. After so many years of losing brought about by bad personnel and business decisions, Mr. Rooney began ceding more and more control to his son, Dan.

By the end of the 1960s, Dan had hired Noll and had laid the groundwork, personnel-wise, for four Super Bowl victories. The formula, which led to two more Super Bowls, is simple: let the coach coach. The Steelers have had only three coaches in the last forty years, so it's obvious that the formula works. Art Rooney II is a smart man like his father and grandfather, so he won't fool with that formula.

I admired Joe Robbie for many of the same reasons that I admired Mr. Rooney, including the fact that both men, unlike many owners who inherited their money (and in some cases their teams, too) were self-made.

The Chief was the son of a saloon keeper and a gambler. Robbie's was a real rags-to-riches success story. He dropped out of high school and joined the Civilian Conservation Corps to support his family. He worked for every dollar he ever made. Maybe he was tough to bargain with, but most people who have worked hard for their money are. It's a lot easier to hand over somebody's else money than it is your own.

I believe that Robbie received a raw deal not just because of his prickly relationship with the press, but because he succeeded where so many others couldn't have and that bothered a lot of people. I'm not just talking about putting a team in Miami. His stadium was financed entirely with private money. He proved many of the other owners, plus the press and politicians who said it couldn't be done, wrong. He showed that it was possible to build a stadium without shaking down the taxpayers and these people didn't appreciate Robbie enlightening everyone to an alternative way of conducting business.

I feel that Robbie might have been one of the most pro-fan owners in the NFL, but he was consistently dragged by the press and the politicians who tried to paint him as the exact opposite. Let's start with the 1974 offseason. Robbie barely had time to celebrate the victory in Super Bowl VIII.

"Our team was held hostage and we were required to re-purchase our players in the open market," he explained. "The WFL seemed intent on dividing up our roster as part of their scheme to get underway."

I recalled that Fran Monaco, the owner of the WFL's Jacksonville Sharks, held daily pressers to report the progress of his negotiations with a dozen or so Dolphins.

Robbie provided me with a copy of the report distributed to the partners. The warning was dire: "as a result of our multiplied payroll, the Miami Dolphins will realize less than half the net earnings in fiscal 1974 than were attained in fiscal 1972 and 1973. ...with the Orange Bowl stadium already sold to capacity, and the television revenue fixed for the next several years, we see no prospect within the foreseeable future of recovering the increased payroll costs or reaching the same earnings we achieved in the past two years."

"Where else in the enchanting world of industry, commerce or business can you produce the best product in all competition, continue to sell at the same volume, and suffer earnings reduced to less than half of what they were the previous year?" Robbie asked, rhetorically. "We are not profiting from success. We are paying for it."

Now, faced with this situation, what do you think most owners would have done? They would have fucked over the fans, of course. Not Robbie. His people had determined that even a substantial increase in ticket prices would not have restored the team to its 1972-73 earnings levels so he wouldn't even consider that option.

"I personally had three choices," Robbie later explained. "I could sell the franchise at its peak of success, settle for competitive mediocrity, or bite the bullet to preserve the championship nucleus and settle for reduced earnings. The first two were really not choices at all. Not after how much the fans had done for us."

Some people may find this statement laughable, but the fans were always foremost in Robbie's thoughts. In September 1974, Robbie did his own survey of Miami season ticket holders and discovered that the fans preferred one o'clock games to four o'clock games by a two to one margin.

"Parents were concerned about coming home, preparing late dinners and getting the kids ready for school the next day," Robbie told me. He communicated that information to the league and while I don't think the league really cared, I commended him for soliciting feedback from the fans and trying to give them a voice.

I also specifically remember when Robbie got a couple of letters from Congressman Skip Bafalis protesting the blackout policy in November of '74. I wasn't with the team when the city of Miami tried quadrupling the team's rent at the Orange Bowl in 1976, but I'm willing to bet a considerable amount of money that Robbie didn't get any letters of support from Bafalis or any other politician that time.

It's unfortunate, for the NFL, for the fans and for the game of football itself, that there aren't more owners like Joe Robbie, Art Rooney, Sr., or Tim Mara, the founding owner of the New York Football Giants and another self-made man from humble origins.

Now, more than ever, that kind of foundational leadership is needed. The NFL has strayed from its working man roots in recent years and I think that's going to hurt the league in the long run.

At one time, the pro teams were the alma maters of the working class. Most pro players were honest, rough-and-tumble characters who worked other jobs in the offseason. Proud, patriotic, hard-working blue-collar fans could identify with them. Not just identify with them, but more often than not you could have a drink with them at the local bar. Today, if you're working in a factory or on a construction site how do you identify with a wide receiver making $10 million and holding out for $12 million?

In the old days, the biggest off-field stories were the carousing exploits of players like Bobby Layne, Paul Hornung, Joe Namath, Larry Csonka and Jim Kiick. They seemed to be regular guys who liked to have a good time. Their behavior endeared the league and its players to the fans more than anything else.

Today, the players who get the most attention are the loudmouths and the lawbreakers. It seems as though every offseason is filled with stories of players being arrested for beating their wives or girlfriends, for violent crimes, or for crimes relating to drugs. When the NFL starts talking about family values, the family I think of is the Manson family.

How many families can even afford tickets today? To get season tickets, you have to take out a second mortgage for personal seat licenses. Super Bowl tickets now cost upwards of $1000 a piece face value, and that's if you can get them for face. Most of the loyal, long-time fans are shut out of the system and have to pay big bucks on the secondary market to scalpers.

And if the NFL cares so much about the fans, why the primetime playoff games in northern cities in January when it's ten below zero? Then there's the debauchery going on in the parking lots, the drinking and fighting that would make Nero blush.

The NFL could really use a few more Don Shulas, too. I'm being serious when I say that. While we had our differences, a good many of them, you'll never get me to say that Shula was a bad person. I believe he was a good human being.

When he retired, he was probably the last coach to have done a hitch in the service. He was probably the NFL's last working-class coach. Even as other, less accomplished teams built expensive headquarters and practice facilities, he never complained about the Dolphins' aging digs, which were admittedly some of the worst in the league. He went to work out there every day with a lunch pail mentality.

And you may not have liked his candor or brusque manner at times, but his unfiltered honesty is sorely missing from the NFL's coaching ranks today. I feel too many coaches are scared to be anything but a mouthpiece for the owner or the commissioner. They all tow the company line.

Another thing I admired Shula for was his standing policy that he would never announce to the press the name of a player that had been cut or traded until he personally talked to the player. I thought that was a very stand-up thing to do.

Of course, then he would turn around and do or say something that would reveal how petty he could be. Like when Nick Buoniconti decided to play in the WFL in 1975, he said Nick "gave up immortality in a Dolphin uniform for a few more bucks." Immortality! Buoniconti was the anchor of the "No-Name Defense." Buoniconti secured his immortality.

It was rich coming from a guy who closely monitored what every other coach made or got. I remember the time Shula and George Allen did some kind of promotional event and Shula found out that Allen got a Bulova watch and he didn't. He made a big stink with the organizers until he got a watch, too.

The one thing I've never waffled on was Shula's coaching ability. My line on Shula was that he was so good, he would even win in the Big 8! Back in the early 1970s, the Big 8 was the most competitive conference in college football. Every year, the league had at least two, sometimes three teams finish in the top ten in the final polls. In 1971, three Big 8 teams finished 1st, 2nd, and 3rd (Nebraska, Oklahoma, and Colorado, respectively) in the final AP poll. That line got back to Shula and I don't think he appreciated it. Maybe he didn't like being lumped in with college coaches. But I intended it as a compliment.

I once told Joe Paterno that the smartest decision he ever made was not taking the Patriots job when it was offered to him. He would have had the Boston media to deal with and he would have had to play Miami and coach against Shula twice a year.

There is no question that Shula is one of pro football's all-time greatest coaches. Now when people try to argue that he's the all-time best, I'll give them all-time wins, but I point out that while Shula did win two Super Bowls, he lost four and he had John Unitas in Baltimore, Bob Griese and Dan Marino. Some coaches go their entire careers without having one decent quarterback, let alone three Hall of Famers.

When I left, I wrote a letter to Shula to get some things off my chest. In it, I was truthful when I said I hoped he'd win the next three Super Bowls, but I knew it wasn't going to happen. I told Hank Goldberg that Shula will never win another Super Bowl because he has too much control. And I was right. Robbie gave him command of the whole ship. If you look at Shula's draft choices through the years, though there were exceptions like Marino, most never worked out. Bad trades and front office turmoil didn't help.

Although Braucher was right and Shula did somewhat come around, the bad days outnumbered the good by a large margin. Our distinct personalities made us incompatible. We fought over the smallest things, the same as John Michelosen and I did.

In one of my earliest reports, I told Robbie that the Dolphins received too much offseason press. I felt it was an oversaturation of coverage and feared the public would get fatigued over football news. Of course, Shula disagreed with me. He wanted the Dolphins, and maybe himself, to be in the news year-round. Robbie agreed with me and so we scaled back what we did with the media in the offseason. That pissed Shula off.

Another example was when we were putting together the media guide for the 1975 season, Bobby Beathard asked us to include the names of the scouts. Both Callahan and I assured Beathard that it would be done. Evidently, this seemingly trivial detail wasn't brought to Shula's attention for him to sign off on and he went and bitched to Robbie.

In addition to dealing with Shula, I never felt at home in Miami. It never seemed like football season down there. Every day in Miami is June 10. Unlike my last job, I think there were actually a few people who were sad to see me leave. There were only three of them, Joe Robbie, Charlie Callahan and the guy at the gas station who got my comps, but that was three more than in St. Petersburg.

In the end, it was the competitiveness of Shula, the competitiveness of the NFL in general, that ruined the job for me. Although I didn't officially leave until June of 1975, I had mentally checked out of the job right around the time of the Dolphins' last-second loss to Oakland in the famous "Sea of Hands" divisional game in late December.

We secured the division in week 10 with a win over Buffalo and finished 11-3. I felt as though I had been holding my breath the entire season, so I was relieved that we had secured a spot in the playoffs. I had exhaled too soon.

The week leading up to the Oakland game was like nothing I had ever seen doing PR in college. The atmosphere in both the administrative offices and over at the coaches' offices was stifling. Everybody was on edge. It wasn't a game. It was a war.

While the writers were painting it as a battle of the Raiders' brawn versus the Dolphins' brains, in reality was Shula's autocratic approach versus Al Davis's scheming and maneuvering. I remember the league sent somebody out to Oakland to make sure the field wasn't being watered to slow down our players. More than anything else it was a war of nerves and by the time kickoff rolled around, mine were totally shot.

We lost in excruciating fashion, but I didn't feel the slightest bit bad. Now if Pitt had lost to Penn State that way, I probably would have committed suicide.

I wasn't as down as everybody else, so I took a commercial flight from Oakland to Miami that had a long layover in Houston instead of going back on the team plane. I didn't want to have to mope around and pretend like the world had ended. Plus, I wasn't taking any chances of Shula blaming me for the defeat.

To this day, I'm afraid that I'll be remembered in Miami as the guy who worked for the Dolphins when they failed to reach the Super Bowl. That I cursed the team. Coaches are incredibly superstitious. I'm certain that somewhere, in the back of his mind, Shula is probably convinced that Beano Cook was the reason why the team didn't win three consecutive Super Bowl rings.

I'm certain that Shula is the reason I didn't try to make a go of it in Miami. It had become obvious that Shula seemed intent on making my life miserable. That's why I decided to quit the Dolphins. I have no regrets. The day I left the office for the last time, I felt as relieved as the guy, bitten by a mad dog, who had just received his last rabies shot.

I just wasn't cut out for pro football. Unlike the coaches, I couldn't treat it like life and death. Due to my experiences at Pitt and *ABC* I thought I knew how bad coaches were going into the job, but nothing could have prepared me for what I found in the pros.

I've never met anybody in any other line of work that is more obsessed with their profession or more dedicated to the relentless pursuit of power and success than a professional head football coach. Not politicians. Not network presidents. It's too bad the people who run the oil companies aren't as competitive as NFL coaches. Gas would be a dime a gallon.

Coaches seem to suffer from a strange single-mindedness that borders on psychosis. They are so ruthless in their pursuit of victory that the end always justifies the means. That, to me, was the only reasonable explanation for Shula's strange behavior, why George Allen had the grounds crew open the door to the stadium tunnel when a Redskins' opponent was attempting a field goal (think wind currents) and why Hank Stram employed a fake photographer to wander around the bench of visiting teams and gather information.

I've never come across another group of people who voluntarily shun their families, friends and contact with the outside world for such long periods and are so happily willing to bend the rules of engagement, blow up any barriers, and torpedo any target that gets in the way of winning.

For the longest time, I couldn't quite come up with the professional parallel I was looking for. Someone else, however, had figured it out.

Some years later, I was having a memorable conversation with the late, great George Young, the long-time league executive and architect of two Super Bowl victories with the Giants, when the subject of coaches came up. Young, who had worked as director of player personnel for the Dolphins for a few years in the late Seventies, knew all about Shula. He had plenty of experience with other coaches, too.

Young would utter many memorable lines – not all of which are repeatable – over the years, but one in particular is entirely appropriate to share with you. When I told him about my experiences with Shula and shared some of my observations about the kind of men who inhabited the coaching profession, Young laughed and, while nodding his head up and down in agreement, said something I'll never forget.

"They're nothing," Young said, "but U-boat commanders."

Kiski graduation photo, 1949.

University of Pittsburgh graduation photo, 1954.

Private Beano Cook, U.S. Army, circa 1955.

With best friend, John O'Connor (left, in uniform), circa 1955.

Clowning it up with West Virginia sportswriter Mickey Furfari (back middle), circa 1950s.

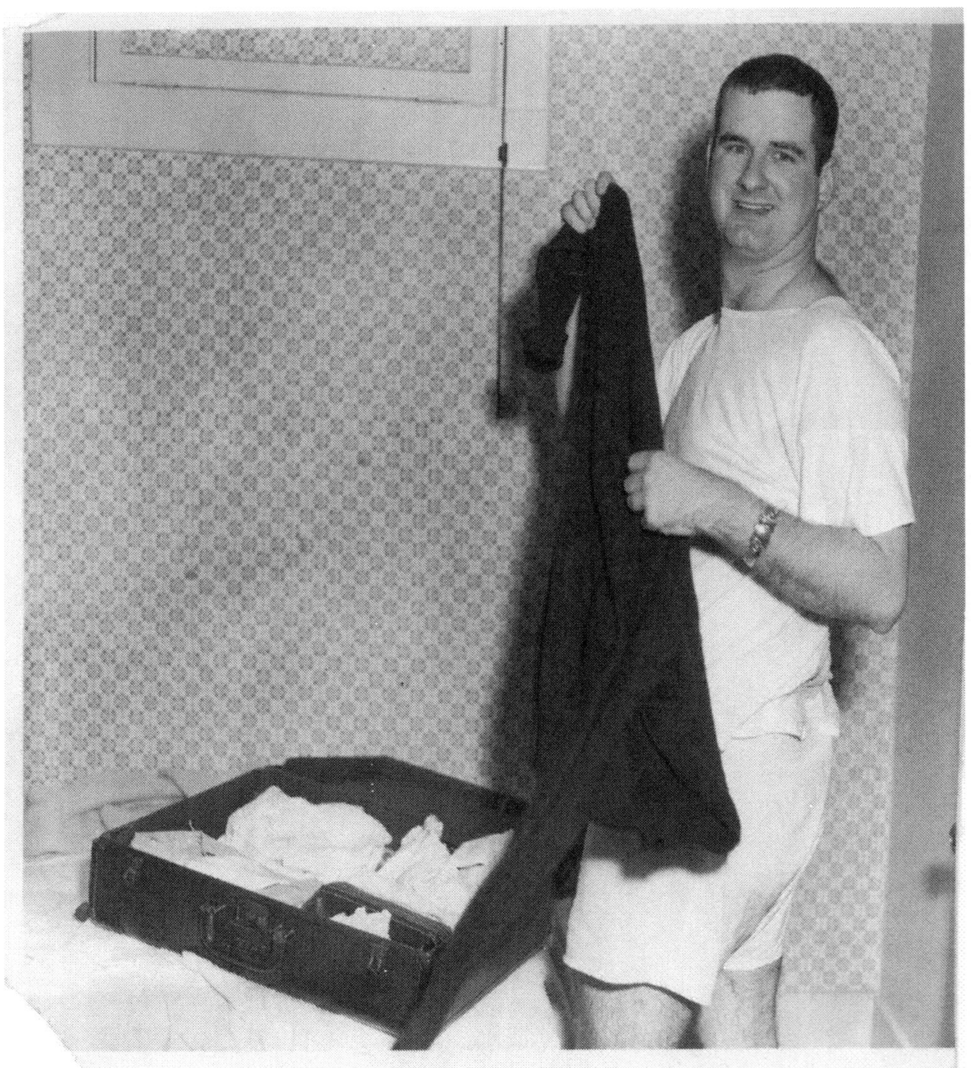

Traveling on the road with the Pitt football team, circa 1956-57. The photographer? Beano's road roommate, legendary writer and future Pittsburgh Steelers' color commentator, Myron Cope.

At Pitt fall football camp, Meadville, Pennsylvania, circa 1950s-1960s.

At Pitt football practice with Mike Ditka (89, left) and Larry Vignali (62, right), circa late 1950s-early 1960s.

On the phone inside the pressbox at Pitt Stadium, circa 1950s-1960s.

Enjoying a smoke inside the pressbox at Pitt Stadium, circa 1950s-1960s.

Collecting money for the (illegal) total points pool, Pitt Stadium pressbox, circa 1950s-1960s.

Inside the pressbox, Pitt Stadium, circa 1950s-1960s. *"...it was usually a minute or two before kickoff. What came next was one of my favorite moments, one of the real highlights of the job...I'd take my seat, light up a smoke and for a few, fleeting moments, quietly soak it all in: the sea of fedoras and waggling pennants in the stands; the clicking of typewriter keys; the muffled sounds of the marching bands on the other side of the pressbox glass. I'd take a drag and exhale a puff of smoke and a sigh of relief."*

Outside Pitt Stadium, circa 1950s-1960s.

With Captain Thomas Hamilton, athletic director at the University of Pittsburgh, 1949-59.

With Frank Carver, athletic director at the University of Pittsburgh, 1959-68.

With Ethel Kennedy at Yankee Stadium, late 1970.

Group photo of all NFL publicity directors taken at the PR meetings in Tampa, Florida in April 1975 (Beano is wearing a dark polo shirt, upper far left).

At work in his office at *CBS* Sports, circa late 1970s.

With friend Susan Nemeroff (left, wearing glasses) at *CBS* Sports, circa early 1980s.

On set with good friend and the first host of *ESPN's* "College GameDay," Tim Brando, circa late 1980s. (Courtesy of Tim Brando)

With his beloved mother, Mary Kennedy Cook, circa late 1980s-early 1990s.

The authors, John D. Lukacs (left, Notre Dame Class of '99) and Beano, at at Pitt Stadium on Monday, November 15, 1999. This photo was taken two days after the final game played at Pitt Stadium, a 37-27 Pitt victory over Notre Dame. Note the scoreboard displaying the final score of the game. (Photo courtesy Brad Spier, aka. "America's Guest")

CHAPTER 6

Honeymooning at Pitt Stadium.

I don't know where exactly I rank on the list of famous men who never married – probably somewhere behind Isaac Newton and President Buchanan and just ahead of Jack Tripper and Sam Malone – but it's widely known that I'm a lifelong bachelor.

Over the course of that lifetime, which is going on four score and a two-point conversion years ago, I've gotten as close to the altar as Vanderbilt has to an SEC title. Like Vandy, I never tried very hard.

Getting married at an early age made about as much sense to me as awarding the national title in August. In the early days of the Associated Press Poll, from the late 1930s through the 1940s, the first vote wasn't taken until sometime in October. I took the same approach with my love life. Why be in a big hurry to vote some chick number one?

When I was thirty-five, I was working for Roone Arledge and *ABC Sports* and living in New York City, so yes, it was a very good year. I didn't come across many blue-blooded girls of independent means, but being a single guy in the Big Apple with an expense account during the heyday of network television sports was the closest anybody gets to being Sinatra.

Now that I'm in the autumn of the year and looking back on my life, I realize that the older a committed bachelor like myself gets, the more he's like an aging, veteran college football coach who is running out of chances to win a national title. For many reasons, both of us will never wear a ring. One is, we are both too tired to recruit anymore.

A matchmaking service? No, thanks. That's like hiring a search firm to fill a coaching vacancy.

Blind dates? No way. With my luck, I'd be set up with a black widow serial killer, or worse, an alumna of Penn State.

Now I'd consider going on "The Bachelor," but only on the condition that all of the contestants are Southern Cal Song Girls.

For a long-time independent like me, marriage has always been a lot like conference membership – a fascinating, but at the same time frightening proposition. We're all familiar with the vows. In the Big Ten, for example, I think "for better or worse" means that going into any given season, you can expect Ohio State and Michigan to be better than you and Indiana and Northwestern to be worse.

As for "in sickness and in health and in poverty and in wealth," here's some advice I give to my single friends thinking about giving up their independence: the three most expensive things a man can have are a mortgage, a wife, and an ex-wife.

While companionship has its benefits, being married for a long time is a lot like going 7-5 every year, which means the same bowl tie-in, same trip to El Paso or Birmingham. When you're single, you at least have the possibility of ringing in New Year's in Pasadena or New Orleans with a new team from somewhere else in the country.

From my perspective, the institution of marriage is really overrated. Kind of like the 1961 Iowa Hawkeyes. For those of you too young to remember, Iowa was the preseason number one in '61. The Hawkeyes kicked off the season with 22 first place votes in the first poll in late September but had completely fallen out of the rankings by Halloween. Many of my relationships resembled that kind of season.

Still, I'm not a complete pessimist when it comes to romance. I don't hold the view, expressed by one of my army buddies who, having been burned on one too many dates, growled that "the word love was invented by Hallmark for the purpose of moving inventory."

While the word has been cheapened by today's society, love is nevertheless a real phenomenon. It's simply a phenomenon I don't have much experience with.

When I think about it, the only things I've ever truly loved are my parents, hot chocolate chip cookies, the movie "Casablanca," getting points at home, and the greatest sport that's ever existed, college football.

My lifelong love affair with college football started on a Saturday in late November 1940. I was nine years old. My father, a Stanford alum, was pacing around the living room in our home in Pittsburgh and I was sitting at the foot of the radio as we listened to "The Big Game" between Stanford and California.

That radio was a behemoth of a Zenith, one of those giant wooden floor models. There was so much static you'd have thought they were beaming the play-by-play from Bombay or Berlin instead of Berkeley. An undefeated season for Stanford was on the line, so it's no surprise dad was unable to sit still.

My father was quite possibly the biggest Stanford football fan the world has ever known. Forget Romeo and Juliet, or Rick and Ilsa. The greatest love story in history was Mills Cook and the Stanford Indians.

The earliest lesson most boys learn from their old man is "the birds and the bees." Not me. Thanks to Stanford football, I learned about the thrill of victory and the agony of defeat right about the same time I learned to talk, which was several decades before "Wide World of Sports" first aired.

"If Stanford loses," I remarked to my mother in early childhood, "it's not too much fun around here."

I never resolved it in my mind whether dad loved Stanford or my mother more.

"It's a pick," she once told me.

I think part of the ferocity of my father's Stanford fandom was attributable to the fact that as someone born and raised on the West Coast, he felt out of place living out East. I imagine that for him, listening to Stanford play was kind of like an American expat hearing the Star-Spangled Banner while celebrating the Fourth of July in Poland.

It was a reminder of a faraway home. We left San Francisco shortly after I was born and he never returned. Well, technically not while he was alive. After dad died, I scattered some of his ashes in two places, near the Golden Gate Bridge and outside the will-call window at Stanford Stadium, in hopes God had left him one on the fifty.

Another reason was that the school's games were rarely broadcast nationally on the radio, plus it was so hard to get scores back then. My father felt there was a bias in the East against West Coast football and he never relented on the opinion. I can still see him on one of his final fall Saturdays, sitting on the edge of his living room chair waiting impatiently, puffing on cigarette after cigarette, for a Stanford score.

"Colgate 7, Cornell 7," chirped the sportscaster on the television.

"You idiot," my dad snapped. "We already heard that one."

Television caused another problem for dad. As he got up in age, the West Coast schools began playing night games for TV. The games ended late, well past his bedtime. Sometimes so late, the scores were no where to be found in his Sunday paper.

One Sunday morning in November 1973, I called my parents from an airport.

"Do you know who won the Stanford-Southern Cal game?" my mother asked. The tone of her voice was like somebody asking if any room remained on the last boat out of Dunkirk.

"Unfortunately, I do. USC kicked a last-second field goal to win, 27-26."

"I'm not going to say a word," she said. "Well, at least not until after breakfast."

I hated to be the bearer of bad news, and a loss to USC was the worst possible news. Although my father acknowledged that Cal was Stanford's biggest rival, he reserved a special antipathy for Southern Cal.

"USC is never any lower than second place as the most-hated team by any West Coast football fan," he once said to me during a memorable lecture in the late 1940s. I'm pretty sure his views were directly related to the fact that Stanford never managed to beat USC while he was in school on "The Farm."

When I was in my thirties and forties, I didn't have the heart to tell my dad that I had developed a crush on the Trojans. Perhaps you've heard that old saying, "the enemy of my enemy is my friend?" Well, USC cost my nemesis, Notre Dame, quite a few national titles.

Even so, I have very fond memories from my youth of my father and I parading around the house, my dad playing the role of drum major, pumping his arm while singing a parody version of USC's fight song, "Fight On!" Feel free to hum along in your head:

Fight on...for ol' SC!
Our halfbacks are on...sal-a-ry.
Our ends...have all been fired,
They've been no good...since they were hired...

I can't believe more than 70 years have passed since the 1940 season. It is still so vivid in my memory. Frankie Albert, Stanford's quarterback, was running this new-fangled offense called the T-formation. Albert and Hugh Gallerneau were the stars on that team. The media called the players the "Wow Boys," a play on the "Vow Boys," as Stanford's previous great teams were known. It was all so exciting because Stanford was a power again and it reawakened a passion in my father that coincided with my earliest memories of college football. It was a helluva ride and what made it so fun, and so special I now understand, was that my father and I were on that ride together.

The Washington game in early November was essentially for a Rose Bowl berth, so when we got the first score, Washington 10, Stanford 0, I thought my dad was childish for being so upset. It wasn't until I got older that I understood his mania. When I get the first Pitt score and the Panthers are down early, I'm agitated.

When the final, Stanford 20, Washington 10, came over the radio waves, my father was ecstatic. You'd have thought he had found a million bucks in the basement.

The only thing that topped that reaction in my memory was when the final gun sounded on the Cal game a few weeks later. Stanford won, 13-7, and my dad picked me up and threw me upon his shoulders, grabbed my mother and twirled her around the living room. I'd never seen him so happy before and, to be honest, I don't think I ever saw the two of them like that again.

At that age I had no idea what real love was, certainly no solid understanding of sex, so to me that scene, brought about by the favorable results to a college football game, that had to be what the adults called "love."

The static-filled soundtrack of marching bands and the cheering of far-off fans wasn't Dooley Wilson playing "As Time Goes By," but it did the trick. Right then and there, I fell head over heels in love with college football.

Our father-and-son football bond cemented, we listened to Bill Stern and Ken Carpenter broadcast Stanford's Rose Bowl victory over Nebraska on *NBC* Radio on New Year's Day 1941, but I sensed that the game wasn't that big of a deal to my dad.

Back then, the bowls were considered exhibitions. Perhaps he'd have felt differently had he known that the 21-13 defeat of the Cornhuskers would be Stanford's last Rose Bowl win for thirty years, until the big upset over No. 2 Ohio State in the '71 Rose Bowl. There was one Pasadena trip in between, but we never discussed the '52 Rose Bowl, a 40-7 Illinois win. Talking about that game was forbidden, like bringing up a relative that was a crossdresser.

Decades later, when dad was dying, I visited him in the hospital. Stanford had beaten Cal the night before and when I brought him the good news, he hardly smiled.

That's when I realized how sick he was. That was his last football season. He died the next February.

A few months later, just as the new college football season – the first of my life without my father – was getting underway I was visiting my mother.

"Do you think dad will know when Stanford wins?" I asked her.

I'll never forget her reply. It's better than any line I'll ever come up with.

"If the Gipper knew," she said, "so will your father."

That joyful scene in our living room was no contrived Hallmark moment, as my lonely, lovelorn army buddy would have had you believe. That's how true love works. That elation, that spontaneity, that spark – in my opinion that's what makes college football different than any other sport on the planet.

I'm convinced that's why Cupid ignored me the rest of my life. He figured he hit the bullseye that night in November 1940 and moved on to other targets.

How have I kept the love affair going all these years? There's got to be an explanation for the powerful hold the sport has over me, and many of you as well.

I'm no scientist, but there must be a connection between the chemical chain reaction behind the forces of attraction and the anticipation of a college football season. You know the feeling. It's almost identical to the one you get in your stomach on your first date or before leaning in for your first kiss.

It first gets ahold of me when the preview magazines come out in June, and slowly builds in intensity and momentum, like a kicker galloping toward a ball on a tee. Just when you feel like your heart is going to jump out of your chest, the preseason polls are released and right around Labor Day, boom – you're watching the first kickoff of the season on TV!

If you're a diehard fan, this feeling happens every summer for the rest of your life. In those years when your alma mater has 20 starters returning, it starts sometime in April.

And I don't know about you, but for me the feeling doesn't dissipate when the seasons change, when the color of the sky here in Western Pennsylvania goes from UCLA powder blue to Army gray, and the leaves slowly change colors from Michigan State green to Georgia red, Clemson orange, Texas A&M maroon and Wyoming prairie gold and brown.

After the season ends in January, when the snow that's as blindingly white as Penn State's road uniforms blankets the ground, I start counting down the days until I'll see the sport again. In a way, it becomes a long-distance relationship. Only in this case, months, not miles, separate me from college football.

In addition to the highs, I know of no other sport that causes heartbreak like college football. At the end of the epic Notre Dame-Alabama Sugar Bowl game on December 31, 1973, our *ABC* cameras captured a shot of a female Alabama student in tears. I was standing in the back of the booth when I noticed Howard Cosell looking at a monitor. He opened his mouth to say something – as always, Cosell's first instinct – but hesitated. I can't remember who, it was either Chris Schenkel or Bud Wilkinson who jumped in with a comment, instead.

There was something in Cosell's pause that intrigued me so much that as soon as we got into the limo to take us to the hotel in the French Quarter, I had to satisfy my curiosity.

"The girl, the Alabama coed," I asked. "Why didn't you say anything?"

Cosell lit up one of his trademark cigars and looked out the window.

"I wanted to say, 'ten years from now, miss, it won't make any difference,'" he said.

To a point, Cosell was probably correct. In ten years' time, the young lady would have probably been married with a family. Then Cosell turned back and looked me in the eye.

"Then I realized on this night, the battle for the championship of intercollegiate football far exceeded anything that had happened in her young life thus far," he explained, exhaling a puff of cigar smoke. "The Crimson Tide of Alabama, plain and simple, broke that little girl's heart. You don't ever trivialize a broken heart. Especially on national television."

At that moment, I couldn't help but wonder if Howard Cosell, the arrogant announcer who would forever be most closely linked with the NFL, the most Madison Avenue and money-hungry of professional sports leagues, might just have been, at that moment, falling for the college game.

I can't say for sure, but the way he turned away to look, reflectively, out of the window suggested to me he didn't want to betray his emotions.

I imagine that my favorite line of 20th Century literature is Thomas Wolfe's observation that "you can't go home again." Yet, as talented a writer as Wolfe was, it is obvious to me he knew absolutely nothing about college football because each year, thousands of alumni return to their alma maters to attend football games.

Homecoming, the closest thing to a mating ritual in sports, is like the swallows returning to San Juan Capistrano, only there is tailgating and beer. And, I guess, no swallows.

Its roots can be traced to the grassy quadrangles of Ivy League institutions, but in my mind it'll always be associated with the cornfields and wheatfields of the Midwest, at schools like Illinois and Wisconsin, where the tradition first began to flourish in the 1910s.

In the South, a desire to return to one's roots and rekindle old loves is expressed not only annually, but on a weekly basis in the fall. I have it from trusted sources that while a good spot for "makin' a little lovin'" on a "Mason-Dixon night" is Alabama's Bryant-Denny Stadium, there's no greater place to be with your girl than inside LSU's Tiger Stadium on a "Louisiana Saturday Night."

In Tennessee, Volunteers' fans sing about a "half bear, other half cat" girl from a special place called Rocky Top who's "wild as a mink, but sweet as soda pop." I've always been partial to classy, well-behaved brunettes, but to each his own!

And then there's the late John Denver, who famously sang about going "home to the place where I belong." For many Mountaineers' fans, that place is called Morgantown and that song is essentially the state anthem of West Virginia.

It doesn't matter whether you take a series of winding country roads, the steep incline of Pittsburgh's DeSoto Street, the scenic mountain byway of Pennsylvania Route 26's backdoor into State College, the Dolphin Expressway and 17th Avenue down to Miami's Little Havana, the asphalt artery of Central Avenue into the heart of New Haven, Connecticut, the Old Greenway Highway which leads to Clemson, South Carolina, or a nameless numerical ribbon of interstate to get there, yes, oh my goodness yes, you can go home again.

You can flirt with other sports, engage in some hanky-panky with hockey or hoops, have a fling with pro football, shack up with skiing or surfing, even race around with a mistress of motorsports, but I truly believe that college football is the old steady, the high school sweetheart, that everybody comes back to every fall.

A few years ago, a serendipitous encounter at a bar in a Las Vegas casino the night before a big fight led to a memorable exchange between two good friends who also happen to be two of the biggest college football fans I've ever known. One was John Lukacs, the guy who I am writing this book with. The other was the late Bert Sugar, the prolific writer and sports historian who was probably more "Runyonesque" than Damon Runyon himself.

Sugar, as most of you know, was best-known for his fedora, his cigars, his wit and his association with baseball and boxing. The public, however, remained largely unaware of Sugar's longtime loyalty to his Michigan Wolverines and his devotion to college football.

Over a drink, Lukacs asked Sugar if he was still a big college football fan. Sugar pushed up his hat, leaned forward and replied with two questions of his own, a fantastic one-two punch combo.

"Am I still a big college football fan?" Sugar shouted. "Does Dolly Parton sleep on her back?"

* * *

In the interest of full disclosure, college football was not my first love. The first sport to capture my heart was baseball. I know. It's quite a revelation.

The title of this book, after all, is my best-known line and it was inspired by my famously public feelings on the national pastime. But don't worry, those feelings haven't changed. I feel the same way today as I did when I uttered those words in February 1981.

Do you know what my three favorite days of the year are? I'll tell you. New Year's Day for the bowl games, the Saturday on which the semifinal games of the NCAA men's Final Four are played, and the last day of baseball season – and not necessarily in that order.

The order of my three least favorite days is pretty much set in stone: April 15, any day Congress is in session, and baseball's opening day.

You might as well add the start of spring training to that list. To me, the four most depressing words in the English language are "pitchers and catchers report." It bums me out when I hear them every February.

But things weren't always this way. See, I was once seven years old. And every seven-year-old boy falls in love twice: with his second-grade teacher and with baseball. The former romance dies quickly; the latter endures much longer.

Much of the appeal of my romance with baseball involved the place where for me the sport literally lived, Forbes Field in the Oakland section of Pittsburgh. There are others of a certain age who grew up in other cities that know what I'm talking about.

When I was hitchhiking around the country as a kid, I saw games at Fenway Park, Braves Field, Wrigley Field, Comiskey Park, Sportsman's Park, Yankee Stadium, the Polo Grounds, Ebbets Field, Briggs Stadium, Griffith Stadium, Cleveland Municipal Stadium, Crosley Field and Shibe Park.

When you reminisce about these old ballparks and your youth, it's a lot like taking a trip back to the neighborhood you grew up in. Most of the people you once knew moved away a long time ago. Likewise, nearly all of the houses that baseball teams once lived in have been razed and the residents have either moved away or else moved into more luxurious living quarters. If you're like me, you probably find these mansions lack the appeal the old houses possessed.

In the end, the ballpark of one's youth is more than just an address or a geographic place, it's really a cosmic intersection of memories. Despite my feelings about baseball today, I wouldn't trade my memories for anything.

I could appreciate the beauty and allure of those other famous ballparks, but none were as attractive to me as the one in my backyard. Like Stefanie Powers, Forbes Field had perfect measurements. It was 300 feet down the right field line, with a 15-foot screen working its way out toward right center. Straight down the left field line, it was 365. The deepest part of the park was left center, where the flagpole was, a staggering 457 feet from home plate. All these years later, I somehow know these numbers better than my Social Security number.

The old-fashioned scoreboard occupied much of the left field wall and, starting sometime around the 1938 season when I first started attending games, it also occupied most of my attention. I was mesmerized by the way the scoreboard operators manually put up the runs, hits and errors and the scores of the out-of-town games by hand. Nothing was mechanical or automatic.

And I got a huge kick out of it when I caught glimpses of these guys, this was in the middle of summer, when temperatures reached 100 degrees Fahrenheit inside that giant sweatbox, shuffling along the catwalks in their undershorts.

I've always been a fan of the stage and going to a ball game was a lot like attending a play. There were the leading players on the field, but I liked watching the supporting cast members and stagehands who worked behind the scenes and between the acts.

Take Myron O'Briskey, for example. O'Briskey ran the concessions at Forbes Field for almost fifty years. I got to know him when I got older. He was a character.

At the Kentucky Derby they sell mint juleps in metal cups with the Churchill Downs emblem etched on the side. That was O'Briskey's idea. They used to sell the mint juleps in glasses, but O'Briskey came up with the idea to sell the metal cups. They were a big hit as souvenirs. Everybody collected them. It was a brilliant idea.

O'Briskey wasn't just an idea guy. He was a hands-on salesman. It was fun to watch him work. He'd appear in a crowded section, one of his vendors following closely behind with a full rack of fresh, hot peanuts. He'd take an empty seat and a minute later flag down the vendor and buy a bag of peanuts.

Pretty soon, after every nose in that section got a whiff of those delicious peanuts, the vendor was besieged with business. After that, O'Briskey and his sidekick would reload the rack and head to another part of the ballpark to continue their hustle.

The more you went to this strange theater, the more you noticed people like O'Briskey. You picked up on other things, too. Like how the Pirates announced the starting lineup only once, and sometimes purposely garbled a few names over the PA in order to drive up sales of scorecards.

At times, the audience was more entertaining than the act on the main stage. There were no luxury boxes, so you had politicians, storekeepers and steel workers all jumbled together. Back then, most of the games started at 3 o'clock, which was so all the city employees, judges, bus drivers and street sweepers, could go.

Between the chatter of the ballplayers on the field and in the dugouts, the hecklers in the stands and the vendors hawking their wares, the dialogue was better than anything Bill Shakespeare – the English dramatist, not the 1930s Notre Dame football star known as the "Merchant of Menace" – ever came up with.

I feel bad most people alive today know Forbes Field, or any of the old parks, from black-and-white photos or newsreel footage. My memories are in brilliant Technicolor with Vitaphone sound.

I remember Greenberg Gardens, Kiner's Korner and attended the '44 All-Star game. There was a giant, fifty-foot wooden statue of a Marine standing at attention out in left field, presumably guarding the park from an enemy attack. They still put out the bunting for the all-star games and the playoffs, but those colors look and feel different, somehow more important, when the country is at war.

I remember the vivid red of the brick outfield walls and the iridescent green of the ivy that covered them. The thousands of insects swarming around the light cages on a sultry summer night. The "whoosh" sound when a vendor clipped off the cap to a bottle of beer or soda pop – everything was in glass bottles back then – and the clink of the bottle cap as it tumbled onto the bleachers.

And the taste of a hot dog at the ballpark. When Humphrey Bogart said that "a hot dog at the ball game beats roast beef at the Ritz," truer words were never spoken.

I feel extremely fortunate for having seen, smelled, heard, tasted, and experienced it all at the age I did. I remember watching one of the Sunday shows, I think it was sometime in the early 1990s, when I heard the political commentator William F. Buckley, Jr. say he never attended a baseball game. At that moment I felt indescribably sad. I felt awful for the guy.

Buckley's admission was a tragedy. If you never got to see a baseball game as a kid, had your heart broken or were fired from a job, you should ask for your money back because you've been cheated out of the three most important experiences of life as an American.

By the time I was about ten, I was so blinded by my love of baseball and that ballpark, I became obsessed with the idea of living there. One night, I actually tried to move into Forbes Field. This is a true story.

After the end of a night game, I hid out in a maintenance room and waited for everyone to go home. Not long after I heard the "clank" sounds of the light towers shutting down, I decided to venture out. I was wandering through the concourse when I ran into two black boys who were about my age. We instantly bonded over the fact that the three of us shared the same hare-brained scheme.

Under the moonlight, we ran around the bases and played in the outfield. When we got tired, we had a dinner of O'Briskey's peanuts and popcorn washed it down with as many free Cokes as we wanted. No dinner, before or since, was as good.

We bedded down in the Pirates' dugout, but we were evicted when one of my new friends went to take a leak in the middle of the night and was discovered by a security guard who called the cops.

Were my parents pissed at that one. Had the decision been up to me, I'd have preferred to have stayed in the back of the squad car that brought me home in the wee hours of the morning.

Forbes Field didn't seem to change all that much over the years, but almost overnight, my adolescence turned into early adulthood. As a kid, I used to study the wool uniforms with their bright colors and intricate stitching, the stirrups, the logos and all the variations in wardrobes between the teams.

Once I reached a certain age, I started paying more attention to the blouses of female fans, which customarily had less buttons fastened depending how on hot and steamy the afternoon was.

I also began paying attention to other important details of the sporting life, such as how the scoreboard operators put up the winning team's score first when posting the final from an out-of-town game. I learned from the wise guys in the stands that this was a serious, though unwritten rule, a courtesy for bettors and bookies. You can imagine the yelling and swearing pouring from the stands if proper protocol wasn't followed.

Much to the mortification of my parents, I completed my bachelor's degree in profanity in those bleachers. Later, I did some post-graduate work under Bob Prince and the city's sportswriters.

While it didn't happen exactly how I had planned it that fun night in the early Forties, I now understand that in way, I did indeed grow up at Forbes Field.

Although I had just turned 29, part of me felt like a little kid again during game seven of the 1960 World Series. Yes, *that* World Series. *That* game seven.

Thankfully, I didn't have to hide out in a broom closet the night before the game. I had a credential and watched the game up in the pressbox. Half of the city of Pittsburgh, it seemed, was crammed in there with me, and we were all afraid to breathe, let alone utter a sound in the bottom of the ninth.

When Bill Mazeroski hit the homer, let me tell you, the "No Cheering in the Pressbox" rule wasn't just violated. It was like fucking V-J Day all over again!

Sometime while Maz was rounding the bases, in the midst of all the hugging and revelry, I yelled over the din, "We're all getting laid tonight!" The sound of the cheers went up a decibel or two. I have only hazy memories of blurting out that line, as well as most of the rest of that evening, but apparently the line wasn't lost to history. Some years later a sportswriter friend told me that my exclamation had become something of a legend.

The way the story was told to me, a writer who had been in the pressbox that historic day in October 1960 relayed my line to another writer, who passed it on to another, then another. As the years went by, the story kept making the rounds, in countless pressboxes and crowded bars, and one way or another, it made its way out to Hollywood and reportedly reached the ears of the guys who wrote the movie "Caddyshack."

I had never seen the movie until just a few years ago. When Rodney Dangerfield yelled "Hey, everybody – we're all gonna get laid!" I had a pretty good laugh. I guess I do have a kind of physical resemblance to Dangerfield. Even so, I'd say the whole thing isn't remotely true. But what the hell – as the newspaper editor says in John Ford's "The Man Who Shot Liberty Valance," one of my favorite westerns, we'll print the legend.

I've often said that the end of the 1960 World Series was the end of my childhood. It was the beginning of the end of my romance with baseball, too. A little over ten years later, they demolished Forbes Field and that wrecking ball destroyed what was left of my relationship with the game.

After everything that followed – Astroturf, concrete, cookie cutter stadiums, the revolving doors of free agency, strikes, steroids, the $200 million contracts – there was no chance for a reconciliation.

Most of the blame, in my opinion, for the falling out falls on the present-day players. Just like their counterparts in the NFL and NBA, they are spoiled by television's money. To me, they come off as greedy and self-centered. They're just not relatable anymore.

Don't believe me? How come none of them have nicknames? Maybe it's just the way things are nowadays. Or maybe there's something more to it. Perhaps the public isn't as enamored with these guys as previous generations were. I think a lack of appealing nicknames has eliminated much of the flavor and character of baseball. For a very long time, the nicknames were part of baseball's lure.

Early on, you had "Shoeless Joe" Jackson, "Georgia Peach," "The Big Train," and "Big Six," Ty Cobb, Walter Johnson, and Christy Mathewson.

In the 1920s and 30s, kids were captivated by "The Bambino" and "The Iron Horse," Babe Ruth and Lou Gehrig, Jay "Dizzy" Dean, Robert "Lefty" Grove and one of my personal, but little-mentioned favorites, the New York Giants' Carl Hubbell, aka. "The Meal Ticket."

Growing up in Pittsburgh in the 1930s and 40s, the brothers Paul and Lloyd Waner, known as "Big Poison" and "Little Poison," respectively, were two of my favorite players, as was Joseph Floyd "Arky" Vaughan. I was devastated when he was traded to Brooklyn.

Again, people are partial to their own era, so for me, the 1940s and 1950s had both the best players and the best nicknames. There was "The Say Hey Kid," Willie Mays, in my opinion the best player in baseball history. You also had Stan "The Man" Musial, who was from Donora, Pennsylvania, Enos "Country" Slaughter and Sal "The Barber" Maglie.

My favorite nickname from this era was the greatest hitter of all-time, "The Splendid Splinter," Ted Williams. People point out that Williams went 0 for 1 in his only trip to the World Series, but I counter that as a fighter pilot in the Marine Corps he never lost a war or a dogfight. That's a much more important legacy.

In the 1960s and 1970s, Ernie Banks was "Mr. Cub," and Pete Rose was "Charlie Hustle," but once the 1980s rolled around, what happened to nicknames? There were a few, but they were far between. My theory is, that's when the emphasis on the word professional in professional baseball started.

My favorite baseball nickname of all-time was "The Yankee Clipper," which also happened to be one of the nicknames of my all-time favorite player, Joe DiMaggio. Funny thing is, I never saw "Joltin' Joe" play in person. I was alive for basically the entirety of DiMaggio's major league career, and I always thought he was a great player, but it wasn't until I got older that I understood that I appreciated him for the way he carried himself, on and off the field, and conducted his business.

I'm not quite sure when I got this feeling for DiMaggio. It was probably sometime in the 1980s around the time of the Pittsburgh drug trials, when the off-field behavior of so many pro athletes started becoming bigger stories than their accomplishments on the field.

DiMaggio didn't have many peers when it came to on-field accomplishments. He made the all-star team every year he played, 13 seasons, and was the cornerstone of nine Yankees' World Series-winning teams.

Here's a stat that is absolutely mind-boggling: DiMaggio had only eight more strikeouts, 369, in his entire career than he had total home runs, 361. I learned that from

Vin Scully. When Vin told me, I was floored. When I tell other people, they don't believe it, either.

Of course, there's also "The Streak," yet, as Ernie Accorsi once commented, "The Streak wasn't the most impressive thing he did in his life." One of the best lines about DiMaggio's marriage to Marilyn Monroe was when she was telling him about the thunderous applause she received from thousands of GIs on a USO tour during the Korean War.

"Oh, Joe," she exclaimed, "you've never heard such cheering in your life."

"Yes," DiMaggio replied, "I have."

My adult appreciation of DiMaggio has little to do with his on-field exploits or the fact that he managed to be briefly married to the most famous sex symbol in American history. It was his relationship with the game of baseball that impressed me the most.

Unlike many of today's players who barely see themselves in a relationship much less as equal partners, DiMaggio understood that the game was bigger than him. He understood he had a moral obligation to conduct himself in a manner which would never bring shame to the game because he remains such an integral part of the history of baseball. DiMaggio, perhaps more than any ballplayer in history besides Ruth, remembered his obligation to the paying public, to the fans. That's something many of today's professional athletes fail to comprehend. Especially when it comes to little kids.

"There is always some kid who may be seeing me for the first and last time," DiMaggio famously said. "I owe him my best."

I wish ballplayers today would read that line and think of all the kids who save up their money to buy their jerseys, before they leave to play for their fourth team in six years.

DiMaggio never embarrassed anybody: his teammates, opposing players, or umpires. There was no theatrics, no temper tantrums. The only emotion the guy ever displayed was when he kicked up some dirt in disappointment.

He treated team management with respect. Sure, one year he got into a contract dispute, and maybe he was bitter, but he never went public with his complaints the way so many ungrateful players do today.

I think there's no better example of the kind of man DiMaggio was than the way he exited the game. Unlike so many other players who hang on well past the time they should have retired in order to keep cashing paychecks and to remain in the public eye, he knew it was Mickey Mantle's turn at Yankee stardom, so he graciously surrendered centerfield. I'm convinced he did so out of his love for the game, for the Yankees and for their fans.

You may not agree with me and maybe you think these observations or opinions are just those of an out-of-touch old man, but I think I'm right. At the very least, Simon and Garfunkel agree with me.

I'm old enough to remember when most players, even some stars, returned to their hometowns and worked regular jobs in the offseason just like the people who paid to watch them. They interacted with fellow citizens at gas stations and in hardware stores.

Nowadays these guys live in mansions in gated communities, walled off from regular folks, and spend all offseason training to be Mr. Universe. I'd love to see a ballplayer try to follow Babe Ruth's training regimen today. He didn't have a personal trainer or drink protein shakes. Ruth guzzled booze all night, got laid, showed up at the park an hour before the game with a hangover, ate two hot dogs and somehow still hit two homers.

Their appearances bother me as much as their attitudes. Too many of them look like slobs in baggy uniforms. And they all have scraggly beards, like 17th century pirates. That, and like all other athletes nowadays, they have too many tattoos. The only guys who had tattoos when I was growing up got them during the war. It was a brotherhood thing. I just don't see any similarities between landing with the Marines on Iwo Jima to fight the Imperial Japanese Army and landing in Seattle for a three-game series with the Mariners.

Baseball has gotten way too scientific with all the metrics and analytics. I remember when the only time you ever saw a shift was for Ted Williams. Now, .200 hitters face shifts.

And don't get me started on the pitch counts. Today, teams use seven or eight pitchers a game, some of whom only face one batter. We'll never see another Don Larsen or Harvey Haddix game again. The days of the indefatigable, iron-armed pitcher have gone the way of twi-night doubleheaders and taking trains on road trips.

The emphasis on strategy is totally out of control. You might as well call the guys who fill out the lineup cards micromanagers. The games probably wouldn't take so damn long and the sport wouldn't be that difficult to watch if the managers just let the players play. Like their counterparts in the NFL, they want too much control and, if the team wins, all the credit.

I've never thought very highly of managers. It wasn't until the 1960s that Gene Mauch reportedly invented the double switch. Talk about slow on the uptake. Knute Rockne or Paul Brown would have come up with the idea on their first day on the job in spring training.

Revenue sharing is a fashionable term today, but in my opinion, the players, the managers, and the owners all deserve equal shares of the blame for ruining the sport. Walter O'Malley, who moved the Dodgers from Brooklyn to Los Angeles, once said that "baseball is too much of a sport to be a business and too much of a business to be a sport." He was right.

The greed of some of the owners of big market clubs who are perfectly willing to buy, rather than compete for, a World Series championship has ruined the game for fans just as much as teams – like my hometown, penny-pinching Pirates – that run their organizations with an eye toward profits, not pennants.

If there was an award for the dumbest and least competent group of people over say, the last 100 or so years, it would be a three-way tie between the general staff of the

French Army, Major League Baseball team owners, and the assholes in Congress responsible for writing the 1.6 gallon per flush toilet rule into the 1992 Energy Policy Act.

As far as top-level leadership goes, Major League Baseball has had an unreal succession of poor leaders. I don't think baseball has had a quality commissioner since Happy Chandler.

To give you an idea of the kind of intellects that have been running baseball for the past fifty, sixty years, I think back to 1974, when Bowie Kuhn was going to suspend George Steinbrenner for making illegal contributions to President Nixon's re-election campaign. Orioles owner Edward Bennett Williams thought Kuhn was being too heavy-handed.

"Bowie," Williams pointed out, "George didn't kill anybody. Look, we've got a current player in the major leagues who shot and killed a woman."

"Yeah," Kuhn replied, "but that was in the off-season."

In any event, baseball and I broke up a long time ago. The game's problems aren't my concern anymore. I moved on with my life and I'm happy with what I got in the divorce settlement: my memories and a short section of the Forbes Field wall, which is still standing in Oakland, right at the edge of Pitt's campus.

I will admit that sometimes, when I take that trip down memory lane – Roberto Clemente Drive goes right by the wall – and I see the ivy-covered brick, I'm reminded of the good times baseball and I had. The relationship was just not meant to last.

The same way, come to think of it, my second-grade teacher and I were not.

*　　　　　*　　　　　*

Baseball might be America's national pastime, but college football, even more so than pro football, is America's national passion. There are a few reasons why I believe this to be true.

To start, college football has ageless beauty. It's the Sophia Loren of sports. It never seems to get old. The sport just turned 140, but to me, it doesn't look a day over 100.

It looks good in black-and-white and in color, in afternoon sun and under the lights, on natural grass and on artificial turf. It's even attractive on Boise State's blue playing surface.

It doesn't have any inhibitions: you can get it on in front of 100,000 fans at Michigan Stadium or in front of a fraction of that inside Idaho's Kibbie Dome.

The more I think about it, though, America's long-term relationship with college football is built to last because it's not based on sex. Sex is the most overrated thing in the world – except when you are doing it. It's 80% anticipation and 20% gratification.

Once upon a time, coaches believed that sex was a distraction from the game. That's why many coaches and schools had rules against players getting married. The thinking was, too much sex sapped an athlete's energy and stamina.

The most famous example might be Notre Dame's "Jumpin'" Joe Savoldi. With three games to go in the 1930 season, which was Knute Rockne's last, the All-American fullback was kicked out of school for being illegally married. It sounds crazy today, but it was a big scandal.

I'll never forget a conversation I had on the subject in the late 1960s with the late Johnny Vaught, the legendary Ole Miss coach.

"Son," Vaught laughed, "how can you wake up in the mornin' and concentrate on football when that thing's winkin' 'atcha?"

I told Vaught he had a point. Whenever women are involved, I've had problems concentrating on college football myself. And now that I've thought about it, I've been known to have said some strange things while under the influence of sex. Chuck Neinas, the former commissioner of the Big 8 and executive director of the CFA, once asked me if I ever told a woman that I loved her.

"Of course I have," I replied. "Just never standing up."

There's no such thing as a bad college football season so the sport has never cheated on me. I'm ashamed to admit this, but I once cheated on college football. I was ten years old.

It was New Year's Day, 1942. Oregon State was playing at Duke in the Durham Rose Bowl, the only Rose Bowl to date played outside of Pasadena. The decision to move the game was due to the hysteria that took hold of the country after the Pearl Harbor attack. Jap submarines were sinking ships right off the West Coast and Nazi U-boats were doing the same off Florida. People were scared that the country was going to be invaded. One of our exalted elected officials, believing the West Coast to be indefensible, demanded that the U.S. armed forces prepare defensive positions in the Rocky Mountains.

The original copies of the Constitution and the Declaration of Independence were removed from display and shipped to the impregnable safety of the gold reserve vaults at Fort Knox. Complementing the nationwide blackouts, bayonet-wielding soldiers patrolled the White House grounds and anti-aircraft guns were installed in Seattle parks, amid the derricks of California oil fields and in New York City's Central Park.

Texan Dan Jenkins, who is three years older than me, told me he learned of Pearl Harbor at a movie house in Ft. Worth and he ran home as fast as he could because he thought that Pearl Harbor was just a few miles west of Amarillo.

I don't remember being as worried. Of course, I was probably too young to understand what the adults were getting all worked up about, as well as the significance of the Rose Bowl being played in North Carolina.

Like it happened yesterday, I recall switching off the radio, rudely cutting Ted Husing off in mid-sentence, and going to see Errol Flynn and Olivia De Havilland in "They Died With Their Boots On" at the movie theater. To this day, I regret the decision. I saw Custer and the Seventh Cavalry get upset by Sitting Bull and the Sioux, but I missed the Beavers beat the Blue Devils, one of the biggest upsets in Rose Bowl history.

Other than that one momentary, solitary lapse in judgement, I've been faithful to college football ever since. Once I got hooked, I listened to every game that I could find on the radio. The West Coast games were special to me not just because of my dad's loyalty to Stanford, but because everything out west seemed so exciting. Whenever you watched the highlights on the newsreels, their stadiums seemed packed to capacity and the student sections were executing those creative card stunts.

The mascot names out there were so exotic, too. You had the Bruins, Trojans, Huskies, Ducks and Beavers. They were different from the East Coast teams like Pitt, Penn State and Princeton, all of which seemed to have been named after a cat.

I expanded my horizons geographically and learned about the Fighting Illini, the Fighting Irish, the Gophers, Hawkeyes, Cornhuskers, Crimson Tide, Sooners, Razorbacks, Yellow Jackets, Gators and Hurricanes. It wasn't long before I memorized them all.

I did the same with the names of the coaches, star players, all the rivalries and rivalry trophies, stadiums, and especially the distinctive names of all the great little college towns that the schools were located in like Lincoln, Pullman, Tuscaloosa, Ann Arbor, Annapolis, Corvallis, Champaign, and College Station. I wanted to visit them all.

Back then, the radio broadcasters used to provide these spectacularly vivid descriptions of the stadiums, the colors of the uniforms and the helmets, the formations of the bands and everything else that the listener couldn't see. I desperately wanted to see all these wonderful places and things with my own eyes.

I took a train to Philadelphia to see my first Army-Navy game in 1948 at the age of 17. When I went away to college at Brown, I hitchhiked all over the Eastern Seaboard to take in games at places like Municipal Stadium and Franklin Field in Philadelphia, the Yale Bowl, Baker Field, and the Polo Grounds.

One of my most memorable hitchhiking adventures was the time I thumbed it from Providence down to New York to watch No. 1 Army play No. 18 Michigan at Yankee Stadium in October 1950. I may be a cold-hearted cynic when it comes to long-term relationships, but I sure as hell believe in love at first sight. That was the first time I saw those glorious, winged Michigan helmets. In living color! In person!

Another reason why college football and I have been together so long is because there are no in-laws. But it does have Notre Dame, which is a lot like having in-laws. Those of you who are married probably understand the analogy. Your spouse's parents were around long before you found your true love, and in a way they actually created the sport you love, so despite their attitudes, the way they often behave, and the problems they cause you, you have no choice but to put up with them.

Now the Fighting Irish didn't actually invent the sport, but they might as well have given birth to the modern manifestation of the game. The things Notre Dame did many years before all of us were born in terms of strategy, marketing, publicity, and business practices are responsible for college football's massive popularity today.

"I don't particularly like Notre Dame or its fans, either," Dan Jenkins once admitted to me. "But what would college football be like without them?"

While we're talking about Notre Dame, this is a great opportunity to clear the air on what I think is a major misunderstanding. The public thinks I love Notre Dame. People couldn't be more off. My close friends know my rule about phone calls: I don't answer after 11 p.m. unless it's Stefanie Powers or someone calling to tell me that Notre Dame lost!

The people that think I'm a Notre Dame homer, just because I talk about the Irish all the time, they couldn't be more off-base. Whether the Irish are winning or losing, Notre Dame is such an integral part of college football and its history you can't ignore the school. It's like teaching American history and leaving out the Founding Fathers, Gettysburg, Thomas Edison, the Wright Brothers, and World War II.

Plus, Notre Dame was dominant during my formative years in the 1940s. I once read an interesting article in the *Wall Street Journal* on how for boys, the teams you associate with, the lifelong relationships you have as fans, are basically cemented during adolescence. Once you hit your teens, you discover girls and for most guys, sports become a secondary obsession. So, for people that complain that I talk too much about Notre Dame, the service academies, and World War II, those were the dominant teams and important events when I was growing up.

The precise moment my dislike for Notre Dame manifested escapes me, but it might have been in November 1943. When I heard the news that Notre Dame lost to Great Lakes in the final moments, I felt like the guy who said, "I built the Titanic, and it's unsinkable."

Notre Dame let me down. I had said it was impossible for that team, which I still feel is one of the greatest in college football history, to lose. It was one of my earliest picks and when Great Lakes upset the Irish, everybody, especially the older guys who were basing their bets off my opinions, let me have it. I wasn't the genius 12-year-old tout I thought I was.

While I'm not anywhere near as rabidly anti-Notre Dame as I was when I was younger, it's still difficult for me to praise the school. That's due to the attitude of the alums, who are an outwardly pleasant, but subconsciously smug bunch.

A Notre Dame alum friend of mine was the late Pete Flaherty, who later became mayor of Pittsburgh. I knew him when both of us were much younger. He went to Mount Mercy College, which is now called Carlow College, and then Notre Dame law school. When I worked at the boat house in North Park, he used to try to cheer me up after yet another Pitt loss to Notre Dame by saying Pitt's players "fought like hell." He was trying to be nice, but as I got older I felt like I was a kid being patted on the head and congratulated for Pitt giving it the old college try.

They're smug not just because of the winning, but because they think Notre Dame is an elite academic school. Don't get me wrong, it's a great school, but it's not on the level of the Ivies, or schools like Johns Hopkins, MIT, Stanford, and Duke, academically.

I used to get into arguments about this with Joe Robbie, the Dolphins owner. Robbie not only sent some of his kids to Notre Dame, he helped raise a lot of money for the school. He was a big Notre Dame fan who regularly called it "the best school in America."

One time, I had had enough. I said that if Notre Dame was truly elite, Joe Kennedy, the patriarch of the preeminent Catholic family in the country, would have sent his boys there, not Harvard.

Robbie had no answer for that one. That line, when I use it now, usually shuts the Golden Domers up – for about a minute. Neither Harvard nor Yale nor any of the other Ivies ever had a Rockne. Or a Leahy. Or a Parseghian. Or a Holtz. Which means you can't keep them quiet for long.

Now I do have a special fondness for a very small, select handful of Notre Dame alums. Charlie Callahan, of course, tops the list. Lou Somogyi is Callahan's contemporary counterpart as a Notre Dame historian. Roger Valdiserri, the longtime Notre Dame SID, is on there. There is a Pittsburgh newspaperman named Terry Shields. Don Ohlmeyer is another favorite Domer. I consider Paul Hornung a good friend.

If not for a Notre Dame graduate, I might never have gotten out of basic training. See, when I went into the army, Uncle Sam wasn't exactly getting a Sergeant York. I'd never handled a gun in my life, so I nervously introduced myself to the crack shot next to me at the rifle range in hopes of getting some tips.

"Where'd you go to college?" I asked.

"Notre Dame," he replied. "Class of '54."

Of course, I said to myself. *Just my luck. Fuckers are everywhere.*

But I truly was lucky. Joe Leonetti, who played baseball at Notre Dame, taught me how to shoot. He became a high school principal in the Cleveland area. I told Joe that I would pay him back one day. If you're reading this, Joe, thank you!

The co-author of this book, John Lukacs, is a Notre Dame graduate from Western Pennsylvania. Early on in our friendship, we had a three-day cooling-off period between phone calls after Notre Dame and Pitt played.

For the most part I've gotten over my issues with Notre Dame, but I'm concerned that Notre Dame and the Catholic Church may not be as understanding with him. I hope he isn't excommunicated for some of these blasphemous paragraphs.

I consider Lukacs one of the best pure writers I've ever known. Like Roone, I've never been very good at giving verbal compliments, so I usually send him notes. I did, however, once tell him that if he had been around in the 1960s, I would have hired him to write for *Pittsburgh Weekly Sports.* At first, I don't think he understood or appreciated the compliment, but I think he does now.

He's the only person I've met whose knowledge of college football history comes close to my own. He's good, but I regularly remind him that he's had the benefit of the Internet, which I never had. Again, you have to keep the Domers grounded.

I am very lucky that he found me because after so many false starts over the years, I almost gave up on this project. It's one of the great ironies of my life that a Notre Dame alum is the reason this book is reality. After I read our first chapter, I knew it was finally going to work. I told Lukacs it was like Rick and Renault heading off to the Free French garrison at the end of "Casablanca." It was the beginning of a beautiful friendship!

"Deep down you really like Notre Dame," Roger Valdiserri used to joke. "We'll convert you yet." Sometimes I worry that Roger's right. But I don't know if I'll ever come around on the Subway Alumni. At one time they were as arrogant as Yankees' supporters and about as well-behaved as English soccer hooligans. Jack Whitaker used to call them "scarlet rednecks."

After Notre Dame routed Army in a game at Yankee Stadium in 1969, George Vecsey wrote about the Irish fans in his gamer for the *New York Times*. But an editor who was a Notre Dame alum got upset and they changed the story so the original version only ran in the bulldog, or early edition. They are fanatics. And there are so damn many of them.

It drove me crazy when half the fans at Pitt Stadium rooted for Notre Dame. Of course, it's like that when Notre Dame plays at other places, too. Notre Dame, I've said it a million times, almost never plays a road game. On the rare occasion when they do, they're confused when the crowd isn't on their side.

One of my favorite Notre Dame losses was the season finale in '71, the 28-8 drubbing at Louisiana State. "There was a lot of noise out there," Ara Parseghian said after our *ABC* telecast while shaking his head in disbelief.

At one time, the Subway Alums had a reputation not only for bringing big numbers and for some occasional bad behavior, but for being a little unhinged. To illustrate that statement, I'll tell you a great story Creighton Miller, a star halfback at Notre Dame in the early 1940s, shared with me.

Notre Dame was playing at Northwestern one year. Miller had been warming up by himself in the far corner of the field and when he looked up from his stretches, he was surprised to find that the team had returned to the locker-room. The famously flaky Miller began to panic. Unable to remember how the team entered the field, he went up into the stands and got into a line of spectators at a concession stand. Miller figured he'd ask the vendor where the visitors' locker-room was. As the line moved forward, a Northwestern fan was complaining to his buddy about all of the rowdy Irish rooters.

"And get a load of this one," he says, while gesturing over his shoulder in Miller's direction, "coming to the game wearing a full uniform. Asshole thinks he's a player."

They're so obnoxious they even worship the people on the periphery of the Notre Dame program. Want proof? Lindsey Nelson told me that about the time he was walking down the street alongside Vince Lombardi, this is sometime in the late Sixties, and someone yelled out in wonderment, "wow – there goes the Notre Dame announcer!" Not so much as a mention of the famous Green Bay head coach. That's unbelievable.

The Greek told me that Notre Dame fans were vicious after the 1978 Cotton Bowl. He thought No. 1 Texas was going to win and picked the Longhorns. Usually, fans kidded the Greek about his bad picks. He started exchanging playful banter with these guys. But he realized they weren't joking and hurried out of there before someone took a swing at him. I told him it had to be Subway Alumni. The alums typically don't behave that way.

All Notre Dame fans, however, take the games too seriously. I remember an interview Chris Fowler did with a Notre Dame student for "College GameDay" before the Notre Dame-Miami game in 1989. The kid said that Notre Dame versus Miami was "good versus evil."

"Do you really believe that?" Fowler asked. "As in a biblical sense?"

The kid thought on it for a second, then said, "Yes, I really do."

Fowler was surprised, but I wasn't. Notre Dame fans think you're not supposed to beat them. When you do it once, it's beginner's luck. When you do it regularly, it's a mortal sin. If you somehow manage to pound Notre Dame, the fucking Crusades start all over again.

The First Crusade started when Army delivered two ferocious beatings upon Notre Dame during the war. Notre Dame students flooded West Point with postcards and hate mail. In Notre Dame's defense, however, Army did take advantage of the war to try to steal Johnny Lujack. A Congressman from Western Pennsylvania secured an appointment to West Point for Lujack, but he declined it because he was set on attending Notre Dame. Army fans and some generals and politicians attacked Lujack's patriotism, which was bullshit. Anyway, given the fights between fans, the ticket scalping and all the betting that accompanied these games, the series had gotten so nasty, Army ended it.

The Second Crusade was launched against USC in the 1960s and 70s, when the Trojans had dominant teams under John McKay. I got a kick out of how much those teams frustrated Notre Dame fans. In typically hyperbolic fashion, holier-than-thou Irish fans called USC back Anthony Davis "the anti-Christ."

The highlight of the 1970s, betting-wise, for me was the infamous '74 Notre Dame-USC game. I had Southern Cal minus four and had all but written the wager off when Notre Dame took a 24-0 lead.

After USC scored 55 unanswered points, 35 in the third quarter alone, I sent the following telegram to John McKay: "Most people will remember Nixon's resignation as the premier television event of the year. Not me. Thank you for the third quarter."

Then came the Miami Hurricanes. Notre Dame had beaten up on Miami of Florida for decades, but when Miami turned the tables on Notre Dame, the latter's fans couldn't take it. Of course, they brought religion into it again, calling the games "Catholics vs. Convicts."

I'll admit that was pretty clever, but Notre Dame's weaponization of religion, whether in recruiting or publicity or anything else, has always bothered me. It's like conducting chemical or biological warfare against the rules of the Geneva Convention.

A co-worker of mine at *ABC* in the 1980s named Carol Lehti told me how she was indoctrinated while attending Catholic grade school. "On Fridays in the fall," Lehti said, "we sang the Notre Dame Victory March and prayed for Notre Dame to win. And if Notre Dame won, we didn't have any homework the following week." That's not fair. It's tough enough to beat Notre Dame without having a bunch of little girls praying against you.

It angered me that Notre Dame used the fact that John Michelosen was a former Catholic against Pitt in recruiting. In the late 1970s, when Dan Marino announced that he had decided to attend Pitt, a disappointed Dan Devine reportedly sent him a picture of the school's grotto and a note that said, in so many words, "how could you?" I didn't think it was fair that any school would use a recruit's faith to try shaming them into signing a letter-of-intent.

Another thing that contributed to my dislike was how Notre Dame refused to play the other Catholic schools. Many years ago, there were a lot of small Catholic schools that used to play big-time football. At one time, they fielded competitive teams.

Duquesne, Fordham, and Santa Clara are probably the most notable examples. Duquesne was consistently ranked in the early years of the AP poll and won the '37 Orange Bowl. Fordham won a Cotton Bowl. Santa Clara went to three major bowls, two Sugars and one Orange, and won all three.

One by one after the war, these cash-strapped schools started dropping down into a lower division. Or else they dropped the sport altogether. Before making these decisions, several of them approached Notre Dame to help them out.

These were proud programs. They weren't looking for a handout. They wanted to play Notre Dame. They'd get killed, but the guaranteed sell-outs, the money from the gate, would keep not only the football program going, in some cases it would basically fund their entire athletic departments for a year.

The late Maurice "Mossie" Murphy, a friend of mine who was the biggest booster in the history of Duquesne athletics, told me that his uncle pleaded with Notre Dame to play just one game. He said that one game could save Duquesne football. Notre Dame dismissed the overtures. "We're not going to help the competition," was the response.

Competition! You've got to be fucking kidding me. I never understood why they wouldn't help their fellow Catholics. I know there's a rivalry there between certain Catholic orders, especially when the Jesuits are involved, but I think it was dishonorable behavior on behalf of Notre Dame's administrators.

After all, they helped out Michigan State at almost exactly the same time. When Biggie Munn left Syracuse to take the Michigan State job, his first order of business, literally, was to get Notre Dame to agree to a series. The Spartans were so desperate, they offered Notre Dame nearly the entire gate. For some reason, Notre Dame's president not only agreed to the series, he said they'd split the gate down the middle.

I still can't figure out why Notre Dame agreed to help Michigan State out. Why be generous to an institution outside the family and not a little brother like Duquesne? In the early part of the 20th Century, Notre Dame was the little guy and had a hard time getting games against national powers. They knew what the Spartans were going through. But why cut them a break?

Most likely, the collars at Notre Dame had some ulterior motives. Perhaps they thought that a strong Michigan State would weaken archrival Michigan or otherwise stick it to the Big Ten? In any event, the minute Notre Dame agreed to play Michigan State, the Spartans were able to get other big games across the country. It gave them instant national recognition. But I'm convinced the move ultimately backfired, because Munn was the only coach to beat Frank Leahy three years in a row, in 1950, '51, and '52.

Now Notre Dame did play one small Catholic school during this time and I know why. Notre Dame played the University of Detroit at Briggs Stadium in 1951. It was the first night game Notre Dame ever played. The public version of how the game came about differs significantly from the real story. How do I know? Because Charlie Callahan told me the truth.

In 1951, Detroit was celebrating the city's bicentennial and somebody at the school thought they should play Notre Dame as part of the festivities. People at Detroit contacted Notre Dame, but Notre Dame at first rebuffed them, just like they did to all the other little Catholic schools.

Well, the game was eventually played and the press gave all sorts of reasons why. To this day people think it was a favor for Gus Dorais, Rockne's quarterback who coached at Detroit for many years, and that priests on both sides and all these city officials and civic leaders got together because all the parties wanted to make it happen. That was bullshit.

What really happened was that one of the wealthiest Catholic families in Detroit, big Notre Dame donors, found out how Notre Dame was behaving and threatened that if the game wasn't played, they would withhold money from Notre Dame. Callahan told me the truth about the ultimatum, grabbed my wrist, as was his habit when he wanted to make a point, and said, "lad, our people understand money."

There is no disputing that statement. But I will never call Notre Dame greedy, like Frank Broyles and Vince Dooley did after the announcement about Notre Dame's exclusive contract with *NBC* in early 1990. Both men were out of line with their comments. Especially since the domino effect that Notre Dame started with the deal, the conference realignment that resulted, got Broyles what he wanted. It got Arkansas out of the Southwest Conference and into the Southeastern Conference.

Ironically, Dooley's Georgia was one of the two schools, along with Oklahoma, that led the charge for deregulation that resulted in the big Supreme Court decision in '84. When Notre Dame took a leadership role to look after its own interests, well, that was a problem for everybody.

All of the vitriol that was directed at Notre Dame from other schools about the deal was something else. These other ADs and coaches, had they been in Notre Dame's shoes, if they had Notre Dame's clout, they all would have made the exact same move.

The media response was terrible, too. It was selective outrage. Everybody wrote that Notre Dame was selfish for leaving the CFA, but everyone forgets that the Big Ten and the Pac-10 left before Notre Dame. *Sports Illustrated* didn't take those conferences apart like they did Notre Dame.

You can say a lot of things about Notre Dame, but you can't say they operate out of greed. Their insistence in taking only their fair share of the gate in the Michigan State series is proof of that. I know our dealings with them when I was at Pitt were always conducted with both schools as equal partners. As far I know, they never tried to strong-arm anybody else, either, when it came to money and scheduling.

Now they did have a reputation for being cheap, I will go on the record saying that. I was upset when Notre Dame didn't send the band to Michigan State in '66. It was a money thing. For the first Cotton Bowl in January 1970, Notre Dame's return to bowl games after the 45-year hiatus, they tried getting the Cotton Bowl to pay for the band's travel expenses. The Cotton Bowl people couldn't believe the request.

And in 1982, when Notre Dame played Michigan under the temporary lights at Notre Dame Stadium, they squeezed a few more bucks out of *ABC Sports* saying that they had to pay cops overtime for traffic control. I think Jim Spence signed off on it rather than haggle. The collars are cheap, but they aren't greedy.

It pains me to say it, but the way Notre Dame handled television and the school's central role in the way the medium grew the sport, I think the school was more than magnanimous in its dealings with the rest of the colleges, with the networks, and then later with the CFA.

When I was at *ABC*, all but one of the top five games we had, ratings-wise, involved Notre Dame. The '71 Nebraska-Oklahoma game was the only one Notre Dame was not involved in. The top five highest-rated games since deregulation and prior to the *NBC* deal, Notre Dame was involved in all but one or two of those as well. With those numbers, and the school's following, why would Notre Dame put up with regionalized telecasts? Why wouldn't the school want to chart its own course?

I thought Joe Paterno was really out of line, too, when he said that Notre Dame went "from an academic institute to a banking institute." That was typical Paterno. The comment was rooted more in jealousy than anything else. He was pissed off because he thought Penn State should have gotten the *NBC* deal instead. The fact that he thought Penn State was even a possibility was ridiculous.

Notre Dame was the only logical choice for two reasons. There is only one school with a truly national following, and that's Notre Dame. Like it or not, that's just the way it is. Nobody can touch Notre Dame's tradition. The campus is one of the most breathtakingly beautiful I've ever set foot on. There's the fight song, which everybody knows the tune of, plus they have a propensity to pull upsets.

All of this is part of the Notre Dame "mystique." I've always said that the movie "Rudy," and I mean no offense to these schools and their alums, but that movie just doesn't work if Rudy played for Minnesota or Mississippi. Hollywood doesn't even make the film if it isn't based on a Notre Dame player.

The other reason is also plainly obvious: if there are fifty million Notre Dame fans in this country who want to watch Notre Dame play and win, there are at least fifty million people, maybe more, on the other side who want to watch Notre Dame play and lose. That's really what it all comes down to. Notre Dame is the only school that can pull ratings, win or lose.

I picked up on this early in my life. I remember in 1950, a friend of mine asked me if I wanted to go watch the Pitt-Notre Dame game. I asked him, where? How? Some Notre Dame games back then, this would have been '50 or '51, were on the old DuMont Network in the Chicago area, but I didn't understand how we could see it.

He said he knew a movie theater in Pittsburgh where they were showing it. A movie theater! It might have been on closed circuit somehow. It was then I realized that people would go to any lengths to watch that team any way, anywhere, anytime. Oh, and of course, half the seats in that theater in downtown Pittsburgh were taken by Notre Dame fans.

Notre Dame football was made for television. For all intents and purposes, college football on television started in 1951. Only national games were televised from '51 through '54. Incredibly, school administrators and the short-sighted suits who ran TV back then were not sure that televising games would be profitable. They were concerned that television would cost everyone money, that TV would lower attendance figures and hurt the gate.

Sure enough, Notre Dame, as a two-touchdown underdog, upset Oklahoma in one of the first nationally-televised games in 1952 and the ratings were through the roof. It got the whole thing started. They started doing regional games in '55.

The reason the NCAA TV committee was formed in '52 was to stop Notre Dame. All the other colleges were scared that Notre Dame would be on every week eventually. If Notre Dame hadn't existed, eventually the NCAA would have taken over, just not as soon as it did. I predicted way back in the 1960s, when the Notre Dame Sunday replay with Lindsey Nelson was a big hit, that Notre Dame would one day have its own network. I'm surprised it took as long as it did for them to work it all out.

All the other schools and coaches were crazy to get all worked up. Especially Paterno. I know for a fact that Miami of Florida was the only other school under consideration by *NBC*. Now if it had been up to me, I wouldn't have picked Notre Dame or Miami. I think the only squad that deserves its own network is the USC Song Girls.

Despite my very strong feelings about Notre Dame, I believe that unlike a lot of people in the media I'm fair in my treatment of the school, its teams, its coaches, and its players. Many Notre Dame fans won't agree with this, but very few of them are aware of some of the things that I've done behind-the-scenes.

In 1970, for example, I told Herschel Nissenson of the Associated Press that Joe Theismann was the best quarterback in the country. Jim Plunkett won the Heisman Trophy that year, but I was convinced Theismann was better. I told Nissenson to look at the stats. Theismann had better passing numbers than Plunkett in basically every important category. He had a higher completion percentage and a better touchdown-to-interception ratio.

If you ask Nissenson, he'll admit that I convinced him to vote Theismann first-team All-American over Plunkett. Many newspapers, writers and scouts thought he was nuts for doing so. It was at my urging.

I pushed Paul Hornung for the College Hall of Fame for what seemed like forever. It was my annual mission for at least fifteen, maybe even twenty years. I still think it was ridiculous that we didn't get him in until 1985.

I didn't push Theismann in '70 because I liked Notre Dame or because I liked Theismann or even as a favor for Roger Valdiserri. I truly believed he was the better quarterback and deserved to be recognized as such by the AP. Although I always got along well with Hornung, I went to bat for him for the same reasons.

This is going to come as a big surprise to a lot of people, but unlike many in the media today who work entirely too hard at being edgy or controversial, I don't say things just to get a reaction. I don't make predictions for show or say something that I don't totally, 100% believe.

Now when I was the SID at Pitt, or when I was putting out *Pittsburgh Weekly Sports*, I did try to create controversy. My job at that time was to generate publicity, get space and play the role of salesman, whether it was selling Pitt players to writers, selling tickets for Pitt athletic events to the public, or selling papers.

Ever since I went on the air, that approach changed. I had already made the pitch to Roone to put me on the air. When I went to work for *ESPN*, I wasn't auditioning. I wasn't chasing headlines or space or trying to make a name for myself.

My original goal with my commentary and material was to be different from the jocks. I wanted to be informative, but in a creative way. When you get to a certain position, people write about your predictions and what you say because you are on the air, not necessarily because the stuff that is coming out of your mouth is controversial or off-the-wall. You get attention by default. Everything I've said or predicted in the past, same as everything I say or do now, it was said and done because I believed it. Which brings us to Ron Powlus.

That particular prediction will almost certainly be the one college football fans remember me for and I can live with that because it's part of the job. As I've said before, the public only remembers the ones you get wrong. You rarely get credit for what you get right.

Not too many people remember that there were three parts to the prediction, which I made on the air the after Notre Dame defeated Florida State in 1993. I said, "let me tell you something about Notre Dame. In the next four years, they are going to win the national title at least twice and Ron Powlus will win the Heisman Trophy at least twice. He will be the greatest quarterback in the history of Notre Dame."

The parts I felt most certain of were the predictions that Notre Dame would win two national titles and that Powlus would go down in history as the school's greatest quarterback. The part about winning at least two Heismans, that line wasn't part of the first draft.

As I was repeating the material to myself before I took my seat on set next to Chris Fowler on our "College GameDay" set, it suddenly occurred to me that my intended line, "Ron Powlus will win the Heisman," sounded underwhelming. So, at the last second, I decided the punch the material up a bit. The line as it came out wasn't intended or delivered that way purposely for shock value. Against my better judgement, I simply overdid it.

For years, I've second-guessed myself for saying two. I'm certain that had I said something like "Ron Powlus will win the Heisman Trophy and be the first overall pick in the NFL draft," it would not have been as big a deal as it was.

Not only did I juice up the prediction too much, I called an ill-advised audible in front of the biggest possible audience. What slipped my mind during that hit was the fact that the camera is always the star. Because those words were uttered on television, the reaction was incredible. Even if I had given the same quote to some writer for a print story, I don't think it would have taken off the way it did. It was delivered on live television, so it stuck.

But let it be known that I don't regret the prediction. I wouldn't take it back if given the opportunity. Why? Because it took guts. Nobody goes on the record with anything like that anymore. People in the media today make predictions or picks in August and then walk them back or else completely change teams midstream. Nowadays, you can barely get guys to pick a game, let alone go out on a limb like I did with the Powlus prediction.

I also still maintain that my rationale was sound. With the exception of that brief, feverish fit of hyperbole, everything I said was the right call for that moment.

Notre Dame had just kicked the shit out of Florida State. The game wasn't as close as the final score suggested. They had the best big-game coach, their own TV network, all that tradition and talent, plus the nation's number one quarterback recruit waiting in the wings. Why wouldn't the Fighting Irish have seemed destined to dominate college football for the foreseeable future?

Although he was an untested freshman, Powlus wasn't the unknown in the equation. The hype that accompanied his arrival in South Bend had, at least on the surface, a solid foundation in fact. I based my predictions on what some trusted sources, football people, told me about his talent.

After the first big scrimmage, Notre Dame people raved that Powlus could spot the fourth open receiver in a pattern. One Irish assistant coach, Joe Moore, told me that going off the film he'd seen, Powlus could play in the NFL as a back-up right away. Moore was a Pittsburgh guy from Upper St. Clair who built all those great offensive lines as an assistant at Pitt and Notre Dame. And people I knew who had followed Pennsylvania high school football for a long time compared Powlus's arm strength to Dan Marino's.

If someone asks me who is going to win the Heisman 100 years from now, I'm going to tell him to bet on whoever is lining up behind center for the Irish. Why not? It's a safe bet. The school has produced four winners at the position and no other position in college football gets more publicity than the quarterback at Notre Dame. It's probably the second-most important position in the Catholic Church behind the Pope. If anybody was going to equal or break Archie Griffin's record, odds are fairly good it would be a Notre Dame quarterback.

I also assumed that Powlus would be surrounded with talent just as his predecessors were. That was the part I got dead wrong. While Powlus didn't turn out to be as good as his advance billing, his record would have been much better if Notre Dame's administration had not begun an effort to deemphasize around the same time he committed. The priests at Notre Dame turned off the talent spigot, as they have a history of doing, when they want to reassert control. They've been doing it since Rockne died.

There's a reason why coaches don't last beyond ten years at Notre Dame and it's not all due to the stress of the job. See, the story of Notre Dame football is more or less the story of a century-long game of tug-of-war between the collars and the coaches.

When Rockne died in the plane crash, it was more than a coach dying. Rockne had tremendous power, which the fathers resented. They got together and decided to never again let a Notre Dame football coach hold that much power. They tied Hunk Anderson's hands during the Depression. Elmer Layden fared better on the field, but he saw the writing on the wall and left to lead the NFL.

Father Hesburgh, who I respect greatly, had grand plans to turn Notre Dame into a top-notch educational institution and for that to happen, Frank Leahy's football factory had to be shut down. Hesburgh cut the number of scholarships Leahy could give out, from 33 to 18 a year. Terry Brennan was a victim of the same restraining measures. Then they pulled the rug out from under Lou Holtz, which led to his resignation before Powlus's final season.

So Powlus had to face Notre Dame's schedules without enough weapons. For example, Holtz signed Randy Moss, but Notre Dame wouldn't let him into school because of a disciplinary incident which I later learned was a bad call by Notre Dame. Can you imagine if Powlus had been throwing to Randy Moss? He might have won three Heismans!

That's a joke, not another prediction. In all seriousness, if I had known the full story of what was going on behind the scenes in regards to recruiting and the power struggle between Holtz and the administration, I'd have scaled back the extent of what I thought Notre Dame and Powlus would achieve.

In any event, I regret the stress I placed on Powlus. It's okay to place stress on pros or knock them when they screw up or fail to meet expectations because they're getting paid for it. It's not fair to heap outrageous expectations onto a college kid's shoulders, especially when that college kid plays such a lightning-rod position. Joe Montana, after all, once told Don Criqui that there is more pressure playing quarterback at Notre Dame than there is in playing the same position in the NFL.

So I'd like to take this opportunity to apologize to Powlus. While it certainly wasn't the first time that I engaged my big mouth before my brain, this time my words didn't only affect me.

Hopefully, both Notre Dame and college football fans will one day appreciate the solid career Powlus put together at Notre Dame despite being hampered by two major injuries, a tumultuous coaching change and all the stress that comes with dealing with the media, the Subway Alumni and the unreasonable expectations that accompany the job of starting quarterback at America's most storied football program. By all accounts he was a good kid who worked hard, and his legacy shouldn't be anchored to my prediction.

And perhaps the most important takeaway from this is that we should all learn to temper our expectations in life. I know I have. For instance, I've always had pretty high hopes for this book. I've been told the material is incredible and that it has a lot of potential, but I have this weird, unshakable feeling that it isn't going to win one, let alone two Pulitzer Prizes.

* * *

No marriage is perfect. The key to a more perfect union, they say, is communication. So, I'm going to communicate some of the issues that I have with the people involved in running, and in some ways ruining, the sport that I love. I'm talking about the college presidents, conference commissioners, athletic directors, bowl officials and television executives that are calling the shots. Some of what I'm going to say is constructive criticism. The rest falls under the heading of much-needed marriage counseling.

For starters, quit playing around with the game's traditional look. I'm not talking about the never-ending fashion show at Oregon with the Ducks' uniforms. I'm talking about rules changes that are making the sport almost unrecognizable from the game I fell in love with in the 1940s.

Look, I understand that times change. College football, however, doesn't need plastic surgery. They've ruined the sport's natural beauty, the things that have made it so appealing for so long. Things like ties.

My boss at Pitt, Tom Hamilton, was the guy who uttered the famous line, "a tie is like kissing your sister" after the 1946 Army-Navy game. As Navy's head coach, he passed up a game-tying field goal attempt and instead tried to score a touchdown before time ran out on the 1-7 Middies. Navy came so close to upsetting No. 1 Army, Notre Dame leapfrogged the Cadets in the final poll.

Interestingly, when I asked Hamilton about the line he told me he didn't remember saying it. Perhaps the emotion of the moment affected him with some sort of amnesia. I understood that Hamilton, like most players and coaches on the subject of ties, was disappointed and would probably want to forget such an inconclusive ending, but as a fan I had a different perspective. Ties were one of the sport's strange idiosyncrasies that led to my infatuation with college football in the first place. I enjoyed the fact that sometimes, there were no winners and no losers.

If you think about it, had they not ended in ties, some of the most famous contests in college football history would not be memorable at all. The legendary 1926 and 1948 Army-Navy games would have no special significance. Neither would the celebrated three consecutive scoreless ties between Fordham and Pitt in the 1930s.

The same with the 1922 Cal-Washington and Jefferson scoreless Rose Bowl, the 1948 Penn State-SMU 13-13 tie in the Cotton Bowl, the 1953 "Fainting Irish" Notre Dame-Iowa game, the 1958 Army-Pitt game, the 1966 Notre Dame-Michigan State game, the 1973 Michigan-Ohio State game, and the 1984 Texas-Oklahoma game. A point here or there, all that history is erased from existence.

I don't know when we got the idea that ties were bad. If I had to bet, it was probably somebody in television who planted the college football overtime idea in people's heads. The longer a game goes, the more money they could make in advertising. We're lucky overtime was just recently instituted.

Donn Bernstein told me that *ABC* and the Sugar Bowl people were playing around with the idea of implementing a special sudden-death overtime period in case the 1979 national title showdown between Penn State and Alabama ended in a tie. I was relieved when I heard that Bear Bryant and Joe Paterno both shot down the idea.

I also don't know when we got the idea that low-scoring games had no drama. I remember listening to the 1946 Army-Notre Dame game, arguably the most famous tie in college football history, on the radio. Imagine listening, not watching, not streaming or whatever they call it now, to a game on the radio in which there was no scoring. Boring, right? Wrong. The tension was unbelievable. It was an exercise in holding your breath.

Today, fans focus too much on long bombs and late kicks. They think only shootouts can be great games. That scoreless Army-Notre Dame game was a matter of every single tackle being meaningful from the first quarter until the final gun. If anybody had reached the open field it would have decided not just the game, but the national title. Arthur Daley wrote in the *New York Times* the next day that "nobody scored any points. But nobody in the huge Yankee Stadium throng asked for their money back."

Overtime. One would think that of all people, I'd be in favor of more college football, but I feel that what we've gained in quantity since the introduction of overtime, we've lost in terms of quality. The quality of play is being diluted. The overtime rules, as they currently stand, favor the offense and they almost completely take special teams out of the equation.

Plus, the possibility of multiple overtimes increases the likelihood that an otherwise well-played game ends in a slew of sloppy mistakes committed by exhausted players. These stretched-out games also present greater opportunities for serious injuries.

If I was in charge, there would only be overtime in conference championship games, bowl games, and – when we finally get a playoff system – games that will decide the national championship or the right to advance in the championship chase. There are some games neither team deserves to win. Other times, neither team deserves to lose. Why can't we just accept that?

I'm probably in the minority on this opinion, too, but controversial championships and split national titles weren't such a bad thing, either. I remember the first real dispute of my lifetime, 1947. It was a bigger deal than '46. Many fans and sportswriters would have liked to have seen Notre Dame and Michigan settle the argument on the field after the unofficial post-bowl AP poll vote taken in January of '48, but not me. It occurred to me that if they played, it would end the conversation.

As someone who loves college football and loves to talk, I've never wanted the conversation to end. I welcomed the debate at the end of the '46 and '47 seasons, 1966, all the talk that resulted from the logjam of undefeated teams atop the polls in '73, the split awards in '74 and '78, and the arguments that followed the controversial conclusions of the '84, '89, '90, '91, '93, '94 and '97 seasons.

In my opinion, not knowing the definitive answer to the age-old question, "who's number one?" is always better than knowing. I've never been a fan of rematches or of manufactured outcomes. Rutgers beat Princeton, six goals to four, in "the Game of the Nineteenth Century," college football's inaugural contest in the autumn of 1869. Not too many people know that Princeton got a rematch, which the Tigers won, 8-0, later that season. I'm not certain it solved anything. Each team could claim a head-to-head victory. I'm sure there was still plenty of debate over which team got to visit President Grant in the White House.

Did many deserving teams lose out over the course of the last 130 years? Of course. But I maintain college football as a sport won. See, these disputes grew the college football conversation, it added voices to it, and kept it going indefinitely. The disputes gave writers something to write about, commentators something to comment on, and fans something to argue about all year-round. Seasons bled into each other without resolution, and, for the longest time, everyone seemed perfectly fine with that.

There's too much emphasis on finality in college football today. Everything has to be settled. Wrapped up nice and neat with a bow in January. I miss college football before the BCS, the arguing, the lively debate about who the best team in the country was.

Once upon a time, there was a certain democratic feeling surrounding the sport that none of the pro sports, or any of the other college sports for that matter, had. Everybody had an opinion and every opinion, it seemed, counted. You had all these people, from college professors to regular fans, who devised rating systems to determine the winner of the mythical national championship. There was Paul Williamson and Parke Davis, Frank Dickinson and Dick Dunkel, Deke Houlgate and Frank Litkenhous, the Helms Foundation, the "Azzi Ratem" system, and many others. Taking my inspiration from them, I even devised my own method, called the "Cook Index," as a kid.

Other kids my age, when they grew up, wanted to be a big league ballplayer, a millionaire or President of the United States. Not me. If you had told me when I was 12 years old that I would one day have a vote in the Associated Press college football poll, I'd have considered it a personal fulfillment of the American Dream!

Although it's one of the honors of my life to have been a voter, I can acknowledge that the AP poll itself came about as a way to fill space in newspapers. Seventy-five years have gone by and the polls are still little more than a publicity gimmick. What it basically boils down to is each AP voter is representing his local area without having seen more than one or two games. For the entirety of its existence, the coaches' poll consisted of a few dozen coaches who horse traded amongst themselves, giving their votes to teams on their schedule or in their conference.

But the polls contributed to the conversation, occasionally turning up the volume on it in January, and in the end they helped keep it going and, in so doing, they served their purpose.

I believe that the way the sport was originally set up, the maddening, imprecise way it determined its annual champion, that's what made it our national passion. We as college football fans didn't just have "hot stove league" chats in the dead of winter. We talked and argued passionately about the polls and national titles all year long.

I'm convinced that the endless conversation that went hand-in-hand with the sport for the first 125 years of the sport was directly responsible for its popularity. I worry that as we move inexorably closer to some kind of clear-cut championship system that resembles NCAA basketball's March Madness or the NFL playoffs, the elimination of the conversation will stunt the sport's growth and reduce its attractiveness to new generations of fans.

Another pet peeve of mine: the trend of playing college games, especially the major bowl games, in pro stadiums. A monster was created with the Kickoff and Pigskin Classics. Now we play the opening weekend games in the Georgia Dome and Jerry World. We have games throughout the season, like Texas A&M-Arkansas, being played at NFL stadiums. Notre Dame has started playing so-called neutral site games in baseball parks and in NFL stadiums. It's ridiculous. College games belong on college campuses. Period.

And don't get me started on the bowls. As long as the original, historic stadiums are structurally safe and sound, the bowls should be played there.

The Orange Bowl should have been played in the original Orange Bowl until the end. I supported the movement in Miami that writer John Underwood was leading to keep the Orange Bowl in the old horseshoe in Little Havana.

I've been a longtime supporter of the Fiesta Bowl, too. I wanted it to stay in Sun Devil Stadium. That place is only fifty years old, but it has more character than the Arizona Cardinals' new, space-age looking facility will ever have.

The Cotton Bowl should be played in the Cotton Bowl. Why? Everybody remembers the '79 Cotton Bowl. If Notre Dame and Houston played indoors, there's no ice and frigid temperatures, no dramatic Joe Montana "Chicken Soup" comeback game.

In 1958, the first and only Bluegrass Bowl ever played took place in Louisville. It was between Oklahoma State and Florida State. The game was basically played on a skating rink, the conditions were so icy.

The 1983 Egg Bowl, although not a postseason game, was another game that comes to mind because of the "Immaculate Deflection," a strange gust of wind that knocked down a short Mississippi State field goal attempt, giving Ole Miss the win.

Weather games are as much a part of the fabric of college football history as ties and split national titles. To me, it seems like officials are trying to eliminate them as well.

The staggered bowl schedule has completely sucked all of the air and anticipation out of New Year's Day. All of the major bowls should be played on the same day, whether it is New Year's Eve, New Year's Day, or January 2.

Two of the greatest days in the history of the sport in my opinion were January 2,1978 and January 2, 1984. On both days, historic upsets in the major bowls propelled two No. 5 teams, Notre Dame and Miami of Florida, respectively, to national titles. Under the current set-up, those types of holiday miracles have been effectively outlawed.

College football used to have its own special presentation, especially on television. Ever since the NFL adopted the two-point conversion and they started playing a lot of games and most of the bowls in these sterile, climate-controlled environments, professional and college football games are beginning to look indistinguishable from each other.

I fully understand that these new stadiums are bigger and have all the modern amenities. I also know college football is a business. But college football is a classy dame. Playing in these shiny, new NFL stadiums is an attempt to sex up the sport too much. It's like putting Grace Kelly in go-go boots. It doesn't look, sound or feel right.

A lot of people are to blame for turning college football into a minor league version of the NFL. We'll start with those running athletic departments nowadays. In the old days, your athletic director was a former head coach or star athlete at your school. These people cared about the wins and losses and perception of the football program as much as the alumni, donors, students, and fans.

Now, you're getting lawyers and professional administrators who aren't alums of the schools they work for. They're glorified accountants, green eyeshades. They care only about maximizing profits and financial matters, not to mention their own financial well-being. They don't even do any work in hiring coaches. They outsource everything to search firms.

Just like many ADs, the university presidents are little more than highly-paid mercenaries with PhDs. They have no connection to their schools or a specific region of the country. You have some woman who is the president of Arizona State one year and two years later she could be at Boston College. And I hate to generalize, but most of these people could care less about the history and traditions of college football.

And then there are the academics. Not all of them are bad, but when I was the SID at Pitt, many of them turned their noses up at me, as if they were too good to share a campus with an athletics publicist who behaved like a bull in a china shop. Little did they know how much it bugged me that I had to share a stadium with them on Saturdays!

It always bothered me that faculty got tickets at discount prices, but many resold the big games at a nice profit. The ones that did show up at the games barely made any noise. I suspect it is like this at many schools.

What made me more angry, however, was the way they turned their noses up at college football, as if it has no place at an institution of higher learning. A lot of it is educational elitism, but jealousy plays a role, too. They resent the notoriety and money that coaches get. I think it was Bear Bryant who said that "60,000 people don't fill a stadium to watch a professor administer an exam." It's one of the great lines.

I've always felt that a certain group of radical academics were one of the biggest existential threats to college football. They'd do away with the sport if they could. They've been trying for years. Any excuse will do.

At the turn of the 20th century, they complained about excessive violence. A few decades later, they argued that giving scholarships to athletes was akin to professionalism. I suspect they're going to use the concussions in this century.

There's a great scene in the 1940 movie "Knute Rockne All-American" in which Pat O'Brien, playing Rockne, gave an animated, heartfelt speech defending the importance of college football as a way to teach the country's young men about character, courage, and the concept of teamwork. I liked how the movie people included legendary coaches like Pop Warner, Howard Jones, Bill Spaulding, and Amos Alonzo Stagg in the scene playing themselves.

The speech resonated with me when I first saw it as a kid, but it wasn't until a few decades later that I understood that O'Brien's words were a call to arms in a fight that I too needed to answer.

In 1962 there was a big fuss going on down in Dallas about the sad state of Southern Methodist's program. The Mustangs had been terrible for the better part of the mid-1950s and early 60s. They went winless a few seasons during that time. Right before the school hired Hayden Fry, some SMU alumni were talking about dropping the sport.

The whole thing, in my opinion, was part of a larger plan, a ploy by radical academics across the country to push for a national de-emphasis. It was a dangerous idea. If one big-time football school folded, then it might be followed by another. And another. It was just like the domino effect that President Eisenhower warned us about with the worldwide spread of communism. I felt as though my favorite sport, an essential part of our national identity and the country's competitive character, was under attack.

As I got older and learned more about World War II, I realized Captain Hamilton's genius in his pioneering of the V-5 program, which later led to the V-12 training program. He believed that athletic competition, especially in a team sport like college football, helped create officers, pilots and leaders. Those programs saved college football at dozens of schools and in the process helped us win the war.

The guy who said "a tie was like kissing your sister" when talking about a football game knew that battlefield losses during World War II were equally unacceptable. I felt the same way during the Cold War, so I typed up an op-ed that was published in papers around the country.

"What is this country coming to?" I asked. "Apparently, some people feel big-time football is more of a threat to our national security than communism. A recent survey by the army showed that the soldiers who show an interest in sports and play them make the best combat troops. Is football a sin? Is it that bad?"

"College football is in serious trouble because of this feeling. I have seen these jokers at work in different universities all over the country. ...I am afraid that the egg heads might prevail – these cynical individuals who are jealous of the publicity the coaches and athletes receive. These types of men our country can give to Russia. If the press, radio, and television do not fight these people, then college football could die."

I wasn't as eloquent as Pat O'Brien was in the movie, but I thought that Rockne, Warner, Stagg, and the others, not to mention Captain Hamilton, would have been proud of me. The powers at Pitt, on the other hand, were a different story.

Chancellor Litchfield received a letter from a professor in the school of engineering at Syracuse named Ralph Swalm. Litchfield wrote, "I think this is pretty poor stuff coming from us" in the margin and forwarded a copy of my op-ed and Swalm's letter to our AD, Frank Carver. Carver didn't say a word, but the look on his face when he handed it to me told me that he approved of my initiative.

"As an academician and, therefore, in the eyes of your publicity director, an egg head," wrote Swalm, "I wish to object to any representative of an institution of higher learning writing such ungrammatical and illogical drivel as that found in the enclosed article. Surely such a release can in no way advance the primary purposes of Pittsburgh – or of other universities. That it comes from an official representative of your college is frightening."

I'm sure a lot of people found the fact that I was employed by Pitt frightening. I found it interesting that the good professor chose to complain about my poor grammar instead of attacking the substance of my letter, so I chalked that one up as a victory.

I've never been very diplomatic or great with the written word, but I love college football so much, I'll defend the sport any time, anywhere, by any means. Well, any means short of dueling, I guess.

There's no denying that college football has enemies and that there are issues that need to be addressed so that the sport can not only survive, but thrive moving forward. And do so without losing any more of its foundational identity.

Now more than ever, the sport needs leadership. Centralized leadership. College football needs a commissioner.

I've been arguing for this for nearly fifty years, ever since I witnessed first-hand the chaos that resulted from the assassination of JFK. Yet it's not just that the sport needs someone with the power to make difficult decisions during a national emergency. Other problems will arise and that because of sectional bias, institutional inertia and politics, the loose confederation of conference commissioners and NCAA councils currently running the show won't be up to the task of finding the right solutions.

I can see that with what's going on with the graduate transfer movement, it's an inevitability that there will one day be some sort of free agency in college football.

On that train of thought, I don't know if college football players will ever be paid, but I predict they will eventually unionize, so you'll need someone with business experience capable of negotiating labor deals and mediating disputes.

There will be a need for someone to negotiate television rights as well as rights for whatever else develops in terms of advancements in the field of telecommunications.

Most importantly, there has to be a strong, singular personality capable of preserving the integrity and unique identity of the game, someone who can safeguard the sanctity of the sport and successfully straddle the fine line between amateurism and professionalism.

Out of all the predictions I've made in my life, and especially the ones that I've made in this book, I am most confident in this one: one day in the near future we will have a commissioner of college football.

While I have a few ideas on candidates, the only thing I am certain of in terms of this prediction is that it won't be me. I'm taking my cue from General William Tecumseh Sherman, who said regarding the presidency of the United States, "if nominated, I will not run. If elected, I will not serve."

Thirty years ago, I'd have jumped at the opportunity. Now, I'm too old. The sport needs someone younger and more energetic. Someone who doesn't mind a lot of travel. Besides, I'm too opinionated and I definitely wouldn't be a fair and impartial arbiter.

Due to the need for neutrality in decision making, I don't think it can be a former coach or athletic director. Nor can it be someone affiliated with the NCAA. That organization is more toothless and incompetent than the League of Nations.

The ideal candidate would be someone who not only loves the sport as much as I do, someone who will be a guardian of its history like I am, but a true fan that's totally independent. I'm thinking of someone who could do for college football what "The Squire," Kenesaw Mountain Landis, did for baseball.

I'm imagining someone with television experience and a charismatic presence, someone like Joe Foss, the World War II flying ace, Medal of Honor recipient and "American Sportsman" host who headed the AFL and negotiated several TV deals before the merger.

The commissioner should have some leadership or command experience, or, at the very least, a commanding personality. Someone like Tom Hamilton checks those boxes. But I'm not so sure a military background is a job requirement. After all, baseball owners picked General Bill Eckert to succeed Ford Frick and his tenure was largely a failure.

Lastly, the candidate should also understand PR and possess a vision that will enable him or her to see future events and problems coming and head them off at the pass. There was no one more emblematic of either attribute than Pete Rozelle.

I don't know if any one person checks all these boxes. But I've thought quite a bit on the idea over the years and have come up with a short list of candidates that meet a good many of my requirements.

Pete Dawkins probably has the best all-around pedigree as a former player at Army, as a Heisman Trophy winner, Rhodes Scholar, decorated war hero, successful businessman and enthusiastic supporter of the game and everything it stands for. The only people who would probably object to Dawkins would be graduates of the Naval Academy.

One of their ranks, Roger Staubach, is another individual who would be perfect for the job. In all honesty, when you're looking at former players, I think someone associated with one of the service academies would be one of the small handful of universally acceptable candidates. I don't see Texas Exes getting behind an Oklahoma Sooner, or Miami of Florida grads feeling good about a Florida State alum.

The entire country could get on board with a legend like Staubach. He did a tour in Vietnam. He's got impeccable football credentials. He's one of only, I think three or four players, to have won both a Heisman and a Super Bowl MVP award. He's an extremely successful business executive. He's got a television background as well.

Two others who I think America would embrace in the role of commissioner are media guys who I've known for the better part of the past 25 years: Tim Brando and Chris Fowler. I got to know both during the early days of "College GameDay" on *ESPN*.

Their names are synonymous with college football. They've been to every college campus in the country. Furthermore, they know everybody in the sport, coaches, ADs, current and former players, media, television executives, etc. They probably have a better view of the contemporary game than anybody else, plus I think that my passion for the game and my appreciation of the history rubbed off on them.

Lastly, I don't necessarily think that being male is a prerequisite for the position. Former Secretary of State Condoleezza Rice would be a great candidate. I've heard that Rice is a big college football fan and I read somewhere that she said that being commissioner of the NFL was her "dream job," so I can't help but wonder if being the first-ever commissioner of college football wouldn't be an intriguing proposition for her.

Rice is the only individual on my list who I've never met, but her résumé speaks for itself. She's accomplished, intelligent and telegenic. Besides, anybody used to dealing with kings and dictators has the experience needed to handle the coaches in the SEC.

* * *

When I was a voter in the AP poll, I believed in transparency. I used whatever opportunity *ESPN* provided me with, whether it was "College GameDay," the Saturday night "Scoreboard Show," "Sunday SportsDay," or the Internet chat I did with Howie Schwab, to share my ballot with the public and explain why I voted the way I did.

In that spirit, I want to share one last ballot with you, my final rankings of the greatest teams, coaches, and players, as well as my favorite fight songs, rivalries, helmets, traditions and all the other things that make the game of college football so special to me.

On these next few pages, I'm going to share some incredible stats, stories and lines that, like Pat O'Brien said before he launched into the Gipper speech in the movie, "I've kept to myself for years." You may not agree with my picks, but remember, no poll, human or computer, is perfect. These are merely one fan's favorites from a lifetime of following college football.

So, who's number one? Which team do I think is the best in college football history? The only thing I hate more than losing a bet by the hook are politicians that flip-flop on positions, so I've tried to be consistent when providing an answer to the writers, producers and people on the street that have asked me this question over the years. If you've heard me talk on this topic before, my opinion hasn't changed. If you haven't, sit tight. Before I give my final answer, Regis, let me explain which team it isn't.

The most physically impressive championship teams I've seen are the 1971 and 1995 Nebraska teams. They steamrolled opponents. But neither is the all-time greatest.

The most accomplished team might be Notre Dame's 1943 team. The '43 Fighting Irish beat five teams ranked in the top ten, three of which finished No. 2, No. 3 and No. 4 in the final AP poll, and played seven of its ten games on the road.

Contrary to popular belief, the Great Lakes team that upset Notre Dame wasn't coached by Paul Brown. In '43, Great Lakes was coached by Tony Hinkle. The field house at Butler University is named for him.

Notre Dame old-timers used to complain that they would have gone undefeated if several of their own players, who had been drafted into the military, hadn't been forced to play for Great Lakes. They had a point. Jimmy the Greek told me that when he learned that Great Lakes would be suiting up ex-Irish players like Emil "Six-Yard" Sitko, he took the 17-point underdog Sailors. Sure enough, Sitko had a big game with a touchdown and an interception. I once told Charlie Callahan, don't blame Uncle Sam for that loss. Blame Admiral Yamamoto.

If Notre Dame fans were upset with losing players to the war effort, imagine how Pitt felt. In 1943, Bill Abromitis was playing fullback for Pitt. Halfway through the season, the Navy assigned Abromitis, a V-12 trainee, to a training course at Penn State. The coaches there immediately drafted Abromitis to play football, and, in a strange quirk of fate, he scored a touchdown for the Nittany Lions in their 14-0 win over Pitt. And then when it came time to award varsity letters, Abromitis received his letter from Pitt, not Penn State!

The most talented teams, as far as future NFL stars, in recent college football history are unquestionably the 2001 Miami Hurricanes and the 1972 USC Trojans. There were 17 future first-round, and 38 total draft picks, on that 2001 Miami team. The Hurricanes' average margin of victory was 34 points. In terms of all-time athleticism, I don't think anybody could match-up with them.

The '72 Trojans suited up 13 All-Americans and had 33 total players drafted. Keith Jackson said the '72 Trojans were the best team he's ever seen.

The '44 and '45 Army teams were juggernauts, but the quality of opponents those teams faced due to wartime manpower shortages has always been a sticking point for me. The quality of college football played in those two years, as opposed to early in the war before the country was fully mobilized, wasn't very good.

The most heavily-decorated team in college football history was Army's 1914 team. One of four College Football Hall of Fame players on that team was Robert Neyland. Omar Bradley didn't make the Hall of Fame, but he ended up doing okay for himself; Bradley became a five-star general and the first Chairman of the Joint Chiefs of Staff. And another guy named Eisenhower, whose earliest claim to fame was tackling Jim Thorpe in the 1912 Army-Carlisle game, would have been on that team, but he tore up his knee and had to quit football.

In my opinion, the best team in college football history, by any measurement, was Notre Dame in 1947. Forty-one players from that team went on to play professional football. In fact, 20 of them were drafted *before* the '47 season. Lou Somogyi told me that. Seven were inducted into the College Hall of Fame. On Notre Dame's roster were two Heisman winners and two Outland Trophy winners. That team was so deep, *Life Magazine* speculated that Coach Frank Leahy had a total of "seven first teams."

I knew all this stuff. What I didn't know, until Charlie Callahan mentioned it off-handedly during one of our many dinners, was that the 1947 team never trailed. You're reading that correctly. They were never behind at any point in any game.

Not only that, they were never even close to being tied with an opponent in the second half. The only time a team got within two scores of the Irish in the second half was when Notre Dame's back-up quarterback, Frank Tripucka, threw an interception that Northwestern returned for a touchdown in the fourth quarter. That was the only game all season that Notre Dame didn't win by double digits.

Think about the sheer impossibility of it. No opponent won the coin toss, got the ball and put a quick score on the board. Not a single bad snap, busted coverage, fluke fumble or communication error put Notre Dame behind for a single second.

The '47 Fighting Irish never came out flat and they never had to come from behind. They dominated every opponent from the first whistle of the season opener until the final gun sounded on the season finale.

It's the greatest stat in the history of college football. It's the sport's version of the DiMaggio hitting streak. No team will ever do it again. The wartime Army teams, the 2001 Miami team, the '72 USC team, the '71 and '95 Nebraska teams, none of those squads dominated every single minute of every game like that Notre Dame team did.

As far as I know, the only team that got anywhere near this record, before or since, was Tennessee's 1939 team which rattled off ten consecutive shutouts before losing 14-0, to USC in the 1940 Rose Bowl.

When I told Johnny Lujack that stat, he didn't realize it. And he quarterbacked that team! When I told Steve Spurrier, he was very impressed. He said he'd never heard anything like it. So was the Greek. And here's an interesting thing he told me in response: according to his recollections, the only game Notre Dame didn't cover during its 39-game unbeaten streak between 1946 and 1949 was the tie with Southern Cal in '48.

That might be an even more ridiculous stat, that Notre Dame covered nearly every single game for four years. Not even Oklahoma during their 47-game win streak covered every game. Presumably, Notre Dame was favored in every game except for the '46 Army game and the lines probably weren't that high, since point spread betting was in its infancy. I have no way of researching or proving this, but since the Greek said it, I'd say it's true.

How anybody can say that a team that never trailed and always covered isn't the best ever is beyond me. However, if you don't agree with me, that's your prerogative. But know that you're not just disagreeing with me. You're also disagreeing with Grantland Rice and "Dr. Z," Paul Zimmerman, both of whom also thought the '47 Fighting Irish were the standard by which all future great college teams will be judged.

What about coaches? I don't mean to shortchange small school coaching legends like Eddie Robinson and John Gagliardi, but for our purposes this discussion will be limited to major college football coaches who consistently won, both big games and championships, on the biggest stage in the modern era.

And there can be no serious conversation on coaches until we first pay our respects to what I consider the "Founding Fathers" of college football: Amos Alonzo Stagg, Walter Camp and John Heisman. They were responsible for the innovations that modernized the game into the phenomenon that we wait all week to watch on Saturdays and Sundays. Stagg invented the huddle, the quarterback keeper, varsity letters and padded goalposts. Camp contributed the snap, the downs system, and countless other innovations. Heisman gave us four quarters and the famed trophy that bears his name. Where do I rank these guys, in order? I can't. It's like trying to rank Adams, Jefferson, and Madison.

There are five coaches, who, though big winners, fall just outside my final rankings. The first are the two greatest defensive-minded head coaches in college football history. Due to the overwhelming emphasis on offense in the game today, I've long felt that what these first two coaches accomplished by placing a strategic priority on defense deserves special mention.

Tennessee's General Robert Neyland won 173 games and logged 112 shutouts. In 65% of the games Neyland coached, the opponent didn't score a single point! That's a staggering stat. Neyland's famed "Seven Maxims" are college football's Ten Commandments.

The only college coach with a better shutout percentage was Pitt's Dr. "Jock" Sutherland, who went 111-20-12 over 15 years with 79 shutouts. He didn't just win, he won by matching wits against a "who's who" of coaching legends. Sutherland defeated his mentor, Pop Warner, three times (twice while coaching at little Lafayette, and once while Warner was at Stanford), and regularly faced Hall of Fame coaches like Knute Rockne, Howard Jones, Dana X. Bible, "Sleepy Jim" Crowley, Bernie Bierman and Wallace Wade.

Barry Switzer won 12 Big Eight titles and three national titles at Oklahoma, but like the case with Sutherland, what's most impressive was his career record against his rivals and contemporaries. He dominated Tom Osborne and was undefeated against Darrell Royal, Bobby Bowden, Joe Paterno, Bo Schembechler and Woody Hayes.

Bobby Bowden won two national titles and 12 ACC titles at Florida State. He finished second all-time to Joe Paterno in total wins among major college coaches. Yet his greatest accomplishment was finishing in the top five in an astounding 14 consecutive seasons. I don't think any coach will ever duplicate, much less beat, that feat.

John McKay won four national titles and in 16 years at Southern Cal, he lost only 17 conference games. What is most remarkable about McKay's résumé was the fact that over the course of his final nine years, Southern Cal played Notre Dame and UCLA 18 times and only lost three of those games. He's also the most quotable coach in college football history.

Okay, the five greatest coaches in major college football history. Why only five? The top five in any poll is all that really matters when you get down to it, so the number fits.

Starting, in ascending order, at five is the late Joe Paterno. Now before Penn State fans complain that I don't have him higher, I want to explain that my personal rankings are based upon my own special selection criteria, not just won-loss records. And emotion, personal relationships, or past history – none of that factors in.

For example, I'm not exactly a fan of John Dillinger's work, but if someone asked me who the greatest bank robber of all-time was, Dillinger would be my answer. Whether I like someone or not is incidental.

That said, Paterno is of course the all-time winningest major college football coach in terms of total wins. In my opinion, he might just be the best gameday coach in the sport's history. In other words, if I had to pick one coach to be on the sideline of a team that I wanted to win a championship game, with no regards to pre-game preparation or any of that other stuff, I'd probably pick Paterno. It would be him or John McKay. One of those two.

Paterno is the best bowl coach of all time. He was 24-12-1 in the postseason and he's the only coach to have won all five major – Orange, Sugar, Cotton, Fiesta and Rose – bowls. One of those victories, Penn State's upset win in the 1987 Fiesta Bowl, was a masterful job of preparation and coaching. If Reggie Jackson is Mr. October, Joe Paterno was Mr. January.

Paterno isn't on my list because of his wins, his collection of bowl rings or his remarkable longevity. It's because he was to Penn State what Rockne was to Notre Dame, the one who started it all. At the time of his death, his 409 wins were roughly half of what the Penn State program had tallied in the entirety of its existence.

Now Joe and I didn't always see eye-to-eye, and, as you're going to read, on many occasions I had issues with some of the things he said and the way he ran his program, but he literally put State College, Pennsylvania on the national college football map and I have the utmost respect for him for that accomplishment.

I've always respected Paterno. No matter what I might have said about him or Penn State on the air over the years, I liked Joe. There's a misconception that because you have a disagreement with someone or call them out or criticize them that you hate them. That's not fair. In fact, I'd venture to say that Joe and I were friends. Not close friends, but we were friends.

Now is as good a time or place as ever to talk about our relationship. Paterno is a polarizing figure nowadays because of the scandal, so his place on my list is probably going to create some controversy. That's appropriate because he's an important, controversial character in the story of my life and career.

I knew Joe for over fifty years, since way back when he was an assistant at Penn State and I was the SID at Pitt. He handled recruiting in Western Pennsylvania, so I used to see him quite a bit. We got along well. Well, except for the time we almost got into a fight at Gustine's in the late 1950s. We had to be separated by people at the bar.

About ten years ago, at Budd Thalman's retirement party in State College, the story came up. Neither of us could remember who started it or what it was about. I think it was over a recruit, probably Ditka. But Paterno was adamant who would have finished it. "I would have kicked your ass!" he laughed. He was probably right.

The funny thing is that back then Joe was an easy-going, laid-back guy. Football to him was fun. I was the one that took the Pitt-Penn State rivalry too seriously and treated football and recruiting like it was life and death. "It's just a game, Beano," he used to tell me. "It's not war."

I was probably the one who started that altercation at Gustine's. But I don't think Joe ever admitted that something changed in him after he got the head job. His ambition to win was something I never thought I'd see. He began treating football like it was war.

It started with the way Penn State handled the media. At first, freshmen weren't allowed to talk to the media. Then it was other players. Pretty soon, Penn State had a controlled press. The people who run China and North Korea would be impressed if they knew what Penn State once got away with.

In 1970, when Paterno benched Mike Cooper, the school's first black starting quarterback, I heard that Franco Harris and Lydell Mitchell skipped practice in protest and some white players were upset. Someone from Penn State asked the *Centre Daily Times* to lay off the story for fear that it would create rumors of problems regarding race relations on the team. The answer from the paper's beat writer reportedly was, in so many words, "don't worry, we won't write anything."

When out-of-town writers weren't compliant, Penn State got combative. Herschel Nissenson, for example, had problems with Penn State. Paterno accused him of being anti-Eastern football. Someone at Penn State supposedly even went so far as to start the rumor in media circles that Nissenson provided favorable coverage of Oklahoma because someone there set him up with a broad. That wasn't true.

What was true was that after awhile, many national writers, not to mention television people, dreaded being assigned a story on Penn State or going there to do a game. When Donn Bernstein left *ABC* in 1991 to take another gig in PR, he told me he was relieved he "didn't have to deal with Penn State anymore."

I got tired of hearing about the "Penn State Way," and all the propaganda that was coming out of State College. More and more, Penn State appeared to be a Potemkin village. For example, Paterno's exalted commitment to academics. Matt Millen revealed to somebody, I forget who told me this story, that Paterno told players to carry briefcases around campus, but he didn't care if there were any books inside them.

Paterno also made a big deal about publicly supporting players' extracurricular activities and off-the-field interests, which propped up the façade that Paterno was different from other coaches because he was willing to let these things take precedence over football. An example was how he made the impression that he permitted Mike Reid to be redshirted to perform in a campus production of "Guys and Dolls." The thing was, Reid got hurt in the opener against Navy in '67. It was a bad knee injury. That's the reason he was redshirted. The way Paterno made it sound, he gave Reid a leave of absence.

Another thing that I couldn't take was when Penn State had the audacity to complain about fairness in officiating when a call went against them. This was the school that beat Nebraska at home in 1982 on one of the worst calls I've ever seen in my life, when the Penn State tight end caught a pass that was clearly out-of-bounds on the go-ahead touchdown drive.

The questionable officiating at Penn State home games wasn't a big secret. Lou Holtz used to say the most difficult thing to do in college football was to take a team to Penn State and finish the game with less penalties than the home team.

There was one memorable game in which Penn State ended up with more penalty yardage than the visitors and that was the 1973 Pitt game. Although Pitt lost, 35-13, the game was memorable to me because of what was said after it ended.

Pitt had been beating the undefeated, sixth-ranked Lions by ten at halftime and no doubt some amount of panic had set in with the home crowd. But the Penn State faithful needn't have worried. The Lucas brothers, Richie and Kenny, were talking to one of the officials after the game. Richie played at Penn State in the late 1950s and Kenny played at Pitt in the early 1960s. "Richie, there wasn't anything to worry about," the official said. "We had them."

We? Are you kidding me?

Then there's Don Guman. It was incomprehensible to me that Penn State thought it was acceptable to have the father of a former player working the sidelines as an official. I'm not saying Guman was crooked. Not at all. By all accounts, he was an honest, solid referee. My argument is that Penn State should have acknowledged that other schools were uncomfortable with the arrangement. But they didn't care.

Pat Sullivan, the Auburn quarterback and Heisman Trophy winner, got married when he was a sophomore to a girl whose father, Joe Hicks, was an SEC official. Hicks requested to be taken off the Auburn-Clemson game one year and never did another Auburn game while his son-in-law was playing.

When the cutthroats in the SEC are concerned about a conflict of interest and the people at Penn State wonder what all the fuss is about, that told me something about Paterno's priorities.

Privately, behind closed doors, other coaches and schools used to talk about what they thought the "Penn State Way" really meant. Woody Hayes, for example, called Paterno a "hypocrite son-of-a bitch" in 1978. See, Ohio State and Penn State had agreed to a home-and-home deal for September games in 1976 and 1978.

Hayes was fucking furious when he learned that Paterno had moved two games up in the schedule before playing Ohio State in '78. The game with Penn State ended up being Ohio State's season opener and the 2-0, battle-tested Lions shut the Buckeyes out, 19-0, in Columbus.

In 1981, Penn State tried to buy the Miami of Florida game. They wanted to pay Miami to move the game to Penn State. It was the last game in a three-game deal; the first two games, in '79 and '80, were played in State College. It had to have been Paterno's idea because he was AD at the time.

Anyway, Miami's cash-strapped athletic department was reportedly receptive to the idea, but Miami's coaches found out and went berserk. Here were the administrators, trying to give up the Hurricanes' homefield advantage. The Miami coaches all threatened to quit. The game was ultimately played in Miami and Howard Schnellenberger's Hurricanes upset No. 1 Penn State, 17-14. It was a ballsy move by the coaches and the players backed them up.

During Paterno's glory years, Penn State would do anything and everything to try to gain an advantage. In November 1980, No. 4 Pitt played No. 5 Penn State in State College. Both teams were out of the national title chase, but there was still a lot at stake with rankings and bowl berths. Most importantly, pride was on the line. So Paterno pulled out all the stops.

My friend Bill Hillgrove, Pitt's veteran radio play-by-play man, headed up to Happy Valley with his crew for the game. Hillgrove took over the job when Ed Conway died of cancer in '74. He does Pitt basketball and play-by-play for the Steelers, too. If there was a Mount Rushmore – technically it would be carved into the side of Mount Washington in Pittsburgh – of Steel City sports media personalities, Hillgrove has to be on it. He's a Duquesne alum, but I think I can speak for all Pitt alums when I say that I consider him one of us, a "Pitt guy."

Anyway, they put in a request to interview Paterno and were told to have their equipment set up in a certain classroom at a certain time and that Paterno would be there. Well, they were all ready to go at the appointed time but there was no sign of Paterno. Everybody kept looking at their watches. They were doodling on their notepads.

Suddenly, Hillgrove's producer, Kerry Richards, saw what looked like a notebook on a desk. He picked it up and showed it to Hillgrove. On the cover was printed, "Pitt gameplan."

"What should we do with this?" asked Richards.

"We're going to leave it right where it is," Hillgrove answered.

It was too good to be true, and it likely was. Hillgrove later said he couldn't believe that a Penn State player would have been so careless to have left a copy of the playbook there. In that room, at that specific time!

To this day, I can't believe Penn State tried such a maneuver. That's as junior varsity as it gets. I don't think Mercersburg, Kiski's rival, would have tried that when I was in prep school.

Paterno was named *Sports Illustrated's* "Sportsman of the Year" in 1986. I laughed when I heard the announcement. Late in the 1985 Pitt-Penn State game, when Pitt was getting blown out, he took the second team out and put the first team back in to preserve the shutout. "I want to bury Pitt," an official heard Paterno say on the sideline. Joe knew Foge Fazio was out. It wasn't necessary to humiliate Foge. That wasn't being very sportsman-like.

Then there's 1977. Nobody knows about this. For years, Paterno had bitched about a perceived bias against Eastern football by the media, but when he had a chance to strike a big blow for Eastern football he chose not to. Why? Because Pitt was involved.

At the time of the Pitt-Penn State game in November 1977, Penn State was ranked No. 9 and Pitt was No. 10. A behind-the-scenes agreement had been proposed by the Orange Bowl committee in which the winner of the game would receive the Orange Bowl bid. Jackie Sherrill said yes, but Paterno said no. Paterno thought Penn State should have received the bid because it was ranked higher. Penn State ended up winning the close game, 15-13, but Eastern football lost out. Arkansas got the Orange Bowl bid instead.

Paterno considered Penn State the standard bearer of Eastern football and by that, he wanted everybody to get in line behind Penn State. When he proposed the Eastern Conference in 1981, I was at first receptive to the idea. Then I learned that under Paterno's plan, Penn State would receive more than just the Nittany Lions' share of the television revenue. The number was somewhere in the vicinity of eighty percent.

Once Boston College, Maryland, Pitt, Rutgers, Syracuse, and Temple read that fine print, they didn't want to be considered junior partners and that's why the whole thing fell apart. For years, Paterno talked like it was Pitt that was single-handedly responsible for torpedoing the plan.

When I pointed out that Paterno held grudges, or when I called him sanctimonious or called Penn State out, I was saying what I believed. I wasn't looking for headlines or attention or trying to get under his skin or even to needle Penn State fans.

Now I will admit that when the latter occurred, it was a bonus. My main issue with Penn State's fans is that they forget their roots. Few remember or know what it was like when Penn State wasn't even a bit player on the national scene. I really gave it to them after they booed Penn State's loss at home to Cincinnati in 1983. Paterno had finally delivered a national title the year before and they were booing. It was a bad look.

Penn State fans, of course, complained about that one. Penn State people took everything personally. I remember at the start of the 1987 Fiesta Bowl, when *NBC* put up the graphics for the starting lineups, I noticed that Penn State's players were majoring in things like tourism and parks and recreation. *No wonder they have these really high graduation rates*, I said to myself.

A few days later, I got a call from Bill Fleischman of the *Philadelphia Daily News* and I repeated that remark to him. Fleischman included the material in his column and I started getting all kinds of letters from pissed-off Penn State professors. Even Jim Tarman took time out of his busy job as Penn State's AD to write Fleischman.

"What you have to keep in mind here, Bill, is that Beano is a Pitt graduate and a former Pitt publicist," explained Tarman. "Try as he might to be an objective 'journalist,' his Pitt background surfaces when it comes to Penn State – more so in highly-successful Penn State years such as 1986."

Tarman cc'd that letter to Paterno and me. I could only laugh. It was a peculiarly Penn State thing. They always had to get in the last word.

When I called Penn State and Paterno out, I did it for two reasons. One, I felt it was my job to use to my unique perspective and sources to inform the public about what went on up there. Nobody else was doing it, or even could do it. It's like the men who see some guy's wife as being a knockout, as being really something, but the husband himself cannot figure out why. He's close, so he sees her flaws and behind-close-doors personality on a daily basis.

I saw things at Penn State, as well as other places, and felt I was duty bound to open my mouth. I've always been this way. When I was the SID at Pitt, writers liked me because I was blunt and honest. I told the truth about what was going on with our teams. Especially about the basketball. It got me in hot water more than once.

The other reason is that in my opinion, Paterno lost perspective on what he used to preach. When we were younger, I thought he was different. We could talk literature or plays or movies. Football wouldn't even come up. I truly believed he more than just a coach. I guess when I was presented with the proof that I was wrong, it was tough to take. I felt as though I had to hold him up to his own purportedly high standards.

I know Paterno and the people at Penn State didn't always appreciate my opinions. And I know that at times, I went too far with some of my comments. There were things I said to or about Paterno, Tarman and Budd Thalman that I wish I could take back.

So yes, there were some bad times and occasionally some bad blood between the two of us. But I think we got past that. It's all water over the Whipple Dam. If we had not been on good terms, would Paterno have let me into his home to interview his wonderful wife, Sue, for a "College GameDay" feature after he broke Bear Bryant's record?

The last time I saw Joe was an interview I did with him for *ESPN* five years ago.

It was like it was in the 1950s again. We had a lot of laughs. When I heard that he passed away, I thought back to that day and was thankful we went out on good terms.

I'm certain many Penn State fans will never bury the hatchet with me. Some will never forgive me for things I've said and many will probably bitch that Paterno is only number five on my list. In all honesty, Paterno would be higher if he'd won more than just the two national titles.

On the other hand, other people will probably feel that Paterno shouldn't even be on the list because of the scandal. I guess it's fitting that me talking about Paterno, even after he's gone, still creates controversy. See, when I was complimentary of Paterno and Penn State, Penn State people and fans would say they were back-handed compliments. I couldn't win. So some things, when it comes to certain subjects, don't change.

Those of you who think Paterno should be erased from history, you're wrong. Every one of us has flaws. Nobody goes through life without making mistakes. Some make big ones. I think Joe's big mistake was not being more forceful and using his power to make sure the AD and the other administrators followed through on the reports and allegations.

Did Joe know? Yes, of course he knew. He got the information from his young assistant coach and he gave it to the right people further up in the chain of command as he was supposed to and he probably expected it to be handled correctly. What were people expecting him to do, circumvent the AD, the university president, all the lawyers and the police and call a press conference and air all of the dirty laundry himself?

In my opinion that wasn't a reasonable expectation. I'm not trying to make excuses, but I have a problem with how Paterno was perceived after the whole sordid affair. The Penn State scandal is college football's Watergate. It might even have been more thoroughly covered than Watergate.

But the one thing that all these writers and commentators and talking heads missed was something that was plainly obvious to me: they assigned Paterno a certain blame while not considering the fact that he was from another generation, a generation of people that was used to handling things in a different way.

Once upon a time, when uncomfortable situations arose, these things were handled in hushed conversations and in a way that didn't bring any attention to anybody, that's the victims, their families, the perpetrators, what have you.

I remember back when I was growing up, when a teenage girl that wasn't married got pregnant, the family would send her to have the baby in a convent. These girls would just disappear for awhile. Nobody ever saw them or spoke of them. That's how things were.

In cases of sexual deviancy, the police were rarely involved. Nor the media. A few men would handle the problem, in many cases with violence. This was a time when a sense of shame took precedence and was responsible for decision-making. Regardless of how the situation was rectified, the story wasn't made public knowledge.

I'm not saying any of this was right, it's just that people weren't always in agreement when it came to dealing with these things. The one thing everybody was certain of was that it didn't need to be everybody else's business. The media didn't rule the roost and people weren't open to having their names, affairs and tragedies laid out for the world to examine.

I have no way of knowing this to be true, but something tells me Paterno, when he got the news of what that pervert did, wasn't thinking like a football coach or a public official in the 21st century. He was thinking like someone who was born in 1926 would have thought.

We have developed a very bad habit in this country of examining history through the perspective of our own time and passing judgment on people from other eras according to our perspective, our opinions, and our feelings.

Paterno shouldn't have been crucified for not handling the situation like a coach forty years younger than him might have. His accomplishments, his life, a life in which he served as a positive role model for the thousands of young men that he coached, shouldn't be erased. He did more good for that institution than any one person will ever do for Penn State. You're kidding yourself if you think you can just wipe that all away.

I honestly don't know what's more bizarre, the people who think you can take down a statue and change history, or the fact that a Pitt guy who has a long and checkered history with Paterno is the one arguing on behalf of remembering the great coach's largely positive legacy.

Unlike Paterno, I never met, nor had any kind of relationship with Glenn Scobey "Pop" Warner, but like every American boy I can attest to having been acquainted with his name at an early age. Warner is the fourth all-time greatest college coach on my list.

Even more so than Camp, Heisman and Stagg, Warner was perhaps the greatest innovator the game has ever known. He is credited with introducing the single-wing and double-wing formations, the bootleg play, the screen pass, the double reverse, uniform numbers, and the use of shoulder pads and tackling dummies. Warner won four national titles, all in the pre-poll era.

To me, Warner is unique among the old greats because he won at geographically distinct places with different admissions standards and under continuously changing sets of rules that governed play. He won at Cornell, Carlisle, Georgia, Iowa State, Pitt, Stanford, and Temple. That's like a coach in the modern era winning in the Ivy League, the SEC, the Big 12, the Big East, the Pac-10, and as an independent. No future coach, no matter how well-traveled, will have a résumé like that.

Oh, and you want longevity? Warner's career started under the Teddy Roosevelt Administration and ended during the Franklin Roosevelt Administration.

Until Paterno surpassed him, Bear Bryant was the all-time winningest coach in Division I-A. But Bryant still holds the record for most wire service national titles, six, all at Alabama. When it came to pure coaching ability, Bryant's skill was almost unparalleled.

That famous line, "he's so good that he can take his'n and beat your'n or he can take your'n and beat his'n," was supposedly uttered by another coach about Bryant, but I'm not totally sure of its origin. It's been attributed to many coaches, including Bum Phillips. I first read it in a story about Bryant written by John Crittenden in the *Miami News* when I was with the Dolphins.

But I was later told by Clemson's Frank Howard that he was the one who said it. Howard said it was a compliment intended for Missouri coach Don Faurot, after Clemson barely edged Mizzou in the '49 Gator Bowl. No matter who gets credit for that famous line or who it's in reference to, there's no question Bryant was moving chess pieces around the field while his opposite numbers were playing checkers.

In my opinion, however, there's more to Bryant's legacy than his reputation and all the wins and championships. Bryant had a swagger about him, a certain charisma, that no other coach had. And that houndstooth hat, it's the third-most famous hat in American history, right behind Lincoln's stovepipe and Davy Crockett's coonskin cap.

Bryant would rank higher if he had been the Rockne or Paterno of Alabama, but he wasn't the school's foundational coach. Wallace Wade and Frank Thomas won big in Tuscaloosa before him.

Even so, one thing I am sure of is that no coach will ever be venerated by Alabama fans like Bryant was. Certainly, no coach will ever be more revered – or feared – by his players. I was convinced of that after hearing the following story from Dr. Z some forty years ago.

Sometime right after Joe Namath quarterbacked the Jets to victory in Super Bowl III, Zimmerman told me that he wrote a story for the *New York Post* in which he quoted Namath as saying, "the Bear always said defense wins games." A day or two later, Namath told Zimmerman he had been misquoted. He wanted Zimmerman to run a correction.

"Wait a minute, Joe, that's what you said about the defense," Zimmerman said.

"Yes, I said that about the defense," Namath explained. "But I never said Bear. I said Coach Bryant or maybe even Mister Bryant. There's no way I said Bear. You gotta fix it."

I never played a down for Bryant, but I never had the guts to call him Bear to his face, either. The handful of times I met him, I addressed him as Paul or Coach. I will also add that while Bryant ranks No. 3 in the Beano Poll, he's probably No. 1 in the Coaches' Poll. Many of his peers, including legends like Nebraska's Bob Devaney and Southern Cal's John McKay, thought Bryant was the best ever. Again, there's nothing wrong with split decisions.

Knute Rockne was not only the most famous college football coach, he was perhaps the most famous American sports figure the world will ever know. When he died, his funeral was broadcast live on the radio around the world. My mother told me that the three greatest national outpourings of grief she recalled in her lifetime were after FDR's death, the assassination of JFK and when Rockne died. She died at the age of 96.

Rockne had Bryant's charisma and coaching acumen, Warner's mad scientist brain, and, with his rousing pep talks, he was the greatest motivational leader and speechmaker in the sport's history, the Winston Churchill of college football.

And he could flat out coach. Notre Dame's 1929 national championship team went 9-0 and didn't play a single home game. Notre Dame Stadium was being built at the time, so Notre Dame played all nine games on the road. Can you imagine a modern team doing that? Most of the big schools today play seven or eight home games.

What I am most in awe of when it comes to Rockne was that nobody saw the big picture like him. Most casual fans know him primarily for his role in popularizing the forward pass and for the Gipper speech, but he was in effect Notre Dame's head coach, athletic director, business manager and SID.

He was the first coach to grasp the importance of radio, was an expert at cultivating relationships with sportswriters and doing PR, and he was way ahead of his time when it came to marketing both himself and the Fighting Irish. Nothing illustrates Rockne's vision better than the conversation he had with Notre Dame's president about the plans for the soon-to-be-built Notre Dame Stadium. Callahan told me this one.

Upon examining the blueprints, the priest noticed that Rockne had set aside sizable tracts of land for parking. This was in the late 1920s, when automobile ownership wasn't nearly as common as it is today. The interstate highway system was still twenty, thirty years into the future.

"Knute," said the priest, "I can't see any reason for reserving such a vast amount of space for parking lots. Nobody drives to football games."

"They will, Father," Rockne assured him. "They will."

Today, 80 years since he last coached a game, Rockne is still the all-time leader among major college coaches in winning percentage. Right behind Rockne's .881 is Frank Leahy's .864. That, and his personality, are the only things Rockne had on Leahy.

Both coached for a total of 13 seasons and Leahy ended up with two more wins than Rockne and also bested him in total national titles, four to three. I truly believe that had Rockne and his prized pupil ever went up against each other, with talent and everything else being equal, Leahy would have beaten Rockne head-to-head.

Not even Charlie Callahan agreed with me on this, so I am probably the only person in the media or in college football who thinks that Leahy was the best pure coach in the sport's history. I'll tell you why.

Leahy can't be the best, people say, because he only coached 11 years at Notre Dame. Well, one year at Notre Dame equals five at any other top school. The job ages you rapidly. If Methuselah had coached at Notre Dame, he'd have never reached sixty.

And the aging process is much more rapid if you worked at the job like Leahy did. No coach in the history of football at any level was, is, or will ever be more dedicated to winning than Frank Leahy. He was the prototype of today's NFL coach, the workaholic who's married to the game and sleeps on his office couch.

Leahy slept on a cot in a room at the university fire house. He only saw his wife and ten kids in the offseason. All he did was watch film and wear out chalkboards. If he were around today, the guy would think the hours that Bill Belichick, Andy Reid, and Jon Gruden put in were not a serious enough commitment to winning.

Leahy's relentless pursuit of perfection had serious repercussions on his health. He collapsed from an attack of pancreatitis during the 1953 Georgia Tech game and his condition was so serious, Father Joyce administered last rites in the ambulance that rushed Leahy to the hospital. When Father Hesburgh forced Leahy out after the 1953 season, he said he thought Leahy's life was completely out of balance. His obsession with winning had completely overtaken him. He was fearful that Leahy was going to die on the field on TV.

At times, Leahy could be such an intimidating taskmaster, he made Bryant and Lombardi look like kindergarten teachers. His spring practices were so notoriously brutal, one injured Notre Dame player being carried off the field during a scrimmage on Good Friday was overheard to say, "now I know how Christ felt."

Johnny Lattner told me the great story about a practice in which Leahy had the first team offense run the same play over and over again.

"Coach Leahy," an exhausted Lattner asked between plays, "why do we have to run this same play one-thousand times?"

"Because, lad, 999 times are simply not enough."

Leahy didn't have Rockne's flamboyant personality and wasn't a cheerleader when it came to motivation. He was strict, but not a screamer, either. He had a dry, Irish sense of humor that was deeply based in his staunch Catholicism.

"Ooh, you heretic, John Lattner," Leahy growled after Lattner fumbled five times against Purdue. "What am I going to do with you? You committed those five mortal sins." Leahy ordered him to go to the Notre Dame Basilica and make a confession to repent for his frequent fumbling. Lattner wasn't sure if Leahy was serious or not, but he went.

Say what you will about Leahy's madness and his methods, he got results. No other coach won like he did. His personal goal when he took the Notre Dame job was to never lose a game. He damned near pulled it off. In six of his 11 seasons in South Bend, he went unbeaten. If you consider the two years he spent as head coach at Boston College in 1939 and 1940, he went undefeated seven times in thirteen seasons. He went 20-2 at BC, was 11-0 in 1940 and beat undefeated No. 4 Tennessee in the Sugar Bowl.

Leahy is officially credited with four AP national titles. The questionable pass interference call in the '48 USC game cost him his fifth and in '53, the polling was done before the bowls. Maryland lost in the Orange Bowl to Oklahoma, which Notre Dame beat, so that could have been six. There's also the matter of the two years he was away serving in the Navy during World War II. I'm not going to say that Notre Dame would have beaten Army in '44 and '45, but they wouldn't have been blown out like they were. So, if not for the war and other circumstances, there's a chance he'd have finished with seven, maybe even eight national titles. That's unbelievable.

Another reason why I think Leahy is the greatest is because he didn't just win, he won playing the most difficult schedules imaginable. There were no directional schools or cupcakes. Then Notre Dame cut the annual number of scholarships he could give out by nearly half in 1948.

Leahy said 1952 was his finest coaching job. Notre Dame went 7-2-1 that year yet finished No. 3 because of how demanding the schedule was. Notre Dame tied No. 12 Penn in Philadelphia, beat No. 5 Texas in Austin, No. 9 Purdue in West Lafayette, No. 4 Oklahoma at home, lost to No. 1 Michigan State, and beat undefeated No. 2 USC out there. He defeated the Southwest Conference champions, the co-Big Ten champions, the Big Seven champs and the Pacific Coast Conference champions all in one season.

Over the course of his short career, Leahy vanquished nearly every great coach from his era as well as coaches from eras that preceded and came after his own. He beat Neyland in that '41 Sugar Bowl. He went 1-1 versus Fritz Crisler, 2-0 versus Bud Wilkinson and he never lost to Red Blaik and Clark Shaughnessy, all Hall of Fame coaches. He was 4-1 combined versus two of Georgia Tech's three most famous coaches, Bobby Dodd and Bill Alexander.

If all this isn't enough evidence to support my opinion, there are two additional reasons why I believe Leahy was the best ever. First, Leahy coached four Heisman winners, more than anybody else, and he has more players in the College Hall of Fame than anybody else. And before you say, well, he had unlimited material at Notre Dame, five of the thirteen inductees he's connected to played for him at BC.

Second, his legacy isn't confined to college football. At the end of every NFL season, the Super Bowl winners hoist a trophy named for the most famous coach in NFL history, Vince Lombardi. Do you know who one of Lombardi's mentors was?

The line coach at Fordham who was responsible for quarrying and developing the "Seven Blocks of Granite," one of whom was Lombardi, in the 1930s was none other than, yes, you guessed it – Francis William Leahy.

Next, let's talk the all-time greatest players in college football history. We're going to do a top five again, but split in two categories, players who I saw play and those who were before my time. Yes, there were players before my time. I'm old, but I didn't have Rutgers season tickets in 1869.

I've probably watched thousands of players in my seventy or so years as a college football fan. And each year, the sport furnishes us with new stars, so it's increasingly impossible to even try to narrow down the list. Still, two names stand out.

I've tried my best to remain impartial, but when it comes to the all-time greats that I've seen with my own eyes, I can't help but be biased towards my alma mater. They are both Pitt legends.

The most electrifying player I've ever watched play college football is Tony Dorsett. He's probably the only player in memory that, when he got the ball, no matter where it was on the field, you expected him to take it to the house. He could dodge eight tackles and dart for fifty yards, but it was a letdown if the play didn't finish in the endzone.

Dorsett's one of the most decorated players ever, a three-time first-team All-

American who owns a Heisman Trophy and the Maxwell and Camp Awards.

The greats save their best performances for the biggest games and that's why Dorsett was one of them. He rushed for more than 750 yards in four games against Notre Dame and with a chance to play for the national championship on the line, he battered Penn State for 224 yards and two touchdowns in his final regular season game.

In my opinion, there is only one player in the history of college football that, when he stepped onto the field for every game of his career, was not only the toughest and most fearsome player out there, but the most athletic, intelligent, and competitive player on the field as well. He's probably the only player capable of being a first-team All-American in all three facets of the game – offense, defense, and special teams – today. That player was Mike Ditka.

At Pitt, he played both ways, most often lining up at end. The black and white films really don't do Ditka justice. Nor do his stats. The best way I can describe Ditka for young people is to imagine watching Rob Gronkowski play tight end for your team on offense, then watch the same player turn around and imitate Dick Butkus and Reggie White on defense. Oh, and he was our punter, too. His leg was like a mortar.

In Pitt's tie with No. 1 Army in 1958, Ditka had an amazing 40-yard catch that got us out of a hole deep in our own territory and then a series or two later, while playing defense, he hit Army's Bob Anderson so hard on one play that he broke Anderson's nose.

I've not seen anybody in all my years of watching college football who could switch gears like that, go from a long-distance scoring threat to a savage defender, so easily and so effortlessly.

Ditka may be Pitt's greatest all-around, all-time athlete. He played varsity baseball and basketball for the Panthers as well. What stood out to me, more than his energy, versatility, and athleticism, even more than his celebrated toughness, was the intensity with which he played. I once said that Ditka had not merely a fire, but a blast furnace, burning inside him. I've never seen a greater competitor, someone who so hated to lose like him. If I'm in a foxhole and a million Red Chinese are coming over the hill, I want to be in there with Ditka. Now he probably wouldn't want to be in there with me, but that doesn't change my opinion.

In the second category, I have Red Grange, George Gipp and Jim Thorpe. The old-timers on the College Football Hall of Fame's history committee, guys like Fred Russell and Pat Harmon, considered those three the sport's holy trinity. You were labeled a heretic if you questioned it. The older I got and the more I thought about it, I understood why.

Most people, when they hear the name "Jim Thorpe," think of his accomplishments in the Olympics. Many know him as a sensational multi-sport athlete that excelled in football, baseball, basketball and track and field. Few, however, know that he became a household name as an early college football star who played for Pop Warner at Carlisle Indian School in central Pennsylvania in the first decade of the 20th century.

But all you really need to know about Thorpe is that in 1999, he was designated

America's greatest athlete of the 20th century by Congress. That and the declaration of war on Japan after Pearl Harbor are probably the only two things Congress has ever gotten right.

George Gipp's legacy is eternal because of his foundational, dare I say supernatural, role in the sport's early lore. Take a second to reflect on this statement: nobody alive today knows what his voice sounded like. No recordings of it exist. He was also something of a strange, secretive bird who disliked being photographed. Yet somehow, every college football fan, it doesn't matter how old they are or what school they root for, knows Gipp's last words and Rockne's Gipper speech. Gipp might have died at age 25, but he's still alive in everybody's consciousness, the most immortal athlete in American sports history.

Unlike the case with a lot of athletes who were cut down tragically in their youth and whose exploits were exaggerated or embellished to enhance their legacies, Gipp didn't need any help. He was the all-time rushing leader at Notre Dame for nearly sixty years. Gipp set that record when jazz was just starting to be popular. When Jerome Heavens broke it in 1978, disco was all the rage. I can't believe that record stood for so long at place like Notre Dame with all the backs they've had. In fact, ninety years after his death, Gipp still holds some Notre Dame records. I predict he'll remain in our hearts – and the record books – for years to come.

I met Red Grange long after his playing career was over, when he was doing television. The reverence with which many people, this is in both athletics and the media, treated Grange was really something. I've gotten to know and been around a lot of the greats at various functions, but nobody could touch – just like when he was playing – Grange. When he entered a room or a pressbox, heads turned. People dropped what they were doing. You felt you were in the presence of a god.

It could be argued that he's not just the greatest football player, at any level, of all-time, he's also the most important player. Grange was the first national college superstar and he's also responsible for single-handedly popularizing and, as some have speculated, saving the pro game.

He was the prototype star American athlete. All of the Heisman Trophy winners and first overall picks in the NFL draft, the big money contracts, the commercials and promotional sponsorship deals, post-playing career media gigs – Grange did it all first.

The old-timers' reverence, however, that had nothing to do with Grange the product. They worshipped Grange the player. From what I was told by those who saw him play, his speed, stamina, power, and vision was unparalleled.

"This man Red Grange of Illinois is three or four men, and a horse rolled into one for football purposes," wrote Damon Runyon. "He is Jack Dempsey, Babe Ruth, Al Jolson, Paavo Nurmi and Man o' War. Put them all together. They spell Grange."

To put Grange's talent into today's perspective, I imagine it would be like taking the individual talents of Tony Dorsett, Raghib "Rocket" Ismail, Johnny Rodgers, and Vince Young and putting them into the body of one contemporary player. The name on the back of the jersey would spell Grange.

Grange is also in possession of college football's best-ever nickname, "The Galloping Ghost." It's slightly ahead of North Carolina legend Charlie "Choo-Choo" Justice, "The Cornbelt Comet," Iowa's Nile Kinnick, and Byron "Whizzer" White of Colorado.

I've always been partial to "Mr. Inside and Mr. Outside," Army's Doc Blanchard and Glenn Davis, too. Pitt's "Dream Backfield" and Fordham's "Seven Blocks of Granite" are my favorite nicknames for a position group. I think "The Four Horsemen" is overrated. But Notre Dame has that photograph of the players on the horses, which is famous.

My favorite unit nickname is "Chinese Bandits," which was what LSU head coach Paul Dietzel called the third platoon of his three-platoon system in 1958. These guys, all inexperienced underclassmen, were essentially the Tigers' second-string defense. They played tenaciously every time they got in the game and helped LSU to the 1958 national title.

My favorite team nickname? Navy's outstanding 1954 team was nicknamed "A Team Named Desire" by someone in the media early in the season after head coach Eddie Erdelatz commented that "every man on this team is filled with desire."

What makes the nickname so special is the bizarre coincidence that occurred at the conclusion of that special season. The Midshipmen went 8-2 and finished No. 5 after beating the SEC champs, Mississippi, in the '55 Sugar Bowl. The Sugar Bowl, everyone knows, is played in New Orleans, where Tennessee Williams' famous play, "A Streetcar Named Desire," is set! The players posed for publicity photos while riding the actual streetcar named Desire during the bowl week. That's unbelievable.

As for coaches' nicknames, for many years the game's best-known coaches had short, catchy nicknames that were synonymous with the sport: Rock, Jock, Pop, Shug, Woody, Bo, Bear, Bud, Biggie, Duffy, JoePa and countless others. Last names were unnecessary. Everybody knew who you were talking about.

My two all-time favorites, though, aren't very well known. Ohio State's Francis "Close the Gates of Mercy" Schmidt and Yale's Raymond "Ducky" Pond, both of whom coached at their respective schools in the 1930s. Put a sticker on your helmet if you've heard of either of them because that means you are a serious fan!

I get asked all the time, of all the college football games ever played, which was the best? I won't bother with any suspense or build-up here. The greatest football game ever played, college or pro, was Nebraska's 35-31 win at Oklahoma on Thanksgiving Day, 1971. Dave Kindred's lede in the *Louisville Courier-Journal* pretty much summed it up: "They can quit playing now. They have played the perfect game."

That game had everything. Buildup. Buzz. Legendary coaches. Lead changes. Drama. Huge ratings. Of the 15 highest-rated regular season games on television at one point from the 1950s through the 1970s, 14 involved Notre Dame. The other one was the '71 Nebraska-Oklahoma classic. For many years, that Sooners and Cornhuskers game was the highest-rated regular season game of all-time.

I had a gut feeling it was going to be big, so I suggested to Roone that we take it, and we did. The decision was made in February or March of '71. When Oklahoma destroyed Texas and Colorado in consecutive weeks in early October, we knew, like Texas-Arkansas in '69, it would be for the national title.

I didn't attend that game. I went home to Pittsburgh instead to spend Thanksgiving with my parents. Out of all the big games we did when I was at *ABC*, that was unquestionably the biggest of them all, but I don't regret the decision. As much as I love college football, a holiday spent with your parents is more important than any game.

As for games that I attended, I'll tell you my five favorites. All had some bearing on the national title, but some are more well-known and more special to me than others.

The best college football game I saw in person was Notre Dame versus Alabama in New Orleans on New Year's Eve, 1973. It was Ara and the Bear, and arguably the two most storied programs in college football history going up against each other for the first time ever with the national championship on the line.

There were six lead changes, special teams scores, trick plays, and the game came down to the gutsiest play call, the incredible Tommy Clements pass to tight end Robin Weber, in the sport's history. I'll never attend one like that ever again.

Number two was UCLA at USC on November 18, 1967 in the Los Angeles Coliseum. It was number one versus number four, McKay versus Prothro, and the Song Girls jumping up and down as O.J. Simpson went, as Chris Schenkel called it, "sixty-four thrilling, captivating, collegiate football yards" in the fourth quarter to give the Trojans a Rose Bowl berth.

Third on my list is one we've already discussed in great detail, Texas-Arkansas in Fayetteville on December 6, 1969.

Coming in at four is Iowa versus Ohio State on November 16, 1957. The Buckeyes were trailing 13-10 in the fourth quarter at home, but fullback Bob White picked up 64 of the team's 67 yards and scored the game-winning touchdown on the final drive.

This one was special because I went with my best friend, my buddy John O'Connor, who was a huge Ohio State fan. The Buckeyes went on to be ranked No. 1 in the UPI poll and shared the national title with the AP No. 1, Auburn.

The fifth and final game on my list, very few people remember this one, but I'll never forget being in the stands when Navy upset No. 2 Army, 14-2, on December 2, 1950. The Cadets not only entered the game unbeaten, they had not lost to Navy since 1943. The Middies, 21-point dogs, shocked the Army.

It wasn't a great game as far as drama, but there was tremendous emotion inside Philadelphia's Municipal Stadium that day. When the game ended, as I stood there watching the teams sing the alma maters, it hit me that I might have witnessed the greatest upset in college football history. All these years later, I still think I did. The only game that might lay an equal claim to that distinction was when Holy Cross pounded No. 1 Boston College at Fenway Park, 55-12, in 1942.

The greatest plays of all-time? I've thought a lot on this over the years and I honestly still don't know where to begin. Just about the only conclusion I've reached is that another beautiful thing about college football is that I can put together a list of famous plays using only the names of players, one of the schools that participated in the game, a famous radio call or the actual call in the huddle itself, and no further explanation is necessary. You don't need the year or any other information. You'll read it and you'll see the play in your mind, as if it's running on b-roll.

Let's give this exercise a try. The following, in no particular order, are my favorite all-time plays: Wrong Way Riegels; The Puntrooskie; Billy Cannon; Right 53 Veer Pass; "Run, Lindsay, Run!"; Stanford band; Doug Flutie; The Statue of Liberty.

Now that I've conjured these memories in your head, you need a soundtrack to go with them, right? I can never hear the following fight songs too many times: "Anchors Aweigh," "The Eyes of Texas," Texas A&M's "Aggie War Hymn," "On, Brave Old Army Team," and the "Pitt Victory Song."

The five greatest songs in American history from top to bottom, are the "Star-Spangled Banner," "God Bless America," "White Christmas," any song by Sinatra, and the "Notre Dame Victory March." The "Victory March" is the most famous fight song because it's the only fight song that is as universally well-known as those other American standards. The chorus is easy to remember and the arrangement is catchy to the point of being infectious.

The "Victory March" is the most famous fight song, but it's not my all-time favorite. That would be Yale's "Bulldog," which was written by Cole Porter in 1913. There's a movie, called "Night and Day," about Porter starring Cary Grant that came out right after the war. I had the song in my head for weeks after I saw that flick. From the opening drum roll, the sound is stirring and the lyrics have that old-fashioned college cadence to them. "Bulldog, bulldog...bow-wow-wow!" I can't help but sing along whenever I hear it.

I enjoy watching Alabama's Million Dollar Band, Tennessee's Pride of the Southland Marching Band, Texas's Longhorn Band and Notre Dame's Band of the Fighting Irish perform. The pre-game flip that the Penn State Blue Band's drum major does is an impressive tradition.

And my father would not forgive me if I didn't include the Leland Stanford Junior University Marching Band. That crazy crew, when they stopped playing at halftime of the Arkansas game in '70 and pulled their pants down, they nearly gave all of us at *ABC* heart attacks. Thank God they were wearing swim trunks underneath. Nobody had any idea they were going to pull that stunt.

My favorite band, college or otherwise, has always been The Ohio State University Marching Band. Their uniforms are snappy and military-looking, and Ohio State has the best catalog in college football. From "Across the Field" and "Carmen Ohio" to the band's rendition of "Hang on Sloopy," it's one great tune after another.

I can honestly say that every Buckeyes' game I've attended, I've looked forward to watching the band more than the actual game. But there's another reason for that. "The Best Damn Band in the Land" is responsible for the best tradition in college football, "dotting the i" in the Script Ohio formation at halftime.

The three greatest honors that can be bestowed on an American are to dot the i, be awarded the Heisman Trophy and be the guest star murderer in an episode of "Columbo." My idea of the perfect weekend would be to take in the Michigan game with Stefanie Powers in Columbus and dot the i at halftime. That wouldn't just be the perfect weekend, I'd want it to be my last weekend on earth. If you dot the i, what else is there left to look forward to?

My other favorite traditions, in no particular order: touching Frank Howard's Rock; Texas A&M's 12th Man; toilet papering the trees on Toomer's Corner at Auburn; Tennessee's checkered end zones; singing second after the Army-Navy game.

Now the greatest rivalries, there are many factors such as the proximity of the schools, the coaches' backgrounds and other things that make a rivalry great, but in my opinion you can narrow it down to three basic ingredients: history, high stakes and hate.

Notre Dame-Southern Cal is the greatest intersectional rivalry in college football because it covers all three of my criteria. You've got nearly 100 years of history. And high stakes? I can't come up with another rivalry game that has decided more national titles and featured more Heisman Trophy winners.

And it's really easy to hate an opponent when it costs you a title, or three. The coaches and players can talk sportsmanship and respect all they want. The fans on both sides know why they circle the date of the game on the calendar. There's nothing wrong with rivals sharing some degree of hatred of each other. As long as the stadium parking lots don't start resembling the OK Corral, heated rivalries are good for the sport.

Michigan-Ohio State and Alabama-Auburn are arguably the two biggest sectional, or regional rivalries in college football. When you consider everything that's been on the line in these games over the years in terms of conference championships and bowl berths, they are excellent examples of how history, hate and high stakes combine to create lasting rivalries.

In a way, both games might be more important, from a fan's perspective, than Notre Dame-USC because some things, believe it or not, are more important than national championships and Heismans. The winners of those games have bragging rights in their states, their neighborhoods, their churches, their corner bars, their workplaces, and in some cases their bedrooms, for a full year.

Going around the country, I consider the next tier of great rivalries to be ones like USC-UCLA and Oklahoma-Texas. These rivalries have got all the hate, history, and high stakes you could want, plus they are truly competitive. Since the creation of the AP Poll in 1936, other than Indiana-Purdue, these two rivalries have featured the most games that have been decided by a touchdown or less.

To me, USC-UCLA is still unique because it's the sport's last big city rivalry. It's college football's version of the Yankees and the Dodgers, back when the Dodgers were still in Brooklyn. But the rivalry is probably on its way out as a big deal due to the falling fortunes of UCLA football the last few years. What killed UCLA football, I try to tell people, was that in 1976, they closed down the journalism school. You wonder why USC gets all the headlines and space? It's because all the writers and TV reporters are USC alums. I'm serious. It's a factor.

When I was at *ABC* in the 1960s and early 1970s, Oklahoma-Texas used to be one of the funnest road trips on the schedule. This game brought the most interesting crowds I've ever seen. You had all these country folks coming in for the Texas State Fair. I've never seen so many good-looking women dressed to the nines in one place than in Dallas the weekend of the Red River Shootout. Or so many ridiculously wealthy people. On a Friday night before one game in the late 1960s, I was at a bar and overheard two fat cat boosters in ten-gallon hats arguing over which of their alma maters, Oklahoma or Texas, had the better squad. They finally decided to bet the game. Only they didn't bet cash – they bet oil wells.

The shenanigans that went on year-round with this rivalry were unbelievable. I'll never forget the story told to me by a friend who worked in the offices of the NCAA. He got a call from a player's mother who wanted to know who would be paying her son's car payments. This was sometime in the 1970s. See, she was confused because the kid was transferring from Oklahoma to Texas, or from Texas to Oklahoma, and wanted to know which school would be responsible for honoring the original, and obviously illegal, arrangement. It's a true story!

I tell fans that you have to see a Harvard-Yale game before you die. The game is like taking a time machine back to college football's early days. It's competitive and there's a ton of history, but there isn't much in the way of hate. The fans are friendly and respectful. The ingenious cheers that come out of the student sections are worth the price of admission, too. It's no surprise that one of those brilliant minds, a staffer on the *Harvard Crimson*, came up with the most famous headline in college football history, "HARVARD BEATS YALE, 29-29," after the famed 1968 installment.

There are two small school rivalry games that I highly recommend: Williams-Amherst and Lehigh-Lafayette. For the former, you should go when the game is played at Williams, in Williamstown, Massachusetts. If the Ephs beat the Lord Jeffs, the entire team, still wearing their uniforms, marches en masse up Spring Street for cold beers and free haircuts at St. Pierre's Barber Shop. It's one of the purest, most delightful spectacles in the sport.

The latter has been played longer than any other rivalry in college football history. The only two rivals who have met more often than Lehigh and Lafayette are Germany and France. It's also the longest uninterrupted rivalry dating back to 1896. There are only three things you can count on in life as a college football fan: death, taxes, and Lehigh-Lafayette.

A sore subject with me is that of dead rivalries. Games that should be played, but for whatever reason or reasons, are not. I still can't believe that nobody had the guts to step up and fight to keep historic rivalries like Pitt-West Virginia, Texas-Texas A&M, Oklahoma-Nebraska, and so many others, alive.

Another great dead rivalry nobody knows about is Maryland-Navy. It's one of the best hate rivalries of all-time. It was an institutional, in-state rivalry. It was civilian versus military. It was blue collar versus elitists. It ended because of the '64 game.

In that chippy, closely contested game in College Park, Maryland, Terps' linebacker Jerry Fishman twice gave the Brigade of Midshipmen the bird. They played the following year in Annapolis to finish the contract and then Navy all of the sudden announced that the series was over. The two teams didn't play again for forty years.

I remember watching the *CBS Evening News* on December 7, 1966, the 25th anniversary of the attack on Pearl Harbor. The network ran b-roll footage of the attack, then showed Japanese officials and American admirals talking like old friends. I have no idea why, but for some really strange reason I couldn't help but think about the Maryland-Navy feud and I began to laugh. It all seemed so absurd. The Navy will forgive Japan for Pearl Harbor, but not Maryland for the finger!

Fast forward a few years, this is around 1980 or 1981, when my good friend Ernie Accorsi was working as the assistant GM of the Baltimore Colts. He didn't particularly have any desire to leave the NFL, but he was asked to interview for the Maryland AD job by a good friend of his, Jack Scarbath, a member of Maryland's Board of Trustees. Scarbath was an All-American quarterback at Maryland in the early 1950s. As a junior, Scarbath led the Terrapins to an undefeated 10-0 record and an upset of No. 1 Tennessee in the Sugar Bowl. He was runner-up for the Heisman behind Billy Vessels.

During the interview in Baltimore, Accorsi met with a faculty representative to the athletic department. Accorsi gave an honest assessment of the state of Maryland's program and suggested two courses of action that needed to be taken. To start, Maryland needed to double the seating capacity of Byrd Stadium to attract home-and-homes with major powers.

"And," Accorsi added, "you don't have a rival."

"Yes, we do," came the reply. "Penn State is our rival."

"You may think they're a rival, but they don't think you are a rival. They've beaten you 20 straight games. You should play Navy."

"We dislike the United States Naval Academy."

"Precisely why you should play them!" Accorsi answered.

Accorsi nailed it. I'm amazed that many people, especially those in high administrative positions in college athletics, refuse to acknowledge how important history and hate are. Again, that's probably because many of the people calling the shots today are clueless when it comes to understanding the game. We're missing out on some great games and the fans and alums are getting screwed.

The rivalry that meant the most to me personally is of course Pitt versus Penn State. It was the city versus the country. Families were divided down the middle. Both schools went after the same players. While the stakes were never very high, there was plenty of hate.

It doesn't matter to me that the rivalry is, for all intents and purposes, dead on the field. It'll always be alive in my heart. There used to be a sign above the urinals in the home locker-room at Pitt Stadium that read "Please flush twice, it's a long way to State College." I still say that to myself on occasion after taking a leak in my apartment.

My favorite rivalry joke is one that used to go around the week of the Penn State game in the 1950s and 60s. It's based on a guy writing a letter to the advice columnist, Abigail Van Buren. It goes like this:

"Dear Abby, I have a problem. I have two brothers. One is a graduate of Penn State. The other was just sentenced to death in the electric chair for murder. Two of my sisters are ladies of the evening and the third is a minor who was just released from the reformatory where she had served time for smothering her illegitimate child to death. My father sells narcotics to high school students. My mother died from insanity when I was only three years old. I, myself, have terminal cancer and the doctors have only given me three months to live. My problem is this – recently I met a beautiful, funny girl and I want to marry her. Do I tell her about my brother who went to Penn State?"

Clearly the schools are interchangeable, so replace Pitt and Penn State with your alma mater or favorite team and rival and use the joke to razz a co-worker, brother-in-law or whomever else you want.

Those who know me well know that my favorite rivalry game has always been Army-Navy. Interestingly, it's the one game that doesn't fit my theory on what makes a rivalry great. It's perhaps the one big rivalry game in all of college football that's super competitive, but there's no hate between the two teams. There's been very little in terms of high stakes in the games over the last fifty years, but that doesn't mean that service academy football isn't important. Let's be honest. The only way we'll ever see Army, Navy and Air Force ranked numbers one, two and three in the AP Poll is if World War III breaks out, and nobody wants that.

Yet no matter how many wins or losses the teams have, the Army-Navy rivalry will always matter. I've always said, Army-Navy is not a game that will affect the national title – it's more important than that.

I took in my first Army-Navy game in Philadelphia in 1948. I took the train, I think it was *The Duquesne* streamliner, which had service from Pittsburgh to Philly then to New York City. Army was 8-0 and ranked third in the country and Navy was 0-8. The final was 21-21. It was a great game with a historic ending, but it wasn't so much the action on the field that pulled me in, it was everything going on around the players that I got swept up in. No other rivalry game has all of the pageantry that Army-Navy has.

Both fight songs are as stirring as they get. Between the Corps of Cadets and the Brigade of Midshipmen, I had never seen so much emotion and energy in the stands. The antics of the mascots, Army's mule and Navy's Bill the Goat, were fun to watch. I later found out that my first Army-Navy game was the last one for Mr. Jackson, the veteran mule mascot named for General Stonewall Jackson, who was retired after that season.

The trip back to Pittsburgh took all night, a red-eye on the rails, and I arrived exhausted but at the same time exhilarated. I went to the '50 game two years later. I've been to probably twenty Army-Navy contests total. That '48 game hooked me for life.

Speaking of the mule and goat, we have to talk about the mascots. That's another reason why I fell in love with college football in the first place. The mascots were something completely unique to college football and they still are. Many are real living animals that are as beloved by the fans and alums and their caretakers as their own pets.

You've got beef, Texas's big bovine mascot Bevo, beautiful birds, Auburn's War Eagle and Air Force's falcon, Aurora, and even a boar at Arkansas, Tusk.

The most fearsome mascot in college football is Mike the Tiger. Before the 1973 Alabama game I passed by his cage, which is purposely parked by the entrance to the visitors' locker-room. If I had been an Alabama player, I'd have found another way to enter the field!

With horses, it's a two-horse race between Southern Cal's Traveler and Florida State's Renegade. I don't know if it's true, but somebody once told me that the first Traveler in 1961 was the brother of another famous horse, Silver, from the "Lone Ranger" television show. And no offense to Florida State's Chief Osceola, the guy who holds Renegade's bridle, but the ranking big chiefs in Tallahassee will always be Lee Corso and Burt Reynolds.

The best human mascot is West Virginia's Mountaineer. I'd say that even if the Mountaineer didn't have a long rifle and wasn't less than an hour drive from my apartment.

While I'm a traditionalist who prefers real animals and people, I don't mind the costumed characters. My favorites are Nebraska's Herbie Husker, Wisconsin's Bucky Badger, Miami of Florida's Sebastian the Ibis and, lastly, Missouri's Truman the Tiger. I know my friend John Walsh at *ESPN*, a Missouri journalism school grad, appreciates that one.

Since I hate to fly, I once told somebody that if *ESPN* ever let me do games regularly, I wouldn't travel in a bus like John Madden. I'd tour the country in Purdue's Boilermaker Special train, Oklahoma's Sooner Schnooner, or the coolest car in college football, Georgia Tech's 1930 Ford Model A Sport coupe, Ramblin' Wreck.

I've always been a dog lover, so it's only natural that four of my top five favorite living mascots are dogs. You've got the two most famous bulldogs in the United States, Georgia's Uga and Yale's Handsome Dan, Smokey, Tennessee's lovable bluetick coonhound, and Texas A&M's beautiful collie, Reveille.

What mascot is my all-time favorite? Colorado's Ralphie the buffalo. Why? It's a good story. I got to meet that big gal briefly on the sideline before the '72 Oklahoma-Colorado game. It was a good game between two top ten teams and Colorado upset Oklahoma, 20-14, but what I remember most was Ralphie charging out onto the field and promptly taking a big, steaming shit on the 40-yard line! I've loved all the Ralphies since.

The Gettysburg Address is the most famous speech in American history and

Knute Rockne's "Win one for the Gipper" speech is second. I'd put President Kennedy's inaugural speech third, Lou Gehrig's "Luckiest Man" farewell fourth and General MacArthur's "Old Soldiers Never Die" retirement address to Congress fifth.

In terms of strictly college football speeches and pep talks, John Cappelletti's Heisman Trophy acceptance speech in December 1973 is not far behind Rockne's speech. I don't know anybody who watched it live on television and didn't tear up.

Nile Kinnick's Heisman speech in 1939 was similarly memorable. Then there was Yale coach Tad Jones, who, before a Harvard game in the 1910s, made this brief, but powerful motivational statement: "Gentlemen, you are going out to play Harvard. Never in your life will you do something as important."

The greatest last words in college football history aren't the Gipper's. They were the ones choked out by a dying U.S. Army officer, Lieutenant John C. Trent, who was killed in action at Wonsan, North Korea on November 15, 1950.

"Big John" Trent was an All-American end and captain of the 1949 Army team that hammered No. 1 Michigan in Ann Arbor en route to finishing 9-0 and No. 4 in the country. Although he made a big catch to beat Penn at Franklin Field in '49, Trent was best-known for his tenacious blocking at the end position.

The night of his death, Trent went on a perimeter check, visiting with his fatigued men in their foxholes. As Trent was making his rounds, the communists attacked the edge of the American lines. All that stood between them and an end-run that would have rolled up the position was Trent. He fought them off valiantly but was mortally wounded.

By the time relief got to him, he had only a few moments, a few pained breaths, left. With them he said, "the bastards didn't circle *my* end." An old West Pointer told me that story a long time ago. It gave me chills when I first heard it and it still does every time I repeat it.

There have been some great lines uttered by players and coaches over the years, but the most gifted storytellers in college football have always been the broadcasters. First, there are names that are synonymous with certain schools. I'm talking about the local radio legends.

At the top of this list is without a doubt Larry Munson at Georgia. Next is Nebraska's Lyell Bremser. He was Big Red through and through, one of the longest-tenured team broadcasters in history. You have to include the longtime voice of the Michigan Wolverines, the late Bob Ufer. Some schools don't even have one legend, but Tennessee had two in Lindsey Nelson and John Ward. Dan Jenkins would be mad at me if I didn't mention Kern Tips, the longtime voice of the Southwest Conference.

Now my personal favorite? That would be the late Joe Croghan, who I thought was great on Navy games. Nobody ever brings him up, however, because when you think of his career, you first think of him as the voice of the Baltimore Colts and the Miami Dolphins, as well as the Washington Senators and Baltimore Orioles.

The national announcers, the radio heavyweights like Ted Husing and Bill Stern, they narrated the college football of my youth. While in many cases these were the same voices that later generations listened to on other sports, I remember them from a college football perspective. For example, if I hear the name Red Barber, I don't associate him with the Dodgers or Yankees. I think of him doing the Orange Bowl.

When I was growing up, my father said that "Graham McNamee will forever be the voice of the Rose Bowl," and I didn't understand because I had never heard McNamee call a Rose Bowl. Now I get it. When I tune into the Cotton Bowl, even though he's been gone for some time, I still expect to hear Lindsey Nelson's voice welcoming me to Dallas.

As for television voices, he's not considered a college football voice, but I loved when Jim Nantz was the No. 1 play-by-play guy for *CBS*. I wish he'd do college games again. To many fans, Brent Musberger's voice is synonymous with college football. Ron Franklin, Verne Lundquist, and Tim Brando are favorites of mine, too.

My former *ABC* co-worker, the late Chris Schenkel, is the second best to ever do it. His name is on the award presented by the National Football Foundation to the best broadcaster for a reason.

Keith Jackson, of course, is the gold standard. He had that wonderful southern storyteller style and on-air personality that meshed perfectly with the sport. Listening to Keith Jackson call a college football game was like listening to Shelby Foote talk about the Civil War.

Perhaps most importantly, Keith knew precisely when to stop talking. After a big play or touchdown, he let the audience hear the roar of the crowd and the band. He knew people wanted to hear the fight songs and soak in the atmosphere. And Jackson, perhaps more than any other broadcaster in college football history, understood the history. He embraced the game's traditions and, as a result, he became one himself.

What's my all-time favorite place to take in a game? Many of the campuses in the Ivy League provide beautiful backdrops. My favorite is Yale. Whenever I visited, I used to walk around and look up at a window in some ancient dormitory and wonder, *is that Nathan Hale's room?* If you attend Harvard-Yale, try to go when the game is in New Haven. No offense to my Hah-vard friends, but I think the Yale Bowl, the first stadium in the country to be called a bowl, is a better venue.

New Haven is nice, yet it's not my favorite college town. Oxford, Mississippi has a strong claim to the No. 1 spot. Athens, Georgia is near the top of my list, too. So is Boulder, Colorado. Lewis and Clark would have a hard time finding it, but State College, Pennsylvania is my favorite college town and the Rathskeller on Pugh Street is my favorite college bar.

If you're talking tailgating, I love the "World's Largest Outdoor Cocktail Party" that takes place prior to Florida-Georgia, but nothing compares to the silver candelabras and the spreads they put out in the Grove at Ole Miss.

Those are fun atmospheres. This next category is fear atmospheres. Even though it only held 59,075 people, Notre Dame Stadium, at one time, was a tough place to play. It's no longer that way.

Although I've never been to Tiger Stadium at night, I feel strongly that one of the toughest things to do in college football is beat LSU at home under the lights when the Tigers are wearing white. Speaking of wearing white, a whiteout night game at Penn State is perhaps the most exciting, visually impressive spectacle in the sport.

The most intimidating atmosphere of all-time was the Orange Bowl. I don't know if any school will ever beat the 58-game home winning streak that the Miami Hurricanes put together from 1985 to 1994. At most schools, you can tell the difference between the student section and the rest of the fans. It wasn't that way at Miami. Every section of the Orange Bowl was a combination of the Raiders' Black Hole and the Roman Coliseum. When the fans started stomping their feet you thought the whole structure was going to cave in. When you add in the sweltering South Florida heat and humidity, it was the greatest homefield advantage in college football history.

My favorite total campus and gameday experience is West Point. Because of the beauty and the history. The third Saturday in October at West Point is probably my favorite football weekend experience in all of sports. The leaves are changing. There's the splendor of the full-dress parade on the Plain. As Army enters the field, you're looking out over the Hudson River and you hear the Corps of Cadets singing "On, Brave old Army Team." It takes your breath away.

Other stadiums in addition to Michie Stadium with great waterfront views are Neyland Stadium in Knoxville and Husky Stadium in Seattle. I'm going to insist that if Washington and Tennessee ever play, it has to be somewhere where the Vol Navy can anchor alongside Washington's flotilla. It would be college football's Battle of Midway!

Ohio Stadium, the historic horseshoe on the banks of the Olentangy River, is up there, too. The façades of the stadiums built in the 1920s are so majestic. The stadiums at Illinois and Nebraska are two more great examples. Another strikingly beautiful structure is Franklin Field in Philadelphia, the first double-decker stadium in the United States.

The most picturesque location for a stadium in all of college football? Kenan Stadium in Chapel Hill, North Carolina. There is nothing like walking beneath those tall pine trees. It's a magnificent setting, the Augusta National of college football.

The best home uniforms in college football are LSU's whites and UCLA's powder blues. I've always been partial to Penn State's and Texas's all-white road uniforms. Georgia's silver britches are sharp.

My all-time favorites are Notre Dame's green ones from the 1940s. *LIFE Magazine* put Johnny Lujack, wearing an emerald jersey and glistening gold pants, on the cover one week in the fall of 1947. The colors were so vivid and eye-catching, kids gathered at newsstands to gawk at that cover. I don't remember the first issue of *Playboy* causing that kind of buzz.

Notre Dame's golden helmets, both for their simplicity and symbolism, make my list of best helmets, too. If helmets are works of art, I'm a minimalist. I love the gray numbers on Alabama's, the big red "N" on Nebraska's, the "U" on Miami's and the "Y" on BYU's. As far as stylized logos go, it's a three-way tie between the Texas longhorn, Florida

State's spear and my alma mater's Script Pitt. To me, Ohio State's silver helmets don't look right in September. When November rolls around and they are half-covered in Buckeye stickers – that's the look.

The undisputed helmet champs? Michigan. Nothing comes close to the Wolverines' winged helmets. I don't know why, but that headgear caught my attention when I was a teenager and it remains my favorite all these years later. Lloyd Carr, when he was the head coach at Michigan, sent me one. When I die, I want to be buried in it.

Now, for the category you've all been waiting for, the cheerleaders! Every red-blooded American male football fan knows that this conversation starts and ends with the schools in the South. If the Civil War had been a beauty pageant, the South would have won. Still, don't count out the schools north of the Mason-Dixon line. There was a cheerleader at Notre Dame in the early 1970s by the name of Terri Buck. She was something. When *ABC* did Notre Dame games, we made sure she got more airtime than Ara Parseghian.

When it comes down to best squad, the Southern Cal Song Girls have always been in a category all their own. Yet there's more to the lure of the Song Girls than the fact that they are all knockouts. If you ask me, the outfit has a lot to do with it. Nearly all of the other squads nowadays wear very revealing get-ups. Southern Cal has stuck with those white sweaters, which are up there with Columbo's raincoat and Fonzie's leather jacket in terms of famous American articles of clothing. They're flattering, sure, but they provide an all-American, girl-next-door look. Every Song Girl looks like the kind of chick you could bring home to your mother. Unless, of course, your mother went to UCLA.

Like with cheerleaders, the SEC schools have, collectively, by far the best-looking coeds. The runner-up league was the old Southwest Conference. My *ABC* colleague Andy Sidaris, the guy who pioneered the "honey shot," swore that his alma mater, SMU, had the best-looking coeds.

In my entire career, only one production meeting stands out. It was at the end of my first season working for *ABC* in 1982. The last show of the year was usually done at the site of a big, season-ending game, and that year we traveled to Austin for Texas and Arkansas. It was a Friday afternoon. The meeting was dragging along when two shapely women entered the room to distribute the press tickets for the crew. Suddenly, some very suggestive music started playing and they began taking their clothes off! We never found out who was responsible for the show or if the strippers were Texas coeds, but there was strong speculation that they were. Just one more reason why I miss the SWC.

The under-the-radar school with the best-looking chicks? That's the University of Colorado. This may be a surprise to many people, but to Chris Fowler, a Colorado alum, it isn't. When I was at *ABC*, I conducted a survey on the subject. All of our crews had Colorado in their top five, if not number one. Even Roone Arledge voted for Colorado. Noting the booming local economy, he told me, "everything is selling well in Boulder. Except bras."

Roone had a strict rule against *ABC* Sports personnel fraternizing with coeds, but rule or no rule, I didn't have much of a chance. I never had much luck with women, old or young, on campus or off. It certainly wasn't for a lack of trying.

My friend Jimmie "Mississippi Red" McDowell, an Ole Miss alum and a great newspaperman who served as the executive director of the National Football Foundation for many years, loves telling the story about the CoSIDA convention in Lubbock, Texas where I fell in love with a hairdresser who worked in a salon near our hotel. I ended up getting a haircut on three consecutive days until she agreed to have dinner with me.

"Hallelujah!" McDowell shouted when I told him the good news. "This siege has gone on longer than Vicksburg."

While a handful of my relationships got serious, none progressed to that most serious of discussions. I'm pretty sure if the women I dated ever put together a Top 25 poll for marriage contenders, I would not be ranked. I'd be found under the heading "Others Receiving Votes."

Part of the problem was my looks. No number of expense account martinis made me appear handsome. When I see photos of myself from the 1970s, with my bushy sideburns, I look like a detective on "Barney Miller." Nor was I ever a decent dresser. Some of the loud, colorful sports jackets I wore, I looked like a cross between an Orange Bowl representative and Herb Tarlek.

Still, I've had my moments. The great Mitch Levy once had the USC Song Girls serenade me on the air during one of our radio segments in Seattle. And how many guys can say they've talked to their two biggest celebrity crushes?

There was the unforgettable night, this is going on thirty years ago, at Runyon's, when I was eating with an executive from *CBS*. The subject of Mary Tyler Moore came up and he asked if I wanted to talk to her. I thought he was kidding, but a phone was brought over and he dialed up her home number. He handed me the phone and I carried on a five-minute conversation with Mary Richards! It was one of the highlights of my life.

Stefanie Powers wished me a happy birthday on the air one year during a hit I did on Todd Wright's *ESPN* radio show. That was the best birthday gift I ever received, and I have the show's producer, the amazing Louise Cornetta, to thank for it.

Truthfully, I don't have any regrets about staying single. I was simply never meant for marriage. While my friends entered one by one into the romantic equivalent of conference realignment, I was destined to be a swinging bachelor, kind of like Notre Dame, stubbornly independent and fiercely protective of both my personal finances and my scheduling freedom, until the very end.

No woman could ever seriously mount a challenge for my affections because the love of my life remains, and always will be, college football.

My mother, to her credit, understood this early on. Over the years, she made some astute observations about my love life, or lack thereof, but perhaps none was more accurate than her prediction in the 1960s that I'd remain among the ranks of the unmarried for the rest of my life. One of her friends asked why she thought that way.

"Because," she laughed, "no girl dreams of honeymooning at Pitt Stadium."

CHAPTER 7

The one I am most proud of.

I have two standing rules regarding employment. First – and I credit this one to Bob Prince, who drilled it into my head when I was young – always be employed. Always be on someone's payroll. After health problems, money problems are the worst to have. "There's no cure for cancer," Prince used to say, "but there is one for poverty."

Of course, to be clear, you shouldn't work just for the money. The accumulation of wealth shouldn't be the basis of one's existence. There are only three reasons for money: 1) to provide for your loved ones; 2) to bet on sports; 3) so you don't have to sit in the middle seat in the last row next to the restrooms on a packed flight.

The second rule is, if you get up Tuesday morning and wish it were Friday, you need to find another job as soon as possible. It's easier said than done, but the old saying, "find something you love for a job and you'll never work a day in your life," is spot on.

Consider these three men, all born in 1926, who are still working because they love their jobs: Fidel Castro, Joe Paterno and Hugh Hefner. One is a dictator who has spent nearly fifty years in power. The other runs the island of Cuba. And I'm not completely sure just what, exactly, Hefner does, but if I were him, I would not be in a hurry to retire, either.

In August 1975, two months after I left the Dolphins, I took a job as director of publicity for the *Mutual Broadcasting System* in Washington, D.C. I wasn't merely on someone's payroll; it was a prestigious position in PR. *Mutual* was one of the grand old networks. I had grown up listening to "The Shadow," "The Lone Ranger," and "Boston Blackie" on *Mutual*. *Mutual* had "Monday Night Football," the World Series, the Cotton Bowl, and many other major sporting events, plus a world-renowned news organization.

Unfortunately, I don't have any good memories or funny stories about this particular job to share with you because every day was a Tuesday morning. That's why I quit. To be honest, I wasn't all that excited about the job when I took it, but I was excited to live and work in the nation's capital. After I got there I learned that they were in the process of moving operations across the river to Arlington, Virginia. That was a downer.

I didn't get along with management, either. Let's just say the CEO wasn't very fond of me. Later on, whenever people asked me what happened at *Mutual*, I said the company's ad slogan, "The feeling's *Mutual*," was accurate.

I had no idea what I wanted to do next, but I knew what I didn't want to do, and that was work in sports, television, print media or publicity. I was exhausted with everything that went hand-in-hand with working with the people that inhabited those worlds.

In what is without a doubt the craziest career move I made in my life, I joined VISTA in January 1976. Some people thought I was having a nervous breakdown or going through a midlife crisis. It wasn't true, but I can't blame them. The secretive way I behaved probably led folks to believe that I had gone off the deep end. I didn't give out a forwarding address or phone number and kept in touch with only a few people over the following year.

"Beano's all sported out," somebody suggested. I can't remember who said it, but the line got back to me and when I heard it, I thought it was an accurate declaration. I really was. Yet it wasn't like I ran off and become a monk. I simply felt the timing was perfect to try something completely different.

"If you would not be forgotten, as soon as you are dead and rotten," Ben Franklin once said, "either write things worth reading, or do things worth the writing." I had proven myself incapable of writing things related to sports worth reading, so I decided to try to do something with my life that wasn't necessarily worth the writing, but something that might be worthwhile for others. That, in so many words, was my main motivation in joining VISTA.

Short for "Volunteers in Service to America," VISTA was created in 1964 as a domestic counterpart to the Peace Corps. I briefly considered joining the Peace Corps, but I decided on VISTA for a number of reasons.

For one thing, it upsets me that Congress sends aid to other countries. Few realize it, but we have poor and disadvantaged people here in the United States, and I think we should help our fellow Americans first.

I was told that I would almost certainly be assigned to a town in the South. That sweetened the deal. I'd always wanted to live, even just temporarily, in a small southern town like those described by my favorite authors, Thomas Wolfe and Willie Morris, in their books.

Finally, while I wanted to get away from some things for awhile, I knew that I wouldn't be able to live without college football. It occurred to me that it would have been very difficult to get the scores in the Amazon rainforest or in some remote part of Africa. In daydreaming about potential Peace Corps adventures I might have imagined myself as a modern-day Dr. Livingstone, but I didn't presume anybody would send Henry Stanley into the jungle to find me and tell me that Pitt had defeated Notre Dame.

I flew to Atlanta in late February 1976 for orientation. When I checked in to the Georgian Terrace hotel, I was disappointed to find that it was no longer the luxury hotel that hosted the premiere party for "Gone with the Wind" in 1939. I had shown up expecting Clark Gable and instead got cockroaches. The place hadn't just fallen on hard times, it was a dump.

My roommate was from Pittsburgh, of all places. His name was Herbie Webster. He was a younger black guy with long hair, dreadlocks, like the singer Bob Marley. He was very friendly and, I could tell, very excited to be in Atlanta. He asked me if I had traveled before. "Before this, I really only traveled once," he said, "but that was to Cleveland. It really doesn't count."

I told him I had traveled a bit, but I didn't say why. I was pretty guarded. It wasn't that I was ashamed of my professional past. I just didn't want to talk about it. In my experience, when you meet strangers and tell them that you work in sports or the media, you end up doing all the talking. Whenever I'd strike up a conversation with somebody on a flight, they'd always want to know what Howard Cosell, or some other on-air personality, was like off-camera. Then they'd ask if I could get them tickets or autographs.

I now understand that I wasn't just "sported out," I needed a break from being Beano Cook. So, for the first time in many years, I made the conscious decision to go by Carroll. I used my real first name during orientation and throughout my time in VISTA. My mother had her doubts about me joining VISTA, but she did like the idea that some people in the world would not know me as Beano.

The first morning, I found myself in the grand ballroom sitting in a circle with 22 other VISTAs. That's what we called ourselves, VISTAs. We did exercises to get to know each other and assess our fitness for the program. They partnered us up with another volunteer and you had to describe yourself to them. Then that person introduced you to the rest of the group. It seemed silly, but it worked. It broke the ice.

In another exercise, the group leader asked us to stand in front of the group and draw pictures to illustrate a certain word. I felt like I was playing charades. I don't know how, but I still remember some of the words: nervous; tipsy; alienated; isolated.

I counted 67 total VISTAs, including myself, at the orientation in Atlanta. Forty were women, and I think six were black. I later learned that female VISTA recruits outnumbered males three to one. There was only one black male in the group, my roommate. There were two married couples who signed up as a package deal. At 44, I was by far the oldest volunteer.

At times, I felt like I was back in the army. We took an oath of allegiance. They took our fingerprints. We watched training films and listened to lectures. There were a thousand rules and regulations to become acquainted with, and a corresponding number of forms to fill out.

During one of the lectures, we were told that by law VISTAs weren't permitted to remain in the organization for more than five years, but there was no need to worry about that. Many volunteers, we learned, did not make it through their one-year enlistment.

We were each issued a "VISTA Guerrilla Survival Manual." "This," the preface warned, "is a basically a conservative document. Its object: to conserve VISTAs." I couldn't help but sense the speakers' underlying pessimism, but I appreciated that they didn't try sugarcoating the difficulties that we would face in our assignments. Even so, on more than one occasion during orientation I watched the cockroaches scurry across the ballroom floor and wondered what the hell I had gotten myself into.

The most interesting part of the training for me was when everyone explained why they had joined. Some said that they couldn't find work and needed a job. One guy, on the other hand, quit a great job at IBM. He was burned out with the corporate world and said there had to be more to life than making money.

One of the volunteers for the local program, a housewife, admitted that she joined to save her marriage. She said she was driving her husband nuts and figured social work would get her out of the house. Several VISTAs were liberals who went on and on about their participation in various protests, sit-ins, and marches. I think they were upset the Sixties had ended.

When it was my turn, I said that I didn't consider myself an activist or a do-gooder. I wasn't there to change the world, but I wanted to try to make it a better place.

Whatever our individual motivations and whatever we expected to accomplish, we were told that none of us would get rich in the process. There were roughly 4,000 VISTAs in the national program and resources were stretched very thin. It was a paying gig, but just barely; I made $57.50 a week. It was a far cry from what I was used to making, but to be honest, I only felt underpaid when I heard Jim Rockford ask for $200 a day, plus expenses.

I had joined VISTA thinking that the experience would be rewarding in other ways, but we were advised to temper our expectations in that regard, too. "What we don't pay you in money," one of the speakers, Waldo Klein, joked, "we make up for in frustration."

Klein's words proved prophetic, but I was still pretty gung-ho when I arrived in Tallahassee a few days later for my pre-service training with the Florida Parole and Probation Commission. I had been detailed to that office by the Southeastern region of ACTION, the government umbrella agency under which service organizations like VISTA, the Peace Corps, and SCORE, the Service Corps of Retired Executives, operated.

In Tallahassee, I received a crash-course in working with lawyers, judges, cops, parolees, and parole boards. My job was to serve as an intermediary between parolees, their communities, and the criminal justice system in order to keep them from becoming repeat offenders.

As a VISTA volunteer coordinator, I would attend hearings, work out disputes, help them manage the requirements of their probation, as well as assist them in finding housing and employment. I would be helping plug a human being back in to society. That, to me, sounded like gratifying work.

The location of my first assignment was Lake City, Florida. After trading Herbie

Webster one of my trunks for two pieces of luggage and a suitcase to be named later, I caught a ride to Lake City, 103 miles east of Tallahassee, with another VISTA, Harold Charles, who was going all the way down to Miami for his assignment.

As we zoomed east along Interstate 10 at seventy miles an hour, both of us got a kick out of the fact that every radio station on the dial was playing Baptist church services, and peculiarly, that the services had sponsors. It wouldn't have occurred to me previously, but I had to admit that yes, God, gospel music and Cannon's fine menswear indeed went together. Charles, a serious Catholic, concurred, but was skeptical that such programming would ever fly in his church, because there was no way to hit listeners up for the collection.

Despite our lighthearted commentary, I could tell Charles was second-guessing his decision to join VISTA, too. Who could say whether his Hail Marys and regular trips to the confessional would have any influence on Miami landlords or the receptionists with Florida Power and Light? Likewise, I had no idea what awaited me in Lake City. I knew nothing about the place other than the fact that Pat Summerall had been born there.

When Charles dropped me off, I imagined myself as Napoleon landing on the island of Elba, heading into exile from my old life. It's one thing to feel excited and enthusiastic when you are sitting in a circle with 22 other people. You feel differently when you're deposited in a small town that's a long way from home with no car, not knowing where you are going to live and not knowing a single soul.

Thankfully, my first steps were reassuring. Lake City appeared to be a quiet, quaint little town. It reminded me of Mayberry from "The Andy Griffith Show." As I lumbered along with all my luggage, I was curious to find small mounds of dirt rising up between the sidewalk cracks. When I bent down to inspect these formations, I made a pleasant discovery: anthills! This was a significant improvement over the piles of dog shit one typically found on the sidewalks in New York and D.C. So far, so good.

Taking a stroll down Marion Avenue, Lake City's Main Street, was like taking a trip back through time. They had a drug store where you could get a chocolate soda. I didn't think those existed anymore. And there was a pretty, picturesque town square called Olustee Park that was full of flowers and trees. On the weekends, if the weather was nice, I would pick up my mail and my stack of newspapers, take a seat on one of the park benches and read all day.

Not long after I arrived, the big story on the front page of the local paper was about a guy who drove off without paying for two dollars worth of gas at a filling station. Two bucks! It certainly appeared that I had found my own Libya Hill or Yazoo City.

Getting used to living in the South wasn't as difficult as I imagined. The accents weren't as strong or heavy as Hollywood made them out to be. The two things that it took time to get used to were how Southerners measured distance and their love of grits.

In the North, distance is typically measured in miles or city blocks. If you provide someone with an address, they'll say, "that's three miles away," or "go two blocks and make a right."

In the South, distance is measured in increments of time. Southerners would tell you it took ten minutes or two hours to get some place. The strange thing is, they were usually right. How they knew how fast you drove or what your method of transportation was, I'll never know.

And grits came with everything. If you ordered two eggs and a cup of coffee, you got a side of grits. If you ordered surf and turf, you got grits. If you asked for change for a quarter for the payphone, you got nickels, dimes and yes – you guessed it – grits.

Part of the job, according to the six goals of ACTION, was "to stimulate interest by the local citizenry in volunteerism." Getting to know the townspeople was basically PR, which I could do in my sleep.

A lot of it was common sense, too. In the early years of VISTA, the first volunteers were radical liberals. They had the fervor of missionaries and looked upon the people who lived in small southern towns as wild natives that needed to be converted. As a result, they were resented.

"There are two things down here you don't do," one of the regional coordinators warned me. "You don't ask people who they are going to vote for, and you don't ask how much they make. If you follow those rules, you'll find the people easy to get along with."

I did, and they were. I was accepted by the community almost overnight. How could I tell? Before I had a car, I got around by hitchhiking. As I got to know more people, I noticed they looked for me to give me rides.

I became part of a group that got together for breakfast and lunch at a place called the Corner Cupboard. A cup of coffee was fifteen cents. A grilled cheese was forty-five cents. A BLT was eighty-five. I couldn't believe the prices. After the meal, there would be a contest to settle the bill. Everyone would guess the check's total, kind of like betting an over/under. Whoever got the closest without going over, they had to pay it.

I thought about the people I had worked with in network television and wondered what they would have thought about my new life. Many of the people I knew in television would have scoffed at the idea of somebody making $57 bucks a week and having fun doing it. Now Chet Forte, he was the lone exception. I imagine he would have enjoyed having action on a lunch check totaling four bucks.

Of course, I wasn't there to sit in the park and read my papers, drink chocolate sodas and hang out with the locals. Even though I got a laugh out of the story about the gas station bandit, I had a feeling the job was not going be easy.

I learned during orientation that Florida's incarceration rate was the highest in the country. While Lake City might have seemed a small, idyllic community to an outsider, it was actually a decent-sized town. In 1976, the population was roughly 10,000 people. It was the seat of Columbia County, which was ranked in the top one-third of Florida's largest counties in terms of land area, and the courthouse was located there. I would be working with parolees from a wide area.

I was told that the two VISTAs who had preceded my arrival in Lake City hadn't lasted very long. One, from New York City, lasted 30 minutes. The other reportedly stuck around a little longer. He made it five days.

My work was clearly cut out for me, so I took a novel approach to the job – which was to not consider it a job in the first place. The thing I tried to do was build personal relationships, make the interaction more man-to-man than anything else. Just because these people had been in trouble with the law, that didn't necessarily mean that they were stupid. If I was in their shoes, I'd wonder, *why does this stranger want to help me? What's the catch?* I remembered Thoreau's line: "If I knew for a certainty that a man was coming to my house with the conscious design of doing me good, I should run for my life."

I had to be both approachable and available. That's one of the reasons I decided to stay in a cheap motel outside of town. I thought it would make me seem like a regular guy, someone they could identify with, not a well-to-do Yankee who was treating VISTA like summer camp. I got in trouble with my boss due to my informal approach and the general way I did things, but I think most of the parolees appreciated my attitude and honesty.

I spent most of my time at the VISTA office in town, at the courthouse, and at halfway houses. A halfway house, if you don't know what I'm talking about, is a place where people on probation live. It's not a confinement facility like a jail, people can come and go, but it's not a resort, either. There are strict rules. The line in VISTA was that "a halfway house was halfway between freedom and the nearest bar."

It was serious work. There weren't many laughs. The work alternated between boring and uncomfortable. Courtrooms were nowhere near as exciting as "Perry Mason" had led me to believe.

I also felt like I was wearing many hats. When I was conducting an interview, I felt like a psychologist. When I administered the Minnesota Multiphasic Personality Test, I felt like a schoolteacher. When a client got into trouble, I felt like a parent.

As for the uncomfortable, there was this one time a cop asked me to accompany him on a trip with a juvenile female. She was a runaway. I joked that she didn't appear to be dangerous, like Bonnie Parker. He pulled me aside and said that wasn't the point. He wanted a witness in case a charge of sexual assault was raised against him. These incidents, he added, go both ways during transport.

The whole ride was very quiet. I felt sick to my stomach thinking about how some cops took advantage of young girls in those situations. I could go on, but I don't think it's necessary to recount all of the most depressing aspects of the job. I also don't think I have a right to.

A few months in, I got this big idea that I was going to write a book about going from working in sports and network television to social work. It was a variation on the format of an excellent book I had read called "Blue-Collar Journal," about a college president who took a sabbatical from the world of academia and spent time doing menial labor jobs such as garbageman and ditch-digger.

My book was going to be titled "Fingerprints," because of the symbolic meaning of the word for those who were booked after being charged with crimes and the important impressions, the figurative fingerprints, that the people I met in VISTA left on me.

I planned to write it like a diary, from the first-person perspective of a Northerner who had lived in big cities all of his life and was transplanted to a small town in the South. I'd tell stories from the point of view of someone who once took limos to major sporting events that found himself hitchhiking to work. I would compare the differences between working with professional athletes and big-time broadcasters with bail bondsmen and small-time crooks.

In between, I planned to discuss subjects like race relations, the criminal justice system, governmental incompetence, and aspects of American culture in general. I was excited about the idea because I figured that while I may not have been the best writer, talent-wise, to take on the project, I was perhaps the only person in the world who could write from first-hand experience when I described, for example, the difference between a Monday morning hearing in juvenile court in Lake City and a Monday Night football game in Miami.

I contacted the author of "Blue-Collar Journal," Haverford College President John R. Coleman, and we exchanged a few letters. He shared some insight and suggestions. Coleman and some friends in New York provided me with some publishing contacts, several of which expressed interest in the project. But things never progressed beyond that point.

I have no problem telling stories about coaches, athletes, and people in television in this book because they made a lot of money and, in a way, they signed up for the attention. That's not the case with the volunteers in VISTA. And the parolees, even if I changed names, they didn't deserve to have their stories shared with the world. It wouldn't have been ethical to profit off the pain, poverty, and misfortune of others. After about a year of planning and research, the idea just didn't sit right with me, so I junked it.

That said, there are two parolees whose names and faces remain imprinted in my mind. These men stood out, and still do all these years later, because they posed questions to me that changed my outlook on life.

The first was a guy who had gone away to prison for ten years. It was on a "B&E," a breaking and entering charge. Nobody was hurt and I don't think a weapon, a gun or a knife, was involved, so the sentence seemed excessive. In my experience on the job, people who committed that type of crime got maybe a year, then probation.

I was in a hurry, moving forward with the interview, so he interrupted me. I think he was hurt that I brushed off the fact that he lost ten years of his life, and, in all likelihood, that he lost it unfairly.

"Do you have any idea how long a time that is?" he asked. "Do you, really?"

I was embarrassed. I thought about it for a good thirty seconds and finally, it hit me. My response probably didn't make much sense to him. "That's ten Ohio State-Michigan games!" I blurted out. "Christ. That *is* a long time."

The exercise put the concept of time and the often arbitrary unfairness of our criminal justice system into much better perspective for me. It also made me think back to when I told people I had joined VISTA. They asked how long the term of enlistment was. One individual, when I answered that it was a year, remarked, "a whole year? You get time off for good behavior?" I felt guilty remembering that I laughed at the line. At the same time, though, I was very appreciative that I was sitting on the side of the table that I was.

Then there was Jim. He had been in the system for most of his life. When I met Jim, he had just done time in the prison in Georgia where they shot "The Longest Yard" and had been released to a halfway house in Florida, his home state.

"Jim," I asked him one day, "how'd you get into this mess?"

I expected him to provide details about the recent crime that got him sent up.

"I was one of seven children," he answered. "The youngest. When I was 12, my parents left us. Never saw 'em again. Where do you, Carroll, think you would be today if that happened to you?"

I was floored. The question, the way he used my first name, the tone of his voice – the combination hit me like a Mack truck. It was unbelievable. I grasped for the right words, any words, but nothing came out. The expression on my face, which communicated equal parts shock and sympathy, was the best that I could do.

In one of his press conferences, President Kennedy said that "there is always inequality in life. ...Life is unfair." I don't know why those words have always stuck with me, especially in light of some of Kennedy's more famous speeches, but it was during that moment in that halfway house that I realized the sad truth in those simple statements. I was grateful for my parents and all the fairness that I've had in my life. Jim's words still haunt me. I often wonder what happened to him.

There were two other people in Lake City who I got to know through the job that I would like to tell you about. They were people on the legal and law enforcement side I worked with. If not for them, I might have been the third VISTA to quit Lake City in under a week.

C. Dennis Roberts was an attorney based in Lake City. Roberts worked as a public defender, which in my opinion is one of the toughest jobs in America. Because of television, the F. Lee Baileys and Johnnie Cochrans of the world have become the faces of the legal profession. That's unfortunate. People like Dennis Roberts deserve more notoriety.

The late Patrolman Harold Roberts (no relation) of the Lake City Police Department was another friend. We had a lot in common. We liked the same television shows, we appreciated the same kinds of jokes and humor, and we both felt the same way about politicians. When I told him about my mother's "Three P's," he shared his variation on the line: "America is tired of politicians, their pious pontificating, and pissin' away our money."

Harold Roberts was primarily a traffic cop, but he occasionally served as my escort. I'll never forget the time we were driving somewhere in a patrol car and he had me open the glove compartment to get a map. When I did, a pistol fell into my lap. I flailed about like it was a poisonous snake. He started laughing uncontrollably.

"And Kojak is one of your heroes!" he roared.

He had a serious side as well. His viewpoint was at times powerfully enlightening. For example, one afternoon we were sitting in Olustee Park waiting for some business in the courthouse to wrap up. I made a comment about the memorial erected in the park in honor of the Confederate soldiers killed in the Battle of Olustee, which took place just down the road.

Years later I learned that the battle was the largest Civil War battle to take place in Florida. At the time, though, the engagement didn't register with me, at least not the way bigger, bloodier battles like Gettysburg or Antietam, did.

"That's a really nice monument," I said, "for such an insignificant battle."

"Perhaps it's insignificant in the history books," Roberts replied, "but it wasn't an insignificant battle for those who fought in it. It certainly wasn't insignificant to the widows it created, to the children who lost their fathers, or to the parents who became childless."

There have been very few times in my life when Beano Cook, with his big mouth, was rendered speechless, yet it happened quite a bit that year I spent in VISTA.

I got along with nearly everybody. The townspeople, the cops and court personnel, and many of the parolees. Everybody, really, except for my boss, Charles Maxwell. He didn't like me from day one and although he never came around, I never disliked him.

Maxwell was instrumental in my transfer to Tallahassee, where I basically did PR for the Florida Department of Health and Rehabilitative Services for the remainder of my time. I didn't like Tallahassee near as much as Lake City, but I had two very good bosses, Jeff Schembera and Doug Maddox. There were only four people who called me Beano in VISTA; along with Harold Roberts and Dennis Roberts, Schembera and Maddox were the other two.

I made it the full year and I was proud of myself for the accomplishment. During the period of time that I served in VISTA, the mid-1970s, the washout rate was roughly thirty-five percent. By comparison, about twenty-seven percent left the Peace Corps early. The Florida-based ACTION offices, I later learned, had the highest turnover in the country.

When I left, I felt the time I spent in the program was well worth it, but I don't know if the government felt that way about my service. Some of the higher-ups probably considered me a problem. There was simply too much chickenshit, like in the army, for me.

I'll admit to being guilty of doing some things that weren't allowed, like lending money to parolees, but many of us felt overwhelmed by all the paperwork, regulations, and directives. I believe the bureaucracy and red tape prevented us from more effectively helping people, and in this way, the entire purpose of the organization was undermined.

A wonderful woman I met in Tallahassee, Minerva Hathaway, was 66 years old when she wrapped up her fifth and final year in VISTA. She spoke for many of us who felt disillusioned with certain aspects of the experience.

"When I first joined in 1971, we were a poverty-fighting organization," Hathaway told me. "We are now doing what all other volunteer organizations do. We are putting band-aids on sores. American do-gooderism treats the symptoms, but never the disease."

Maxwell and I didn't always see eye-to-eye, but one thing we agreed on was that top-level leadership was non-existent. "Washington," Maxwell once said, "might as well be the lost city of Atlantis." The money and mandates came out of D.C., but little else.

A high-ranking member of ACTION once said, "if a VISTA leaves only a memory of himself or herself in a community, then he or she has failed." Those were the vague marching orders we got. How can one possibly define success or failure in such a way? It's not like a football coach, who can be rated in terms of wins and losses.

I may not have been undefeated when it came to keeping my clients from going back to prison, or universally well-liked at all levels of the organization, but I don't consider my time in VISTA a failure. I believe that I positively impacted many of the people I came into contact with. And I must have left more than a memory in Lake City because I kept in touch with people there, and they with me, for several years.

One thing is for certain. When I look back at this strange year of my life, I now understand that I got more out of it than I put in. I learned a lot.

Like geography. I learned that there are two different Souths. There's the South, and there's the Deep South. Southerners don't consider Texas part of either, but Texans do. And Florida is essentially two states. When I worked for the Dolphins and lived in Miami, I might have been in the southern part of the state geographically, but I was in the part of the state that more closely identifies with the Northern U.S. culturally. Northern Florida is considered the South.

I learned that the desire for community is stronger in the South than in any other part of the country. Charles Maxwell told me something else I'll never forget. "In New York, you probably didn't know your next-door neighbor or really anybody else in your apartment building," he said. "Down here, on the other hand, your closest neighbor might be five miles away. And if he's in trouble, you don't think twice about running over to help him."

They do take care of their own in the South. In more ways than one. One of the great VISTA stories was the one where this VISTA had a client, a parolee, that had been on the run for three months. He couldn't track the guy down. The people in this parolee's hometown knew of his whereabouts, but said nothing. He was one of them. That was, however, until he shot his dog and a neighbor turned him in. I don't know what the guy's original crime was, why he was on parole in the first place, but if I had been his VISTA, I'd have recommended that the judge gave him the electric chair.

The whole VISTA experience was eye-opening. Not because I was conducting ground-breaking research or making insightful observations like the great, amateur American anthropologist I thought I was when I was pitching New York publishers my book idea. It was because I had gone in with a lot of dumb misconceptions and my experiences set me straight.

The first misconception was about the poor. I learned that nobody wants to be poor so that they can get welfare checks. That's a myth. Nobody wants to be on food stamps. So let's give our less fortunate brothers and sisters a break. It's not right to pass moral judgment on applicants seeking some type of welfare aid.

That said, those that try to scam the government their entire lives should be ashamed of themselves. There is only one day anybody should pretend to be poor. That's April 15.

The second misconception I had was about Southerners. I was surprised I didn't find people disliking me because I was a Yankee. Although they certainly knew I was one. "Don't take it personally, son," one older gentleman told me. "We consider anybody from north of the South Carolina-Georgia line a Yankee."

My early opinions of the South were based on "The Adventures of Huckleberry Finn" and later, from books like "North Toward Home," but I found that even those great works of literature came up short when it came to presenting an accurate portrayal of life in the South. It's my opinion that the negative perceptions about the South that many Americans in other parts of the country have are perpetuated by the federal government and the media.

One individual in ACTION, someone very familiar with the workings of Washington, D.C., told me that he sincerely believed that Congress colluded with the media to focus attention on the South, on things like racial unrest and poverty. This created tension in the South, and at the same time shifted attention from the problems in the North.

It was an interesting theory, that Appomattox was only an armistice. While the shooting might have stopped, the Civil War was still being fought in other ways by certain segments of the country. Of course, I found that what I was told about the South still not being over the Civil War was true. The South still hasn't gotten over losing the war, but I'll add that the North hasn't accepted the South winning the peace.

By far, the biggest misconception I had about the South was on the subject of race relations. I had grown up thinking that race problems were confined to the South. When I joined VISTA, I brought those misconceptions with me, and I was proven dead wrong.

Early in my enlistment, this is right after I got a car, I picked up a black hitchhiker on the highway. After we exchanged some small talk, I posed a question to him: "Is it hard being black in the South?" His reply? "It's hard being black anywhere, man."

From what one heard back then on the evening news or read in the magazines and in the major metro papers, you'd have thought that people in southern towns joined the Ku Klux Klan like their counterparts in northern towns join the Elks. Only through first-hand experience did I learn that this was untrue.

And if I hadn't become friends with Officer Roberts, I might have maintained the misconception that every white cop in the South resembled Rod Steiger's character, Chief Gillespie, in the movie "In the Heat of the Night."

Perception, of course, depends on who is doing the perceiving. I'm not arguing that the conditions in the South were great, especially since I probably I didn't see the worst of it. Lake City was racially diverse, but my experiences, as a white VISTA, were probably much different from those of minority volunteers, especially those who worked in the poorer areas of places like Jacksonville and Miami.

The biggest difference between racism in the North and in the South, from my viewpoint, was the way it was expertly camouflaged in the North. We saw segregation in the South on our television sets every night in the Sixties, but few of us were aware that we walked past it everyday in the North.

I wasn't made aware until a conversation I had with the late William "Mugsy" Moore which took place around the time I returned home for my two-week vacation during the Bicentennial summer of 1976. Moore, who would become Pittsburgh's first black police chief about a decade later, told me that when he started out on the force, this is right around the same time I started working at the *Pittsburgh Press* in the early 1950s, he wasn't allowed to drive a patrol car. That wasn't all he told me.

Moore talked about the secret arrangement that existed between the politicians who ran the city and black community leaders for many years. The politicians said they couldn't give blacks city jobs, for fear of alienating blue collar white voters, but in exchange for the people in their communities remaining reliable Democrat voters, they would let the whore houses and numbers rackets in black neighborhoods operate freely. In other words, if you keep voting for us, we're not going to help you better your lives, but there would be no raids.

I planned to use this interesting (and sure to be controversial) material in my VISTA book. There are times, even now late in my life, I wish I had proceeded with the project. But it wasn't meant to be. It wasn't meant to be me who wrote about these issues. These were subjects much too important for me to tackle. While I sincerely cared about these issues, I didn't have the credentials.

Years after I gave up on the book idea, I thought I would try pitching a piece about my experiences to a newspaper or magazine, but I felt it would not be taken seriously. Or, perhaps more precisely, that I wouldn't be taken seriously as the author of it by a public which, by that point in my life, knew me predominantly as an eccentric sports television personality.

So, this might be the only written record of what was one of the most fascinating years of my life. I can live with that. Now after I'm done living, I don't know if my obituary will be in the *New York Times*. If it is, it will be an honor. As for what material will be included in it, I suspect that it will contain a run-down of the places I worked, and probably some combination of the Salk story, the roster story and a handful of my best lines.

Part of me hopes that somewhere in there, there will be at least a mention of VISTA. Of all the titles I've had in my life – Private Cook, Pitt SID, NCAA press director at *ABC* Sports, director of public relations for the Miami Dolphins, Cosell's "unmade bed," even the Pope of College Football – VISTA volunteer coordinator might be the one that I am most proud of.

CHAPTER 8

Pull out the driver.

The first week of 1977 was a memorable one. My alma mater, Pitt, won the national title by demolishing Georgia in the Sugar Bowl on New Year's Day. Two days later, on January 3, I learned that Thomas Wolfe had been wrong. That was the day I joined *CBS* Sports as an associate director of publicity. Apparently, you can go home again.

When I left *ABC* in February 1974, I was certain I would never work in television again. The egos, the backstabbing, the petty office politics – all of it had gotten to me. At first, I wasn't sure I had made the right decision in coming back. Some friends thought my return was a bad omen, too. Two months after I showed up at *CBS*, "The Mary Tyler Moore Show" ended. One month after that, America's other sweetheart, Phyllis George, got married and was taken off the market. I was blamed for both of these national disasters.

I thought I would never live in New York again, either. Yet when I got back into town, it was like I had never left. They were still running the same stories, on crime, corruption, and transit strikes, in the papers. The sidewalks were still minefields of dog shit. And the average cost of a phone call was still three dimes. That's because the first two pay phones you tried were invariably broken. But it felt good to be back.

And I had to laugh. Not only was I back in Manhattan and back in television, three years and four jobs later, I had moved a grand total of half a block! Still, I felt I had come a long way. Maybe I was older and wiser, or perhaps it was due to the perspective-altering experiences I'd had in VISTA. Whatever it was, I felt much better prepared for my second stint doing publicity in television when I arrived at Black Rock.

One person I have to thank for my changed outlook was the late, great Charles Kuralt, who was one of the first individuals to welcome me to the company. I asked Kuralt, has it, as in the television business, gotten any better?

"Well, people don't stab each other in the back anymore," Kuralt explained. "Everybody is going around stabbing each other in the chest!"

Jokes aside, the most important thing I learned from Kuralt was the fact that I wasn't weak-willed for having felt the way I did three years earlier. Everybody in the business, he said, goes through a rough patch. It doesn't matter whether you're a top executive or talent, a publicist or a young PA, everybody feels disillusioned or disgruntled at one time or another. Nobody is immune.

For another example, fast forward ten years. Dick Ebersol's 40th birthday party. Everybody in television was there. I was talking to Don Ohlmeyer and suddenly his eyes seemed like they were going to pop out of their sockets as he scanned the crowd.

"What's wrong, Don?" I asked him.

"I've never been in a room this large, with so many people," he said in that measured, reflective speaking style of his, "who hate each other so much."

Ohlmeyer was a seasoned veteran by this point, but I found it interesting that he was 42 years old when he had that revelation. I told him he was almost exactly the same age as I was when I got fed up and left *ABC* in '74 and advised him not to lose a minute of sleep over whatever was bugging him. That it happens to all of us.

Since I was employed by two of the three legacy networks and *ESPN*, I've been asked on several occasions to describe what each company was like to work for. The similarities and differences between how the organizations were run, how the bosses and big names behaved – that sort of thing. We'll get to *ESPN* in a bit. Right now, I'm going to share some observations and compare my experiences working for *ABC* Sports and *CBS* Sports.

Let me preface these remarks by saying that of all the jobs I've had in my life, all the organizations that I worked for, *CBS* was far and away the best from an employee's perspective. The corporation, one of the first to institute the policy of pensions, showed a genuine concern for its employees. The general health plan ranked with the best in all of corporate America. The investment plan was more than fair. It was generous.

As for everything else, I won't attempt to speak for everybody who worked at both networks. But I'm probably not the only alum of both outfits who would tell you that while these divisions were basically next-door neighbors, at times it seemed as though they were located on different planets.

The first thing I noticed was the difference in public perception by outsiders. When I worked at *ABC*, friends asked, "what is Howard Cosell really like?" When I went to *CBS*, the first question was, "do you know Walter Cronkite?" *ABC* was seen as the country's top sports network and *CBS* was known for its vaunted news division.

When I told people I worked for *ABC* Sports, they were impressed. When I told people I worked for *CBS*, they took me seriously. Part of that was a little routine I used to pull. Whenever I had trouble checking into a hotel or at the airport, I would pull out my *CBS* identification card and announce, so that everybody within twenty feet could hear me, that "I work for '60 Minutes.'" The issue would be resolved immediately! I got a kick out of that.

Did I know Cronkite? Not in any real sense. Our paths crossed a few times. But I have a pretty good feel for people and I could tell that he wasn't a phony. I found out that Cronkite's 25th anniversary party in 1975 was held in the cafeteria at the broadcast center because he wanted the technicians and engineers to be able to attend. That's a stand-up move. He refused attempts by the higher-ups to make it a VIP affair. He wanted no part of "21."

I feel lucky that I can say that I worked for *CBS* when Cronkite was sitting in the chair. I believe he's the best to ever do it. That line, "the most trusted man in America," that was good PR and marketing. There was something to it, though. I used to tell people, this was back during the Cold War when the bombs could start dropping at any moment that if the world is going to end in thirty minutes, to hell with the President – I want to hear the news from Cronkite.

There wasn't any funny business permitted in the news division under Cronkite and I saw that carried over to sports. I have no way of knowing for sure, but I'd say the company-wide obsession with doing things in a straight-and-narrow fashion was due to the influence of the network's legendary founder, William S. Paley.

For example, I noticed right away that *CBS* Sports didn't employ gimmicks with scores on any of their productions. On *ABC's* "College Scoreboard Show," they used to turn the counter as if they just got the score. In reality, they might have had it for ten minutes.

CBS strove for consistency. We didn't get college football until right around the time I left, but I noticed that after I was gone, *CBS* used one poll and stuck with it the entire season. I admired them for that. When I was NCAA press director at *ABC* Sports, we used the AP Poll for a team one week, then might use the UPI for that team the next week. We used whatever poll provided the higher ranking in order to juice up the promos for our games.

I remember in 1973, *ABC* didn't use the AP Poll for basically the entire season because Oklahoma was on probation. The Sooners couldn't go to a bowl or appear on TV, but they were still ranked in the AP, unlike in the UPI, or Coaches' Poll, where they had been excluded. But there was one "Monday Night Football" game that we used the AP Poll in the promos for the following Saturday's game because there had been a shake-up that week in the top five that provided one of the teams in our game with a higher ranking.

A lot of the things that *ABC* Sports did would not have flown at *CBS*. The most notable example, in my opinion, was when *ABC* execs admitted to the *New York Times* that one reason the network put Howard Cosell on the air was because many Americans disliked him. He pissed people off, but that drew viewers and big ratings.

CBS would never have taken that approach. Paley wouldn't have permitted it. Paley was an empire builder and a visionary, of course, but there were certain things, ways of doing business, I think he felt were beneath the "Tiffany Network."

In the 1970s, bars used to hold contests during "Monday Night Football" where patrons could throw a brick through an old TV whenever Cosell was on the screen. Paley probably found the notion of pulling numbers due to a personality who made those kinds of stunts possible revolting.

To me, *CBS* Sports operated like a blue bloods club. Productions at *ABC* Sports, by comparison, were geared to attract the blue-collar sports fan.

For better or for worse, no division in the history of television better embodied the famous quote, "winning isn't everything, it's the only thing," than *ABC* Sports under Roone (oh, and that line? It's always attributed to Vince Lombardi, but the football coach who deserves proper credit for it is UCLA's "Red" Sanders). As a result, *ABC* Sports personnel, everyone from producers to publicists, had much more freedom in their jobs than their counterparts elsewhere.

People at *ABC* Sports were expected to be aggressive. If you went and did something to try to be innovative or beat the competition and failed or fucked up, it was more acceptable to come back and ask for forgiveness than it was to ask for permission in the first place. You were expected to be on offense all the time.

Remember the story I told you about how I manipulated the rankings to pump up our Iron Bowl promos at the end of the '71 season? Roone was pissed, but I believe the chewing out I got was much less harsh than it could have been because he liked my initiative.

Now when I got to *CBS*, I noticed right away that the network's lawyers occupied the 36th floor at Black Rock. Paley's office was on the 35th floor. What does that tell you?

At *CBS* Sports, I found a regimented work environment, a strict managerial hierarchy and an organization really set in its ways. To start, there were a bunch of weird rules you had to familiarize yourself with. One was, if two persons occupy an office, the one with seniority sits in the back. Everyone had his place in the food chain, and you didn't forget it. I always felt out of place on those rare occasions I got off the elevator on or above the 30th floor, where the execs were officed, at Black Rock.

The familiar refrain I heard when I made a suggestion was, "we've never done it that way." That took some getting used to. At *ABC*, even a lowly publicist like yours truly was free to approach the great and powerful Oz, Roone, with ideas and suggestions.

Traditions, I discovered, died hard at *CBS*. Take production meetings for NFL games, which were held at 5 p.m. on the dot on Saturdays. Why? Because back in the '60s, Vince Lombardi met with *CBS* people at exactly 5 p.m. in his office in Green Bay.

And then there was "The Keeper of the Eye." That's what Jay Rosenstein, the long-time VP of Programming at *CBS* Sports, called him. The Keeper was a *CBS* lawyer whose only job was to make sure the logo, the all-seeing, never-blinking "Eye," was reproduced correctly.

Once, the design department was slightly off on a rendition of the logo that appeared on some promo materials. There is no way anybody out of house would have noticed it, but Rosenstein got a call.

"It must be fixed immediately. If Dr. Stanton were still here," the Keeper added in a deathly serious tone, "he would have you destroy every piece of paper the Eye is on."

Then there was a click. No explaining. No ifs, ands or buts.

The Keeper was referring to Dr. Frank Stanton, the longtime network president who had retired more than ten years earlier. While I found that sort of reverence to certain individuals and strict adherence to institutional rules to be somewhat strange at first, I didn't think much of it. But it wasn't long before I saw that the rigid structure of the organization was affecting our programming. There wasn't a priority placed on innovation or experimentation at *CBS* like I had seen at *ABC*.

Now it hadn't always been this way. At one time, *CBS* Sports had the most brilliant and innovative people in the business working on the production side and they were given a lot of freedom in their jobs.

I want to talk about four of them that I worked with that I don't think have been given their due. They were all well-known inside the business, but regular sports fans don't know these names. They should. These men are largely responsible for the way we watch sports on television today.

The first was Tony Verna. He could do it all, every sport, both as a producer and a director. You name the event – the Olympics, the Kentucky Derby, the '67 Ice Bowl, basketball, figure skating – he turned it into a work of art. After leaving *CBS*, Verna directed the Live Aid concert, as well as interviews with U.S. Presidents, Pope John Paul II and Mother Teresa.

Nobody understood television technology better than Verna. He was a real genius, one of the smartest people I met in my career, so it's not surprising to me that he was the individual who invented instant replay. He used it on the touchdown run by Army quarterback Rollie Stichweh in the fourth quarter of the 1963 Army-Navy game.

Pat Summerall gave the industry-changing technical trick its name a few weeks later, at the '64 Cotton Bowl. Try to imagine watching a sporting event, any sporting event, today on television without instant replay. You can't do it.

It bugged Verna that *CBS* never gave him any recognition for his invention. I think he finally left the network in 1981 because he was fed up with management and felt unappreciated.

It's also always bugged me that for a long time, *ABC* tried taking credit for instant replay. There was a long-standing argument regarding which network used it first. The fact that *ABC* even attempted to make an ownership claim was ridiculous.

I once read a book on the history of *ABC* in which it was written that the network did it during a Texas-Texas A&M game. Another source from *ABC* claimed that they had showed it as part of the halftime highlights during the 1961 Boston College-Syracuse game. When I worked for *ABC*, I kept hearing from some people about a game between the then-New York Titans (the franchise now known as the Jets) and the Denver Broncos in which it was done. Well, if the idea was so good, how come they didn't use it again until after Verna did it in '63?

The best story involving Tony Verna is one that he's only indirectly involved in. Duke Struck told it to me. Struck is another television heavyweight that few people outside the business know anything about. He was the first director of "The NFL Today" in 1974, when Jack Whitaker was doing the show. This was right before Brent Musberger,

Phyllis George and Irv Cross were hired.

Like Verna, Struck could do everything – the Olympics, Super Bowls, college football, the NBA, the World Series – and do it well. His talents extended beyond sports, too. He directed the "MacNeil/Lehrer Report" on *PBS* for a few years, then returned to *CBS* and "The NFL Today" in 1980. He was the director of "The *CBS* Morning News" and later worked on "The Oprah Winfrey Show" and *ABC's* "Good Morning America."

Struck, as this story illustrates, was successful because he was great at thinking on his feet. Here's the background. Verna once lived with a woman named Maureen Kane. He wanted to marry her. After awhile, Verna gave up and moved on with his life. Maureen Kane ended up marrying John Dean, the White House lawyer who flipped on Nixon and became a key witness for the prosecution during the Watergate investigation.

Struck was directing the Watergate hearings and he was having a helluva time trying to get a reaction shot from Mrs. Dean, who was seated behind her husband. She was just sitting there; there was no emotion. It wasn't good TV. Finally, he sent her a note. A page quietly handed the note to her and Struck ordered the camera to zoom in on her face right when she opened it. As she started reading, she began fluttering her eyes and scanning the room nervously. Bingo!

You want to know what the note said? It said, "right about now, don't you wish you had married Tony Verna?" That's it. There was no signature. Fucking Struck! What a maneuver. That tells you how good, how creative, these guys were.

When I think of a fall Sunday, I think of God, Charles Kuralt and "The NFL Today" – and not necessarily in that order. No offense to the Almighty, but churches, after all, changed worship schedules because of Kuralt and "The NFL Today."

"The NFL Today" was and will forever be the best studio and pre-game show in history. There are three things in my life I hated to see come to an end: any good blow job, any bad blow job, and "The NFL Today." There will never be anything like it again.

There are four people, in my opinion, who deserve the credit for the show's popularity. One was executive Bob Wussler, who created the show. Another was the director, Bob Fishman. The third was Jimmy the Greek. The fourth was my good friend Mike Pearl.

Every pre-game show on the air today is a direct descendant of "The NFL Today," and that makes Pearl a founding father of modern sports television. Pearl had worked on the show for the first year with the new cast, then took over as producer in 1976. The first big decision he made was to hire the Greek, and that's the real reason why the show took off. The show was pulling a five, maybe a six, in the Nielsens. Once the Greek was on board, it started pulling an eight consistently.

People can say what they want about the other talent, about the popularity of pro football, but viewers tuned in in such large numbers because of betting and because of the Greek's picks, even though he wasn't allowed to mention the spread.

I had gotten to know Pearl when I worked for the Dolphins. He had dropped out of Miami of Florida during the 1960s to join the sports department at *WTVJ*, the *CBS* affiliate in Miami. He was one of our gang, a group of bettors that included Rich Podolsky and Hank Goldberg. At the time, Goldberg was working for the Greek, writing the latter's columns which were syndicated in newspapers across the country. People called him "The Greek's Ghost," as in ghostwriter. That's how Pearl picked up on the Greek.

Pearl's other contributions to the success of "The NFL Today" included wrangling the egos of the talent, coordinating the story lines, and expertly monitoring all the moving production parts of an NFL Sunday. But at *CBS* Sports, the director occupied a more prominent role than the producer. At *ABC*, it was the other way around. Pearl wanted to do, and was capable of doing a lot more, so Roone snatched him up.

At first, I was sad when he left us in 1980 for *ABC*, but I ended up being very thankful he made the move two years later because was my producer when Roone put me on the air in 1982. I can say with complete certainty that the experiment would not have worked if not for Pearl. Pearl would eventually produce all the big events for *ABC* and enjoyed a hugely successful career that also saw stints in top leadership roles at *ESPN* and with *Turner Sports*.

The fourth face on *CBS* Sports' production Mount Rushmore has to be the late Frank Chirkinian. In my opinion, The Masters is the marquee event that it is because of Chirkinian. He was the best golf producer in the history of the medium of television. Nobody juggled the shots, the graphics, and the commentary better. He was an innovator and a perfectionist.

And when he was in the truck, he was one of the biggest pricks of all-time. To say he was abrasive, that would be putting it mildly. Nobody swore or chewed people, talent, subordinates, and even pro golfers, out like Chirkinian. He wouldn't get away with half the things that came out of his mouth if he was in the business today. He was so demanding, such an authoritarian, Pat Summerall called him "The Ayatollah." The nickname was perfect.

Some people had issues with Chirkinian, but I liked the guy because I like people who are blunt. My only issue with his work, I told him, were his cut-aways. Linger a little longer. Let the crowd enjoy the scenery, especially at places like Augusta National. "If teachers covered history the way you cover golf," I once told him, "it'd be Patrick Henry said, 'Give me liberty'...now over to 16."

I got a grunt instead of a "fuck you" in reply, so I think Frank might have somewhat respected me and my opinions. He gave me some valuable advice when I was at a crossroads of my career, which I'll tell you about in a bit.

Right around the time I left *ABC* in '74, I said that "the television industry is a 40-story 'Peyton Place.'" "Peyton Place" was America's first prime time soap opera. The show was a hit in the 1960s. If I had only known what working at *CBS* would have been like! There were more characters and there was more drama at *CBS* Sports than at any other place I worked in my career.

Many people will find this declaration surprising, but that's probably because *CBS* had always done an excellent job showing its best face, or rather faces, to the public.

The personification of the trustworthy, no-nonsense newsman, Edward R. Murrow, spent thirty years with the company. Eric Sevareid was there even longer. Cronkite was America's favorite uncle. Andy Rooney was America's lovable curmudgeon. Charles Kuralt, he was everybody's idea of the perfect next-door neighbor.

I always felt that *CBS* had a reserved, refined, WASP-ish image and the reputations of management, people like Paley and Stanton, as well as certain sports programming properties like The Masters, reflected that.

Nobody outside the business knew about characters like Chirkinian or some of the other people we had working behind-the-scenes. A good example of *CBS's* all-star supporting cast was my friend, the late Bill "Catfish" Brendle.

"I'm not quite sure what Billy Brendle does," *CBS* network president Bob Wood once said. "But whatever it is, he's indispensable."

Brendle did publicity for the network. He is not just one of my favorite all-time co-workers, he was one of the funnest human beings I ever met. You could be down in the dumps all day, but when you walked into a packed Runyon's and heard that voice of his over the crowd, your mood instantly improved.

Brendle was one of those jolly, good-natured, glass half-full guys, and chances are, the glass was more than half-full because the company was paying for it! When it came to the subject of expense accounts, which we're going to get to, he's considered one of the best entertainers in network television history. That's partly because of the way he freely spent the company's money. It was also due to his unique sense of humor. It was off-the-charts.

I once asked Brendle about his length of service at *CBS*.

"Seventeen years," he replied. And then, after a brief pause, he added, "if you don't count the lunches, eight."

There's also the time Pat Summerall spent an hour driving Brendle around the stadium parking lot after an NFL game in Tampa. Brendle had had a little too much to drink and couldn't remember where he had parked his rental car.

Summerall said they had done so many laps, he thought he was driving in the Daytona 500. And Pat was probably half in the bag himself. Finally, he stopped the car.

"Okay, Bill," he said. "The game's been over for two hours. There aren't many cars left out here. Let's narrow down the search. What kind of car is it?"

"Hertz," hiccupped Brendle.

If I could pick anybody to narrate the story of my life, I'd want Summerall to do it. When you heard that baritone in the open, you knew it was a big game or a big-time event. Everybody knew he was a real pro, and sadly, everyone knows about his battle with alcoholism, too, but few know that another part of his job at *CBS* Sports was playing the role of peacemaker.

Sometime in the late 1970s, Summerall and Billie Jean King were partners in the booth during an event. The producer was Chirkinian. It was the first time King had ever worked with him. I don't know all the details regarding the incident, but Chirkinian told her off. Frank was, well, just being Frank. King was ready to walk off the broadcast.

"Is he always like that?" an angry King asked Summerall during a break.

"Most of the time," he laughed.

Summerall then slowly small-talked King back into her chair and the broadcast went off without a hitch.

I'll never forget another time Summerall literally saved the day, and by that, I mean saved the publicity department from having to do a lot of damage control work.

You might remember that the team of Summerall and tennis great Tony Trabert covered the U.S. Open for *CBS* for many years. During the 1980 tournament a Polish player, Wojciech Fibak, made a mistake that cost him his match. He lost in the quarterfinals. In his commentary, Trabert said something like, "well, what do you expect? He's Polish."

The next day, we had a visitor at Black Rock: National Security Advisor Zbigniew Brzezinski. Oh, was he pissed. He wanted Trabert's head and was threatening to call the papers. Until now, nobody has ever heard this story. That's because it never became news. Summerall, who happened to be in the office, stepped in and soothed Brzezinski's feelings. It was really something. By the time the elevator doors opened to the lobby and Summerall was waving goodbye, Brzezinski had probably forgotten why he was there in the first place.

There wasn't much difference between the talent at the two networks. In television, talent is talent. It doesn't matter where you work. Every network has its legendary voices.

Over the course of my two stints at *ABC*, I worked with Cosell, Chris Schenkel, Keith Jackson, Jim McKay, and Jim Lampley. During my time at *CBS*, I got to know Summerall, Dick Stockton, Brent Musberger, Tom Brookshier and Gary Bender, among several other great voices.

And behind-the-scenes, every network has its oversized egos, down-to-earth personalities and a scattering of everything in between. On one end, you've got Schenkel, who is widely considered to be the all-time nicest guy, talent-wise, in the business. Nobody ever said a bad word about him, and nobody ever heard him knock anybody. Well, except for Billy Packer. I don't know why he disliked Packer.

Chris was very, very easy to get along with. That was to his detriment. For years, he didn't even have an agent. He just took whatever the suits offered him. Then he hired Barry Frank, which was good, because he finally started making the money he deserved.

If you're talking about good people in the business, in addition to Summerall and Schenkel, no conversation is complete without Jack Whitaker. Whitaker is a first-class television personality and, more importantly, a first-class person. He worked at both *CBS* and *ABC*, and his writing ability was never matched by anybody at any network. His essays were unbelievable. We'll never see another writer like Whitaker on television again.

On the flip side, if *CBS* Sports would never have put Cosell on the air, it's my opinion that Roone wouldn't have hired Brent Musberger during the glory years at *ABC* Sports. Why? He would have been too damaging to team chemistry. I never met a more aggressively ambitious announcer in my career than Musberger. And I wasn't the only one who saw it.

After the 1985 Masters, a group of regulars on the PGA Tour summoned the courage (after a few drinks, I should add) to corner Frank Chirkinian and ask that Musberger not be used on future broadcasts for two reasons: he didn't add anything and he received too much airtime.

Dan Jenkins, as is usually the case, had the best line on Brent. "His ambition is to be on all three networks," Jenkins said. "At the same time."

Musberger had a reputation of being a cutthroat co-worker. I can't say whether it was deserved or not. Rumor had it, he'd use your material or steal your lines. I could understand how that might piss people off.

During the whip-arounds for NFL games, the on-site announcers tell the control room what they plan to say. This goes on during a commercial. Well, Musberger got the announcers upset because he used to listen in on the conversations.

One NFL Sunday, Summerall got some late, inside information that Terry Bradshaw wasn't starting for the Steelers because of a sore arm. So Musberger throws it to Summerall and says, "now let's go out to Pittsburgh and Pat Summerall. So Pat, Bradshaw's a late scratch. It sounds like that arm is giving him problems." Summerall was fucking furious. He told me Musberger stole his scoop.

Everyone knows about the time Musberger and Jimmy the Greek traded punches at Peartrees, which was a hangout on New York's East Side. This was in late October 1980. The public story was that the fight was over airtime, that the Greek thought Musberger wasn't giving him enough on "The NFL Today."

Behind-the-scenes, there were two competing stories, or reasons, regarding the altercation. The first was that the Greek was pissed because Brent reportedly jumped his scoop that Dan Devine's successor at Notre Dame would be a high school coach. A month later, Notre Dame confirmed that Gerry Faust, a high school coach in Cincinnati, was the new coach of the Fighting Irish. I wouldn't be surprised if this was the case since the Greek probably had plenty of sources in his home state.

And then I heard that the reason the Greek took a swing at Brent was because he was upset that Brent had supposedly leaked to Tom Shales, the TV writer for the *Washington Post*, that the Greek had reportedly made some politically incorrect comments off-camera.

I am using ambiguous adverbs because have no way of verifying these stories. I merely remember what people in the office were saying at the time. I didn't work on the show and since I wasn't present for any of the background, build-up, or the main event itself, I'm not making a definitive statement on the actual cause for the dust-up. But my experience tells me that fistfights typically start over things more serious than airtime.

Or who knows, perhaps the whole thing had been planned by Musberger as a way to get his name into the papers and build a reputation as a tough guy or something. The Greek was from Steubenville, Ohio. People from places like that, with backgrounds like Jimmy's, they don't just let slights, real or perceived, slide. Brent had to expect that there would be some kind of retaliatory move. Maybe he wanted it. Maybe that was the point of the exercise.

Hell, maybe the Greek was in on the act, too. Neither of these guys, mind you, ended up with a scratch. If you think about it, for two people who worked on a such a high-profile show, it doesn't make much sense to risk a black eye or a broken nose when you have to go on the air in a few days.

Another rumor I heard was that in 1985, Musberger allegedly tried to get the producer of "The NFL Today," George Veras, off the show because Veras was going through a divorce. He claimed Veras wouldn't be stable enough to do the work.

Look, television is a super stressful business. There are big bucks and egos and livelihoods at stake. But Veras, by all accounts a good guy who had never been anything but dependable, was the producer of a TV show. He wasn't piloting the fucking space shuttle.

I never knew what to think of some of these stories, but there's no mistaking the fact that they all have one thing in common, Brent Musberger. They illustrated his need to be in front of the camera, on the front pages and front and center when it came to being in control.

Don't read too much into my comments. I don't hate the guy. I don't consider us enemies. I've just never been able to stand big egos and, in my opinion, his is the biggest the business has ever seen. Even bigger than Cosell's. It's my right to share that opinion.

And he did something, or was a part of a group of people who did something, that at the time hurt me very much. While I got over it, I won't forget it. Let's just say while I've always respected his talent and liked his work, sometimes he's made it difficult for me to respect and like him.

Truth is, there are a couple of things I've always admired Brent for. One is his drive. "We will catch 'Wide World' in two years. Cosell is yesterday's news," he once boasted. "Arledge and *ABC* Sports are yesterday's news." The exact date he said those words was April 28, 1981. I wrote it down on my clipboard because I wanted to remind him of his prediction when it didn't come true. Yet I can't help but wonder, if everyone at *CBS* Sports had been wired like Brent, it just might have.

I've always been envious of his camera presence. His ability to appear so calm and comfortable on the air. He's unflappable. You have all these people, producers and directors, yelling in your earpiece – it's not easy doing television. Especially live television. But he's always made it look easy. That's talent.

Another thing was Brent's blunt honesty. Over the years, he's said things on the air that have gotten him into hot water. But he's always been that way. He talked the same way to his castmates and the PAs as he did the suits. A former newspaperman himself, he was a straight-shooter with columnists. Why they hammered him, I couldn't figure it out.

Talking about Brent's blunt manner, nobody printed it, but I remember when a writer asked why we were bringing Phyllis George back after Jayne Kennedy left "The NFL Today" he said, point blank, "we need tits."

I understood that he wasn't being crude. He realized that the business had changed and that was just his way of saying it. Phyllis's ground-breaking role on the show meant that sports television was no longer a male-only fraternity. A female presence on set was no longer a gimmick or an experiment. It had become a prerequisite.

Which brings us to another difference between the two networks. When I worked in publicity at *ABC* Sports, Howard Cosell barged into my office to bullshit and to bitch about the media, management, and everybody else under the sun. When I went to *CBS*, Phyliss George took over that role. At least Phyllis usually knocked first.

Let me tell you, while Phyllis was of course much easier on the eyes than Howard, she was more than just a set of tits. She had the total package. She was genuine, well-spoken, warm-hearted, and unpretentious. She might have been a former Miss America, but she had a certain girl-next-door way about her. She was kind of klutzy, too, and that further endeared her to many of us who knew her and worked with her.

My friend Bob Quincy, a newspaperman who also spent some time as the SID at North Carolina, once told me, "if you would put everything you wanted, looks, personality and charm, into one girl to marry, that would be Phyllis George."

My friend Pete Axthelm once did a feature on Phyllis for John Walsh's *Inside Sports* magazine. Ax was so intoxicated by her charm, he would have done anything for her – even quit drinking. If you knew Ax, or know anything about him, you understand the seriousness of that statement.

She was the irresistible force that could budge even the most famously immovable objects. When Roger Staubach retired in 1980, he briefly joined *CBS* to do some color work on our NFL telecasts. It was then I learned that the "Captain America" persona was the real deal. Unlike many big-name pro athletes, Staubach never fooled around. The devout Christian even went so far as to have it written into his *CBS* contract that his wife would travel with him on the road. Contrast this with the behavior of others in the business who didn't want their wives anywhere near them when they went on the road. I also learned that there was an escape clause in that contract. Sort of.

"If I could get permission from two persons," Staubach said, "I would run off with Phyliss George for a weekend."

Who were the two? I asked.

"My wife and Jesus Christ," laughed Staubach.

My office at *CBS* served more or less as the company clubhouse. Working the door was my incredible secretary, Josephine. I nicknamed her "Whips and Chains," but she was actually easy to get along with. People from publicity, production, advertising and other departments would hang out there. Out-of-town sportswriters, as well as former athletes, guys like Paul Hornung and Johnny Unitas, dropped in, too. I'd light up a Winston and open a can of TAB and away we'd go.

I honestly don't know how Phyllis came to be sitting in there with us, or how our one-on-one bull sessions started. But I do know that the talks I had with Howard were different than the ones I had with her.

While Howard wanted sympathy, Phyllis wasn't looking for a shoulder to cry on. I think she merely wanted someone to listen. I'm glad I did. She had a lot to say. Until I got to know Phyllis George, it had never occurred to me to try walking a mile in the heels of a woman who worked in sports television.

While I'm from the "old school" in many ways, and I was an SID in an era when press tickets were stamped "No Women Allowed in the Pressbox," I never considered myself a chauvinist. There weren't many women working in sports or sports media when I started, but I didn't bar them from Pitt's facilities or treat them any differently.

As proof, many women over the years will attest that I didn't always watch my mouth around them. Some might have thought it was disrespectful, but I looked at it another way. In so many words, I was saying, "I have no problem with you being here or doing the job. That's just the language we speak around here and I'm going to talk to you and treat you the same way I do everybody else."

When she started on "The NFL Today," I thought the bad reviews Phyllis got in the papers were overreactions. The glowing ones were off-base, too. I thought the comparisons between Phyllis and Jackie Robinson were ridiculous. You couldn't equate cat calls and lewd behavior with death threats. More importantly, not only was she not even the first woman to talk pro football on television, she wasn't even the first woman to do it for *CBS*!

That was Jane Chastain. Chastain covered sports for *WTVJ-TV* in Miami, the same station Mike Pearl worked at as a producer. She did good work in Miami and then was hired at *CBS* the year before they hired Phyllis. She worked on NFL and NBA games and covered some bowl games as well. Every woman in the business today owes Jane Chastain a debt of gratitude for blazing the trail for them, but tragically, few have ever heard of her.

Right around the time I was finishing up with the Dolphins, an editor at *TV Guide* called me and wanted me to recommend a local writer to do a feature on Chastain. The working title of the piece stemmed from a letter-to-the-editor titled "Get that Broad out of the Booth." I recommended Rich Podolsky, because he had just left the *Palm Beach Post* and I knew he could use the payday, plus I thought he would treat Chastain fairly.

Now before you go off thinking I was enlightened, I'll also freely admit that for some time I didn't think women were technically qualified to report on a contact sport like football. And I've never really understood the whole sexual equality movement. I once read somewhere, I think it was in the *Wall Street Journal* or *Forbes*, that women control something like 65 percent of the world's wealth. Women have more than half of the money, they control 100 percent of the world's supply of pussy, and yet they complain about inequality?

Phyllis, to her credit, laughed at that line. The more we talked and laughed, the more I listened, and the more I understood her perspective, a much bigger supporter of hers I became.

It was hard not to once you understood that she was fighting a two-front war. Sexism goes both ways. Men and women can both be guilty of it and in various degrees. For instance, she told me she quit "Candid Camera" because she got fed up with Allen Funt asking, "where is that cunt?" If you think that's bad, you should hear how she was treated by the feminists from the women's lib movement who protested beauty pageants. They called her a traitor. Then there were other women, those who considered themselves real sports journalists, that considered her a trespasser on their AstroTurf and derided her as a Barbie doll with a microphone.

If it sounds a lot like a lose-lose situation, that's because it was. Unlike their male counterparts, women in television have to straddle fine lines in everything they do. Especially if you're talent. You can get hired because of your looks, but if you try keeping and doing the job solely on that premise, that's what people, both men and women, will focus on, not your work. Once you're labeled as nothing more than a pretty face, you're screwed. On top of that, everybody is either trying to screw you, thinks that they can, or else thinks that's how you got your job. Good looks are both a blessing and a curse.

Summerall told me about the time he took a seat next to Phyllis on a flight. She was going to work one of her first games for *CBS* as a sideline reporter. It was probably the first time the two of them had actually met. Just as the plane leveled off, she blurted out, "I didn't fuck to get this job. Everybody thinks I did."

I guess she felt the need to dispel any rumors in order to start their working relationship off on the right foot. After that earnest admission, in true Phyllis fashion she promptly spilled ice water on herself. "Now," she sighed, "I have a cold crotch."

"I believed her and after that, I believed in her," Summerall said.

The first female television sports reporter in Pittsburgh was a woman named Lee Arthur. This was in the early 1970s. She was kind of kooky, and didn't know much about sports, but she was a knockout. And, apparently, she took the job seriously.

When she joined *KDKA-TV,* the *CBS* affiliate in town, she made a promise to Bill Currie, the long-time station sports director. "I'm not going to fuck anybody in the office or any athletes," Arthur said.

The late Currie was another great Pittsburgh character who possessed a personality as colorful as his collection of sports jackets. The North Carolina-native was known as "The Mouth of the South" for good reason.

"Then, Lee," Currie famously replied. "You are going to miss some of the best cock in town. Whatever or whoever you do off the clock is your own business."

It was a great line, but a fundamentally incorrect observation. The sex life of a woman in the television business never stays private. A guy would never have to make a statement like Phyllis did to Pat. The line I've used is that "true equality in this business will only be achieved when women can fuck whoever they want, whenever they want, and nobody calls them whores."

I think it's one of the best lines and observations ever. Only it's not mine. I didn't come up with it. One of my closest friends at *CBS* – a woman – did. Susan Nemeroff started out working in publicity for us and she eventually became responsible for coordinating all on-air talent matters for the division. I want to make sure she gets credit for it. Susan nailed it.

One of these days, although I won't be around when it happens, a woman will be the lead play-by-play announcer on whatever network has the Super Bowl. That same woman will one day make the same, or perhaps even more money than the highest-paid male broadcasters. But she still won't be equal.

Like Susan said, not until she can run around and behave like any man does and not be held to a different standard. We might as well also add, not until she can drink, gamble, or get divorced without being labeled damaged goods. All the things a man gets away with.

Sex has always been an issue in the business. For women, smarts are the next obstacle. If you're a woman and you appear unprepared or less-than-knowledgeable, you're considered a bimbo. If you're too knowledgeable, you're labeled a know-it-all. If you are too ambitious or are viewed as too hard-charging and hell-bent for success, you run the risk of rubbing co-workers and everybody else the wrong way.

Take, for instance, Andrea Kirby, who I worked with at *ABC*. Kirby, a pioneer herself, was an intelligent, talented on-air personality who worked on the "College Scoreboard Show" and on "Wide World" in the early '70s. But she never allowed herself to relax for one moment and even try to be one of the guys. In fact, we used to joke that Kirby was so relentless in her approach to the job that she might actually kill someone to get ahead.

"If you catch me on top of her, it's not what you're thinking," Dave Diles once said. "I'm just holding her down until the police arrive."

I'm convinced that Phyllis was the first woman to succeed in network television sports because she was the first one that figured out how to behave like both a woman and man whenever the situation called for it. Countless local sports reporters, beauty queens, wannabe actresses and weather girls never tried behaving like anything but a woman.

One minute Phyllis could be Miss America, next she could be one of the guys. She could be sweet, but she could also hold her own in my office. She was persistent, but she didn't have an over-the-top personality. She was prepared, but didn't come across as a walking sports encyclopedia. She accepted advice and constructive criticism, but she stood her ground and didn't let anybody change her look or her style, which is something Chastain reportedly let Wussler and her bosses get away with.

And she disarmed her detractors with her charm, rather than lash out at them.

While she wasn't the first female to talk NFL football on television, in a way she did have something in common with Jackie Robinson: she didn't automatically call out every football fan or television writer that panned her performances as sexist the same way Robinson didn't tear off into the stands to punch every jerk who shouted a racist epithet at him. I don't want to make it sound like I had anything whatsoever to do with her success, but perhaps she kept her head because she let off steam with me during our chats.

The great Roger Kahn told us in his book "Boys of Summer" that the Robinson experiment was ensured success because Robinson first won over most of his teammates. It didn't matter if Robinson won over the media, or the fans, any of his opponents or anyone else in America if he first couldn't win the hearts and minds of the guys in his own clubhouse.

Phyllis's teammates, I won't speculate what her "The NFL Today" co-stars thought about her. I do know that the writers and production staff were all behind her.

As for the two of us, Phyllis and I weren't as close as Howard and I were. I don't want to give the impression that we were. We were teammates distantly and by default; we both worked in the same division at the same network. I definitely wasn't Dixie Walker, but I wasn't Pee Wee Reese, either.

We lost touch over the years, so I never had the chance to ask her what she really thought of me, but the fact that she knew the door to my office was always open to her, that makes me happy. It tells me all I need to know.

* * *

We had great production people and top-notch talent. We had valuable properties such as the NFL and The Masters. So why couldn't *CBS* Sports get over the hump? Why couldn't we knock *ABC* Sports off the top spot? There were a couple of reasons.

This statement might anger some of my former *CBS* colleagues, but I think *ABC* Sports had a better organizational work ethic. That came from the top. As I've said, Roone demanded we take viewers out of their living rooms to the game. You were also expected to take your work home from your office into your living room. If you went home at all.

There was one July evening, I had been with *CBS* maybe a year or two at this point, when our offices were empty except for the cleaning crew and a few younger publicity and production people. I gathered everybody in front of a window and motioned across the way to *ABC* and, one by one, pointed to the three offices that still had lights on: "Martin. Spence. Howard. That's why they are number one."

Of course, this dedication had its drawbacks. It's common knowledge in the business that *ABC* Sports didn't just rack up Emmys. During its heyday, it probably had more divorces than any other division in television history.

I remember telling Frank Smith when he was president that we shouldn't let the receptionist go at 5 o'clock since *ABC* Sports had someone that came in late and that, like most of my unsolicited suggestions, was dismissed. It wasn't until after Smith was canned that I was somewhat successful in convincing the higher-ups to keep our receptionist until at least 6 p.m.

To whomever would listen, or whomever I could corner in an elevator for a minute or two, I talked about the things that Roone did to become, then stay, number one. I probably pissed people off by doing these things, but I wasn't trying to embarrass anybody. I was trying to motivate our people and help us gain ground. I wanted *CBS* Sports to be number one.

Another thing. When I was at *ABC*, our properties were viewed as equal partners. We were sensitive to certain things, but we didn't let anybody dictate what stories we covered or how we did our jobs. It was a different story at *CBS*, where some of our senior production people and others in management displayed Stockholm Syndrome. They behaved like they were hostages.

In March 1982, this is right around the time I left *CBS*, Notre Dame head coach Digger Phelps made some public statements about widespread corruption in college basketball a few days before the Final Four in New Orleans. Kevin O'Malley, the executive producer for college sports on *CBS*, didn't want to touch the subject. Probably because he had been instrumental in getting the NCAA basketball package for the network. He didn't want to piss Walter Byers and the NCAA off.

But it was a story. We couldn't just ignore it. One of our producers, Ted Shaker, went over O'Malley's head to Neal Pilson, who a year earlier had begun the first of his two terms as president of *CBS* Sports. Pilson told Shaker that Brent Musberger could interview Phelps.

A year later, in early February 1983, the only undefeated men's college basketball team left in the country was Nevada-Las Vegas. That week in the coaches' poll, four coaches didn't vote for Vegas. Not only that, a team with three losses, North Carolina, was voted into the top spot. At the planning meeting held early in the week, a staffer suggested a sit-down with Jerry Tarkanian to get his thoughts on the snub. O'Malley quashed the idea. "No, we are going to give our weekly poll," he reportedly said. "It's a better way to promote college basketball." Nobody in the room could believe it.

"It wasn't our job to promote college basketball," one of the individuals present later told me. "Our job was to cover stories like this!"

Not once during the weekend of the 1985 Final Four did *CBS* mention the Tulane point-shaving scandal. And during the 1987 tournament, the NCAA asked *CBS* to tell its announcers not to identify which conference the officials came from in each game. Amazingly, they went along with the request. Well, for the first two rounds. That's when the criticism started coming in from the media.

It wasn't just college basketball. For a number of years, the Greek only picked NFC games which prompted somebody to say, "we shouldn't call this show 'The NFL Today,' we should call it The NFC Today." Because of mounting in-house criticism, the

Greek started to pick AFC games. It was never the Greek's decision to pick only NFC games. In fact, he resented it.

I also remember the time, I think it was during the 1983 NFL season, when *CBS* wouldn't do a piece on Cliff Stoudt (who took over for an injured Terry Bradshaw as the Steelers' starting quarterback) because he played for an AFC team. Chuck Milton, one of the show's producers, couldn't believe it. "It's promotional hype," he told me, "over journalism."

In the pregame show for Super Bowl XXI between the Giants and Broncos in January 1987, I was surprised – I won't say shocked – that *CBS* didn't once mention the Mara feud. That was another story they tip-toed around. I've already told you how *CBS* refused to interview Mike Reid for a commentator position after Paul Brown called the network. And how they wouldn't give Larry Csonka a tryout, either.

To me, the people calling the shots lacked guts. They wouldn't stand up to anybody or any organization. They wouldn't tackle any difficult stories. In my opinion, this hurt the credibility of the division.

For the record, *ABC* Sports wasn't perfect in this regard. I know of several instances when individuals in positions of power backed down from running something that would have created controversy or caused friction with some organization or league. Most of these, however, were very minor and don't warrant discussion.

Now one time, Howard Cosell's magazine show was going to do a feature on Bob Vorhies, the Virginia Tech football player who died of exhaustion after reportedly being forced to run punishment drills after a practice in 1977.

The crew did the interviews and were in the process of editing the piece when either Virginia Tech or the NCAA contacted the network and warned *ABC* not to run the piece. I wasn't working there at the time, but from what my sources told me, only after the lawyers hired by the Vorhies family threatened to subpoena the interview tapes did *ABC* have the guts to put on the show.

I know of only one instance where *ABC* Sports appeared to have genuflected in front of the altar of the NCAA. My friend Jim Lampley did some incredible investigative work on a story about improprieties in the Oklahoma football program. This was in the early 1980s, when I was working for *ABC*. Lamps even got two Oklahoma players to admit on camera that they got $3,000 each. The NCAA learned of this bombshell report and called Jim Spence directly. The piece never made it on the air.

Just why, I have no idea. Perhaps Spence knew something the rest of us didn't. Sometimes in these situations, players might have a beef with the coach and think they can get even by going public with damaging material. Since I don't have all the details, I can't say if Roone would have run the story or not. I only know that due to his epic battles with Walter Byers, he wasn't afraid of the NCAA.

Back to *CBS*, there was also the relationship with The Masters. I don't know if it's still like this, but at one time the relationship between *CBS* Sports and the Masters people was one of the most bizarre in the history of television sports. As Kevin O'Malley once said, "having the Masters is like having a crazy aunt in the attic."

The Masters people were more than crazy. One year, they wanted us to paint our production trucks green so everything on the club grounds would match.

Everybody knows the story about how Augusta National president Clifford Roberts banned Jack Whitaker from working the tournament after he called the crowd swarming around Jack Nicklaus on the 18th green after the Monday playoff a "mob" in 1966. Not only was it a chaotic scene, Whitaker was getting an earful from Frank Chirkinian, who was being pressured by the people back in New York since it was time for Cronkite. Roberts' behavior was absurd. It would be like Churchill banning Murrow from London for using the wrong choice of words while reporting from the middle of a Luftwaffe air raid.

At one time, out of all the major sporting events, the people who ran the Masters were the stingiest in terms of issuing press tickets. So as a publicist working the Masters, you spend most of your time working on finding extra press tickets. You really have to use your ingenuity with the requests. The key is to keep them believable. For example, no lighting director is needed at the Masters, but we used to tell them one is needed. The name *CBS* used? Ray Dark.

One year I worked the tournament a technician was picked up in town for soliciting a hooker. When Chirkinian sent someone to bail the guy out, the cop in charge said, "you know, some of our people would love to see the Masters." We scrounged up a few passes and they were "donated" to the precinct. The technician was released. No charges, no court date, no nothing. Now that's American justice!

Masters press tickets are probably the third-toughest ticket in sports. In my experience, the second-toughest is the semi-finals of the men's basketball Final Four. The toughest? By far a Masters parking pass.

Not long after I left the network, I had heard that *CBS* Sports was giving serious consideration to increasing the number of golf tournaments it would cover. This was an abrupt departure from a few years earlier, when Van Gordon Sauter was president of the division and the decision was made to decrease the number of tournaments televised.

A deal was almost set with the PGA negotiating committee when at the eleventh hour, Hord Hardin, the chairman of the Masters and the Augusta National Golf Club, called Neal Pilson. The way I understood it, *CBS* wasn't legally obligated to tell the Masters people that they wanted to televise other tournaments. And everyone knew that the Masters would remain the centerpiece of the network's golf lineup. I think Hardin just wanted to let everyone in New York know that the Masters people had eyes and ears everywhere.

Hardin reminded Pilson that *ABC* had long coveted the Masters. It was a veiled threat. The end result was that *CBS* Sports buckled. The deal was shot. The people at the PGA couldn't believe it. They had walked away from *NBC* in the first place to work with *CBS* and then had to return to *NBC* with hat in hand.

The business practices at *CBS* Sports were befuddling. We lost $1.5 million every year on the Cotton Bowl and kissed their asses. We made $300,000 annually on the Blue-Gray game and treated them horribly. We somehow lost $2 million on the first Ali-Spinks heavyweight title fight in February of '78. I heard that Neal Pilson's contract with Jack Nicklaus supposedly cost the company around $2 million over 20 years. Unreal.

In February 1983, *CBS* spent a ton of money to send a crew to Finland one weekend for a speed skating competition. When the crew went to West Germany to send the edited work over the satellite, the West Germans refused to send it. It seems a bill was overdue by a year. When somebody got on the horn to Jim McKenna, the VP of Finance, he reportedly said, "I sent a check Thursday. I can't understand it. The check was sent Thursday."

The bill was a year late and he sends it the Thursday before the weekend *CBS* wants to use the satellite! Are you kidding me? But that's how business was conducted at *CBS* Sports. The crew in Europe, to their credit, worked like hell in attempting to line up other satellites, but they had no luck. Brent Musberger covered up the fiasco as best he could saying, "sorry folks – due to satellite problems, we won't have the speed skating from Finland."

There are many examples that point toward the problems *CBS* Sports had. One that always boggled my mind was the difficulty with commercials. There was this one time a golf tournament was rained out, so a tape was shown. There was an over-run, which the affiliates couldn't believe, and two commercial positions, 90 seconds each, never made it on the air.

One weekend in 1983, a college basketball game was running late. Not just late, 22 minutes late. With 13 seconds left, West Virginia was up 13 points. The game's over. Yet O'Malley refused to put in the last commercial. Frank Chirkinian, who is down in Florida for a golf tournament, is yelling into producer Terry O'Neil's ear. "They are already 22 minutes into my show and now I have to do the fucking commercial!" he screamed. After O'Malley decided to roll full credits, Chirkinian gave up. I never found out if he got the spot on or not. I didn't envy the producers who had to scramble like that, or the folks in advertising who had to deal with irate sponsors after these screw-ups.

Truly, many of the wounds were self-inflicted. I learned that at *ABC*, when sports pre-empted a show, the loss of profit in the original show wasn't figured into the cost. At *CBS*, it was. This is called pre-emptive cost. It hurt *CBS* Sports when it attempted to match *ABC's* bids. I was not in the least bit surprised to learn that for nearly two decades, until sometime the mid-1970s, *CBS* Sports annually lost money.

Some of the losses, you couldn't assign a dollar amount to. Have you ever seen film of the first use of Instant Replay? No one has since December 7, 1963, when it aired on live television. Do you know why? Because the tape that Tony Verna used no longer exists.

Bootleg footage of only the race has been used in documentaries and by various networks over the years, but no one has seen the full *CBS* Sports broadcast of the 1973 Belmont Stakes, when Secretariat famously blistered the field by 31 lengths, since June 9,

1973, either. That tape is gone, too. You're probably wondering, how is this possible?

One of the first things I did after joining *CBS* Sports was pay a visit to the archives department to watch the Instant Replay tape. I didn't get to see it live because Pitt played Penn State in football that afternoon and then we played Duquesne in basketball later that evening. I was shocked when the curator told me that they didn't have it. I was even more shocked when he told me why.

Apparently, in 1974 some executive decided to destroy all of the old tapes and films of sporting events that had aired on the network. That's how we lost the only visual record of the first use of Instant Replay, the '73 Belmont broadcast, and God only knows how many tapes, film reels and radio recordings of old football, baseball and basketball games and other historic sporting events going back to probably the 1920s or 30s.

All this sports history, priceless material, like the Library of Alexandria, gone for good. And for what? $15 a can. Unbelievable.

Without a doubt, the single biggest thing holding *CBS* Sports back was the revolving door at the top level of management. I spent just over five years with the network and during that time, I think we had four, no five - maybe even six - different people serve as president. Between all the promotions, the different titles, "acting," "interim," and so-forth, it was hard to keep track. The leadership at *CBS* Sports made Italian governments look stable.

Too many executives, in my opinion, used the division as a stepping-stone. Their counterparts at *ABC* Sports had no desire to move, whether it was upstairs, across the street to *CBS*, over to 30 Rock and *NBC*, or anywhere else. At *CBS* Sports many of the upper management people were so busy maneuvering for the next job, they didn't do the one they had right. It was the most hypercompetitive atmosphere one could possibly imagine.

I remember when the company earmarked one entire floor at Black Rock to four executives in the division. There would be one office in each corner. Now because of plumbing issues, only two of the offices would have executive bathrooms. All four individuals fought like little kids over the bathrooms, so the idea was cancelled.

When Frank Smith became president of *CBS* Sports in '78, there was literally a line of people waiting in the hallway to be promoted to vice president. "Everybody here thinks they're entitled to move up," I remember saying to Rich Podolsky that day. "I'm just glad to have a fucking job."

And without fail, the wrong people were always the ones being promoted. "The trouble here at *CBS* Sports," somebody told me when I arrived, "is that 90% of the important decisions are made by people who don't know sports and wouldn't know how to get a show on the air or off it."

In my five years at *CBS*, I was never completely sure just who was in charge in any division or at any level. Consider April 24, 1980. The day of the failure of the Iran hostages rescue mission. It's 6:59:55 p.m. The other networks are leading right into President Carter's address to the country, but *CBS* ran a promo for "Dallas."

I heard "J.R. has an affair with Sue Ellen's sister," and I cringed. Mercifully, after maybe ten seconds, I heard that *CBS* beep and Carter's speech, already in progress. "We couldn't do anything about it," one of the technicians said. "It was the computer."

At that moment, I found out that person in charge wasn't actually a person at all – the computer was running the show. In fact, automation might have been a good idea considering some of the alternatives.

While a bunch of us were standing around watching Carter's speech on a monitor, somebody suggested to one of our VPs in sports that our NBA game might be pre-empted because of the news special. "I don't think so," he said confidently. "This will be old news by then." Jay Rosenstein and I looked at each other in disbelief.

I want to make it very clear that I'm not knocking everybody at *CBS* Sports. The rank and file, most of the producers, directors, PAs, technicians, engineers, and the secretaries, were dedicated, industrious workers. They just had no leadership.

The first weekend of the 1984 NCAA tournament, Kevin O'Malley reportedly messed things up so badly that seven commercials were missed. The next day, nobody could find him. I heard that the commercials were made up the following weekend, but that's not the point. He didn't take responsibility and worse, nobody above him made him take responsibility.

I once said some things about O'Malley to *Newsday's* Stan Isaacs, who had one of the country's first columns devoted solely to sports television. These remarks were classless and tasteless on my part, although they were indicative of the way I felt. I had high hopes for O'Malley. It took me a few years, but I learned that he was nothing but a polished fraud. As somebody at *CBS* once said, "he's great at meetings."

So was Neal Pilson, in my opinion. I didn't dislike him personally. I just didn't have much faith in his decision-making capability or leadership credentials when he ascended to the top spot at *CBS* Sports. "Three things I fear," I told a writer, "is Notre Dame getting points at home, the Moral Majority and Neal Pilson."

Many people were enamored with Bob Wussler. I wasn't one of them. He was the very definition of a suit. And in his case, they were all pinstripes.

I first met Wussler at the '60 Winter Olympics and he helped reinforce my early negative opinion of the kind of people who worked in television. It wasn't until later that I understood why Paley and the honchos at *CBS* had Cronkite anchor the coverage and why the news division basically ran things in Squaw Valley. It's because other than Tex Schramm, they didn't trust anybody in sports. Anyway, Wussler should have been a politician. It seemed like he was always scheming. I'll give you a few examples why I thought that way.

One of the few higher-ups I liked was Barry Frank. He was the individual responsible for bringing me to *CBS*. Frank didn't run the show for very long, but I guess the fact he got the job at all was something in and of itself. When Frank appeared set for the number one job, a mysterious telegram was sent to the FCC from someone known only as "McCarthy." This shadowy character questioned Frank's integrity. Nobody knows for sure, but many people believe it originated in-house. Somebody tried to sabotage Frank. That's how much of a madhouse the place was.

Unlike much of the senior management at *CBS*, Barry knew sports. Specifically, sports and sports-related programming as entertainment. Barry is probably better known now as an agent, but he was the guy responsible for getting shows like "Battle of the Network Stars" and "American Gladiators" on the air.

He also knew when he was being used. When Wussler hired Frank, he gave him his first assignment: fire Bill Brendle. Frank, to his everlasting credit, rebelled. See, it was Jack Schneider, the president of the network, who wanted Brendle out because Bob Wood loved Brendle, so Wussler tried to get Frank to do Schneider's dirty work.

On another occasion, Wussler wanted Frank to hire Don Ohlmeyer. Frank was unsuccessful and Ohlmeyer eventually went to *NBC* Sports to head up their Olympics coverage. A few years later, Barry learned from a high *NBC* Sports official that if *NBC* had failed to land Ohlmeyer, Wussler would have been given the job. Always scheming.

I have nothing bad to say about Gene Jankowski, the chairman of the *CBS* Broadcast Group, but typical of the ways things were at *CBS*, he occasionally meddled in areas in which he had no expertise. For example, God only knows why, but Jankowski got it into his head that *CBS* needed Frank Gifford to be a top-flight sports network. You're not going to believe this, but in 1984 *CBS* and *ABC* almost made a trade, Gifford for Summerall and Madden. Thankfully for *CBS* Sports, it fell through because Madden wanted too much money.

The only bigshot in corporate that I liked was Jim Rosenfield, the president of *CBS* Television. He was a stand-up guy who wasn't afraid to say what was on his mind.

One of the last events I attended while working for *CBS* was Super Bowl XVI, played between Cincinnati and San Francisco, in January of '82. The game remains the highest-rated Super Bowl, with a 73 share, in history. The highlight of the week for me, however, wasn't the game. It was the party thrown by the network the night before the game and something Rosenfield did there.

That reminds me, another difference between *CBS* and *ABC* was that *CBS* threw much better parties. It wasn't even close. They had these parties in New York that were star-studded affairs. All of the actors that were on *CBS* shows would show up.

The fall of my first year with the network, 1977, I went to the NFL season kickoff party. I had been there only a few minutes when I spied one of my favorite television characters of all-time: Detective Captain Steve McGarrett of "Hawaii Five-O." I have never been a drinker, but I had a few to try to loosen up. Even so, I couldn't work up the courage to go over and say hello to Jack Lord. It remains one of my biggest regrets.

The people at *CBS* outdid themselves with the Super Bowl party in Detroit. The party had everything – plenty of laughs, good food and high-quality booze and even some unscheduled entertainment.

At some point in the evening, there was a commotion at the door. Apparently, one of the city commissioners from San Francisco had shown up without an invitation and was upset that he wasn't being allowed into the party. What happened was, the mayor of San Francisco, Ms. Dianne Feinstein, went up to Rosenfield and expressed her displeasure. Anybody, she said, should be able to attend the party.

"You have lots of freeloaders here," she complained.

Rosenfield was boiling. He looked at Feinstein, composed himself, then said something that effectively ended the conversation.

"This party is for the people who are spending $22 million dollars on *CBS* tomorrow afternoon for the Super Bowl. You, mayor, are the freeloader."

I had never heard anybody put a politician in their place like that before. Feinstein started apologizing up and down. I was disappointed, but not at all surprised, to learn that the taxpayers of California later sent this woman to Washington as a U.S. Senator. The biggest freeloaders always find their way to the biggest trough.

Another thing I respected Rosenfield for was the way he treated Carl Lindemann near the end of the latter's life. Lindemann was a longtime *NBC* Sports employee and respected executive who joined *CBS* Sports as a VP in June of '78.

A couple of years after I left, this was sometime in '85, I heard that Neal Pilson reportedly called Lindemann, who was dying of cancer, and told him that he'd exceeded his sick days and would be taken off the payroll. Pilson was desperate to reduce the head count because of pressure from above. I never found out if Pilson knew that Rosenfield had called Lindemann a few days earlier and told Lindemann not to worry, that he would remain on the payroll. I'd hate to think that he did. It could have, and probably had just been an honest mistake on Pilson's part, but I felt awful for Carl, to be terminally ill and to have had his emotions being pulled in a tug-of-war like that. It was so unnecessary. These stories just show you how dysfunctional the day-to-day operations on the upper floors at Black Rock were.

And while the lines of communication were often down in-house, outsiders always got through. There was the time Barry Frank wanted to fire Sonny Hill, a commentator on the "NBA on CBS." Jesse Jackson went to Wussler, president of the network at the time, and pressured Wussler to countermand Frank's decision. Wussler caved and so Hill remained an extra year.

On another occasion, Pete Rozelle once undermined Frank Smith by calling Gene Jankowski directly concerning overruns of NFL games. I never thought highly of Smith, but I felt bad for him. His VPs were really angry, and they were right to be.

Adding to this chaotic work environment was the scandal involving the "winner-take-all" tennis tournament in 1977. We lost the Kentucky Derby and the Preakness to *ABC*. Our golf and NFL telecasts were rapidly losing ground in the ratings. We were airing stuff like "The Human Fly," "World's Strongest Man," and "taped trashsports," as Steve Wulf called them in *Sports Illustrated.* We finally hit rock bottom by the summer of 1980. We were behind not only *ABC* Sports, but we were in third place behind *NBC* Sports as well.

And then came the promotion that corporate finally got right. On July 11, 1980,

Van Gordon Sauter was named president of *CBS* Sports. It was like Lincoln, after trying countless incompetent commanders, promoting General Grant. That was the exact moment when the tide of the ratings war turned.

After what Van did during his three separate stints as president of both *CBS* Sports and News, the company should have built a statue of him. He turned around two floundering divisions and did so in record time.

He did it by being a leader. He wasn't afraid to ruffle feathers and didn't care who he pissed off. He called out our own people publicly, remarking that our anthology show, "*CBS* Sports Spectacular," was "neither sports nor spectacular." He shuffled broadcast teams, cleaned house of deadweight executives, and aggressively pursued new properties, like college football and basketball. And he kept everybody apprised of what he was doing by sending out these insightful, wonderfully well-written memos.

Van reminded me of Roone. Both were pipe-smokers and neither were sports experts. Roone was no slouch intellectually, but I don't think he was near Van's level. Van was extremely intelligent and well-read. And he was worldly; he had been a correspondent in Vietnam for the *Detroit News* and had been chief of the network's Paris bureau. He once said that had he not gotten mixed up in newspapers, radio, and television, he might have dedicated himself to becoming the world's foremost authority on the Crusades.

We had a very good relationship. It was a lot like my relationship with Roone. In fact, it probably started the same way. Word got to Van that I was coming into the office on weekends, but he probably didn't know that I was there to run up the company's phone bill!

Like Roone, Van listened to me. He paid honest attention, not just lip service, to what I said. He did a few things and promoted a few people based upon my suggestions. I know it pissed off certain people, like Neal Pilson, that Van would take my opinion over his. Van, unlike so many other high-ranking people I met in television, was title-blind. If what a publicist was saying made more sense than what a VP thought, so be it. What it basically came down to, I later learned, was that Van trusted me.

Some years ago, Van and I caught up on a phone call. I'll never forget what he said. "You are the most honest person who ever worked for me," he told me. That was one of the greatest compliments I received in my career.

Thanks to our relationship I was able to do three things that were noteworthy in terms of having a lasting influence on *CBS* programming.

The first thing was maybe even more important than my role in setting up the '69 Texas-Arkansas "Big Shootout" at *ABC*. Looking back on it, it was probably a much bigger deal than I realized at the time.

The second was no where near as monumental as the first in terms of the big picture and what it meant financially to the company, but it was very important to me, personally.

And the third, I thought it would be one of the proudest moments of my career in publicity and television. Instead, it led to my departure from *CBS*, my return to *ABC* and the start of my second career as an on-air commentator.

Let's start with the NFL maps. Some of the stuff we put on the air was ridiculous, but what was more ridiculous was the way we were bungling the most popular, profitable property *CBS* Sports had, the NFL. For years, I'd taken calls from friends, both bettors and regular football fans, about the haphazard way the network seemed to assign games to our affiliates across the country. It occurred to me that this might be affecting our ratings, so I looked into it.

In 1980, I went to one of the map-making meetings and observed the decision-making process first-hand. It was a joke. If these executives had pulled games out of a hat and randomly assigned them to certain stations or markets, they could have done a better job. They knew nothing about pro football or, more importantly, about the people who watched it.

I explained to them that people in Green Bay, for example, wanted two things, to watch the Packers win and to watch the Bears lose. And in Chicago, the feelings were the same, just reversed. Love may always conquer hate in the Bible, but hate holds it own in the NFL's black and blue division.

So instead of giving Green Bay and Chicago fans the chance to watch their hated rival lose, these clueless suits usually sent them some hyped match-up that on paper appeared to be a big game according to won-loss records or the league standings.

Yet sometimes, when a better game was available, they persisted in giving these fans the home market team, no matter how lousy or how far out of the playoff chase that team might be. It was like going to a restaurant and having someone else order your food and they fucked up every single time.

Another thing I told them was that team loyalties and fandom didn't necessarily follow the lines on maps. State borders, city limits, even time zones – throw all that stuff out the window. For example, it was a colossal mistake to keep assuming that people living in central and southcentral Pennsylvania, in the vicinity of places like Hanover, Hershey, and York, were either Steelers or Eagles rooters. In actuality, I said, there is a huge contingent of Baltimore Colts fans who inhabit this particular part of Pennsylvania.

Another example was the little-known fact that a sizable chunk of the Southwest, in Arizona and New Mexico, is considered Pittsburgh Steelers country. Why? Because of Dallas. For years, viewers in the Southwest had been sent Dallas games because of geography and the lack of an NFL franchise in this area. This was long before the Cardinals relocated from St. Louis to the desert.

Nobody in New York knew that a lot of these people resented having the Cowboys shoved down their throats. And what was the one team that always beat Dallas in the late 70s? Pittsburgh. Again, love-hate. In this case, hatred of "America's Team" created an unknown, untapped market for Pittsburgh games in a strange part of the country.

The basic problem was that for years, the people making these important decisions had only a superficial understanding of sports. What appeared to these execs to be cut-and-dried decisions made using traditional maps and common sense were actually anything but. They consistently made the wrong calls and as a result, the network was losing out on viewers, advertising bucks, and ultimately, profits.

I didn't think I had shared any brilliant revelations. It was merely the same kind of knowledge, a real football fan's perspective on rivalries and rooting interests, that I brought to the table in our dealings with the NCAA television committee when I was working at *ABC*. But back then, Roone or some other exec had the guts to say, "wait a minute. Beano's onto something here." At *CBS*, the suits told me to get lost. One time, I was actually told to "get the hell out" of one VP's office.

Undaunted, I resumed the fight the following year. And since we had just hired Terry O'Neil to be executive producer, I now had a powerful ally. O'Neil was a Pittsburgh guy I had worked with at *ABC*. I told his mother when he came to work for *ABC* that I would look out for him. I didn't have to. The kid had his head on straight. He got a Masters in English from Columbia and he became a top-flight producer under Roone's tutelage. He started out as a researcher for the '72 Olympics and by 1980 was producing "Monday Night Football."

One day, I wandered into his office to enlist him in the cause. O'Neil later glamourized the exchange and our subsequent efforts in his book, "The Game Behind the Game." I don't remember if it actually happened this way, but in his telling of our subsequent efforts to get the bottom of things with the NFL maps, he made the two of us look very hard-working and heroic, like Robert Redford and Dustin Hoffman in the movie "All the President's Men," so I'm okay with it.

"O'Neil," I addressed him, "do you have any idea how many millions of dollars these guys have wasted over the years?"

"What?"

"The NFL ratings, O'Neil. Do you have any idea how much advertising money they've let get away? Forget that. Do you think the stockholders know? Do you think they know about the fucking idiots who've been doing their NFL maps?"

Neither the stockholders nor anybody else at the company had any idea what I was getting after. But O'Neil picked up on it immediately. And so did Van. At his orders, O'Neil took control of the process from the suits.

Here's the dramatic part of the movie: the two of us pored over maps; we crunched Nielsen numbers; we asked our affiliates to survey their viewers; we talked to sportswriters, station managers, broadcasters, bartenders, bookies, team publicists, you name it.

Through our polling, which was on-going throughout the season, we learned what fans in what areas rooted for which teams, disliked which teams, and, most important of all, which fans and viewers in which areas felt underserved by the current arrangement.

Once we digested all this research, we divided the country into two dozen regions and laid out something that resembled a battlefield map. There were some clearly demarcated front lines separating the AFC and NFC areas but plenty of pockets of unoccupied territory, football no-man's land, interspersed in between.

When the season kicked off, we consulted our new map and plugged the games into our formula on a week-to-week basis. Often, the decision was an easy one. Occasionally, some educated guess work was involved. And in those neutral areas where we really didn't have a clue what game to go with, we had a default setting.

"The two most important people to *CBS* are J.R. Ewing and Tom Landry," I was quoted as saying in *Sports Illustrated*. "We have a rule we go by when planning NFL telecasts. ...When in doubt, give them the Cowboys."

It was impossible to get every single game correct since we had to make the choice to pair the right game with nearly 200 *CBS* affiliates each week, but we were right a lot more often than we were wrong. The proof was in the numbers.

According to O'Neil, during the 1981 regular season, our NFL telecasts pulled an unbelievable average weekly rating of 17.5 and the network raked in $48.7 million in profits. That was an increase of more than $20 million over the $28.4 million *CBS* made during the 1980 season.

Those numbers vindicated me. They were proof that I had been right. I later learned that not only had I gotten the last laugh on some of the people who occupied the executive suites on the floors above me, our efforts had gotten the attention of people in Congress. O'Neil cc'd me on his correspondence with Louisiana Senator J. Bennett Johnston, who wrote *CBS* in late November at the request of some constituents in Shreveport who were displeased with our decision to bump some Saints games for the Cowboys.

"You should know, Senator, that our Shreveport affiliate, *KSLA-TV*, has surveyed its viewers and found a preference for the Dallas Cowboys over the Saints when the two teams are playing in the same time period," O'Neil wrote in reply.

"When Dallas games are not available to Shreveport viewers, we often weigh regional interest in the Saints versus games of importance to the NFL post-season playoff picture. This weekend, for instance, we find that many viewers are more interested in San Francisco (10-3) at Cincinnati (10-3) than they are in a game involving the regional club which has been eliminated from playoff contention."

O'Neil, shrewdly sticking the needle into a politician like that, that was the cherry on top of the sundae! That's why he's one of the best writers I've ever known.

To be sure, Terry deserves a lot of the credit for the network's banner NFL year. He made some significant changes, from both technical and production standpoints, that undoubtedly brought more eyeballs to our telecasts. The new pairing of Summerall and John Madden as our No. 1 broadcast team had a lot to do with our success, too.

We had a lot going for us in '81. The Giants made the playoffs for the first time in 18 years, and the Jets also made their first post-season appearance since 1969. Both teams gifted us great numbers in the New York market. The eventual Super Bowl champion 49ers, with Joe Montana, were an exciting, up-and-coming team and our decision to expose a lot of the country to Bill Walsh's exciting new brand of football boosted our numbers as well.

I'm thrilled to have been not only a part of a highly successful season for the network, but one of the prime movers behind it. It's no exaggeration to say that we changed the way in which *CBS* televised pro football and, in the process, we truly changed sports television history. Every network televising NFL games today is working off the original blueprint for coverage maps that Terry O'Neil and I drew up.

The second noteworthy accomplishment I had a hand in occurred in 1983, after I had left *CBS*, but the story actually starts in 1950. Let me explain.

I've always had a dislike for redundant phrases. This feeling goes back to when I was a freshman at Brown and was called out in front of the class by my English professor. He was one of those old, stuffy, Ivy League language purists.

"Mr. Cook," he said, reading from my composition, "complete sellout. What do you think a sellout is? Incomplete?"

I was embarrassed. I still catch myself using redundant phrases, but it doesn't happen near as much because I'll never forget that lecture.

I feel that redundant phrases such as "devious lawyer" and "crooked politician" have earned their places in our lexicon. But the overwhelming majority of redundant phrases are cop-outs, crutches we resort to. I don't like it, but I get it – people use them for effect.

We hear way too many redundant phrases in sports. When an announcer says, "largest crowd ever" or a color commentator mentions "basic fundamentals," it's like fingernails on a chalkboard to my ears.

The two people who shared my feelings on redundant phrases were Curt Gowdy and Jack Whitaker. While Whitaker was a fanatic behind-the-scenes in purging these phrases from his copy, Gowdy was the only one I knew who embarked on a public crusade to change the way we spoke.

A number of years ago, Gowdy decided to describe a football game in overtime as "sudden victory" instead of "sudden death." "I believe it's better to be positive than negative," Gowdy told the media. He offended some people, but when you look at the terms, both are correct. I told Gowdy it didn't get rid of the overused phrase itself, but it was a start.

Where am I going with this? For some reason, the redundant phrase that always bothered me the most is "new record." In sports, for example, it can be a "Major League record," an "NCAA record" or "NFL record," but it's never a new record. A record by itself, after all, is new.

Back to 1983. The stock market started booming that spring. I still had Van's ear, so I pestered him to order *CBS's* anchors and reporters to quit using "new record" when the Dow Jones hit another milestone.

One afternoon in April, Van called me and told me to make sure I tuned into the

"*CBS* Evening News." That night, I heard a reporter use "record high" in a story on the stock market. I jumped up from the couch and did a little jig in the living room, I was so excited!

I immediately thought of my English professor at Brown. He was probably long gone, but I imagine that he would have been pleased to know that one of his students had helped engineer a minor victory for the English language.

I still wasn't anywhere close to being a decent writer, and I worked in what he'd have probably considered the dreadful, low-class medium of television, but at least I wasn't a complete sellout.

* * *

Around the time the calendar was flipping from 1981 to 1982, I had arrived at not just another crossroads in my career, but perhaps the most pivotal point of my entire life. I had a decision to make. In all likelihood, it meant I'd have to leave *CBS*.

It wasn't an easy one. I felt that I had done some of my best work for the network, especially in getting publicity for some of our new hires. I had more fun at *CBS* Sports than at any other place I worked in my career. Apart from a small handful of suits, I loved the people I worked with.

We had survived the Summer of '77, the chaos and the blackouts, as well as all of the turmoil that had occurred at the company. Among the many things Van did, he also boosted morale. The management merry-go-round showed no signs of stopping, but *CBS* Sports appeared to finally be trending in the right direction.

The country was coming out of a recession, and I had just begun to recover financially myself. When I worked as a copy boy at the *Pittsburgh Press* in the early 1950s, I never understood why newspapers ran obituaries or an entire page full of little numbers related to the stock market. Years later, when I put money into the market, I finally understood the importance of those little numbers. Over the previous five years I had managed to withdraw from the market and at the same time, break even.

And now that some of my friends were dying, I understood why papers published obituaries. I also learned that there was no such thing as breaking even in that department. Whenever I read about someone younger than myself who died, it made me squirm over my expense account breakfast.

I shared these thoughts, as well as my intention to leave *CBS*, with my best friend, O'Connor. I had no idea that O'Connor himself would be dead in three years at the tragically young age of 49.

"I don't know if it's a good idea. You're always talking about your mother's Three P's," O'Connor said. "Maybe you need to start thinking about another set of P's."

"And those are?" I asked.

"Pussy, plastic and pension. Without any money, you're not getting any of the first and you'll be living off the second. And at your age, you need to be thinking more about the third than anything else."

He brought up a subject that I had been avoiding for months. A major milestone was approaching. Barring any unforeseen circumstances, I would turn 50 on September 1. We had a saying at *CBS* Sports that when you reach 50, you are playing the back nine.

I didn't feel old, but I knew I was getting older. The first warning sign was that while I still enjoyed watching "Charlie's Angels," I found myself following the plots!

Truthfully, the previous year had aged me a lot. In 1980, I learned that I had diabetes. I went through nine months of hell with a department boss who thankfully got the boot in August. My trunks, with my past inside of them, got ransacked at a storage facility during the riots in Miami. Both literally and figuratively, I felt as though I had nothing to show for my life.

For the first time, I started seriously thinking about both mortality and my legacy. Who was I? What did I intend to do with the rest of my life? What will I be remembered for?

There were three very important events that occurred in 1981 that brought everything into perspective and helped me make my decision.

The first was the death of Bill Brendle. As I stood outside of the church on that cold brisk Friday in January, it occurred to me that Brendle died at 58. That seemed so young. He had just made the turn to the back nine.

That night at Runyon's, I reflected some more on that saying. In some ways, I envied Brendle. He went out on top, at the pinnacle of the publicity profession. And he'd never have to worry about office politics or about getting fired.

"I would feel sorry for Brendle except for one thing," somebody at our table said. "He's not missing a fucking thing."

And pretty soon, I discovered, nobody missed him. Brendle was beloved in the business, so I was shocked how quickly people forgot about him. It was then that I realized that the only people in television who are remembered are talent, or else the biggest of the big-shot executives. If I didn't do something, and soon, I ran the risk of being known as little more than a good PR guy who had some funny one-liners.

A few weeks later, I found myself in the lobby of a hotel located near the Richfield Coliseum, which was halfway between the cities of Cleveland and Akron, Ohio. It was the morning of February 1, 1981. I was in town for the NBA All-Star game.

A writer asked my thoughts on the news that Commissioner Bowie Kuhn was giving the returning Iran hostages lifetime Major League Baseball passes. To this day, I don't know where the line came from. I hadn't heard a word about Kuhn's decision until I was asked the question. I hadn't had any time to think on it or rehearse an answer. I guess my dislike of baseball was so strong, my reply was a reflex act.

"Haven't they suffered enough?" I laughed.

It was like that episode of "Seinfeld" when Jerry gave Kenny, the struggling comedian, some material: "That's gold, Jerry! Gold!" As soon as the words left my lips, I knew the line was gold. I knew it would be a hit. Everybody around me cracked up.

Nobody knows this, but there was a second part to that line. I was waiting for the laughter to die down, then I was going to add "and if the NBA gives them lifetime passes, they're going to want to go back to Iran." Thankfully, my brain disengaged my mouth before I blurted that part out in front of a bunch of NBA people. I don't know how the words didn't escape. Subconsciously, my fear of not working must have overruled my ability to tell a joke.

The line appeared in stories and columns in papers across the country. My one-liners had always been popular with writers and sports and television people, but when cab drivers, people at airports and strangers on the street started repeating the line back to me, it occurred to me that segments of the public knew who I was. My stand-up, more accurately sit-down act, was no longer confined to bars, restaurants, my office, or pressboxes and press lounges.

The notoriety reinforced a belief that I'd had for some time. I always felt that if given the opportunity, I'd make a decent college football commentator on television. I didn't necessarily want to call games, but I thought I'd be a good fit for studio work.

By the early 1980s I had gone from thinking, *you could be on television* to *you should be on television.* I knew I wasn't experienced, but I came up with material that was both different and definitely as good as, if not better, than anybody else's.

When I told my mother that I wanted to be on television, she shrugged her shoulders.

"If Phyllis George can be on TV, Carroll," she said, "I don't see why you can't be."

It wasn't exactly a ringing endorsement.

Other than my mother and O'Connor, there were only a handful of people I discussed my feelings, as well as any future plans with. One of them was Frank Chirkinian. He wasn't a friend, much less a trusted confidant, but that was why I felt comfortable asking him his opinion. I knew he'd be his typically gruff, bluntly honest self and would tell me what he really thought, not what he thought I wanted to hear.

During the advance work for a golf tournament, I told him that I wanted to be on the air, to talk college football. I also told him I had no idea how to go about asking for a tryout or if I even should.

While I'd never had any issues pushing another person for a promotion or gig, or to make my opinions known when I felt someone was fucking something up, my own insecurities typically prevented me from talking about myself. On top of it all, *CBS* didn't even have college football at the time.

Chirkinian didn't say that he thought it was a great idea, but he didn't say it was a dumb one, either. Basically, his advice was, if I was serious I needed to quit thinking about it and try to do it.

"Look, there are times to play it safe," he told me, "and there are times you just have to say, 'fuck it' and pull out the driver, okay?"

I probably hadn't played a round of golf since I was in prep school, but I knew the analogy and understood was he was getting at. You can't worry about failure, or that someone will think your ideas or dreams are out-of-bounds.

My opening came in the summer of 1981. Van, after landing the NCAA men's basketball tournament, had set his sights on the college football package. This was an incredibly lofty ambition. Not only had no network ever had both major college sports, football had been the sole property of *ABC* since 1966. Getting college football wasn't going to be as easy as the hoops deal was. In that particular case, *CBS* didn't really win the rights. *NBC* lost them.

But if there had been a way to bet on *CBS*, I'd have done it. I felt like my entire career in publicity and college athletics had prepared me for just such a moment. I had worked on rights deals when I was with *ABC* and I knew everybody at all levels of leadership in the sport, including all the ADs and administrators on the NCAA TV committee. In my mind it was a done deal. It was going to be one of the most important things I had ever done, professionally.

"When we get the NCAA package," I told my roommate, Rich Podolsky, "I'll have found my Holy Grail."

I had another reason to be supremely confident. In 1977, I came up with a split-network plan that I discussed informally with members of the TV committee. I wasn't acting in any official capacity on behalf of *CBS*. My thoughts were just those of one diehard college football fan.

I told them that it would be in the best interest of college football to divide television coverage of the games between at least two of the three networks. In my opinion, the growth of the sport was hindered by confining college football to one network.

Pete Rozelle had increased the popularity of pro football throughout the 1960s, I explained, by negotiating three different packages with the three networks. All three, as a result, weren't just televising NFL games, they were constantly promoting them as well.

Since only one network had controlled college football for so long, that meant that the other two networks weren't talking about the sport at all, other than for one week around Christmas in order to promote the handful of bowl games that existed at the time.

My pitch was designed to appeal to three different types of people: a network president, a college athletic director and a college football fan. What network wouldn't want more viewers and more advertising revenue? What AD wouldn't want more money for his school's coffers? And what fan wouldn't want to be able to watch more games on television? No matter who you were or how you looked at it, it made too much sense.

Word reached Roone about my plan and it made perfect sense to him, so he moved quickly before anybody at *CBS* or *NBC* had the chance to look into the feasibility of what I was proposing. *ABC* Sports paid $120 million to lock up the exclusive rights for all regular-season games from 1978 to 1981.

By the time that rights deal was reaching its end, there had been some significant changes across both the college football and television landscapes. These factors combined to present the perfect opportunity for *CBS* to get college football.

The folks in charge at the NCAA and of its member schools were no longer as concerned about attendance as they had been in the 1950s and 60s. They understood that television, or television's money, was going to be the main revenue source for athletic departments moving forward.

Formed in 1977, the College Football Association had amassed quite a bit of clout on behalf of the sport's biggest and most powerful schools and had been threatening Walter Byers that it would begin negotiating its own deals with the networks.

The arrival of cable television changed the calculus as well. As we would see, Ted Turner's *WTBS* would end up a surprise winner in the 1981 negotiations. That provided a path for other cable channels, including an upstart outfit in Connecticut called *ESPN,* to secure a foothold in the market with college football a few years later.

When we got to Denver, I learned that I had sold the folks at the NCAA on my idea years earlier. They opened negotiations on the premise that the deal would be a split-network one. It was just a matter of which networks would be part of it. We basically picked up in in 1981 where my informal conversations with the TV committee had left off in 1977.

The talks were at times incredibly heated, but that was due to Byers, who hadn't mellowed a bit over the past two decades. Most of the fireworks were between Byers and Jim Spence, who had replaced Roone as *ABC's* head negotiator.

Our problems in the *CBS* camp were easy by comparison. We just had to play our cards close to the vest to keep our own senior people in New York from getting wind of what was going on. We knew they wouldn't let us enter a bidding war, and they might even have forced us to withdraw just when we were on the verge of sealing a deal.

For example, one of our principal provisions was that each carrying network would be free to divide its fourteen exposures between national and regional exposures, as delineated in the ground rules. We had heard a rumor that *NBC* was willing to do something that at the time was completely unheard of.

"Don't let the word out that *NBC* is willing to do 13 games in prime time," Van told us in one of our private pow-wows. "If the guys on the 35th floor hear this we'll all be back on the first flight to New York."

As you already know, we prevailed. *ABC* and *CBS* each agreed to pay roughly $132 million for the rights to all the regular-season college football games from 1982-85. *WTBS* would pay $17.6 million over a two-year period from 1982-84 for the right to choose from the scheduling scraps the two bigger networks left on the table. Our people signed off on the deal because the NCAA upped the amount of time allotted for commercials from 21 to 26 minutes per telecast, which enabled us to sell additional advertising.

The record – not a new record, mind you – deal was announced to the media on July 30, 1981. Everybody came out a winner.

College football fans would be seeing a lot more games on television, 70 total national and regional games per season.

The individual schools were big winners. The features of the deal included an increase in exposures and substantially bigger paydays. Under the previous deal with *ABC*, a school received $210,000 for a regional game and $300,000 for a national television appearance. The fee structure under the new deal started at $700,000 for a regional appearance and would increase to $800,000 as the contract progressed.

An appearance on national television would mean an escalating payday of between $1 to 1.2 million dollars per game. These numbers may sound like chump change today, but consider that at this time there were just 15 bowls and only the Rose, Cotton and Orange had payouts that surpassed $1.2 million.

The irascible Walter Byers and the NCAA won again, too. The organization had wanted to keep the CFA and the blue bloods at bay and it did that, albeit temporarily.

WTBS struck a blow for cable. *ABC* didn't retain its stranglehold on the sport, but it didn't lose college football, either. And *CBS* Sports now had the unique opportunity to become the country's network home for the two most popular college sports.

The only loser in the whole deal, at least the way it looked on the surface, was the individual who probably did the most to make it happen for *CBS*: me.

After we got the NCAA package, I inquired about the possibility of helping anchor our coverage of college football as a studio commentator and was told, flatly, to forget about it. That was it. There was no discussion, no chance to make a pitch. I wasn't told why. I couldn't believe it. I didn't ask for a five-year contract. All I wanted was an audition. An opportunity.

I'm convinced Neal Pilson and Kevin O'Malley, and perhaps some others, didn't want to give me that opportunity. To me, it felt more like a personal, rather than a personnel decision. Whatever the case, they really blew it.

No one at the company was better at getting his name in the papers, and the network publicity, than me. *CBS* was going into this contract having to learn how to cover college football on the fly, but I knew the entire *ABC* playbook front and back.

I knew every AD and SID in the country, my way around every campus from West Point to Washington State, and where to put the cameras in every stadium from West Virginia's Mountaineer Field to Cal's Memorial Stadium.

I was hands-down the most knowledgeable individual on the subject of college football employed by *CBS*. Perhaps at any network. I knew people at the NCAA. I knew nearly all the coaches, not to mention the team trainers and support staff at every school. Every beat writer in the country found his way onto my expense account. My network of confidential informants put Kojak's to shame.

Perhaps most importantly, I knew stories. I knew feel-good ones and how to dig up dirt. As my good friend Donn Bernstein later said, "Beano knows where all the skeletons are hidden in college football."

I had even been the network's voter in the AP Poll for a few years, until my vote was taken away from me due to a "conflict of interest." When I asked for an explanation from one of our vice presidents, I was never given an honest, satisfactory answer. This same VP (whose name I won't share), however, promoted a woman who slept with him.

I don't hold Van responsible for the decision or the way I was treated. By late 1981, he already had one foot out the door in sports and was concentrating on his new impossible mission, the resurrection of *CBS* News.

Nevertheless, I felt betrayed and unappreciated. It was my original idea and format for the split-network plan that the TV committee liked. I selflessly employed my contacts and relationships on behalf of the company. I felt I was one of the main reasons we got the fucking package.

At that moment, it was beginning to look like all my work at *CBS* was for naught. Nobody seemed to care, and nobody would ever know the vital role I had played in bringing college football to *CBS*, my work on the NFL maps, or any of the other things I had done to help change the culture at *CBS* Sports. It looked as though my legacy at the network would be limited to one tiny footnote, that of convincing the higher-ups to keep the receptionist until 6 p.m., instead of letting her go home at 5 p.m. So much for my Holy Grail.

As I headed out on to the back nine of my life, I looked up at the proverbial leaderboard and made a fateful decision. I knew I had to make a move. I sat down at my desk and began typing out a letter to the one person in television who I knew would take me and my desire to be an on-air college football commentator seriously: Roone Arledge.

It was time to say fuck it, and pull out the driver.

CHAPTER 9

Under snacks for crew.

The date: sometime in the late 1970s. The location: the 26th floor of *CBS* headquarters in New York City. The protagonist: Jerry Robbins, one of the green eyeshades at *CBS*.

I remember the scene like it was yesterday. Robbins was standing in the hallway outside his office, waving a fistful of paper slips above his head. He reminded me of a runner on the floor of the New York Stock Exchange. And oh, was he ever pissed off.

"Everybody in this division," he yelled, "must hate each other!"

The papers in Jerry's hand were expense account forms, or vouchers. Seven of them, to be precise. A few days earlier, a *CBS* Sports crew had covered an NBA game in Chicago. After the game, these seven individuals took seven separate cab rides from Chicago Stadium to the airport. At least that's how the expense accounts, the way they were written and submitted for reimbursement, told the story.

Here's what really happened: these seven guys piled into two or three cabs and two or three of them footed the bill for the rides, but each one of them put in for cab fare on their individual expense account.

Robbins approved everything, but he wasn't condoning the practice. His outburst that day wasn't an act. He knew exactly what was going on and he wanted everybody to know that he wasn't a dope. Basically, he was warning these guys not to do it again. That was wishful thinking.

Padding an expense account is an American tradition dating as far back as, well, probably the first American expense account itself. After being appointed commander-in-chief of the Continental Army in 1775, General George Washington magnanimously declined Congress's offer of a $6,000 annual salary. Instead, he offered to serve for free and keep a record of the nominal expenses he expected to incur and submit it to Congress for reimbursement at the conclusion of the Revolution – if the United States won the war and still existed, that is.

After resigning his commission right before Christmas in December 1783, Washington filed a whopper of an expense account, one for an astounding $449,261.51 in

1780 dollars. Considering more than 200 years of inflation, that figure is now closer to $5 million. How could Washington have racked up such a tab?

According to the original document, our future first president regularly feasted on veal, oysters, and Madeira wine. He hired a band to celebrate his birthday. Other expenses included saddles made from Russian leather, an imported crate of limes and hundreds of other items for which Washington conveniently "misplaced" the receipts. Nevertheless, Congress approved everything, establishing a precedent that exists to this day. This explains why the Pentagon pays a thousand bucks for a toilet.

Following in the footsteps of Washington, the "Founding Fathers" of the expense account, in the history of sports media that is, were no less an ingenious and talented group of individuals than those powder-wigged patriots who penned the Constitution and the Declaration of Independence.

In our business, padding an expense account is called "creative writing," and all these characters that I'm going to tell you about were true masters of the craft. Their work doesn't quite measure up to the scripts from "All in the Family," but in some cases it comes close.

The late Joe Aceti, the great director who was probably best-known for coordinating "Wide World of Sports" and directing the famed Ali-Frazier "Thrilla in Manila" heavyweight fight, was one of the best when it came to both innovative production concepts and padding expense accounts.

While working at *ABC* Sports early in his career, Aceti's uncanny skill at creative writing became the stuff of legend. He used to work the College All-Star Football Classics in Chicago every summer.

To give younger readers some background, they started playing these exhibition games between the reigning NFL champions and a squad of college all-stars in the 1930s. As you can imagine, once pro football got big, the games stopped being competitive. The last time the college kids won was in 1963.

Aceti worked the very last all-star game in '76, the game that was called in the third quarter with the Steelers leading 24-0 because of a huge rainstorm. It was a monsoon.

Every year Aceti submitted an expense account filled with eyebrow-raising expenses. In '76, I heard he put down $38 for bug spray! Like the all-stars, Aceti gave it the old college try but apparently, he didn't get away with that one.

Joe's best work of fiction was one that he did get away with. In this particular case, Aceti was overseas with an *ABC* crew working the British Open one year. Back then, "The Open" was filmed, not aired live, and wrapped up on Saturday, not Sunday. On Monday, a production assistant brought the film back to the States to be edited and aired on "Wide World" the following week.

Well, upon his own return to New York, Aceti submitted an expense account listing a sizable sum for tree trimming. This took balls, because, as everybody knows, British Opens are typically played on links courses that don't have any trees.

But Aceti told me that the accountants were good with numbers, not sports. He realized that few of them watched the events we televised. Sure enough, they rubber-stamped the expense account and Aceti thought he was in the clear.

Yet a few days after "Wide World" aired, Aceti was ordered to report to *ABC's* accounting department to discuss his expense account.

"Joe," said the one accountant, "We were reviewing your expense account and noticed you had $740 for cutting down trees."

"I watched our show and I didn't see any trees," added another accountant.

"Obviously, (the trimmers) did a great job!" Aceti announced. "They were worth every penny."

To the legendary publicist Bill Brendle, creative writing was an art form, like painting. His *CBS* Sports expense account was his canvas. And like any artist, he wanted others to enjoy his work. He simply employed his expense account to ensure everyone had a good time. Sometimes, the good times got ahead of him, but Brendle was very adaptable.

One night at Runyon's, he gave his credit card to the waiter. As the waiter headed toward the machine to stamp the check, Brendle yelled out in a tone reminiscent of the actor Andy Devine. He had this great, gargling, laughing voice that you couldn't forget. The whole bar heard him.

"Date the receipt tomorrow," he instructed the waiter. "I spent today's (as in per diem) last night!"

Truthfully, if anyone deserved a free meal, it was Brendle. Brendle wasn't just a hero of mine, he was a genuine, decorated American war hero. During World War II, Brendle saw combat in Europe. And one day in October 1957, he was sitting in a chair in New York's Park Sheraton Hotel barbershop next to gangster Albert Anastasia when the notorious "Lord High Executioner" of Murder, Inc. was gunned down in a mob hit. Talk about close shaves.

An *ABC* Sports employee whose name I won't share was sent to Munich to prepare for the network's coverage of the 1972 Olympics. At the time, this individual was having some problems with his girlfriend who was back in New York. He was constantly on the phone trying to smooth out the relationship. When he checked out of the room, he was astonished to find a $3,500 phone bill tacked onto his room charge. Ouch.

From what I understand, it took him a few months of creative writing spread out across several dozen separate expense account submissions to cover that one with company cash. I don't know exactly what he wrote, but F. Scott Fitzgerald or Thomas Wolfe couldn't have surpassed the effort.

There are instances when too much creative writing in an expense account backfires. A producer was once called into Tex Schramm's office at *CBS* Sports in the late 1950s to explain a recent expense account.

"I see you spent a lot of money for entertainment last Saturday night," Schramm said. "You were at a restaurant until four in the morning with Paul Brown. You expect me to believe that? If you would have had Bobby Layne's or Paul Hornung's name on there, I would have believed it. But not fucking Paul Brown."

That one was not approved. But sometimes, name-dropping does work. It took him two tries, but the late John Mosedale figured out how to swing it.

Mosedale was a fantastic television writer and, as this story illustrates, an extremely talented creative writer as well. Mosedale joined *CBS* in the early 1960s. He was the first full-time writer hired by *CBS* Sports, but he spent his long career shuttling between both *CBS* Sports and *CBS* News. He wrote for Harry Reasoner, Walter Cronkite, Charles Kuralt, Brent Musberger, and Jimmy The Greek, too.

The greatest thing Mosedale ever wrote, in my opinion, never made it on the air. He once submitted a list of legitimate expenses for things like lunches and dinners. It was rejected. That pissed him off.

He went back to the drawing board, only this time he included the names of dead actors and actresses. A huge Shakespeare enthusiast, he used the names of The Bard's characters, too. The resubmitted version was hilarious. According to his accounting, he went out to dinner with Tyrone Power, Carole Landis, and a mysterious Mr. Falstaff. Incredibly, this time it was approved. The accountants didn't recognize any of the names.

Sportswriter George Kiseda once described expense accounts as "welfare for the middle class." I think Kiseda was right. Back in the old days before writing, TV and talk radio gigs paid big salaries, people compensated by taking advantage of the special opportunities expense accounts offered because they had to. They needed to make ends meet.

I remember spending a day in New York with Dan Jenkins sometime in the late 1960s. He couldn't believe the difference in the cost of living between New York and his hometown of Fort Worth, not to mention the amount of time it took to get anywhere. "If you work in New York and don't live in Manhattan, you might as well live in Omaha," he said.

Later that evening before dinner, he lowered his menu and shook his head in disbelief at the prices. "You can make a million bucks a year," he laughed, "but if you don't have an expense account, you can't make it here."

Back then, many media members not only depended on expense accounts, they had to take money or services, such as meal money and team-covered transportation, from the organization they covered, too. That's a practice that's long gone in sports media.

Kiseda once remarked, regretfully, during his time on the Philadelphia Phillies' beat he that "felt like a whore when they came around with the meal money." It put him in an uncomfortable position. In other words, he felt as though it obligated him to lay down and provide positive coverage of the team, ownership, and front office.

Younger people in the business, especially anybody born after Watergate, probably have no clue what I'm talking about, because that's when it all changed. With Watergate, everything became adversarial. Writers and media personalities no longer do dinner and or drinks with politicians, athletes, owners, or anybody they cover. Potentially damaging stories aren't killed because of personal friendships or professional courtesy.

Once upon a time, these things were commonplace. In the sports world, teams expected good news to be trumpeted and bad news buried by the media men who were, in a way, on their payroll. The consequences for not playing by these rules were harsh. I told you about the problems Bill Roeder had. Roeder wasn't just removed from the Yankees' beat for a critical story, he was booted out of the sports department at the now-defunct *New York World-Telegram*. The teams had much more clout back then.

Let's get something else straight while we're at it. Most of the writers and TV guys from that era, very seldom did they steal the money outright from teams, their papers, or networks. None of the guys I'm talking about, like Brendle and Aceti, were thieves. They were honest, hard-working guys. They didn't pocket the cash.

Take Aceti. While he definitely didn't spend $700 bucks on tree trimmers at the British Open, he probably just took care of his crew. Back then, this was before networks paid for caterers, whoever was in charge would order pizzas, buy snacks, or cases of beer for the guys. Or else he tipped the local help, paid off some cops or had to grease some palms somewhere just to do his job. That money came out of his pocket and those things add up. These guys spent the money and simply had to find ways to legitimize it because the bean counters back in New York didn't understand how things worked out in the field. That's where individual creativity comes in.

There was an *ABC* News reporter stationed in Moscow during the Cold War. This reporter wanted to buy a refrigerator for his spartan Soviet apartment, but the bean counters at *ABC* News repeatedly refused his request. Fed up, he decided to turn his expense account in every couple of months, during which time he would quietly fabricate enough other expenses, such as transportation or translation services, to be able to purchase his cherished refrigerator. Finally, he filed an expense account with a little note paperclipped to it. "The refrigerator is in there," read the note. "Find it."

For a time in the late 1960s, some *ABC* employees would take their shirts on the road and send them out to be dry cleaned. It would always appear on their expense account as "laundry," so in one way, they were telling the truth. In reality, people would take five or six shirts - some got greedy and took every item in their closet - on the road to be cleaned, but they would only be gone on assignment for two days. After awhile, *ABC's* accounting department got wise. The practice was eliminated.

One individual, I can't remember if it was someone I worked with at *ABC* or *CBS*, took this idea one step further. This guy had enough nerve to take his drapes on the road, send them out to be cleaned, and then put it on his expense account!

Work-related transportation was paid for across the board by all the networks. As the Robinson story suggests, padding an expense account with cab fare was the most common practice.

I remember that when *ABC* did NBA games, the network always set its production crews up at Detroit's Pontchartrain Hotel for Pistons' games. This hotel was right across the street from Cobo Arena, the Pistons' home at the time. It was a two-minute walk. Of course, everyone still put in for cab fare and the claims were always approved. It was our version of an uncontested lay-up.

Sometimes, however, cherry picking these easy expenses could cause problems. I knew a sportswriter who covered the New York Mets for the *New York Daily News*. When on the road, he took the team bus, but of course put in for cab fare. Well, during one road trip, a fight broke out on the bus.

Unfortunately, he was unable to write the story via a first-hand account because his editor would then know that he was taking the bus and putting in for cab fare. He had no choice but to let another paper's beat writer break the story. It killed him, but it was better than having to fess up to his boss and to the bean counters.

If I had to bet, I'd say that limousines were the most frequently expensed travel expenditures in the history of network television. I used to take limos to and from the airport when I did publicity for *ABC* Sports in the 1970s and I was a nobody. I didn't feel bad about putting in for it because that's the way everybody traveled. There was so much money to go around back then, it wasn't considered a big deal.

One of my friends, the late Mike Letis, was into limos more than anybody else. Remember how Bob Prince advised me to put in for cab fare when visiting the men's room? Well, Letis would take a limo to take a leak.

Letis, a Dartmouth grad, was one of the best sports marketing guys ever. A big horse racing guy, he was involved in the Olympics, the Breeders' Cup and helped develop "This Week in Baseball." Letis was a lot of laughs. Yet I think I got the last laugh on him. "Letis," I told him one time, "when you die, you're showing up at heaven's gates in a limo." I'm certain that God approved his final expense account.

While we're talking about travel expenses, everybody knew that Dick Ebersol, the current president of *NBC* Sports, was going places at a young age. In one notable case, however, I just couldn't understand how he was getting around.

It was in 1967 that Ebersol took two years off from Yale to work as a researcher for *ABC* Sports for the Olympics. He was the first Olympics researcher. I was intrigued by this kid from the beginning. He was 19 when Roone hired him. He seemed to run in celebrity circles. I watched him lead a donkey up Sixth Avenue for a birthday party being held for Teddy Kennedy. And there was a rumor going around the office that he was subletting Faye Dunaway's apartment.

Anyway, I learned that Ebersol worked all week in the city then returned to New Haven on the weekends in a rental car paid for by *ABC*. Limo rides were one thing, but no network paid for a rental car for a researcher back then. Hell, I was in charge of publicity for college sports and they wouldn't okay a rental for me.

"How are you doing this?" I asked him.

"Well," he replied, "I volunteered to take Roone's mail to him on Sunday after he's been out of town. I pick up the car on Friday, go to Yale, hang out with some friends, and then deliver Roone his mail on Sunday."

Aha! It was at that moment that I knew that Ebersol would make it big. There were people, really smart, aggressive ladder-climbers, who had been at *ABC* for years that hadn't thought of doing what he had. Roone rewarded his ingenuity by signing off on the rental car.

Ebersol is a brilliant television executive, but when it came to working the system and expense accounts, he had an amazing teacher. Few people could top Roone. He might come back from a trip to Europe, hand in the hotel receipt, pull out some crinkled receipts for entertainment or dinner, and his poor secretary would have to find a way to legitimize $2,000 in expenses. I know it wasn't easy for her, but she always got the job done.

It isn't that Roone put the money in his pocket. Oh, no. He spent it. He liked to entertain, and he liked to have a good time. For Roone, entertaining was essential not only to deal-making but for maintaining both his empire and his friendships.

Someone once interviewed Don Ohlmeyer and asked him what was the most important thing he learned working for Roone. I'm sure the interviewer was expecting an answer about some technical aspect of television production or negotiations and was surprised at the reply.

"The most important thing I learned from Roone Arledge," Ohlmeyer answered, "was how to use other people's money to take care of your friends."

I know of very few instances in which people stole money outright. Most of the time, people would simply use their expense accounts to eat and drink beyond their means. One example was the late Bob Drum, a colorful sportswriter and 19th hole regular, who was up there in Brendle's league. I got to know Drum while working as a copy boy at the *Pittsburgh Press*.

Work cut into socializing, so the Drummer wasn't one to waste words or time. He typically attended just one of Pitt's football practices a week, spent the least amount of time necessary there, and each of his stories followed the same predictable formula: "Pitt practiced offense, defense and polished up its kicking game." Drum then went to the bar to get polished up himself.

When it came to expense accounts, Drum's advice to me was similarly concise and to the point: "Pick up all checks before noon." Let everybody else pick up the checks after that. Breakfast and lunch tabs were usually less expensive than dinner checks because of the booze. I quickly learned what Drum was talking about. Sportswriters, see, are like vampires. Both have deadlines and both do their drinking after sundown.

Often, when on the road entertaining assorted media members late at night, I'd look around at a table full of cocktails and T-bones and think of the poor blue-collar guys who work their tails off and never get to experience that kind of royal treatment. The average fan has no idea how well those in the sports media eat and drink. Or how they do it.

Norm Vargo, a longtime Pittsburgh-area sportswriter, is well-known for plundering the buffet line in the pressbox at Steeler games. Vargo spent several decades on the Steelers' beat for the *McKeesport News* and remains one of the best to ever cover the team.

One evening he was at The Meadows, a horse track outside of Pittsburgh, for a working dinner. At least that's what his bosses were led to believe. After poring over the menu, Vargo's interview subject was ready to order.

"What are you going to have?" he asked.

"I think I'll have the surf and turf," answered Vargo.

Confused, the guy re-opened his menu for further examination.

"I don't see that on the menu," he said. "Where is it?"

"Right here," said Vargo, pointing to two separate sections of the menu. "I order the steak here and the lobster there." Vargo just ordered two separate, extremely expensive entrees, but expensed it as a single meal.

Vargo earned his reputation. Other sportswriters, often unfairly, get theirs from colleagues. Consider the case of Gordon White.

One of the things you constantly do in network television is entertain people from the *New York Times*. As long as you have someone from the *Times* on your expense account, it doesn't matter how you spent the money. It will always be approved.

Gordon White covered college sports and golf for the *Times*, and his name was a staple on my expense account for years. The funny thing is, he appeared on dozens, maybe even hundreds, of other people's expense accounts, too.

"If the I.R.S. ever looked into it," Jim Tarman joked, "they would think that Gordon White weighed at least 600 pounds."

When my friend Geoff Mason was with *NBC* Sports, he once entertained members of the International Olympic Committee in Geneva, Switzerland. When he got the check, he was shocked. The bill was somewhere in the vicinity of $1000 for three or four people. And that's not counting the tip.

Mason knew that he was headed for a showdown with the suits so a few days later, a surprised *NBC* accountant received an expense account to which the enterprising Duke alum had stapled a menu from the restaurant proving he was telling the truth.

I never ran up any ridiculously large tabs, but one of my regular tricks was putting in for dinner with my friend Ernie Accorsi, during his time as general manager of the Colts and the Browns, when I merely flew over Baltimore or Cleveland on my way somewhere else.

I also fulfilled one of my greatest life ambitions when I successfully put dinner with a dead man on my expense account and had it cleared. That was in 1967. My posthumous partner in that ruse was Charlie Bartlett of the *Chicago Tribune*.

Another benefit of having an expense account is using it to get out of trouble. The best story I have in this regard concerns one of the many adventures of the famed "Wrecking Crew," a crazy collection of four hard-partying *ABC* Sports employees who wreaked havoc on dozens of road assignments throughout the late 1960s and early 70s.

The Wrecking Crew – it was Mason, another Duke alum named John Martin who became a vice president under Roone, Fred Hutchison, and Don Ohlmeyer – was in Akron, Ohio one summer to work the World Series of Golf.

They threw a massive party in their suite, one of their all-time best. The room was completely trashed. The motel manager was so pissed off, he called the police and after a tension-filled, early morning caucus, the Wrecking Crew agreed to pay for the damages. As the manager exited the room, Hutchison crept up behind him and tapped him on the shoulder.

"Excuse me, sir," he said. "On the bill, could you put the damages under 'room service'?"

I don't know if that expense account was approved, but if I had to bet, I'd say it was. At one time, the sky was the limit when it came to spending in network television.

There was a big motorcycle race in Houston that *ABC* Sports covered one year. In addition to their individual rooms, the crew set aside a block of four rooms for a post-race party. One room served as a lounge for talking, one was for drinking, another was for smoking marijuana and the last one was for fucking.

It was approved. The accountants didn't say a word. After all, what's a few hotel rooms when on pavilion night one year at the U.S. Open tennis tournament, *CBS* Sports spent $6,000 on flowers! Yes. Six grand. On flowers.

That was for a real event. The business was a such a big party back then, you could get almost anything approved. I'm going to tell you a great story about what I think might be the most interesting sporting event in *ABC* history. But it wasn't on "Wide World" or "Monday Night Football." It wasn't the Olympics or a college football "Game of the Century." It's one that only those of us who were there know about.

In late 1970, *ABC's* college football production staff and announcers played their "Monday Night Football" counterparts in a pick-up, touch football game at Yankee Stadium. Imagine the Turkey Bowl games you play with your buddies around Thanksgiving. It was like that, only the players and coaches were some of the most famous television sports personalities in the world.

This was a very, very big deal. Company bragging rights were on the line. That day was a blast. If the tapes of this game still exist in a vault somewhere, I'd pay good money to watch them.

On the pro sideline, Keith Jackson, Howard Cosell, and Don Meredith were calling the game, only it wasn't like a typical broadcast. Since it wasn't really on the air, we didn't have to worry about the FCC, so there was plenty of profanity and laughs.

I think Chris Schenkel was our captain. As you know, when the ball gets rolling on things like this and competitive juices start brewing, ideas start snowballing. It got to the point where somebody decided that we couldn't play for the company championship without having our hall of fame coach, Bud Wilkinson, on the sideline.

To get Wilkinson to the game, he was picked up in a private charter at an airport in Oklahoma and flown to Dallas, where he boarded a commercial flight for New York. It was a complex, expensive operation, but we got Bud to the Bronx in time for kickoff.

I was assigned the role of sideline reporter. With an *ABC* mic, I conducted playful interviews with the cameramen and PAs that were playing, as well as with some of the execs and celebrities that found their way onto our private field of dreams. One of the interviews I did was with Ethel Kennedy, who stopped by after a meeting at our offices regarding the Robert F. Kennedy Pro-Celebrity Tennis Tournament.

Here's where the expense accounts come in. The company, actually the accountants, paid for the whole thing. They just might not have known that they did! The whole event, the booze, rental fee for Yankee Stadium, Wilkinson's flights, none of it was legitimate business. It was all done for a good time. The total cost was probably creatively written into a number of expense accounts by the bigger names like Cosell and Schenkel and was therefore approved without question.

Those really were the good old days. That was the era when the major networks, during primetime, were getting a 95 share. The money was just pouring in. Now there's cable and Internet streaming services and a lot more competition for America's eyeballs, so they're getting a 60 share on a good night. That's a big difference. Because of this, the networks have gotten serious and started clamping down.

The beginning of the end of the golden era of expense accounts can most likely be traced to the decision made by *CBS* to issue their employees American Express corporate cards in the early 1980s. *CBS*, in my opinion, had been the most lax of the networks when it came to financial oversight. Bill Paley, without knowing it, probably fed more people than Christ did with the loaves and the fishes.

Under the corporate card system, any meal over five dollars had to be put on the card and the bill went straight to the accounting department. All of us who worked at *CBS* were pissed. We had been eating everywhere for free and putting in for meal money, and now, we couldn't play around anymore. It didn't take long, however, for people to figure out how to work around the card system. And I had something to do with it.

Unbeknownst to me, Rich Podolsky started making arrangements to hold a 50th birthday party for me late in the summer of 1981. First, he talked Joe Healey into closing Runyon's down at 8 p.m. for the private party. Next, Rich went around the offices at *CBS* and got a dozen people to commit to splitting the cost of the party amongst themselves.

It was one of the greatest surprises, not to mention nights, of my life. You couldn't move in there. There were so many of my friends, people from the sports and media worlds, that showed up.

There was Howard Katz, Dick Ebersol, Don Ohlmeyer, Gary Bender, Pat Summerall, John Martin, and Roger Valdiserri. Val Pinchbeck came and brought Pete Rozelle and a bunch of NFL people from the league's Park Avenue headquarters, too. It was unbelievable.

My favorite part of the whole story is how they settled the monster tab that we racked up. Healey gave Podolsky a portable AMEX charge machine to take home and the next day, half the office lined up to run their corporate cards through the machine. That's the story of how *CBS* paid for my 50th birthday party!

That's one of the best, but not the best. In my opinion, when you're talking expense account stories in sports media, nothing – I mean absolutely nothing – tops the Howard Rothstein story.

I don't remember the exact date, but for some strange reason I recall that it was a particularly hot July afternoon sometime in the early 1970s. There was a group of *ABC Sports* employees huddled around the coffee wagon on the 20th floor of the network's Manhattan headquarters. We somehow got to talking about all the strange things that we had cleared on our expense accounts. There were some great examples of creative writing discussed on this day.

The chatter was interrupted when one of the younger guys posed a question that made everybody sit up and take notice. It might have been theoretical. Then again, it might not have been.

"How do you put hookers on the expense account?" he asked.

Everybody knew about Roone's rules when it came to gambling and fooling around with coeds. When it came to drinking and prostitutes, though, things were, how should I say it, a little more permissive.

"If *ABC Sports* ever goes out of business," Roger Valdiserri once said, "the hookers in this country have problems."

And if we're being honest about the way things once were in the business, it must be stated that *ABC* wasn't the only place where this sort of thing went on. It was like this at the other networks as well. I know for a fact that at *CBS*, the answer to the question was typically "TPA," under the heading of "talent payment authorization." But *ABC* is the gold standard for a good reason, Harold Rothstein's all-timer.

While we were pondering the query, the inimitable Rothstein, a creative writing legend, already had an answer. Without hesitation, he nonchalantly delivered his classic reply, one that sounded as though it had almost certainly been used before.

"That's an easy one," Rothstein said. "Under 'snacks for crew.'"

CHAPTER 10

People are going to be disappointed...

There are three jobs in this country that one needs no real talent, training nor experience for: member of Congress, prostitute, and sports television personality.

If you think you've heard that line before, you have. Howard Cosell said it. But Howard stole it from me. I want it on the record that I was the one who came up with it.

Now that that's settled, I am going to try to explain how a PR guy, liberal arts major and non-jock with no significant broadcasting experience landed a job as a college football studio commentator with *ABC* in 1982. Considering the outrageously competitive business that is network television, it almost defies explanation, like a $5 a day extra landing a starring role in Cecil B. DeMille's epic "The Ten Commandments."

When I asked the people at *CBS* to give me a shot, they laughed at me. And I later found out that a few did more than laugh. Perhaps they thought it was a ridiculous idea. And maybe today, nearly three decades later, a lot of college football fans will agree with their assertion that I didn't belong on the air.

Luckily for me, my old boss at *ABC* Sports, Roone Arledge, didn't feel that way. Roone had a reputation as a risk-taker, as being someone who thought unconventionally, so I knew he'd at least listen to what I had to say. Even so, I was shocked at what he did. He hired me sight unseen. There was no audition process. To this day, I don't know why. He never told me the reason. It certainly wasn't because of my résumé.

I did a few short sports shows on assorted Pittsburgh radio stations in the early 1960s, and I mean short. One, on *KQV*, aired sometime between 8:02 and 8:07 a.m. The money wasn't very good, and I always had the feeling that I was being cheated, but I was just happy to be on the air.

My only local television credits included a brief stint as the host of a weekly sports show on Pittsburgh's *WIIC-TV* in 1962. I was relieved of my duties at *WIIC* because, of all things, I didn't smile enough. So thought the title and only sponsor of my show, Gilbert Furniture, which had me ousted.

I worked as the second man in the booth for a handful of ABC regional college football telecasts in 1970-71. Roone approved that experiment, too, but it didn't amount to much. I received no feedback, hate mail or fan mail. None of the games were memorable, either, except one I did with Dave Diles that was filled with penalties. "There are more flags here than there were at Appomattox," I cracked. Diles liked that line and kidded me about it for years.

Perhaps what Roone thought I lacked in experience, I made up for with my unique sense of humor and my uncanny ability to generate controversy. The latter talent, as I would later discover, proved an indispensable gift.

You know about my releases at Pitt, and the U.S.S. Arizona cover controversy with *Pittsburgh Weekly Sports*. I found that talent was universal. It worked in print and on the airwaves.

During one of my early radio bits on *KQV* in 1963, I cracked that Donn Clendenon, the Pittsburgh Pirates' free-swinging first baseman, "left more men on base than the German army did on the Russian Front during World War II."

Within a few days, the city was abuzz with the news that I had made a racial remark on the air. I guess several black listeners believed that I singled Clendenon out because of his color. Race had nothing to do with it. There were plenty of Pirates who left men on base, but Clendenon was the most visible target because he struck out a lot. In fact, he would go on to lead the National League in that ignominious category, the first of two times in his career he would accomplish the feat.

Later that season, as the strikeout epidemic spread throughout the lineup, the club's publicity department eliminated the entire team's strikeout total from its daily stat sheets. In response, Roy McHugh penned a column in the *Pittsburgh Press* suggesting that local papers could improve on that line of thinking by printing only winning box scores. That way, he argued, tongue planted firmly in cheek, losing and poor play could be eliminated altogether. Surprisingly, several readers thought McHugh was serious. They even wrote letters to the editor suggesting that he was an idiot.

If I had to bet, I'd say Roone hired me because he needed something to make *ABC's* coverage of college football stand out when compared to that of its new competitor, *CBS*. The timing of my sales pitch could not have been more perfect.

Part of that pitch was that sports television had gotten stale. It needed a fresh face with new ideas, but one accompanied by a perspective that was grounded in an expert understanding of the game's history. The two sports in which history matter the most are college football and baseball, and in college football, the old soldiers, the Lindsey Nelsons of the business, were rapidly fading away. Few of the younger, up-and-coming broadcasters possessed an appreciation for the pageantry and history of the game.

I also thought that the ex-coaches and ex-athletes regurgitated the same monotonous material week after week. Their ad nauseum recitation of the game's technical aspects was, in fact, nauseating. I figured that by 1982, the viewing public was educated in the intricacies of the game, you run to set up the pass, score more points than the other team to win, and what have you.

Plus, these guys were all members of a close-knit fraternity. Coaches typically don't knock other coaches. The same could be said of athletic directors and college presidents. I didn't plan to practice that kind of self-censorship, I told Roone. I planned to speak my mind.

I didn't care if the guards pulled or not, who I offended, and I didn't think that the majority of fans cared, either. I wanted to examine the unique facets of what I believed was the most unique sport on the planet and talk about things that would make a college football fan, dozing in his La-Z-Boy in Montana, wake up and take notice.

My intention was to talk about the same things that I did whenever I was holding court in my office or some bar. My material would include subjects such as scheduling, leadership at all levels of the sport, both historic trends and hot-button issues, as well as provide some subtle information that might be helpful to viewers wagering on the games.

The most important thing to me was to offer commentary from a completely new perspective. I wasn't going to be talking from the perspective of someone who used to stalk the sidelines, or from that of someone who was in the huddle. And I wasn't going to be a clone of another *ABC* employee.

Some writers wrote that Roone hired me to be another Cosell, and while I will go to my grave believing that one of the reasons he hired me was because of Cosell's success, it was a ridiculous assumption. There will never be another Howard Cosell just like there will never be another Thomas Jefferson.

Besides, Cosell was everywhere and did everything for *ABC*. According to the plan, I'd be limited to segments on *ABC's* college football pre-game, halftime, and post-game shows. "Beano will not be on significantly at all, in terms of time," my good friend Donn Bernstein, *ABC's* press director for college football, told the media before the season, "but what he says in two minutes might be the most significant two minutes of our telecast."

I never intended to emulate Cosell, the Greek, or anybody else. And while I loved college football, I decided I wasn't going to be a cheerleader, either.

For too long, the NCAA and the administrators who ran the show had gotten away with sidestepping important issues, treating athletes like cattle, and projecting a wholesome image of the sport that was increasingly distanced from reality.

My buddy O'Connor was famously grouchy about the promo spots that schools aired during the games. You know the ones, where they had these kids looking into microscopes. Every college produced a variation of these commercials, just like every team ran the counter play.

"You'd think we'd have a cure for cancer by now with these All-American running backs working in the lab after practice," O'Connor grumbled.

The NCAA and its member schools didn't know it yet, but those days of marching bands and microscopes at halftime were coming to an end. Roone Arledge had decided to put the loudmouth at the end of the bar in front of a camera, and he was waiting for the red light to come on.

I would be talking first and foremost as a fan, perhaps the biggest, most passionate, and most opinionated college football fan in the country. That was my angle.

It all sounded good to Roone. He didn't want college football's Cosell, a cheerleader, another coach, or a camera magnet with movie star looks and perfect hair.

"Just be Beano," he told me.

I imagine there were times over the next four years he resented saying that.

There was probably no place besides *ABC* that I could "be Beano." I joked that I knew I was back at *ABC* Sports when I saw a secretary fly through the air to pick up a call before the third ring, but in all seriousness, I truly felt at home because only at *ABC* could an experiment like me have been attempted. The culture at *ABC* was built on the foundation of creative freedom. Even if *CBS* had put me on the air, I doubt it would have worked because of how rigid things were there.

Being Beano meant I would voice my opinion and say what was on my mind, just like I had always done. This probably caught many of the country's college football fans, those who were introduced to me for the first time due to my new gig, off-guard.

For instance, I had never approached preseason predictions using conventional wisdom. That's why, for my first preseason prediction with *ABC*, I picked the University of Florida to win the national title. Not only that, after Florida beat a 15th-ranked Miami Hurricanes team in the season opener, I said they would thump Southern Cal at home the following week. Many people thought I was crazy.

I thought the situation was right for Florida to win the national title. They had talent, like future all-pro linebacker Wilber Marshall, and a productive short passing attack. The schedule has always been the most important factor for me and most of Florida's big games were at home. They had the cocktail party in Jacksonville, of course, but they had hung with Georgia powerhouses each of the two previous seasons, losing by identical 26-21 scores. They seemed on the verge of getting over that hump.

It was more than a good pick; it was a good pick in which to make a big splash. I talked to Buddy Martin, my friend, former boss at the *St. Petersburg Times* and a Florida alum, and he agreed. Plus, I had a great line to pair with the pick: "Moses only had to wander forty years to get to the promised land. Those poor Gator fans have had to wander through the SEC for fifty years. They're due."

I drowned in the Red Sea with that one. The Gators did beat Southern Cal, but they finished 8-4. The point I was trying to make, though, was that anybody can pick one of the blue blood schools to win it all every year. And most of the talking heads on television at the time did. Most of them still do. I never understood it. Just like in betting, where do you get playing massive favorites all the time?

That's why for much of my career, whether I was on television or in my online or print work, I tried to find a dark horse contender that I thought had a legitimate chance.

My standard formula was to pick a team that had finished the previous season strong, either with a rivalry game or bowl victory, and had a significant number of starters returning. Sometimes this would be a brand-name team, yet more than often than not it wasn't going to be a traditional power.

Secondly, the schedule had to be set up for success. This meant a big non-conference or rivalry game at home and perhaps a well-placed bye week.

Another factor was coaching. A head coach with a reputation as a winner was a very important ingredient as well.

Finally, my gut played a big role in the process. There were times I threw the schedules and depth charts and all the intangibles out the window because I could sense that a school was due for a magical year.

I picked Arkansas, led by Lou Holtz, to win the national title in 1980. I voted Johnny Majors and Tennessee the preseason No. 1 in *Sport* magazine in 1983 when nobody else had the Volunteers in the top 20. I picked Arizona State in 1984. Those were big losers.

But in 1985, I nailed the national championship game and the winner before the season started. I picked Oklahoma No. 1 in my *Sport* column because I felt the Sooners played incredibly well against the toughest schedule in the country in 1984. I picked Penn State to play for it all on the air on *ABC* in September because I had a feeling that Joe Paterno was itching to turn in a great performance coming off a 6-5 season.

And then there was 1988. I nailed both picks. There were two of them that year due to some unique circumstances. And as luck would have it, both teams, Notre Dame and West Virginia, played for the national title in the Fiesta Bowl.

I picked Notre Dame to win the 1988 national title all the way back in August 1987. I said Notre Dame would go 8-2-1 in 1987 (they ended up going 8-3 in the regular season and then lost in the Cotton Bowl to Texas A&M) and then win the national title the following season. Lou Somogyi printed the prediction in *Blue and Gold Illustrated.*

And I did it again on the air on "College GameDay" on January 1, 1988. The pick made sense to me. Notre Dame had been down for the better part of the decade, but they had material. The schedule was tough, like all Notre Dame schedules, but the Irish had seven home games that year, including the two toughest games on the schedule, Michigan and Miami.

Then there were the intangibles. The 1988 season would be the 100th anniversary of Knute Rockne's birth, plus there was the Notre Dame third-year coach variable. All the coaches who won national titles at Notre Dame – Rockne, Leahy, Parseghian and Devine – won it in their third year on the job. If Lou Holtz was going to turn the Notre Dame program around and join those coaching legends, the forces of fate indicated that it would be in that third year.

So, why did I at the last moment take West Virginia to go all the way in my *ESPN* prediction in August of 1988? It's because I hate flying.

The only thing I hate more than commercial air travel is paying taxes, but the airlines are rapidly gaining ground on the I.R.S. The seats keep getting smaller. You get less and less leg room. Not that the food was ever any good, but they've all but eliminated meal service. At the same time, the prices keep going up. Lastly, it's hardly a reassuring sight when the first word you see when you get to the airport is terminal.

I was all set to meet up with a crew from *ESPN* at Notre Dame when someone from the travel office in Bristol called to tell me that the only airline that had a direct flight from Pittsburgh to South Bend had just cut that route. I'd had a handful of cramped, turbulence-filled flights on the puddle jumpers from Chicago to South Bend over the years and I was determined to avoid another one of those experiences at all costs.

I went back to the list of my other preseason contenders. Miami of Florida, Florida State and UCLA were out because those were very long-distance flights. So was Norman, Oklahoma, which would have required me to make connections in Dallas and Tulsa. That left one team whose campus, incidentally, was only an hour drive away. That settled it. Let's go to Morgantown. Let's go, Mountaineers!

Now WVU wasn't just a default pick. Coach Don Nehlen had a lot of starters back from a gutsy team that lost the rivalry games, to Pitt, Penn State and Syracuse, plus the bowl, by a grand total of ten points. They also had an outstanding dual-threat quarterback, Major Harris, who I thought was going to be a dark horse Heisman Trophy contender. The Mountaineers had never been close to the rarified air of a national championship, they hadn't really done much of anything since Pappy Lewis's 1953 and '54 teams won back-to-back Southern Conference titles, so they were really, really due.

In a way, I'm glad things happened the way they did with the flights because the WVU pick got a lot of buzz nationally. It started with the folks in Vegas. A friend in the desert called and told me that Caesar's Palace had WVU 70-1 before I made the pick. He said the Mountaineers moved to 50-1 immediately after my pick. Each week, as West Virginia kept rising in the polls, those odds changed. Notre Dame was a 4.5-point favorite going into the Fiesta Bowl.

The 1988 season, incidentally, was one of my best years in betting. I was popular with both the public and the sharps. I got every big game right, except for UCLA over USC. I said in September that you could take it to the bank that UCLA would end it's four-game losing streak to Nebraska and sure enough, the Bruins blasted the No. 2 Cornhuskers. I never wavered in my belief that Notre Dame would upset Miami. I picked Notre Dame, even when it was announced that several Irish starters would not be making the trip to the coast for disciplinary reasons, to defeat Southern Cal 27-17. The final was 27-10.

The pick also made me quite popular in Morgantown. I exchanged letters with a big Mountaineers fan in Wheeling named Frank Joanou who printed up t-shirts with my name on them. My pen pal told me that his crew of WVU boosters attended all the games wearing them. And after the Fiesta Bowl matchup with Notre Dame was announced, the City of Morgantown proclaimed December 9, 1988, as "Beano Cook Day" in my honor.

The following year, I picked Arkansas over Notre Dame, Nebraska, Miami, and Southern Cal because *ESPN* paid for a private jet to fly me to Fayetteville.

In 1990, I picked Ohio State because Columbus was a four-hour drive from

Pittsburgh. From that season forward, I don't think I ever picked another team, this was while I was still obligated to shoot the pick on campus, that wasn't within driving distance.

It wasn't a perfect formula. It was basically a crapshoot. At times I looked like a genius and others, like an absolute moron. But that never bothered me. I think most of the people who make picks for a living take themselves much too seriously. The only two things you truly must bat 1.000 in are flying and heart transplants. Everything else, you can go three for four.

And to be honest, it didn't matter to me whether I was right or wrong. I considered myself successful every preseason because I always accomplished my goal of setting myself apart from every other talking head in the business.

And while we're at it, the other important thing I want to make clear is that contrary to popular belief, none of my picks were ever guesses. Some of them might have been out there, but there had been plenty of research behind them and thought put into them. They were risks, but calculated risks.

While my preseason predictions and weekly picks were intended for the consumption of the fans and the media, I aimed my commentaries at organizations and people in positions of power. On Monday, September 6, 1982, I came out with my guns blazing. That weekend, Jack Whitaker, Jim Lampley and I headed down to Athens, Georgia for a primetime Labor Day night showdown between the defending national champion Clemson Tigers and Vince Dooley's highly-rated Georgia Bulldogs.

The scene was surreal. Here I was between the hedges, under the bright lights, wearing that canary yellow *ABC* Sports blazer. I couldn't believe it was really happening.

I was very lucky to be teamed with Whitaker and Lamps during my inaugural season. Whitaker, the Eric Sevareid of sports, is intelligence personified. He was another *CBS* cast-off that Roone signed. I can't believe *CBS* let him get away.

And Lampley, who in 1982 looked like he was young enough to be on the General Electric College Bowl academic quiz show (that's the way my mother described him), remains one of the best personalities in the business. I've always felt that the best college football studio show in history was the team of Dave Diles and Lampley.

I also discovered, to my relief as a rookie, that Jim's talent was equaled only by his patience and unique ability to improvise, both on the air and off. In the middle of a studio show one fall Saturday, Lampley received a telephone call from his wife informing him that she had located a suitable address for the couple on Long Island. They had been in the market for a house for some time.

"It's $400,000," she said.

"Great," replied Lampley, "we'll take a look at it."

"Well," she added, "we already bought it."

I had no idea whether the viewing audience was going buy into me, and neither did the network brass, so to be safe, my segment that night was pre-recorded. Some people at *ABC* were concerned that I might freeze on the air, and to be perfectly honest with you, I didn't mind the decision. I was so fucking nervous, I felt like it was my first affair, and the husband was going to come home from his business trip early! It's one thing to be on the radio in Pittsburgh; it's something completely different to be on live national television in primetime.

For my debut segment, I addressed what was then (and still is occasionally) a hot topic in the college football world, parity. I argued that parity was not a recent trend, a losing season at Notre Dame or even a rash of recent upsets of the haves, the traditional powers, by the game's have-nots.

Parity, by my definition, was Vanderbilt winning the ultra-competitive Southeastern Conference. The only way the Commodores could make it to the Sugar Bowl, I said, would be if nine teams (at the time, there were ten teams in the SEC) went on probation.

The resulting furor my remark created throughout the South, especially in Nashville, was something I'll never forget. For starters, Vanderbilt issued a complaint, saying that my remarks could hurt recruiting. I said I didn't care. That wasn't my problem or responsibility. That pissed more people off.

So many Southern writers and columnists, probably at the behest of the SEC commissioner's office, tore me apart. All for merely telling the truth. Vanderbilt, although a premier academic institution and a charter member of the league since its inception in 1933, has never won an SEC football title.

Of course, Vanderbilt surprisingly put together it's first winning season since 1974 that year. The Commodores went 8-3, played both Alabama and Georgia tough, and landed a bid in the Hall of Fame Bowl. I still don't believe they will ever win the conference or play in the Sugar Bowl, at least in my lifetime, but that isn't the point of the exercise here.

Until I spoke out publicly, nobody had had the balls to say on the air what every college football fan in the country knew, that Vanderbilt only maintains its membership in the SEC so that the conference can claim some semblance of academic legitimacy. And also, because the Commodores can be counted on for a guaranteed win by the other schools.

In retrospect, the controversy over my debut could have been a much bigger conflagration. I had intended to say that the only way Vanderbilt could win the SEC would be if nine planes crashed, but wisely changed it after testing the line out on a few friends. Their responses were uniform, with no dissenting votes: "Beano, we want to see you on the air more than once." I don't like focus groups, but I'm glad I listened that time. The only person who could have gotten away with a line like that was Don Rickles.

I was just getting started. In November, I broached another taboo topic. To me it was becoming obvious that the Big Ten was no longer the dominant conference in college football. I thought the league was vastly overrated and said so on the air. It's no secret that I've never been a fan of the Big Ten – it's the most arrogant organization since the Third Reich – but this argument wasn't predicated on any personal beliefs.

Again, I was simply stating the truth, and for some people, the truth hurt. The Big Ten's poor record in non-conference play (8-14, with three victories over Mid-American opponents and two versus an awful Syracuse team) that year, in addition to its general absence from the national championship picture and its dismal won-loss record in the Rose Bowl over the course of the past decade, provided me with cold, hard evidence.

I said that it was time to reevaluate the Big Ten's arrangement with the Rose Bowl, that the conference's champion wasn't deserving of its automatic bid to such a prestigious post-season bowl any longer.

Part of my argument was based on current events and part of it was my knowledge of the Rose Bowl's history. Teams like Alabama, Pitt, Nebraska, Tennessee, Duke, Tulane, and SMU had once played in the Rose Bowl, and some great intersectional games had taken place in that stadium, and I felt that fans from other areas of the country were being deprived of future classics due to the current contract.

The late Wiles Hallock, commissioner of the Pac-10 and chair of the NCAA Football TV Committee, sent *ABC* a letter complaining about my dogging of the Big Ten and the way I wore my "prejudices" on my "rumpled sleeve." According to Hallock and the folks on the TV committee, I should not have been "given the opportunity to downgrade any portion of the product for which *ABC* is paying $131,750,000, particularly as substantial a portion as the Big Ten's appearances represent."

"He's been around long enough to know all teams and conferences enjoy and suffer up and down cycles," added Hallock. "I guess he'll never understand diplomacy, or tact, however, and despite what I believe your right to be with respect to editorial freedom, in your own interests, as well as ours, exercise your right to blue-pencil an employee's script, please."

When I read the full letter, I had a hard time getting through the double talk. Who wrote what I had read, Wiles Hallock or Joseph Goebbels? In the same sentence the NCAA stated that it respected *ABC's* right to editorial freedom, but it also wanted *ABC* to censor me?

Donn Bernstein asked me if we should leak the letter to the press. I told him that under no circumstances should it be leaked. Remember what Ben Franklin said: "Three people can keep a secret, but only if two of them are dead."

So yes, it was leaked anyway. I know Bernstein didn't do it. It was probably done by someone at the Big Ten to try to get a response from Roone, as well as a public reprimand of yours truly. Within no time, I was getting calls from the media asking for a comment.

"They want to blue-pencil my script," I said. "But everything's ad lib so they'd have to blue-pencil my tongue."

To hell with apologies, diplomacy, tact and whatever else Hallock was talking about. I realized early in the experiment that I didn't want to second-guess myself. If it didn't work out, fine. But I wanted to make sure I did it my way, like Sinatra.

Besides, the only opinion I cared about was Roone's and I hadn't heard a word from him or from anybody else regarding his displeasure. But that didn't mean that he wasn't aware of what was going on.

Two weeks later, the late Chuck Howard, a former director who became vice president of production, sent a reply that served as *ABC's* official defense of my comments. It was a surprise to me since Chuck and I never got along really well. He had a prickly personality. He was the kind of guy who got upset when elevators stopped on other floors. I have no proof, but I believe that he was told to write the letter by Jim Spence, who in turn had probably gotten his orders from Roone, the Wizard.

"In the opinions of everyone concerned at *ABC* Sports Beano was correct in his assessment of the Big 10," Howard wrote. "...we cannot be in a position where we are telling our commentators that in effect they can only make positive statements about the NCAA, its members, a conference, a game or an individual athlete or coach involved in a game. If we do that our announcers and we at *ABC* Sports have lost our credibility."

A few weeks later, with Christmas drawing near, I stuck the needle in a little deeper and twisted it some more. For one segment, I put together a wish list for certain people and teams in college football. I asked Santa Claus to bring the Big Ten and Commissioner Wayne Duke a much-needed Rose Bowl matchup against the Ivy League champs. See, the Big Ten had lost seven of the last eight on New Year's Day in Pasadena.

I would not have gotten away with my comments or behavior a few years later, when an individual named Dennis Swanson took over *ABC* Sports. Swanson was an Illinois graduate and a Big Ten fanatic. The first thing one noticed upon entering his office was the Illinois football helmet on his desk.

It was another season, but once again, the Big Ten was faring poorly. A researcher named Jerry Klein wanted to put up a graphic illustrating the Big Ten's abysmal non-conference showing, but Swanson heard about it and vetoed the idea.

During my last season at *ABC* in 1985, I ruffled some more feathers in the Big Ten when I chastised Iowa for running up the score in a drubbing of Northwestern. I could understand wanting to pour it on a team like Michigan or Ohio State whenever you had one of those rare opportunities, but Northwestern?

Of course, the Big Ten and the entire state of Iowa didn't appreciate my comments and threw a fit. I got hate mail from every town from Dubuque to Sioux City. Interestingly, the one person in Iowa who did agree with me was legendary Iowa coach Forest Evashevski. During a later encounter, he told me that what I said was right.

As proof that I am an equal-opportunity offender, I also incurred the wrath of the Atlantic Coast Conference. This time, the offended party was Dick Schultz, who was then the athletic director at the University of Virginia. Schultz wrote Roone a letter complaining that I referred to Virginia's excellent head coach, George Welsh, on the air as "Georgie." He wanted me fired for the remark.

Despite the fact that I considered Welsh to be one of the five best coaches in the country, and often said so on the air, Schultz implied that I had disrespected Welsh on national television. My offense, in reality, was using one of Welsh's old nicknames.

Years earlier, I had heard people at Penn State, where Welsh worked as an assistant under Joe Paterno, call him Georgie. Welsh himself told me that he wasn't bothered by what I said and in fact thanked me for giving his program recognition and national exposure.

Years later, I spoke at the same banquet as Schultz, who was by that time executive director of the NCAA. I reminded him that he tried to get me fired and he said he didn't remember anything about it. I didn't believe him.

I think the real root of Schultz's contempt stemmed from some additional comments I made about the improbability of Virginia ever seriously competing for the national championship in football. Although Welsh's Cavaliers did briefly hold the top spot in the polls for one week during the 1990 season, I still feel that they are perennial national title longshots. And that would be with Georgie Welsh or Mister Jefferson on the home sideline.

Roone never said a word. He sent me a copy of Schultz's letter, which was his way of saying, "FYI. Carry on." The affair was dismissed.

Occasionally during my second stint at *ABC*, I earned the disfavor of other organizations, several of which had nothing to do with college athletics.

One memorable dust-up resulted from the time a sportswriter asked why I was figuratively divorcing Mary Tyler Moore, my longtime celebrity crush, and shacking up in my dreams with Stefanie Powers.

Without thinking, I responded, "well, Mary is getting older." The next day, the line appeared in the paper. The very next business day after that, a formal complaint from NOW, the National Organization of Women, arrived at *ABC* headquarters demanding that I be censured for sexist comments.

Although I was taken aback, it shouldn't have surprised me. The political correctness movement was really starting to gain momentum by the early 1980s. And I guess it was partially my fault. I kept forgetting that I was no longer just a rumpled publicist. I was now an on-air television personality who wore his prejudices against certain conferences and older women on his rumpled sleeve. Once you are on TV, everything changes. You wear a much bigger target on your back.

My name has appeared in print quite a bit over the years for my one-liners, but I had no idea of the amount of ink I'd get once Roone made the decision to put me on the air. When *ABC* officially announced my hiring in March 1982, it received a substantial amount of media coverage because I was the first non-athlete, non-coach, and non-professionally trained journalist to be analyzing football games in the studio.

Howard Cosell, the first to do so from the booth, suggested that I would be "the first unmade bed on television." I know he loved using that line, but I also think it was his way of trying to insulate me from the inevitable criticism that would be coming my way.

I did dozens of interviews with television writers across the country, but one of the pieces that resulted stands out. It was a column written about me by the *Washington Post's* David Remnick. While many writers focused on my appearance, Remnick was the most objective of all the writers when it came to analyzing my work thus far.

"Unfortunately, Cook's TV stints can occasionally resemble Bo Schembechler's bowl game performances. Cook has an admitted tendency to tighten up on the air, and what comes across to the global village is not the smartest-guy-in-the-saloon persona that is truly Cook's, but rather a slightly stiff recital of a well-reasoned thought."

I probably appeared tight and uncomfortable for two reasons. First, because of my inexperience with the technical aspects of the job, dealing with things like earpieces and mics. And second, because I was terrified of making factual errors. Too many people on television today, in my opinion, are more concerned with being clever and witty and delivering a funny line or creating controversy instead of making sure that what they are saying is correct. Facts have become casualties of the ratings wars.

I don't know why it's stuck with me all these years, but I'll never forget the time Chris Schenkel, this was during my first stint at *ABC* doing publicity, got the name of Bear Bryant's hometown wrong on national television. The next week we were flooded with letters. Whenever things like that happened, I realized two things: one, the smaller the town, the bigger the pride; and two, never forget that somebody is always paying attention to what you say.

So yes, in my pursuit of perfection I made quite a few rookie mistakes my first year, like looking at the wrong camera and other beginner's errors, but I took solace in John Wooden's observation that "the camera has made a fool out of all of us."

For the most part, the critics were kind. And when they weren't, I remembered my mother's advice when I was putting out *Pittsburgh Weekly Sports*: "Don't be like Hearst." Several of my colleagues, namely Cosell, were like the paranoid publishing magnate. He and many others imagined purported conspiracies and spoke openly and unabashedly of the double-standard that existed for those in the media. I didn't always agree with Cosell's tirades against the print media, but often, his views were correct.

As a fallible critic myself, I never put much stock in critics, especially after only one season on the job. After all, some of history's greatest successes endured less than complimentary initial reviews.

When Beethoven premiered his Fifth Symphony in 1808, the critics were unimpressed. It's now considered one of the greatest pieces of music ever written.

I remembered that the play "The Fantasticks," when it opened in 1960, received a poor review from the *New York Times.* Who knows, without that review, the play might have lasted 50 years on Broadway instead of only 42.

There was one particularly brutal review for a play in the 1940s. It went something like, "no jokes, no women, no chance." The play was "Oklahoma!"

My favorite flick, "Casablanca," was called "tolerable" by *The New Yorker*.

I remember reading in the *New York Times* a review of the country music variety show, "Hee Haw." The critic called the show "'Laugh-In' in a cornfield" and "ghastly." It aired for 25 years.

"I Love Lucy?" At first, the critics didn't. Early on, Lucille Ball received mixed results from the pundits.

And what about the little kid in Memphis who got a "C" grade in music and despite his passion for singing and playing the guitar, was told by a professional musician to not quit his day job, which was truck driving? Yes, that was Elvis.

Indeed, "it's not the critic who counts," said Teddy Roosevelt, "but the man in the arena." As my first season progressed, I learned some important lessons about critics and how to deal with both success and embarrassment.

Burt Lancaster once asked Lawrence Olivier how he ignored bad reviews.

"That's easy," said Olivier. "The tough part is ignoring the good ones."

I think that's great advice. In other words, don't take reviews or critics or yourself too seriously. That's important, especially when dealing with hate mail and fan mail.

I like to think that at this point of my life I am well insulated from most forms of criticism, but I will admit that one thing that did bother me tremendously was when I learned the reaction of some people at *CBS* when *ABC* hired me.

A triumvirate from *CBS* – Brent Musberger, executive Kevin O'Malley, and producer Ted Shaker – told Mike Francesa to watch me every time I was on the air and catalog all the mistakes I made. Francesa came to me. "They wanted me to give to them every mistake you made," Francesa told me. "They planned to give (the list) to members of the media."

That really pissed me off. These guys were trying to get people to knock me in print in hopes that a bunch of bad reviews would force Roone and *ABC* to fire me. But their plan ended up backfiring. Once I found out, I worked harder than ever to prove them wrong.

One media member they planned to give the list to was Rochester (NY) *Democrat and Chronicle* sports editor Rudy Martzke, now the media columnist for *USA Today*. Someone at *CBS* made the remark that the over/under on my stay at *ABC* was six weeks, and Martzke, who is basically a good guy, but cautious, advised to bet the under.

I enjoyed the last laugh at the end of the 1982 season. William Taaffe, in his "TV/RADIO" column in *Sports Illustrated*, paired up both networks in what he called the "TV Bowl" and attempted to decide the national champion of network television college football coverage. According to his scoring system, which awarded points for game coverage, announcing, pregame and halftime shows, *ABC* was the winner by the final score of 14-3

Due to my "shaky start" I was no where near in the running for MVP of the "TV Bowl," but I was happy to read that Taaffe considered me "the conscience of the college game." "The establishment's ire proves his merit," Taaffe added.

Most important of all, each of my four years at *ABC*, we had higher ratings than *CBS* for both the pregame and postgame shows, even the one year out of the four that *CBS* won the ratings for the games themselves. I don't want to make it sound as though I was personally responsible for these ratings victories, but it was a team effort and I felt I was an important member of that team.

I remember during the first two seasons, the game selection by *CBS* puzzled us. We thought they knew something we didn't. As it turned out, the people at *CBS* had no idea what they were doing. Again, that's something I could have helped with, but they didn't want me.

That network's incompetence aside, I think we beat *CBS* in the ratings because we focused on promoting college football as a sport, whereas *CBS* employed a tunnel-vision approach where they single-mindedly promoted nothing but *CBS*'s coverage of college football.

For example, in September 1982, Notre Dame played Michigan in the first night game in Notre Dame Stadium history. In their pregame show, *CBS* didn't say a word about the game. And they had a former Notre Dame coach, Ara Parseghian, there in the studio. Why? Because it was an *ABC* game. They pretended the game wasn't happening. It was ridiculous.

The following year, Auburn was playing Alabama in the first Iron Bowl after Bear Bryant's death. A Sugar Bowl berth was on the line for Auburn, too. Again, because *ABC* had the game, *CBS* ignored it. Yet the following week, we led off our pregame show with a discussion on the Nebraska-Oklahoma game even though it was a *CBS* game. I think the fans and viewers appreciated the fact that we put them, and the games, ahead of television politics.

Although I had attracted the attention of a whole slew of critics throughout my first few months, I had no idea where I stood with the most important one, Roone. I had received not so much as a single note from the Redhead. To tell you the truth, I was nervous. The one thing that comforted me was the knowledge that Roone would make a decision on his own. He didn't pay attention to the critics.

Finally, during a commercial on a Saturday afternoon late in the season, I heard the voice of my producer, Mike Pearl, in my earpiece. He sounded serious. He told me that he just got a call from Roone. I gulped and asked him what was said.

"Well," said Pearl, "he asked why you weren't on more."

Pearl, that motherfucker! Here I was, sweating my ass off, thinking that this was finally "the call." That was the first idea that I had that the Redhead was happy with me. You have no idea the amount of weight that this news lifted off my shoulders.

I got a two-year contract for 1983 and 1984. Not only that, my role was going to be expanded. "We feel one flaw was that (Beano) didn't have enough time to develop, elaborate and substantiate his points," Jim Spence told members of the media. Instead of being in the unemployment line like the guys at *CBS* and at the NCAA and Big Ten offices had hoped, I was going to get more airtime! It was a delicious development.

After '84, I got another one-year deal taking me through the 1985 season. It was only a one-year contract, but that was okay. All I ever wanted anywhere I worked was as many one-year contracts as Walter Alston got. Alston, the long-tenured manager of the Brooklyn and Los Angeles Dodgers, famously signed 23 consecutive one-year contracts to skipper the club from 1954 to 1976.

I can't thank Pearl, and Peter Englehart, my producer from '83 to '85, enough. I was very fortunate to have outstanding producers who were willing to put up with me, a neophyte. The secret of a great producer is not knowing what someone can do, but understanding what he can't do. Pearl and Englehart were excellent examples.

Despite the critics, the flubbed lines and dumb mistakes, the efforts at sabotage from my former colleagues at *CBS*, the letters from NOW, all the minor PR skirmishes and related entanglements, my four years on the air at *ABC* were a wonderful whirlwind.

When I landed in New York (I flew in from Pittsburgh every Thursday to work) there was a limo waiting to take me to the hotel, and when I returned on Sunday, there was a limo waiting to take me back to the airport.

At first, I shied away from the royal treatment. But after one weekend of taking a limo, I did some thinking and said to myself, *you'd have to be an absolute fool to turn this down.* And I really couldn't even if I had tried. With Roone, things were always first class across the board. You didn't have a choice.

I have a decent vocabulary and I can't come up with the right words to explain it all. There was nothing like working in network television in the 1980s. It was the highwater mark of the business in my opinion. At least it was for me. I am going to all these big games, staying in the nicest hotels, doing interviews, taking pictures with fans and signing autographs. And on top of it all, I had an expense account! It was unbelievable.

One moment in time does stand out for me. It was one of the biggest thrills I've received in this business. It took place while I was at *ABC*, during one of our late season road trips. After our show before the Auburn-Alabama game at Legion Field in 1983, a college student approached me and told me that when I came on the air, everybody in his fraternity house stopped what they were doing and listened to what I had to say. I was flattered, but immediately remembered Lawrence Olivier's wise words about the good reviews.

All good things must come to an end at some time, and for my run with *ABC*, that time was in early 1986. By the end of my fourth season at *ABC*, I could tell that some changes were in the air. Capital Cities Communications was purchasing the network and with that announcement, something told me my chances of a fifth campaign were slim.

I immediately thought back to the day Roone hired me in the spring of 1982. I didn't have any contract demands. I told him that he had every right to fire me, all I asked was that I was told of the decision before reading about it in the newspapers.

That's how I found out that I was fired from *KQV* in Pittsburgh in the Sixties. I read a brief in one of the Pittsburgh papers that the station was starting a new sports show with Pie Traynor at 8 a.m. I put the paper down, and a few seconds later, it finally registered. "Hey, that's when I'm on," I said out loud. Or, I sadly realized, used to be on. The long-time station manager, John Gibbs, didn't even have the courtesy to call me. Of course, what happened to me was better than what happened to Nellie King.

King, the former Pittsburgh Pirates' right-hander, also worked for the station after he retired from baseball. This was before he was paired up with Bob Prince on the Pirates' broadcasts on *KDKA*. King finished up work at *KQV* one day then went to play golf. Gibbs called his home and when King's young daughter answered, told her to tell her father that he had been fired. That's the lowest of all the low moves I've heard of at any level of the industry.

Getting fired is never an easy experience in any profession, but the way firings are handled in television has always been one of my biggest beefs with the business. One firing of mine that I still don't understand was when Joe Valerio kicked me off *ESPN's* "Sports Reporters" show. Apparently, he wasn't happy with my commentaries. I say apparently, because I never got a straight answer or explanation why I was booted from the show. I can only speculate.

If he wanted to get rid of me, he should have at least had the courtesy to tell me why. Or, prior to that, he could have told me what I was doing wrong or what he was unhappy about. Then if I don't change or we can't work it out, go ahead and fire me. That's his right. It's these kinds of things that boggle your mind. And it wasn't like we were strangers. I had worked with Valerio at *ABC*. Not only that, I helped him get his first job with the *New York Post*. So much for loyalty or appreciation. But that's television for you.

Back to 1986, my gut was right. On Friday, February 21, I got my phone call, as requested, from Roone and was told I was done. When I asked for a reason, I was told that management felt that there were too many voices on set. Mine needed to go.

I wasn't upset. The decision wasn't personal. It was a matter of the times. Besides, I couldn't be upset with *ABC* or Roone. The network took a chance on me. A big chance. When I got the job, I was probably the first guy over 50 to catch a break since Casey Stengel.

The first media member to solicit my reaction to the news was longtime *New York Post* columnist Phil Mushnick. In explaining my time at *ABC*, Mushnick was more gracious than any other writer and for that, I was grateful.

"Cook put substance over style," he wrote. "He worked to enlighten the viewer, not to please the NCAA. He took shots. He made bold, but highly calculated, predictions. He was newsy. He was offbeat. He cracked wise. He was a devout follower of the game. He was lots of fun. He was different."

If that was going to be the obituary for my on-air career, I couldn't have written it any better myself. At the time, I didn't know if that was the end of my on-air career. Linda Ellerbee, the talented and outspoken journalist, once said, "I don't listen to anybody in this business who hasn't been fired at least once." Although not by choice, I was now a member of that club.

It always hurts to be told you're not wanted, but *ABC's* decision didn't hurt me financially. I knew what I was getting into and planned accordingly. Since my new career had a level of job security similar to that of a leader of a South American country, I decided to defer part of my salary. It made sense. Although I didn't have to worry about being assassinated or the target of a coup, I was an old novice, having turned 51 just five days before my national TV debut. I knew it might not work out.

I could afford to defer my *ABC* salary because I had been working another job at the same time. After his pro career, Paul Martha, the All-American Pitt running back, worked as an attorney for the DeBartolos. He was basically Ed DeBartolo, Sr.'s right-hand man. When I moved back to Pittsburgh, Martha asked if I would be interested in doing PR for the Civic Arena Association. I would be doing publicity for events at the Arena, plus things involving the building's two tenants, the NHL's Penguins, and the Pittsburgh Spirit of the Major Indoor Soccer League, both of which were owned by the DeBartolos.

Since my *ABC* work was confined to weekends during football season, I thought it would be a perfect opportunity to pull two salaries at the same time. Martha set up an interview for me with both Senior and Junior over lunch. It went well until the part when I told Senior that maybe it wasn't illegal to raise ticket prices for 49ers games, but it certainly was immoral because of the big rise in television revenues. Poor Paul Martha almost choked on his sandwich. All I can figure is, Senior liked my blunt approach and my honesty because he ended up hiring me.

I worked for the DeBartolos for two largely uneventful years as vice president of public relations. About the best thing I can say about the job was the fact that it was the first and only time in my life I was a vice president of anything.

And outside of a few meetings I had to attend, I didn't have to report to an office regularly. I worked mostly from home, which made it easier to do radio and television hits during the day. In a way, I felt like a hooker. I never left the apartment and made money by using my big mouth. The only difference was, I usually had underwear on. That, and I paid taxes.

The most interesting part of the job for me was the opportunity to observe the day-to-day operations of a family dynasty like the DeBartolos up close. At times they could be frugal, and they ran the enterprise with iron fists. "My father and I would rather be in the soup line than have stockholders," Junior once told me.

I appreciated their commitment to honesty and especially the importance they placed on good public relations. They didn't put up with any bullshit. There was one memorable time Senior heard about suppliers giving two of his employees a kickback in the form of a trip to London for these men and their wives. When they got off the plane in London, a telegram was waiting for them. "You're fired," was all it said.

My best line of the experience was when I told a writer that the Penguins weren't as bad as people believed.

"They only lose two places," I said. "The United States and Canada."

I don't think I was well-liked by anybody affiliated with the Penguins, Spirit and then later the DeBartolo's ill-fated USFL franchise, the Pittsburgh Maulers. I was fired in 1984 when the organization hired a "money guy" to go over the books and find unnecessary expenses. Somewhere in the report, under the heading of "unnecessary expenses," it must have said "Beano Cook."

On my last day, there was a poem circulating around the office. I never found out who the author was, but it's one of the funniest things I've ever read.

"He came to us one day on a complimentary pass
And for the next two years would be a pain in the ass.
He dropped names by the bushel, like Cosell, Gifford...and Roone
And every Thursday he was home packing his clothes by noon.

He has helped turn three franchises completely around
One of them up and the other two down.
His secretaries can count on his call without fail
To see if he got any newspapers, checks or mail.

Now a lot of people think he is riding in on a white horse
To save the Maulers, who have steered off course.
But dear friends, for Beano has no remorse.
His first job with the Flashdancers is intercourse.

Now a few people will be choked up and cry
As they turn to him and say good-bye.
But you must remember that Mr. Cook is no jerk.
Who else can fall out of bed and wind up at work?"

I didn't have much time for reflection after getting my pink slip from *ABC*. Within two weeks, I had job offers from two different cable networks. Both looked inviting.

I weighed my options, balanced the pros and cons of each gig, considered my experiences over the previous four years, and reached a decision. I told my mother that I had accepted one of the offers and had decided to give the television business another shot. I'll never forget her response.

"A lot of people are going to be disappointed," she cracked, "that you're returning."

CHAPTER 11

One long coffee break.

The two cable networks that offered me jobs after I was fired from *ABC* were *CNN* and *ESPN*. At the time, *CNN* might have been the more prestigious gig, but I had a gut feeling that sports would always take a backseat to news at *CNN*. Working for Ted Turner didn't seem like it would be very much fun, either. Neither of those reasons, however, factored very heavily into my decision.

On the other side, I didn't decide on *ESPN* because I was confident that a 24-hour, all-sports cable channel was going to succeed. The folks up in Bristol, Connecticut were seven years into the experiment, but I still wasn't sold on the idea.

The opportunity to get some measure of revenge after being fired from *ABC* was appealing. See, when I went to *ESPN* I was technically working for the same company. Capital Cities, the new parent of *ABC*, owned 85% of *ESPN*. In a way, I felt like I had divorced one sister, broken into the house again, and somehow married the other.

And while I needed a job, the decision wasn't about money. *CNN* offered me a few bucks more than *ESPN*, but the amount was inconsequential. What both outfits offered in the way of salary was a lot more than I'd make pouring concrete, yet probably less than what an All-American running back commanded in the Southwest Conference at the time.

I declined *CNN's* offer for the same reason I declined the Lakers' PR job when it was offered to me in the early 1960s. It would have involved too much flying. In case I haven't made it clear enough already, I hate flying.

Now I'm not scared of flying like John Madden. I don't like turbulence, but who does? I simply dread everything that goes along with air travel. I can't stand the traffic at airports or the crowds. The gates are three miles apart. I always imagined myself as O.J. Simpson galloping through the concourse with his briefcase in those old Hertz commercials, but with my clipboard and papers flying everywhere I probably looked more like Bronko Nagurski rumbling through a blizzard.

You're always hurrying and waiting, two things I hate. Airports reminded me too much of the army, where we had a saying, "hurry up and wait." That's all you do. You hurry up and wait for taxis, at the ticketing counter, to get through security, to board, and to pick up your luggage. That's if it shows up.

By the time I reached my middle fifties, it had gotten to the point that every decision I made could be traced directly or indirectly to how much flying was involved. Every decision.

Believe it or not, the only person I consulted on this important, career-altering decision in March of 1986 was the woman at the Delta Airlines ticketing desk at the airport in Pittsburgh who answered when I called to ask what the differences in distances and flight times were when flying from Pittsburgh to Atlanta and Pittsburgh to Hartford. The flight from Pittsburgh to Hartford, I was told, was shorter by about an hour.

That one hour, plus the fact that I wouldn't have to deal with the airport in Atlanta, was why I went to work for *ESPN*. That airport is so big and always so insanely busy, every time I connected in Atlanta I felt like I was participating in the fucking fall of Saigon. So, it was more or less pure luck that I got involved with *ESPN*. Looking back on how things worked out, I think it was a providential development for both parties.

How and why the folks in Bristol came to offer me a job, that's another good story. It's a convoluted one and, like many of the best stories in my life, it involves college football and sports betting.

The two individuals responsible for bringing me to *ESPN* are two of the people who I think deserve a lot of the credit for creating the *ESPN* empire, Steve Bornstein and Bill Creasy.

I got to know Bill Creasy about a decade before I went to *ESPN*. This was when I was working for *CBS* in New York. Every Friday during this time, this was in the late 1970s, a group of people used to get together at Mike Manuche's place on West 52nd Street. One of the great hangouts, it was a steak joint, a magnet for people in sports and the media.

This group was basically a collection of sportswriters and television people. On the surface, everybody got together because of sports and our jobs, but when you got right down to it the real reason was betting. Creasy showed up because he liked to bet. He was looking for tips.

I've been involved in lunch groups my entire life. We had a little lunch gang at Kiski when I was in prep school. There were pow-wows at luncheonettes in Pittsburgh when I was the SID at Pitt, and at various places in New York when I went to work for *ABC* Sports in the 1960s. I told you about the group in VISTA, too.

I have a group in Pittsburgh I get together with even today. We eat in a deli in the building on Stanwix Street where the studio I shoot my weekly hits for *ESPN* News is located. We have writers and editors from the Pittsburgh papers, individuals like Terry Shields, Chuck Finder, Colin Dunlap, Kevin Gorman, Brian O'Neill, and Paul Zeise, plus radio personalities like Mark Madden and Ellis Cannon. There are other regulars like Kenny Scholtz, Upper St. Clair football coach Jim Render and his son, J.T.

Betting isn't the sole reason this particular group exists, it's built more around the conversations and the camaraderie, but I like the lunches because they provide an opportunity for me to get out of my apartment and engage in my personal pastime, which is holding court.

These groups were more common many years ago. It was what you did back before the Internet and cell phones. Part of it was because people liked getting together to bullshit without their wives looking over their shoulders.

Another part of it was that people who bet were worried that the Feds were looking over their shoulders, or rather listening in on their phone calls, because of how Bobby Kennedy started using the Interstate Commerce Act to go after organized crime and betting. Back then, we shared information by word of mouth, whereas people do that online today.

One of my favorite lunch groups was the small gang of bettors that I was a part of when I worked for the Miami Dolphins. Every Friday during football season, myself, Rich Podolsky, Mike Pearl, Hank Goldberg, and Jim Johnson, who handled promotions for the team, got together for lunch at a place called the Everglades Hotel. It wasn't far from the Dolphins' front office headquarters on Biscayne Boulevard.

It was a working lunch. The work, of course, was the weekend's games. I gave the college picks for Saturday and Goldberg did the pro picks for Sunday. We each picked five games. It was a small group, but with my flair for dramatics, I turned it into a big production.

I gave my first four picks one after the other, then habitually paused right before giving out the fifth, which was my special, or lock of the week. I needed my ice cream to make my final pick. At that fateful moment, in order to create as much suspense as I could, I hollered for our regular waiter, Emilio, to bring out the ice cream. "Emilllio," I would yell, rolling the l's for effect. Everybody in the joint could hear me. It was a great gag.

One weekend I caught fire. I went four for five. Right after, Rich Podolsky ran into Pearl, who was down in the dumps. Podolsky asked him what was wrong, but he couldn't get a word out of Pearl.

Pearl, as most of his friends and colleagues know, has always been an interesting individual. Part of it is due to his appearance. Nobody would ever mistake him for the kind of guys who appeared in *GQ*. He typically wore ill-fitting suits or khakis and shirts that looked as though they'd never been introduced to an iron.

And the guy is unusually quiet. For example, I remember hearing about one famous meeting that took place regarding the Olympics during the 1980s. It might have been for the Sarajevo or Calgary games when Pearl was at *ABC*. There were a bunch of TV people, plus a handful of Russians, present. Pearl was so quiet, and looked so serious, some of the media people who didn't know who he was were so unnerved they thought he was with the K.G.B.!

Podolsky found Pearl looking more disheveled and serious than usual.

"What's bugging you?" Rich asked him. "Beano went four for five."

"Yes," groused Pearl. "But what Beano giveth on Saturday, Goldberg taketh on Sunday."

Back to New York and Manuche's, there was one Friday in the fall of 1978 when I delivered a virtuoso performance that surpassed my acts with Emilio at the Everglades Hotel. My lock of the week was No. 5 Penn State, which was getting six points at Ohio State. I loudly proclaimed that not only would Joe Paterno's Lions cover, they'd win straight up. And they did. They shut out No. 6 Ohio State, 19-0. Creasy, who won $5,000 on Penn State, went out of his way to thank me for the pick the following Friday.

Okay. It's a year later, and *ESPN* is in its infancy. Who's one of the first people the network hires? Creasy. And who does he bring with him? Bingo – Bornstein.

I'm convinced that Penn State pick had something to do with my landing at *ESPN* seven years later. Bornstein might have hired me on account of a strong recommendation from Creasy, the basis of which was his confidence in my ability to pick games. As I'm going to explain in a little bit, this would cause some friction between Creasy and myself when he came up with the idea for "College GameDay," but it put me on his, and by extension Bornstein's, radar.

By early 1986, Steve Bornstein was the SVP, senior vice president, in charge of all programming and production at *ESPN*. He got his start in television working at a station in Columbus and later produced Ohio State football games in the 1970s for an early cable operation. He knew college football. It made perfect sense to these two guys, when I was fired from *ABC*, to go after me. The timing, I might add, was absolutely perfect for all involved, too.

When *ESPN* went on the air in 1979, there was very little live programming because they didn't have enough money to pay rights fees for the major sports. In the early days, the network survived on Australian Rules Football, bass fishing, ping pong tournaments and other obscure sports.

ESPN slowly started growing its subscriber base by thinking outside-the-box in terms of supplementing its programming with highlight shows, airing tape delay games and televising non-traditional sporting events like the NFL Draft.

Yet things weren't happening fast enough for Steve Bornstein, who had a fucking temper. He could be a real ballbuster. And he exhibited plenty of bravado when he boasted that *ESPN* would one day have the NFL, MLB, and many other major sporting events, but what made him in my mind such a brilliant executive was that he knew that the network needed to summit some smaller mountains before conquering those professional sports peaks. He understood that the first steps on the company's climb to the top were college sports.

It's no exaggeration to say that it was college sports, not "SportsCenter" nor any of the other marquee shows, not the NFL Draft or anything like that, that built *ESPN* into the powerhouse it is today. After all, *CNN's* "Sports Tonight" was killing "SportsCenter" in the ratings. That's why John Walsh was brought in as a consultant.

The network first tasted success with college basketball. *ESPN* expanded into college football by airing tape delay games, but after the landmark Supreme Court ruling in 1984, now had the option to televise games live. And that's when things really started taking off.

"The CFA on *ESPN*" was the network's highest rated series in 1984 and 1985. When my hiring was announced on March 11, 1986, *ESPN* and the CFA were already in negotiations for an extension of their agreement that would call for *ESPN* to start doing prime time games as well. This deal would go through the 1990 season.

It was a pivotal point in the network's history and bringing me to Bristol was a big part of the plan. My role was to do for *ESPN's* college football coverage what Dick Vitale had done for the network, in terms of increasing national visibility, with college hoops.

I liked what I was hearing. Who wouldn't have? Bornstein wanted *ESPN* to be the network of college football much like Roone did when he got the package for *ABC* in 1966, and I was basically going to be the face of our coverage. The season preview show was titled "Beano Cook on College Football" and I would be doing pregame and postgame shows, too.

My first season went reasonably well. We enjoyed good ratings, no major hiccups, and I got plenty of good press thanks to Rosa Gatti, Mike Soltys, and the hardest-working publicity department in television.

We didn't make the big splash everybody was looking for until the following fall. That's where Creasy comes in again. Over the years, various sources have credited me for the creation of "College GameDay," but that's probably because I was the show's most enthusiastic defender during its early years. Creasy, though, deserves the credit for coming up with the idea for the show.

We had a pregame show in 1986. It was called "College Football Scoreboard." Larry Burnett and I did the show. My problem with the show was its length. It was only thirty minutes. One of the things that attracted me to cable in the first place was the belief that I'd have more time to talk. I wanted more time for features and for commentaries.

Creasy and I were both singing from the same hymnal here. He realized that we had a late morning window of programming opportunity to grab viewers since *ABC* and *CBS* had largely given up on the idea of a college football pre-game show. To those networks, only the games mattered.

Bornstein greenlit the idea and "College GameDay" went on the air for the first time at the start of the 1987 season. Today it's one of *ESPN's* flagship productions, but it wasn't a slam dunk success from the start. Early on, one unimpressed sportswriter told me it looked low-budget, "like something filmed in somebody's garage."

Nobody knew what time the show was on, and with the exception of my mother, Tim Brando's wonderful wife Terri, a handful of bookies and the fanbase of the Orlando Renegades, nobody knew who was on the show, either.

So, how did "College GameDay" become the phenomenon it is today, one of the highest-rated shows on the network year in and year out?

It started with people. We had not just high-quality people working on the show, but the right people working on it. That makes a world of difference in television. You can have the best and the brightest in the business, but if they all aren't on the same page, and committed to a common goal, it doesn't matter.

On the production side, Terry Lingner, Mike Vettor and Tom Reilly were the perfect choices to fuse Creasy's vision and Bornstein's direction with my ideas. We had so many outstanding people working on college football, on games and studio production, during this time, names such as John Wildhack, Marc Payton, Fred Gaudelli, Dave Miller, and Chip Dean.

The hiring of Lee Corso, the only original cast member on the show today, was extremely important. I'll never forget the first time I met the former Louisville, Indiana, and Northern Illinois head coach.

"There are three things I will not talk about under any circumstances," Corso said while shaking my hand. "Politics, religion and pass defense!"

We hit it off immediately. I loved working with Lee. Out of all the former coaches and athletes I've worked with, he stands out as a coach the way Doug Flutie (who I worked with briefly at *ABC*), Craig James and Mike Adamle stand out as former players. None of them took themselves so seriously that we couldn't have a good time.

And not to take any credit away from Lee and his many important contributions to the show over the years, but what you see on "GameDay" today in terms of Lee's role on the show, that might have been a result of some of the things I did. Part of me and my shtick, that had to have rubbed off on him. In those early years, Lee played the straight man while I handled the comic relief. I was the one who dressed up in the mascot outfits and did the silly skits.

I might also add that what you see now when Lee makes his famous headgear picks at the end of the show, that was a very close approximation of what Creasy originally intended for "GameDay." He wanted to recreate the way I used theatrics and suspense in making my picks at Manuche's and the Everglades Hotel on television.

I felt he wanted the show to be the college football version of "The NFL Today." I understood that it was a successful formula to copy, but I didn't want to do something that's already been done. When Creasy wanted me to do more picks, I made it clear I didn't want to be pigeonholed in that role. I didn't want to be Beano the Greek. Eventually, we came to an understanding and Norm Hitzges was brought on as the show's handicapper.

The guy who made it all look like a smooth, well-oiled operation (when in reality it was anything but) was my good friend Tim Brando. He is one of the most versatile talents the business has ever known.

Whether he's in the studio or the announcer's booth, doing radio or TV, he can do it all. From the beginning, I knew he was a five-tool player, that he would do it all. I felt like an old journeyman on the San Francisco Seals who would be able to tell people years later that he had spent a season or two playing with DiMaggio.

Brando, who was hand-picked by Bornstein to be his "college guy" at *ESPN*, was the perfect first host for the show. A southerner from Shreveport, SEC country, he knew college football. He had great screen presence. I called him "Baby Brent" due to his poise, which reminded me of Musberger's.

There was more to him than what people saw on the air, too. Brando made significant contributions to the lay out and organization of the show. The two of us logged many long hours putting the show together.

A typical college football weekend at *ESPN* in the late 1980s started on a Thursday or Friday. I used to fly up from Pittsburgh and Howie Schwab would pick me up at the airport with a 12-pack of Diet Dr. Pepper, my fuel for the weekend.

Tim and I would hammer out the scripts on Friday. Early on Saturday morning, we'd go over last-minute changes and rehearse some lines over breakfast at the Holiday Inn. We did the show, then after a full day of games the whole crew went to the White Birch Bar. We typically closed this joint down at two o'clock in the morning.

For all intents and purposes, what you watch on Saturday mornings today stems from all the experimenting we did and conversations we had during those grueling, but incredibly productive and fun 20-hour days.

I used to say that "College GameDay" was *ESPN's* Manhattan Project. Me, Brando, Corso, Lingner, Vettor, Reilly and a few others were the mad scientists out in the desert who built the first, primitive atomic bomb. The people who worked on the show after it went on the road and exploded in popularity, they continued our work and developed the H-bomb.

Brando and I got along very well. He liked to laugh and have fun. He didn't take himself seriously and since neither Corso nor I did, that made him an ideal teammate. "GameDay" wasn't the top of the mountain to him, either. He wanted to do play-by-play more than anything else, so he wasn't concerned about being the star of the show or putting his stamp on it, making it his personal property, at the expense of everybody else.

He did the sideline reporter gig, he did "GameDay," he did "SportsCenter" with John Saunders, he did everything asked of him at *ESPN* and he did it well, but he always had his eye on another goal, and I respected him for that.

Even more than his innate talent and easy-going attitude, I appreciated Brando because he wasn't a know-it-all who would try to change me. He knew I was a goofball, what my limitations were, and worked around them.

For his part, he was a great student. I don't want to make it sound like I taught him anything, but I could tell he paid attention when I was talking. For example, he listened to what I said about scores.

There are three things American male sports fans can't get enough of: scores, sex, and late scores. One thing that all announcers should do, I used to tell him, was when giving scores, give the score of the winning team first. People who bet appreciate this. In the big picture it's a small thing, but small things are the building blocks to big things.

Brando paid attention, worked at it and that's how he became the best at giving scores, doing highlights, since Cosell. He took the same approach in crafting his trade doing play-by-play and that's why he's one of the most recognizable voices in all of sports broadcasting today.

I'll admit that when Chris Fowler took over as host of "GameDay" in 1990, I had my doubts that it was going to work. Now I wasn't doubting his ability or his work ethic (both of which were evident from the get-go), but how he'd fit in terms of team chemistry. He seemed so much more serious than Brando. He wasn't the natural-born entertainer that Brando was. I don't know if he would have flown out to South Bend and belted out the Victory March in front of the Notre Dame team like Brando did after losing our on-air bet on the outcome of the Notre Dame-Miami game in 1988.

I thought he was just another articulate young gun out to make a name for himself. When you're an older guy on television and you get paired up with some young kid, there's a strong urge to think, whether it's Lampley, Brando, Fowler, or anybody else, that they're a prima donna. In each of those cases, I was proven dead wrong.

In Chris's case, I quickly learned that he was a big college football fan. He was a true student of the game and everything that made it so special. I discovered that we had that love of the sport in common. That's why, as I've said in these pages previously, that I think both Brando and Fowler would be ideal in the role of college football's first commissioner. They genuinely care about the game.

The show survived in those early years because of the camaraderie and chemistry exhibited between the hosts and the commentators. And, I think more than anything else, because of our passion. On the production side, the pieces can be interchangeable. Talent-wise, "College GameDay" has never been a one-size-fits-all deal. I've said it a million times: baseball might be the national pastime, but college football is our national passion. To cover it, it must be in your blood. No matter how talented, you can't just plug the best columnist at the *New York Times* or the Capitol Hill reporter from the *Washington Post* into the college football beat at *Sports Illustrated* and expect them to be Dan Jenkins.

Likewise, you can't host "GameDay" as a reserved observer with a monotone voice, like you're Chet Huntley anchoring election night coverage in the 1960s. You've got to display energy and passion for the game, and Fowler did. His energy and passion were authentic.

Fowler's father was a professor at Penn State, so he got hooked while going to games at Beaver Stadium in the early 70s. Many years later, after Joe Paterno diagrammed a play he had run at Brown in 1949 on the back of a paper placemat during a lunch in State College, Fowler surreptitiously swiped the placemat, folded it up and put it in his pocket. He owns an original Catholics vs. Convicts t-shirt and other artifacts. He appreciates the history.

I think that Fowler is *ESPN's* MVP – most valuable personality. Not just in college football coverage. I mean at the company. Across all sports. Over the years, a lot of people at *ESPN* have gotten quite a bit of notoriety and acclaim. And at the same time Fowler has been overlooked. That's probably because he's never depended on catchphrases or other gimmicks in his work.

Fowler was hired four months after me in 1986 and I think it was the most important talent hire in the history of the company. Nobody else could do so many different things like college football, college basketball, horse racing, Grand Slam tennis tournaments, and "The X Games," and at the consistently high level at which he's done them over the past 25 years.

Even if you ignore all that and focus only on "GameDay," that would justify whatever he's paid. Just like Brando, he never tried to be the star. I, for one, am glad he's stayed in that chair as long as he has. He's been a constant, guiding voice for the show for 20 years.

And speaking of voices, for the record, Chris does the best impression of yours truly. If you ever run into him, ask him to do it. I don't know where I'll be, but rest assured that like the Gipper, I'll know about it. And I'll hear him!

Bob Carpenter took over for Brando. He was the show's host for one year, before Fowler settled into the role like FDR settled into the Oval Office. I don't think Bob did a bad job, not at all, but we just didn't have the same chemistry that I had with Brando and Fowler.

In addition to chemistry, continuity is a big deal in this business. Bornstein getting the Brando, Fowler and Corso hires right meant nothing if we didn't get the Craig James and Kirk Herbstreit hires right, too. A bridge is built in sections that must connect. Just by watching them I could tell that a seat on the "College GameDay" set wasn't merely a job or a rung on the employment ladder for those two former players – it was an honor and a privilege.

The same can be said on the production side. Taking over for Lingner, Vettor and Reilly, Barry Sacks and Steve Vecchione led the show to arguably its greatest heights. Researcher Chris Fallica has been a cornerstone of the show for going on 20 years. Producers like Craig Lazarus, Lee Fitting and Michael Fountain, a fellow Pitt alum, maintain the show's founding principles and high standards today.

My only complaint with the show in its current form is that the suits who give the orders from on high seem intent on monkeying with our original formula. They have a lot more money to work with than we had, so obviously production values are much higher, but to this fan watching at home there's too much reliance on the carnival and tailgating atmosphere and too much of an emphasis on style over substance in terms of the pieces we do.

They have a lot more time than we had, too, but I don't think they are using it wisely. They don't think the history is important, at least not important enough for a full feature, anymore.

More than anything else, really, they are playing mainly to the sport's younger, diehard fans, instead of trying to attract new viewers across a wide spectrum of demographics. When I was on the show, and even later after I left Bristol but still had the ear of the people running it, it was important to me that we had a little something for everybody each week.

As anybody who ever sat in on the production meetings or conference calls will tell you, my recurring line was, "when we get to the Ds, there's some guy in Missouri who is thinking about going outside and cutting his grass before the early games come on. Our goal should be to keep him watching for a few more minutes. Because if he does, he'll tune in for the full hour next week. And he'll tell his brother-in-law to tune in, too."*

Every week, we worked hard to serve a smorgasbord of content. I remember one year, we put together a montage of big hits in the lead-up to the Miami-Florida State game to the "New Kids on the Block" song, "Hangin' Tough." That was for the younger fans. We then pivoted to older viewers and did a great interview piece with Johnny Pont and Weeb Ewbank prior to the 100th anniversary of the Miami of Ohio-Cincinnati game.

We made sure we blanketed the country geographically by touching on all the conferences. We even tried to attract female viewers. I remember a short feature we did on the Duke quarterback who worked as an extra in the movie "Bull Durham."

One of my favorite features was the one we did on the origin of the famous "Puntrooskie" trick play that Bobby Bowden pulled out to beat Clemson in 1988. I said that the play was the best since "My Fair Lady," but I had no idea where it came from.

Thanks to Lee Corso, we found out that Bowden got the play from Kentucky coach Jerry Claiborne, who in turn got it from Bum Phillips, who had first used it when he worked for Bear Bryant in 1952. We got Phillips in front of a camera and, as always, Bum provided great sound.

Pieces like that, that had homespun stories, humor, history, and chalkboard material, are a great example of how you can please the fanatics, but not overwhelm the casual viewers with so much technical content, X's and O's, that you scare them off.

Interspersed throughout the hour, there would be a clip of me leading the Arkansas cheerleaders in the "Wooooo, pig! Sooie!" cheer or dressed up in the Penn State Nittany Lion mascot's costume while being hunted in the woods by West Virginia's Mountaineer. I believe that kind of campy content endeared the show to viewers.

And while I didn't want to be a tout, I'd make sure there was a reason for the bettors to tune in. I used to pick three or four games a show and I was right quite often. When I was wrong, we made fun of my picks through some funny segments.

---

* I don't know if it's still the case, but at one time scripts for sports television pre-game shows were typically laid out in alphabetical blocks in order to arrange content according to available air-time. The content at the top of the show is found in the "A" block, aka. the "As." The "Bs" commence after the first commercial, and so forth.

Yet if I had to list my most valuable contributions to "College GameDay," the picks wouldn't even make the list. The editorial guidance and supervision that I gave, my emphasis on history, the way I pushed for longer features, the funny gags that I did, all of that is my "GameDay" legacy.

There is one more thing I'd also like to be remembered for, and that's my unwavering faith. At times, I might have been the only individual at *ESPN* who believed in the show and its potential. That might just be the reason why the show is still on the air today.

The rumors that the show was foundering in the early 1990s were not true. My opinion was that the show's growth was being stymied, not that it was dying. To the best of my knowledge, we were not in danger of being canceled. Not that it couldn't have happened. I wasn't so much concerned with any knee-jerk decisions our people might have made with the show. The thing I feared most was that we would become just popular, or successful, enough that somebody at *ABC* or *CBS* would take notice and then one of those networks would put a competing show in the same time slot and pound us because they had unlimited resources.

So, I began pushing to take the show on the road. To me that was the only way to ensure the show's growth, and therefore its survival. We had already succeeded in doing something that had never been done before, a one-hour pre-game and magazine show devoted exclusively to college football, but we needed to double down on the idea, to take it further.

Taking a pre-game show on the road on a weekly basis during the regular season was something that had never been done before on television with any sport, but I believed that college football was the sport that could make it work. Why?

Consider that college football is the only major sport in which schedules are released 10 to 15 years in advance. That's because college football fans are the only fans that plan their lives around their sport. They first consult the schedules before planning homecoming trips, holiday travel, vacations, and even weddings.

Plus, there's a uniquely festive atmosphere for college football games that not even the tailgating in pro football can match. Other sports have seasons and games; college football has events. I knew college football fans, especially the students, would go wild for the idea.

And it wasn't just some gut feeling on my part. I had numbers to back me up. I had seen our ratings at *ABC* when we took our pre-game show on the road for big, season-ending games between ranked teams, such as Arkansas at Texas in '82 and Alabama-Auburn in '83. They were significantly higher than what we got in the studio in September and October.

And technically, we had done it before at *ESPN* and pulled good numbers. Contrary to popular belief, the Florida State-Notre Dame game in 1993 wasn't the first time "College GameDay" was shot outside the studio. We did the show in Miami when Miami and Oklahoma played for the 1987 national title in the Orange Bowl. The following

January, we did the show from Tempe, Arizona when Notre Dame played West Virginia in the Sunkist Fiesta Bowl.

I also thought taking the show on the road would be a boon to the company at large. Being on-site at the game of the week would send a message – to our viewers, to the fans, to the NCAA, to America – that *ESPN* was committed to being the network of college football. I knew how the people on the NCAA football TV committee thought. It would show them that we meant business. And business is, after all, what everything comes down to. Such a move could have big benefits for the company in terms of future rights deals and building *ESPN's* brand.

Of course, the decision-makers at *ESPN* weren't thinking about future rights deals or branding. Pre-occupied with the rollout of *ESPN2* and other expansion efforts, they were thinking in the present-day and were worried about the company's bottom-line at that moment. They believed that it would have been prohibitively expensive, and a drain on our limited physical resources, crews and trucks and what have you, to do the show remotely week in and week out.

I understood those concerns, but if you remember the story about the CoSIDA convention in Lubbock, when I got three haircuts in three days from a beautician to get her to agree to go out with me, or the way I hammered the suits at *CBS* about the receptionist or the NFL maps, you know that I don't give up easily. I kept badgering everyone who would listen to me, as well as many who didn't want to, and eventually Steve Bornstein, now president of *ESPN*, signed off on the idea in the fall of 1993.

What ultimately triggered the decision? I don't know for certain. Mine wasn't the only voice crying out in the Connecticut wilderness (Bill Creasy had been arguing to take the show on the road, too), but it was definitely the loudest. Perhaps it was a case of my persistence finally paying off. Or maybe I'd just finally found the right set of ears.

Unlike many in this business, I have enough humility to understand that none of my most monumental accomplishments in television would have been possible without the assistance of some good friends and high-ranking allies.

Texas-Arkansas in 1969 wouldn't have happened without Roone. I wouldn't have succeeded in changing the NFL maps at *CBS* without Terry O'Neil and Van Gordon Sauter. And I don't think I would have been successful in convincing *ESPN* to take "College GameDay" on the road if my friend Howard Katz hadn't been working for *ESPN* at the time.

I've known Katz since he started in television, when he came to work for Roone as a PA at *ABC* in 1971 after graduating from Colgate. Katz, one of the great minds and great guys in the business, was working his way up the production ranks at *ABC* when Barry Frank lured him away to work at IMG's Trans World International. There, he was responsible for putting blockbuster shows like "Battle of the Network Stars" on the air.

The executive experience Katz gained at TWI was very attractive to Don Ohlmeyer when he hung out his own shingle and started Ohlmeyer Communications Company in the early 1980s. Katz ran OCC for ten years until Ohlmeyer sold the company to *ESPN*. After six hugely successful years in Bristol, Katz ascended to Roone's old job, the presidency of *ABC* Sports, less than 20 years after he had first joined the company out of college.

Katz rebuilt and rejuvenated the *ABC* Sports brand by renewing some key rights deals and making major personnel moves, and once his mission there was accomplished, he went to work for the NFL. He is now known as the NFL's master scheduler. If you built a Mount Rushmore of the most important sports TV executives of the latter half of the 20th Century, Katz's face would be on there with Roone, Ebersol, and Bornstein.

For me, the timing of Katz's arrival at *ESPN* was divine intervention. See, when *ESPN* acquired OCC, it also acquired Katz. He was named EVP, executive vice president, of production at *ESPN* in May 1993. That meant he was in charge of all remote and studio productions for the company's domestic and international activities.

The only person that Bornstein deferred to, and this might have been in his entire career, was Don Ohlmeyer. And here to my rescue, after years of running into a brick wall, comes the greatest of godsends, Ohlmeyer's guy. It was unbelievable. I probably strained our friendship to the limit by bugging him about taking "GameDay" on the road, but I'll always be grateful that Katz never hung up on me.

So, besides Howard Katz's heavyweight influence, how and why did it all finally happen in November 1993? We needed a big enough game to justify the leap of faith that I was asking our people to take. The stars finally lined up that year when No. 1 Florida State traveled to South Bend, Indiana to play No. 2 Notre Dame.

The hype for the game started in the summer and just kept building until it finally reached a crescendo in November. By the time the match-up of the two undefeateds was locked-in, we were going to have plenty of people and resources committed to covering the game anyway, so it made sense to go all-in and do the first regular-season road show there.

We did the show live from inside the Joyce Center across the street from Notre Dame Stadium the morning of the game and did hits on "SportsCenter" throughout the weekend. The crowd huddled around our set wasn't sure what was going on, and the media reviews were mixed, but a turning point had been reached. The feeling among those who worked on that telecast, as well as those back in Bristol, was that the show's future was on the road.

"GameDay" returned to Notre Dame the following September, the first of six road shows *ESPN* would do in 1994. The show would wander farther and farther from Bristol in the coming years, averaging roughly ten remotes per season for the remainder of the decade.

On November 8, 1997, "Judgment Day," another historic milestone was reached when *ESPN* sent a crew to each location hosting the two games involving four top-five teams. The regular "GameDay" crew of Fowler, Corso and Herbstreit traveled to Chapel Hill for No. 3 Florida State at No. 5 North Carolina.

A few hundred miles north in Central Pennsylvania, myself, Mike Adamle, and

Steve Cyphers set up shop with a satellite "GameDay" set to cover No. 2 Michigan versus No. 4 Penn State. It was an impressive feat of logistics and production prowess that I was proud to be a part of.

It was also as great a "told you so" moment as I've enjoyed in my career. After the resounding 34-8 Michigan victory, Wolverines fans crowded our set and began singing "The Victors." Between hits, as we're bouncing from Bristol to Chapel Hill to State College, I turned around and waved my arms like a conductor during a symphony. These were fans from the road team, it was a cold, damp night, and they were having a blast. I was right. People were going wild for the road shows.

On the ride home to Pittsburgh the next day, it occurred to me that the show was now ten years old. I was one of only two people, along with Lee Corso, who had been on the first show in 1987, the first road broadcast from the 1988 Orange Bowl, the first regular-season road show at Notre Dame in 1993, and the only dual-set telecast in the show's history.

Not long after the dawn of the new millennium, "College GameDay" would be on the road every week of every season starting in late August through the BCS title game. It took a decade for everyone and everything to catch up to my vision, and some invaluable assistance from Howard Katz, Bobby Bowden, and Lou Holtz, but the show was now being beamed from sets teeming with college kids into millions of living rooms, dorm rooms, fraternity houses, sportsbooks, bars, military bases, and other far-flung places around the planet.

Not bad for something that once looked like it was shot in somebody's garage, right?

* * *

In my opinion, the three greatest places and eras to work in television history were at *CBS* News under Murrow and Cronkite, *ABC* Sports under Roone Arledge in the 1960s and 70s, and at *ESPN* from the late 1980s through the early 1990s. I consider myself extremely fortunate that I can say that I was a part of two of those legendary operations.

Now I didn't feel that way about *ESPN* from the beginning. At first, after spending all my life in television working in New York and especially after working for Roone at *ABC* where you took limos everywhere and stayed at fancy hotels, I felt like a veteran who had been sent down to the minor leagues.

That was mainly because of Bristol. Small and sleepy, it was the opposite of the show, the Big Apple. I was used to walking down Sixth Avenue among the skyscrapers when I went in to work at *ABC* and *CBS*. One of the first things you noticed when you showed up at the *ESPN* compound, other than the satellite dishes, was the junkyard across the street.

I don't mean to knock the town, the company or anybody with these comments. I'm merely communicating my observations and personal feelings. Perhaps a more appropriate analogy was that I had been traded to an expansion team. Of course, by the time I got there in 1986, *ESPN* wasn't the '62 Mets. Far from it.

The front office was staffed by experienced executives like Bill Grimes, a *CBS* alum, and Chet Simmons, who had helped Roone develop "Wide World" and was later the first president of *NBC* Sports.

There were senior production people who had built impressive résumés at the legacy networks. People like Bill Fitts, who worked for Jack Dolph and Bill McPhail, and Scotty Connal, who made the call at *NBC* News to televise Lee Harvey Oswald's prison transfer, which is why we have footage of Jack Ruby shooting Oswald.

Most of the talent, apart from guys like Jim Simpson, was at this point still largely unknown, but as the world would eventually find out, it was major league caliber. Every person in every department, across the board, was hard-working and extremely hungry.

I felt that I fit well with this group. Norman Chad wrote in the *Washington Post* that I looked more comfortable on the air at *ESPN* than I did at *ABC* because my "rumpled on-air presence seems to suit cable TV better than network TV. He actually looks like he should be installing your cable TV rather than starring on it."

One of the reasons *ESPN* succeeded early on was because they hired people who looked like me. I'm talking about people who weren't necessarily made for TV, but were experts in their field, people who knew what they were talking about. Roy Firestone, Dick Vitale, Mel Kiper and Corso are some other names who fit this mold. None of us are handsome enough to be cast as the villain on "Columbo."

Another is Pete Axthelm. Ax was a phenomenal writer who knew his stuff, but his disheveled appearance, somebody once said, was "more appropriate in front of the windows at Aqueduct and Yonkers than it was in front of a camera." Yet he helped *ESPN* win one of the network's very first sports Emmys, for "NFL GameDay," now called "Sunday NFL Countdown," in 1988.

As *ESPN* started growing by leaps and bounds, I think the suits fell into the predictable trap of hiring prominent jocks, perfectly-groomed personalities and good-looking women.

While some things might have been low-budget and took a little getting used to after my previous work experiences, I truly loved the work environment at *ESPN*. There was a sense of teamwork and togetherness that I hadn't felt since I was at *ABC* Sports in the late 1960s. Most of the employees were upbeat, happy workers excited to be part of what was being built in Bristol. Now it was a highly competitive environment as well, but to paraphrase Oddball in the great 1970s World War II flick "Kelly's Heroes," there were no negative waves, man.

Everybody worked hard and they partied hard. There was a lot of drinking and betting going on. Fucking, too. The atmosphere was, how should I say it, very permissive. In some cases, probably too permissive.

I'm not going to get into the stuff regarding the drugs and sexual harassment because I didn't have any involvement in either of those things and because I wasn't there full-time. Remember, I was only in Bristol on the weekends. Besides, others have wrote extensively on that stuff. Again, I'm not writing a "tell-all" book here. It's a "tell-some," with my primary purpose being to share some great stories, behind-the-scenes information, and laughs.

Another reason that I – someone who has clashed with authority his entire life, from the headmasters in prep school to the officers in the army, with my bosses at Pitt, the supervisors in VISTA, basically everywhere I've ever worked – liked the environment at *ESPN* was that permissiveness. You could get away with things. As long as you didn't kill anybody, the suits never said a word to you.

I remember the time I was in the studio readying for one of my first appearances. It was during "SportsCenter." The great Gayle Gardner was one of the anchors and she was unhappy that the shot of her wasn't high enough. During a commercial, she threatened the individual behind the offending camera.

"I'm going to knock your fucking lights out!" yelled Gardner.

The person doing the camera work? It was a woman! I looked around the set, yet nobody else so much as flinched. Nobody said a word. No reprimands. No big deal.

Another reason I probably fit in with this gang was because I've always been competitive, not to mention something of a hothead, myself. The little-known skirmish that I started down in Miami right before the '88 Orange Bowl is a good story.

A few days before the game, Tim Brando and I were watching Oklahoma practice when I spied a contingent of people from *NBC* Sports down at the other end of the field. It was Don Criqui, Bob Trumpy and Michael Weisman, who was executive producer of *NBC* Sports at the time. Seeing them was the spark that re-ignited a grudge that had been smoldering for a little more than a year.

On November 29, 1986, I said on *ESPN* that Miami of Florida coach Jimmy Johnson was Texas's No. 1 target to replace fired Longhorns' coach Fred Akers. I felt Johnson was the logical candidate, plus according to what some of my sources were telling me, he would accept the Texas job if offered. I didn't consider it a real scoop, however, because I never made the outright claim that Johnson was leaving Miami and taking the Texas job. It wasn't my story. I was merely the first person to talk about the developing situation on the air.

The following day, on *NBC's* NFL pre-game show, Bob Costas reported that Johnson was leaving Miami after the Fiesta Bowl against Penn State and that all indications were that he was headed to Austin. I guess this was what the people at *NBC* had come up with.

Of course, Johnson never left Miami for Texas. Well, not until he took the Dallas Cowboys job a few years later. Weisman and the people at *NBC* made a call and it blew up in their faces. It happens. But *NBC* tried to shift responsibility for their bad call, their mistake, onto me.

First, Costas weaseled his way out of the mess, saying it wasn't his report. "I conveyed it," he claimed. Then someone, I'm fairly certain it might have been Costas again, at *NBC* later said on the air that "Beano Cook of *ESPN's* report was wrong" or something to that effect. It was bullshit. They were trying to make me look bad. I never said Johnson was definitely going to Texas.

It's a common occurrence in television. You're not doing a good job, but instead of worrying about your own house, you try to focus people's attention elsewhere. To me, it felt a lot like what Musberger, O'Malley and Shaker tried to do by cataloging all my early mistakes at *ABC* in hopes of getting TV writers to write about me instead of the poor college football product they were putting on the air.

I didn't appreciate that maneuver when those guys tried it in 1982 and I didn't like what *NBC* tried doing to me, either. So I called Weisman out. I don't remember exactly what was said, but it was probably something unflattering about him, his network's programming and God only knows what else. Words were exchanged, and next thing I know, I am going after him, wielding my clipboard as a weapon.

"You fuckin' cocksucker!" I yelled. "Fuck *NBC*! Fuck that little shit, Costas, too!"

I was a man possessed. I put on a powerful display of pass rushing skills until, thankfully for everybody involved, I ran out of breath and Brando and some others stepped in to make sure the clipboard didn't claim its first victim. I'm surprised Barry Switzer, upon seeing the commotion, didn't produce a letter-of-intent for my signature.

My behavior, my language, the whole outburst; it wasn't one of my finest moments. I was embarrassed. Nowadays, this sort of thing would be all over the news. I would have heard about it from somebody at *ESPN*. I almost certainly would have been fired. But nothing happened. I never heard a word. That's how much the business has changed.

The only result of the whole affair was that it started something of a running joke at *ESPN*; whenever I picked up the clipboard at a production meeting or made some vaguely threatening move with it, people laughed that I was armed and dangerous.

When I arrived at *ESPN*, the network was no longer in danger of failure. The new, and in a way more difficult challenge was keeping up with the incredible pace of growth. Everyone was under a lot of stress to succeed. The talent, to make a name for themselves. The executives, producers, researchers, engineers and technicians and everybody else to keep their jobs or to get promoted. It was as pressure-packed an environment as I've ever been a part of.

I took it upon myself to help everyone relax and have some fun. In the late 1980s, there was a commercial for Michelob beer that used Frank Sinatra's song, "The Way You Look Tonight," as the theme. When it came on the television, I'd get a technician to turn it up loud in the newsroom. Then I'd start grooving to it and singing along. It would be sometime in the late afternoon on a Friday, people would be working on deadline, getting ready for "SportsCenter," but I didn't care. It was showtime.

As part of the act, I'd change the lyrics to reflect those present. For example, instead of "lovely...don't you ever change," I'd point to Bob Ley, swap out "lovely," and sing, "Bob Ley...don't you ever change..."

Ley would crack up. Brando sang along. Everyone realized that it was time for a break, and they followed in line. Chris Berman, Gayle Gardner – one by one, they all joined in. It was great to see a room full of stressed-out people stop what they were doing, push away from their desks, and start laughing and singing along. The night might have belonged to Michelob, but the afternoon belonged to Beano!

The Bristol era came to a close for me in August 1990. That's when I asked permission to scale back my workload in order to take care of my mother. She was 94. I knew she was getting up there in age, but I didn't recognize that something was wrong, that she was that seriously sick, until she started calling me Beano instead of Carroll. She hated the nickname with a passion.

My mother refused to go into a nursing home, and I couldn't blame her. I had to be close by. I was surprised that the people at *ESPN* were so understanding about the whole situation. They were very nice about it. In fact, they were more than nice. They said I didn't have to travel to Bristol anymore and that I could shoot my segments in Pittsburgh.

Even better, they would keep paying me the same amount as they had when I was commuting. That doesn't happen very often in television, that the bean counters wouldn't try to renegotiate things. I would have been perfectly willing to have taken a pay cut if asked. I'm not in the same class as Al Michaels. Pittsburgh isn't Brentwood, or Santa Monica, or wherever it is he lives.

It was a great arrangement. I did "SportsCenter," "College GameDay," Dick Schaap's Sunday morning show, and "The Sports Reporters," and since I lived only six blocks from my mother, I could check up on her and make sure she was taking her medicine.

My timing couldn't have been any better at *ESPN*. I wasn't there for the beginning, the real growing pains, and while I didn't officially leave the company, in a way I was out of the picture before Disney bought *ABC* and took control. Which I'm thankful for. In my opinion, the company changed too much, and not for the better, once Mickey Mouse was in charge.

I felt there was an emphasis on the entertainment part of *ESPN's* acronym and programming was increasingly geared towards an almost exclusively younger audience. Worse, it seemed like the company was selling its soul for money.

There was one well-known incident about a year after Disney took over, when Michael Eisner called and wanted *ESPN* to do a piece about a yacht race. It was because Roy Disney owned the winning yacht. It was an obscure event, something we definitely would not have covered. For the record, a lot of our people were pissed off. Somebody leaked the request to Phil Mushnick, in hopes the resulting bad press would dissuade the Disney people from making future requests that would compromise our editorial integrity.

Yet there were worse things than doing vanity pieces or favors for big shots.

Once *ESPN* began securing the rights to the major pro sports, objectivity all but went out the window.

"SportsCenter," for example, became a whore for MLB. One of my contacts in Bristol told me that one late September show, instead of leading off with a college or pro football story, we showed highlights from meaningless baseball games. It wasn't a slow news day, either. There are meaningless games, then there are late September baseball games, which are more meaningless than any other games in sports.

Whenever I heard about things like this, I thought back to 1988, when I was removed from doing commentaries on "SportsCenter." John Walsh told me that to him, "SportsCenter" was first and foremost a news show. He wanted to abolish commentaries and remove straight opinion pieces. He said the commentaries seemed "out of place and unsophisticated."

I never found out just who was responsible for the decision. It could have been a focus group. Walsh loved focus groups. Focus groups in the 1980s said that *USA Today* and *CNN* weren't good ideas. The irony of the situation is that a focus group in 1979 probably wouldn't have liked *ESPN*, either.

If I had to bet, I'd say it was Steve Anderson's decision, not Walsh's. Whatever the case, I wasn't happy, but I respected Walsh's opinion and decision. He's one of the legendary names in sports journalism. Walsh had a distinguished career on the print side working for *Rolling Stone* and the *Washington Post* and he is without a doubt one of the main reasons why *ESPN* is the "Worldwide Leader." If something wins an award at *ESPN*, chances are he had a hand in it. I consider him a friend.

Yet to me, over the years "SportsCenter" wasn't laboring to be a news show, serious or otherwise. It had basically become a circus act of catchphrases and a very popular vehicle for self-promotion.

Outside influences, just like they had at *CBS* and other places, wormed their way in at *ESPN*. For example, CFA director Chuck Neinas tried to get me fired from *ESPN*, as well Mel Kiper. He was successful in getting Kiper kicked off the Thursday Night "Halftime Blitz."

And, of course, it was only a matter of time until the scourge of political correctness started influencing things at *ESPN* just like everywhere else.

One of the best projects I did for *ESPN* was the series of Heisman Trophy winner interviews. Jean McCormick was the producer. A Wellesley graduate, she was the first female producer at *ESPN*. She did some great work on "Outside the Lines." She had a mind for sports history.

The problem was, we clashed on a matter of priority. She wanted to interview the first black winners first. I argued that we needed to do the oldest winners, the guys from the 1930s and 1940s, first. To me, it wasn't racism or favoritism, it was common sense. We needed to get these guys in front of a camera before they died. We ended up doing only a half-dozen pieces. I wish we had been able to do more.

Doing interviews is probably the thing I miss most about not being on television anymore. It was one of the best parts of the job. I got to pretend that I was on "60 Minutes." Now I wasn't interviewing world leaders, movie stars or titans of industry, but I enjoyed picking the brains of these athletes and coaches and the give and take. I wasn't Mike Wallace (nobody is), but I had a lot of fun with it, and I think I got to be pretty good at it after a lot of trial and error.

Pretty soon, the family atmosphere that had once been *ESPN's* hallmark was gone as well. I remember when Tom Mees died in the drowning accident in 1996, it wasn't the lead story on "SportsCenter." A lot of people were upset. One of our own had died and I don't think it was even mentioned until much later in the show.

Things like that were falling through the cracks and I don't know if it was done purposefully or not. I suspect some things were. When Larry Kelley, the second winner of the Heisman Trophy, died, his death wasn't even mentioned on "SportsCenter." It was unbelievable. Very few people at *ESPN* today care about history anymore. They think that if something happened before 1979, it isn't important. How the suits can think that way, when "SportsCentury" was not only the best, but highest-rated series the network ever aired, is beyond my comprehension.

I predict that three things will affect *ESPN's* bottom-line in the near future: political correctness, the ignorance of sports history and the addiction to b-roll.

I remember one episode of "College GameDay," Norm Hitzges made a pick and said that the last time team A defeated team B, President Kennedy was in office. And we ran b-roll of JFK giving a speech! That was frightening. Would we, as a country, not know who Hitzges was referring to?

I'm convinced that *ESPN* could land a scoop on the exact time and date of the Second Coming, but wouldn't run the story unless the Vatican provided b-roll of Christ.

Slowly, steadily, but hardly surprisingly, my influence in Bristol dimmed. In 2003, I was taken off the Saturday night college football scoreboard show. They said I'd still be doing commentaries for *ESPN* News and the radio, but for all intents and purposes, that was the end of the road for me in terms of my on-air career.

I've never taken firings very well, but this time I wasn't too broken up about it. For two reasons. One, I'd had a damn good run. I thought back to 1982, when somebody at *CBS* made the remark that the over/under on my on-air career was six weeks. I not only covered that bet, I covered by 21 years. That's like a big underdog winning by three TDs.

The other reason why I wasn't too upset was because I had a new outlook on life. Five days before getting that call, I almost died. My blood sugar dropped really low and I lost consciousness. I went into a diabetic coma. My neighbor sensed something was wrong and when he got into my apartment, he found me passed out on the living room floor.

Thank God he did. I didn't want to go out like that. I want to die the following way: at approximately 9:58 p.m. EST on a Saturday in late October as I learn that I picked six out of seven games (I'm not greedy) and I'm leading in two West Coast games.

I'd had triple bypass surgery in 1999 and I've since lost a toe to diabetes, but nothing came close to that near-death experience in 2003. It really put things into perspective. When you are younger, you think you're indestructible, that you're going to live forever. Before this event, I'd only thought about death, really reflected on it, a handful of times, such as when my best friend O'Connor died, or when Bob Brendle passed away.

Another time was when my mother died in 1993. I was 61, going on 62. I did the math and concluded that if I lived as long as my mother, I'd have another 35 years left. At first the thought of getting close to 100 intrigued me. Then it occurred to me that would mean 35 more years of hate mail from Notre Dame fans. I doubt I'll ever reach that ripe old age, but if I do, I've accepted my fate. King Henry the VIII had Sir Thomas More. Seinfeld had Newman. I have Notre Dame and its fans.

While I was recovering in the hospital, I did a lot of thinking on mortality. For some reason I thought back to when I lived in the Bigelow Apartments in Pittsburgh. There was a much older woman who also lived there named Hilda Levine. She had a very, very sharp wit. She reminded me of my mother. And she got around well for her age. I once asked her why she was so intent on keeping active.

"There are two types of old people," Hilda answered. "Dead and alive."

I never forgot that. Thanks to sugar, I'm not that mobile anymore, so I try to exercise my brain as much as I can. I read a lot. I play gin with my friend Lee Yovanof in the back of his place, Yovi's Hot Dog Shop, on Liberty Avenue in Pittsburgh. We play for ten cents a point. It's not like Pitt playing Penn State, but we're competitive.

Work-wise, I really enjoy doing the college football podcast with Ivan Maisel on *ESPN.com* each week during the season.

And I still do a lot of radio. I think in my lifetime I've done every radio show in the country. I've always enjoyed doing Paul Finebaum's show in Birmingham. We both wrote columns for Scripps-Howard many years ago. He looks like a professor, but I consider him the dean of the SEC.

I have a lot of fun when Mitch Levy has me on his show in Seattle, when I'm on with Tony Bruno, Colin Cowherd, Scott Ferrall, Jason Smith and Todd Wright, too.

I've tried to remain as positive as possible in retirement, but the milestones keep coming. When I turned 80, I started thinking about the things I never got around to doing. That, and my regrets. It was a perfect time to sit down and write out the list. When I finished, I was pleased to discover that it was a very short one.

I would have liked to have traveled some more. To have visited a handful of foreign countries. Foremost among them is Ireland. The one place that doesn't interest me in the slightest is France. If there's another world war, I want France on the other side this time.

I would have liked to have interviewed Fr. Hesburgh. I begged *ESPN* to let me do it. Repeatedly. They didn't think he was an interesting enough individual.

At one time, I thought that when I retired, I'd go into the restaurant or bar business. I probably got the idea from watching "Casablanca" one too many times. Or else the thought stemmed from the time *Newsday's* Stan Isaacs suggested I open a bar called "Beano's." I imagined it would be fun to run a place that would be like the Pittsburgh version of the fictional Cheers, or Runyon's.

Once I thought it through and did some research, I determined it would be too much work. Not to mention money. Isaacs conducted an informal survey among the country's sportswriters, broadcasters, league, and television executives about the feasibility of a "Beano's." To a man they all said the same thing: "I wouldn't invest in it, but I'd drink there."

So I'll never be a saloon keeper like Rick Blaine. I'll also never be a conference commissioner, either. Not very many people know this, but in 1977, I was one vote shy of becoming the commissioner of the Eastern Eight, the precursor to the Atlantic 10. They came after me and I was interested. I didn't get the job. Those things happen.

It would have been an exciting challenge because we would have been creating something totally new. It would have been interesting to have tried to make it work doing things my way. I would have given the games away free to the networks, with no rights fees, and then we'd have shared the profits.

A big regret is that I didn't push harder to create the office of a commissioner for college football when I might have been in a position to have helped make it happen. I should have done it while I still had an extensive network of contacts in college sports, and when I still had a voice, when I was on the air regularly.

I wish I had worked to get a commissioner because in all honesty, I'm not optimistic about the future of my favorite sport. About twenty years ago, I did a commentary for *ESPN*. It was called "The Obsession With No. 1." I argued that the obsession with the national title would ultimately destroy the sport because fans and alums would consider a ten-win season, or one that didn't result in national championship, a failure. It pains me that this prediction is coming true.

Once upon a time, when a coach went 11-1 or 10-2, he got a raise. Now, if a coach goes 11-1, but doesn't finish No. 1, the fans and alums are calling for his head. Please put things into their proper perspective, people. If an air traffic controller goes 11-1, he gets fired! Celebrate the good and great seasons, not just the ones that end with your coach hoisting the national championship trophy. As I've said many times, the emphasis on finality and crowning a clear-cut champion is ruining the sport.

As a result of this all-or-nothing mindset, it seems inevitable to me that there will be a playoff in college football. It'll start small, with maybe two or four teams, but television's money will ruin this endeavor, too. It'll grow to eight and then sixteen teams, and then pretty much every team will somehow qualify just like every school, even teams with losing records, gets to play in a bowl game now. But at that point who cares, because I'll be dead. And, unlike Brent Musberger and Howard Cosell, I'm not expecting to return in three days.

Don't get me wrong, no matter what happens, college football will always be my favorite sport. If I end up in hell, rest assured that I will work to make a deal with the devil to return every fall to attend a few college football games. I'm sure, however, that in return he'll force me to sit through a late September doubleheader between Pittsburgh and Cincinnati. As long as I don't have to sit through batting practice, I'll probably take the deal.

The biggest "what if?" in my PR career was the Salk photo. I still think about it every now and then. If I could have just gotten Dr. Salk to pose for the photo, it would have made the front page of every paper, sports section at least, in the country.

The biggest regret of my life, in any category, is that I'll never dot the i. I almost got to do it once. Christ, it still kills me to think about it. I was invited by Ohio State to do it at a game in September 1986, the 50th anniversary of the first Script Ohio formation, but it was my first year working for *ESPN* and I had to be in the studio in Bristol. You can't start a new job and ask for one of the first weekends of the season off. Yet I was asked, so I consider the invitation one of the greatest honors of my life.

In terms of the games, I don't have any regrets. I've seen all the bowls, all the rivalry games, and all the major sporting events like the Super Bowl, the Masters, the Final Four, and the NBA Finals. I've probably been at more big games than the Goodyear Blimp.

Yet I wish I could have gotten to see an LSU game on a Saturday night in Tiger Stadium. The one other game I had always wanted to attend and never did was Wabash-DePauw. I would have liked to have taken in Andover-Exeter, too.

I thought it would have been neat to have done a Georgia game on the radio, to have been the third man in the booth with Larry Munson.

I've always wanted to see a high school basketball game in a small Indiana town in the middle of January.

I'd have liked to have to spent one night in a room on Virginia's Lawn. Maybe Mister Jefferson's ghost would have paid me a visit.

I'd also always wanted to sit with the Duke students for a big basketball game at Cameron Indoor Stadium. But I doubt they'd have let me. My IQ is only two digits.

I don't have to attend it, but the one thing that I want to see happen more than anything else right now is to see my alma mater, Pitt, win the national title in men's basketball. Failing that, I would settle for the Pitt hoops team going on probation because, like Dan Jenkins famously said about the football program at TCU, "at least I'd know they were trying."

I'll admit it's a little depressing to know that because of my rapidly failing health, I'll probably never do or see any of these things. Not in this lifetime, at least. Perhaps I'll be reincarnated. General Patton believed in it. My mother said she hoped it wasn't possible, because she didn't know if she could handle a second round. To be honest, I don't know if I could, either.

But if reincarnation is possible, I'd like to put in my request now: I'd like to be a doctor or a detective for the next go-around. But not just any doctor or detective. My preferences for the former would be Dr. Quincy, M.E. and for the latter, Detective Columbo. If I can't come back in human form, I'd settle for being Morris the Cat or a Michigan football helmet.

In terms of jobs, I regret not taking the Lakers' PR job. I don't think I would have enjoyed the job very much, but you don't get many chances to live in sunny Southern California. I didn't know it at the time, but that was my one and only opportunity.

The greatest employment "what if?" in my life remains my brief stint with the *St. Petersburg Times*. I don't know what I could have done differently. To this day I regret that I failed, but I don't regret that I tried. If given the chance, I'd do it all over again in a heartbeat. It would be like if Stefanie Powers sat down in the seat next to me on a flight. It would be a longshot, but I'd start up a conversation with her.

It's hard to give up on your dream, so I tell young people not to do so until the last possible minute. That's probably why, all these years later, I still foolishly hold onto mine. I understand, however, that maybe my dream of being a newspaperman doesn't come true until after I die. Maybe for me, heaven will be a big, old-fashioned open air pressbox where I get to take my seat alongside all the famous sportswriters of the past. I can't say for sure.

The only thing I am reasonably sure of regarding the afterlife is that if I go toward that light and the first thing I encounter when I arrive on the other side is a television with nothing but local news on every channel, well, I can only conclude that I somehow found my way to hell.

Whenever I used to do regular interviews, a writer or radio host would invariably ask, "What's burning Beano today?" At this writing, it's most definitely local news. The three worst inventions of the 20th century were the I.R.S., Astroturf and local news – and not necessarily in that order. I say this even though some of my closest friends in Pittsburgh – Myron Cope, Bill Hillgrove, Alby Oxenreiter, John Steigerwald, Stan Savran and Guy Junker – have worked or else still work doing sports for local news.

I just can't put lipstick on a pig. It's unwatchable. If local news producers ever got a hold of "60 Minutes," it would be 20 two-minute stories, ten minutes of weather, two minutes of sports and eight minutes of promos for "Divorce Court."

They do the same stories every night, every week, every year. The best example is the fucking salt story. Every fall they do it. They send some reporter out to interview the head of the public works department to ask him if we have enough salt for the roads for the coming winter. You can set not only your calendar to it, but your watch as well. October 2, 5 o'clock.

Anymore, you've got a better chance of hitting the lottery than you do in watching a real, honest-to-goodness news story. I remember when Dr. Salk died in 1995, only one of the three stations in Pittsburgh led off with the story. One of the three channels, in fact, opened with a piece about a teen dance club opening in the suburbs.

The only outfit that understood the importance of Salk's death was *KDKA-TV*, the *CBS* affiliate. I suspect that was due to influence of my friend Stacy Smith, the city's best and longest-tenured news anchor, who had a personal connection because of polio.

If I only go around once, and I'm done with local news for eternity, I'll sign on the dotted line right now. But I'm not in a hurry to go anywhere. I have my good days and bad, yet on the whole I feel a lot like Lou Gehrig, when he made his famous retirement speech in 1939. As my bookie will attest, I'm not the luckiest man on the face of the earth, but if you take into account things in life other than betting, I'm damn close to it.

I am truly lucky to have made so many friends. I've made enemies, too, but it's a given that you're going to make enemies in your life. My advice has always been, if possible, make sure your enemies are younger than you. That way, when you make it, you can tell them to go fuck themselves. If your enemies are older, by the time you make it, they will be dead.

On the subject of enemies, I am very lucky that I never had to go to war. Our armed forces and our country are lucky in that regard as well.

I wasn't any good at sports, but I'm fairly certain that when all is said and done, I can say I batted 1.000 in my lifetime in something – flying. It's hard to believe, but every flight I took on landed safely.

When I was a little kid, my father told me that he hoped I would do two things in my life: keep my name out of the newspapers and out of the courthouses. I'm batting .500 in that.

I never got married, but I also never went through a divorce. Which means my love life basically ended in a scoreless tie, like Notre Dame-Army in 1946. I can live with being technically undefeated.

I'm fortunate that I've never had to worry about money. An added benefit of that is when I die, some deserving kids at Kiski Prep and the University of Pittsburgh will receive some financial help.

Actually, there will be two benefits. My life's savings will go to those two institutions tax-free. In the last game of the long rivalry between the I.R.S. and Beano Cook, I'll be ending the all-time series with a win. To me, that's better than winning the Apple Cup, the Bronze Boot, the Commander-in-Chief's Trophy, the Old Oaken Bucket, or the Little Brown Jug.

I've met, befriended, and worked with some of the most famous people that ever inhabited the worlds of sports and media.

I've watched and experienced more sports history, especially college football history, than anybody else alive. I was going to say, "alive today," but that sounds too much like a redundant phrase. It might not be, but I'm not taking any chances. I don't want to resume that bad habit.

F. Scott Fitzgerald famously said there are no second acts in American lives. I might be the lone exception to that statement. I think I had successful careers in both PR and television. Anybody that comes after me will be hard-pressed to beat my record. I've accomplished some important things in both fields.

I'm not bragging. Believe me, I know I was lucky to have survived and stayed on people's payrolls as long as I did. On many occasions, I got away with things that would have, and probably should have, gotten me fired.

My timing for job openings and firings was extraordinary. For every door that closed, another – and almost always the right one – opened exactly when I needed it to. I didn't spend any substantial period of time in the unemployment line. I can't help but think someone was looking out for me in this regard.

There's no doubt in my mind that I was lucky to have been born in the era that I was. I wouldn't have had the career I had in today's world.

In PR nowadays, the job is damage control, not actually working with the media. It's no fun. They want yes-men and robots, not comedians. I doubt the people running things at Pitt today would put up with someone like me. The networks sure wouldn't.

And I know for certain that nobody would put me on television today. There aren't any Roone Arledges in the business anymore. Nobody takes chances. If Cosell, Kuralt, the Greek and I applied for a job in television today, none of us would get by the receptionist.

Not only did I get to do all these amazing things and meet all these incredible people, I had so much fun. I had a lot of laughs.

Three things are constant in everybody's life: death, taxes and laughs. And I don't think we laugh enough anymore. I've said this many times over the years: we need another Will Rogers. That's basically the role I've tried to play in this life. If everyone whose paths crossed mine thinks of me that way, and will remember me that way, that would make me very happy.

To tell you the truth, I honestly don't feel as though I worked a day in my entire life. As the wise old sage of the Bigelow, Hilda Levine, once told me, "your life has been one long coffee break."

Acknowledgments

Although one or two names are typically featured on the cover of a book, it's common knowledge that book projects are team efforts. A small team of dedicated individuals helped Beano begin this project and helped me complete it, so to recognize their invaluable contributions, I'm going to give you the roster in a familiar format: alphabetical.

Accorsi, Ernie
Borghetti, E.J.
Brando, Tim
Coleman, John R.
Hillgrove, Bill
Howard, Chuck
Merchant, Larry
O'Brien, Jim
O'Connor, John
O'Neil, Terry
Podolsky, Rich
Smizik, Bob
Verna, Tony

Courtesy of the University of Notre Dame

BEANO COOK was the University of Pittsburgh's athletics publicist from 1956 to 1966. He worked as NCAA press director for *ABC* Sports from 1966-74 and for *CBS* Sports from 1977-82. Cook also worked as a sportswriter for the *St. Petersburg Times*, did PR for the Miami Dolphins and *Mutual*, and spent one year out of sports with Volunteers in Service to America, or VISTA. From 1982 to 1986 he was an *ABC* college football commentator. In 1986, he joined *ESPN*. Cook died at the age of 81 in 2012.

Photo by Osvaldo Equité

JOHN D. LUKACS is a writer and historian whose byline has appeared in the *New York Times*, *USA Today*, *World War II Magazine* and on *ESPN.com*. He was the historical consultant to *ESPN* "College GameDay" from 2002-2010. The author of "Escape From Davao: The Forgotten Story of the Most Daring Prison Break of the Pacific War," he lives in Western Pennsylvania. Follow him on *Twitter*: @JohnDLukacs

Made in the USA
Coppell, TX
17 December 2021

69225290R00245